CARLO STARNAZZI

LEONARDO

FROM TUSCANY TO THE LOIRE

Foreword
by Carlo Pedretti

Cartei & Bianchi
Publishers

Editorial Coordination: Margherita Melani
Editing: Veruska Picchiarelli
Translation: Claudio Pedretti
Computer Graphics: Simone Bogani
Press and Promotion: Elisabetta Giudrinetti

©2008 C.B. Cartei & Bianchi Publishers
Via A. da Sangallo, 17/H - Foligno (PG) - Tel. fax 0742 320623
Via Magenta, 40 - Campi Bisenzio (FI) - Tel. 055 891063 Fax 055 8940843
www.cbedizioni.com - info@cbedizioni.com

ISBN 978-88-95686-01-1

Photographic references: Photographic Archives of the «Armand Hammer» Centre of Studies on Leonardo at the University of California of Los Angeles; National Edition of the Manuscripts and Drawings of Leonardo da Vinci (Roma, Libreria dello Stato, 1923-1941); photographs by the Author and Sergio Cartei.

Every effort has been made to trace owners of copyright material. However we would be glad to hear from any further copyright owners that may have been overlooked. The Publisher declares to be willing to pay any amount due for those photographs of which it has been impossible to determine the source.

Our special gratitude to the Rossana and Carlo Pedretti Foundation, Los Angeles.

Summary

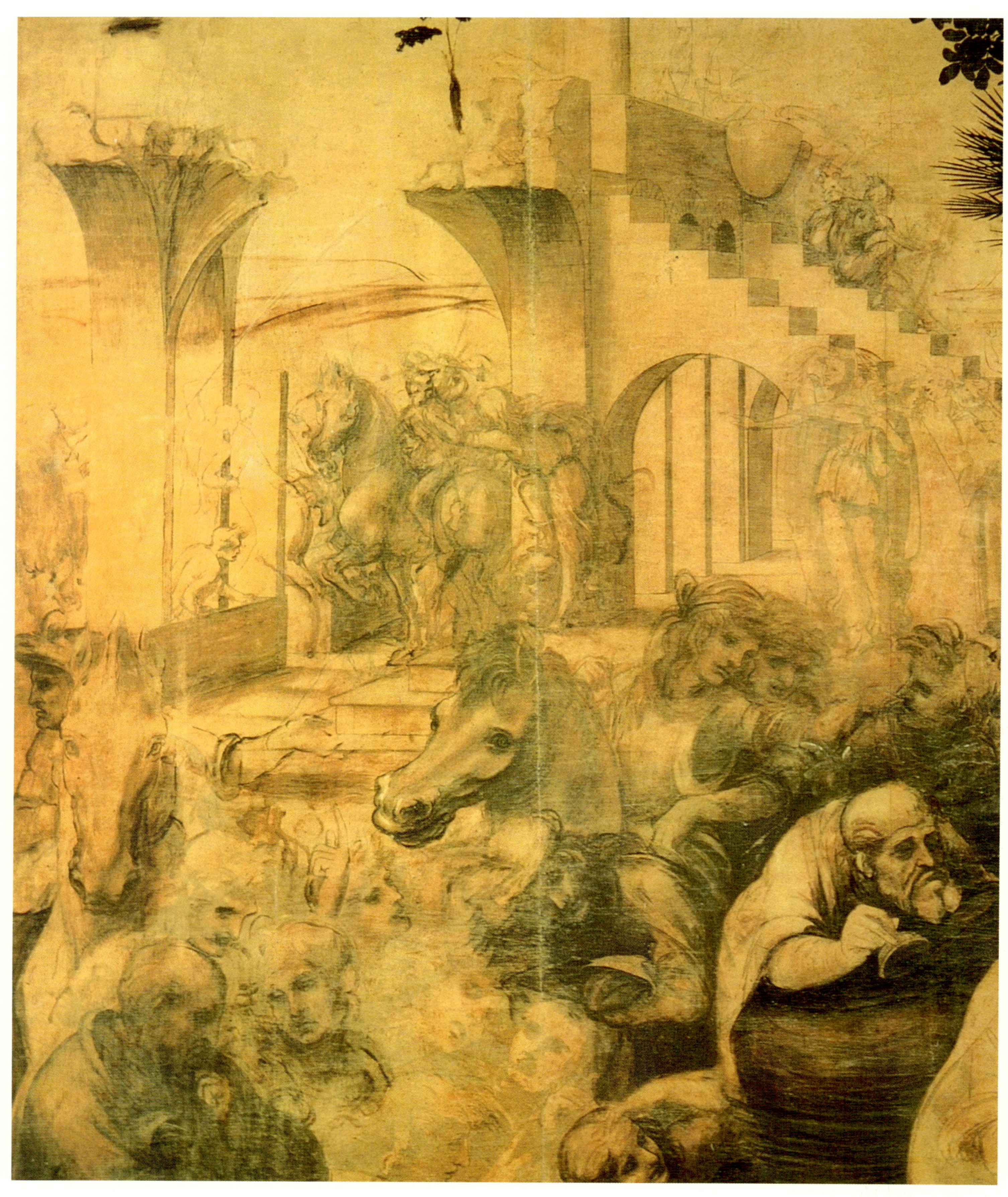

LEONARDO DA VINCI, *Adoration of the Magi*, 1481. Oil on table, 246 x 243 cm. Florence, Galleria degli Uffizi. Particular

FOREWORD

This new book by Carlo Starnazzi can be considered as the third and then the conclusive one of a brilliant trilogy on the relationship of Leonardo with the region of Arezzo. As such, it assumes immediately, even in the title, a European aperture that in an opportune way amplifies, on a historical and scientific ground, its rigorous territorial structure. The so to speak dynamic part of the organization and articulation of the single chapters, just as a leading line in the story-writing sequence, is placed programmatically in evidence by the opening theme, Leonardian itineraries, that places the accent on the main phases of the development of the chasing activity of Leonardo during his frequent movements on the large and complex political, economic, cultural and artistic chessboard of Central Italy, not far from 1500 to 1516. And it is in this historical and geographical context that the three focal points of the research of Starnazzi emerge with spontaneous emphasis: Florence, Cortona-Arezzo and Rome, just like in a triangle rectangle that with a simple overturning can be transformed in a square offering therefore another angle rectangle with which to designate the final goal of Leonardo, Amboise, and therefore the France of the last years of his life, from 1517 to 1519. From here, the fourth focal point is related to the one of Cortona-Arezzo because of the diagonal of our emblematic square.

From the same Leonardo, furthermore, analogous suggestions of geometrical-symbolical configurations could come to our author. They are any thing but the air lines with which the localities, indicated with small circles, are joined each other, like suggesting the passage from the one to the other in a regional sense, and therefore with cartographic inference. I shall mention two examples of this type of quick leonardian mnemonic annotation: the first one on a sheet of the Codex Atlanticus, datable about 1499-1500 (f. 224 v-b [608 v]), with topographical outlines of water and street connections between Milan, Lodi, Pavia and Binasco; the second one - an analogous outline, but without toponyms - placed at the bottom of one page of the Ms. A of 1492 (f. 84 v), better known for the representation of the studio of the painter.

It is not surprising therefore that also in this book Starnazzi is dealing with vincian cartography not only in the Tuscan area, on which he has insisted in the past with remarkable contributions to problems of geology and palaeontology examined with acumen and competence, but even European, from the project of drainage of the Pontine Marshes to the colossal programs of fluvial management of the Arno in Tuscany and the Adda in Lombardy, to which there must be added the still mysterious plan of obstruction of the River Isonzo in Friuli in order to face the feared invasion of the Turks in the year 1500, which followed a device of «mobile enclosure» that the same Leonardo would have proposed again many years later in France on the occurrence of the plan of a new royal residence in Romorantin.

From here the new examination that Starnazzi proposes of well known but still problematic architectural topics that were finding their place side by side, in Italy like in France, to those of the hydric reorganization within urban or regional areas; from here new proposals on the relationship of Leonardo with Francesco di Giorgio, both having roots, as well as all the Tuscans, in the then and still today enigmatic Etruscan tradition; and from here at last also the delicious interval of a legendary flight over the Lake Trasimeno - where moreover Leonardo meets again with the Perugino - that has as a protagonist a singular personage — it is not important whether it is only imagined as the erudite considerations of the Boffito seem to confirm - to which it is irresistible to place side by side Leonardo with his flying visions half way between the audacious and the pragmatic. That is, after all, an excursus like the one even more precious on «Leonardo and the physiognomy» that starts from Vasari to arrive to Mariette, according to an axis traced this time to join Arezzo to Paris.

A book therefore of which anybody can have an immediate idea even by skimming its summary, where its fascinating course, customary to Starnazzi anyway, can be perceived exactly, while it grows towards its impressive end, in this case the majestic image of

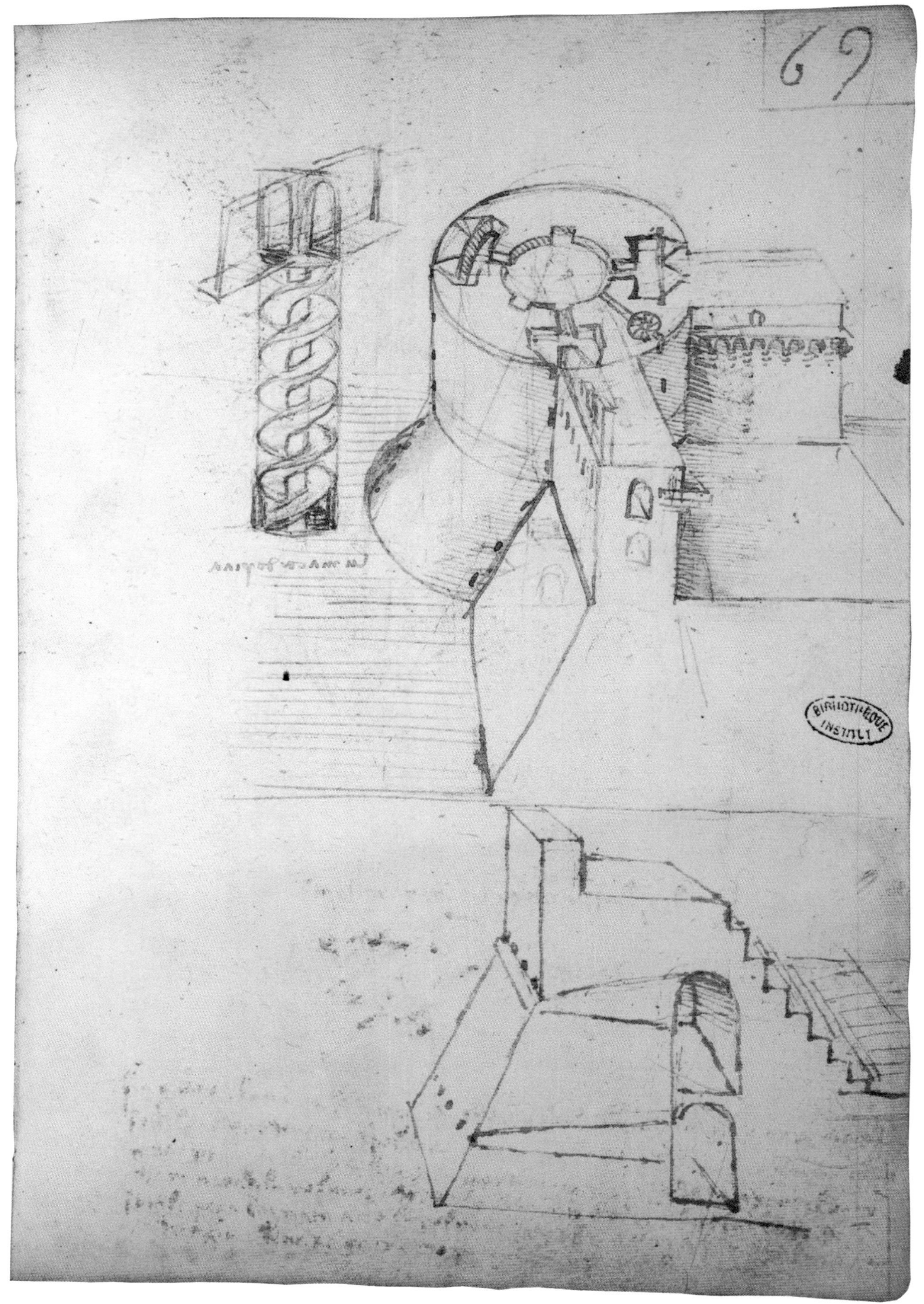

Leonardo da Vinci, *Drawings of stairs, c.* 1484–86. Pen and ink, 231 x 167 mm. Ms B, f. 69 *r.* Paris, Institut de France

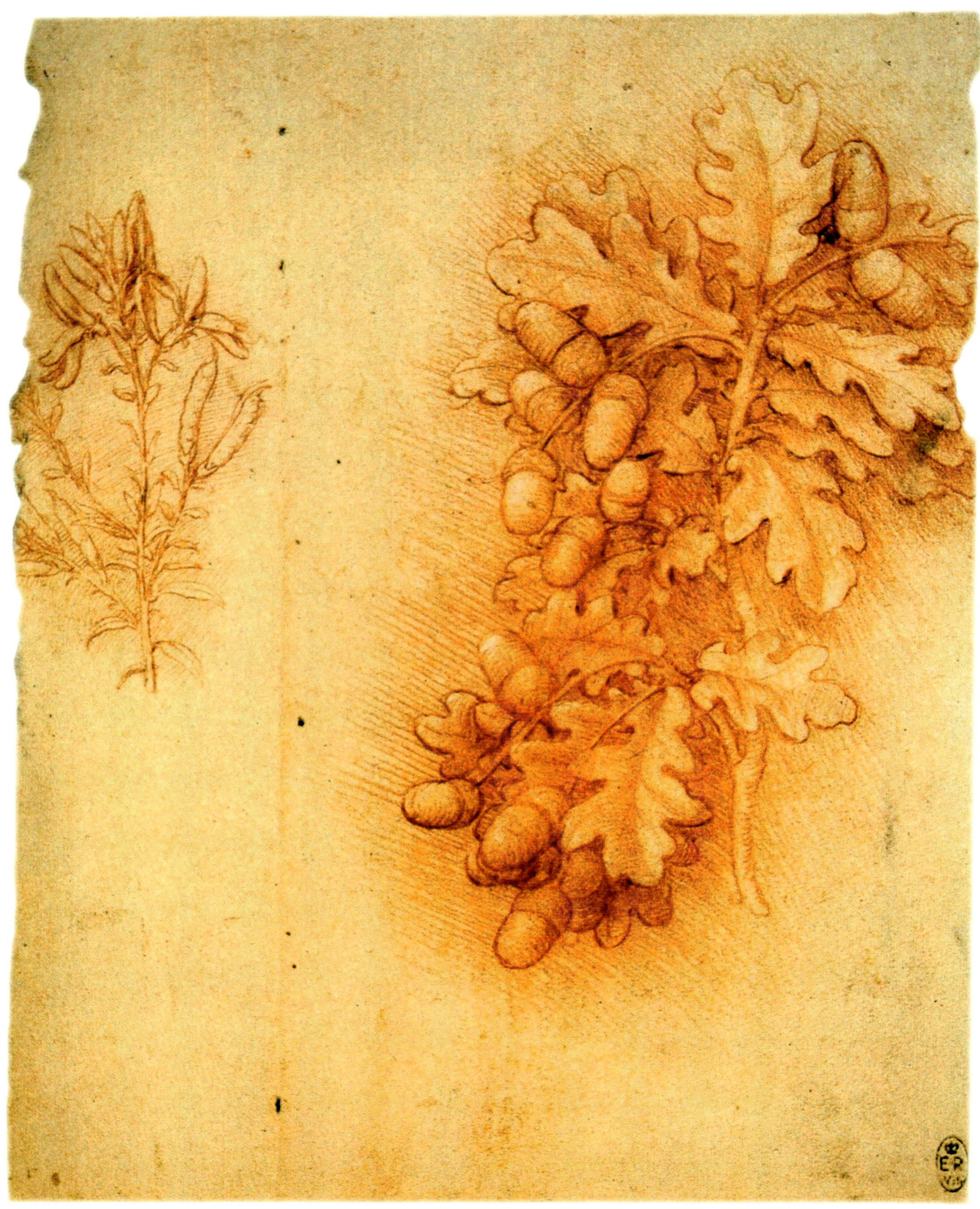

Leonardo da Vinci, *Quercus robur and Genista tinctoria*, *c.* 1506–08. Sanguine with touches of ceruse on paper prepared in pink, 188 x 154 mm. Windsor, RL 12422

the «leonardian» Castle of Chambord, which rises in 1519 when Leonardo dies. It goes back to 1913 the first proposal of Marcel Raymond to attribute to Leonardo the original conception of the Castle of Chambord, the most famous architecture of Renaissance in France, that in its style and in its principles of proportionality, clearly present in plan and elevation, finds its response in the graphical reflections of Leonardo back at the time of his architectural activity at the service of the Sforza family in Milan, when among other things, in the Ms. B datable about 1490, he draws a system of double staircase with counter-clockwise spiral, exactly like the monumental stairway at the centre of the Castle of Chambord, where one flight is used to go up and the other to come down.

To give body to the proposed attribution it helped also the participation to the plan of another Italian architect, Domenico Bernabei da Cortona, known as Boccadoro, for a long time operating in France and of which a wood model of the Castle of Chambord existed right in Amboise. That was a problem that would have been discussed over for a long time, and again in 1952 the role of Domenico da Cortona would have been recognized and proposed again by Lesueur as a result of the clarifications of Heydenreich on the project of Leonardo for Romorantin: on which project, then, it would not have been possible to add anything more to what I managed to supply, also on the basis of new documents, with my publications of 1962 and 1972.

Assessed that in 1518 the King arranged the financing of the plan of the channel of Romorantin, there remained the impasse that the name of Leonardo did never appear in the related documents, and it is only known that the following year, when Leonardo died, an epidemic in Romorantin forced the King to move the plan for the new royal palace to a different place. In addition, fate decreed that right then the Castle of Chambord began to be built up more northwards, replacing a pre-existing hunting lodge. The foundations of the new palace of Romorantin were still visible in the eighteenth century for a height of approximately four meters and indeed the walls of the abandoned construction can still be noticed in prints and plans of that time.

If Leonardo had time enough to be informed of the intentions of the King, it is quite probable that he did advise him, directly or through his architects, on the new plan for Chambord. It is known that Domenico da Cortona was also present in Amboise, but no document could provide evidence of any of his contacts with Leonardo. In 1972, collecting all that had to do with the plan for Romorantin, I indicated a sheet of the Codex Atlanticus with geometrical studies undoubtedly of the French period on which, written from another hand, like a pen test, there is the note, not transcribed in the first edition of the Codex: «Memory to us Master Domenico», that I without more ado proposed to relate to Domenico Bernarbei. However, it was Starnazzi, more than thirty years later, to pick up that tenuous clue in order to tell the rest of the story, enriched of every possible documentary historical contextualization, exposing it with pressing reasoning of stylistical nature made still more convincing through his undeniable scientific sterness.

There is here then a lesson of method on which it is appropriate to insist also because it is a way to go back to reflections of the same Leonardo. Some time ago, I had to assert, I do not remember where, that history is made also of clues. Now I might specify, on the example of the work of Starnazzi, that the clue is exactly the «little spark» of Dante that «generates great flame». In order to be little, the spark is best suited to the weak embers that live for a long time in the ashes. Moreover, such it is the one that Starnazzi finds again in a book of mine of 1972, so that, once exposed and revived, it is all of a sudden ready to favour the great flame.

Leonardo, that already had noticed how «the counterbalance that falls begins in nothing and ends up in great power» (Ms. M, f. 93 r), or that the power of shadow operates on the contrary of the «things carried out by time from small principle into a great increase,

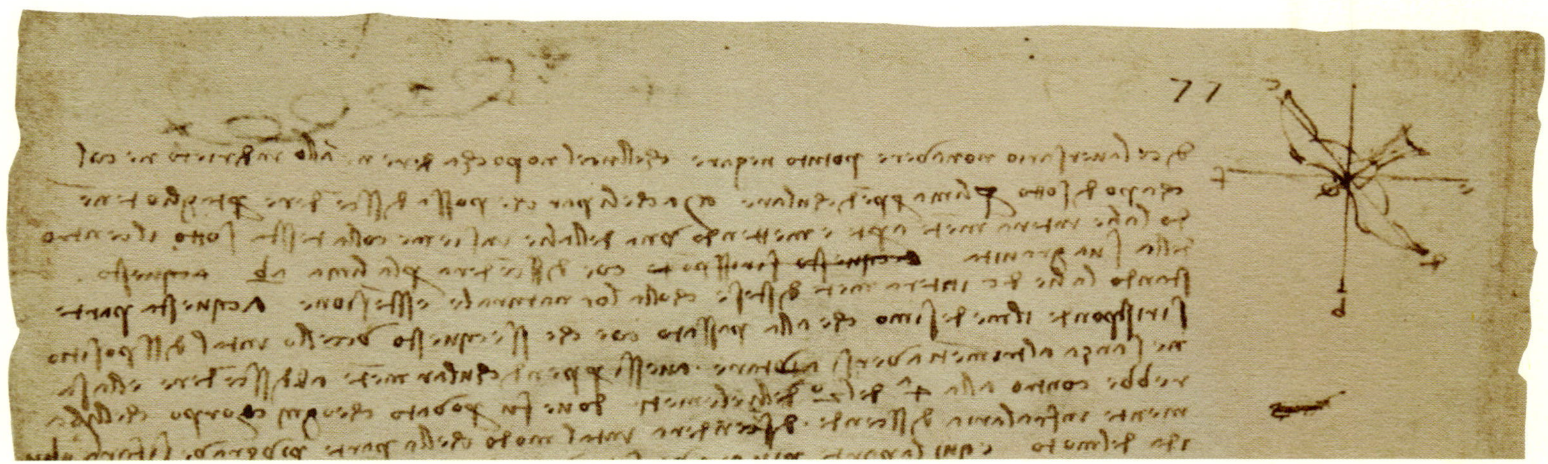

LEONARDO DA VINCI, *Study on the changing of position and direction of birds*, c. 1505. Pen and ink, 290 x 227 mm. Codex Atlanticus, f. 845 *v.* Milan, Biblioteca Ambrosiana

as it would be a large oak which had a weak principle from a small acorn» (Libro di Pittura 548), he would not have hesitated to recognize the same principle of mechanics in the flight of birds, and that precisely five centuries ago: «Being all the principles of things many times the cause of great moments, as we see a small motion, nearly insignificant, of the rudder to have the power to turn a ship of wonderful largeness, loaded with the greatest weight, and in such a quantity of water, that from every side it burdens it, and against the course of the impetuous winds, with the embrace of such great sails, consequently we can be sure with a small motion of their wings or of the tail to enter under or over the wind, for those birds, that over the course of the winds without beating of wings they sustain themselves, it is proper and sufficient to prohibit the descending of the afore mentioned birds» (CA, f. 308 v-b [845 v]).

Carlo Pedretti
Director of the «Armand Hammer»
Centre of Studies on Leonardo at the University of California of Los Angeles
and of its European Centre at the University of Urbino

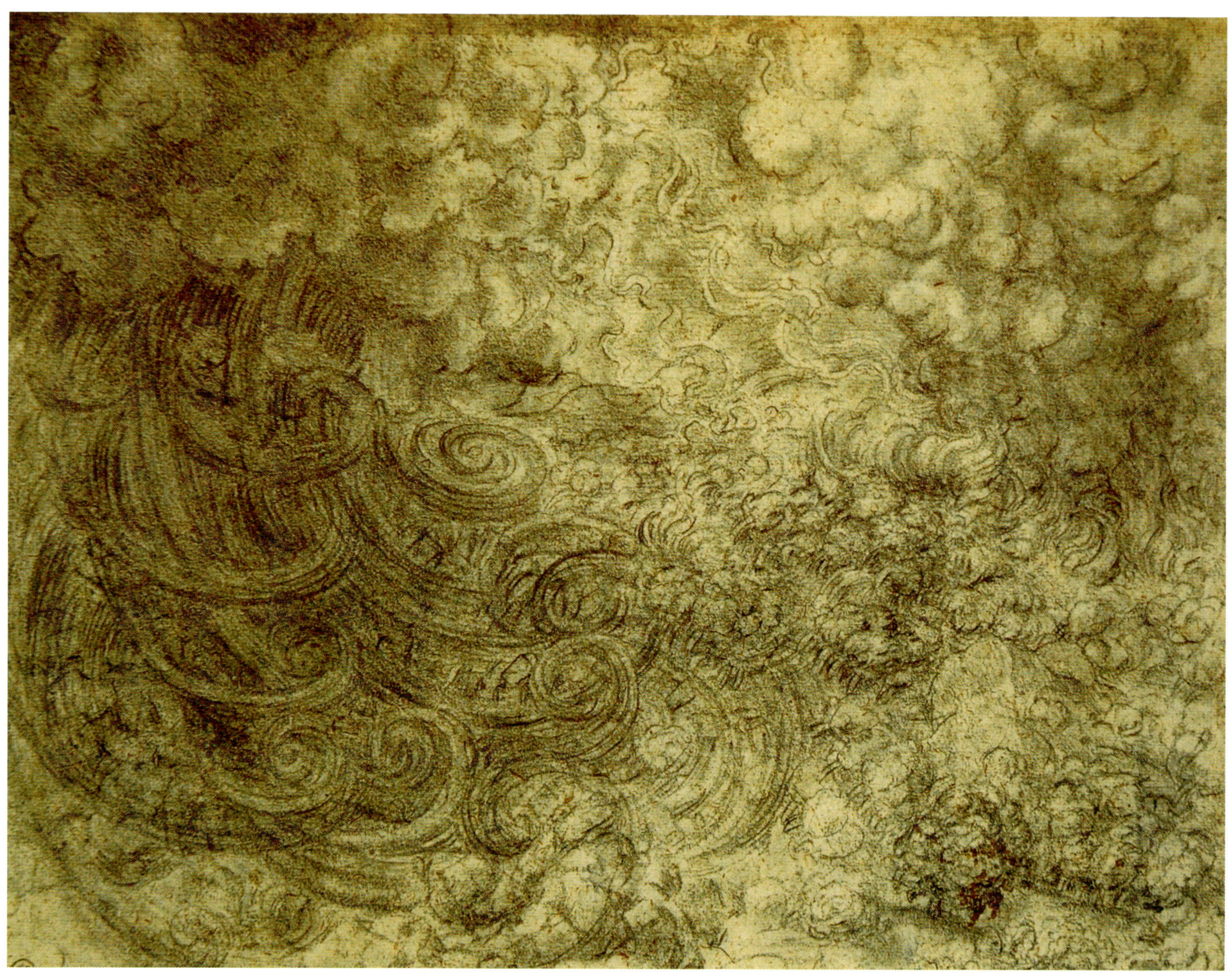

Leonardo da Vinci, *Deluge*, c. 1517-18. Charcoal, 165 x 204 mm. Windsor, RL 12384

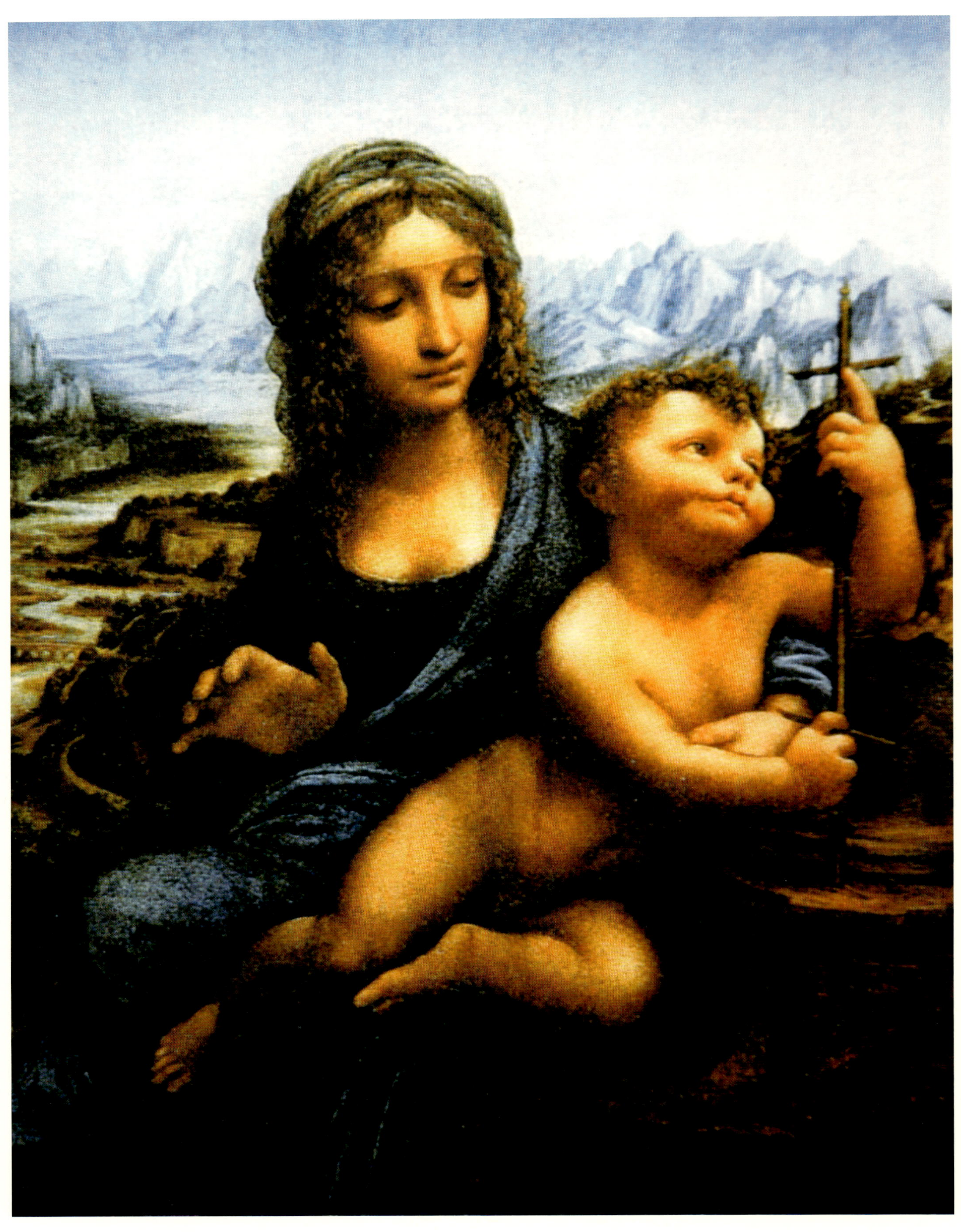

Leonardo da Vinci, *Madonna of the Yarn-winder, c.* 1501-07. Oil on plate, 50,2 x 36,4 cm. New York, private collection

INTRODUCTION

The indication of this precise historical-geographical course, «from Tuscany to the Loire», could provoke the impression that we are now face to face with a reading that sends back to an analysis, in a chronological succession, of the interest of Leonardo for the mechanics of fluids or for the world of the waterways, that he studied as artist-scientist, or that at least might send back to the contextualization of those places which animated his mind in devising and realizing huge hydraulic plans, from 1500 to 1519. In fact, this series of studies faces an entirety of topics so complex and variously articulated, as much as delicate in the facet of the proposals, that concern, on a theoretical and historical plan, both the world of architecture and urban planning, as well as the one of sculpture and painting. Hence we have determined to let emerge from the foundations of the real experience, after a wide work of recognition and by correlating all the numerous historical sources, the cultural ties between Leonardo and the artists who have operated, according to the figurative Tuscan tradition, with more or less clear accents also in Arezzo and its surroundings, from Donatello to Masaccio and Piero della Francesca, from Francesco di Giorgio to Bramante, from Signorelli to Perugino and to Raphael.

Moreover, it has become necessary to illustrate also unknown relationships arisen between Leonardo and personalities who have taken shape and consistency, suddenly exiting from a shadow cone, now as a result of the deciphering of one small marginal note in a sheet of the Codex Atlanticus (f. 174 va), like «memory to us master domenico», with relation to Domenico Bernabei da Cortona known as «Boccadoro» (Pedretti, 1970; 1972), that actively operated in Amboise preparing scenographies for the court festivities and realizing the leonardian devise of the magnificent Castle of Chambord (Reymond, 1913), now examining closely by means of historical criticism the thesis of Vasari of 1568 of a Leonardo who, agnostical and irreligious in the torrentinian edition of 1550, is converted on his death-bed to the catholic faith (Ciardi, 1997), developing the reasoning from the simple testamentary record of the figure of Francesco da Cortona, mentioned by the royal notary Guillaume Boreau, as witness of the last will of the great artist.

In the course of the work, it does not remain in the background the relationship that Leonardo had also with the world of the Roman classical antiquity in his interest both for the statuary, and for the several architectural shapes, that he could admire in a travel made to Tivoli and Rome at the beginning of the sixteenth century (Pedretti 1991; Marani, 1995). And the charm of the ancient works was renewed, in an experience for «itinera Etruriae», in the year 1507, when, visiting the majestic tumulus of Montecalvario di Castellina in Chianti and inspiring to the archaeological remains of that sepulchral monument (Martelli, 1972), from the circular shape and from the particular structural system of the underground tombs, he elaborated the model of a particular «Mausoleum», a perfect building with central plan, that, heading with its language to the motive of the «theatre of the world», where «the whole converges and centres» (Heydenreich, 1962; Firpo, 1971; Garin, 1972), it would have become the standard canon par excellence of the architecture of Renaissance, from Bramante to Palladium. And the theme «Leonardo architect» (Pedretti, 1978; Marani, 1982), beyond covering again over the studies undertaken by the artist-scientist on the dynamics of flight (Giacomelli, 1936; Laurenza, 2004), is proposed again by examining the relations and the experiences that he shared with Francesco di Giorgio in Milan, since the realization of the model in wood for the lantern of the Dome. From here the proposal advanced on the possible employment by the engineer of Siena of a leonardian idea, grown «in a profitable exchange of ideas» and, after a short while, turned to define the architectural outlines of the dome of Santa Maria delle Grazie at the Calcinaio of Cortona, following the tradition of Brunelleschi. And the extraordinary ability in drawing, where Leonardo poured all of his creative power, also to give 'true knowledge' of the limbs and their functions, is remarked in the chapter dedicated to the study of the physiognomy, where the line creates faces in order to define their beauty or it deforms them in their particulars up to the grotesque and to the caricature, participating of those «mental motions», in which the comedy and the tragedy stretch subtly to penetrate in the historical vicissitudes of humanity. This book is therefore the result of a long historical investigation, but certainly also the outgrowth of the enthusiasm and the constructive support that my friend Carlo Pedretti has endlessly known how to transmit to me with the experience and the intellectual energy that distinguishes him. To him my affection and my sincere gratefulness. A particular appreciation goes also to Antonio Paolucci, who has expressed encomiastic judgments on my researches every time we met and who has allowed the use of photographs of the works of art kept in the museums of Florence; and gratitude goes as well to the Military Geographic Institute for the fecund relationship of collaboration that has been lasting by now well beyond a decade. An indispensable mention is due to the Institution «City of Arezzo» Library and particularly to its President Adua Bidi Piccardi, always devoted to the promotion of culture and to the formative growth of new generations. A deferent and affectionate homage goes then to Cartei & Bianchi Edizioni, a publisher who has confirmed itself in the international arena for its valuable publications; while my mind and my heart turn to my wife and to my sons who, although between joy and suffering, knew how to fill my life with participated enthusiasms: to them I dedicate this new work.

Carlo Starnazzi
Arezzo, July 2006

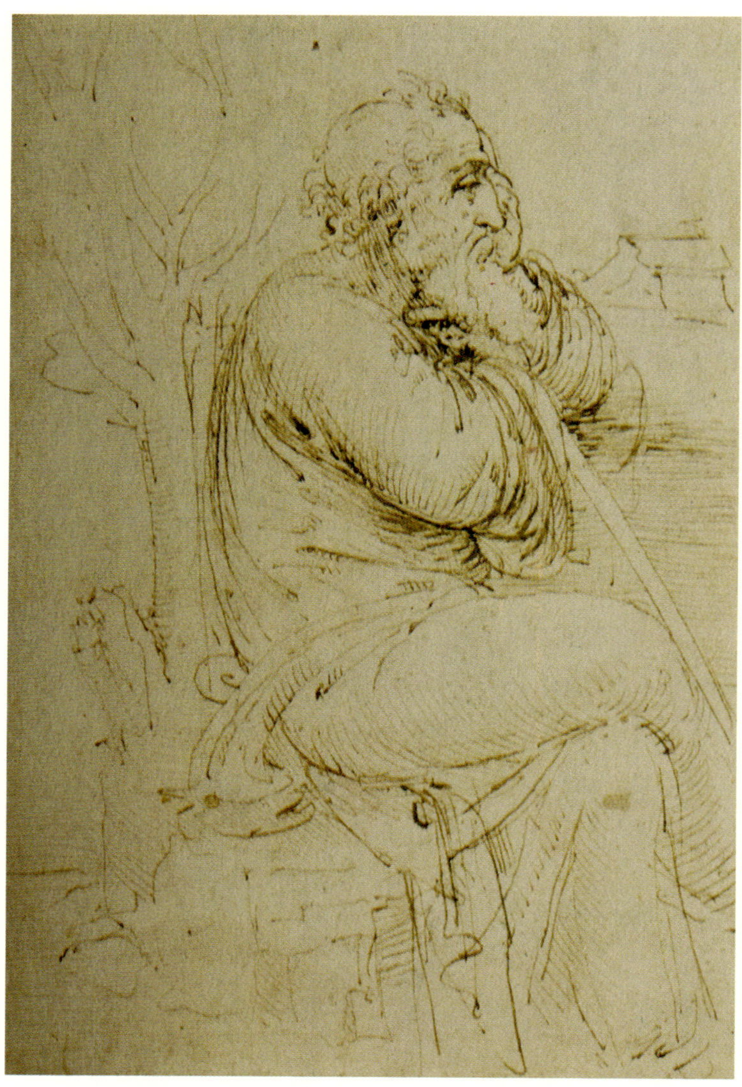

Leonardo da Vinci, *Study of an old man, c.* 1513. Pen and ink, 154 x 127 mm. Windsor, RL 12579

Leonardian itineraries

I. Water, origin of life and death

IN LEONARDO, the topic of water appears in an obsessive way in his activity both of artist as well as of scientist.[1] Water is the foundation of life in the world of Nature and through movement it expresses its eternal and dynamic vital force, leading to the comprehension of the mysteries and the laws that animate the universe:

> *What is water. Water is among the four elements the second less heavy and the one of second fickleness. It never has rest until it does not join up to the marine element, where, not being annoyed by the winds, it settles down and rests with its surface equidistant from the centre of the world (Ms. C, f. 26 v). Water the vital humour of the terrestrial machine moves itself by means of its natural heat (Ms. H, f. 95 r). It consumes the high tops of the mountains. It puts out of their place and removes great stones. It drives the sea away of its ancient coastline, because with the carried earth it raises its bottom. It shakes and ruins high shores; no firmness in her is ever seen, that all of a sudden it might corrupt its nature. With its rivers, it searches every slope of the valleys, and where it takes off and where it puts on new land (Cod. Arundel, f. 57 r). Water is the carrier of nature (Ms. K, f. 2 r).*

Therefore water, become in his mind a theme of subtle and constant naturalistic and scientific investigation, overflowed as a dynamic and metamorphic element of reality the world of his landscapes, from the view of the Arno Valley realized «the day of Saint Mary of the snow/on the 5th of August 1473» (Florence, Uffizi), to the maps of the Val di Chiana (Windsor, RL 12682; 12278) and of the course of the Arno (Windsor, RL 12278; 12277), from the *Annunciation* of the Uffizi to the extraordinary cosmogony of the *Mona Lisa* (Paris, Louvre Museum).

Leonardo discovered there the harmony and the geometrical regularity of reality, the singing of life, but also the blind uncontrollable force of nature that, in its ruinous assault, destroys all that man has built, until it transmute itself, in the powerful apocalyptic vision of the *Deluges* (1517-18), into an expression of death and cosmic dissolution:

> *Among the irreparable and harmful furies, definitely the flooding of the ruinous rivers has to be placed before every horrible and frightening damaging (CA, f. 108 vb [302 r]). There it could be seen the remains of the mountains, already put out of their place by the course of their rivers, to collapse over the same rivers and to close their valleys; which rivers, stopped up, flooded and submerged the much numerous lands with their peoples [...] And the lands covered with water showed their waves in great part covered with tables, bedsteads, boats and other various instruments made out of necessity and of fear of death, over which there were women, men together with their children, with various lamentations and crying, scared by the fury of the winds, which with greatest storm the waters turned upside down and together with them the dead drowned in that one [...] Darkness, wind, tempest of sea, deluge of water, forests burning, rain, thunderbolts from the sky, earthquakes and collapse of mountains, levellings of towns (Windsor, RL 12665).*

There came into being therefore, in a continuous interrelation between art, science and technique, his studies on the motion of water, on the dynamics of vortices, on the capacity and the speed of currents in channels and in rivers, on the distribution of water from the mouths of channels, on the percussion of water on the banks of rivers, on its employ-

---

[1] See K. Clark, *Leonardo e le curve della vita,* «Lettura Vinciana», XVII, Firenze, Giunti Barbèra, 1979; F. Fehrenbach, *Licht und Wasser. Zur dynamik Naturphilosophischer leitbilder im Werke Leonardo da Vincis*, Tubingen-Berlin, Wasmuth, 1997; C. Starnazzi, *Leonardo. Acque e terre*, presentazione di C. Pedretti, libro-catalogo e mostra a Cesenatico a cura di C. Starnazzi, 6 luglio-8 settembre, Firenze, Grantour, 2002.

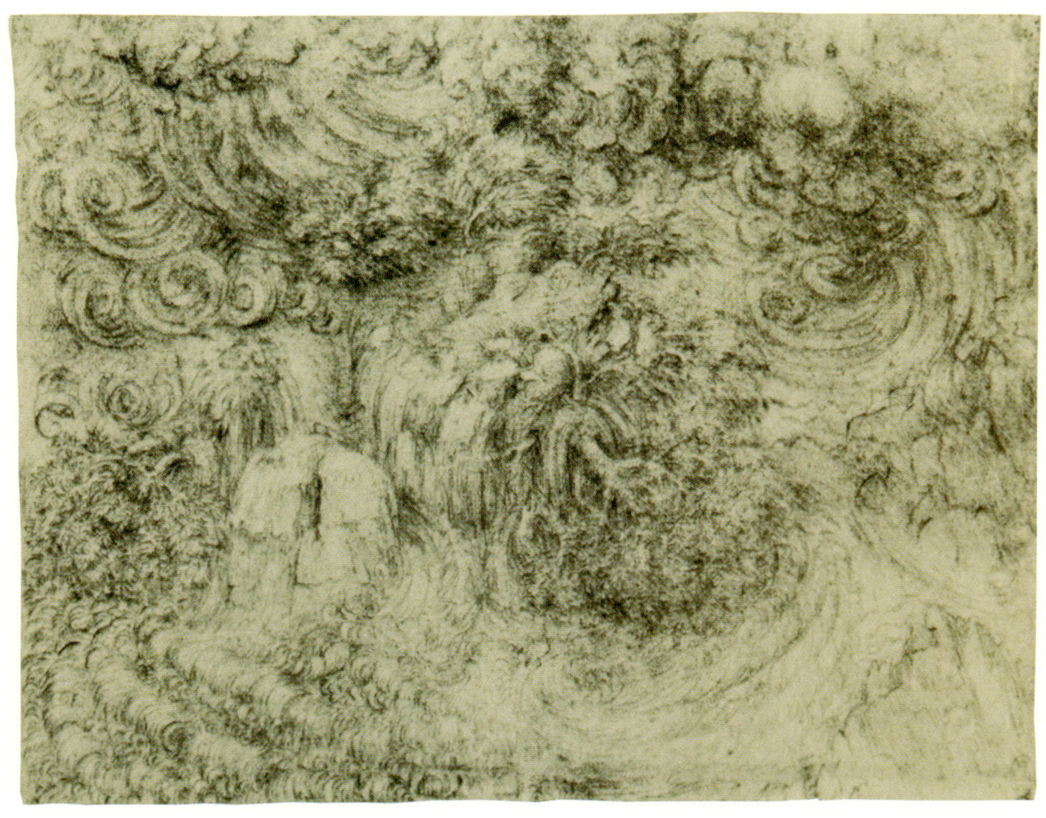

Leonardo da Vinci, *Collapse of a rock wall due to the erosion of water, c.* 1515. Pen and black and yellowish ink, on charcoal and watercolour, 162 x 203 mm. Windsor, RL 12380

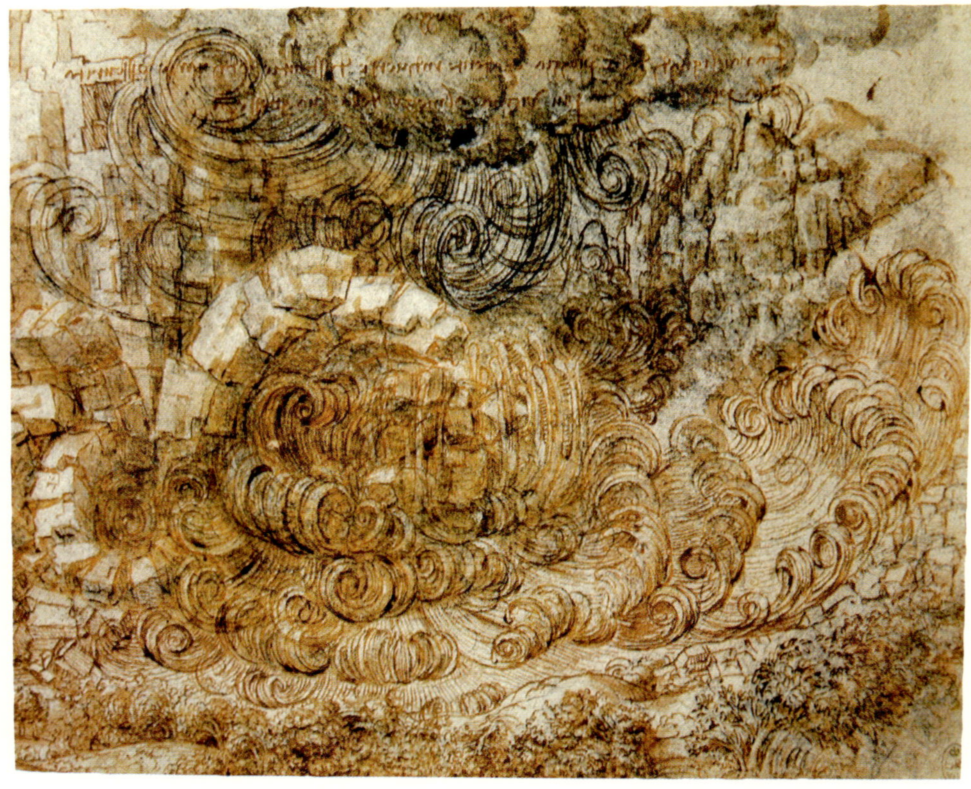

Leonardo da Vinci, *Hurricane, c.* 1517-18. Charcoal, 161 x 210 mm. Windsor, RL 12386

ment in operations of military strategy, on its erosive force and on its implicit function of alteration of the contours of reality. Since his first Florentine period, he had nourished an early interest for all, which concerned the world of hydraulics, the machines and even the «water instruments». In his drawings a great number of hydraulic devices was proposed, among which some types of pumps and particularly the employment of large cochleas or screws of Archimedes (III cent. b. C.), at an angle of 45°, in order to push water, with the spinning motion of a helicoidal surface inner to the tube, now from the current of a river up into a high depot, now, with continuous flow even up onto the top of two towers (CA, ff. 386 *rb* [1069 *r*]; 7 *va* [26 *v*]). Hence, studies made for the raising of water from wells or rivers, in order then to take advantage on a dynamic plan also of their fall effect [2] or in order to examine the weight of a waterfall: «way to weigh a fall of water» (CA, f. 5 *r-a* [19 *r*]). And still, in order to estimate the supply of the amount of water flowing from the mouths of channels, Leonardo planned and made really build the first hydraulic meter for the humanist and Medicean orator in Milan, Bernardo Rucellai (CA, f. 84 *r-c* [229 *r*]), as in his notes and technological drawings, transcribed from his son Benvenuto, Lorenzo della Golpaia (1446-1512) reports: «an instrument that Lionardo sent to Bernardo Rucellai from France made there from a peasant from Dom Dassoli which can be seen represented here» (Codex Marciano it. IV 41 = 5363; f. 7 *v*).[3]

Of Archimedes, the scientist who par excellence had rooted in the collective imaginary since antiquity for his inventive genius, Leonardo had studied with passion the prodigious discoveries: the relationship between circumference and diameter (the π) in the formula 22/7 (a relationship achieved by the Syracusan scientist subdividing the circumference in 96 parts and which Leonardo will want to subdivide in a million parts in order to demonstrate in vain the squaring of the circle; Cod. of Madrid II, f. 122 *r*; CA, ff. 118 *ra-va* [325 *rv*]); the study of levers and the application of forces, destined to the world of machines and to the calculation of their opportune mechanical advantage (CA, ff. 8 *vb* [30 *v*]; 216 *vb* [579 *r*]), the study on the parabolic mirrors, able to concentrate in just one point the solar beams (CA, f. 277 *r-a* [750 *r*]; Cod. Arundel, ff. 86 *v*-87 *r*)[4] and the study on the floatation of

bodies[5] and the «de centro gravitatis» (Ms. F, f. I cop. *r*), with the related problems of hydrostatic basis in calculating the advantages during the phases of construction of boats (CA, f. 153 *rb-rc-ve* [413 *rv*]).

Therefore, in the course of time, Leonardo diversified his interest for the employment of water, adhering to the traditional technical-scientific knowledge, consulting even works, among the wonders of mechanics of the masters of ancient times,[6] like the treatise of Phylos of Byzantium (end of III cent. b. C.) on the *Pneumatica* or science of the compressible fluids, based on phenomena provoked only artificially and derived from the researches of the talented Ctesybius of Alexandria (III cent. b. C.), from which Leonardo would have also learned, through the description made by Vitruvius (I cent. b. C.), the invention of the water-clock-hourglass with alarm (CA, f. 288 *ra* [782 *r*]), around 1508-10.[7]

Another treatise well kept in mind by Leonardo was the later *Spiritalia* by Heron (I cent. b. C.): a work that, containing indications for the construction of pumps, organs and automatons, would have allowed him, adhering to the experimental method, also to realize fountains (CA, ff. 292 *v-c* [798 *br*]; 293 *r-b* [800 *r*]), able to squirt with force a water spray as a result of the employ of a siphon (Windsor, RL 12690; 12691).

And the knowledge of the steam machine of Heron or 'aeolypila' («door of the wind»),[8] mentioned by Vitruvius,[9] would have influenced him in a decisive way during his research on the sources of energy for the construction of the «architronito» ('the steam cannon'; Ms. B, f. 33 *r*), already de-

---

[2]   See M. CIANCHI, *Le macchine di Leonardo*, introduzione di C. Pedretti, Firenze, Becocci, 1982; P. GALLUZZI, *Prima di Leonardo. Cultura delle macchine a Siena nel Rinascimento*, Milano, Electa, 1991; Id., *Gli ingegneri del Rinascimento, da Brunelleschi a Leonardo da Vinci*, Firenze, Giunti, 1996; C. STARNAZZI, *Leonardo. Codici e Macchine*, presentazione di C. Pedretti, Firenze, Cartei e Bianchi, 2005.

[3]   See C. PEDRETTI, *La macchina idraulica costruita da Leonardo per conto di Bernardo Rucellai e i primi contatori d'acqua*, «Raccolta Vinciana», XVII (1954).

[4]   Some topics of Archimede's *Catoptrica* are listed by Apuleius in *Apologia* (XVI).

[5]   In his treatise *On floatings* (I, 6), ARCHIMEDES looks for the calculation of the line of floatation of the solid ones in equilibrium dipped in a homogenous liquid, driven by reasons of naval engineering, enunciating the following postulate, from which his famous «principle» will derive: «Portions of liquid between them contiguous and at the same level are not in equilibrium if they are compressed in different measure […] and every portion is compressed by the weight of the liquid that is over it in vertical, provided that the liquid is not contained in something or compressed by something else».

[6]   An anonymous manuscript of the second half of the fifteenth century (*Additional Manuscript* 34113, British Museum), related to *Macchine idrauliche, di guerra* […], beyond to excerpts of the work of Vitruvius, contains the transcription of the *De ingeneis* by Mariano di Jacopo known as Taccola from Siena, based on the writings of Phylos of Byzantium and devoted to pneumatics and to military technology.

[7]   See M. E. ROSHEIM, *Leonardo's Lost Robots*, presentazione di C. Pedretti, Munich, Springer, 2006.

[8]   HERON, *Pneumatica*, II, XI.

[9]   VITRUVIUS, in his *De Architectura*, offers a complete representation of the scientific technology reached by the world of the Hellenistic civilization in the techniques of construction of buildings, of war machines, of automatons, of clocks and even of organs, as well as in the construction of reduction gears, clutch devices, pistons, escapement mechanisms, precision screws, cog-wheels, propellers, chains of transmission, machines for threading, which will be widely illustrated by LEONARDO in the Codex Atlanticus and in the Codices of Madrid, as «mechanical elements». To the work of Vitruvius and of Phylos of Byzantium was interested also FRANCESCO DI GIORGIO MARTINI, that in his *Trattato di architettura, ingegneria e arte militare* drew hydraulic wheels, suction pumps, endless screws, rack mechanisms. See P. GALLUZZI, *Prima di Leonardo… 1991, op. cit.*

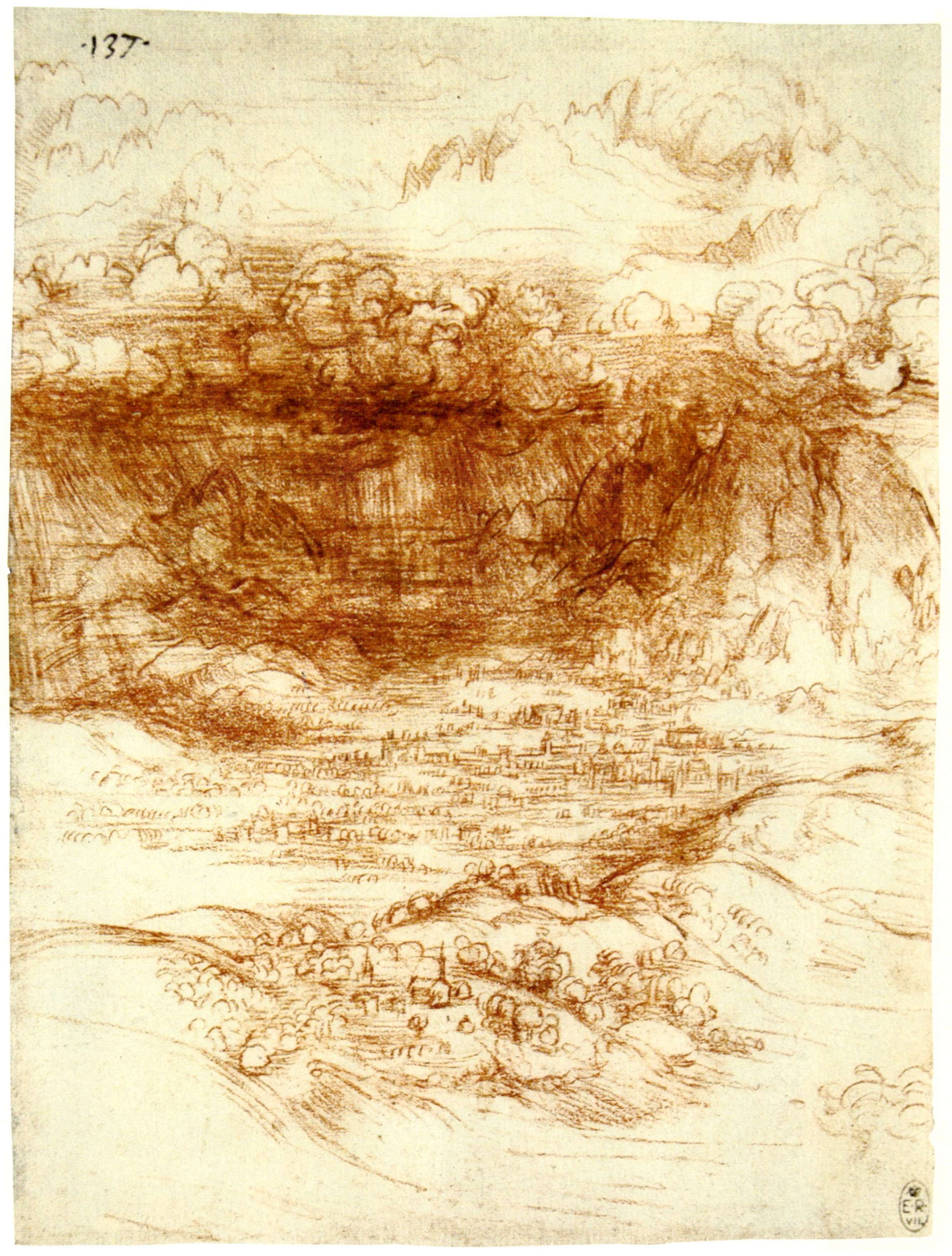

LEONARDO DA VINCI, *Thunderstorm on a valley, c.* 1500. Sanguine, 200 x 150 mm. Windsor, RL 12409

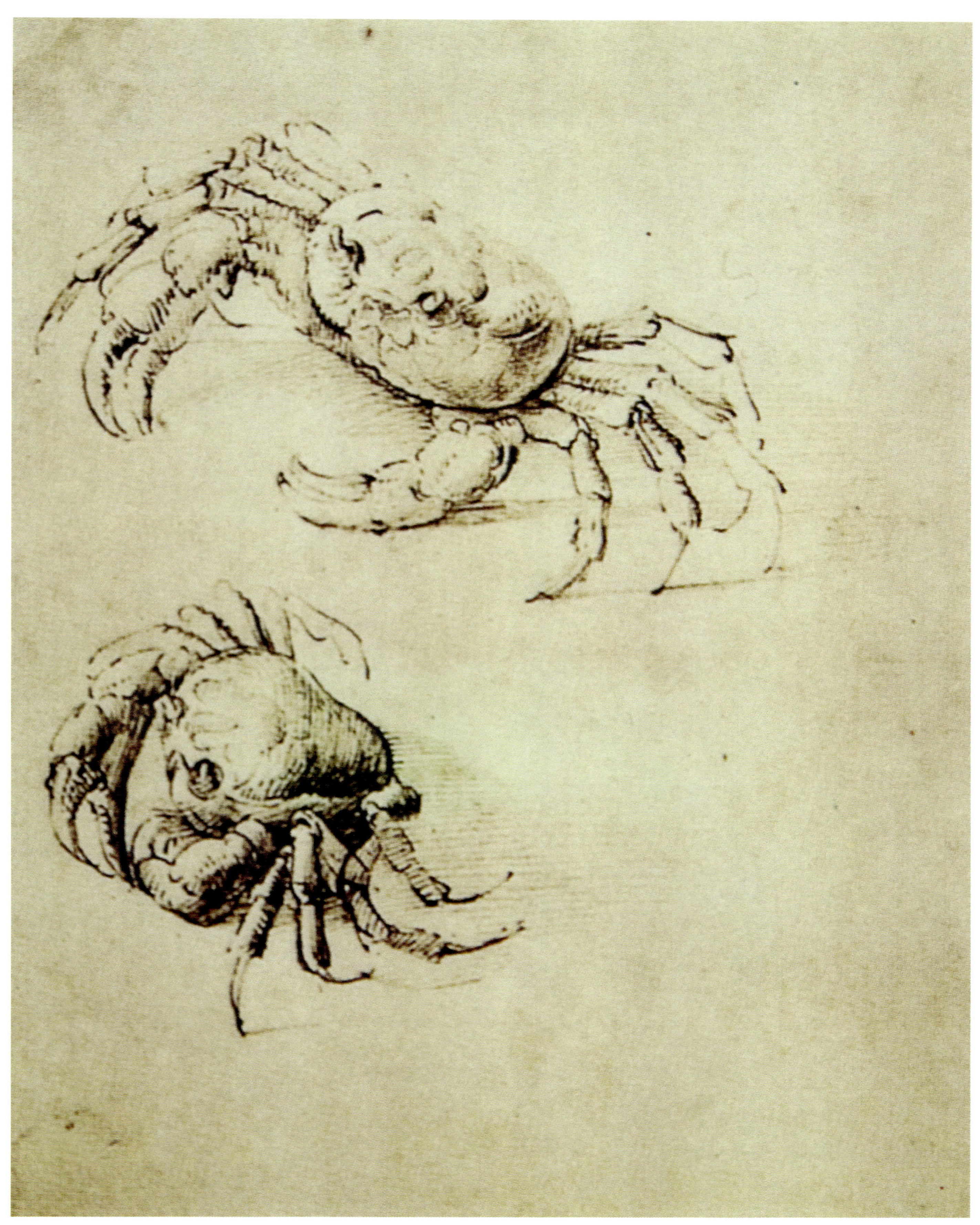

Leonardo da Vinci, *Study of crabs*, c. 1480. Pen and ink. Colonia, Wallarf-Richartz Museum, inv. N. Z2003 *v*

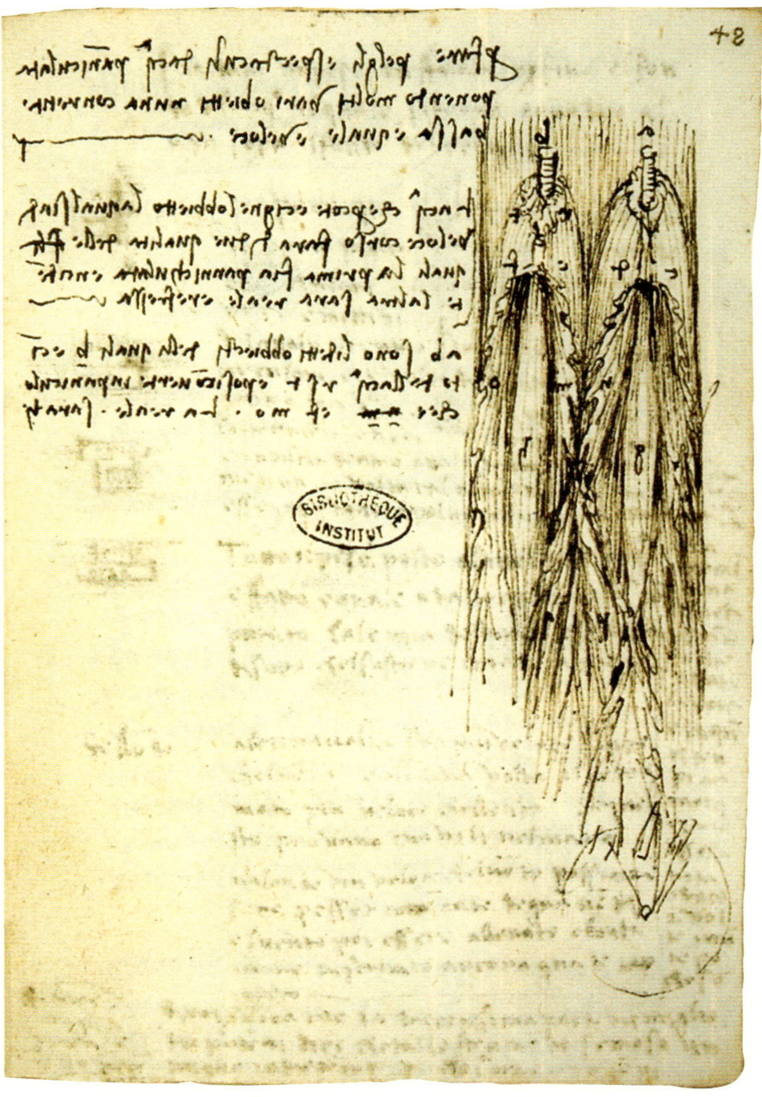

Leonardo da Vinci, *Studies of the lines of force in the currents of «paniculated water»*, 1508. Pen and ink, 145 x 100 mm. Ms F, f. 48 r. Paris, Institut de France

as a result one of the rare machines that take advantage of warm air as a source of energy. On the top of a vertical bar, placed at the narrowing of the flue, is positioned a propeller with four shovels. Turning faster or slower according to the intensity of the produced fire, the propeller moves a pulley in a completely automatic way by means of a gear formed with the coupling of a spindle and a toothed wheel. The pulley then transmits the rotatory motion to the spit. Under this drawing, Leonardo writes: «This is the true way to cook the roasts, since as the fire is moderated or strong, the roast is turned slowly or rapidly». He will remember then in the Codex Hammer the properties of vapour, applying them once again for the good operation of this instrument: «the water that blows through the narrow opening of the vase where it bubbles, blows with fury and it all is converted in wind: and with this [wind], the roast is turned». In the other drawing, placed in the upper part of the same sheet of the Codex Atlanticus (f. 5 *v-a* [21 *r*]), he explains a different type of spit, which can be set to action as a result of the falling of a weight, while its speed is moderated by a whirlwind provided with feathers. Thus the knowledge of Leonardo, as of the other contemporary artist-engineers (Giovanni Fontana, *Bellicorum instrumentorum Liber*; Mariano di Jacopo known as Taccola, *De ingeneis* and *De machinis*; Francesco di Giorgio Martini, *Trattato di architettura*; Vannoccio Biringuccio, *De la pirotechnia*), had been founded on experience, in close relation with science and technology and in full awareness of the necessary conjunction between practice and theory, and for that reason to estimate the motions and the qualities of water meant to comprehend the secrets and the universal principles of nature, in order then to bend them to the advantage of man: «When you gather the science of the motions of water, you must remember to put under every sentence the advantages it has, so that such science is not useless» (Ms. F, f. 2 *r*). Among his investigations of applied hydraulics, also the «sluices» (CA, ff. 46 *va* [126 *v*]; 361 *rb* [1007 *r*]) have a place of great importance, for the original technical solutions devised by his inventiveness. Leonardo planned their improvement, at the time of his interest for the Navigli of Milan (CA, f. 305 *ra* [831 *r*]), but in a particular way for the Martesana, in order to connect it to the inner Moat of the city, through the locks of Incoronata and of San Marco. Leonardo, in fact, in order to keep constant the level of waters in the channels, had devised to favour the strong hold of a sluice, making recourse to the use of angular shutters, while the inferior door, could be manoeuvred from above to diminish or to increase the capacity of the lock (CA, ff. 240 *rc* [656 *a-r*]; 341 *vb* [935 *r*]). For a similar door, Leonardo devised also a hinge placed off its centre, with the aim to guarantee a gradual opening under the push of water. Even in France, planning to drain the

vised by Archimedes and employed first in modern times just about 1865, during the American Civil War (the Winans cannon).[10]

Therefore, the knowledge of the qualities of vapour (Cod. Hammer, f. 10 *r*; Ms. E, f. 16 *v*) will allow him to devise various mechanisms in order to favour practical activities, like in the event of the vapour blower or of the way to transform water in vapour (CA, f. 400 *v-a* [1112 *v*]) or in making move the spit with a sort of warm air turbine (CA, f. 5 *v-a* [21 *r*]). Exactly the devising of the spit, expression of his continuous search addressed by Leonardo also in his juvenile years to the interaction between theory and practice, will have

[10] The possibility to take advantage of steam as a motive power will be reconsidered by G.B. Della Porta in his *Tre libri de' spiritali* (1606), derived from the *Pneumatica* of Heron.

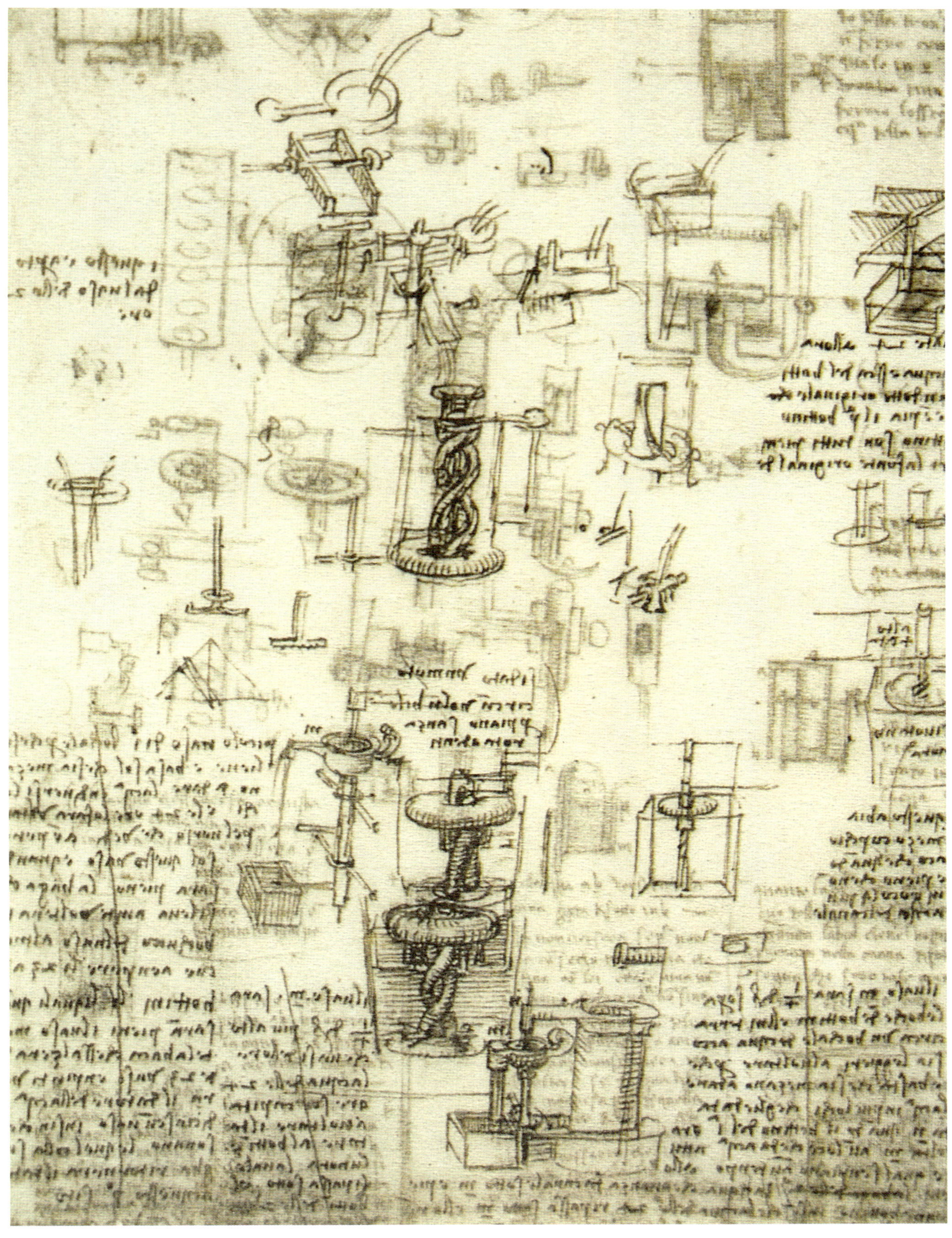

Leonardo da Vinci, *Water-clock-hourglass with alarm*, Pen and ink, 300 x 212 mm. Codex Atlanticus, f. 782 *r*. Milan, Biblioteca Ambrosiana. Particular

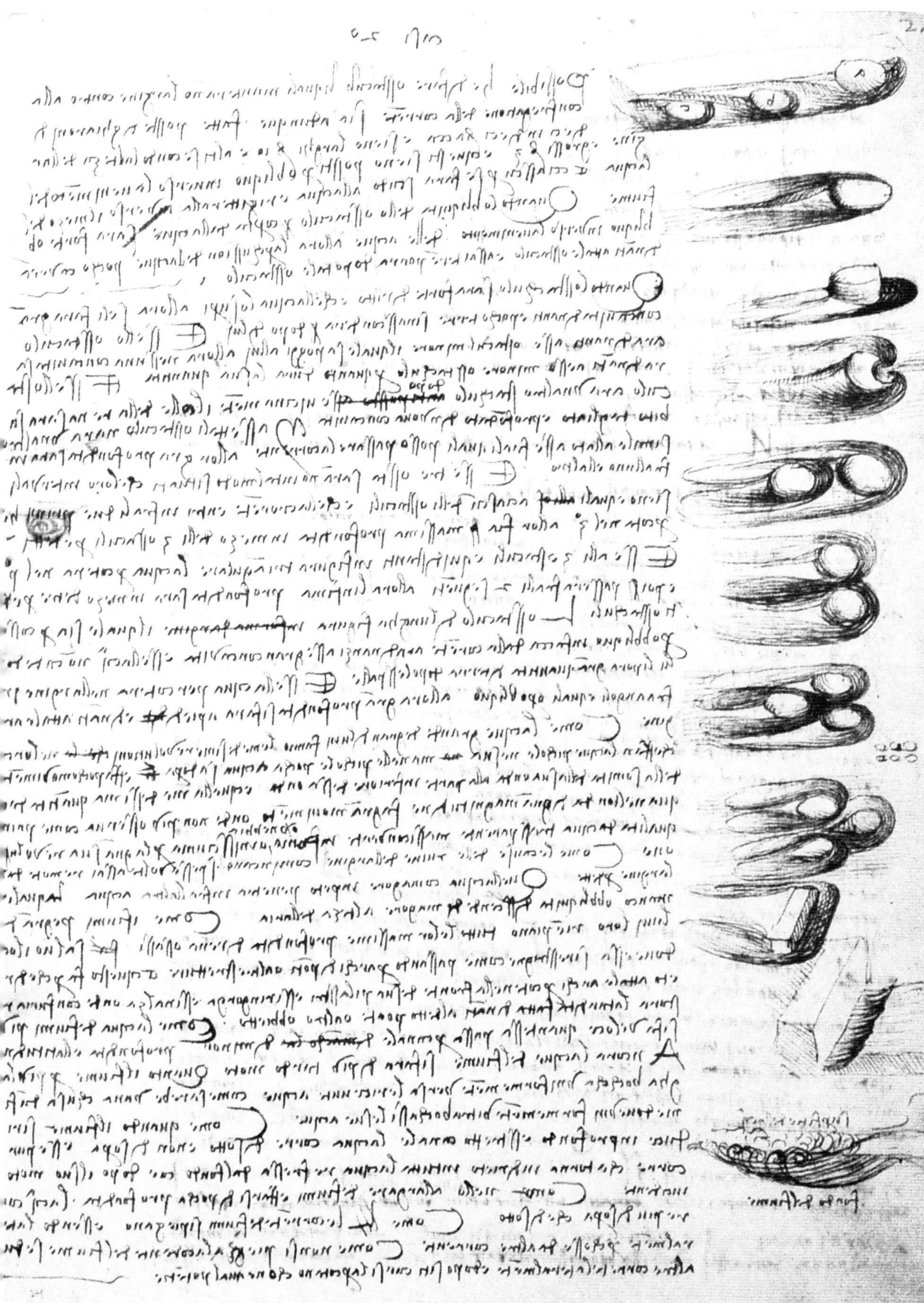

Leonardo da Vinci,
*Study of various shapes
of water flows*, c. 1509.
Pen and ink, 218 x 295 mm.
Hammer Codex,
f. 13B, 13 *v*–24 *r*

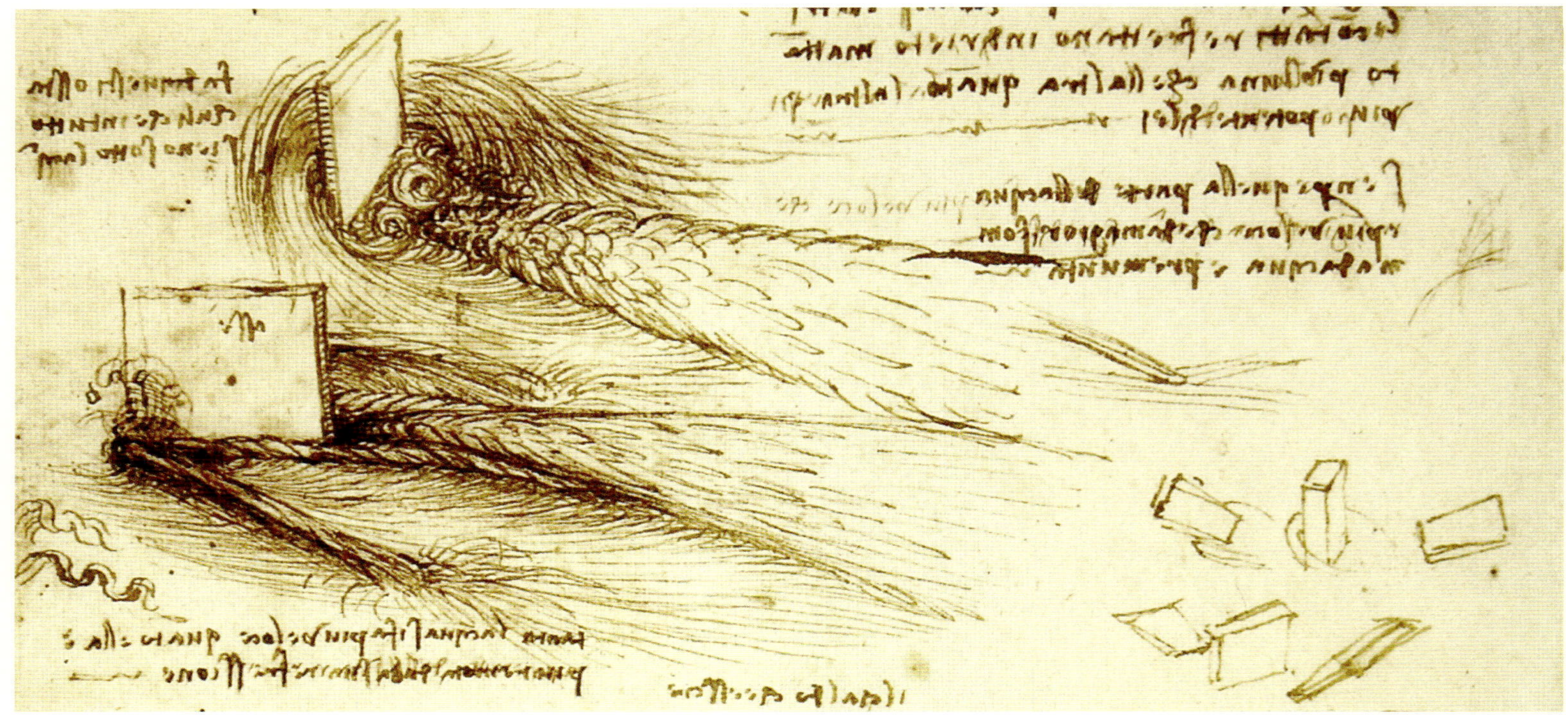

LEONARDO DA VINCI, *Study of hydrodynamics, c.* 1509-11. Red pencil, pen and ink, 290 x 202 mm. Windsor, RL 12660

Romorantin territory, the artist would have assumed to employ with great usefulness, along the course of the Cher and Sauldre rivers, the enclosure with rotating floodgates, that in the spring of 1500 he had already devised in Friuli, when he had to make recourse, on invitation of the Venetian Senate and for strategic purposes, to appropriate interventions of defence, that integrated the fluvial obstruction of the Isonzo with sluices and inundations.

Besides, other initiatives of military engineering (transport of artilleries), perhaps for the expedition of Francis I to Italy, in 1515, had been planned with the method that had been previously adopted in the fortifications of Gradisca, facing the feared invasion of the Turks («Bombards from Lyo<n> to Venice with the way that I gave to Gradisca in Friuli and in…»; CA, f. 79 *r-c* [215 *r*]):

The cataracts […] have to be many, so that it opens and it makes greater force […] And the mobile enclosure has to be made, the one that I ordered in Friuli, of which, opened one cataract, the water that of that one came out took away the ground (Cod. Arundel, f. 270 *v*).

Studies therefore also about the navigation locks that were destined, beyond regularizing the flow of water in the channel itself, to allow establishing the better technical solutions, so that the boats could go beyond strong unevenness and might then be able to pass through directly into the waterways. In planning them, Leonardo considered the related problems of the mechanics of fluids, revealing a perfect mastery of the «fundamental principle of hydrodynamics», that will be enunciated by Daniel Bernoulli (Cod. of Madrid I, f. 169 *r*), of the «principle of Pascal» and of the «principle of Archimedes», so much that he wrote with reference to it:

The great weight of the boat that passes through the river supported from the arc of the bridge, does not increase the weight to the bridge, because the boat weighs precisely, how much the weight of the water that such boat drives away from its place (CA, f. 361 *rb* [1007 *r*]).

Similar technical and technological investigations had accompanied also his grandiose plan to realize at the «Chiane of Arezzo», at the confluence of the Main Channel into the Arno and at a very short distance from the Bridge of Buriano, subsequently consecrated for its symbolic valence in the background of the *Mona Lisa* and of the *Virgin with the Yarn Winder,*[II] a work of high engineering: a bridge-channel, that might allow to put in communication the two water courses

---

[II] See C. STARNAZZI, *Leonardo in terra di Arezzo*, «Studi per l'Ecologia del Quaternario», 17, Firenze, 1995; ID., *Leonardo ad Arezzo. A. D. 2000. La Madonna dei fusi di Leonardo da Vinci e il paesaggio del Valdarno Superiore* (a cura di), con un contributo di C. Pedretti, Tiferno, Città di Castello, 2000; ID., *Leonardo e la Terra di Arezzo. Storia, Miti e Paesaggi*, presentazione di C. Pedretti, Cortona, Calosci, 2005.

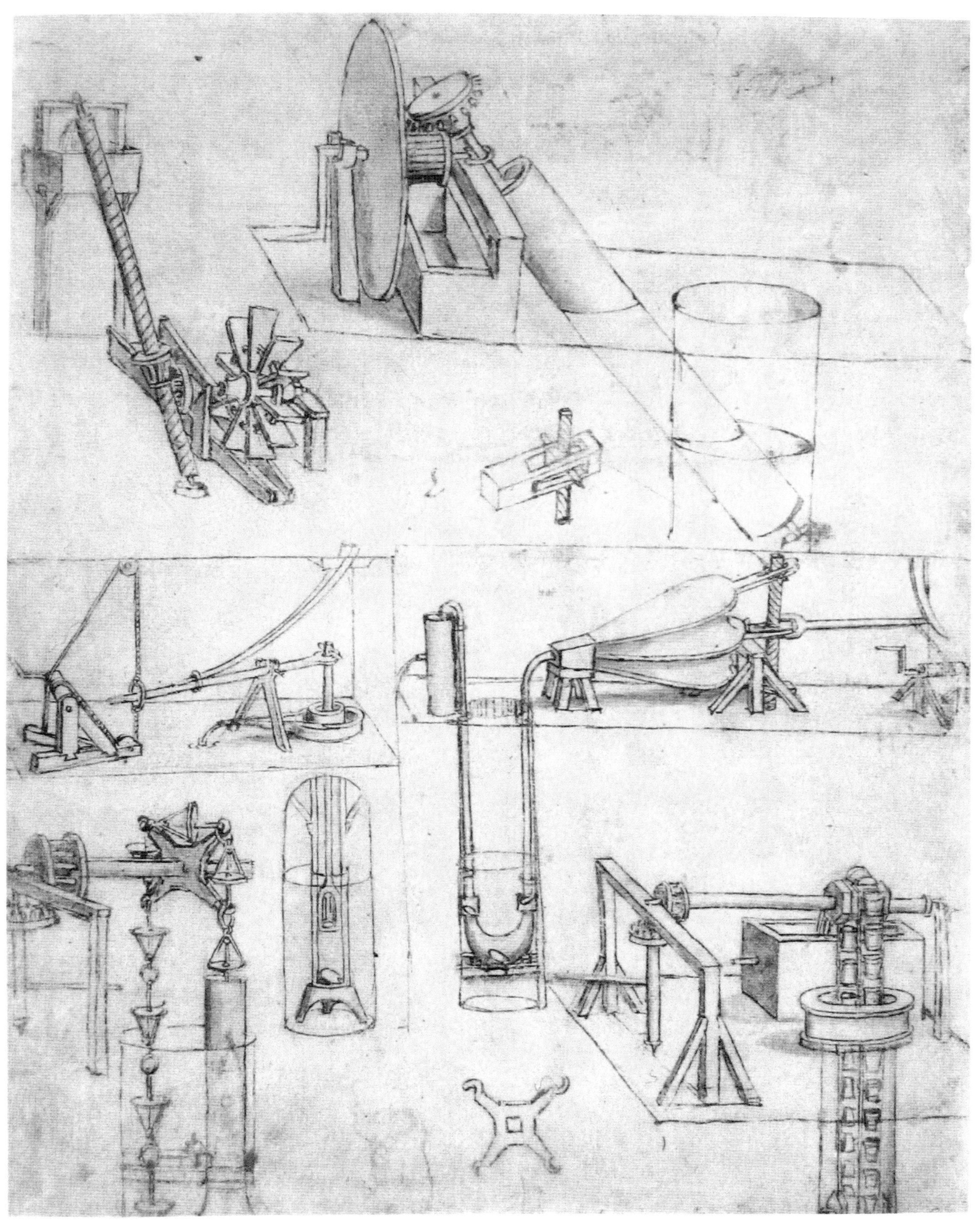

LEONARDO DA VINCI, *Studies of water pumps and of devices to lift water, c.* 1480. Pen and ink, 279 x 216 mm. Codex Atlanticus, f. 6 *r.* Milan, Biblioteca Ambrosiana

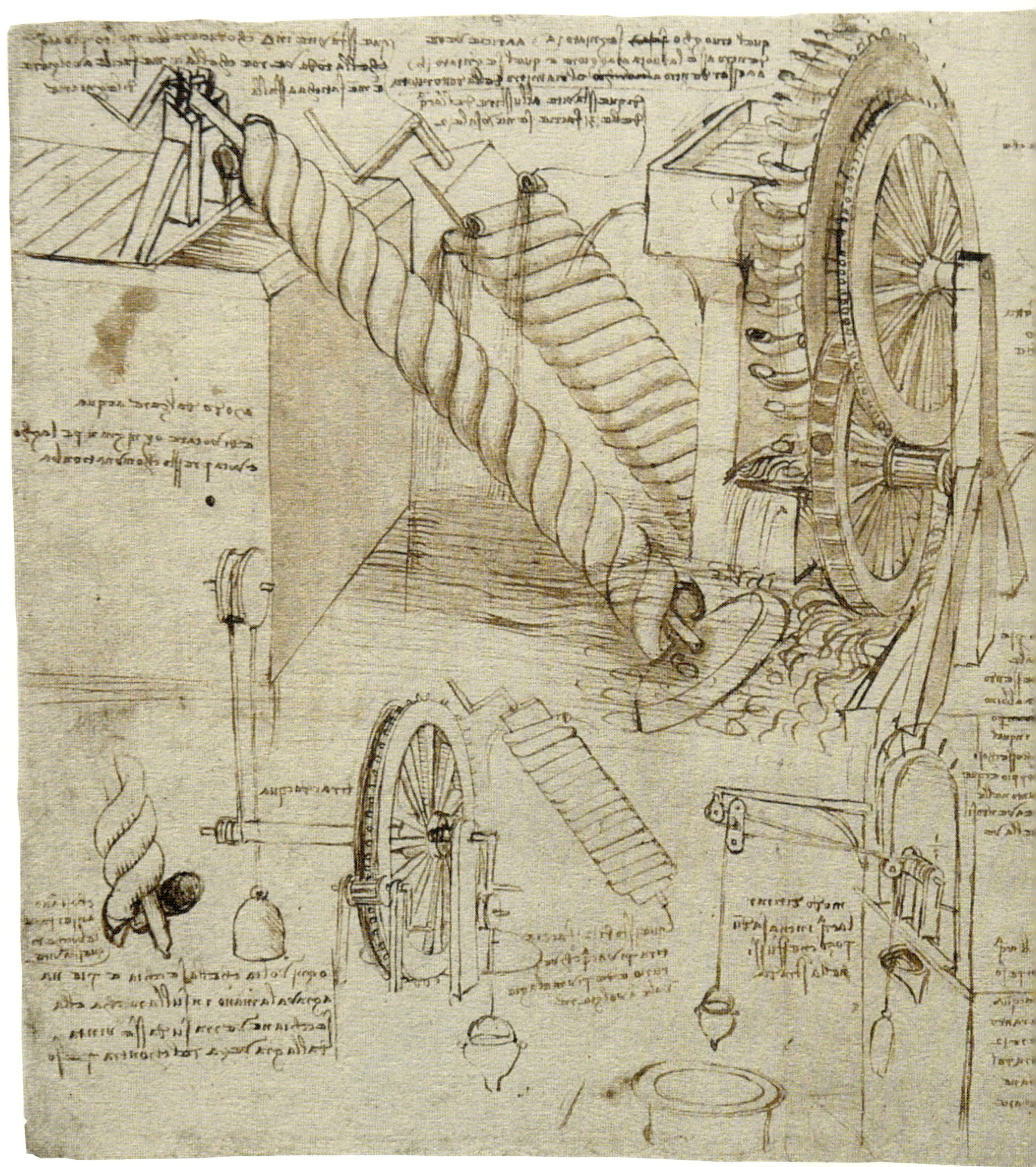

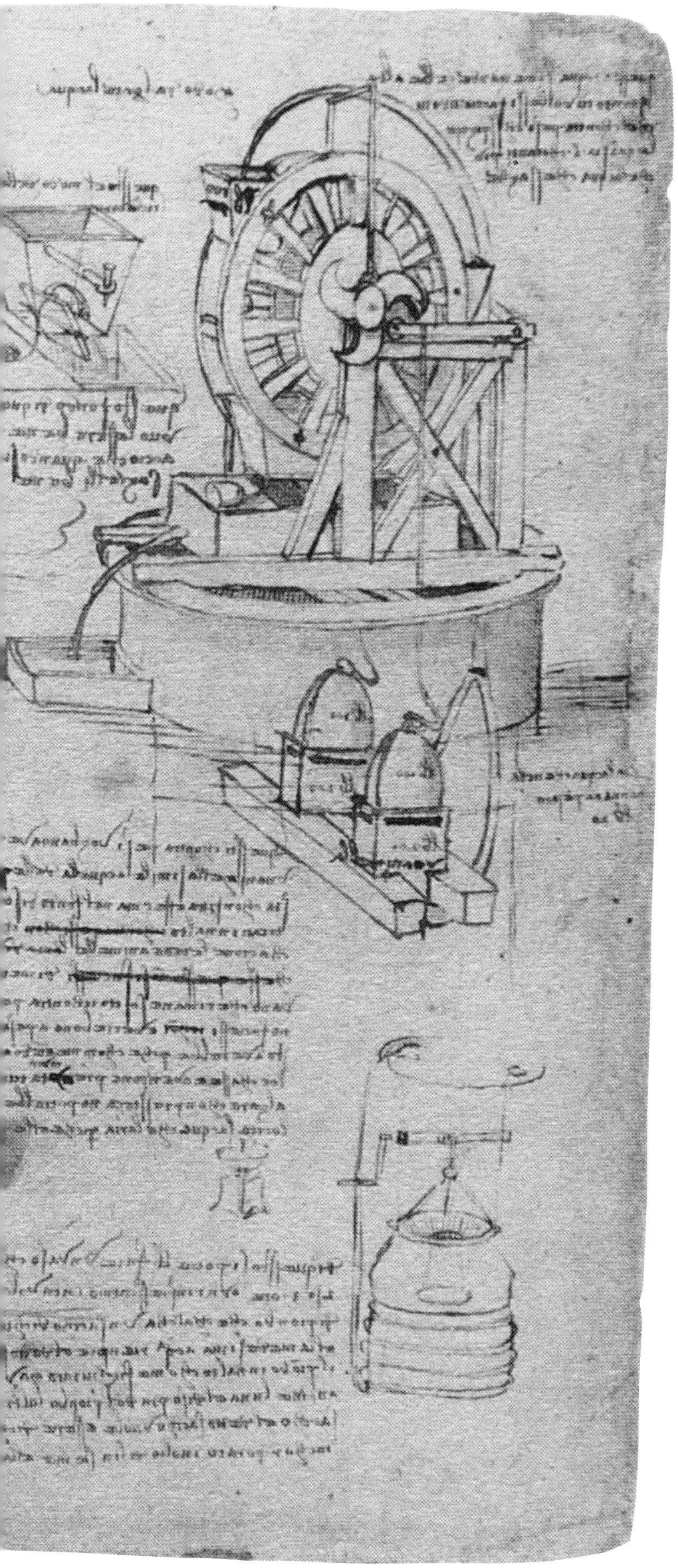

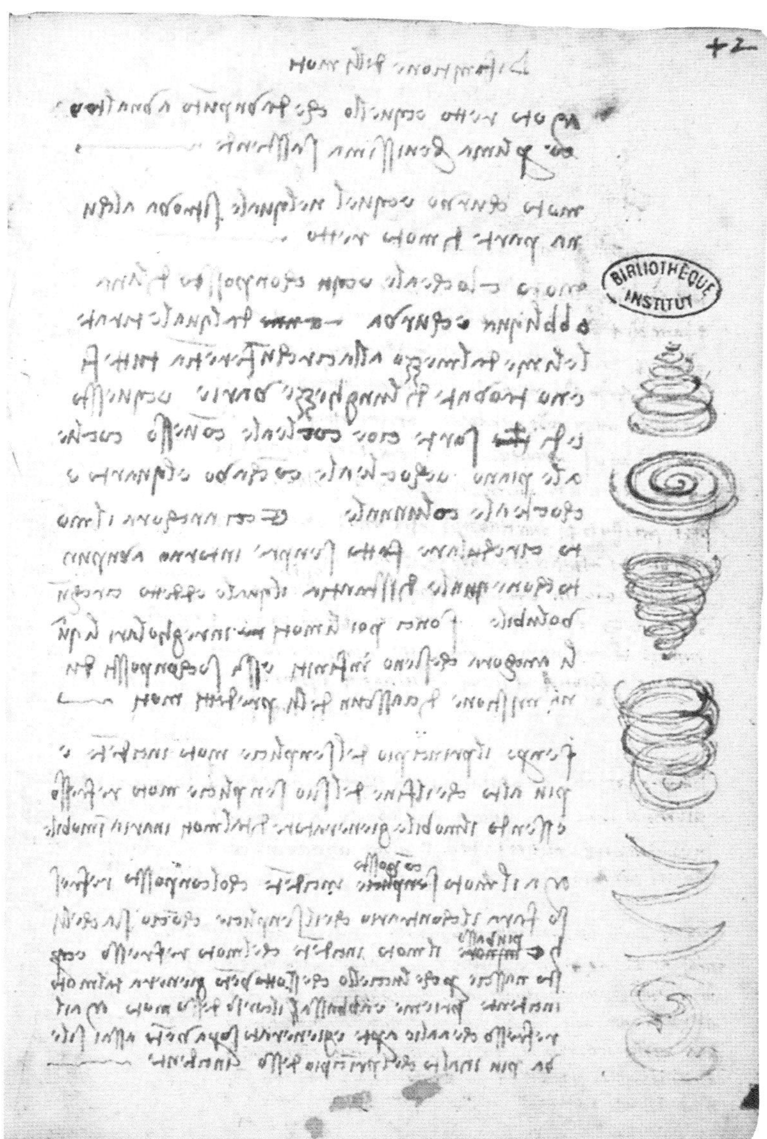

Leonardo da Vinci, *Examples of cochlear motion*, c. 1513-14. Ms E, f. 42 *r*. Paris, Institut de France

Leonardo da Vinci, *Archimede's Screws*, c. 1480. Pen and ink, 291 x 400 mm. Codex Atlanticus, f. 26 *v*. Milan, Biblioteca Ambrosiana

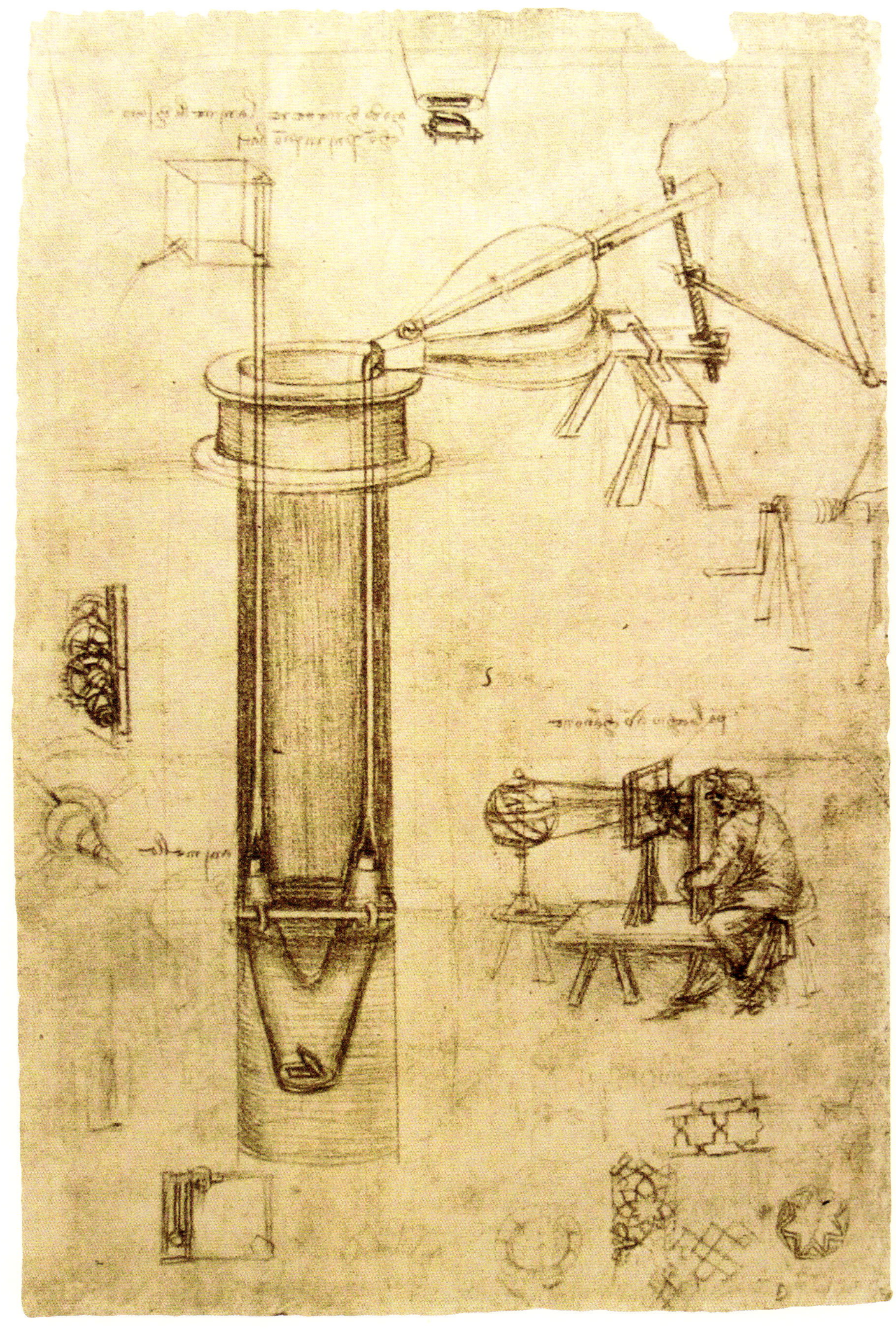

Leonardo da Vinci, *Machine with bellows to lift water and man with a perspectograph*, c. 1480. Pen and ink, 276 x 216 mm. Codex Atlanticus f. 5 *r*. Milan, Biblioteca Ambrosiana

(CA, f. 46 *va* [126 *v*]).[12] In the sheet, Leonardo, referring to matters of hydraulic activity for the digging of the channels and the crossing of the river with a suspended channel, recommended to make recourse to workers, to employ for a better efficiency and a lesser cost with a precise seasonal scansion that is from the period that goes from half March to half June, because «the villains, being out of their ordinary work, can be hired at a good price, and the days are great and the heat does not exhaust them».

In this extraordinary work (CA, f. 46 *rb* [127 *r*]), the artist-scientist had planned also the employment of sluices both in order to allow the passage to a wider number of boats and in order to favour a continuity of navigation with the intention to improve the outflow of waters towards the main river and to maintain constant their level in its canalization, that he was planning for the interests of the Wool Guild from Florence to Pisa. From this operation, on which Leonardo made an estimate of the expenses, it was not separated the idea of the drainage of the entire region, with the result of enormous economic advantages also for all the other Tuscan cities:

Channel of Florence. Florence - Prato - Pistoia - Serravalle - Lake - Lucca - Pisa. At the chiane d'Arezzo, such cataracts have to be made there that, lacking water in the Arno on summer, the channel does not remain dry. And such channel has to be made wide at the bottom 20 and 30 at its mouth, and always 2 arms of <wa>ter or 4, so that two of these arms <are> used by flour mills and fields. That will reclaim the country; and Prato, Pistoia and Pisa together with Florence it will be the year better two hundred thousand ducatoes and they will give their hands and expense to this assistance, and the inhabitants of Lucca the same. So that the lake of Sesto may be navigable, I wanted to follow the way of Prato and Pistoia and to cut through Serravalle and to exit in the lake, because it does not need locks or supports, which are not eternal, and indeed we are always at work to operate them and to maintain them. In addition,

you must know that if digging the channel where it is deep 4 arms, it costs 4 pieces of money for square arm, in double depth it costs 6 pieces of money. If you make 4 arms, they are only 2 banks, that is the one from the bottom of the ditch up to the surface of the edges of the ditch, and the other one from these edges up to the top of the earth that rises from the shore of the embankment. And if it were of double depth the embankment would increa<s>e only of one bank, that is 4 arms, that increases the half of the first expense; that is to say, that where before for two banks they received 4 pieces of money, for 3 it costs 6 pieces of money, at 2 pieces of money each bank, being the ditch at its bottom of 16 arms. Still if the ditch were wide 16 arms and deep 4, costing 4 pennies each work, 4 pieces of money of Milan the square arm, the ditch that at the bottom will be 32 arms, it will cost 8 pieces of money the square arm.

The same Giorgio Vasari (1550; 1568), highlighting the high mastery of the science of waters of Leonardo and his technical ability in preparing original solutions in works of hydraulic engineering, would have annotated that «every day he made models and drawings to be able to easily unload mountains and drill them in order to pass from a plane to another and by means of levers and winches and screws he showed that great weights could be raised and pulled and [showed] ways to empty harbours and pumps to take low waters away of places». And then that intelligence, continued in his praise the historian of Arezzo, as it had already emphasized the Neapolitan humanist Pomponio Gaurico in his *De sculptura* (1504),[13] where he had recognized his well known virtues of «archimedaean genius», it never ceased dreaming up, to such an extent that since when he was young he had meant to divert the course of the river Arno and «to put it in a channel from Pisa to Florence».

---

[12] See G. CALVI, *I Manoscritti di Leonardo da Vinci in ordine cronologico, storico e biografico*, Bologna, Zanichelli, 1925; C. STARNAZZI, *Un ponte-canale presso il Ponte di Buriano*, in ID., *Leonardo cartografo*, introduzione di C. Pedretti, Firenze, I. G. M., 2003.

[13] «Et ipse Alverochii discipulus Leonardus Vincius, equo illo, quem ei perficere non licuit, in Bois maximo, pictura Symposii nec minus et archimedaeo ingenio notissimus», P. GAURICO, *De sculptura*, Firenze, Giunti, 1504. See P. GAURICUS, *De sculptura*, edited by A. Chastel e R. Klein, Genève, Droz, 1969. [«And the same Verrocchio's disciple Leonardo da Vinci, much renowned for that huge horse, which he was not allowed completing, for his painting of the Symposium not less than for his archimedaean genius». Tr. N.]

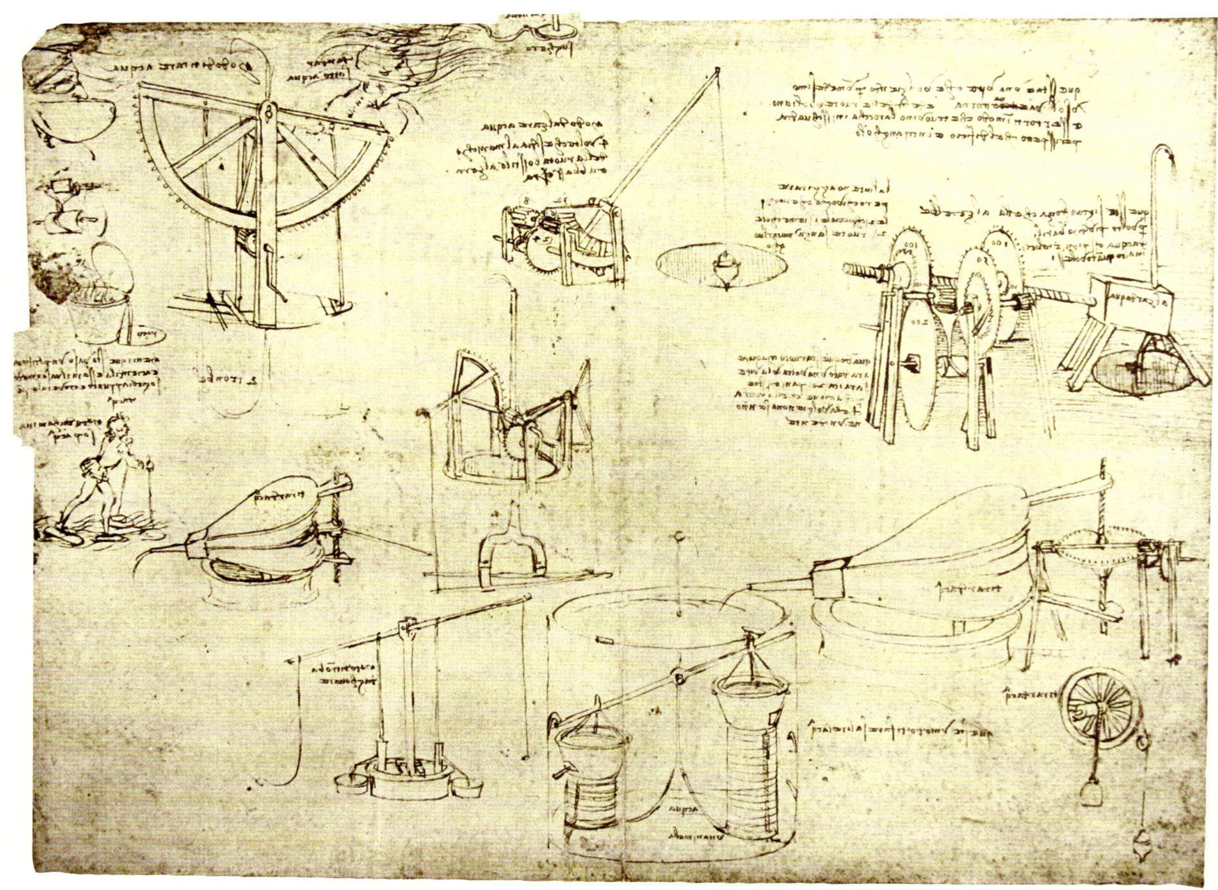

Leonardo da Vinci, *Use of water as an energy source. Studies on the way to walk on water and to breathe under its surface,* c. 1480. Pen and ink, 230 x 165 mm. Codex Atlanticus, f. 26 r. Milan, Biblioteca Ambrosiana

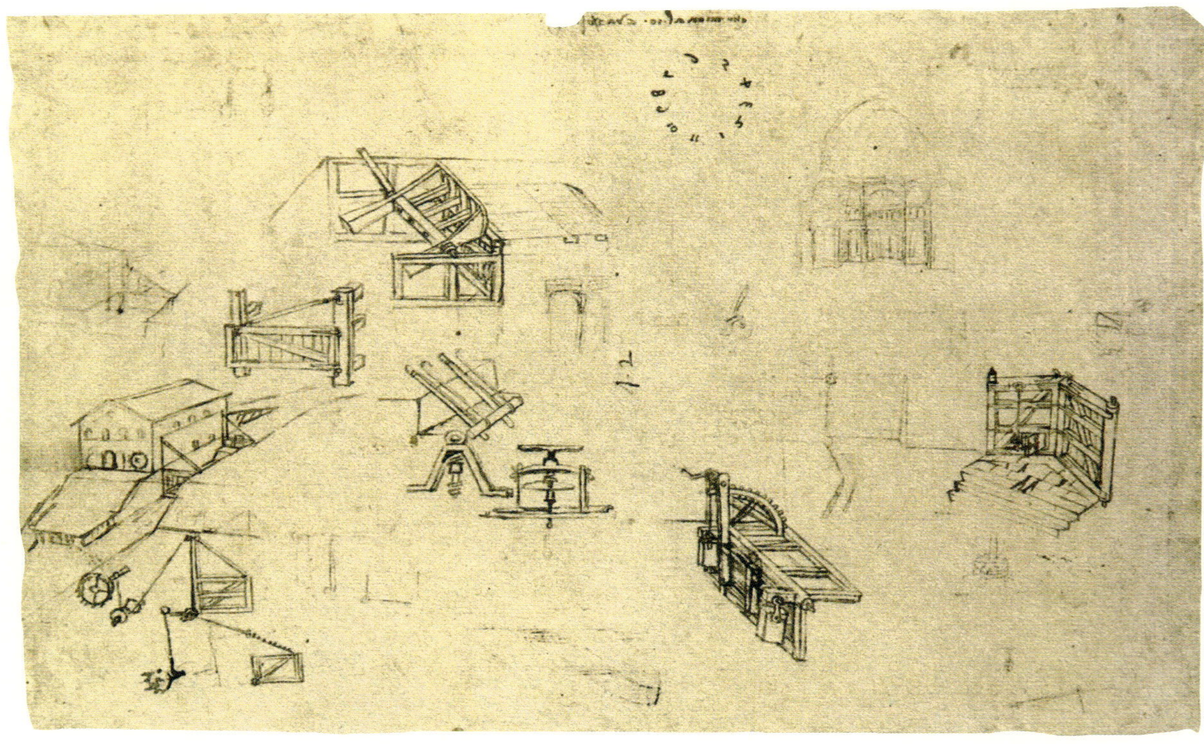

Leonardo da Vinci, *Systems of locks for fluvial navigation,* c. 1485. Pen and ink, 196 x 282 mm. Codex Atlanticus, f. 28 r. Milan, Biblioteca Ambrosiana

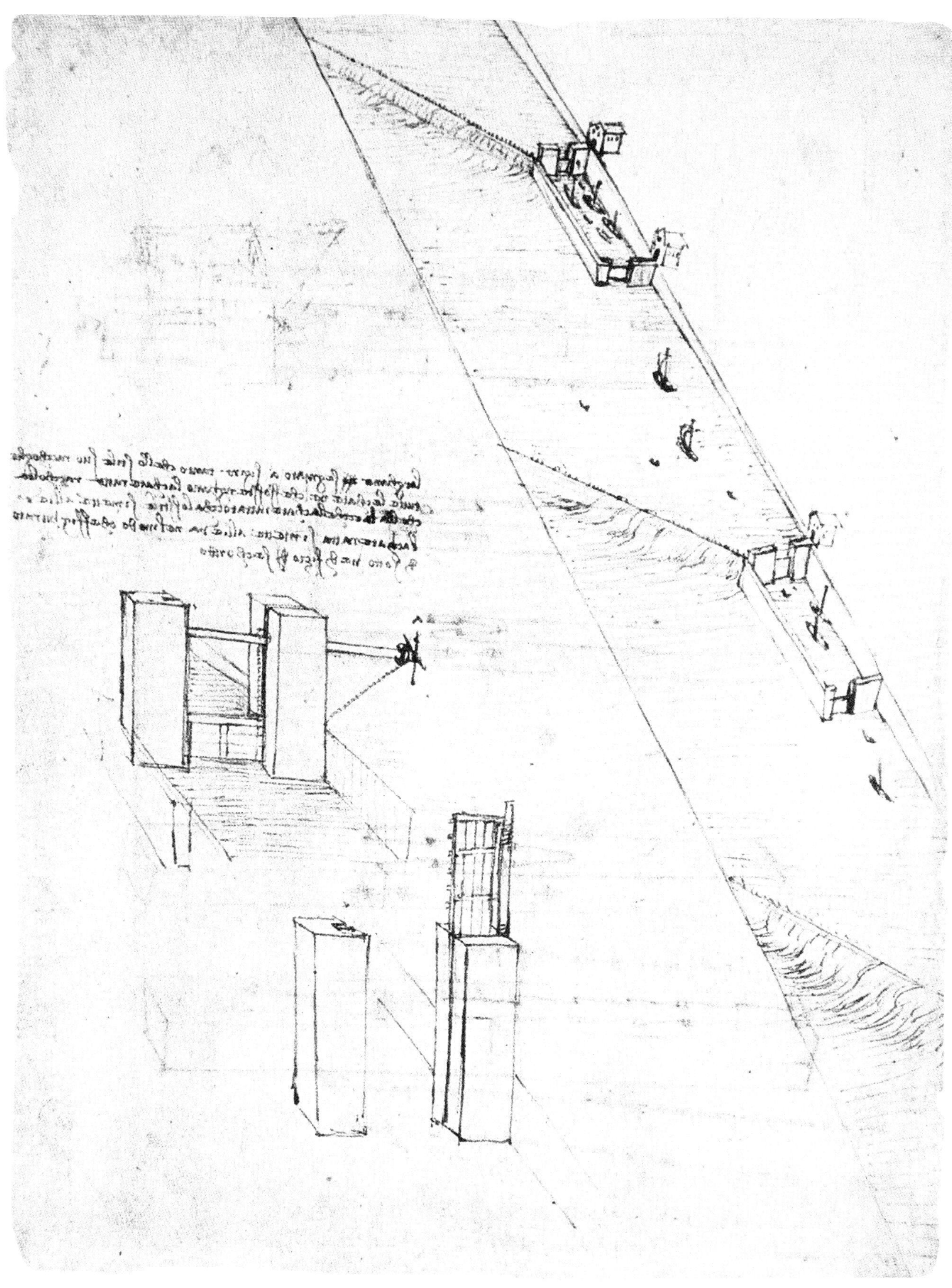

Leonardo da Vinci, *Systems of locks for river navigation*, 1480–82, Pen and ink, 284 x 212 mm. Codex Atlanticus, f. 90 *v*. Milan, Biblioteca Ambrosiana

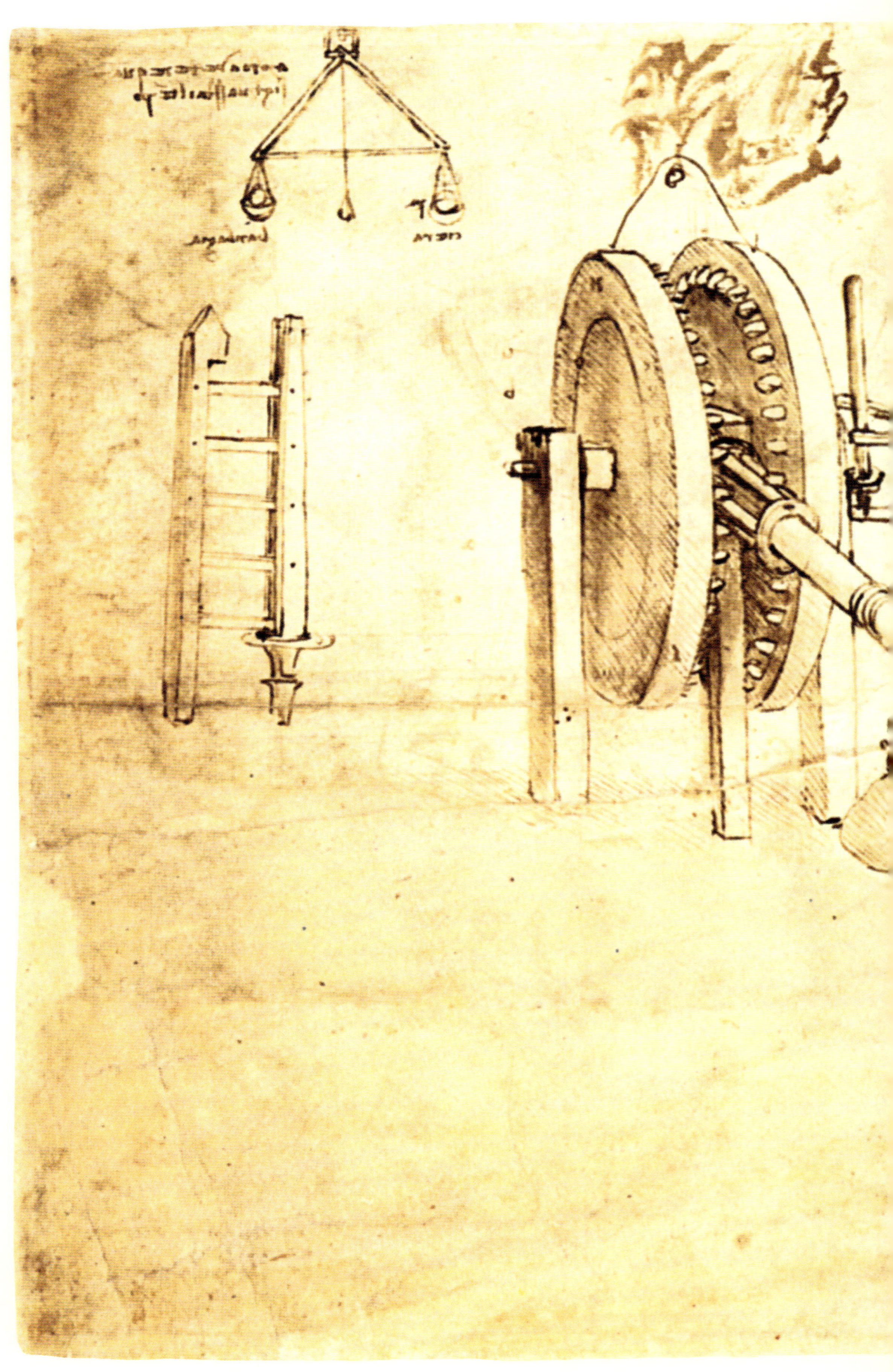

LEONARDO DA VINCI, *Hygroscope and device with transformation of alternated motion into continuous motion*, c. 1478-80. Pen and ink, 278 x 385 mm. Codex Atlanticus, f. 30 *v*. Milan, Biblioteca Ambrosiana

CARLO STARNAZZI

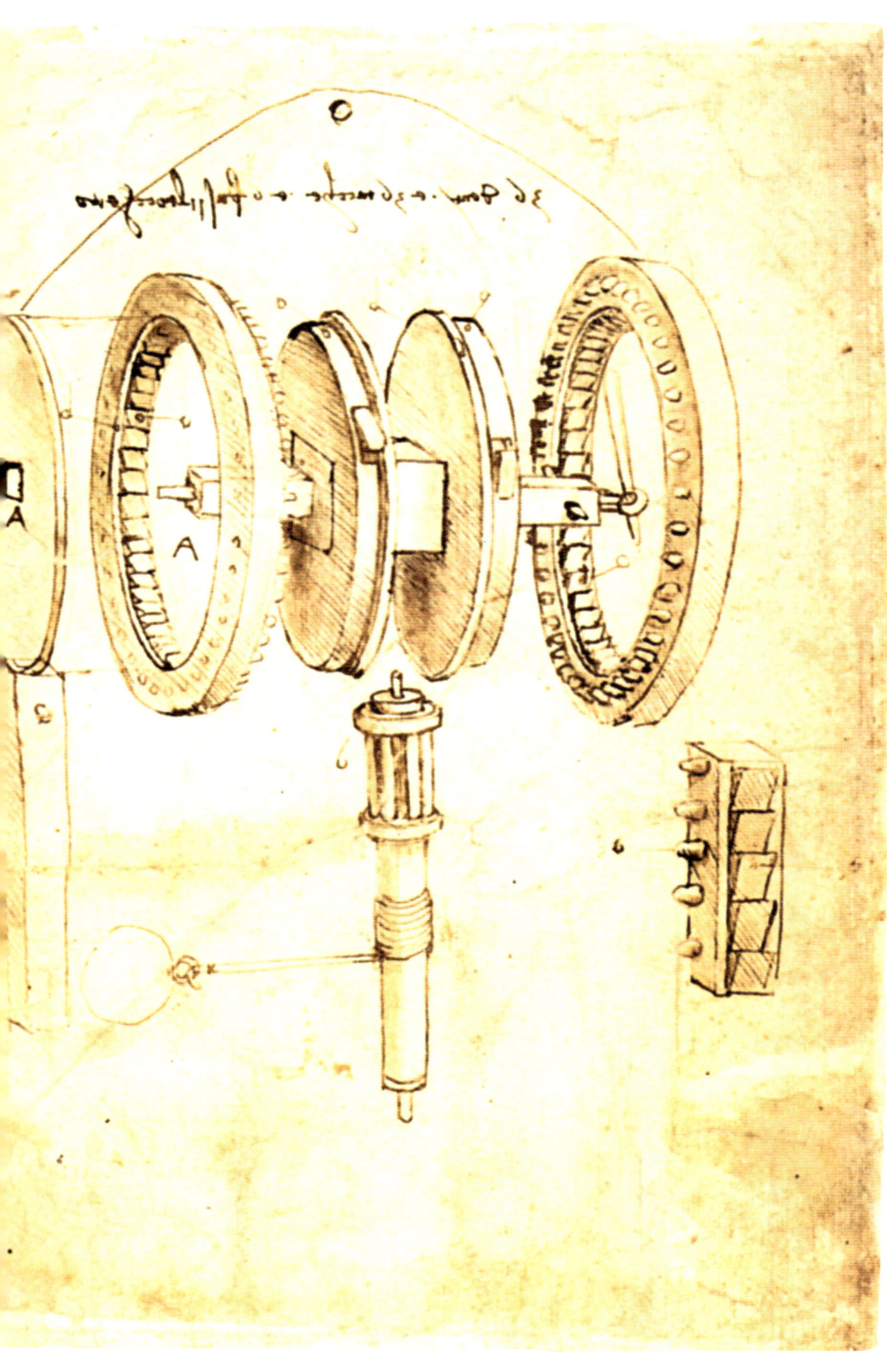

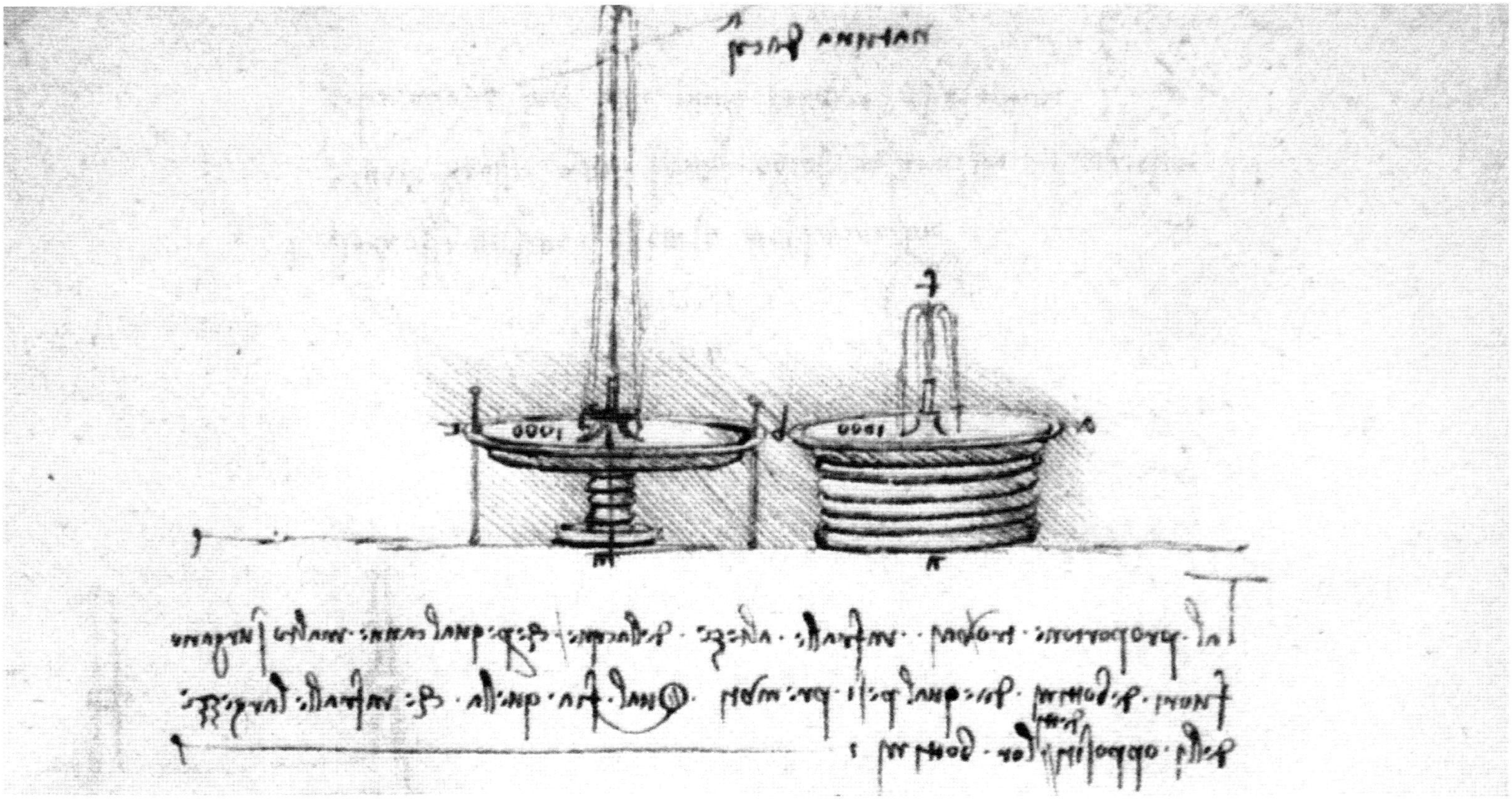

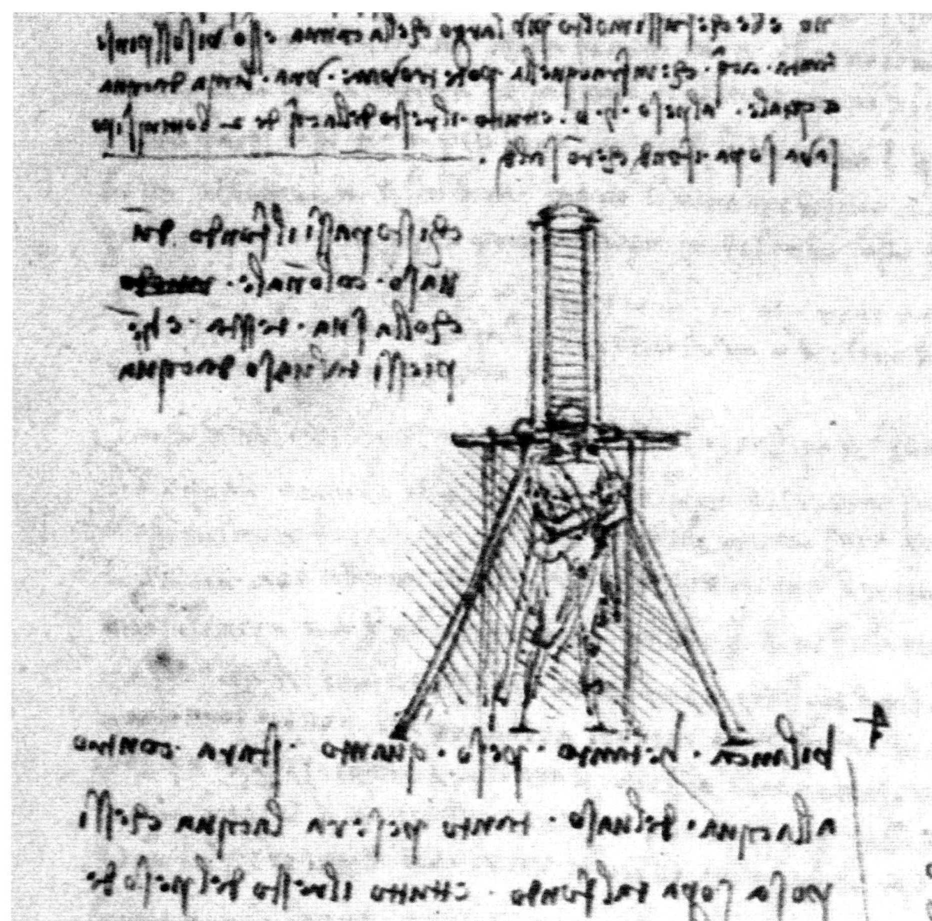

Leonardo da Vinci, *Studies on the pressure of water,* c. 1492-1495. Codex of Madrid I, f. 124 *v*. Madrid, Biblioteca Nacional

Leonardo da Vinci, *Study on the pressure made by a column of water over the head of a man submerged at its basis, c.* 1492-95. Codex of Madrid I, f. 150 *r*. Madrid, Biblioteca Nacional

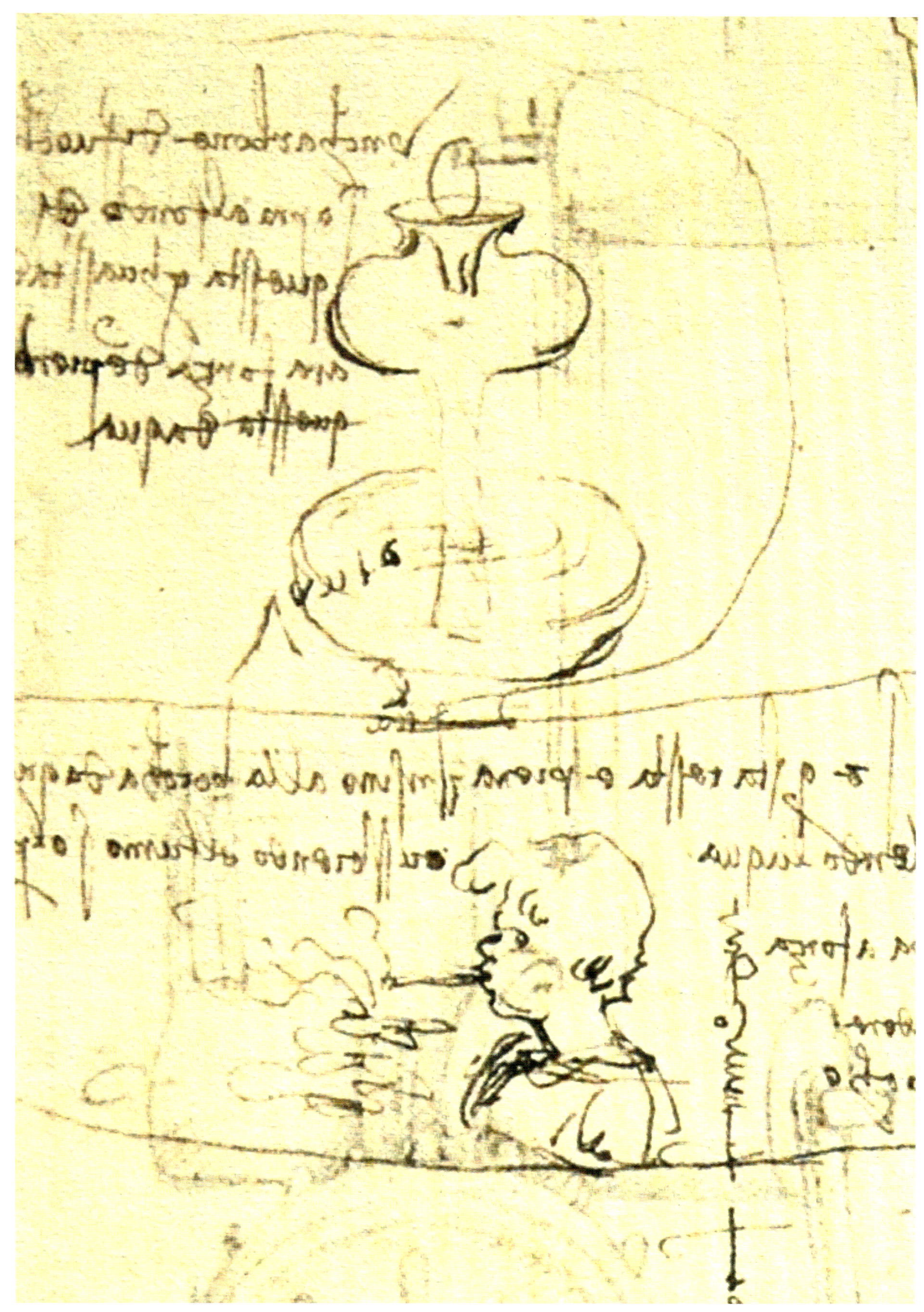

Leonardo da Vinci, *Steam blower to light a fire, c.* 1480. Pen and ink, 203 x 286 mm. Codex Atlanticus, f. 1112 *v.* Milan, Biblioteca Ambrosiana. Particular

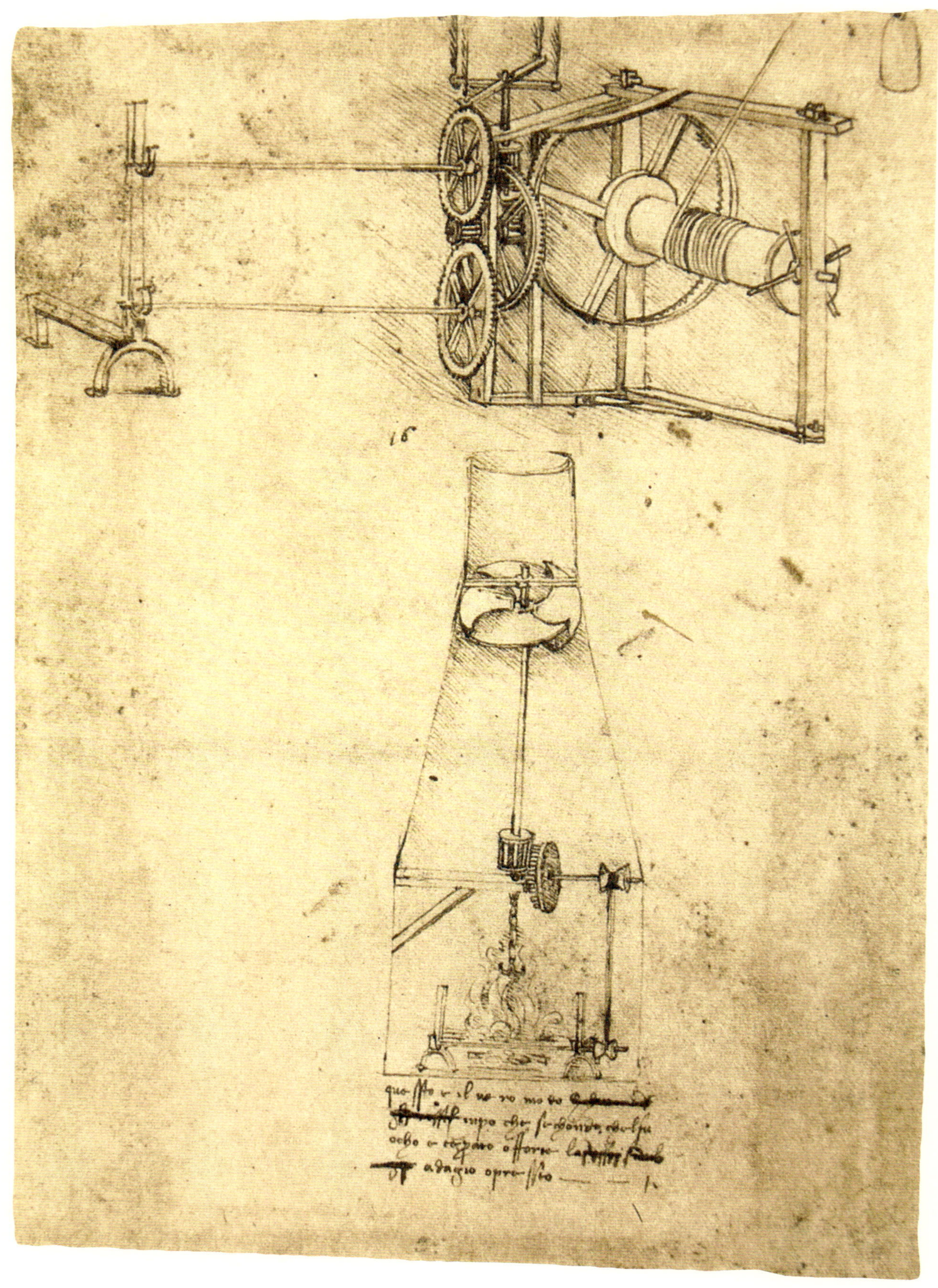

LEONARDO DA VINCI, *Spit moved by hot air*, c. 1480. Pen and ink, 255 x 191 mm. Codex Atlanticus, f. 21 r. Milan, Biblioteca Ambrosiana

 CARLO STARNAZZI

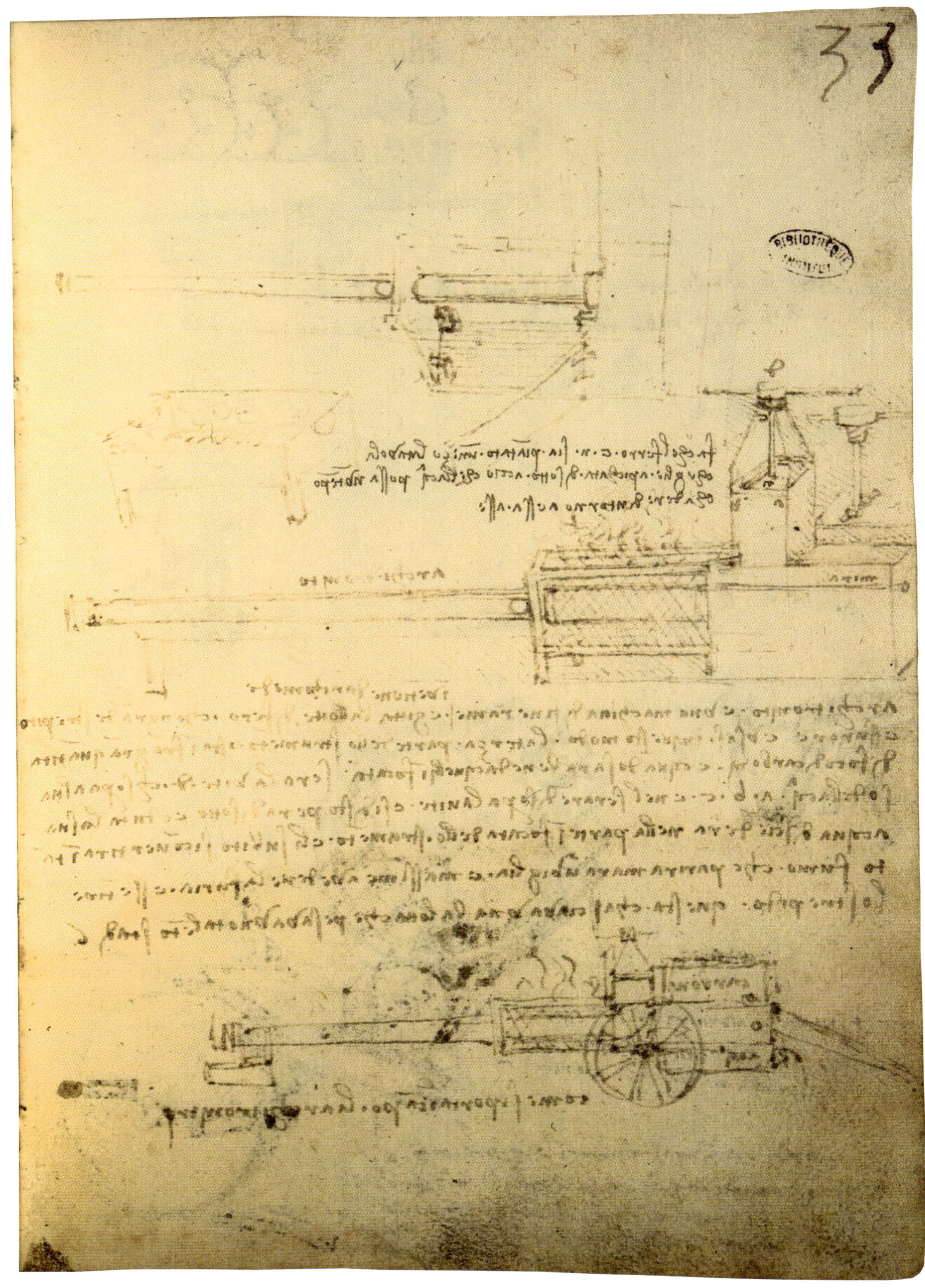

Leonardo da Vinci, *Steam cannon or «architronito»*, *c.* 1487-90. Pen and ink, 231 x 167 mm. Ms. B, f. 33 *r*. Paris, Institut de France

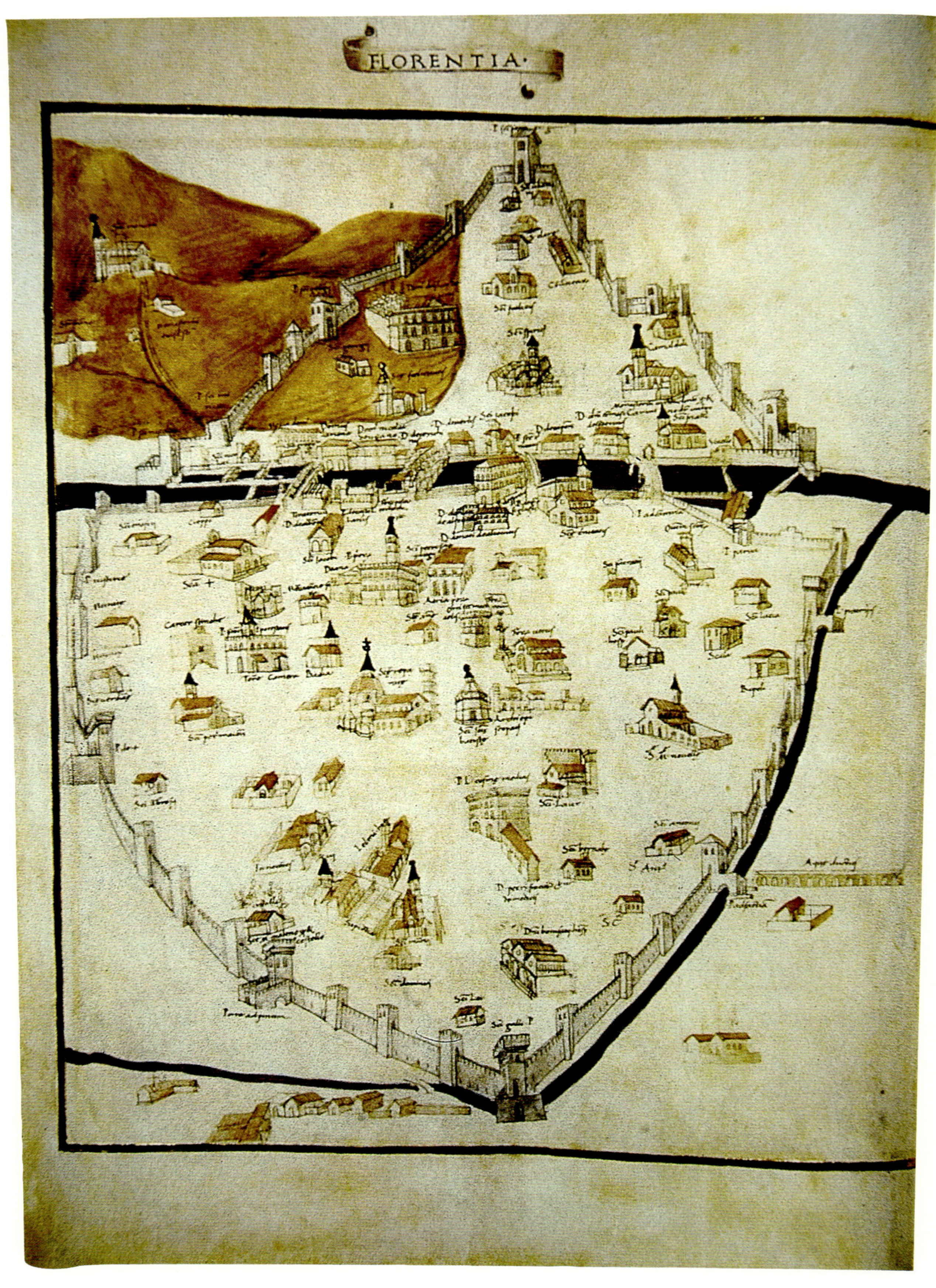

Piero del Massaio, *View of «Florentia»*, c. 1472. From the *Cosmographia* by Claudius Ptolemaeus, in the writing by Jacopo d'Angelo. Urb. Lat., 277, c. 130 *v.* Rome, Biblioteca Apostolica Vaticana

II. Leonardo and the workshop of the painter-cartographer

IN THE second half of the fifteenth century it had become established in Florence the workshop of the painter-cartographer, specialized in the realization of elegant nautical and of the mainland maps, as well as of urban and regional plans that, forever abandoned the iconographical formulation of the medieval maps of the world, written more on a philosophical-religious basis than on a scientific one,[14] will be printed and will be sold to enrich the libraries of the most important Italian courts.

This rebirth of cartography was essentially due to the rediscover during the Humanism of the literary and scientific texts of the ancient authors, among which Claudius Ptolemy, the greatest geographer of the Graeco-Roman antiquity.

The *Cosmographia* by Ptolemy, considered a «Bible» by all the geographers of the fifteenth century, is present in Florence from the very beginning of the century, as property of Palla di Nofri Strozzi. In 1397, the Byzantine Manuele Crisolora, who had reached Florence on invitation of the chancellor of the Florentine Republic, Coluccio Salutati,[15] to teach the Greek language,[16] will bring to the city the work of Ptolemy, which will receive, after the translation in Latin carried out by the humanist Iacopo Angeli from Scarperia (*c.* 1409), several and elegant editions.

The Ptolemaic maps for the first time placed the West in front of a systematic illustration of the known world, but they were also the occasion, above all in the Florentine environment, where a strong interest for geography had diffused among the humanists,[17] to begin to portray with scientific criteria a diversified and more correct geomorphological description of the territory, executing some corrections to the same Ptolemaic calculations both on the plan of the longitude «versus oriens»,[18] than in relation to the outline of the coasts, that turned out to be too much inaccurate in comparison with those of the nautical maps, fruit of the work of modern cartographers who had taken advantage of the direct experience of navigators.

For the cartographical writing of the maps of the world, in conical projection, and of the various regional sectors, in orthogonal projection,[19] it had been taken advantage of the mathematical rules established in the book I of the *Cosmographia* by Ptolemy with the subdivision of the world in meridians and in parallels and with the assignment to the various localities of a longitude and a latitude, whose measures required, in truth, careful observations and complex astronomical calculations.

To this correction took part the same mathematician and astronomer Paolo dal Pozzo Toscanelli that, with Francesco Lapaccini and Domenico di Leonardo Buoninsegni, producers of Ptolemaic texts with maps and translators into Latin of the Greek toponyms, participated of that circle of humanists that in Santa Maria degli Angeli gravitated around the personality of Ambrogio Traversari,[20] friend of Niccolò Niccoli[21] and subsequently general of the Camaldolensians.

Among the most original examples of the «tabulae novae» of the Florentine Ptolemaic Codices, that enriched

---

[14]   Medieval globes representing the world were generally of rectangular or oval shape with a deformed and schematic geographical profile. In use in monasteries or more often destined to the faithful, they showed clear iconographical influences derived from the Bible, like the positioning of Jerusalem at the centre of the world, whose subdivision in three parts was determined by the number of Noah's sons.

[15]   SALUTATI, author of *De fato et fortuna*, was a great humanist who supported in Florence the institution of a public library. POGGIO BRACCIOLINI, writing in 1426 to Leonardo Bruni, so annotated (*Lettere*, Firenze, Olschki, 1884): «How much often I mourn our Coluccio! His books were his no more than of all the scholars».

[16]   The manuscript of the *Geographia* by Crisolora has been identified with the Ms. Urbinate gr. 82 of the Biblioteca Apostolica Vaticana, archetype of the Ptolemaic manuscripts with tables. In his *Vite*, Vespasiano da Bisticci reports that being the city of Florence in the will to make the Greek letters learnt, Palla di Nofri Strozzi «made every thing he could, so that Manuello Chrysolora, Greek, could pass to Italy, paying good part of the expenses. After Manuello had arrived to Italy in the way mentioned with the favour of master Palla, there was a lack of books, and so without books it could not be made anything. Master Palla sent to Greece to get countless volumes of books, all at his expenses: the *Cosmographia* by Ptolemy with the painting which he made to come as far as from Constantinople, the *Lives* by Plutarch, the works by Plato and countless books of the others».

[17]   It is with FRANCESCO PETRARCA (PETRARCH) that began, about 1350, the humanistic interest for the ancient toponymy and the geographical topics, since as the poet annotated in the Codex of Vergil (Milan, Biblioteca Ambrosiana), he wished to know with topographical precision the places visited by Aeneas in his travel towards Italy; which interest was collected and continued in Florence by GIOVANNI BOCCACCIO in his *De montibus, silvis, fontibus, lacubus, fluminibus, stagnis seu paludibus et de nominibus maris liber* (1355-74), a work of great erudition of antiquities, founded on the *De fluminibus* by Pomponio Mela, and that L. Rombai has defined as the «first Italian geographical dictionary». See L. ROMBAI, *Alle origini della cartografia toscana. Il sapere geografico nella Firenze del Quattrocento*, Firenze, Istituto Interfacoltà di Geografia, 1992.

[18]   See S. GENTILE, *Firenze e la scoperta dell'America. Umanesimo e geografia del '400 fiorentino*, Firenze, Olschki, 1992.

[19]   It is traditionally indicated in the Byzantine scholar MASSIMO PLANUDE, at the end of the thirteenth century, the executor of the cartographical apparatus, that had gone lost, of the text of the *Geographia* by Ptolemy.

[20]   AMBROGIO TRAVERSARI was a refined humanist, who made the translations of many theological works of the patristic (Cyril, Athanasius) and of the *Lives of philosophers* by Diogenes Laertius. He was given the task to write up in Greek and in Latin the Bull *Laetentur coeli* [«The skies rejoice» Tr. N.] for the achieved unity of the Eastern and Western Churches during the Council of Ferrara-Florence (1438-39).

[21]   In the first will dated 11 June 1430 of NICCOLÒ NICCOLI, for the restoration of the Codices of his property and the erection of a library that could keep them in Santa Maria degli Angeli, there was defined the legacy of an amount of three hundred gold coins. To carry out such wishes it was indicated a group of friends («optimi et peritissimi viri») [«excellent and most skilful men» Tr. N.], among which appear Carlo Marsuppini, Franco Sacchetti, Leonardo Bruni, Poggio Bracciolini, Domenico Buoninsegni and Paolo Toscanelli. See E. GARIN, *La biblioteca di San Marco*, Firenze, Le Lettere, 1999.

the geographical patrimony with the 27 regional tables in orthogonal projection, a number that become gradually a standard, the maps of *Italia Moderna*[22] and of the chorography of Tuscany, contained in the writing of the *Tuscia Novela* (*c.* 1456)[23] by Piero del Massajo, «painter» and heir of the cartographical work of Francesco Lapaccini and Domenico Buoninsegni, which will be followed, with some variant, by the *Etruria Moderna* (*c.* 1469)[24] and by the *Descriptio Etrurie Nova* (*c.* 1472),[25] have a position of primary importance.

Also Francesco Rosselli, after he had realized in the *Veduta della Catena* (1471-72 / 1480), with the albertian method of survey to measure distances and depth, the first complete depiction of the city of Florence, without just granting a privilege to the sole monumental element within the town-walls, revealed himself as a cosmographer and author of splendid Ptolemaic planispheres, printed on his own, as an expression of his collaboration with Piero del Massaio and his frequentation of the workshop of Vespasiano da Bisticci (1421-1498), where the art of miniature will reach its higher expression in the renowned *Bibbia* (1477-78),[26] transcribed by Ugo Com-

[22]   Biblioteca Medicea Laurenziana, pl. XXX 1, cc 113 *v*-114 *r.*
[23]   Cod. of 1456, kept in the Biblioteque Nationale of Paris: Parigino Lat. 17542, ex 4802, ff. 127 *v*-128 *r.*
[24]   Cod. of 1469, kept in the Biblioteca Apostolica Vaticana: Lat. 5699, ff. 121 *v*-122 *r.*
[25]   Cod. of 1472, kept in the Biblioteca Apostolica Vaticana: Urb. 277, ff. 125 *v*-126 *r.*

[26]   The great *Bible* of FEDERICO DA MONTEFELTRO (cm 44,2 x 59,6), with 24 maps in the first volume and 311 in the second, is kept since 1657 in the Biblioteca Apostolica Vaticana (Cod. Urb. Lat. I-II).

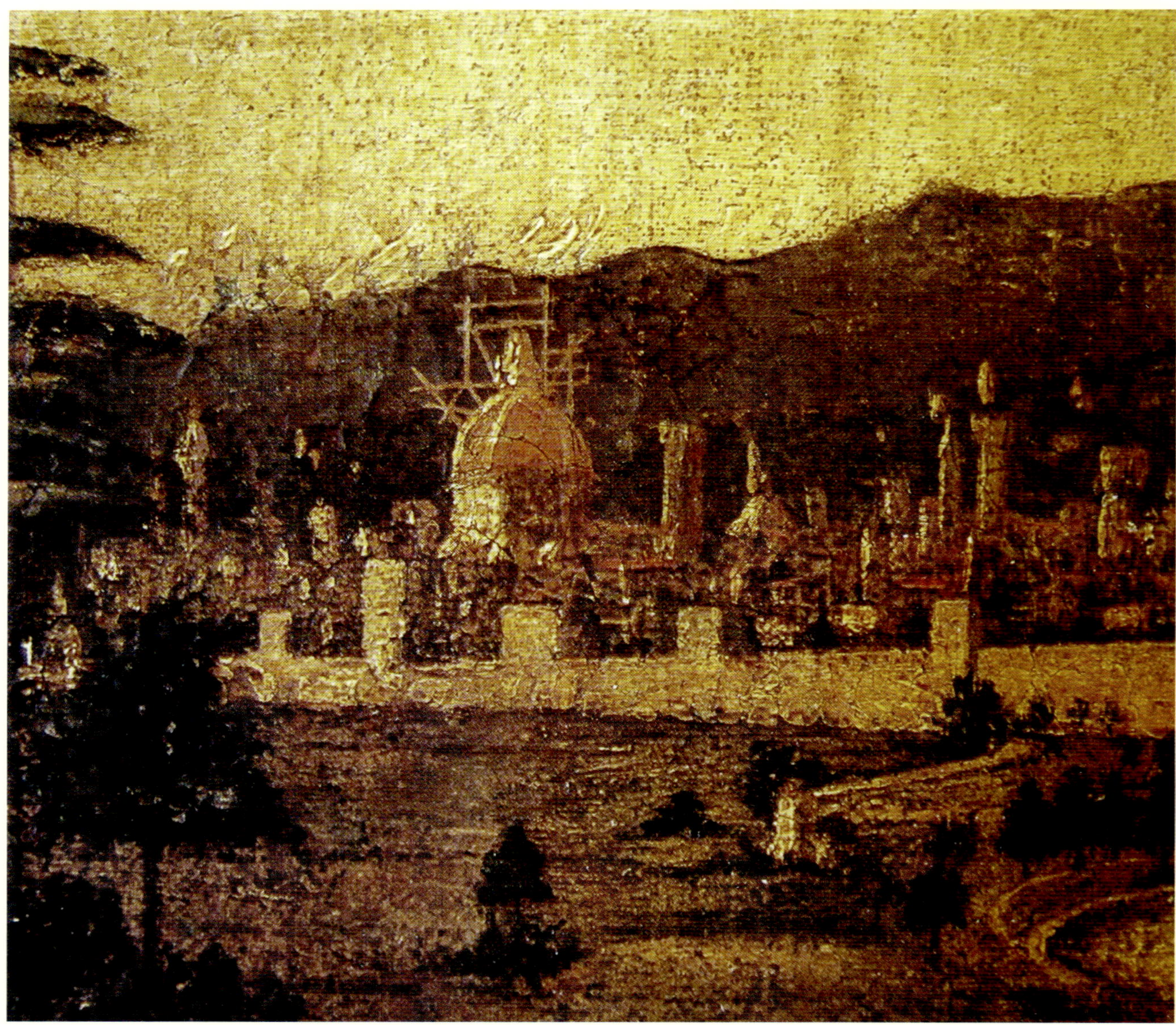

BIAGIO DI ANTONIO, *Tobias and the Archangels*, *c.* 1470. Florence, Bartolini Salimbeni collection. Particular

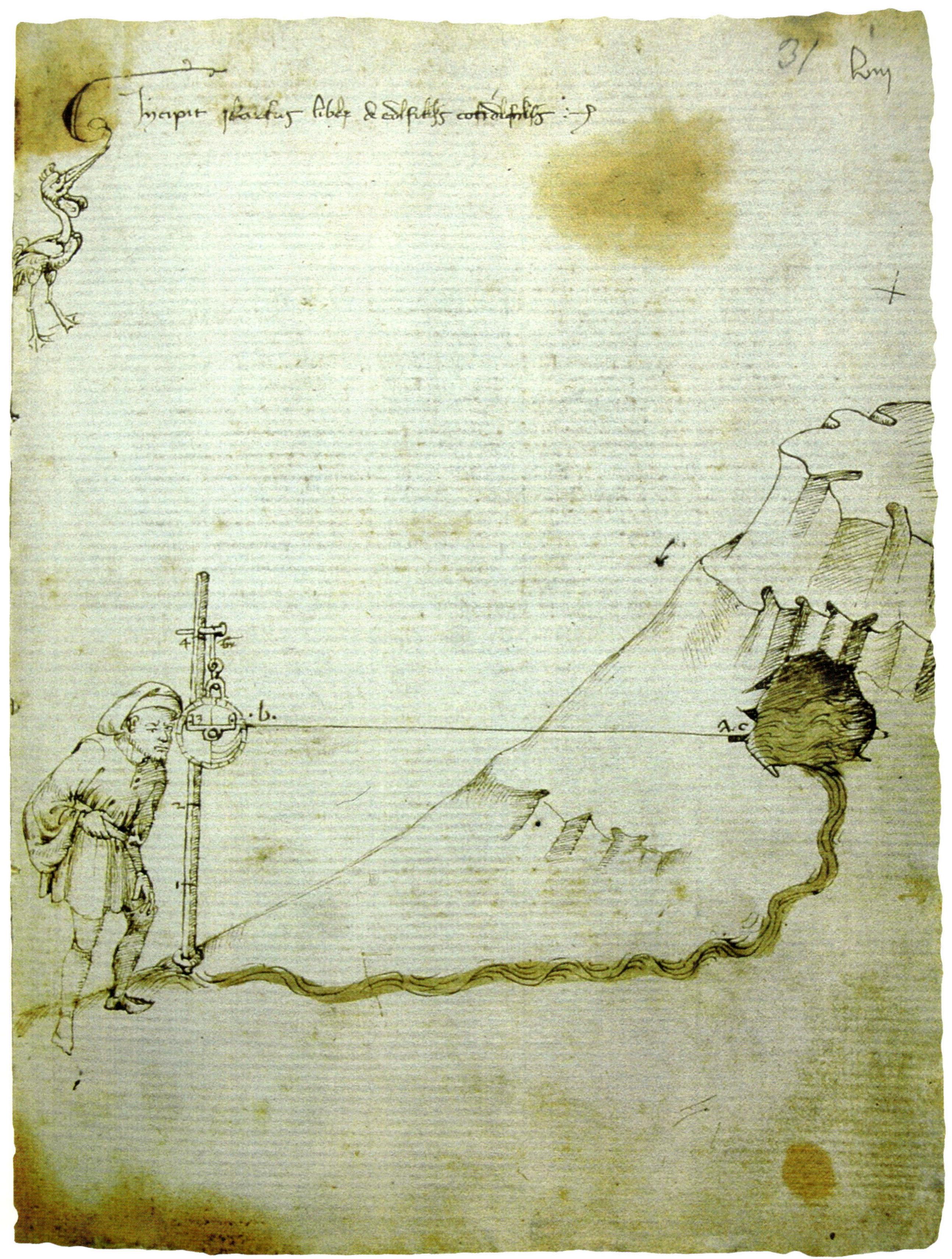

Mariano di Jacopo known as Taccola, *Use of the astrolabe. Liber tertius de ingeneis ac edifitiis non usitatis*, Siena, 1433. Ms. Palatino 766, c. 31. Florence, Biblioteca Nazionale Centrale

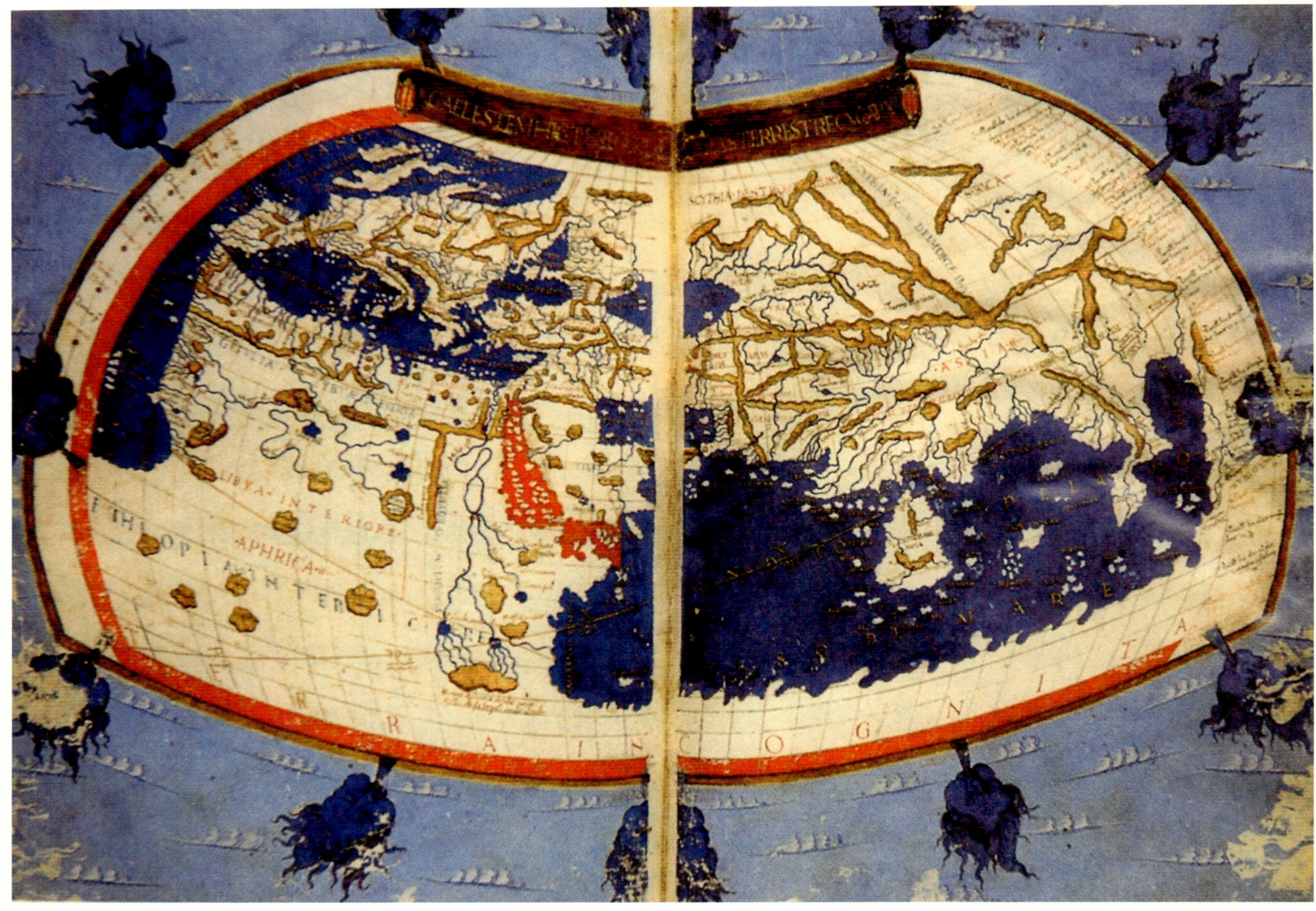

Francesco Berlinghieri, *Map of the world from the 'Septe giornate della Geographia'*. Ms. AC XIV 44, cc. 141 *v*–142 *r*. Milan, Biblioteca Nazionale Braidense

minelli da Mézières and decorated by Francesco Antonio del Chierico on commission of Federico da Montefeltro.

In 1482, also Francesco Berlinghieri, realized his Florentine edition of the *Geographia* of Ptolemy that, popularized in third rhyme, he will enrich, beyond the twenty-seven maps of Ptolemaic tradition, with the four modern tables of Spain, France, Italy and Palestine.[27] To that must be added, for its his-

torical importance, the edition prepared by the German humanist Niccolò Germano («Dominus Nicolaus Germanus»), astrologer and cartographer who was active for a long time in Florence. In the third writing of the Ptolemaic manuscript,[28] where he maintained unchanged the traditional values of the scientific elements, he added, as an innovation, the homeoter

---

[27] The work of the Berlinghieri has three typographical variants of which two copies, very well decorated, were destined to the sons of Muhammad II: the first to Bayazet II (Istanbul, Topkapi Sarayi Muzesi, ms. G I 84), the second to Gema (Turin, Biblioteca Nazionale, Inc. XV I 42, with letter of dedication dated 31 May 1484). His *Septe giornate della Geographia*, printed in 1482, undoubtedly constitute the synthesis of all the ancient and modern geographical knowledge in the fifteenth century. It was composed in triplets, according to a model of geographical production that had started in the previous century with the *Ditta-mondo* by Fazio degli Uberti. See S. Gentile, *La rinascita della Geografia di Tolomeo nel Quattrocento fiorentino*, in *Leonardo Genio e Cartografo*, Firenze, I.G.M., 2003; L.

Rombai, *Geografia e Cartografia nel Rinascimento italiano. La figura del cartografo e le rappresentazioni spaziali nel '400 e nel primo '500*, in *Leonardo Genio e Cartografo*, Firenze, I. G. M., 2003.

[28] Of the three writings of the *Geographia* of Ptolemy by Niccolò Germano, the first two (the first one in honour of Borso d'Este and the second one in honour of Pope Paul II) were published, the one in Rome in 1478, edited by Domizio Calderoni, preceded in time by the publication printed in Bologna by Domenico de' Lapi (1477), and the other one in Ulm (1482), published by Lienhart Holle, with the apparatus of illustrations engraved by Schnitzer de Armsshein, then reprinted in 1486 by Johann Reger. See S. Gentile, *Firenze e la scoperta dell'America…*, 1992, *op. cit.*

                                                             Carlo Starnazzi

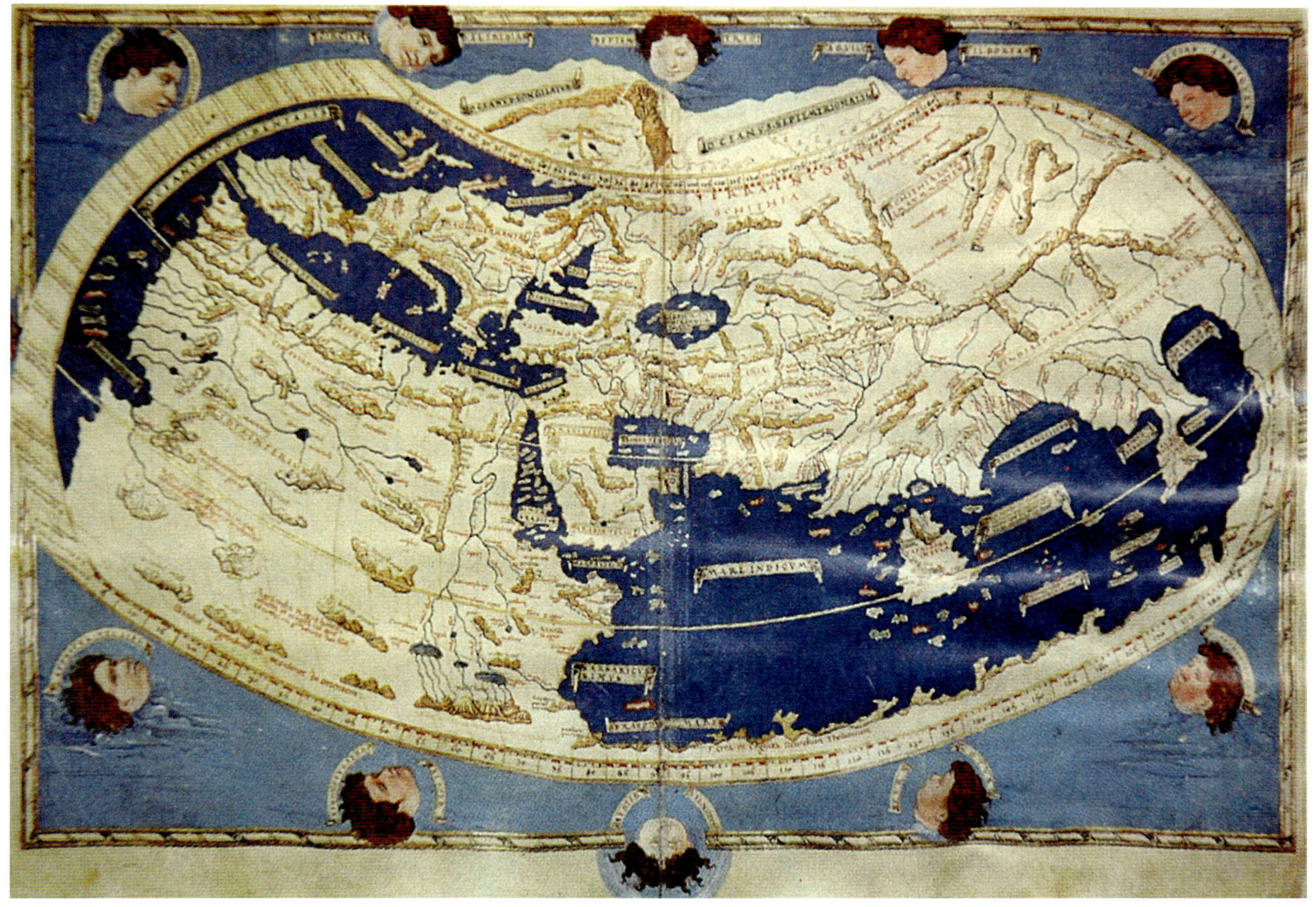

Enrico Martello, *Map of the world*. Ms. Magliabechiano XIII 16, cc. 88 *v*-89 *r*. Florence, Biblioteca Nazionale Centrale

projection of the map of the world and, to the illustrative apparatus derived from the Codices of the years 60-70, five modern regional maps in trapezoidal shape (France, Spain, Italy, Scandinavia, Palestine).

But the eminent geographer will be object of great admiration also for the part of Leonardo da Vinci that, participating to the fecund and consolidated cultural climate that animated the workshops of the Florentine artist-craftsmen, will mention, in the list of his books, that he wrote in Florence about 1503, the *Cosmographia* by Ptolemy (Cod. of Madrid II, f. 3 *r*), not present in the first inventory of his books, that he had made in Milan, about 1495-97, (CA, f. 210 *ra* [559 *r*]). The work of the Alexandrine awoke in him a great fascination and an interest that would have accompanied him until the years of the Roman stay, when, in 1515, in a series of sketches he still revealed the attempt to acquire the method

to develop in plan the surface of a sphere, disposing the four sectors of each hemisphere so as to cover the surface of the terrestrial globe (CA, f. 279 *ra* [757 *r*]).

And other drawings still will reveal this intellectual tension of his, animated by «obstinate stubbornness», now turning his mind to a spherical body subdivided in two parts by the equatorial circumference, now representing its image with partitions in meridians and time zones to develop in plane with perspective depictions or foreshortened alignments (CA, ff. 178 *va* [485 *v*]; 191 *rb* [521 *r*]). In other drawings the vincian intention to dedicate to perspective projections for development or to portray the terrestrial globe without meridians and parallels or having them connected in a bundle of convergent lines in transversal conical projection shines through as a hint, maturing the following opinion, pronounced with the certainty of a postulate of geometry (Ms. M, f. 5 *v*):

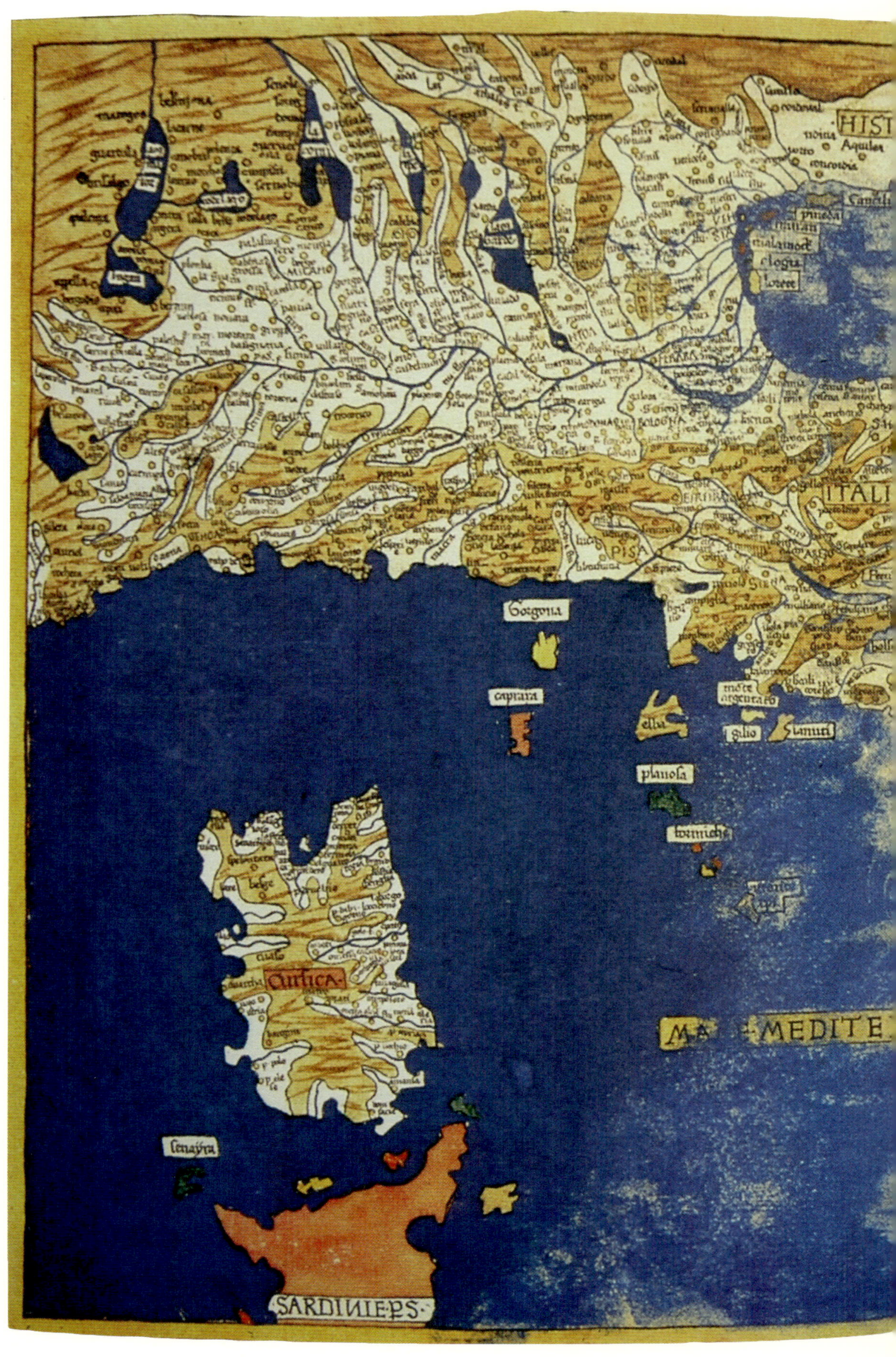

HIST
PISA
ITALI
MA MEDITE
Gorgona
capraia
elba
gilio
Sanuti
planola
SARDINIE PS
Curfica
fenaria

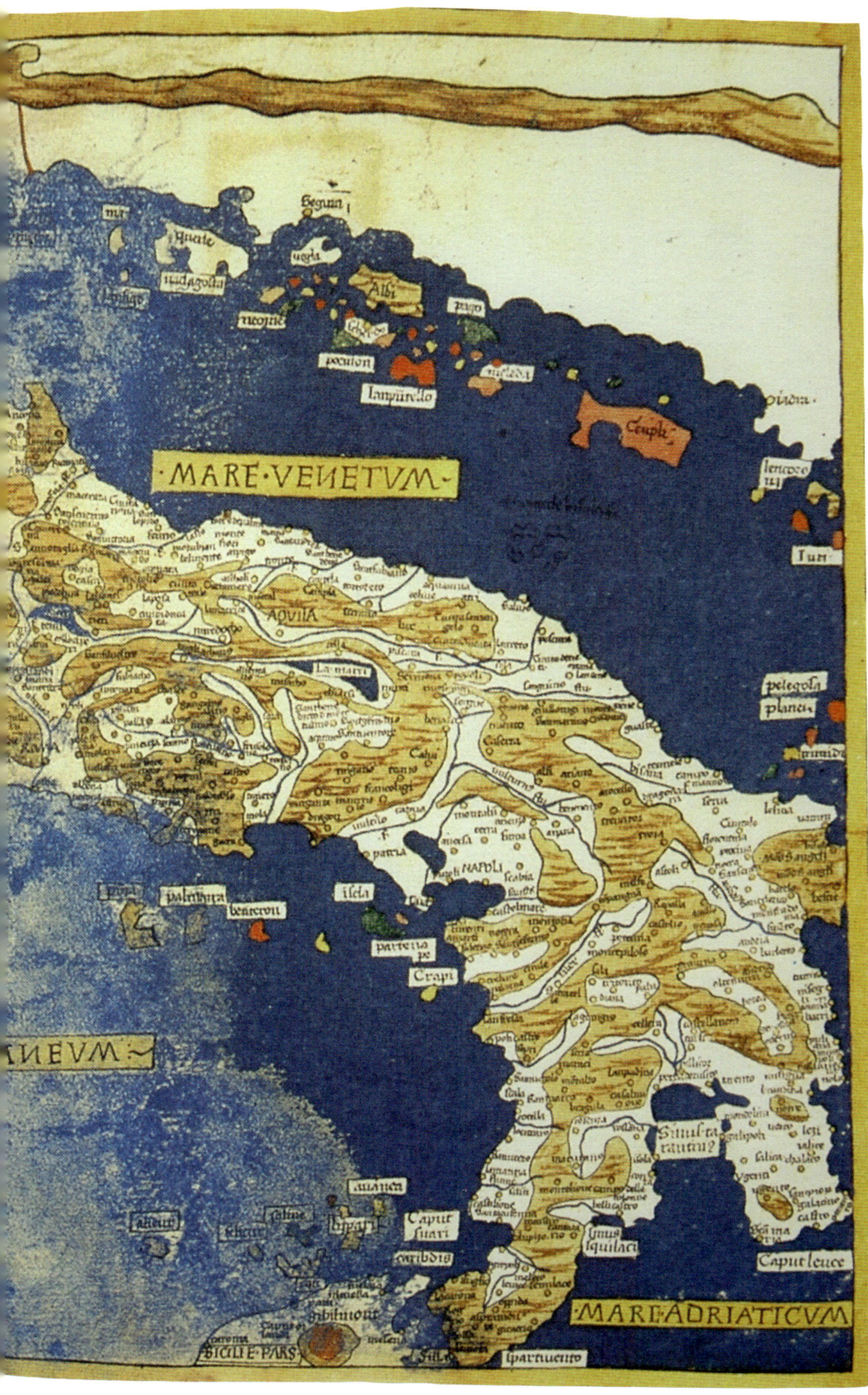

Niccolò Germano,
Tabula moderna Italiae,
1482. 425 x 295 mm.
Inc., I.I, cc. 90 *v*–91 *r*. Florence,
Biblioteca Medicea Laurenziana

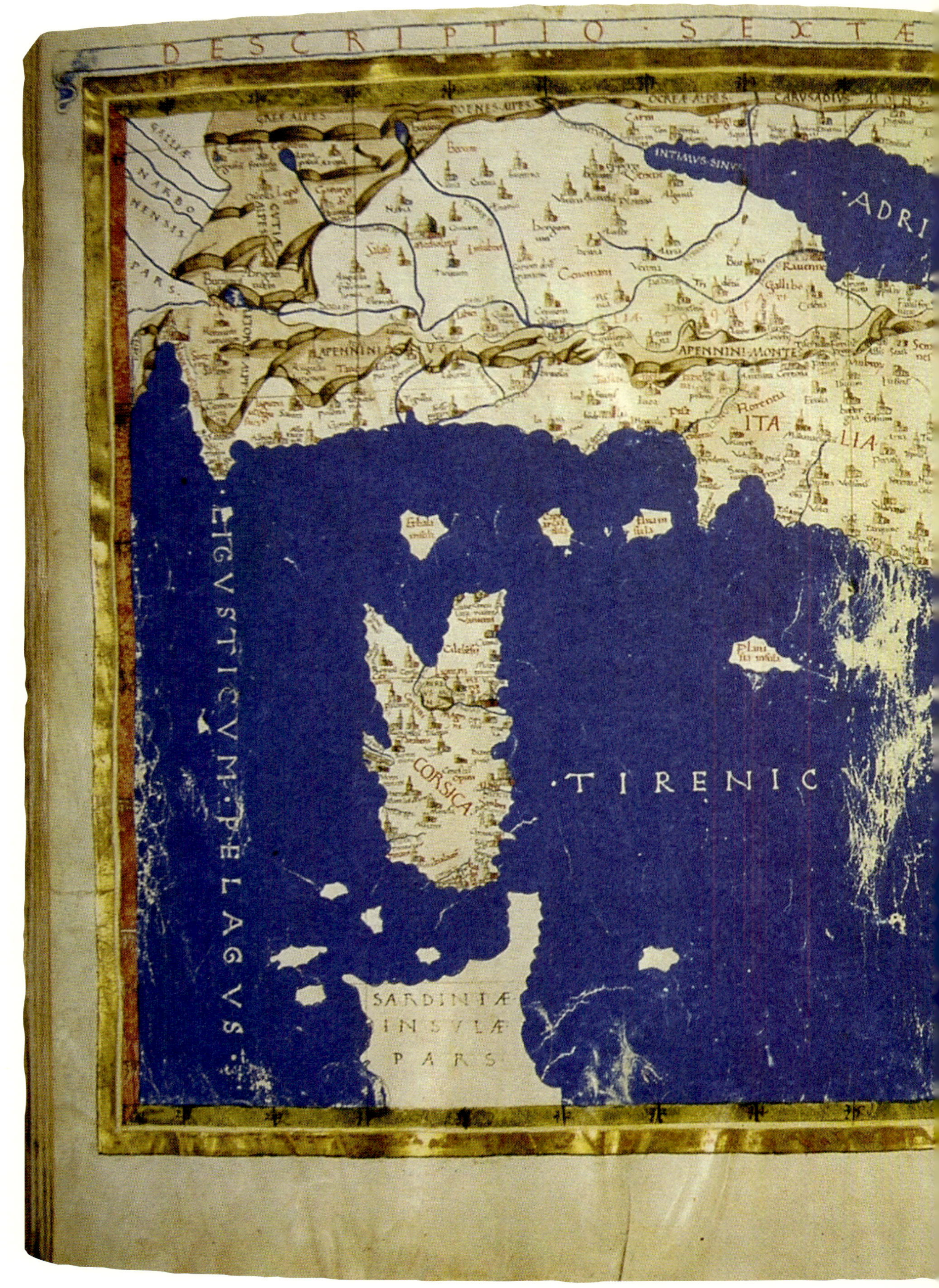

Piero del Massaio,
Modern Ptolemaic Italy,
c. 1460. 560 x 420 mm.
PL XXX 2, cc. 113 *v*-114 *r*.
Florence,
Biblioteca Medicea
Laurenziana

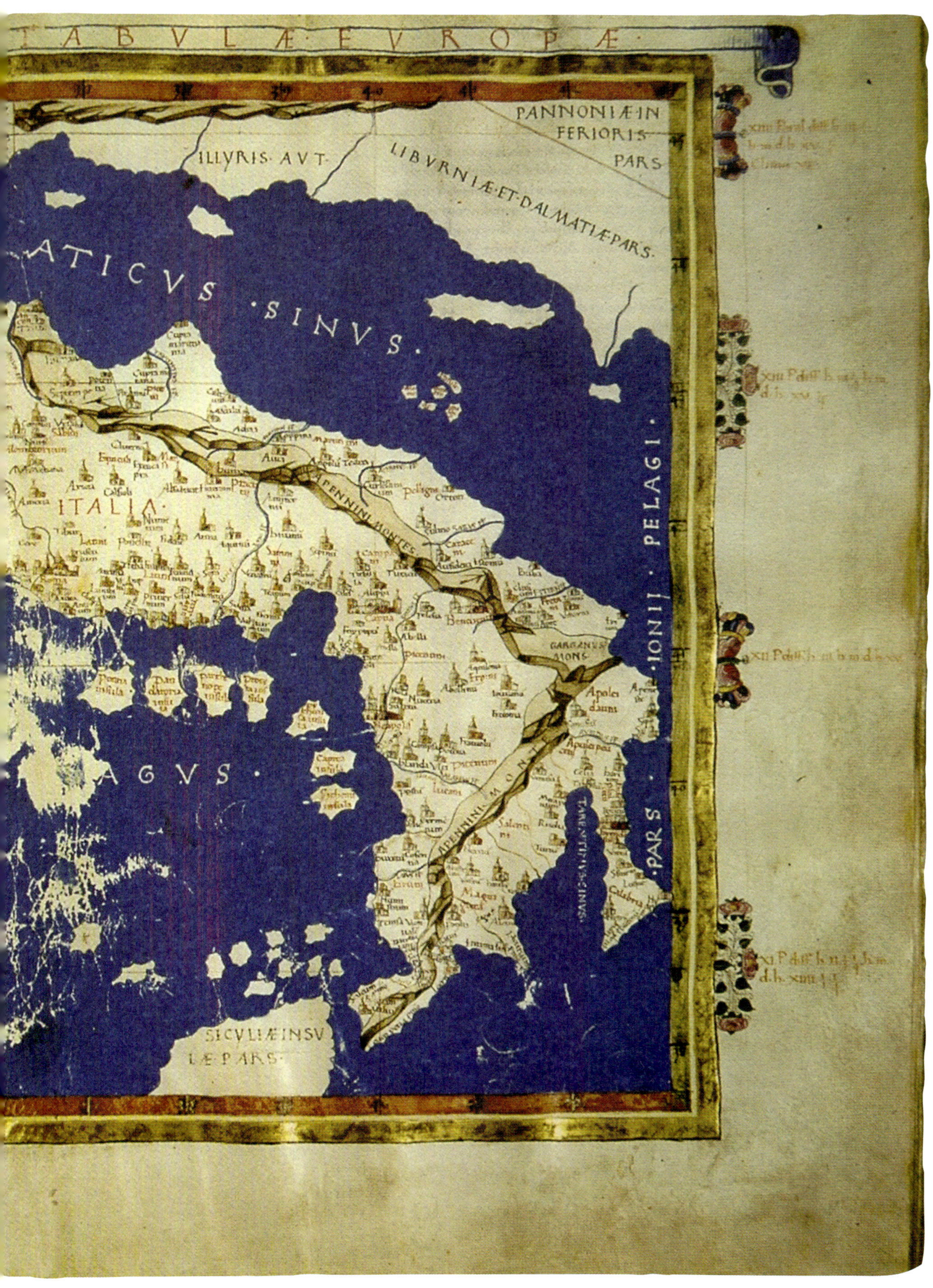
PANNONIÆ IN
FERIORIS
PARS
ILLYRIS AVT
LIBVRNIÆ ET DALMATIÆ PARS
ATICVS SINVS
ITALIA
APENNINI MONTES
IONII PELAGI
GARGANVS MONS
PARS
SICVLIÆ INSV
LÆ PARS

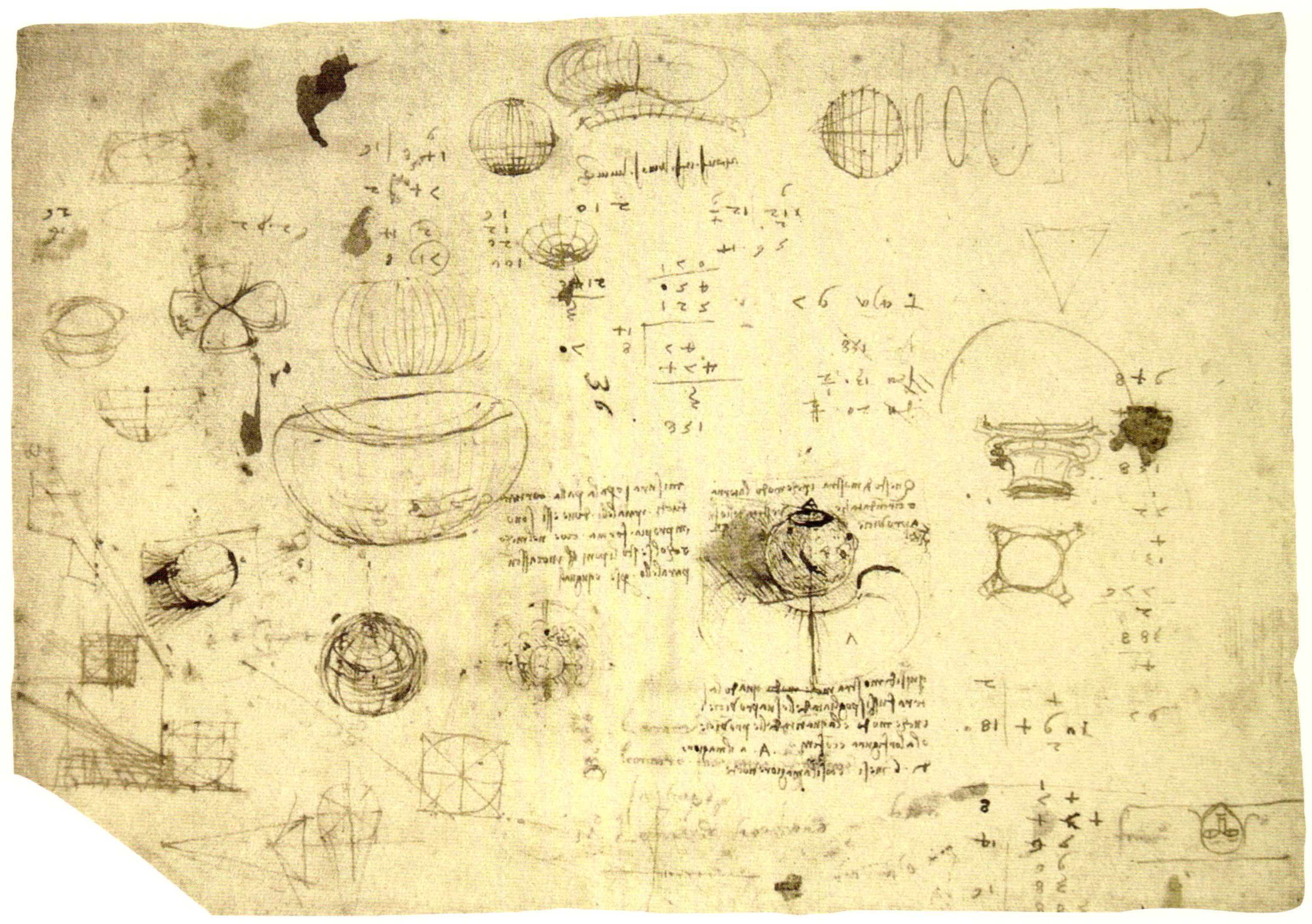

Leonardo da Vinci, *Studies on the way to represent the spherical surface of the Earth on a plane*. Pen and ink, 205 x 284 mm. Codex Atlanticus, f. 521 *r*. Milan, Biblioteca Ambrosiana

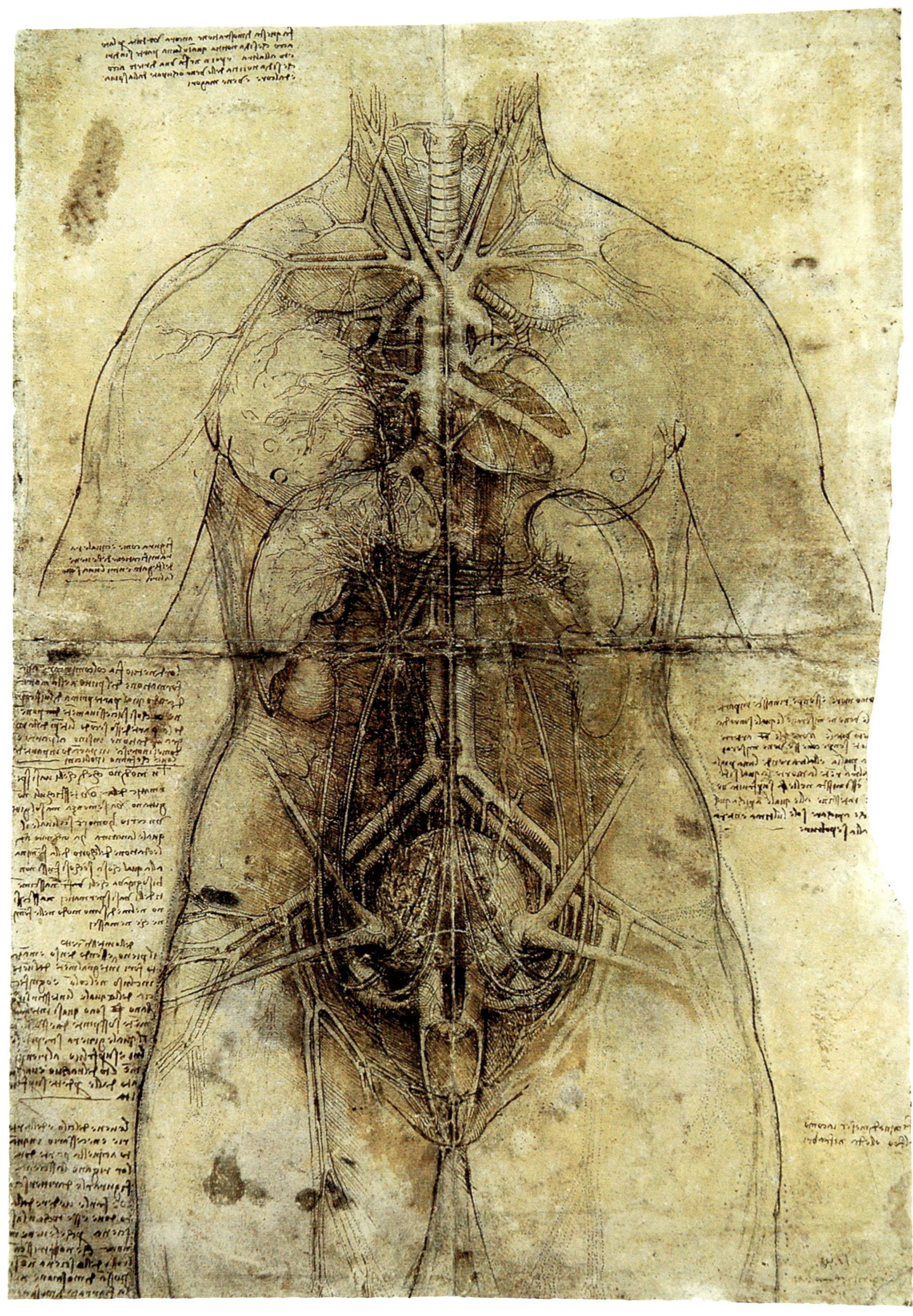

Leonardo da Vinci, *Anatomical table with representation of the female organs, c.* 1508–10. Pen and tawny ink, watercoloured in colour on charcoal, 488 x 333 mm. Windsor, RL 12281 *r*

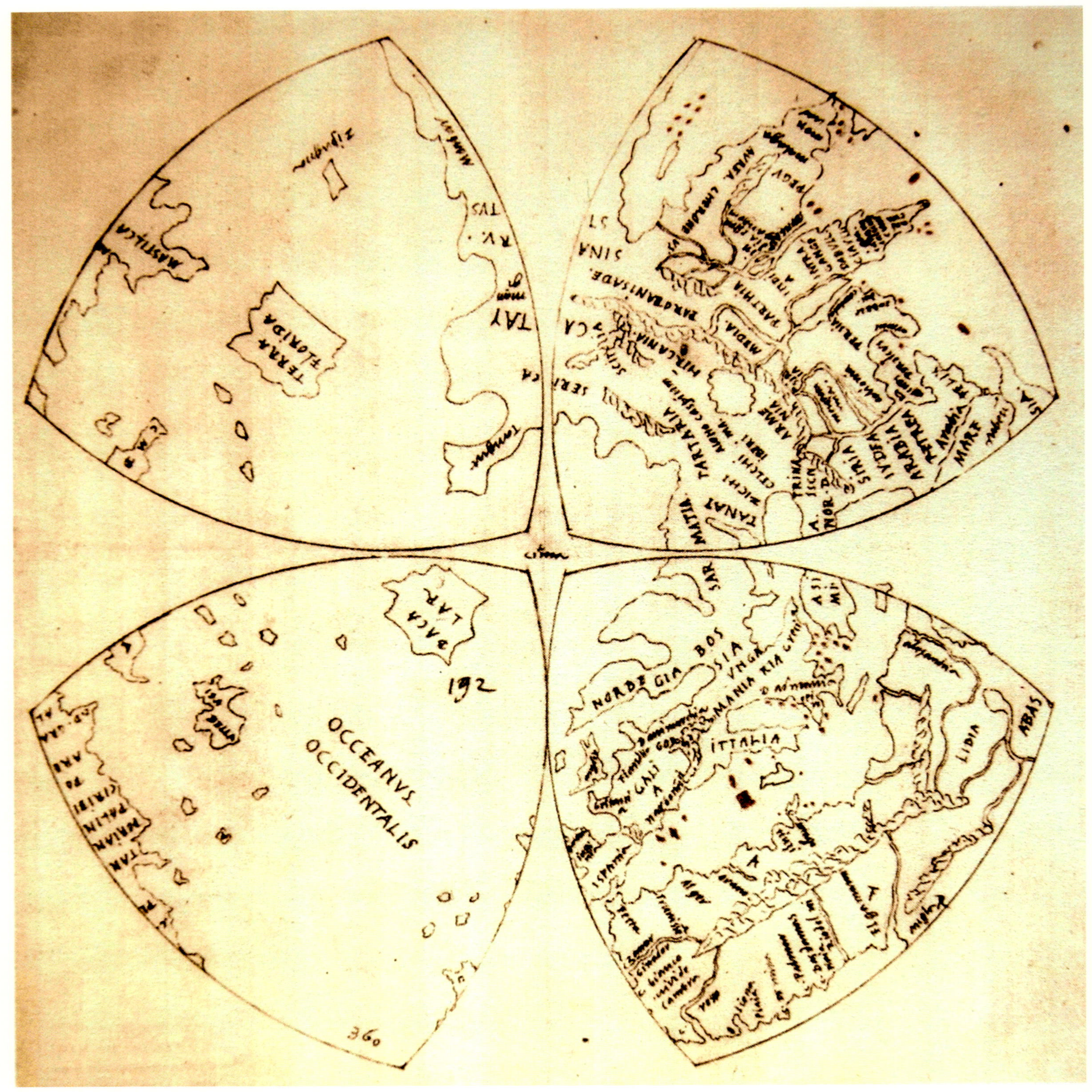

FRANCESCO MELZI (?), *Map of the world, c.* 1515. Pen and ink, pencil, 277 x 276 mm. Windsor, RL 01393

After all, the vigour expended by the artist in representing all the spherical surface of the Earth was motivated by the desire to realize, following the scientific criteria of Ptolemy, a map of the world of his own, like the one that, around 1504, he had lent to his friend Giovanni de' Benci, of the important family of Amerigo de' Benci, father of Ginevra, to whom he had left, when he left for Milan, the *Adoration of the Magi*: «My map of the world, which has Giovanni Benci», (CA, f. 120 *rd* [331 *r*]).[29]

Leonardo, using an analogy of classical and medieval derivation between macrocosm and microcosm, between the human body and the body of the Earth, had compared the circulation of blood to the whirling and capillary flowing of water in the fluvial branches, the hovering in the air of the mountains to the formation of the bony structure of the Earth: «if man in himself has bones, supports and armour of the flesh, the world has stones as supports of the earth. If man in himself has the lake of blood, where the lung grows and decreases in breathing, the body of the Earth has its Ocean sea, which as well grows and decreases every six hours for the breathing of the world», (Ms. A, f. 55 *v*). Therefore, he did not fail, during his experience of dissection of human limbs, to go back and praise the scientific work of Ptolemy, which first had carried out an organic decomposition of the anatomical structure of the body of the Earth. Therefore, while he planned his treatise of anatomy rich of illustrations and while he meant to entrust to the images of the single parts of the «human machine» a visual scientific communication, with which to find a remedy to the «tedious and confuse length of writing» and to supply «true knowledge» of the limbs, the figure of Ptolemy came back to his mind as an unrivalled master of methodology. He had created relationships of

unity and harmony in the illustration of the single parts and their consequent relationship with the terrestrial entirety, between the geographic maps of the single regions and the integrity of the planisphere, in analogy to what he was now about to define in the structural and morphological study of the human body, among the single limbs and their unitary reconstruction:

> *Then here with fifteen entire figures it will be displayed to you the cosmography of the minor world, with the same order that before me it was realized by Ptolemy in his Cosmography; thus I will then divide those limbs as he divided everything in provinces, and then I will say the function of the parts from each side, putting before your eyes the knowledge of all the figure and value of man, since he has local motion by means of his parts. Therefore might it like to our author that I could show the nature of men and their customs in the way that I describe his figure* (Windsor, RL 19061).

Facing therefore the methods for a correct cartographical and pictorial representation of a determined territorial context Leonardo, beyond indicating, in his *Libro di Pittura* (f. 41 *r*, *cap.* 90), «Of the corrected way to portray a site», proceeded to examine grade by grade the correlated topographical operations: «Relief. Altitude. Composition. Site» (CA, f. 155 *re* [421 *r*]). It was a matter of preparing a classification of real data that would have allowed the artist to free himself of the world of mental representation to reach up an objective depiction of nature. The same image of the draughtsman, that employs a transparent plane for the representation of an armillary sphere (CA, f. 1 *vb* [5 *r*]), confirms us how Leonardo, was not only interested to astronomy and the reduction of the Earth and of the sky, but he made recourse to the use of the perspectograph, which he invented, in order to establish a conception of harmony between the painter and the world, founded on an ordering not generic, but rather measured, of the data of experience, that allowed in perspective the transposition of a space to a plane.

These results would have been entirely achieved by Leonardo after having studied for a long time, under the guidance of the great mathematician Luca Pacioli, the Euclidean trigonometry, fundamental for a more scrupulous representation of the territory, and then reconsidered in the accuracy of the detail like a topographical space.

---

[29] GIOVANNI DE' BENCI is mentioned by Leonardo in more than one occasion as «Giovanni d'Americho Benci et chomp.» (CA, 320 *rb* [879 *r*]) or for the «book of Giovanni Benci» (Ms. L, f. I *v*) and still «Giovanni Benci, my book of jaspers» (Cod. Arundel, f. 190 *v*). In addition, a certain Tommaso de' Benci, which gravitated around the world of Marsilio Ficino, had made the popularization of an important text of the *Corpus Hermeticum*, the *Pimander*, which, for the myth of androgynous and its meanings of cosmic revelation, would have exercised a great influence on Leonardo.

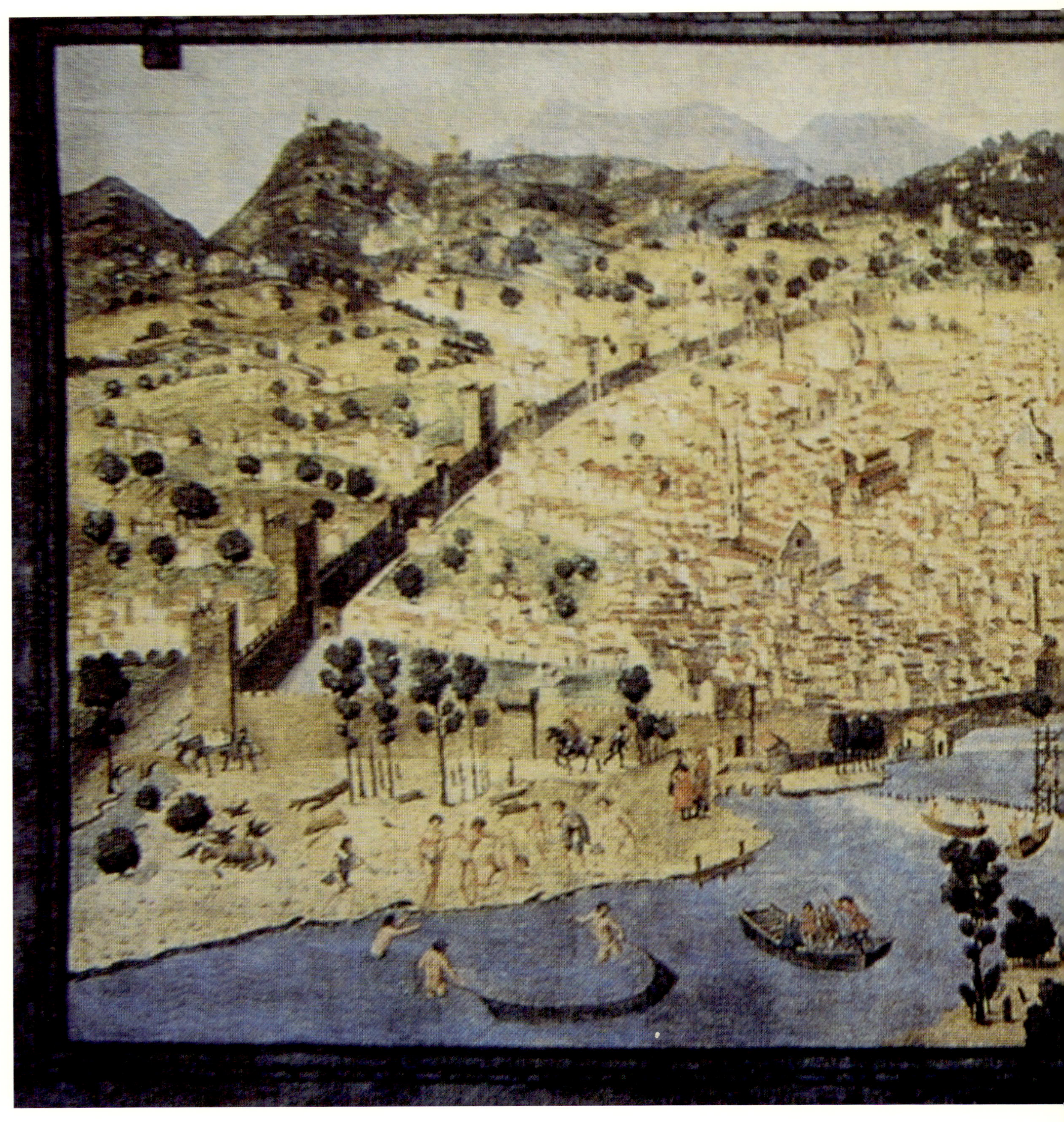

FRANCESCO ROSSELLI, *Perspective view of Florence, known as «Catena»*, 1471-72/1480. Florence, Museum of 'Florence as it was'

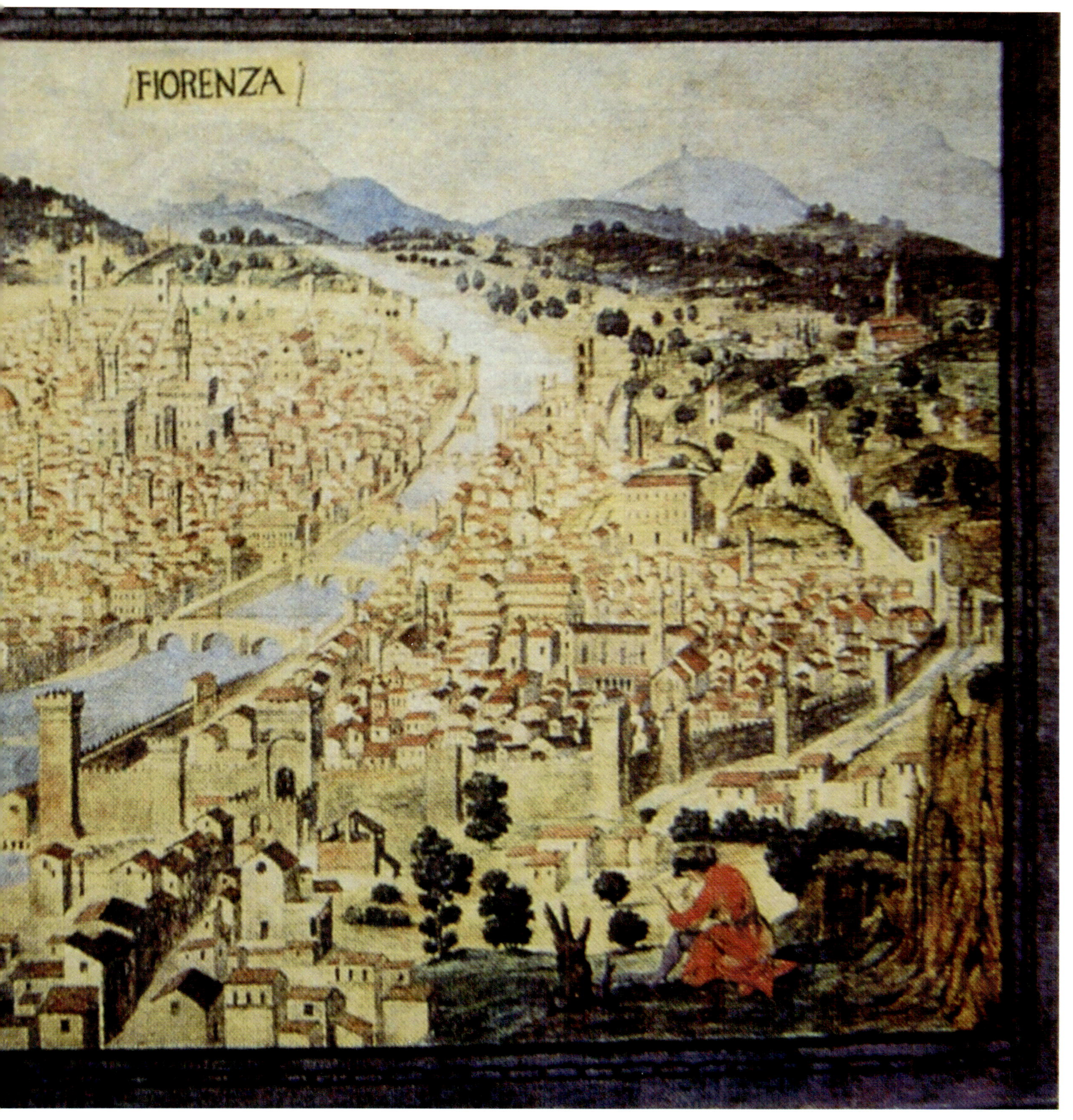

FIORENZA

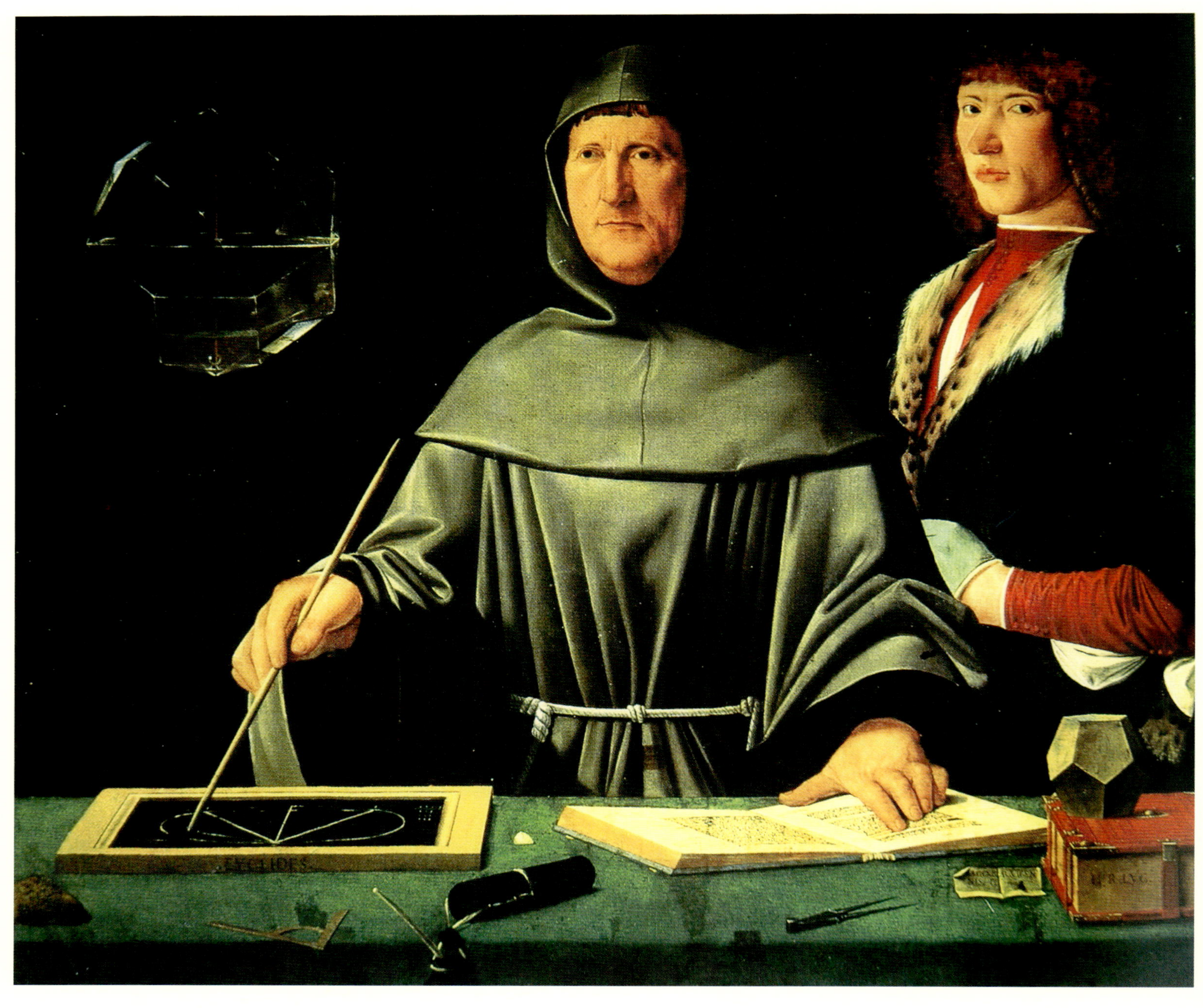

JA. BARB. VIGONNIS, *Portrait of Luca Pacioli*, 1495. Naples, Museo e Gallerie Nazionali di Capodimonte

III. The maps of Leonardo

RECEIVED ON summer 1502 from Cesare Borgia the assignment to work at his service as «architect and general engineer», beyond «considering the places and the fortresses», Leonardo would have also had «to measure and to evaluate» all the conquered regions and cities.[30]
That would have involved not only the highest competence in military engineering, but also the acquisition of fast and detailed information of contingent usefulness, in order to realize immediate planimetries and chorographical syntheses all through the turbulent travel amongst Marches, Romagna and Tuscany. Moreover, the maps of Leonardo point towards just this route, completed in the job of a deep territorial investigation, that, after Arezzo and the Val di Chiana, advanced as far as the cities of Urbino, Pesaro, Rimini, Cesena, Cesenatico and Imola. Selected one or more points for direct observation, he proceeded to the construction of the map raising himself with the mind in aerial perspective at bird flight, in order then to put in connection every single topographical and oro-hydrographical element, with careful proportionality and in a unitary way, to the surrounding environment. The survey of the linear distances among the various towns and villages, emerging from the plane, as it can be deduced from the indications annotated at the bottom of the map of Windsor (RL 12682), was taken from above a tower of Foiano («from Foiano to Cortona 8 miles; from Foiano to Lucignano 2; from Foiano to Marciano 3») and, for the sector of the opposite valley, from above the Castle keep or from one of the towers of the walls of Castiglion Fiorentino, making use perhaps of a mathematical instrument, like the compass or the quadrant, in use for surveys on a territorial scale:

> *from the valley between the Brolio and Castiglione there are 2 miles, from Castiglione to Montechio one mile, from Castiglione to Mami one mile, from Castiglione to the Montanina 4 miles, from Castiglione to Cortona 5 miles, from Castiglione to Vitiano 2 miles, from Castiglione to Robuttino 3 miles, from Castiglione to Ppulicciano 5 miles, from Castiglione to Pigli 6 miles, from Castiglione to the Olmo that is the cutting of the hill which goes as far as Arezo 8 miles.*

Also in the following map of the Val Chiana (Windsor, RL 12278), which looks like the finished outcome of the previous cartographical sketch, beyond demonstrating that he had a profound knowledge of the territory of Arezzo, Leonardo highlighted the innovations of the techniques he had adopted as the multiplication of the points of view and above all his «shading off» technique, with which he managed to realize a learned distribution of the orographical masses, suggesting the variations of altitude and a certain three-dimensionality of the entirety of the spaces, with the artifice of the highlighting («clarity» and «shadowiness»).
Both the attention reserved to the realistic representation of villages, Castles, towns, as well as to the various itineraries and the annotation, written out in the conventional manner from left to right, of three hundred and eight toponyms, suggest a motivation initially tied to strategic needs, associated to movements of troops and to the transportation of artilleries from Arezzo towards Anghiari or Cortona, as well as from Perugia towards Siena and Bolsena, after that, in January 1503, Cesare Borgia came to the decision to eliminate all the commanders that, in the Castle of Magione (9 October 1502), had conjured up against him. The toponyms indicated in the map are as follows:

> *Ponte a Prie, Sceggia, Monte Acuto, Badia de' Tedaldi, Caprese, Montedogli, Pieve a San Stefano, Anghiari, Borgo a San Sepolcro, Citerna, Monterchio, Cielle f., Ranco, Pratomagno, Monte a Santa Maria, Montani[n]a, Pierli, Montone, Larciano, La Serra, La Stratta, Mercatale, PERUGIA, La Magione, Monte Cologna, Pasignano, Torricella, TEVERO FL., Qui sbocca il lagho [The lake ends up here], Chiaveretto, CHIASSA FL., Monte Giovi, Castelnuovo, Rondine, Quarrata, AREZO, Fontiano, Pieve, Pigli, Puliciano, Rughettino, Vitiano, Cazano, Mammi, Castiglione Aretino, Cilone f., Bragone f., Cenella, Montechio, CORTONA, Malborghetto, Minore, Isola Polvese, Isola magiore, Castiglione del Lago, Monte Pontignano, Marciano, NESTORE FL., Ponte a Levane, AMBRA FL., f. Chiani, Mulino, Bucine, AMBRA FL., f. Chiani, Mulino, Bucine, AMBRA FL., Mulino, Chiani, Ponte a Chiani, Ponte alla Nave, Vingone, Bastardo, Pogiole, Battifolle, Ponte a Pietra, Civitella, Cigiano, Gargosa, Monte a Ssansovino, Cesa, Marciano, Calcione, FENA RL., Foiano, Rugomagno, Castel di Bertoccio, Poggio a S. Ciecilia, Armaiuolo, Lucignano, FENNA FL., Farnetella, Asinalunga, Torriti, Fossonico, Petroio, Monfalonico, Montechio, Treguanda, Monte Pulciano, Ponte a Vagliano, Panicale, Castel della Pieve, Lione, Ponte a Carnaiolo, CHIANI FL., Ficule, Ponte a Becatiquello, CHIUSI, Corsignano, Chianciano, Cetona, Sartiano, Roca Chena, PAGLIA FL., Tocato, Roco, Vignone, Castiglione, Capanne, PAGLIA FL., Radicofano, Bagno a San Filippo, Acquapendente, San Lorenzo, Montevarchi, Castel San Giovanni, ANTELLA FL., Monte Scolari, Lapeggio, Lignano, Montione, EMA FL., GRASSINA FL., Strata, Certosa, GRIEVE FL., Santa Maria Impruneta, Mercatale, Lamole, Monte*

[30]   See C. PEDRETTI, *Documenti e memorie riguardanti Leonardo da Vinci a Bologna e in Emilia*, Bologna, Fiammenghi, 1953; M. KEMP, *Leonardo da Vinci. Le mirabili operazioni della natura e dell'uomo*, Milano, Mondadori, 1982; P. C. MARANI, *L'architettura fortificata negli studi di Leonardo da Vinci*, Firenze, Olschki, 1984; C. STARNAZZI, *«Architecto et Ingegnero» al servizio di Cesare Borgia*, in ID., *Leonardo cartografo*, 2003, op. cit.

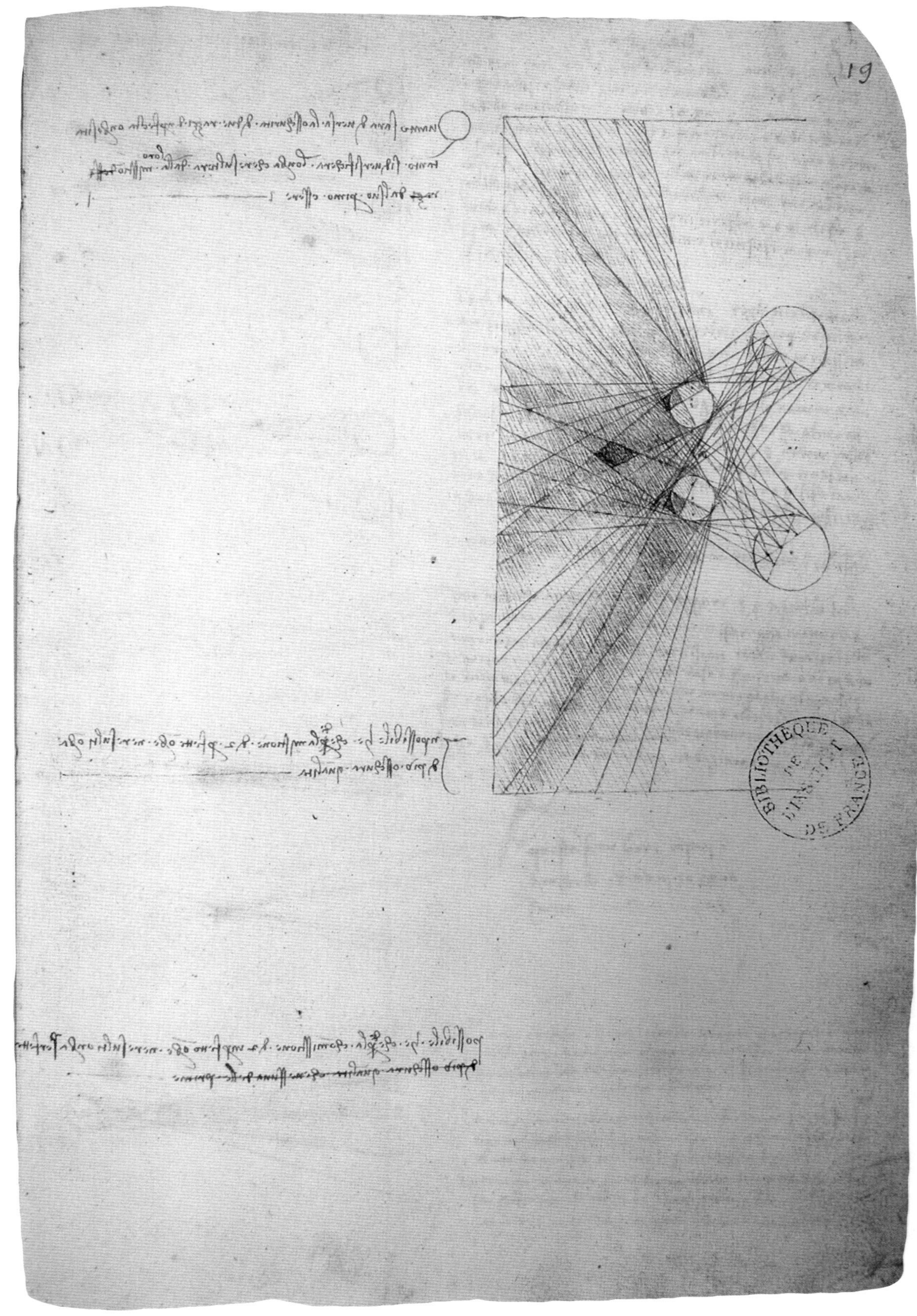

Leonardo da Vinci, *Perfect and imperfect shadow*, 1490-91. Pen and ink, 310 x 222 mm. Ms C, f. 19 *r*. Paris, Institut de France

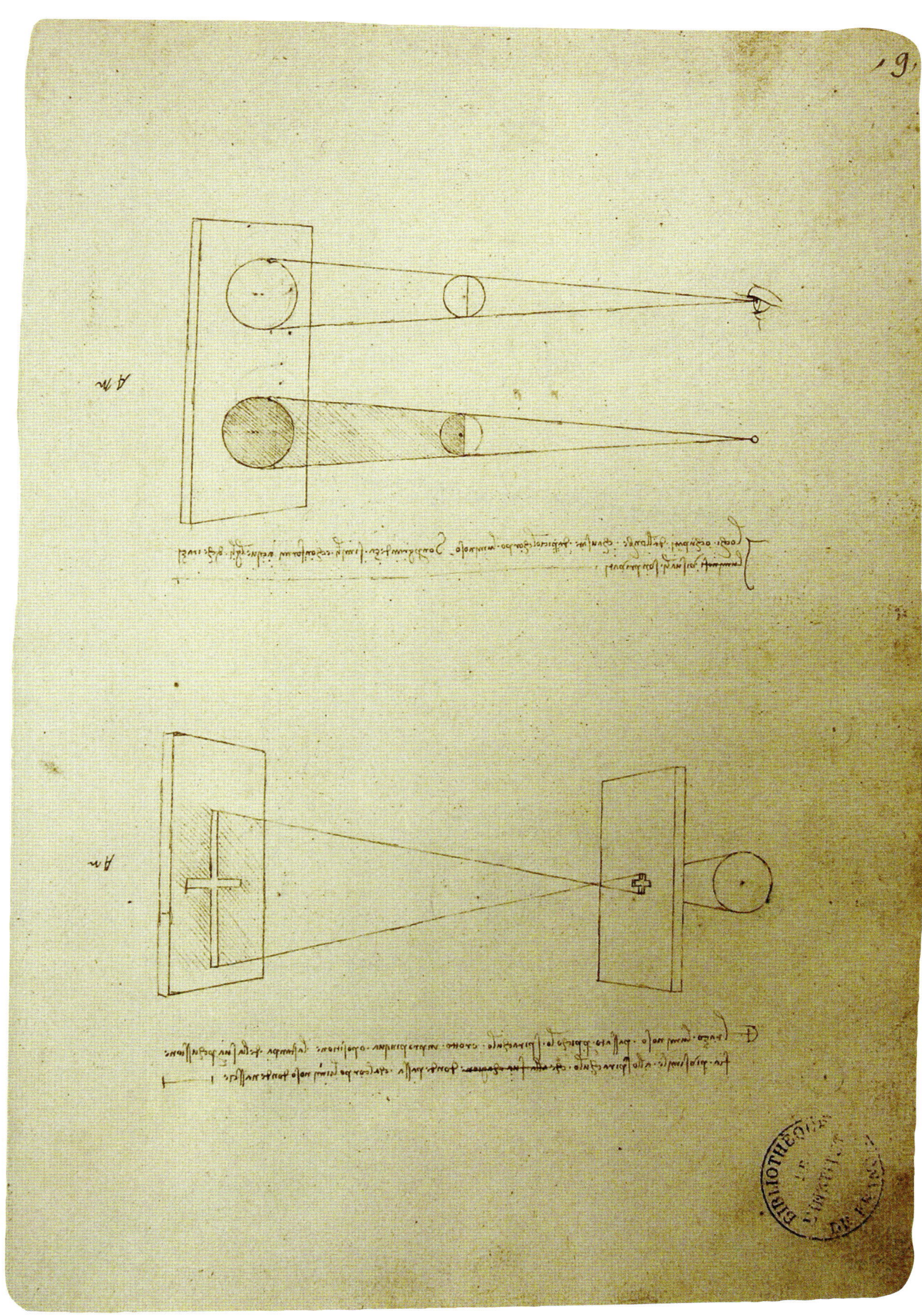

Leonardo da Vinci, *Studies of the luminous rays*, 1490-91. Pen and ink, 310 x 222 mm. Ms C, f. 9 *r*. Paris, Institut de France

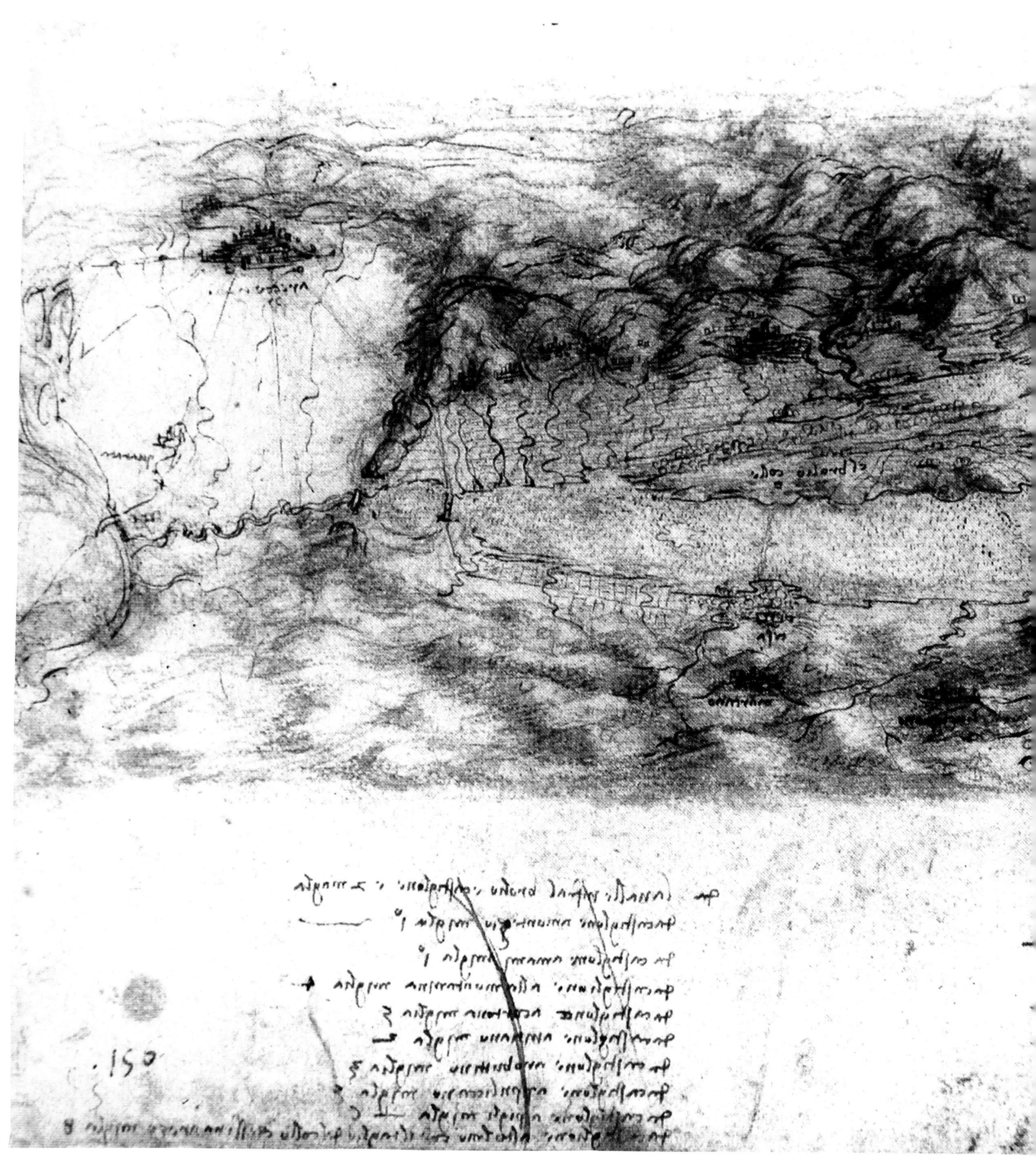

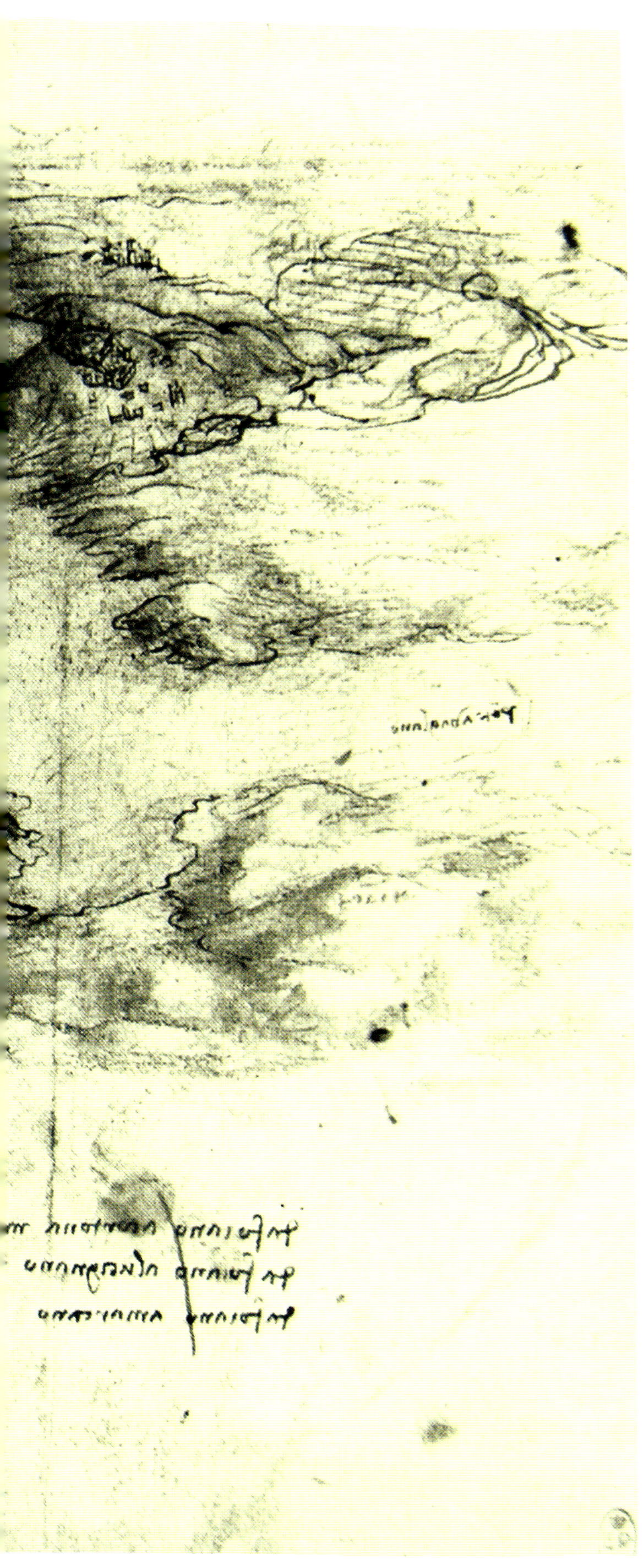

Leonardo da Vinci, *Sketch of the Val di Chiana*, 1502. Charcoal, pen and sepia ink, watercolour of bistre, 209 x 281 mm. Windsor, RL 12682

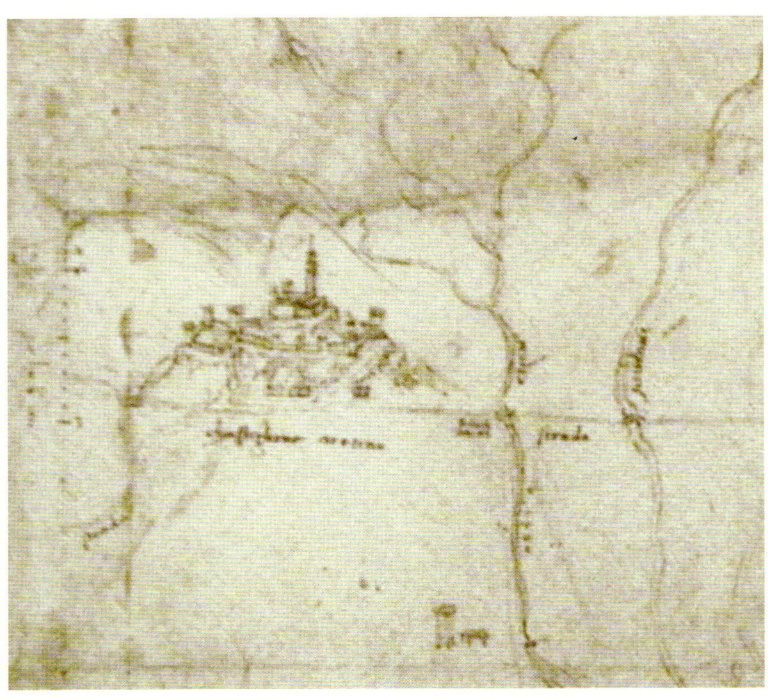

LEONARDO DA VINCI, *Castiglion Fiorentino («Chasstiglione Aretino»)*, c. 1502. Black pencil, pen and ink, 451 x 310 mm. Codex Atlanticus, f. 918 *r*. Milan, Biblioteca Ambrosiana

Ficalle, Malmantile, Montelupo, PESA FL., Sancasciano, Monte Gufoni, Spertoli, VERGIGNO FL., Pasignano, Santa Maria Novella, Lucardo, Rignano, Sambuca, Pansano, Volpaia, Stinche, Gaiole, Vertine, PESA FL., Radda, Pontormo, Empoli, Monterappoli, Granaiolo, Camian, Chastel Fiorentino, Certaldo, Caneto, San Gionettino, Castelnuovo, Castel Varna, Catignano, Pietra, Vico, GHIENNA FL., Marcialla, Barberino, Linari, San Donato in Poggio, Pietrafitta, Castiglione, STAGGIA FL., Castelina, Laleccia, Monte Reggioni, Poggibonizi, Staggia, Rencine, Badia a Isola, Santa Giulita, ELSA FL., Pietrafina, San Miniato al Tedessco, [To]iano, Bichieri, Buciano, Barbialla, EVOLA FL., Valcollevisi, Santo Stefano, Collegale, Fabrica, Montaione, Tonda, ERA FL., Ganbassi, Mumilla, VOLTERRA, Caporbiano, Feltraio, CIECINA FL., Castelvecchio, Monte Mictoli, ERA FL., San Gimignano, Castelnuovo, Casoli, Montecerboli, PASSERA FL., San Dalmazio, Castelli, Sillano, Berignone, SELLA FL., Menzano, CIECINA FL., S. Dalmazio, PAGON FL., Monte Castelli, Castelnuovo, ARBIA FL., Monistero, Montebonichi, Pieve a San Polo, Brolio, San Fedele, Cachiano, San Leonino, Quercegrossa, Cerreto, Sovicule, Fontebecca, Selvaie, Castelnovo, La Torre a Castello, SIENA, Radicondoli, Fossini, CORNIA FL., El Sasso di Volterra, Laleccia, M. Ritondo, Crevole, Murlo, Munistero, VAL D'ARBIA, ARBIA FL., Torti, Travale, Rossia, Cuna, Lucignano di Val d'Arbia, Monterone, Montemurlo, GORA, Montepescino, MENSA FL., GORA, MENSA FL., Macereto, Monte Acciano, M. Capraio, Foiano, Petrio, Petriolo, L[a] FARMA FL., Pari, Pa-

ganico, Tochi, Campagnatico, OMBRON FL., Santa Maria Castelli, Rapolano, Elsciano, Serre di Rapolane, Monte Lifrè, Monte Ghisi, Treguanta, Buonconvento, Montalcino, Camignano, ORCIA FL., Bastiantone, Montecchiello, ORCIA FL., San Quirico, FORMONE FL., Sasso di Maremma, Cinigiano, OMBRE FL., Alberese, Monte Nero, SUANA, Caparbio, M. Argentario, Orbatello, Porto Ercole, Vicorello, LAGO DI BOLSENA, STURLA FL., MAR TIRENO.

This great number of indications about the towns and about the main roads of the entire region, but above all about the hydrographical network and about the great basins, composed of the immensity of the marshes of the Chiane and of the Lake Trasimeno, all let us assume a subsequent reuse of the map for an ambitious hydraulic project related to the reclamation of the Val di Chiana and to the canalization of the Arno from Florence to Pisa.

To this grandiose hydraulic project it is connected the realization of the hydrographical map of Tuscany (Windsor, RL 12277), according to an hypothesis of Susan Kish,[31] Leonardo could have consulted in the Library of Federico da Montefeltro the *Descriptio Etrurie Nova* written by Domenico Buoninsegni, when he reached Urbino, 30 July 1502, in order to put himself in the retinue of Cesare Borgia. But the document of the Codex Atlanticus (f. 334 *rv* [910 *r*]), that is the copy on which Leonardo should have worked for the definition of the mentioned map of Windsor, brings already defined both the hydrographical basin of the Arno and the transcription of the localities of the high Valley of the Casentino,[32] visited by Leonardo with the troops of Vitellozzo Vitelli in June-July 1502, before rejoining the Duke Valentino in Urbino. Therefore, it seems to be more likely that Leonardo had known and held present, for his definitive drawing up of the map with the hydrography of the entire region, the iconographical outcome of a Florentine edition of the maps by Piero del Massaio, rather than the one by Buoninsegni. Leonardo, in this cartographical writing, fixes all his scientific interest onto the oro-hydrographical course of the Appennines and the entire course of the Arno, from the spring to its mouth near Pisa, defining the borders of the entire territory according to the chorography, in approximate scale 1:570.000, of the *VII regio augustea*: «Tuscany is defined by the sea and the river Magra, the river Tiber and the Alp». The Tyrrhe-

[31] See S. KISH, *Leonardo da Vinci: the Map-maker*, in *Imago et mensura mundi*, «Atti del IX Congresso Internazionale di Storia della Cartografia», Istituto della Enciclopedia Italiana, Firenze, Paoletti, 1985.
[32] See C. STARNAZZI, *Un viaggio tra leggende e castelli*, in *Leonardo in Casentino. L'«Angelo incarnato» tra archeologia e leggenda*, mostra ideata e curata da C. Starnazzi (Stia, 1 luglio-28 ottobre 2001), catalogo a cura di C. Pedretti, Firenze, Grantour, 2001; Id., *Leonardo e la Terra di Arezzo…*, 2005, *op. cit.*

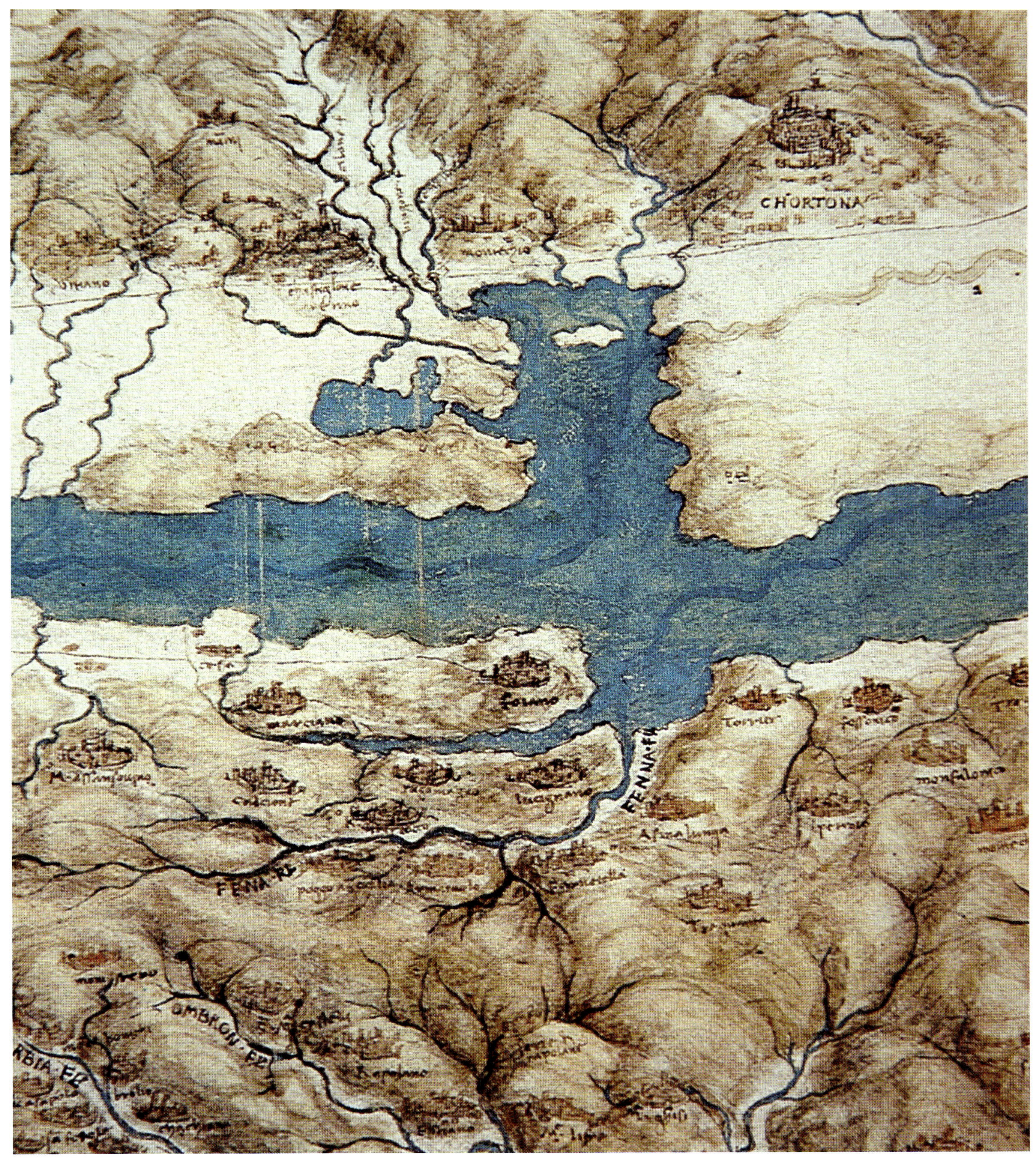

LEONARDO DA VINCI, *Map of the Val Di Chiana*, c. 1503. Charcoal, pen and ink and watercolour, 333 x 488 mm. Windsor, RL 12278 *r*. Particular

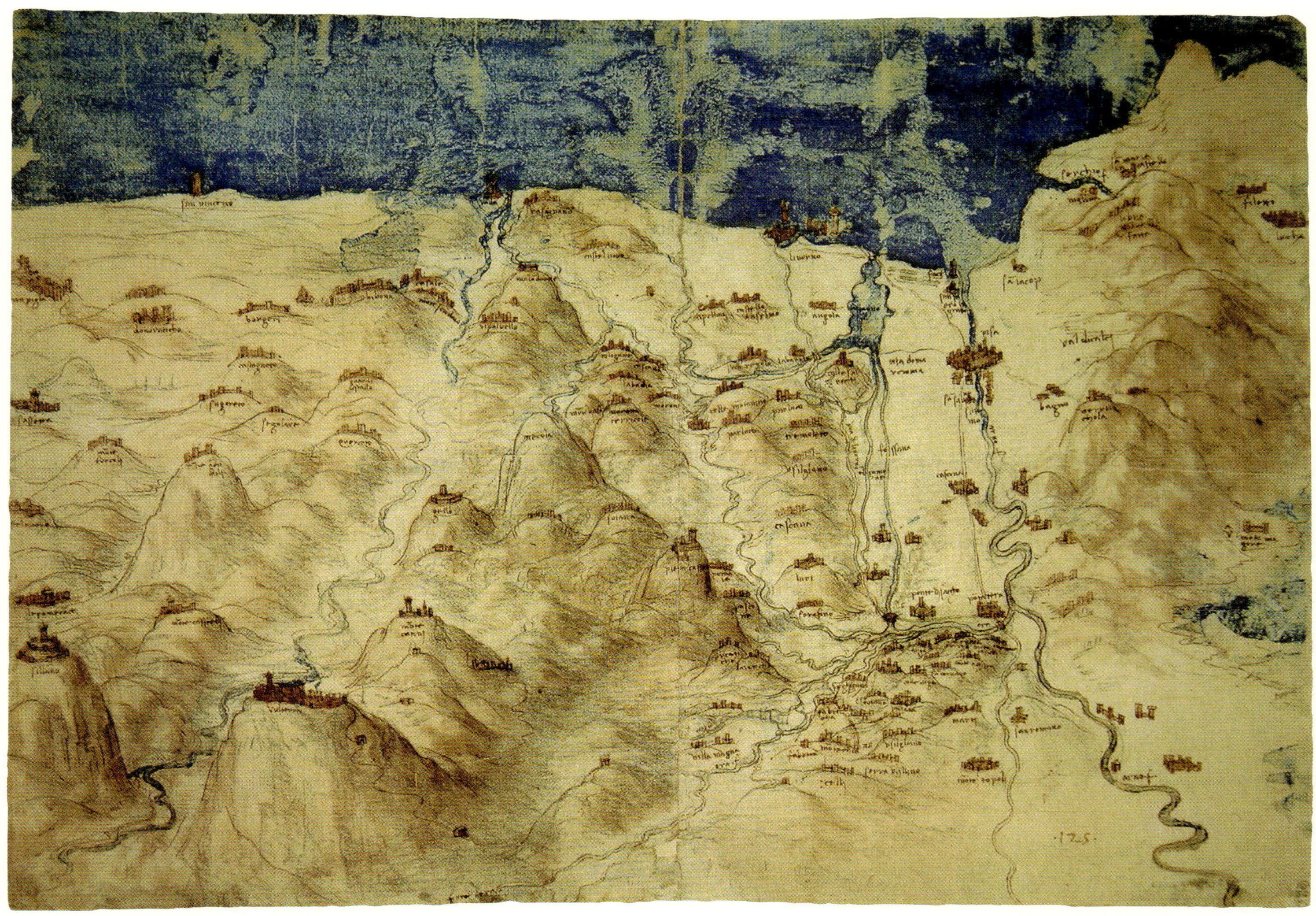

LEONARDO DA VINCI, *Map of Western Tuscany*, c. 1503-04. Charcoal sketch, watercoloured in brown and blue, 275 x 401 mm. Windsor, RL 12683

nian coasts, enough faithful in their morphological course to the model of the Florentine manuscript, extend for approximately 170 miles from the Gulf of La Spezia («Golfo della Spezie») until Civitavecchia, while the inner area is marked on north-west with the lakes of Bientina and Fucecchio, and on south-east, with the spindle-shaped marsh of the Chiane, in connection with the Lake Trasimeno through a supposed channel, never realized («Braccio da Montona closed it so it is lacking»), while a gallery indicates, on the right, its connection to the Tiber; and, further down, the Lake of Bolsena. On the top, there are indicated the towns and the entire hydrographical network of Emilia-Romagna and Marches, from the Po until the Metauro, but the attention is captured by the accuracy reserved to the entire outline of the course of the Arno with its greater tributary, the Sieve, and to their most numerous tributaries. The high hydrographical definition is derived from the direct and profound knowledge that

Leonardo had of all the Valdarno, also because of the studies that were involved in the plan for the canalization of the main river. The structural and geomorphological analysis of the territory in fact would have allowed the acquisition of a hydraulic control of the river, by estimating carefully also its inclination, the roughness of its bed and the speed of its water. This map therefore, together with the one of Imola (Windsor, RL 12284), for the wealth of the geographic data contained and the vitality conveyed from the learned employment of the brown colour, more or less intense for the course of the mountains and the offshoot of the hills, is the best vincian cartographical result, indeed that «crowning and synthesis of his cartographical studies»,[33] that led him to sur-

---

[33] See M. BARATTA, *Leonardo da Vinci e i problemi della terra*, Milano, Bocca, 1903; ID., *Leonardo da Vinci e la Cartografia*, Voghera, O.A.G., 1912; ID., *I disegni geografici di Leonardo da Vinci conservati nel Castello di Windsor*, Roma, Libreria dello Stato, 1941.

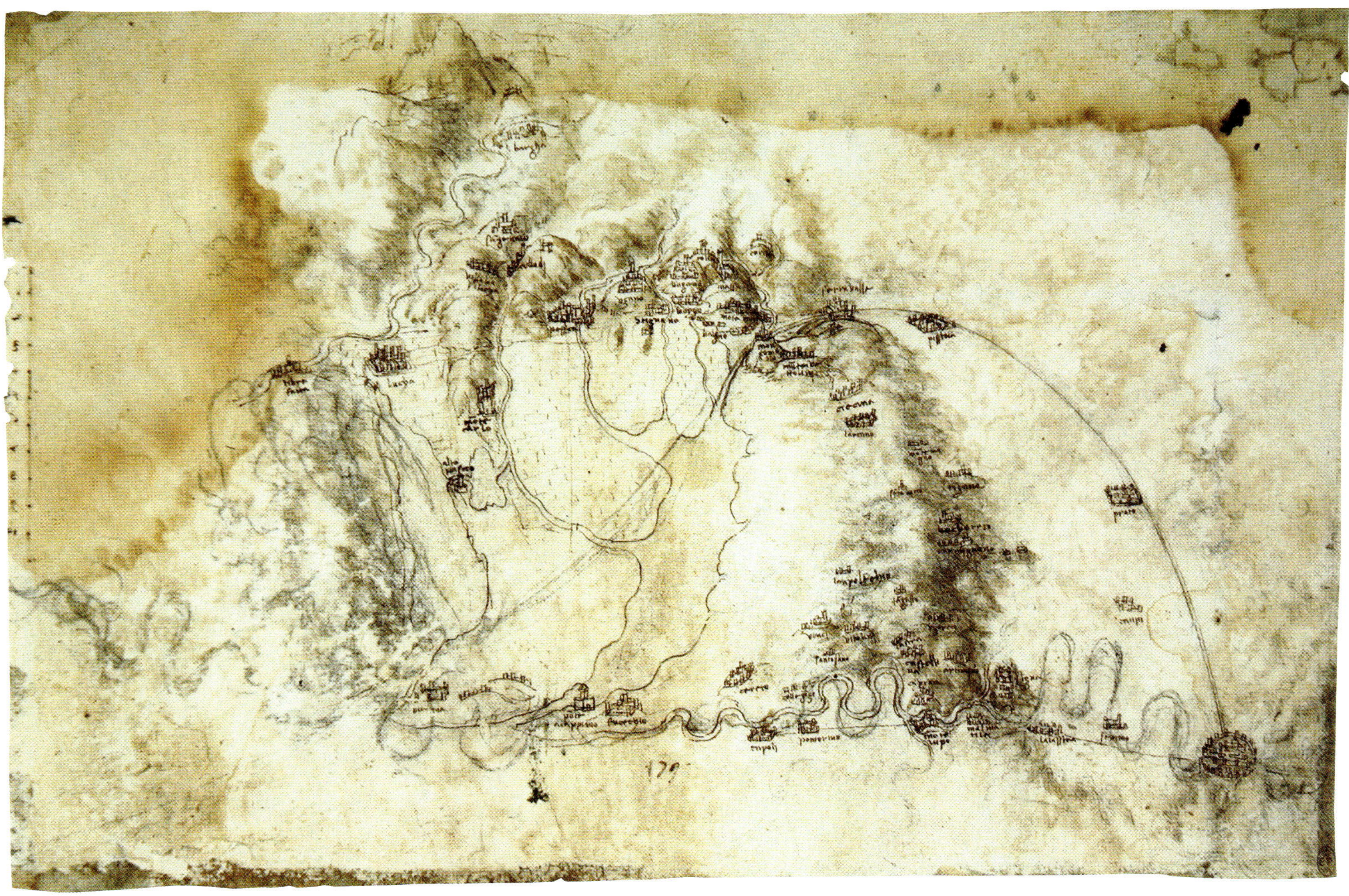

Leonardo da Vinci, *Map of North-Western Tuscany with studies for the diversion of the Arno, c.* 1503. Charcoal, pen and ink, 240 x 367 mm. Windsor, RL 12685

pass every type of previous experience. In this organic vision of central Italy, seen from above like in an air photograph with its animated «naturalness», appear, though with some repetitions, two hundred and twenty-five hydrographical and topographical indications:

Golfo della Spezie, Magra f., Rosano f., Laulel F., Lausella f., Lausella, Lurano, Tavarone f., Bagnon f., Monichia f., Lorgella f., La Toscana è finjta dal mare e dalla Magra, dal Tevere e da l'Alpe [Tuscany is defined by the sea and the river Magra, the river Tiber and the Alp], Salto della Cernia, Frigido f., Lago di Masaciucoli, Serchio, Lima f., Ponte a Serchio, Ponte a la Nave, Fegamo f., Ania f., Forriti f., Lapolla f. Ponte acosi, Luca, Monte Pisano, Arno f., Pisa, Calci f., Alechio f., Lago di Bientina, Caldanella f., Era f., Chiesina f., Gascana f., Lago di Fucechio, Pescie f., Fievole f., Bori f., Vinci f., Streda, Elsa f., Chiena f., Stagra (?) f., Usa (?) f., Ormo f., Monte Albano, Pesa f., Verrgin f., Pesa f., Ombrone f., Sella f., [Canale]

Baratti, Stagno, Massiera, Corna f., Stagno, Lago, Onbrone, Grosseto, Orcia f., Formone f., Orcia f., Lafarna f., Mensa f., Gora, Mensa, Gora, Arbia f., Siena, Onbrone f., Verrgin f., Pesa f., Ombrone f., Stella f., Pistoia, Vingon, Bisenzio f., Prato, Marina f., Grieve f., Grieve f., Ema, Grassina, Entella, Terzolla, Mugnone f., Africo f., Mensola f., Ambra f., Sieci f., Ponte a [Sieve], Ponte, Ruffina f., La Moscia f., Ponte a tonda, Decumano f., Ricane f., Botena f., Rimaggio f., R[o]sena f., Marcione f., Pessciola f., Strulla f., Elsa f., Fisstona, Faltona f., Carza f., Liversone f., Taviano f., Stura f., Lora f., Sieve f., Arno f., Anbra, Lorena, Labegna f., Rondine, Chiani f., Arezo, Ponte della Chiassa, Chiassa f., Castelnuovo, Ponte a Caliano, Belforte, Bagnena, Caloenzano, Salutio, Santa Mamma, Bonano f., [Ta]lla f., Socana f., Socanella f., Rassina, Rassina f., Corsolone f., Vessa f., Arnchiano f., Tegnia f., Rignano f., Rovilo, Solano f., Stagia f., Caldara, Arno f., Arno f., Chiane d'Arezzo, Fenna f., Stagno, Livorno, Porto Pisano, Lafina f., Cecina f., Sterza f., Trossa f., Passera f., Volterra, Pagone f., Ciecina f., Sella f., [Canale] Baratti,

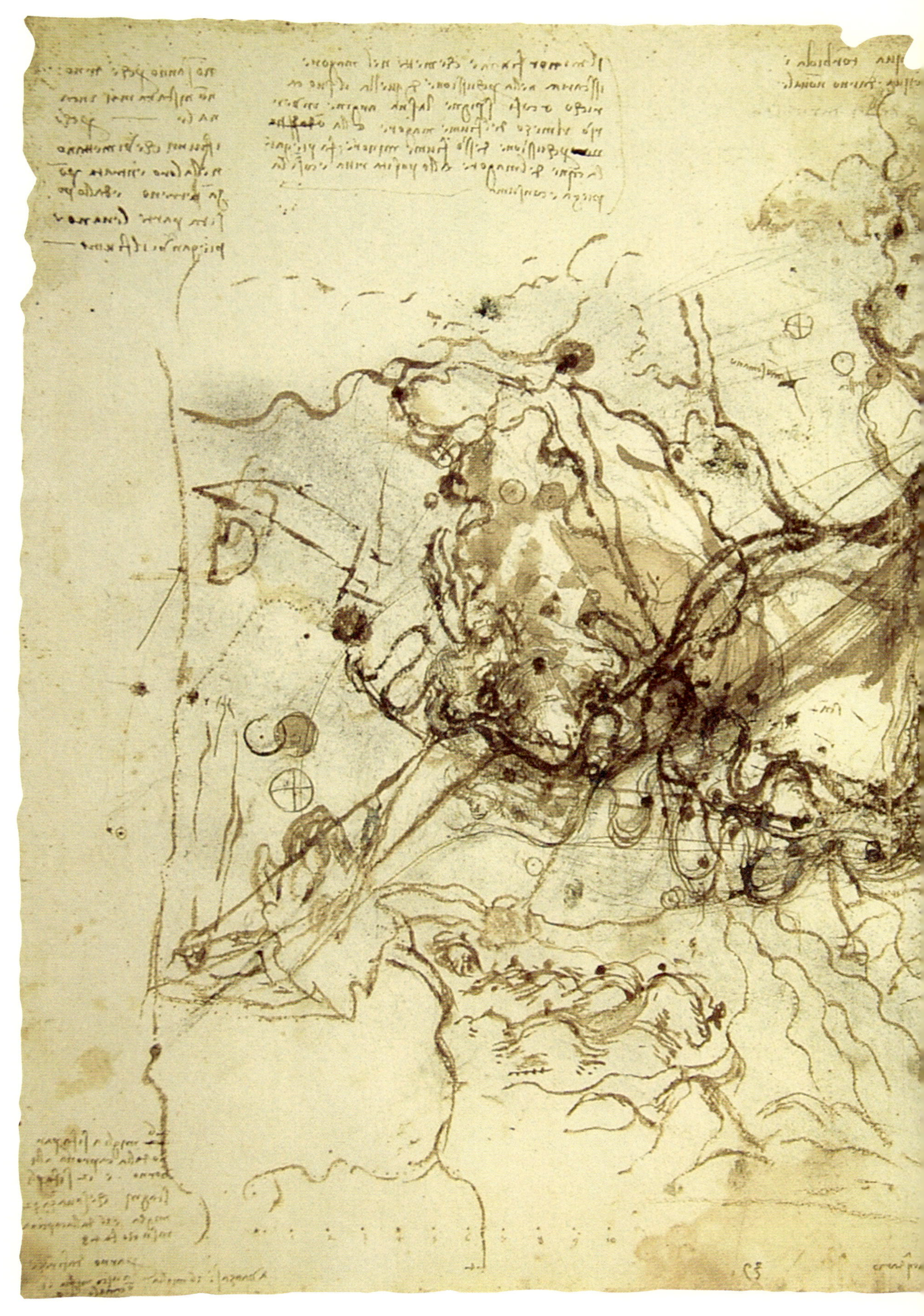

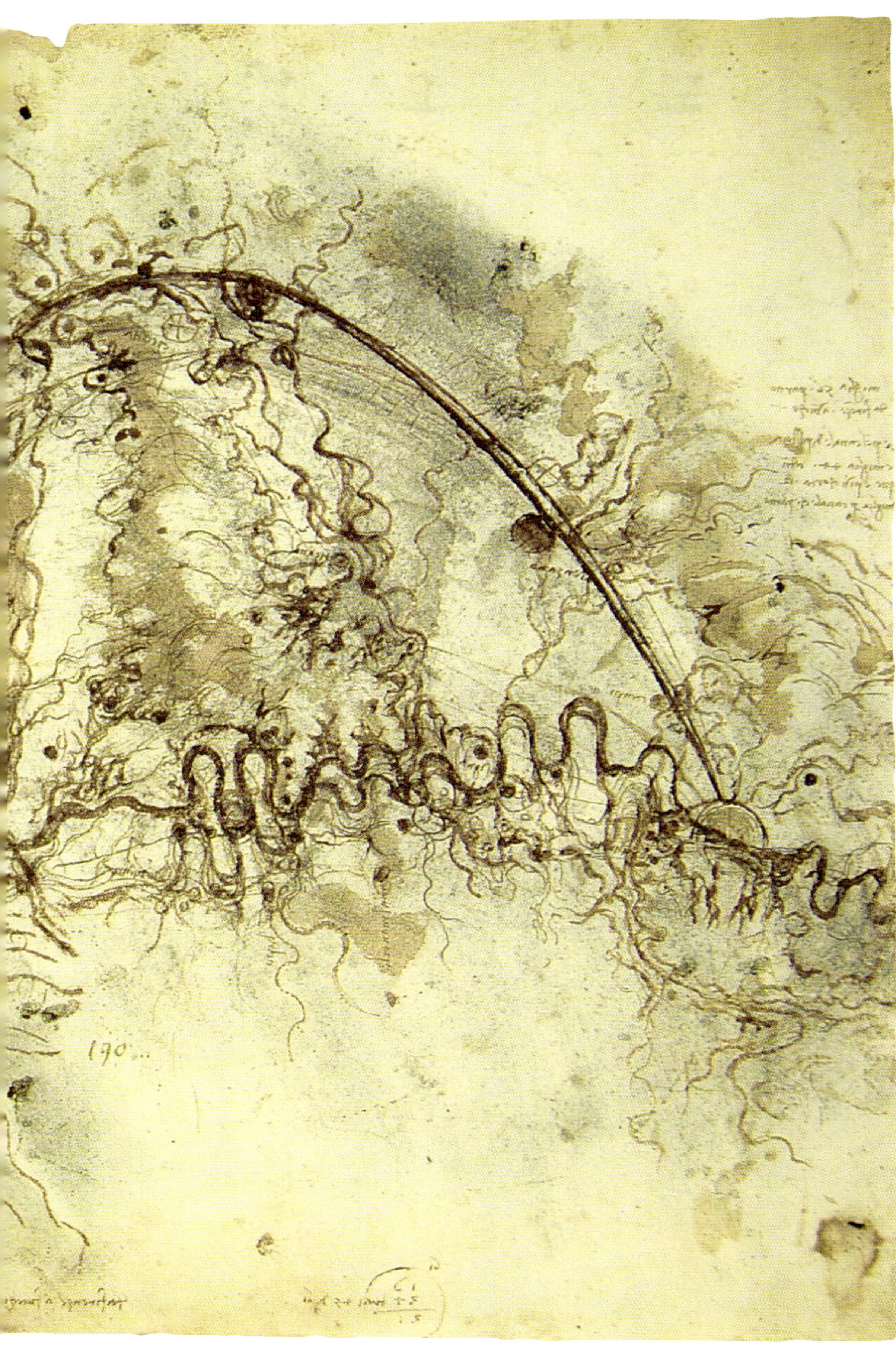

LEONARDO DA VINCI, *Study for the diversion of the Arno,*
c. 1503. Charcoal, pen and ink,
watercolour, 335 x 482 mm.
Windsor, RL 12279

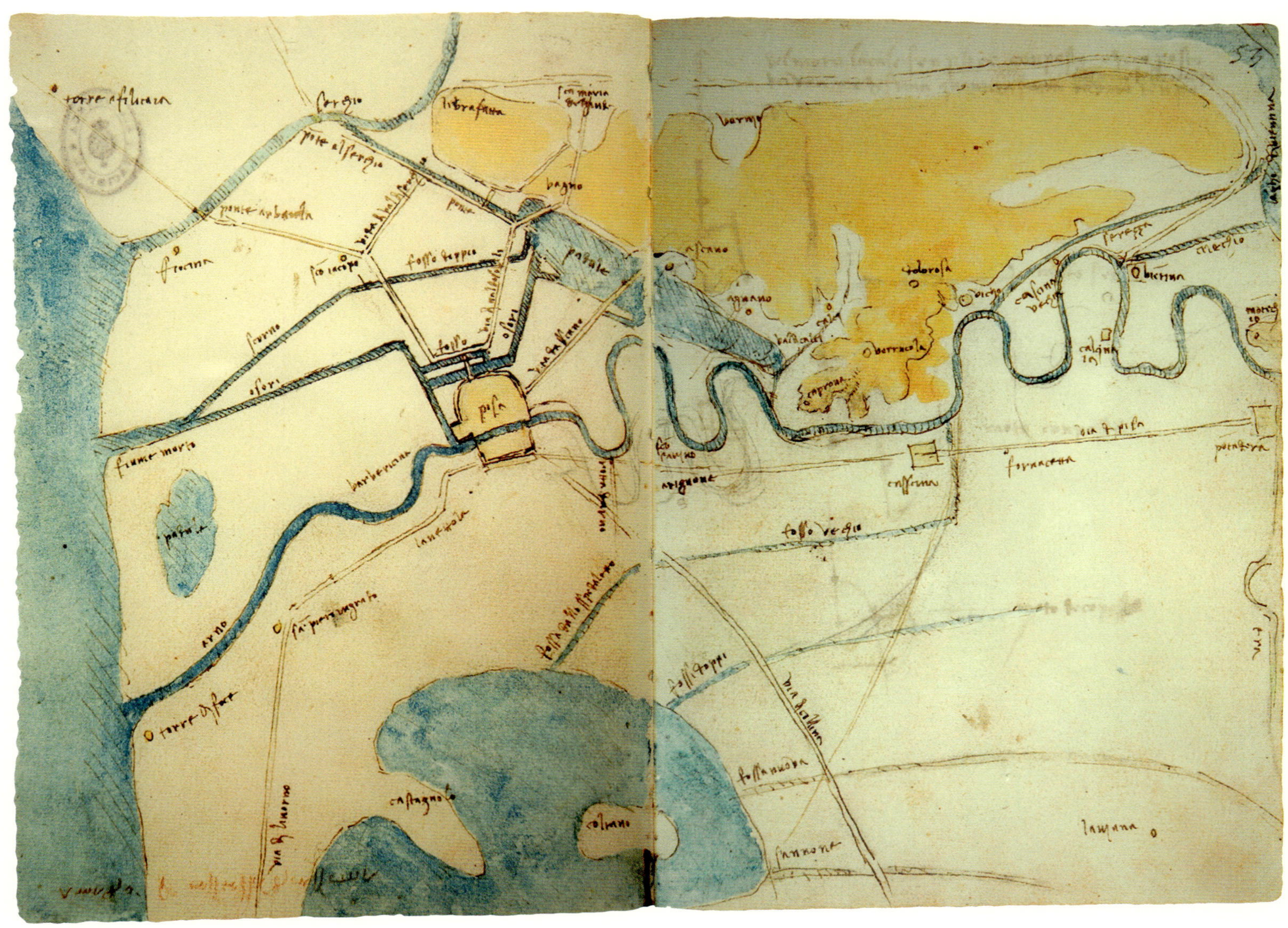

LEONARDO DA VINCI, *Map of the surroundings of Pisa*, 1503. Pen and ink and watercolour. Codex of Madrid II, ff. 52 *v*–53 *r*. Madrid, Biblioteca Nacional

Stagno, Massiera, Corna f., Stagno, Lago, Onbrone, Grosseto, Orcia f., Formone f., Orcia f., Lafarna f., Mensa f., Gora, Mensa, Gora, Arbia f., Siena, Onbrone f., Monte Argentario, Suana, Montamiata, Lago di Bolsena, Castro, Corneto, Civita Vechia, Toscanella, Viterbo, [La]go di Vico, Nepi, Tevere f., Sovara f., [Cer]fone f., Città di Castello, Scatorbia, Tevere f., Perugia, Lagho di Perugia, Trasumeno f., Cortona, Trasumeno f., Braccio da Montona lo chiuse ond'è mancato [Braccio da Montona closed it so it is lacking], Topino f., Chiaccio f., Topino f., Chiaccio f., Nestore f., Paglia f., Chiane cioè la Fenna f., Orvieto, La Parma f., Parma, Closcolo f., Reggio, Po f., Secchia f., Formicone f., Samogia f., Pariazo f., Modona, Reno f., Lamino f., Reno f., Po f., Ferrara, Canale di Reno, Bologna, Po f., Argenta, Saviana f., Ledice f., Sellero f., Santerno f., Imola, Lamone f., Faenza, Montone f., Furlì, Ronco f., Marchia f., Cesena, Marchia f. divide la Romagna da la Marca [divides the Romagna from the Marches], Rimini, Pesero, Canonica f., Metauro f., Fano.

Consequence of a series of direct reconnaissance, carried out along the Tyrrhenian shoreline and the plane of Pisa, there comes the map of Windsor (RL 12683), written up in not mirrored writing and therefore destined to be used, as an instrument both technical and of memory, for precise strategic and military interests.

Leonardo has made use of black chalk, pen and ink, water, and as for colours of ochre and intense blue. It is here represented in aerial perspective a panoramic view of the western sector of Tuscany, further than twenty miles on the west of Florence, from Lucca to Pisa, from the hills of Volterra to Livorno, with a scale a little greater of 1:200000. It is the expression of an empirical knowledge, founded on the meticulous observation of the territory that can be disassembled in its different units, coupled to detailed surveys about the configuration and nature of the territory, where mountains,

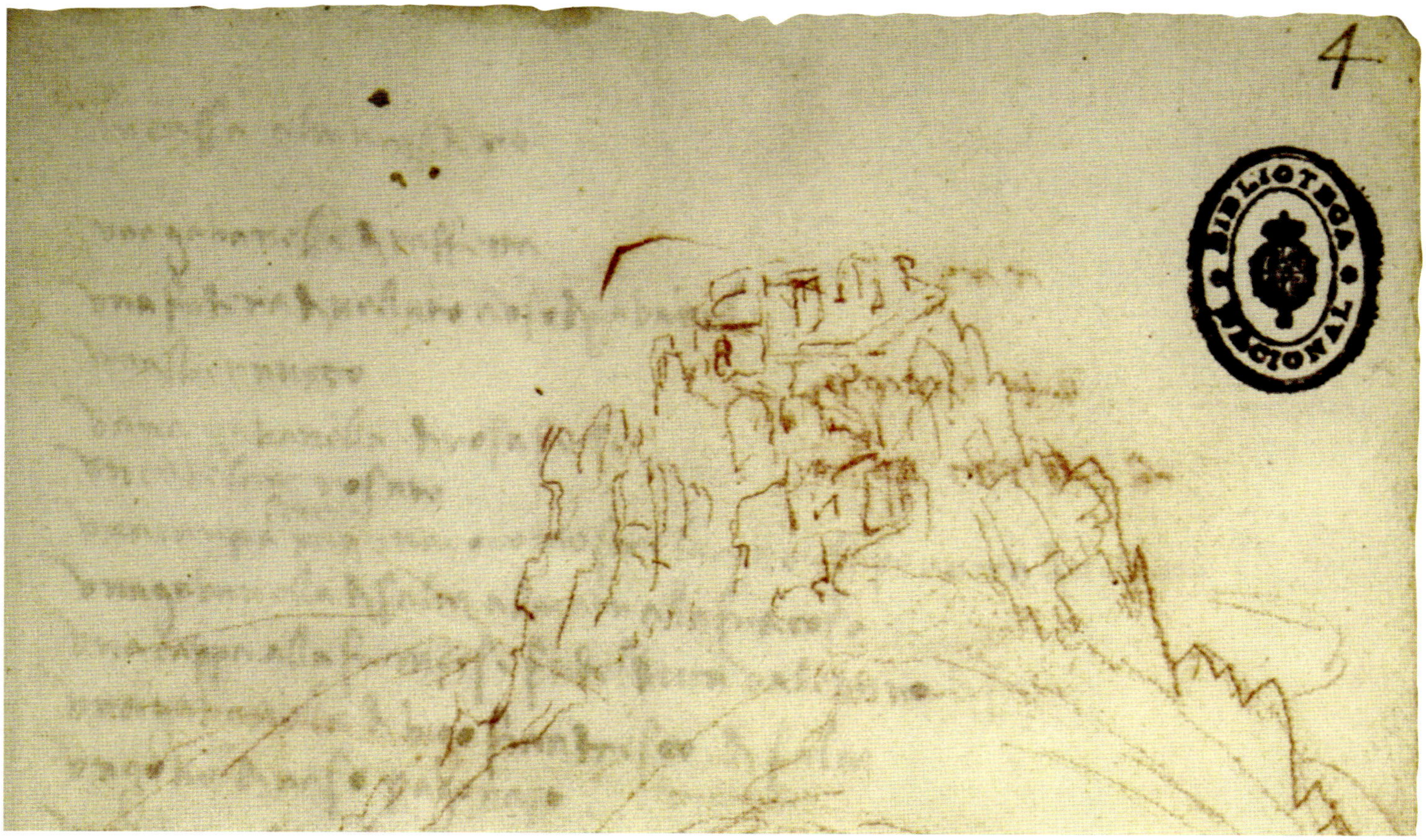

LEONARDO DA VINCI, *The Mountain and the Fortress of the Verruca*, c. 1503. Red pencil on paper. Cod. of Madrid II, f. 4 *r*. Particular

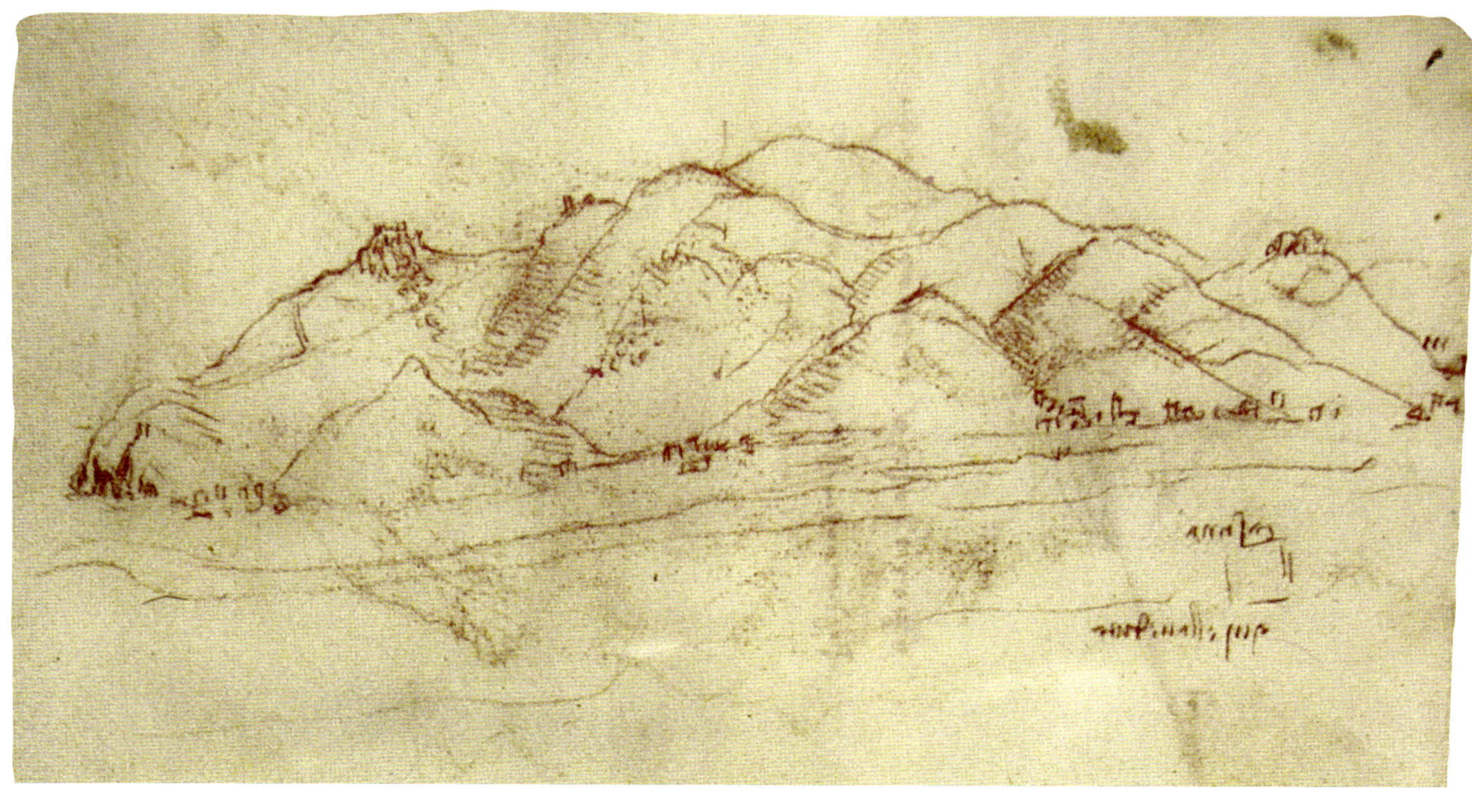

LEONARDO DA VINCI, *The Mountains of Pisa*, c. 1503. Red pencil on paper, 211 x 300 mm. Codex of Madrid II, ff. 7 *v.*

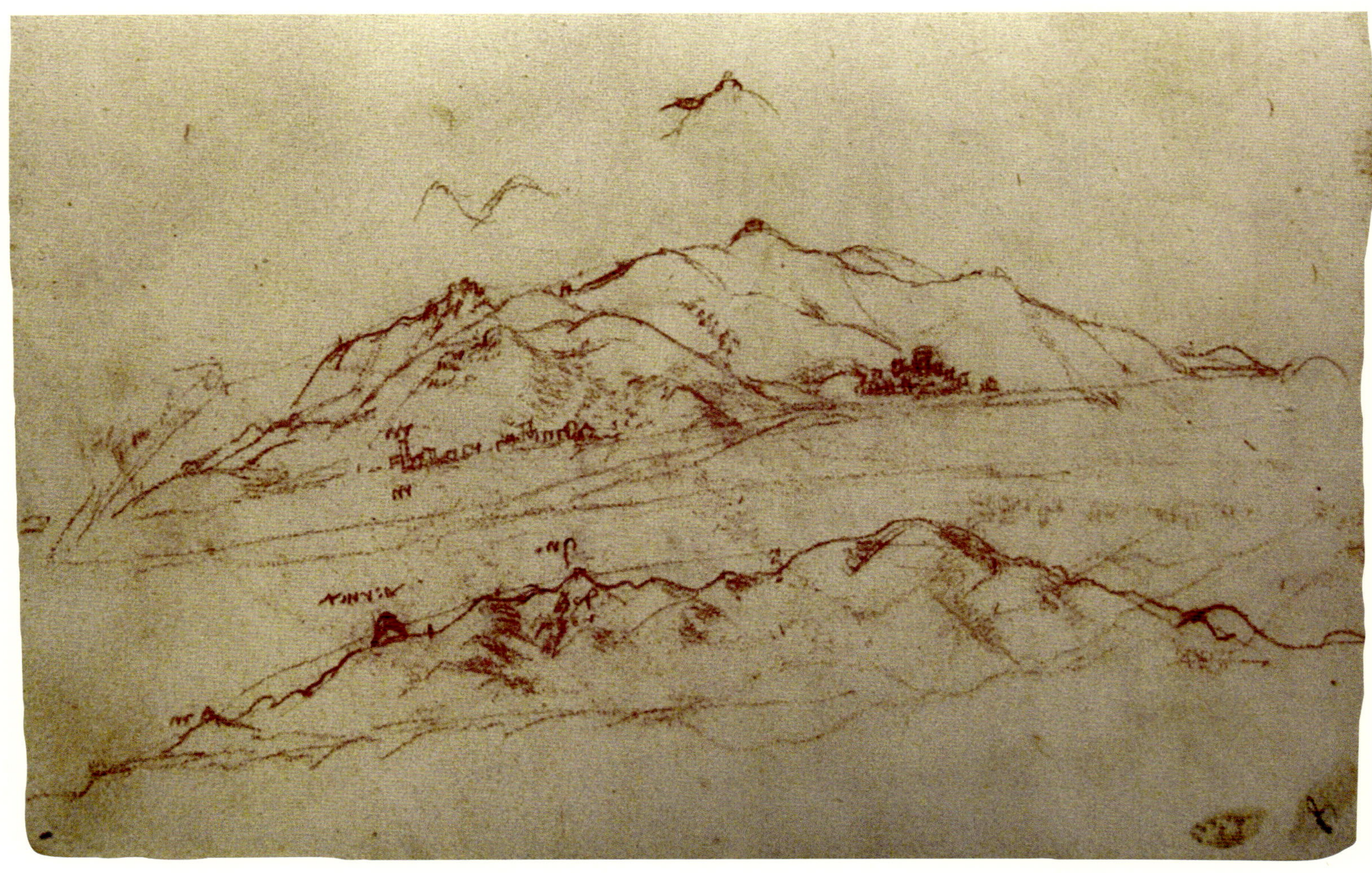

LEONARDO DA VINCI, *The Mountains of Pisa, c.* 1503. Red pencil on paper, 211 x 300 mm. Codex of Madrid II, ff. 8 *r.* Madrid, Biblioteca Nacional

rivers, lakes, ponds, towns and fortresses are emphasized. The map depicts the region in a conventional way with dome-shaped hills «mole-hill-like», on whose top are represented the various cities, making us assume its derivation from pre-existing cartographical documents, though made more lively by the pictorial solutions adopted.

There are here transcribed one hundred and three toponyms, sometimes repeated, and the entire geographical area seems relevant to explain the plan of diversion of the Arno towards the Pond of Livorno, in order to obtain the capitulation of Pisa.[34] The works had started in August 1504, but then, the riotous character of the Arno and the missed payment of the wages, caused the abandon of the realization of the plan within two months:

San Vincenzio, Canpiglia, Donoratico, Borgeri, Bibona, Casale, Montescudaio, Castagneto, Sassetta, Sughereto, Guardistallo, Segalare, Monteforcoli, Montegenmoli, Querceto, [C]astelnuovo, Le Pomerance, Monte Castelli, Sillano, Volterra, Vada, Rasignano, Castelnuovo, Malandrone, Ripalbello, Colognola, Casciana, La Badia, Monte Vaso, Terriciola, Morona, Mecola, Gello, Soiana, Montecatini, Pietracassia, Pomaia, Pastina, Orciatico, Laiatico, Villa Magna, Era f., Fiume Era, Livorno, Capellina, Castello, Anselmo, Nugola, Stagno, San Regolo, La Badiola, Colle Salvecti, Colle Montanino, Parlaco, Parlaco, Tremolato, Via di Livorno, Usilgliano, Alzamone, Casciana, Lari, Serafino, Via di Maremma, Fossana, Ponte di Saco, Foce, San Piero in Grado, Pisa, San Savino Settimo, Arno f., Cascina, Pontatera, Forcoli, Aliga, Collelungo, San Cervagio, Monte Achita, Monte Castelli, [To]glia[no], Ghizano, Fabrica, Foiano, Palaia, Fabrica, Montechio, Usilgliano, Marti, Celli, Serravallino, Monte Topoli, San Romano, San Iacopo, Serchio f., Santa Maria in Castello, Molina, Librafatta, Filetto, Lucca, Val di Calci, Bagno, Verrucola, Vᵃ· Monte Magiore, Arno f.

---

[34] See G. CASTELFRANCO, *Il canale Firenze-mare nei progetti di Leonardo,* «Civiltà delle macchine», III, 1955; C. PEDRETTI, *La Verruca,* «Renaissance Quarterly», XXV, 4, 1972; ID., *Il primo Leonardo a Firenze. L'Arno, la cupola, il Battistero,* Firenze, Giunti Barbèra, 1976.

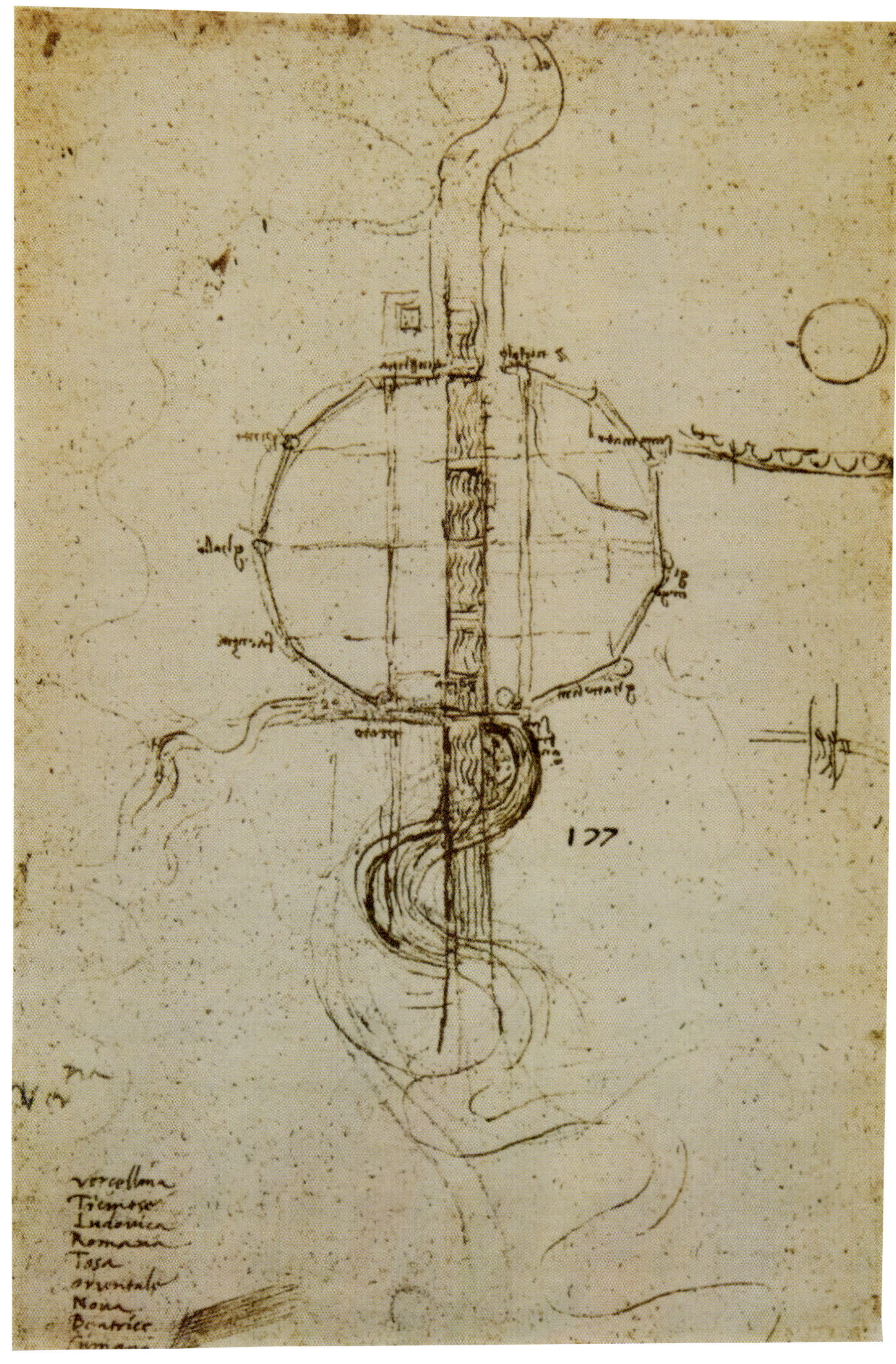

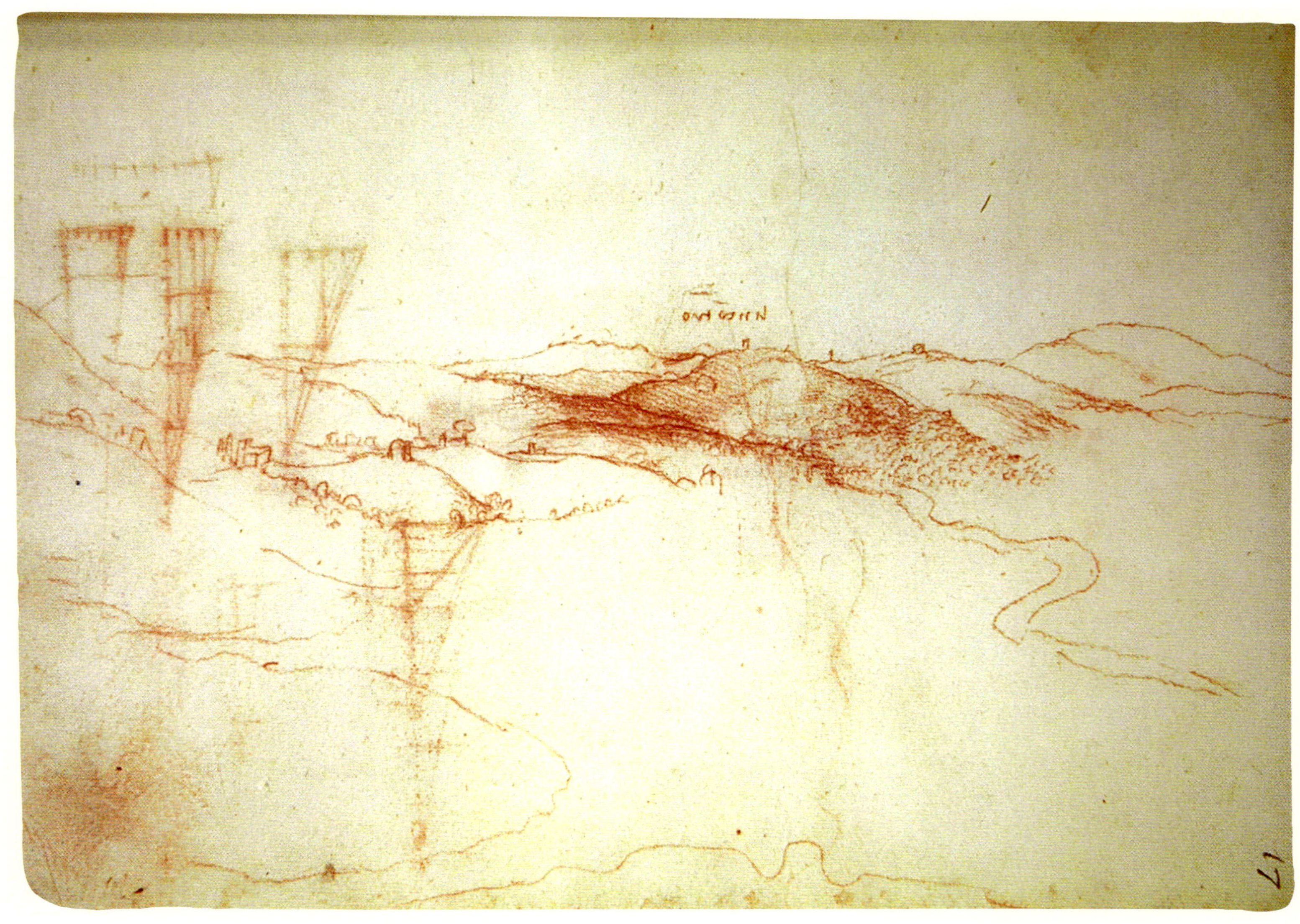

LEONARDO DA VINCI, *The hills around Pontassieve, c.* 1503. Red pencil on paper, 151 x 210 mm. Cod. of Madrid II, f. 17 *r*. Madrid, Biblioteca Nacional

The predominance of the military interest connected to this map is subordinate to the political vicissitudes, which at the end of the fifteenth century involved the ancient and powerful maritime city of Pisa, when with the descent to Italy of Charles VIII, king of France, it had rebelled to the Florentine hegemony (1494). After years of devastating war, carried out under the guide of Antonio Giacomini, the Republic of Florence, guided by Pier Soderini and Niccolò Machiavelli, made use of the advice of Leonardo, in order to bring to an end the plan to divert the course of the Arno and in such a way to force Pisa to surrender (1503-1504). Leonardo, on 21 June 1503, received the assignment of military adviser, inspected first the fortress of the Verruca, in order to make it impregnable (Cod. of Madrid II, f. 4 *r*), and then the hills and the structural situation of the surroundings of Pisa, with the Castles and the fortified villages. Correlated to the investiga-

tion it is the map of the environs of Pisa (Cod. of Madrid II, ff. 52 *v*-53 *r*), where Leonardo carries out a hydrographical study of the entire territory, to prepare the various hydraulic strategies that were necessary «to level the Arno in the area of Pisa and take it out of its bed». In this map, the toponyms have been indicated with not mirrored writing, from left to right, revealing thus its cartographic utilization for an illustrious addressee of the political or military world:

Torre a Filicaia, Serchio, Sancta Maria del Giudice, Librafatta, Ponte al Serchio, Bagno, Ponte, Ponte Arbavolla, Padule, Fucina, Fosso Doppio, Via di Val di Serchio, Sancto Jacopo, Scorno, Fosso, Via di Valdasoli, Osori, Osori, Via d'Assciano, Barbericina, Pisa, Rotta d'Arno, Fiume Morto, Padule, La Vettola, San Piero in Grado, Arno, Torre di Foce, Castagnolo, Fossa dallo Spedaletto, Via di Livorno, Coltano, [in sanguine and turned over] Amodio f. castelli

CARLO STARNAZZI

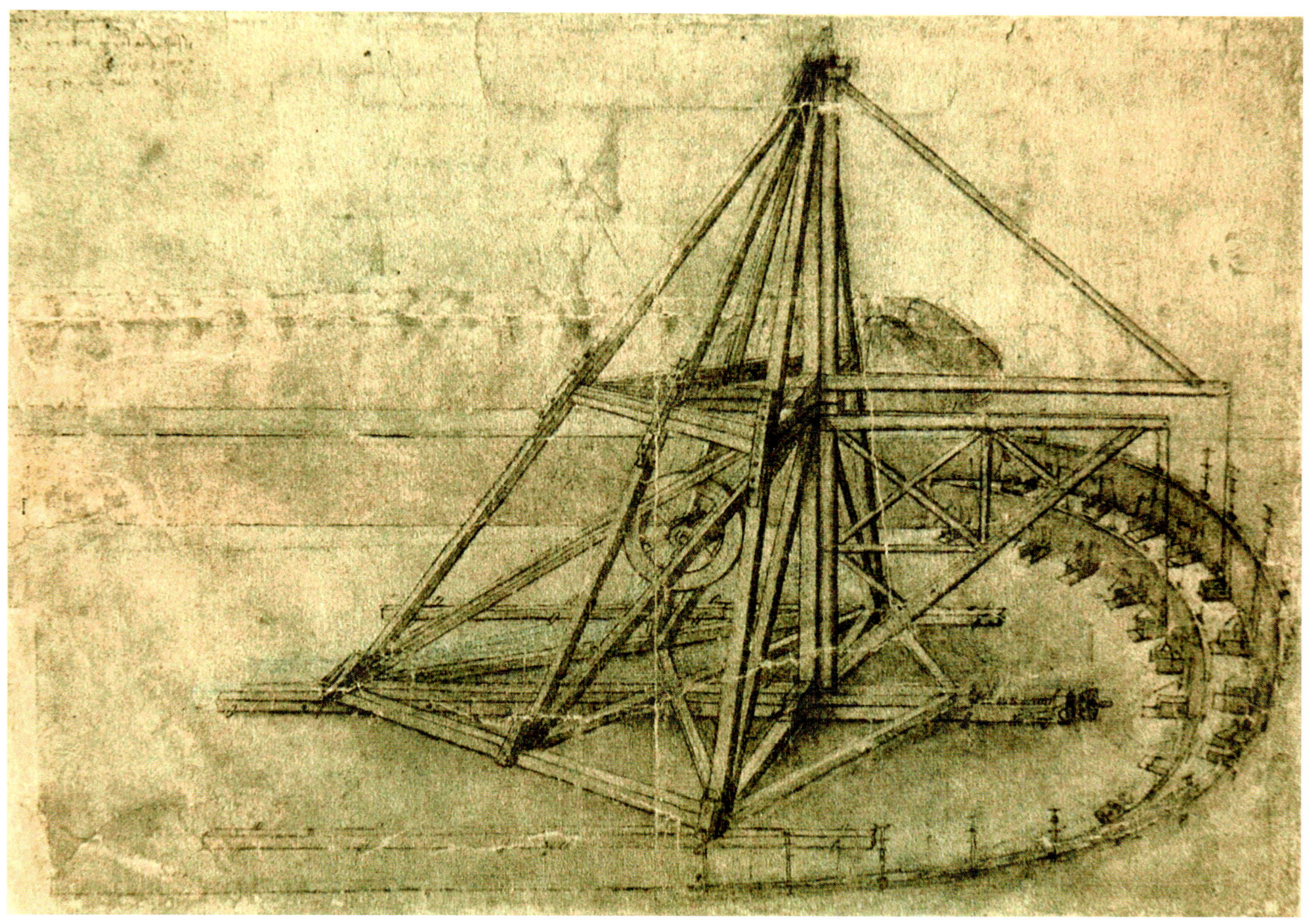

LEONARDO DA VINCI, *Excavating machine, c.* 1503. Pen and ink, 280 x 400 mm. Cod. Atlanticus, f. 4 *r.* Milan, Biblioteca Ambrosiana

di Casscina, Vornjo, Asciano, Dolorosa, Laghi di Bientina, Agnano, Serezza, Calci, Nechio, Vico, Bientina, Val di Calci, Cascina Vecchia, Verrucosa, Calcinaia, Montechio, Caprona, Sancto Savino, Via di Pisa, a Rignone, Cascina, Fornacetta, Pontadera, Fosso vecchio, Era, Fossi Doppi, Via di Collina, Fossa nuova, Sannone, Laviana.

On 20 August 1504, the Florentine Republic deliberated «about turning the Arno at the tower near Fagiano», assenting to the beginning of the works, in which it was planned the construction of a retaining dam along the course of the Arno and the realization of two man-made channels, turned the one towards the river Serchio and the other towards the marshes of Stagno (Cod. of Madrid II, ff, 52 *v*–53 *r*), while the coast would have been controlled by galleys recruited to prevent provisioning by sea.

Testimonies of the setting up of this leonardian project by the Florentine engineers have come out also from recent excavations, that have brought to light foundations of bridges, not far away from where the diversion of the Arno had been planned.[35]

---

[35] See J. ROBERTS, *Il Codice Hammer di Leonardo da Vinci* (a cura di), presentazione di C. Pedretti, Firenze, Giunti, 1982.

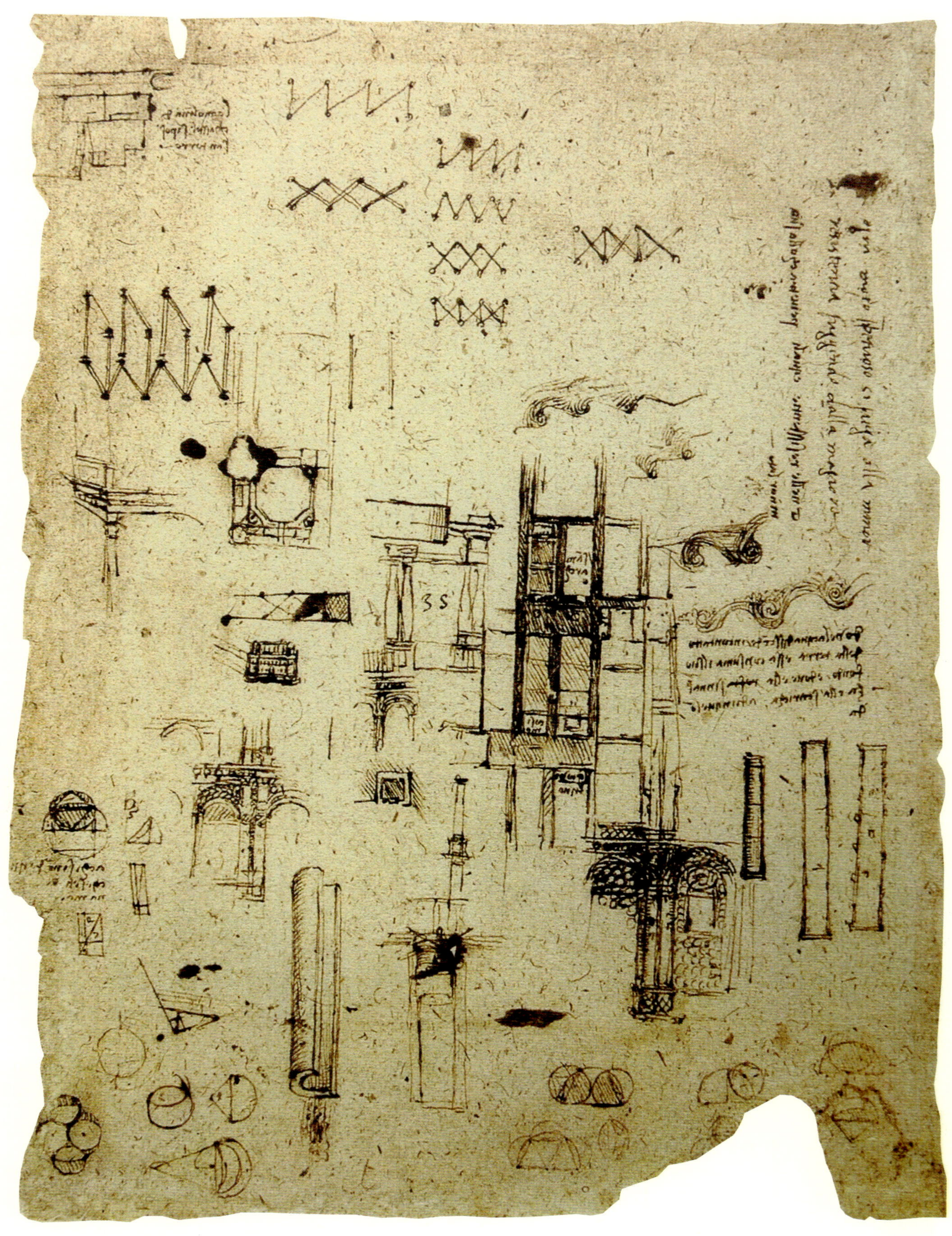

Leonardo da Vinci, *The motive of the «branch»*, c. 1515. Pen and ink, 281 x 220 mm. Codex Atlanticus, f. 865 *r*. Milan, Biblioteca Ambrosiana.

IV. Leonardo and the Rome of Leo X (1514-16)

log of laurel that set out green leaves, almost to demonstrate that the name of the forefather refreshed and revived.

THE COMMITMENT of Leonardo as a cartographer will continue also at the service of Giuliano de' Medici, that, after the raising to the papal seat of the cardinal Giovanni, his brother (11 March 1513), had moved to Rome, lodging near Castel Sant' Angelo, heart and symbol of the military power of the State, where he will be named General Captain of the army.

The triumphal celebration of Leo X as a pontiff took place in Florence under the auspice and the feeling of a renewed Golden Age. It could be perceived everywhere in the city, in a general delirium («it seemed that the city was going upside down»),[36] the sense of a political and cultural rebirth, symbolically suggested, in the counterpoint of a carnival song of Jacopo Nardi, by the parade of the magnificent allegoric wagons, decorated by Jacopo da Pontormo, among which stood out the one of the triumph of the Age and Century of Gold «with a very beautiful and very rich artifice», where the «large dry branch setting out new leaves», would have meant to allude to Lorenzo di Piero de' Medici, duke of Urbino, since the «branch» with the vegetal motive or log of laurel that becomes green again (CA, f. 315 *rb* [865 *r*]) or, like the ring with the diamond (CA, ff. 13 *r* [44 *r*]; 114 *v-b* [316 *v*]), other Medicean heraldic emblem, already adopted by the Magnificent, had been by him brought back to be a symbol of the familiar prestige:[37]

Being all Florence in feast and in joyfulness for the creation of the aforesaid Leo the Tenth, many feasts were ordered and between the others two very beautiful and of greatest expense by two Companies of Lords and gentlemen of the city, of the one of which, that was called the Diamond, it was head Mr. Giuliano de' Medici, brother of the Pope, who had entitled it thus for having been the diamond the motto of Lorenzo the Elder his father, and of the other one, that had for name and standard the Branch, it was head Mr. Lorenzo son of Piero de' Medici, which I say had for motto a branch, that is a dry

Leo X and Giuliano intended to continue the high tradition of the Medici House in the promotion of arts and humanities and therefore, the future Duke of Nemours, convened to his court Leonardo, predisposing his lodging in the Villa of Innocent VIII in the Belvedere of the Vatican, partially restructured and adapted to his requirements by the papal architect Giuliano Leno, assistant to Bramante and Raphael: «Things that have to be done at Belvedere in the rooms of master Lionardo da Vinci» (*Libretto dei Ricordi 1513-A*, Città del Vaticano, Archivio della Fabbrica di San Pietro, ff. 23, 28, 31, 33). The affective connection between Leonardo and Giuliano de' Medici was deep, so much that Benedetto Varchi, in 1564, in the funeral oration for Michelangelo, would have remembered that Giuliano behaved with extreme courtesy towards him, and since he was «gentleman of unheard goodness and ineffable value, he loved him so much that he dealt with him more as a brother than as a companion».

Arrived to Rome, Leonardo continued his life of investigation and of solitude, curved in geometrical-mathematical studies on the transformation of surfaces, on the question of the squaring of the circle, on the «lunettes», finalized perhaps to the realization of a great parabolic mirror (CA, f. 279 *ra* [750 *r*]), on the series of mathematical games that were characterizing his studies «About the geometric game: finished the day 7 of July at hours 23 at Belvedere, in the study made for me by the Magnificent 1514» (CA, f. 90 *va* [244 *v*]). To all that, there had to be added the reflections and the experimentations conducted near Castel Sant'Angelo on the questions about water and about acoustics (CA, f. 65 *ra* [183 *r*]), while with the same enthusiasm he made palaeontological observations on the slopes of Monte Mario: «make you illustrate where are the shells at Monte Mario» (CA, f. 92 *vc* [253 *v*]). And it is on a sheet of the same period that, unexpectedly, Leonardo pronounces with Lucretian epic inspiration his singular observation on the necessity to know the palaeogeographical aspects of the Earth, in order to admire with the eyes of the scientist and of the poet its vitality and breath, its changes in the course of the millennia: «the knowledge of pas<t> times and of the site of the earth is ornament and food of human minds» (CA, f. 373 *v-a* [1040 *v*]). Therefore, scientific surveys on the slopes of Monte Mario, where, around 1517, Raphael would have planned for the leisure of cardinal Giulio de' Medici, that will be Pope Clement VII (1523), a suburban villa conceived with courtyards, porches, baths, theatre and gardens, adhering faithfully, for the love reserved to the models of antiquity, to what was described to such purpose by Pliny the Younger in his *Epistles*,

---

[36] See L. LANDUCCI, *Diario fiorentino dal 1450 al 1516*, Firenze, Iodoco Del Badia, 1883.

[37] See J. SHEARMAN, *Pontormo and Andrea del Sarto, 1513*, «Burlington Magazine», 109, 1965; M. CAMPBELL, *Il ritratto del Duca Alessandro de' Medici*, in *Giorgio Vasari, tra decorazione ambientale e storiografia artistica*, Convegno di Studi (Arezzo, 8-10 ottobre 1981) a cura di G. C. Garfagnini, Firenze, Olschki, 1985. In the Medicean heraldry, the two recurrent emblems are the ring with the diamond and the large branch on which come up new leaves, with allusion to the Glory that revives. Giuliano de' Medici would have added the writing GLOVIS that, read backwards, reveals its intrinsic message of «Si volg» («it turns round»), because after so many defeats, explains Paolo Giovio in his *Ragionamento* (1564), good luck seemed to be again on the Medici's side. See C. PEDRETTI, *«li medici mi crearono e desstrussono»*, «Achademia Leonardi Vinci. Journal of Leonardo Studies and Bibliography of Vinciana», VI, Firenze, Giunti, 1993.

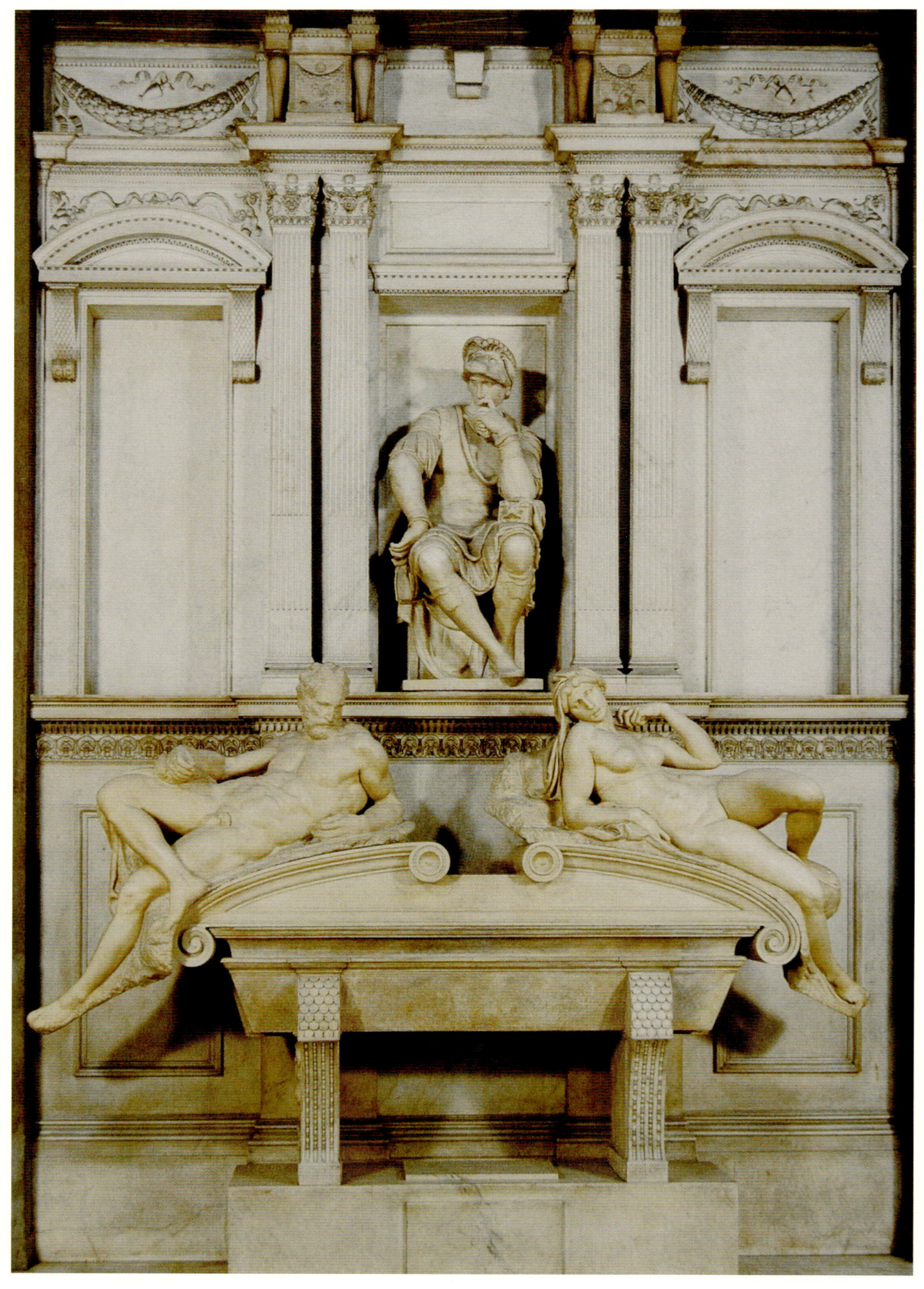

MICHELANGELO, *Tomb of Lorenzo de' Medici Duke of Urbino*, 1524-34. Marble. Florence, Basilica of San Lorenzo, Sagrestia Nuova

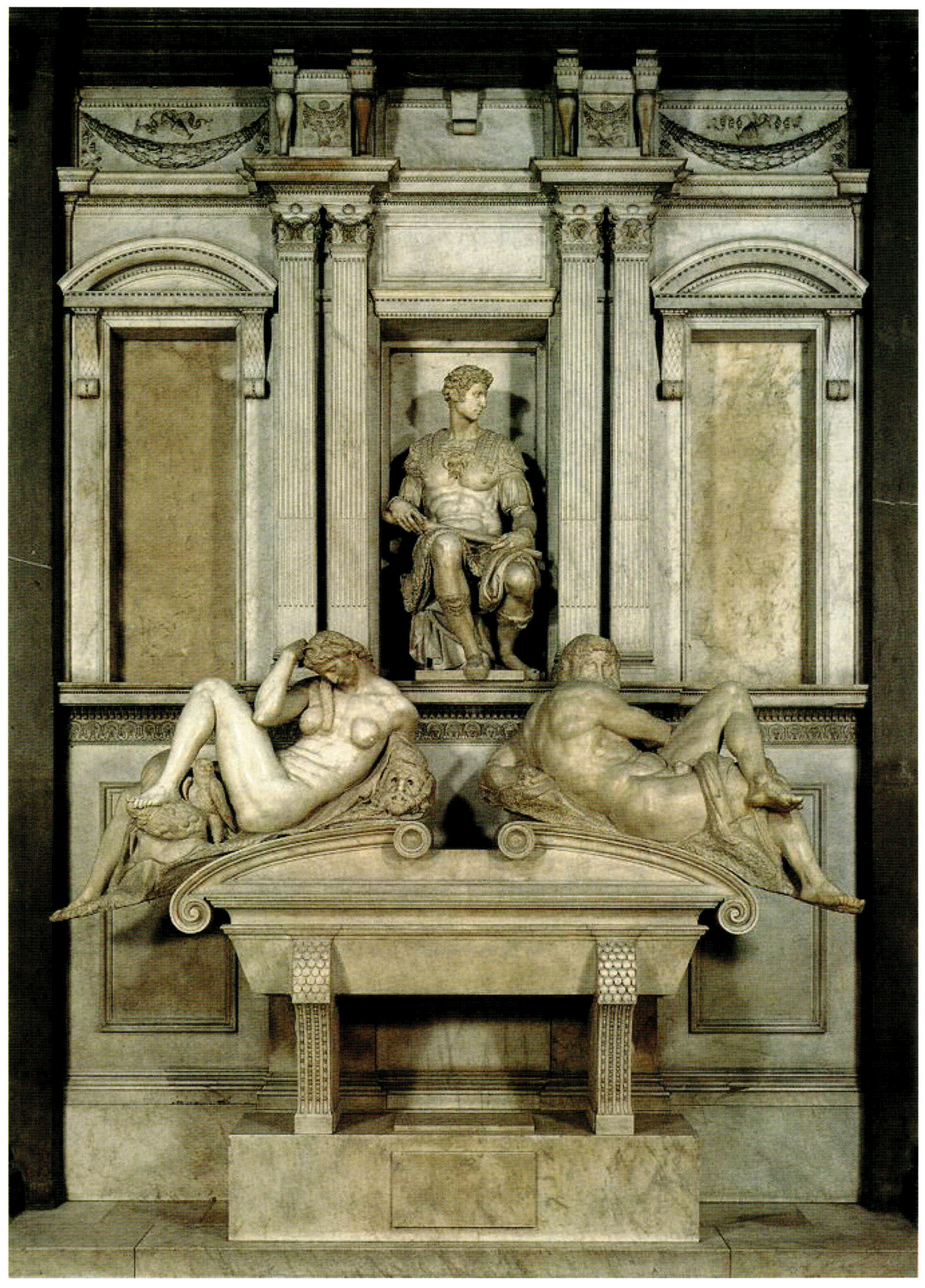

Michelangelo, *Tomb of Giuliano de' Medici Duke of Nemours*, 1524-34. Marble. Florence, Basilica of San Lorenzo, Sagrestia Nuova

consulted also by Leonardo, to study the masonry systems and the shapes of the harbours of the ancient Romans, in a synoptic view with the canonical statements of Vitruvius (*De Architectura*), during the inspection to the port of Civitavecchia in spring 1514 (CA, ff. 63 *vb* [180 *v*]; 271 *rf* [733 *r*]). And, right here, Bramante, under the pontificate of Julius II, had begun the rebuilding of the Castle, employing the «multiple gun-embrasures», invented by Leonardo in his studies of fortified architecture since 1502-03 (CA, ff. 48 *v-a* [134 *r*]; 48 *v-b* [135 *r*]).[38]

At the arrival of Leonardo in Rome, the Eternal City was swarming with the greatest architects and painters of the time: Bramante, after having planned its restoration, was focusing on the Fabric of Saint Peter's, where it was supervisor Atlante Migliorotti,[39] with a complex central plan project (the circle and the square of Vitruvius), of which there will remain, at his death (11 March 1514), the four powerful great arches of uphold of the dome and in phase of completion the western cross arm. An ideal plan, considered as perfect in the Renaissance, and that for its semicircular apsidioles, the four cupolas and the great central dome, reminds closely the projects of churches with central plan devised by Leonardo, around 1487-90, during his first Milan stay, when he worked in close collaboration with Bramante. And then, his perpetual competitor Michelangelo, who had already admired the work of Luca Signorelli, performer of a *Last Judgement*,[40] finished on the vaults of the Sistine Chapel (1508-12), between *Prophets* and *Sybils*, the epic cycle of the history of humanity, from the *Genesis* to the *Deluge*, instilling in the majestic bodies of the *Naked* his powerful concept of beauty.

Signorelli in fact, anticipating Michelangelo in the posture and in the attitudes of the nudes, had faced with talent the topic of the *Apocalypse* in the Chapel of San Brizio in the Dome of Orvieto, where Leonardo, arriving from Foligno (Ms. L, 94 *v*), stopped together with the army of Cesare Borgia, in January 1503 (Ms. L, f. 10 *v*), when the Valentino decided to cut short, after the plunder of Montefiascone and Viterbo, the last resistances of the Orsini House at Cere and Bolsena.[41]

To the anthropocentric conception of Signorelli and Michelangelo, that had placed aside the interest for natural world, Leonardo definitively replaced the macrocosmic dimension of nature, claiming its supremacy and cancelling, in his wonderful and imposing apocalyptical syntheses, orchestrated between vortices and destructions, the figure of man, impotent before the mysteries of a world that he was no more in a position to dominate.

Therefore, on the opposite also of Michelangelo, Leonardo had pushed towards a radical conclusion the artistic aspects of an art meant as philosophy and of which, already in 1504, the young Raphael, that had moved from Siena to Florence,[42] had precisely admired its innovative drive, that is that language so solemn and that «terrible foundation of concepts and greatness of art, in which few have been equal»:

> *Therefore, seeing he the works of Lionardo da Vinci, which in the postures of heads, as well of males as of females, did not have equal, and in giving grace to the figures and in their motions surpassed all the other painters, remained all stupefied and amazed; and in brief since he liked the way of Lionardo more than any other he had ever seen, he commenced to study it, and leaving, though with great fatigue, little by little the way of Pietro, he tried, as much as he knew and the most he could, to imitate the way of Lionardo. However, in spite of any diligence or study he made, in some difficulties he could never pass Lionardo* (Vasari, 1568).

In this period, Raphael was at the apex of his success, after the frescoes in the «Room of the Signature» (the *School of Athens*, 1509-10, in which Leonardo could have admired his

---

[38]   See L. H. Heydenreich, *Studi archeologici di Leonardo da Vinci a Civitavecchia*, «Raccolta Vinciana», XIV, 1930-34; A. Bruschi, *Bramante, Leonardo e Francesco di Giorgio a Civitavecchia*, in *Studi Bramanteschi. Atti del Congresso internazionale*, 1970, Roma, 1974.

[39]   According to the Gaddian Anonymous, Atlante Migliorotti had accompanied Leonardo to Milan, in 1482, in order to introduce to Ludovico the Moor a lyre, of which he was a rare player, on mandate of Lorenzo the Magnificent. The presence of the Migliorotti among the supervisors of the Fabric of Saint Peter's, between 1513 and 1516, is testified also by a letter of Michelangelo, sent to Francesco Fattucci, in 1524, where the same Cardinal Bibbiena is mentioned as a benefactor of the artist: «Returned to Rome I put myself to draw cardboards for the afore mentioned work, that is for the heads and the faces all around of the before said chapel of Sixtus, and hoping to have money and to end the work. I could never obtain anything: and complaining one day with master Bernardo from Bibbiena and Attalante, of how I could not stay any more in Rome and that I had to go off; master Bernardo said to Attalante that I had to remind him about it, that he wanted to make me give some money in any way. And he made me give two thousand ducatoes of Chamber's; that are those, with the first one thousand of the marbles, which they give me as payment for the burial; and I estimated to have more for the lost time and for the works already done. And of the mentioned money, having master Bernardo and Attalante resurrected me, I donated one hundred ducatoes to the one, to the other fifty».

[40]   For Signorelli, the following studies are recommended: G. Mancini, *Vita di Luca Signorelli*, Firenze, Carnesecchi, 1903; M. Salmi, *Luca Signorelli*, Novara, De Agostini, 1953; L. B. Kanter, *Luca Signorelli, Piero della Francesca and Perugino*, «Studi di Storia dell'Arte», I, 1991; M. Lenzini Moriondo, *Signorelli e Perugino*, in *Nel raggio di Piero. La pittura nell'Italia centrale nell'età di Piero della Francesca*, catalogo a cura di L. Berti, Venezia, Marsilio, 1992.

[41]   See C. Starnazzi, *Leonardo ad Arezzo. A. D. 2000. La Madonna dei fusi di Leonardo da Vinci e il paesaggio del Valdarno Superiore* (a cura di), con un contributo di C. Pedretti, Città di Castello, Tiferno, 2000; Id., *Leonardo, il Trasimeno e le Chiane*, in *Leonardo cartografo*, 2003, op. cit.; Id., *Leonardo e la Terra di Arezzo…*, 2005, op. cit.

[42]   After Michelangelo had returned to Rome, in 1506, in order to enter the Pope's service, and Leonardo, at the end of May of the same year, after a request of the governor of Milan, had abandoned Florence, Raphael hoped to replace them in the decoration of the Hall in Palazzo Vecchio, but already on September 5 he too reached Rome, in order then to pass between 1507 and 1508 to Urbino, where property interests recalled him, and then to Perugia, for the Pala Baglioni.

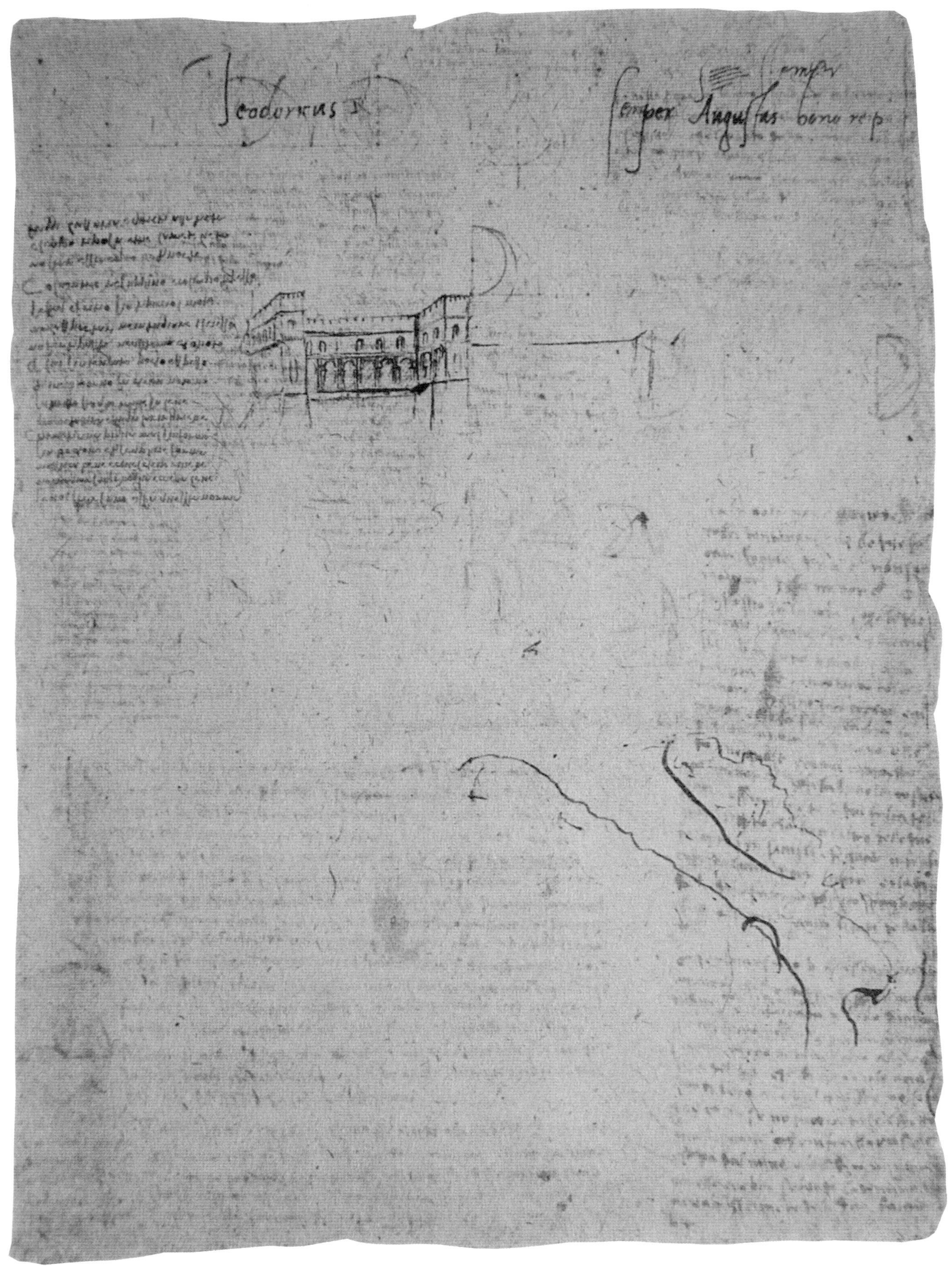

Leonardo da Vinci, *Sketch of the Villa of Innocent VIII at the Vatican's Belvedere*, *c.* 1514. Pen and ink, 282 x 214 mm. Codex Atlanticus, f. 213 *v*. Milan, Biblioteca Ambrosiana

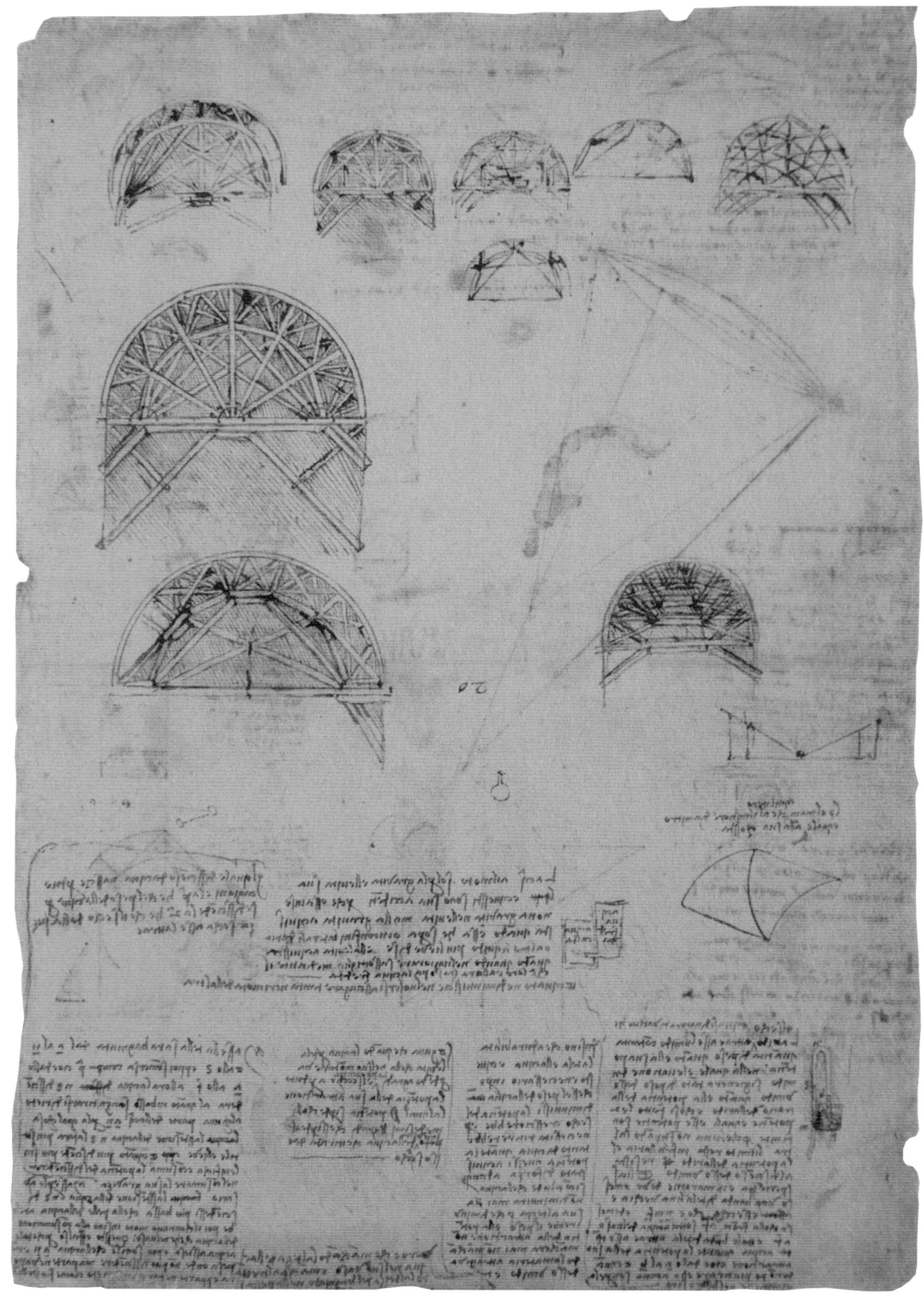

Leonardo da Vinci, *Studies of centering*, c. 1515. Pen and ink, 340 x 240 mm. Codex Atlanticus, f. 537 *r*. Milan, Biblioteca Ambrosiana

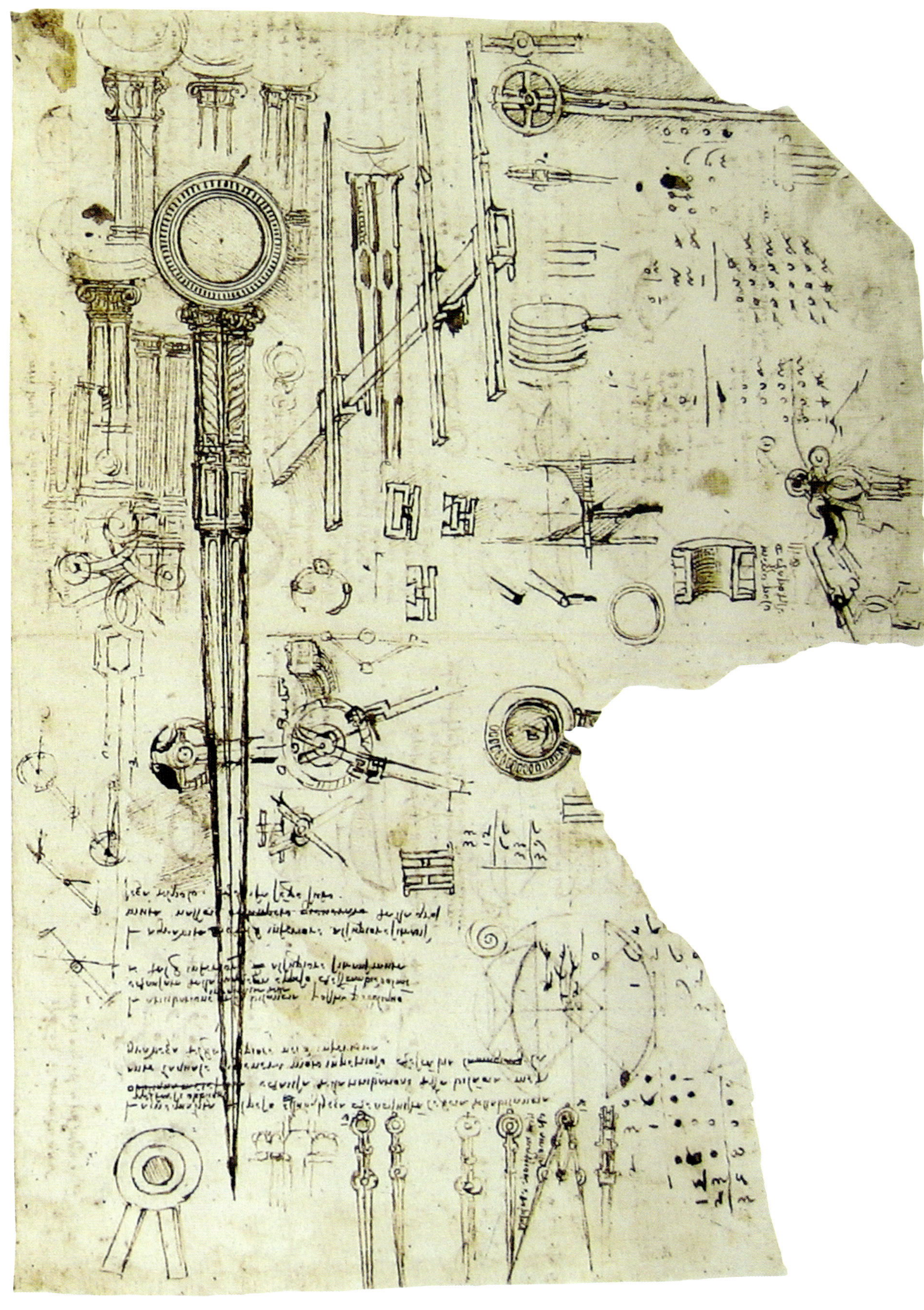

Leonardo da Vinci, *Compasses with branches*, *c.* 1514-15. Pen and ink, 422 x 295 mm. Codex Atlanticus, f. 696 *r*. Milan, Biblioteca Ambrosiana

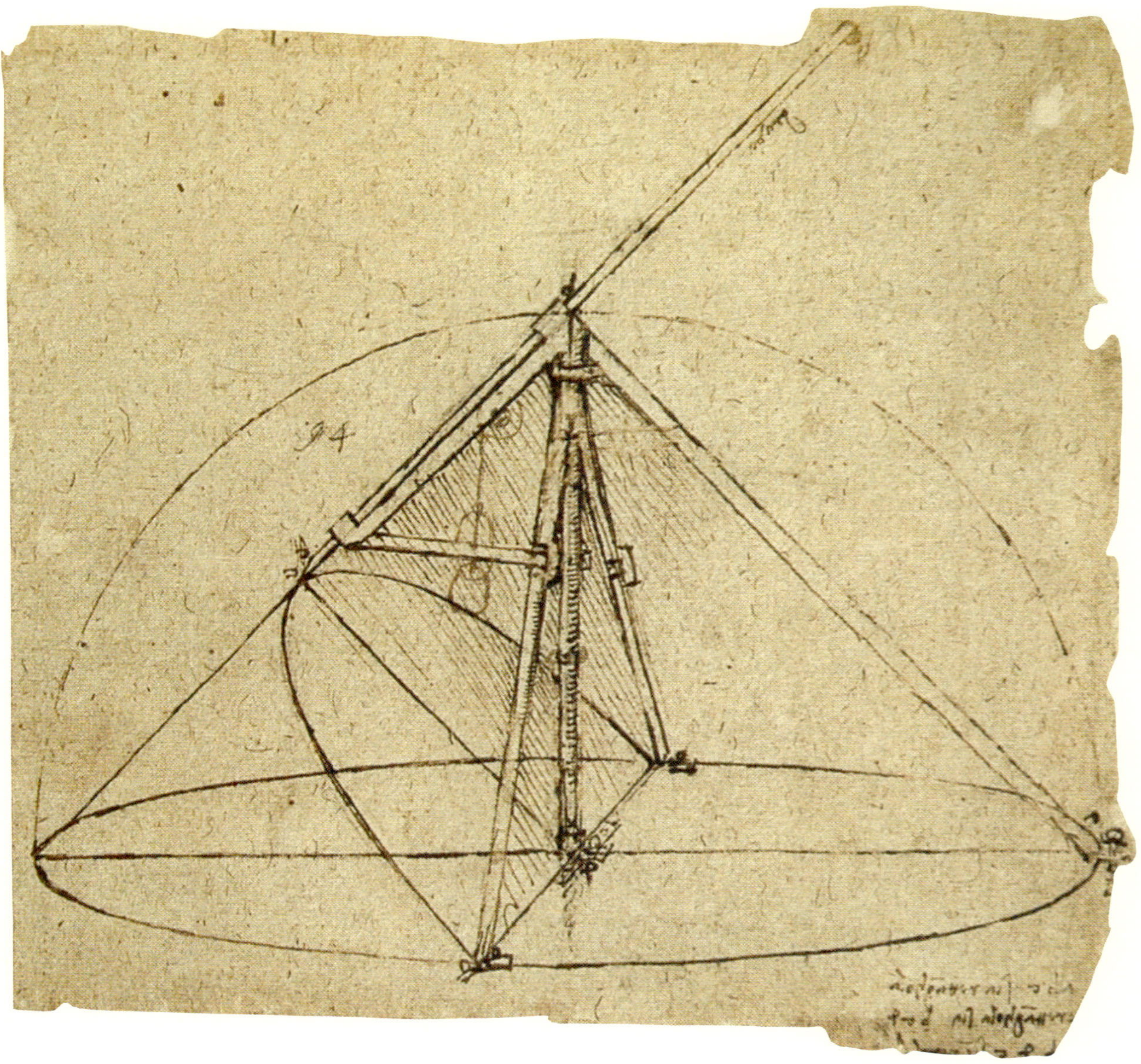

Leonardo da Vinci, *Compasses for parabolas*, c. 1513-14. Pen and ink, 380 x 194 mm. Codex Atlanticus, f. 1093 *r*. Milan, Biblioteca Ambrosiana

resemblances in the figure of Plato, that indicates how to arrive to the Truth)[43] and would have shortly after replaced Bramante as architect in the works of the Fabric of Saint Peter's (1514), supported by Giuliano da Sangallo and Friar Giocondo da Verona.

However, the relations of Leonardo with Raphael, attending both the same environment of the Vatican and the court of Giuliano de' Medici at Montegiordano, would not have been carried out in an attitude of mutual indifference. Raphael, named by Leo X supervisor to the Antiquities (1515), with an absolutely new task, could since then have taken advantage of the experience of Leonardo, involving him as an expert «geometrician and cartographer» also in his program of «master of roads».

Recently, new studies on the drawings by Raphael have documented a direct examination, by the painter of Urbino, of the roman works by Leonardo like the *Saint John the Baptist*, the *Angel of the Annunciation*, the *Pointing Lady* and his studies of anatomy.

[43] In his *School of Athens*, Raphael, recuperating ancient Greek thought, consecrated the myth of harmony and of the «pax philosophica», indispensable premise for religious and political peace, in the encounter between Plato and Aristotle, the one, as Vasari says, with the *Timaeus* in his hands and the other with the *Ethics*. See A. Trendelenburg, *Raphaels Schule von Athen. Ein Vortrag*, Berlin, Bethage, 1843; D. Redig de Campos, *Raffaello e Michelangelo. Studi di storia e d'arte*. Roma, Bardi, 1946; A. Chastel, *Arte e umanesimo a Firenze al tempo di Lorenzo il Magnifico. Studi sul Rinascimento e sull'Umanesimo platonico*, Torino, Einaudi, 1964; E. Garin, *Raffaello e la 'pace filosofica'*, in *Umanisti artisti scienziati. Studi sul Rinascimento italiano*, Roma, Editori Riuniti, 1989.

CARLO STARNAZZI

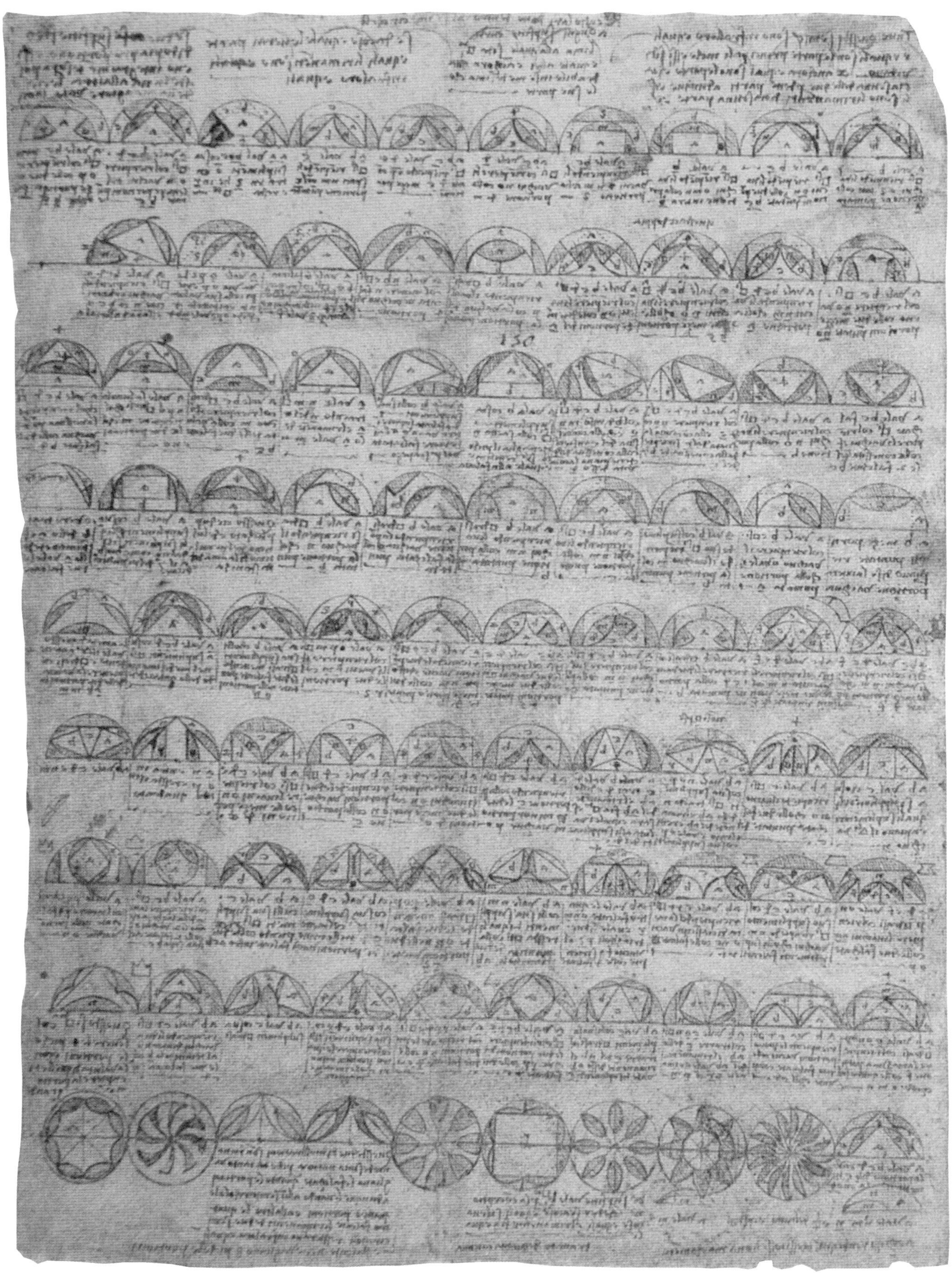

Leonardo da Vinci, *Studies on the lunulae, c.* 1515. Pen and sepia ink, 289 x 217 mm. Codex Atlanticus, f. 455 *r.* Milan, Biblioteca Ambrosiana

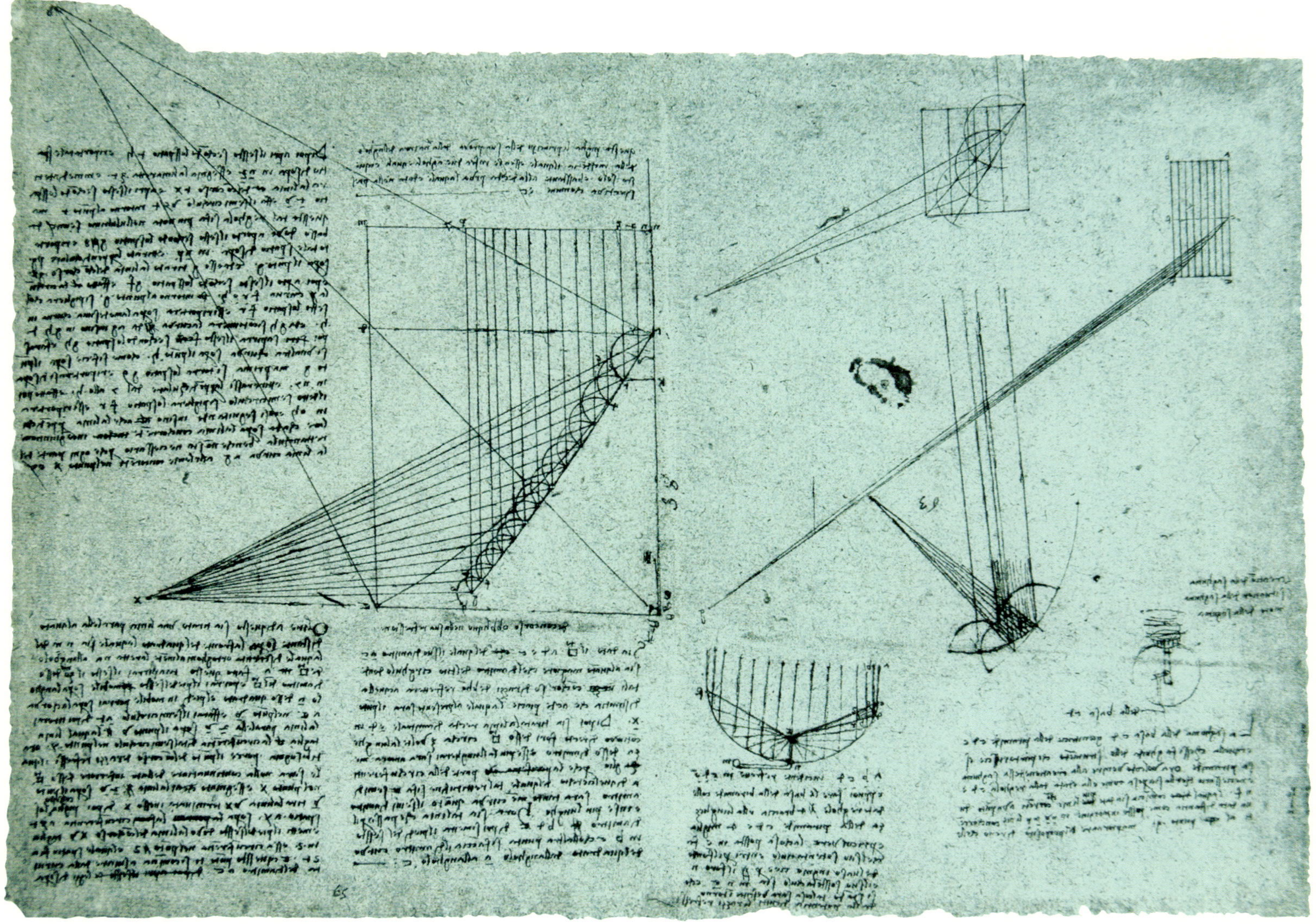

LEONARDO DA VINCI, *Studies of parabolic mirrors of great diameter for the utilization of solar energy, c* 1513-15. Pen and ink on rough blue paper, 400 x 283 mm. Codex Atlanticus, f. 750 *r.* Milan, Biblioteca Ambrosiana

Raphael would have also recovered from the *Adoration of the Magi* by Leonardo the dynamism and the entire orchestration of the gesticulation of the characters that, together with the study of the attitudes and of the physiognomy, would result to be at the foundation of the iconic intensity of his *Transfiguration.* New evidences therefore appear on the field of the research, indicating possible directions to follow, in order to investigate a moment in the life of the two artists still little known up to the present day.[44] Besides, it seems that, for the same *Fornarina,* Raphael has taken inspiration from a *Bare-breasted Magdalene* by Leonardo, replicated by Giampietrino (*c.* 1515), like expression and unveiling, in its seducing sensual beauty, of the *pistis sophìa,* that is of the revelation of the cos-

---

[44] See C. PEDRETTI, *A chronology of Leonardo da Vinci's Architectural Studies after 1500. In Appendix: A Letter to Pope Leo X on the Architecture of Ancient Rome,* Genève, Droz, 1962; M. KEMP, *Leonardo's Leda and the Belvedere River-Gods. Roman Sources and a New Chronology,* «Art History», 1980; D. A. BROWN, *Leonardo and Raphael's Transfiguration,* in «Atti del convegno "Raffaello a Roma" (1983)», Biblioteca Hertiana, 21-28 marzo 1983, Roma, Elefante, 1986; D. LAURENZA, *Leonardo e Raffaello a Roma: nuove evidenze,* in *Leonardo nella Roma di Leone X [c. 1513-16]. Gli studi anatomici, la vita, l'arte,* «Lettura Vinciana», XLIII, Firenze, Giunti, 2003. If D. A. Brown has supported the hypothesis that Raphael had examined the drawings of Leonardo, for the leonardian citations contained in the *Transfiguration* (1518-1520), Laurenza examines two studies for one *Resurrection* (*c.* 1514) related to the announcing angel (Bayonne, Musée Bonnat, 1707 *r*; Oxford, Ashmolean Museum, 558 *r*) and correlates them to the *Saint John the Baptist* and the *Saint John-Bacchus* of the Louvre. The same sheet of Bayonne, in its back, would contain anatomical studies by Raphael of scientific and not of artistic type, perhaps realized after having seen the drawings of Leonardo related to the human trunk, examined from the front, in profile and from the back (Windsor, RL 12636 *r*; 19038 *r*; 19033 *r* e *v*; 19032 *r* e *v*, 19044 *r*).

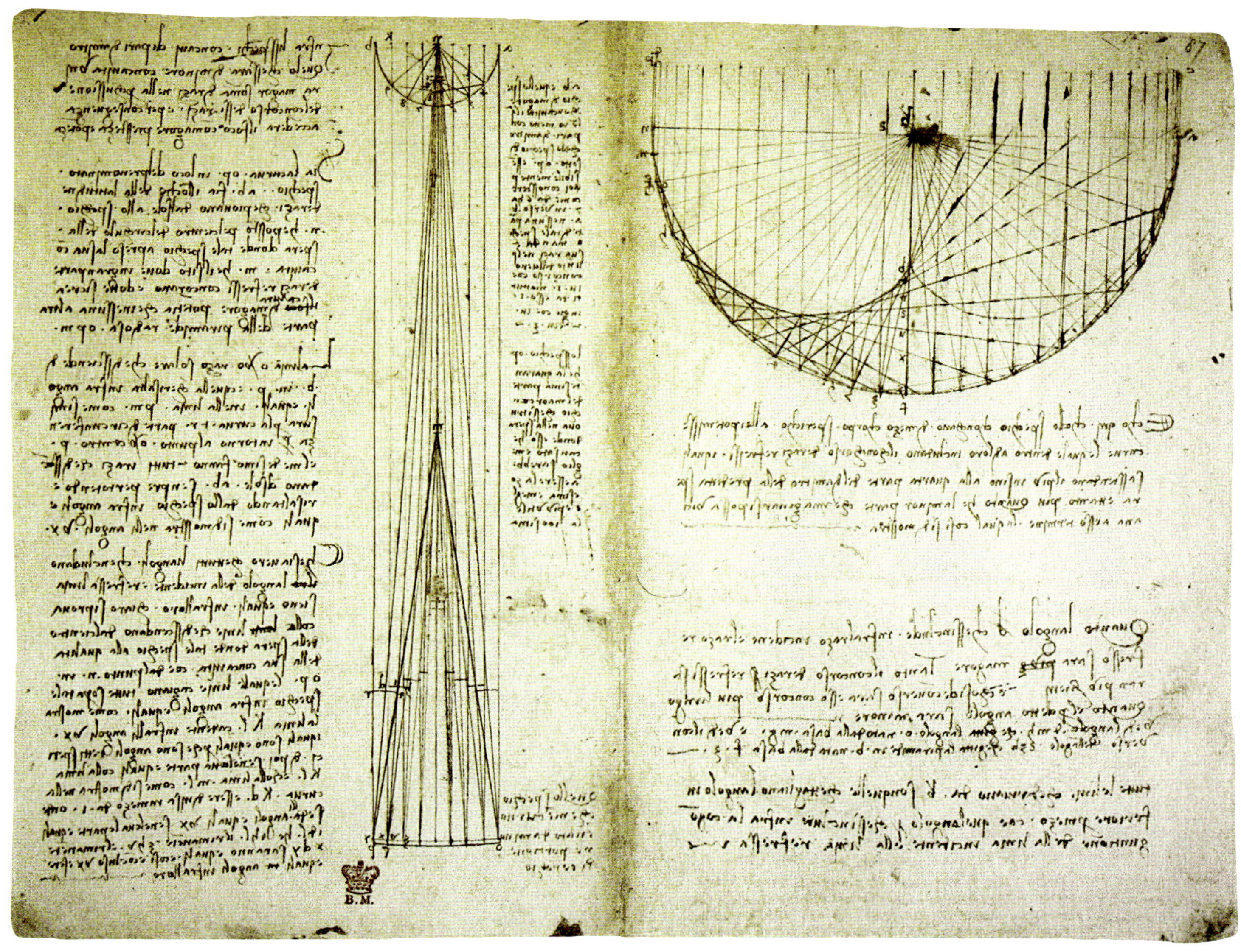

Leonardo da Vinci, *Studies on the caustics of reflection, c. 1503-05. Codex Arundel, ff. 86 v-87 r*. London, British Library

mic secret, evoked with subtle recalls by the rising of a remote landscape, much vanishing and indefinite.[45] Such erotic appeal, tied in an impudent way to a sacred subject, seems to translate what Leonardo would have transcribed in a note of his *Libro di Pittura* (*par.* 25): «And it already happened to me to make a painting that represented a divine thing, which, bought from its lover, he wanted to take off the representation of such deity to be able to kiss it without suspicion, but in the end his conscience was triumphant over the sighs and lust, and forced him to get it out of his house».
Giuliano de' Medici, obtained the Pontine Marshes, for a «motu proprio» of Leo X (14 December 1514), had involved Leonardo in the grandiose project of reclamation of the entire territory («totum et omne territorium, quod putridis stagnatur aquis et Palus Pontina inundat»).[46] The conditions imposed by the pontiff for the land allocation required that Giuliano took care at his expenses of their reclamation and made them flourishing, eliminating the disputes that had risen among the various owners of the lands placed between the hills and the humid zones, particularly with Guglielmo Caetani, duke of Sermoneta. With this intention, the Duke of Nemours had given the assignment to his representative

---

[45] See C. Pedretti, *Leonardo. Genio e visione in terra marchigiana*, Firenze, Cartei e Bianchi, 2005.

[46] «the whole territory, where putrid water stagnates and inundates the Pontine Marshes»

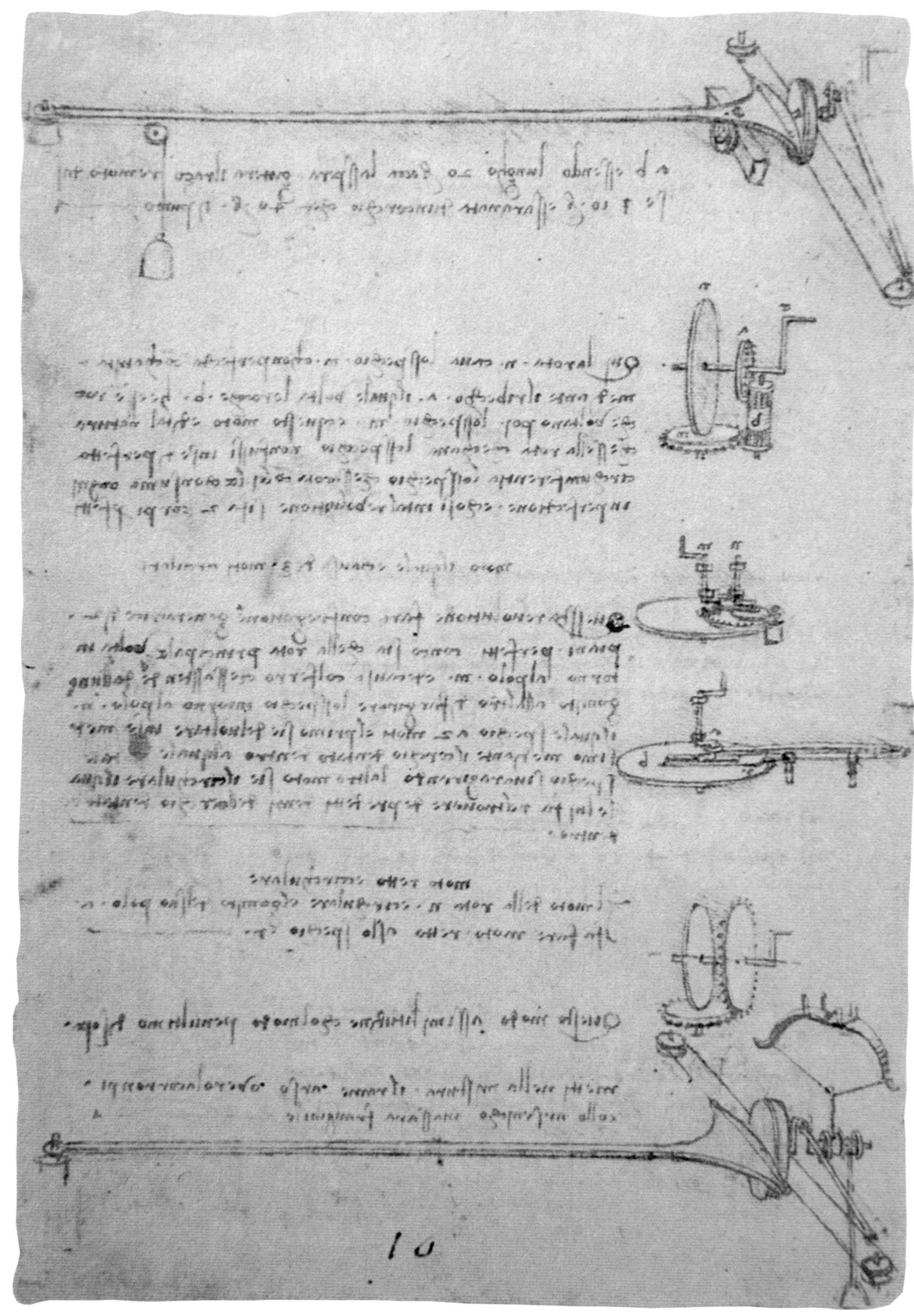

LEONARDO DA VINCI, *Machines for the making of concave mirrors*, c. 1503-05. Pen and ink, 197 x 137 mm. Codex Atlanticus, f. 1103 *v*. Milan, Biblioteca Ambrosiana

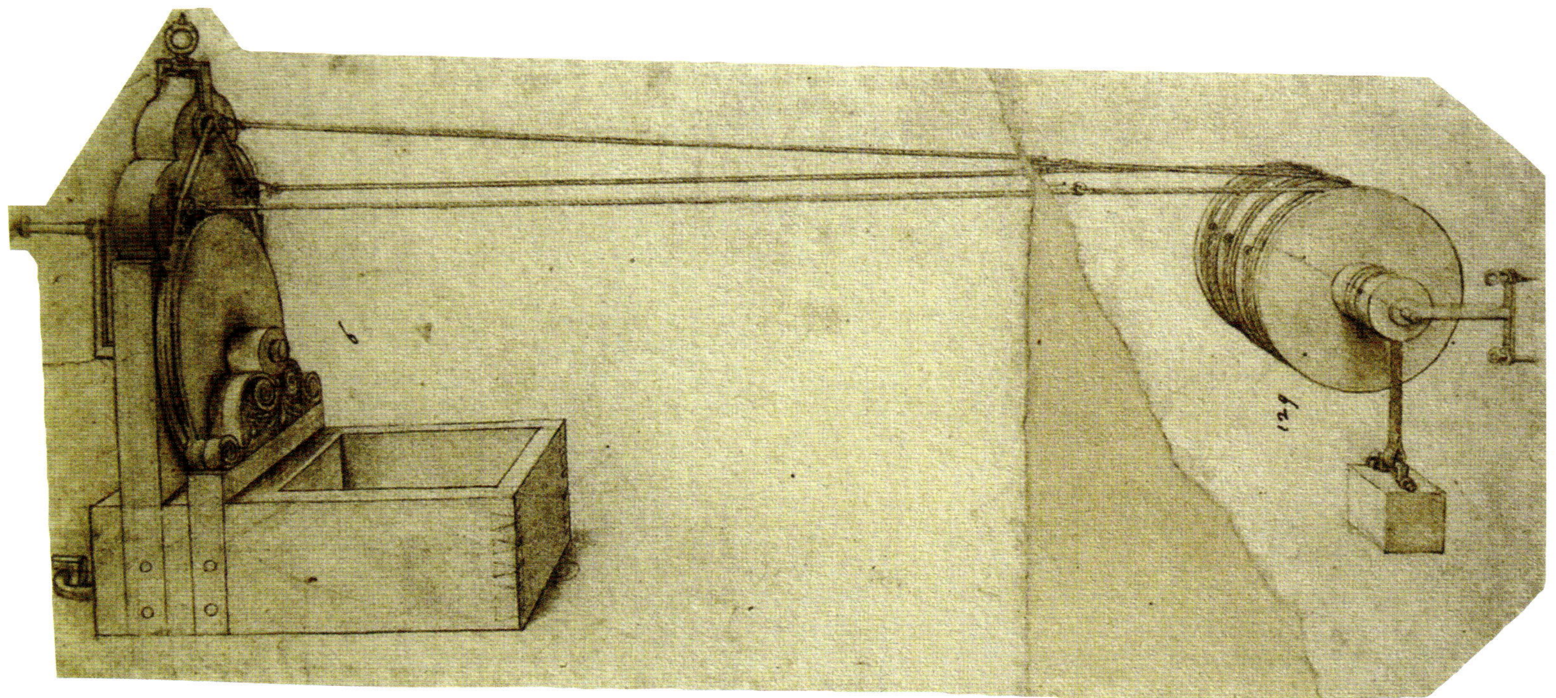

LEONARDO DA VINCI, *Machine to twist ropes, c.* 1513-15. Pen and ink, 169-158 x 384-375 mm. Codex Atlanticus, f. 13 *r.* Milan, Biblioteca Ambrosiana

Master Domenico de Juvenibus, secretary to the Apostolic Camera, helped by a series of «most skilful surveyors».
The technical-hydraulic skill of Leonardo was widely known, since it had revealed itself in the reclamation of the swampy zones near Vigevano, in 1494,[47] and in projects of great importance as the territorial rearrangement of the Val di Chiana and the rating of the fluvial flow of the Arno between 1502 and 1504,[48] so that, in such an important plan-

ning initiative, he could not help being involved in it with precise responsibilities. That is confirmed in the writing of the same topographical map of the Pontine plain (Windsor, RL 12684), realized with stylus, pen, ink, watercolours and charcoal in spring 1515 and subtended to the planning of the project of reclamation of the entire region, with the draining of the marshes and their conversion to immense and fertile prairies. If, in sheet 15 *r* of the Ms. F of the Institut de France, Leonardo reveals the careful study he reserved to the construction of pumps to drain marshes or ponds that border the sea, in the Ms. E, written up in a period comprised between 1513 and 1514 and containing studies of mechanics and of geometry, but also of hydraulics, Leonardo described precisely, beyond to a machine for the drainage of channels (f. 75 *v*), the techniques of «filling», that had to be used to carry out operations of hydraulic rearrangement and of reclamation of a swampy ground by making descend earth in the depressions of the ground below (f. 5 *r*):

The covering with earth of the swamps will be made, when into the swamps will be directed turbid rivers. This is demonstrated, because

[47] In 1494, Leonardo would have carefully studied in Vigevano, in the ideal farm of the Moor, beyond the experimentation of new agricultural techniques, as the protection of vines from the winter frosts by putting them in the ground («Vines of Vigevano on the day 20 of March 1494, and when there is a frost, they are placed under the ground», Ms. H, f. 38 *r*), also the every day productive capacity of the flour mills, in order to improve their output («Mill of Vigevano. 5 heaps of good grain», Ms. H, f. 94 *v*). Then, with the intention to reclaim the territory surrounding the town, he would have made the meticulous description of a staircase of water; an innovative hydraulic technique that consisted of the transportation of an abundant amount of earth, fundamental to carry out a filling of swampy lands and to make them in such a way fertile: «Stairway of Vigevano under the Sforzesca, 130 steps, high 1/4 and wide 1/2 of an arm, along which water falls and it does not consume anything in its last percussion. And along such stairway so much earth has come down, that it has dried out a swamp, to be precise filled up, and it has been made prairies, out of a swamp of great depth» (Cod. Hammer, f. 32 *r*, 5B). This agricultural farm, which Ludovico the Moor had made transform into an elegant suburban villa, would have been celebrated in couplets by Ermolao Barbaro.

[48] In addition to the splendid maps of the Val di Chiana (Windsor, RL 12682; 12278), to comprehend the studies started by Leonardo on the reclamation of the Valley, it is very important to examine the sheet of the Codex Atlanticus (f. 336 *r* [918 *r*]), which is then a magnified detail of the mentioned map (RL 12278), where some toponyms are in mirrored writing and some other in normal course from left to right. An aspect highlighted for the first time by Anton Giuseppe

della Torre Rezzonico in 1777, whom, in his *Vita di Leonardo*, published by Santo Monti in 1914, dwells on the project of the canalization of the Arno, connecting it to the one for the reclamation of the Val di Chiana and starting exactly from the Val di Chio with the smaller streams like the Renello. Even this singular interpretation remained unnoticed among the scholars of Leonardo, to be then emphasized only by Carlo Pedretti in his *Commentary* to the Richter's anthology, in 1977.

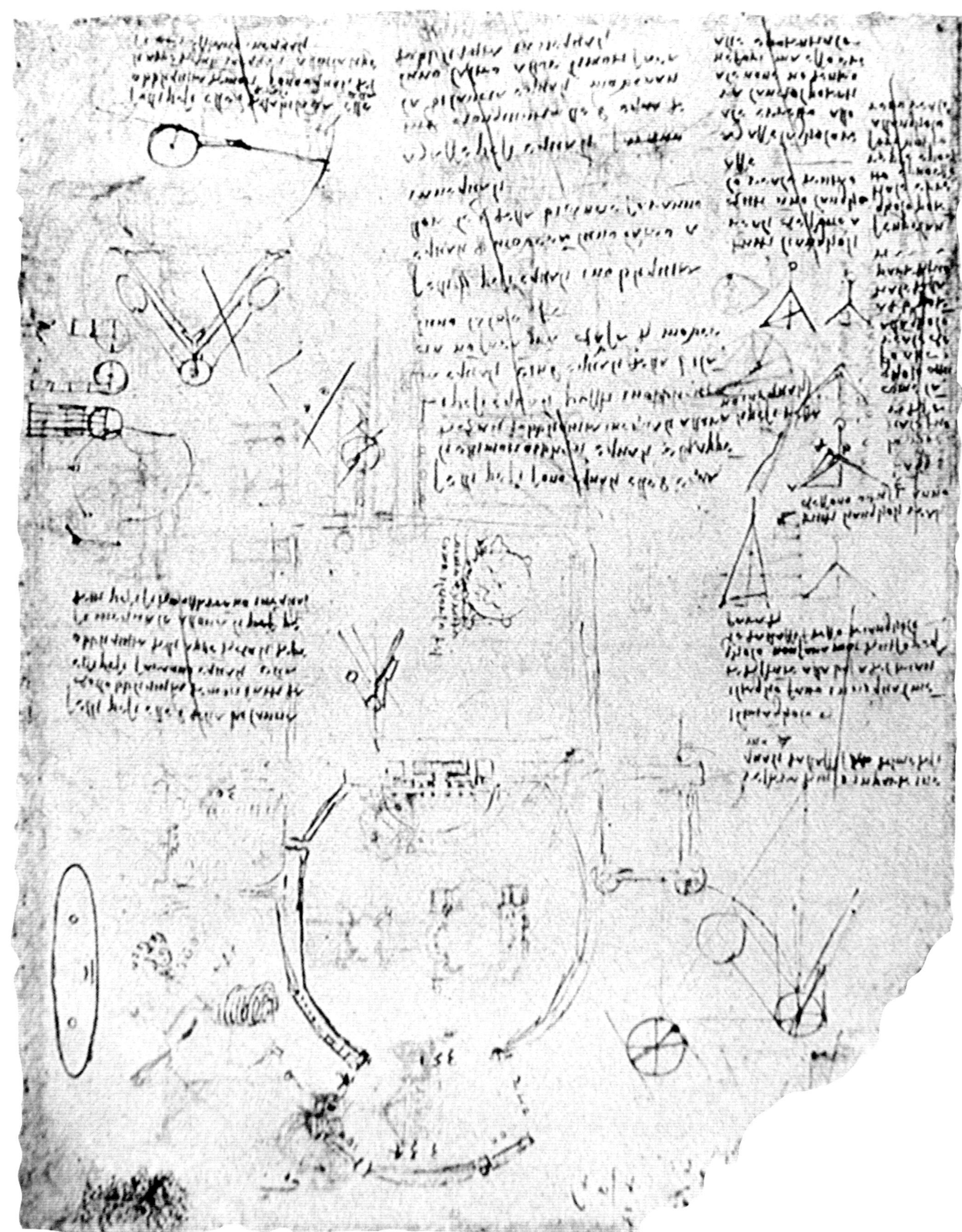

Leonardo da Vinci, *Project for the Civitavecchia Port*, c. 1514-15. Pen and sepia ink, 282 x 220 mm. Codex Atlanticus, f. 733 *r*. Milan, Biblioteca Ambrosiana.

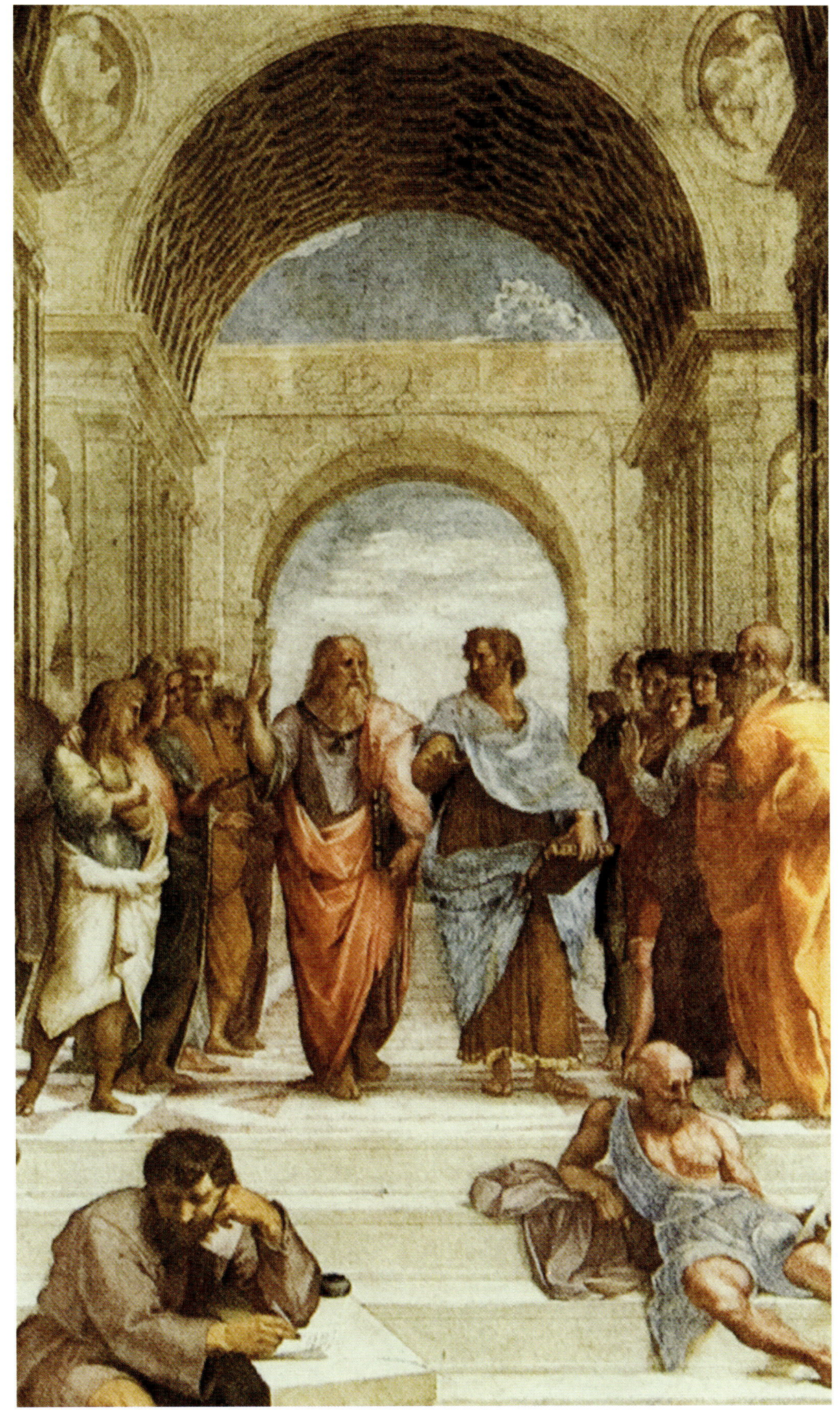

RAPHAEL, *The School of Athens*, 1509-10. Fresco. Vatican City, Palazzi Vaticani, Stanza della Segnatura. Particular

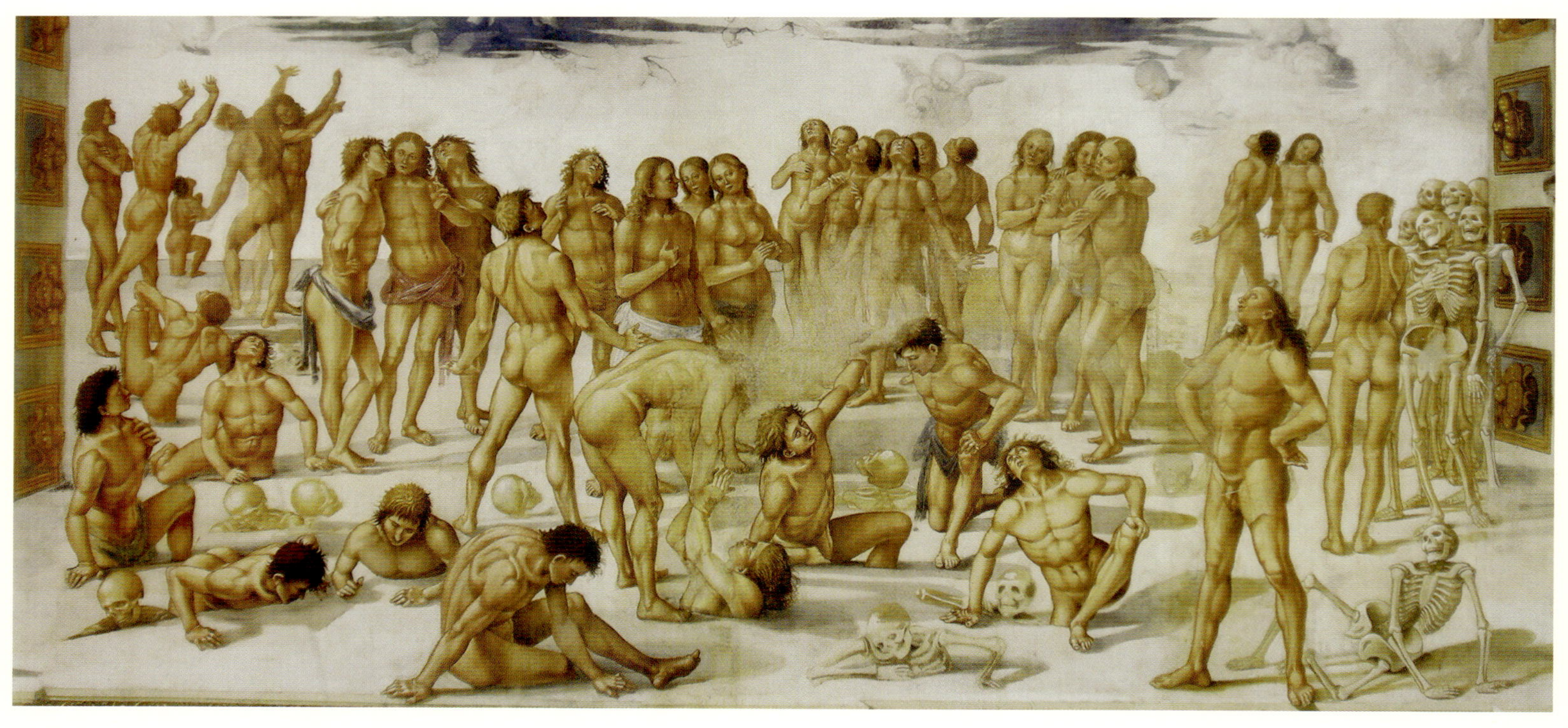

Luca Signorelli, *Resurrection of the Flesh*, 1500-04. Fresco. Orvieto, Dome. Chapel of Saint Brizio. Particular

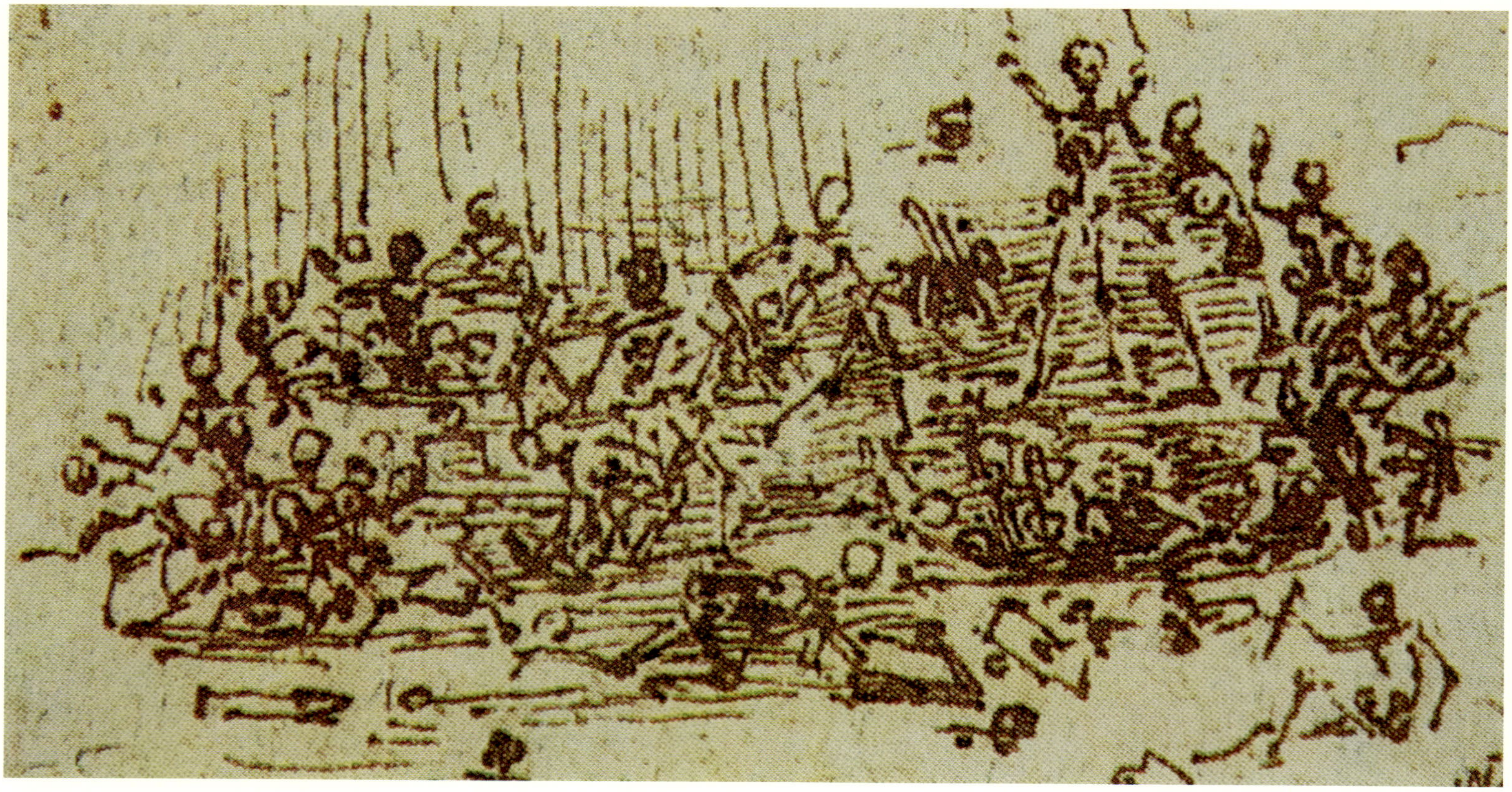

Leonardo da Vinci, *Scenes from the Apocalypse*, c. 1517. Charcoal, pen and ink, 300 x 203 mm. Windsor, RL 12388. Particular

CARLO STARNAZZI

where the river runs, from there takes the earth off and where it is delayed, here it leaves its turbulence, and that happens, because water is never so delayed in the rivers like in marshes, whose waters are of insensitive motion. But in these marshes the river has to enter through a limited place, low and narrow, and has to go out through a wide and of little depth space, and this is necessary because the running water of the river is more vigorous in the lower than in the upper part and the slow water of the marshes still is similar, but the upper lightness of the marshes it is a lot different from its lower gravity, than it is in the currents of the rivers in which the upper lightness is little different from the lower gravity. Then it can be concluded that the marsh will be covered with earth, because from underneath it receives turbid water and from upside it sends out clear water from the opposite part of the marsh, and because of this, such swamp for necessity will raise its bottom by means of the earth, that it is continuously released over it, etc.

The map, though focussed on the malarial and marshy area, reproduces for thirty miles, in aerial perspective at bird flight and with a high definition, the entire region and the coastal line, even if a little simplified, south of Rome, from the Circeo to Terracina, until the plain of Fondi.

It is the result of an inspection led with analytical concern and directed to an organic and decisive interpretation of the emergencies to deal with, adapting to the circumstances, where the artist is planning his strategies and is documenting his geomorphological, anthropogeographical and archaeological knowledge of the region.[49]

The wide curved profile of the coasts, even if well defined, turns out however to be too emphasized and the depiction of the mountainous part is reduced to the sector of the investigations that concerned the description of the altimetric progress of the land and the course of the torrents, whose waters had to be rationally distributed and driven through draining channels up to the sea («Rio Martino» and «Badino»). Leonardo, as instrument of practical geometry, once again used the compass bound together to a simple thread of lead, already used in 1502 for the map of Imola with the method of the «progression» (Windsor, RL 12284 *r*; 12686 *r*),[50]

that recorded the magnetic azimuths with the various distances of the localities, and that continued to be, in the first decades of the sixteenth century, the most followed method, so much that the same Raphael, in the second part of his famous *Letter to Leo X* (1519), who had given him the assignment to prepare a great map of «ancient Rome», will mention it as recurrent apparatus with which to proceed to the survey of the monumental plan («having I been much studious of those such antiquities and having placed not little care in searching them meticulously and in measuring them with diligence»).[51]

The denominations of the single settlements, defined in the map with perspective outlines, have been transcribed with calligraphic elegance by the hands of the pupil Francesco Melzi, the same compiler, around 1540, of the *Libro di Pittura* by Leonardo, whose participation appears also in the transcription of the toponyms of the so-called «map of the world of Leonardo», kept in the collection of Windsor (RL 01393).[52] And a «Map of the world», on whose northern hemisphere a royal eagle has implanted its claws, appears in the drawing of the *Allegory of navigation* (Windsor, RL 12496), with the same naturalism existing in the map of the world of the fresco by Bramante of Eraclitus and Democritus (Milan, Pinacoteca di Brera).[53]

---

north-west with a space of 7 miles. Faenza is seen from Imola between east and southeast exactly in the middle, at a distance of 10 miles. Similarly does Furlì with Imola, with a distance of 20 miles; and Furlinpopoli does the alike with Furlì with a distance of 25 miles. Bertinoro is seen from Imola at 5/8 of east, towards south-east, with a distance of 27 miles» (Windsor, RL 12284 *r*).

[51] In the *Letter to Leo X*, written by Baldassar Castiglione «in person» of Raphael, it was defined the concept of «Renaissance» and for the first time there were faced the complex problems connected to the protection of historical and artistic heritage. Raphael revealed also a great knowledge of the classic art, from which he had taken inspiration also for works of traditional, but for some aspects uncertain attribution, like the Loggia with the *Stories of Love and Psyche* at the Farnesina, the Logge of Leo X and the Stufetta of the Cardinal Bibbiena in Vatican. With moved participation, he denounced to the Pope the state of total abandonment of ancient buildings: «how many, I say, pontiffs have committed themselves to ruin ancient temples, statues, arches and other glorious buildings! [...] How much lime has been made out of statues and others ancient ornaments! That I would dare to say that all this new Rome that now we can look at, how much great it is, how much beautiful, how much adorned of palaces, churches and other buildings, all is manufactured of lime of ancient marble». Drawings by Raphael for the «map of Rome», according to two documents of the Archives of State of Florence, related to the inventory of the family assets of Alessandro Rosselli, son of the famous cartographer Francesco, there would have been find out in their workshop, among a great number of geographical charts and maps of towns, also «some printed sheets of the drawings of Rome by Raphael from Urbino». See F. P. Di Teodoro, *Raffaello, Baldassar Castiglione e la lettera a Leone X. Con l'aggiunta di due saggi raffaelleschi*, Argelato (Bo), Minerva, 2003. We must add that the use of the square, an apparatus derived from the land-surveyor's instrument and used in topography and agronomy to determine perimeters, tracings and alignments on the ground, would be established for the first time by Feliciano da Lazise, in 1518, after the publication of his *Libro di Aritmetica e Geometria speculativa e praticale intitolato Scala Grimaldelli*.

[52] See E. Carusi, *Quel che c'è di Leonardo nel mappamondo a lui attribuito*, in *I disegni geografici di Leonardo da Vinci*, Bergamo, Istituto Italiano d'Arti Grafiche, 1919.

[53] The images of Eraclitus and Democritus in this fresco, like in the *School of*

---

[49] See E. Solmi, *Leonardo da Vinci e i lavori di prosciugamento delle Paludi Pontine ai tempi di Leone X (1914-16)*, «Archivio Storico Lombardo», XXXVIII, 1911; M. Baratta, *Leonardo da Vinci e le paludi pontine*, «La Geografia», 1-4, Novara, De Agostini, 1928; A. Pettorelli, *Le Paludi Pontine e Leonardo da Vinci*, «Salsomaggiore Illustrata», XXXI, 11, 1936; M. Clayton, *Leonardo da Vinci. A Curious Vision*, London, Merrell Holberton, 1996; Id., *Leonardo da Vinci. One hundred Drawings from the collection of Her Majesty the Queen*, London, Merrell Holberton, 1996; C. Starnazzi, *Le Paludi Pontine*, in Id., *Leonardo. Acque e terre*, 2002, *op. cit.*; Id., *Un progetto di bonifica delle Paludi Pontine*, in *Leonardo cartografo*, 2003, *op. cit.*

[50] Leonardo carried out with meticulousness the determination of the topographical particulars and the description of the territorial organization of the city of Imola: «Imola sees Blegna at 5/8 west towards north-west with a distance of 20 miles. Casstel Sanpiero is seen from Imola in the middle, between west and

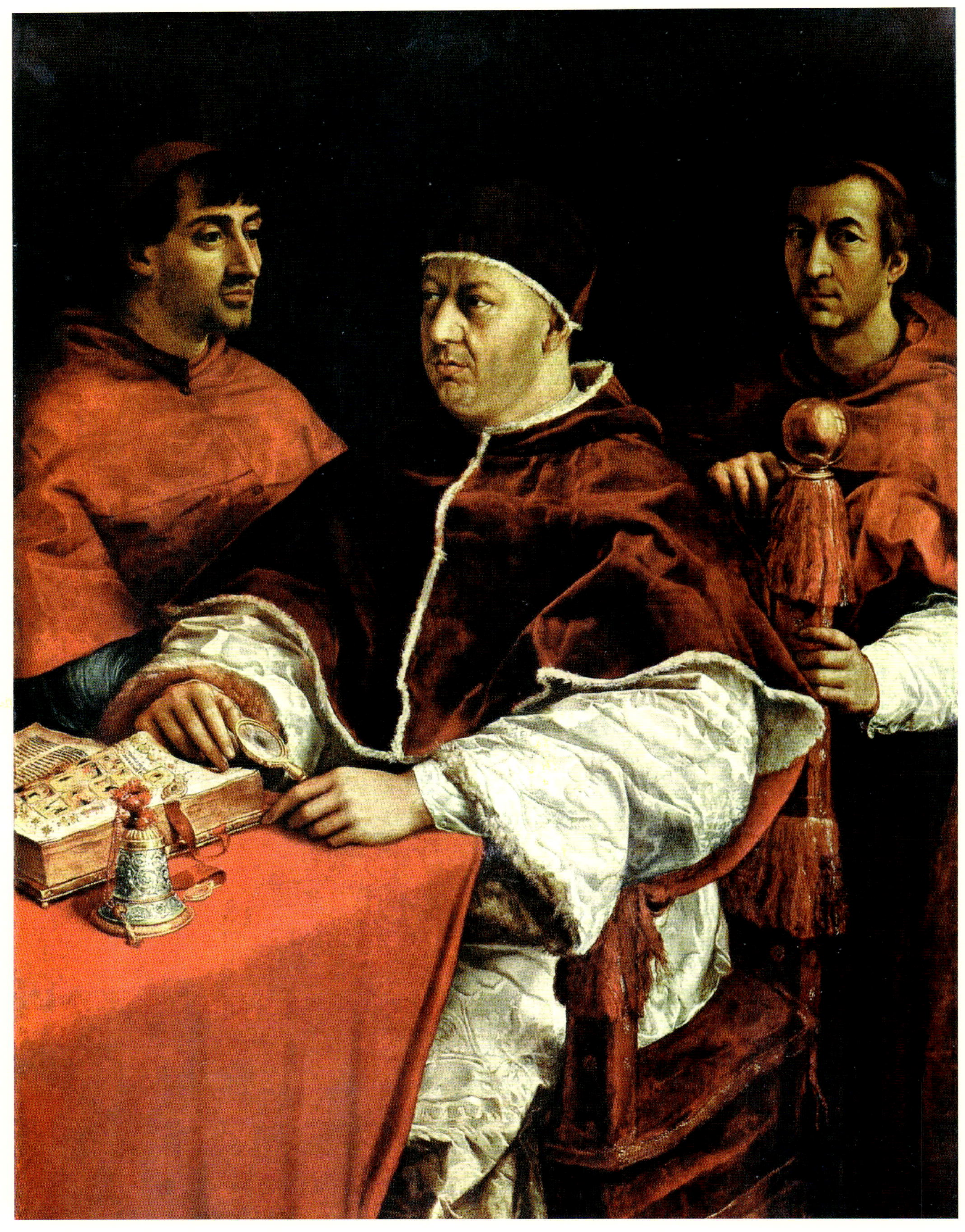

RAPHAEL, *Portrait of Leo X with cardinals Giulio de' Medici and Luigi de' Rossi*, 1517-18. Table, 154 x 119 cm. Florence, Galleria degli Uffizi

CARLO STARNAZZI

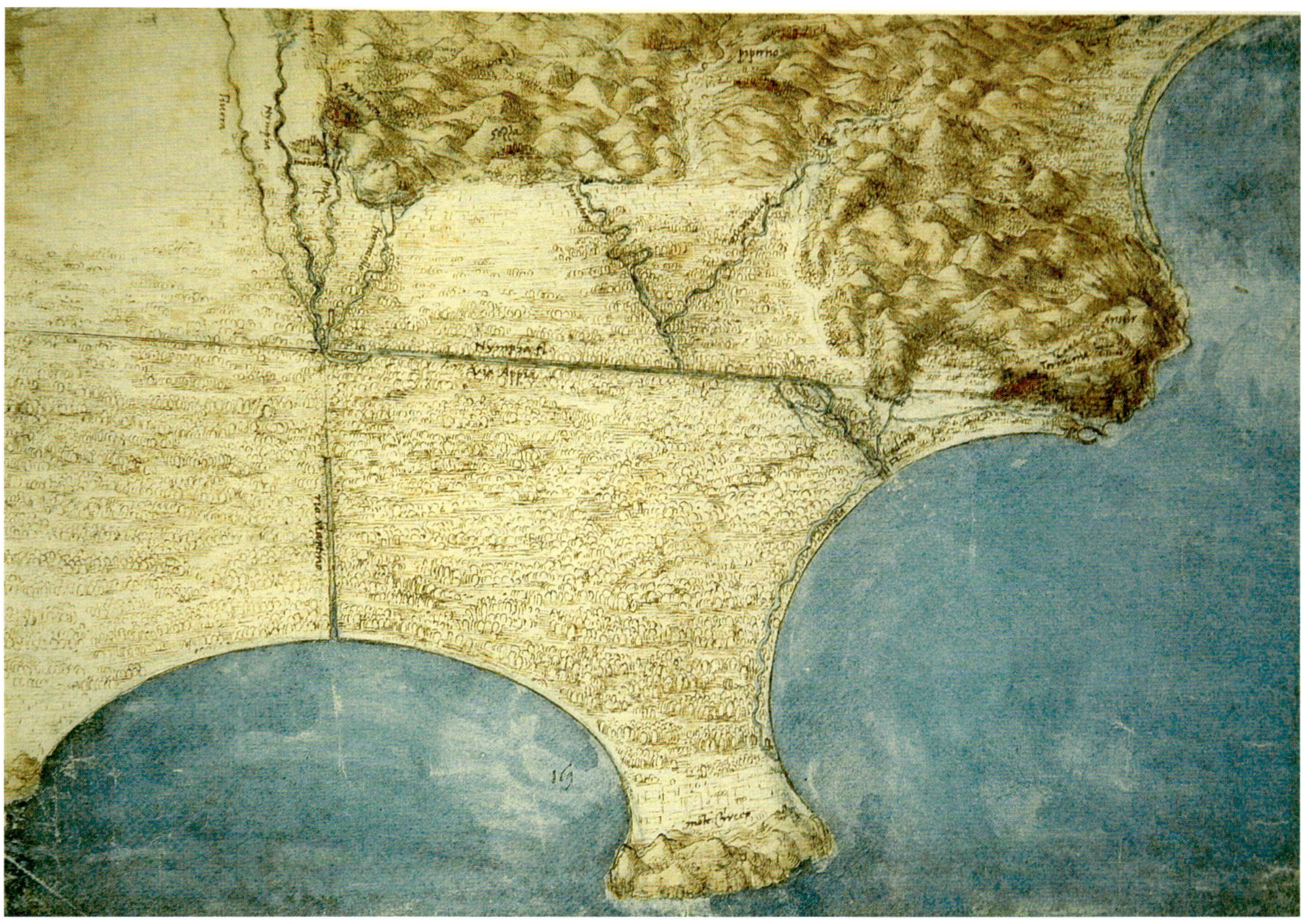

<Leonardo da Vinci, *Pontine Marshes*, 1515. Pen, ink and watercolour, 277 x 400 mm. Windsor, RL 12684>

In the leonardian drawing, the wolf-steersman, exploiting the favourable wind and taking advantage of a rudder supplied with a compass with the winds rose, is heading for his magnetic pole. The allegory, perhaps destined to the decoration of some scenery apparatus, meant to allude to the new concordat signed with a solemn consistory in Bologna, in December 1515, between Leo X and the «Most Christian King» of France, Francis I, winner of the battle of Marignano (13-14 September 1515)[54] and moved by «imperial» ambitions, whose protection the roman Church, steering towards a pro-French politics, needed. And the wolf, intended like avarice and root of every evil, could allude to the difficult relationship between Leonardo and Leo X (see what reported about such topic by the Vasari); a Pope patron, but beside considered eager because of his avaricious demand of money in exchange for indulgences to manage the expenses of the Vatican and that, shortly after, would have provoked the dissent of Martin

Athens by Raphael, find their foundation in the variety of compendiums of the work of Diogenes Laertius, popularized after the version of Ambrogio Traversari († 1439), general of the Camaldolensian order, and mediated by the Academy of Ficino. Ficino in fact had made to paint in a picture or in a fresco on a wall of his Academy their figures, very well known for the two different attitudes in considering reality and human history, weeping and laughing, crying Eraclitus and smiling Democritus: «Had Marsilio, writes an ancient biographer, in his Academy, where he read, made painted the sphere of the world and on one side Democritus who laughed and on the other Eraclitus that sobbed». The literary source for the decoration of the Academy has been recognized from Blankert (1966-67) in the *Epistulae* by Sidonius Apollinaris, where it was advised to decorate certain environments with images of philosophers, like «Heraclitus fletu oculis clausis, Democritus riso labris apertis » [«Eraclitus with the eyes closed by tears, Democritus with the lips open by laughing» Tr.N.]. C. Pedretti, after a suggestion of P. O. Kristeller, proposed that the painting is a juvenile work by Leonardo, for the strong ties that he had with Ficino in the humanist Florence and that E. Garin had so synthesized: «The magical point of union between the science of the painter and the science of nature [...] - which is the very essence of the thought of Leonardo - finds its root exactly in the platonic-ficinian philology». See C. Pedretti, *Eraclitus and Democritus*, «Achademia Leonardi Vinci. Journal of Leonardo Studies and Bibliography of Vinciana», VI, Firenze, Giunti, 1993.

[54] See E. Solmi, *Le fonti dei Manoscritti di Leonardo (1908), e Nuovi contributi alle fonti dei manoscritti di Leonardo (1911)*, in Id., *Scritti vinciani. Le fonti dei Manoscritti e altri studi*, presentazione di E. Garin, Firenze, La Nuova Italia, 1976.

Luther, that, on 31 October 1517, posted up, according to the legend, his 95 *Theses* to the doors of the Castle of Wittenberg, beginning the Reformation.[55]

Leonardo would have still remembered the well-known battle of Marignano, in which the Swiss soldiers at the dependency of the Sforza and of the Imperial forces had been for the first time defeated, during one of the festivities that, in spring 1518, were carried out at the Castle of Amboise in honour of Francis I. Here, counting on the surprise factor in the preparation of the scenographies, he meant to provoke wonder and astonishment in the court, as he had already done for the triumph of Louis XII on his arrival to Milan on 14 June 1507. The matter was to represent in the courtyard of the Castle of Amboise, transformed in a hall, with even stages and galleries, the onslaught and the taking of a false Castle constructed in wood and adorned with clothes, combining to the blows of mortars and arquebuses a series of unusual oddities, that in fact were the result of the scientific studies he had carried out in the Roman period on the expansion of inflated bodies:[56] «Over the merlons and the defences there were many arquebuses; on the embankment there might be seen some mortars of wood hooped with iron, that launched, with powder and with fire, with great loud noise, deflated baloons in the air which falling on the square rebounded with great amusement of everyone and without damage: a new thing and ingeniously well directed».[57]

Before the historical encounter in Bologna, Leo X, according to the diary of the official reporter of the travel, Paride Grassi,[58] in the days of Saturday 17, Sunday 18 and Monday 19 November, changing direction from Acquapendente to Città della Pieve, instead of continuing along the road from Siena to Florence («Cassia Adrianea»), went to Cortona, where it was bishop the cardinal Francesco Soderini, brother of Piero, already gonfalonier for life of the Florentine Republic, but for the occasion named his vicar to Rome, while apostolic datary was Silvio Passerini from Cortona, that had made to come Guglielmo de Marcillat, occupied in executing the stained-glass windows of S. Maria del Popolo, to decorate artistically his residence (formerly Palazzo del Popolo), be-

fore the arrival of the Pope, with 44 windows with glasses decorated with historical scenes. Then, from here, continuing along the «Via Clodia» («Castiglione Aretino») and the «Cassia Vetus» (Arezzo), Leo X reached Florence where, after a pause in a suburban villa, so that the preparations for the celebrations in his honour might be completed, on 1 December, he held a consistory in the city, to discuss the procedures to follow in the encounter with Francis I.[59]

The event will be described and idealized by Vasari in a fresco in Palazzo Vecchio under invitation of the same Cosimo I:

> *I have portrayed of the natural and that can be recognized there in the part far away of the history, out of the order of the consistory, the duke Giuliano de' Medici and the duke Lorenzo his grandson, that are speaking with two of the most clear talents of their age, the one, that old man with curled and white long-hair is Leonardo da Vinci, greatest master of painting and sculpture, that speaks with the duke Lorenzo who is at his side, the other one is Michelangelo Buonarroti.*[60]

In Florence, Leo X will meet also the most famed artists of the time (Andrea Sansovino, Antonio da Sangallo the Elder, Andrea del Sarto, Jacopo da Pontormo), that had been informed by the governor of the city, Lorenzo di Piero de' Medici, of the determination of the Pope to carry out a urban renovation, above all in the Medicean sector placed between the Basilica of San Lorenzo, that will become the «Pantheon» of the Medici House, and the convent of San Marco. This Florentine passage will allow Leonardo to meet many old friends: «Francesco del Morano shoemaker / master Alessandro canon of Fiesole / Sansavino / if priest Alessandro Amadori is alive or not / Martino Octonaio / take Peruzo inflater / the plan of Pisa from Giorgio chart-seller / blue glasses» (CA, f. 83 *ra* [225 *r*]),[61] staying at his friend's house,

---

55 The wolf, as a symbol of avarice and of lust of the worldly possessions, is present in the Sacred Writings and repeatedly in Dante (*If* VII 8; *Pg* XX 10-12), where the demonic figure of Pluto is defined «cursed wolf» for its «endless hunger».
56 About such matter the Vasari wrote in his *Lives*: «He often used to make meticulously remove fat from the bowels of a wether and to make them to come so thin, that they would have been kept in just one hand; and he had put in another room a pair of blacksmith bellows, to which he put an end of the mentioned bowels, and by inflating them he filled up with them the room, which was very large, where it was necessary that who was there should move apart, demonstrating that those transparent and full of wind from occupying at the beginning a little space, they had come to occupy a lot of it».
57 See E. Solmi, *Le fonti dei Manoscritti di Leonardo…*, 1976, *op. cit.*
58 See Delicati-Armellini, *Il diario di Leone X di Paride Grassi*, Roma, 1884.

59 In the *Diario* by Paride Grassi, in the translation by E. Mori (1993), we can read: «The first day of December a secret consistory was held to discuss all that had to be observed in the course of the encounter with the king of France. In that consistory the Pope named two cardinals legates and at the same time, he named four curial legates that were the archbishop of Naples of the Caraffa House, the one of Reggio of the Orsini House, the bishop of Rieti of the Colonna House and the Florentine protonotary De Rubeis consanguineous to the Pope. This last one renounced and to his place was designated De Gozodinis from Bologna. All had to go towards the king and it was arranged that the prelates had to reach Parma and the cardinals legates proceeded not beyond Reggio. In the same consistory it was discussed also about the gifts to offer to the king in occasion of his arrive and the Pope, considered the thing with the cardinals, resolved to donate him the gold cross adorned of precious stones of the value of 15000 ducatoes, belonging to the treasure of Pope Julius, that before was of cardinal Ascanio».
60 See G. Vasari, *Ragionamento terzo*, in *Le opere di Giorgio Vasari*, con nuove annotazioni e commenti di G. Milanesi, pres. di P. Barocchi, Firenze, Sansoni, 1981 [rist. dell'ed. 1906; I ed. 1878-85]
61 Repeatedly Leonardo shows his interest for the construction of glasses with frames and lenses that could facilitate reading and writing (CA, ff. 83 *vb* [226 *v*];

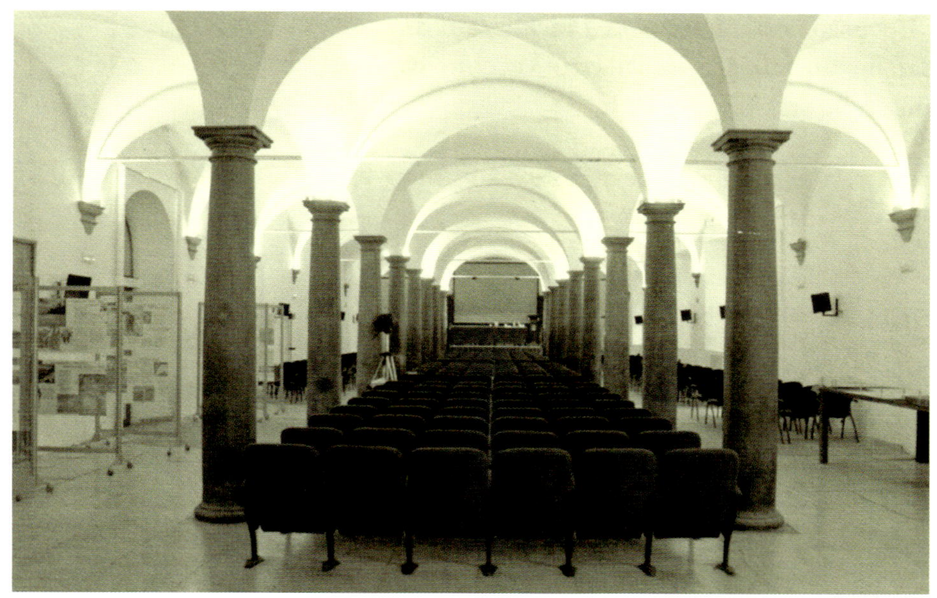

De Vecchi Room. Florence, Military Geographic Institute

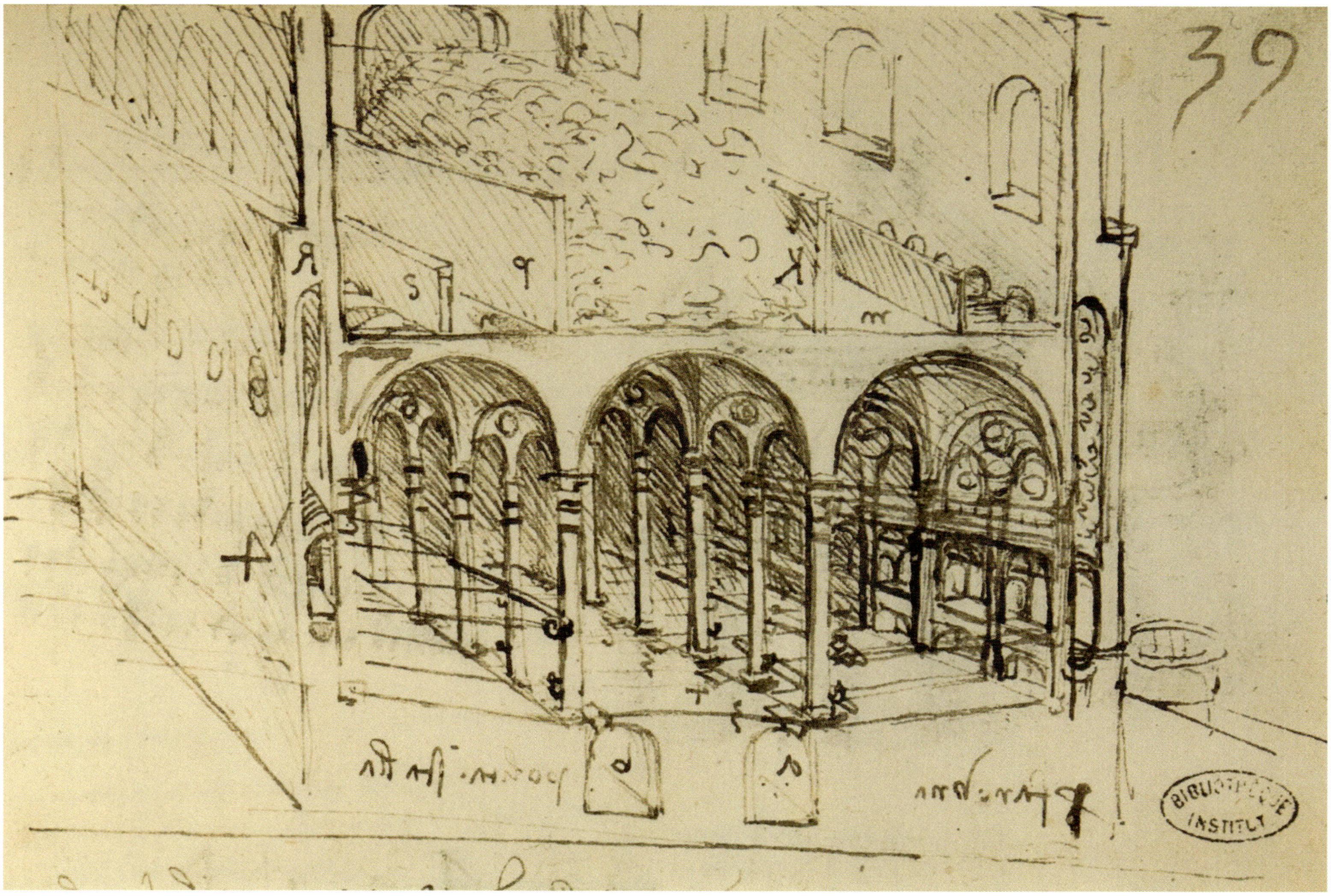

Leonardo da Vinci, *Project for the «model stables» of the Moor, c.* 1487-90. Pen and ink, Ms. B, ff. 38 *v*-39 *r*. Paris, Institut de France

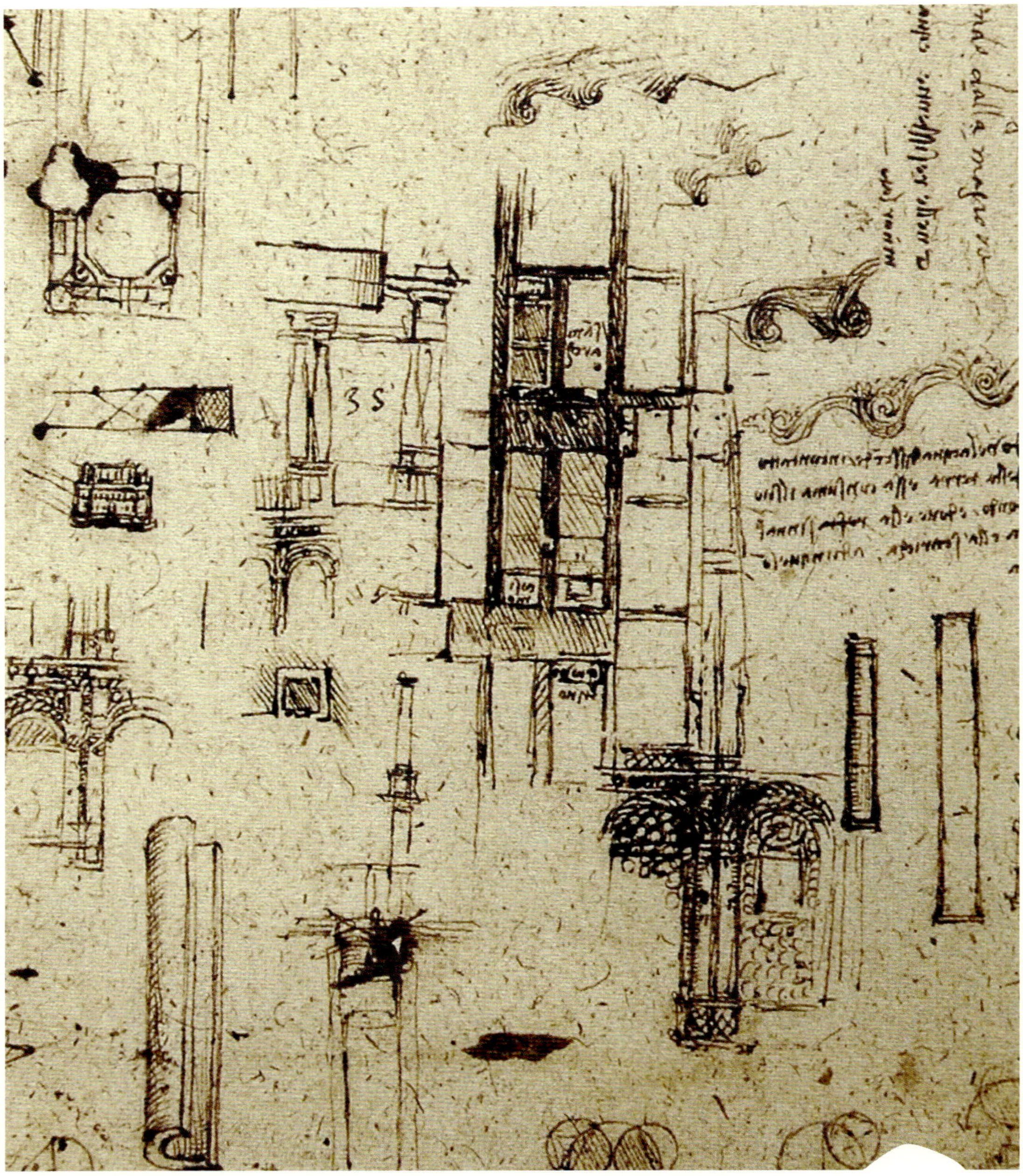

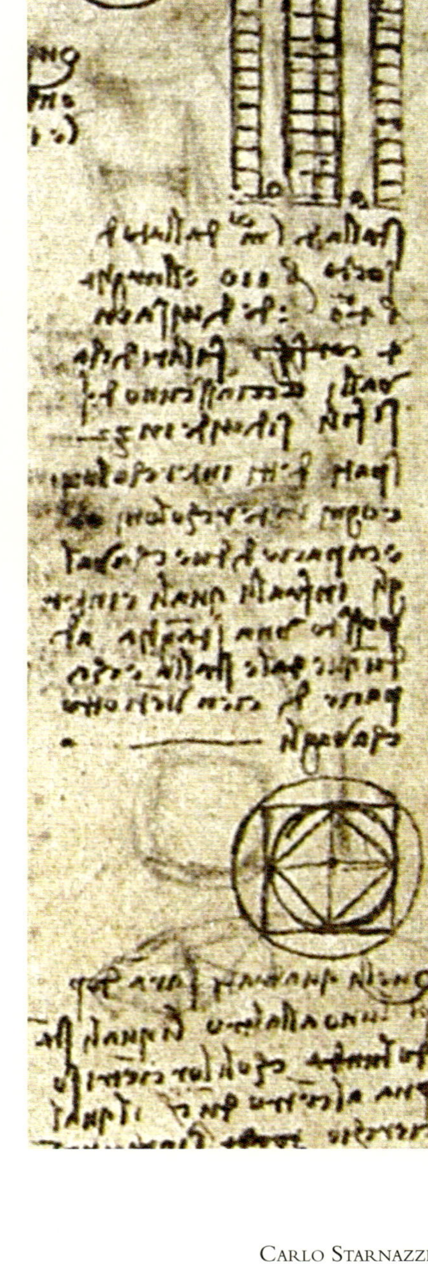

Leonardo da Vinci, *Project of reorganization of the medicean lodgings, c.* 1515. Pen and ink, 281 x 220 mm. Codex Atlanticus, f. 865 *r.* Milan, Biblioteca Ambrosiana. Particular

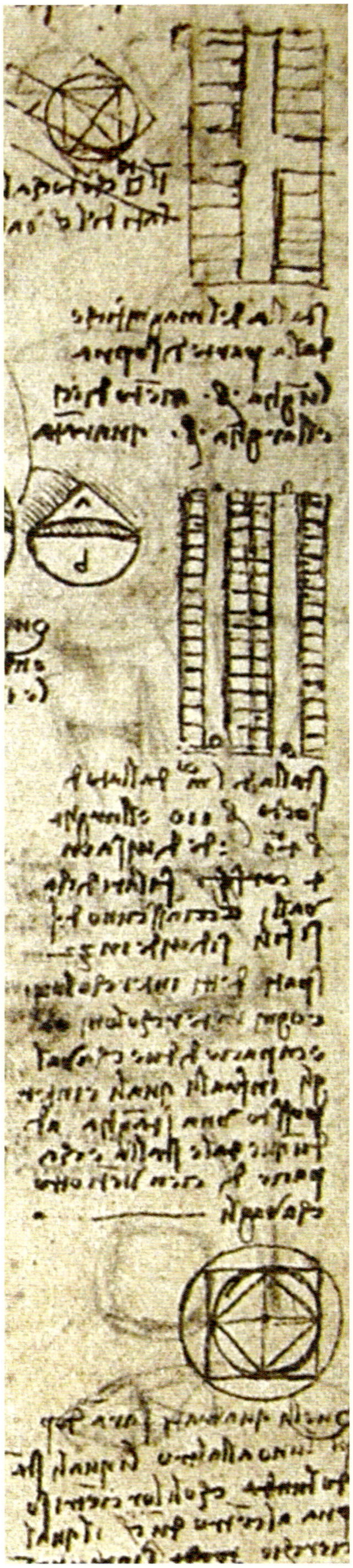

Leonardo da Vinci,
Planimetry for the «Stables of the Magnificent», c. 1515-16.
Pen and ink, 295 x 221 mm.
Codex Atlanticus, f. 264 *v.*
Milan, Biblioteca Ambrosiana.
Particular

the humanist and mathematician Piero di Braccio Martelli, as it had already happened in 1508, when he stayed there in communion and unanimous collaboration with the sculptor Gianfrancesco Rustici.[62]

While all the artists (engravers, painters, sculptors) participated realizing sumptuous apparatuses and ephemeral architectures, as the construction of a four-faced arch, later redesigned by Leonardo (CA, f. 3 *rb* [15 *r*]), or planning the settlement of the facades not yet finished of the Dome and of San Lorenzo with temporary wood models, Leonardo devised a true town-planning scheme, drawing a new facade for the Basilica of San Lorenzo, according to the taste of the classic shapes studied in Rome, and inserting it in one immense public square (CA, f. 315 *rb* [865 *r*]), obtained with the demolition of the various surrounding blocks, in order to allow the majestic Palazzo de' Medici (indicated with the word «Cosimo», the Elder) to have on that side its main entrance, and no more on the ancient Via Larga. The Medicean Palazzo appears again pointed out in the sheet 315 *ra* [864 *r*], with reference to the more famous Medicean emblem «balls» and the Church of San Giovanni («Giovannino»). Under these planimetries, there are an eye and a lock of hair drawn in pen and ink that remind the Mona Lisa very much. Beyond the old Medicean Palazzo, work of Michelozzo, Leonardo sketches also the image of a new palace in elevation, with angular towers (CA, f. 315 *rb* [865 *r*]), as he would have devised shortly after in France for the Castle of Chambord. Subsequent to this plan, he carries out the designs for the «stables of the Magnificent» (CA, f. 96 *va* [264 *v*]): a building, capable of accommodating 100 horses, endowed with an automatic refuelling for the hay, with an advanced system of channels of drain for the inner cleanings and already devised in its

structural elements for the Moor, around 1488 (Ms. B, f. 39 *r*; CA, f. 96 *va* [264 *v*]). The construction was planned between San Marco and the Annunziata, like in fact it will happen in the course of 1516 (today transformed in the reception Hall, the «Room De Vecchi» or «Room of the columns», with the overlooking Library of the Military Geographic Institute). The building, placed at that time in front of the Orto dei Semplici and characterized inside by columns and archivolts and by an extraordinary functionality and innovative technological drive, would have been celebrated by Michel Eyquem de Montaigne (1533-92) in his *Diary*, during the travel he made to Italy at the end of the sixteenth century.[63] On the occasion of the encounter in Bologna between the Pope and Francis I,[64] Leonardo came into contact with the dignitaries of the French court, and for one of them, the master of room Artus Boissif, on Friday 14 December, before the King decided to leave Bologna, he made a portrait in sanguine on a sheet, where Francesco Melzi annotated: «portrait of M. Artus master of room of the king Francis I in the Council with Pope Leo X, which, denying him the union with his arms that he had engaged with the king of Naples for many years, pleased him of naming immediately his brother cardinal».[65]

Meanwhile, the project of reclamation of the «lethal Pontine marshes», started in 1515, was carried to an end by the engineer friar Giovanni Scotti from Como in 1521, year in which they were, for a short time, but with success, cleared. The new lands were in part transferred to Lorenzo de' Medici, duke of Urbino, that for will of Leo X had replaced Giuliano, after his death (17 March 1516), and in part, in compliance with the contract, to Domenico de Juvenibus, while to friar Giovanni Scotti from Como were lavished important donations. The success of this reclamation would have met, in the same year, also the approval of the pupil of Donato Bramante, Cesare Cesariano, that, in his commentary to the *De Architectura* by

---

303 *vb* [829 *r*]), but that also could favour scientific experiences. Reaching an old age in fact he discovers the importance of glasses (CA, f. 244 *ra* [663 *r*]), but he studies at the same time coloured lenses to examine the theory of colours or to observe, once mounted on a telescope, the Moon: «Make glasses to see the Moon great» (CA, f. 190 *ra* [518 *r*]).

[62] In 1508, Leonardo will benefit of the liberality of Piero di Braccio Martelli, that generously gave hospitality to him in his own house (today Via de' Martelli, next to Via Larga, where decades before it had been received also Donatello). Here he began the compilation of his studies of mechanics in the Codex Arundel and to arrange in a systematic way the stuff for a «treatise on waters» and the one for the «Book on painting», as well as he took up again his interests for optics and perspective, for sculpture, anatomy and for the technology on the flight of birds: «Begun in Florence, in the house of Piero di Braccio Martelli on the day 22 of March 1508. And may this be a collection without order, taken out of many papers which I have copied here, hoping then to put them in order in their places, according to the subjects that they will deal with; and I believe that before that I am at the end of this, I shall have to replicate the same thing many times; and so, reader, do not blame me, because the things are many, and the memory cannot keep them and say: «I do not want to write this, because I wrote it before». And if I did not want to fall in such an error, it would be necessary that for every moment that I wanted to copy on it, in order not to reply it, I always had to reread all the past, and especially setting to write at such long intervals of time, from one time to another» (Cod. Arundel, f. 1 *r* = P 115).

[63] See C. PEDRETTI, *Leonardo architetto*, Milano, Electa, 1978; ID., *Presentazione*, in *Leonardo da Vinci, genio delle macchine*, a cura di S. Cremante, Firenze, Cartei e Becagli, 2005; ID., *Un «mirabile artificio» in omaggio al re di Francia*, «L'Osservatore Romano», Giovedì 26 Maggio 2005.

[64] The Grassi so describes the encounter in Bologna between Leo X and Francis I: «Tuesday 11 December the cardinals in number of twenty were convened in the palace of the Pope in Bologna to then go towards the king solemnly at S. Felice's Gate. So large was the crowd in the consistorial room that the same king could hardly go ahead towards the Pope. As he was near, kissed according to custom the foot, the hand and the face of the pontiff, he stated in French that he declared himself beloved son ready to execute every his order. To which the Pope benignly and humanly answered that he transferred to God all that the king said in his regard. Then the chancellor of the king, dressed of a long gold garment, down on his knees lent obedience in the usual form in the name of the king who was present. The king, bending his head and shoulders, approved all that was said by the chancellor and the Pope gave an elegant answer to the declared public manifestation of faith of the king».

[65] See DELICATI-ARMELLINI, *Il diario di Leone X…*, 1884, *op. cit.*

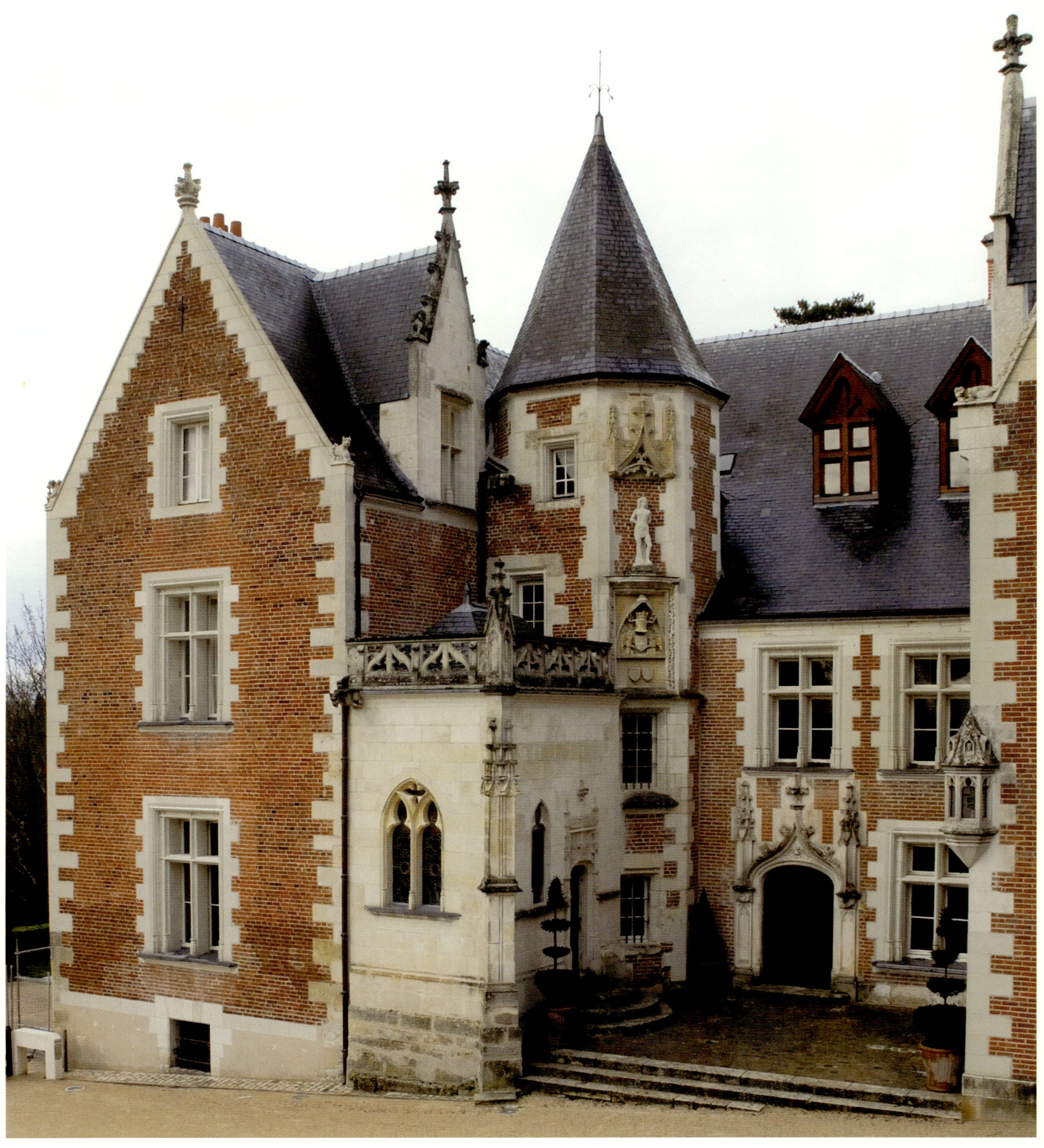

The Castle of Clos–Lucé near Amboise

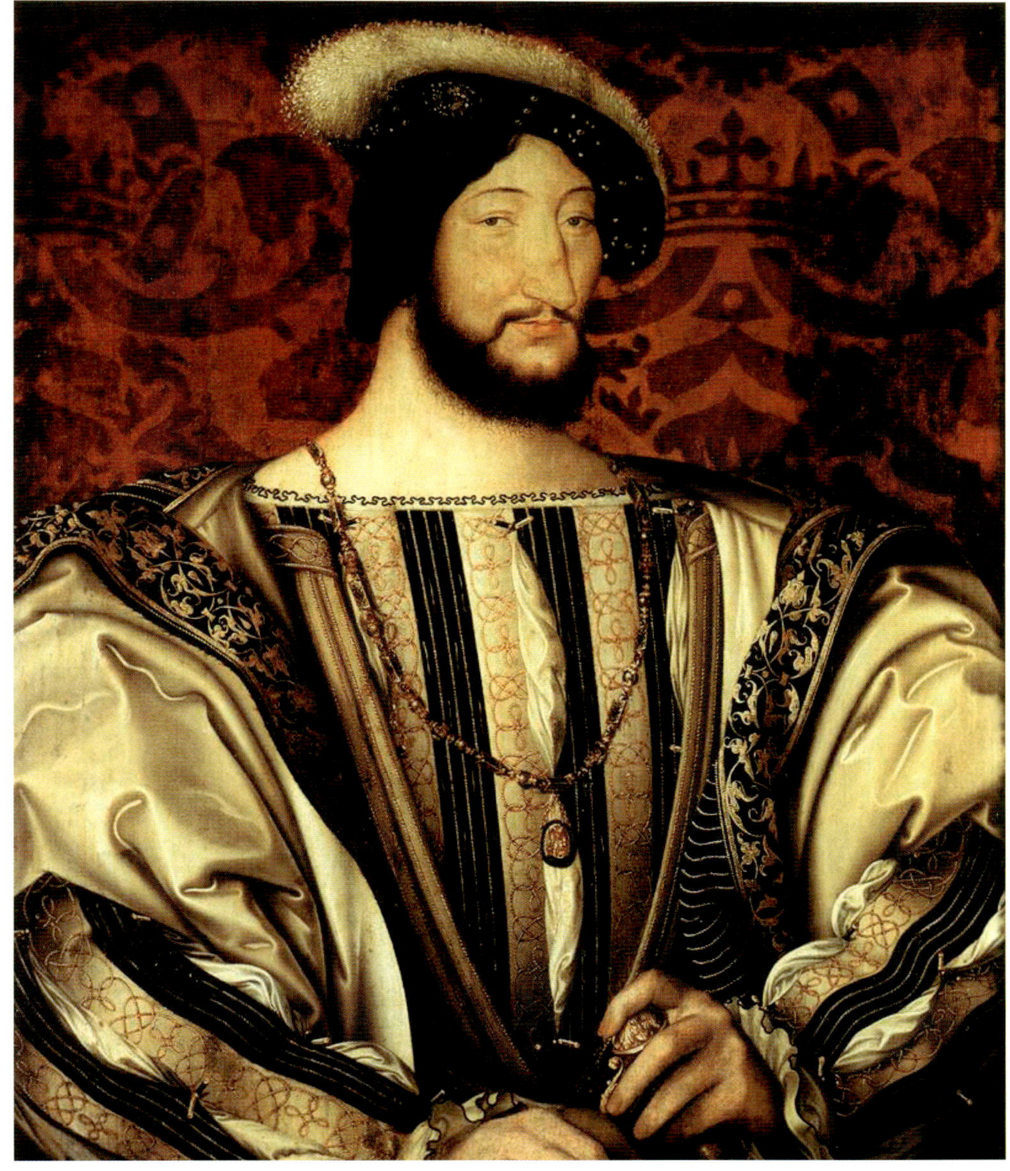

JEAN CLOUET, *Francis I, c.* 1525. Paris, Musée du Louvre

Vitruvius, would have remembered with great admiration how «these Pontine marshes have been purged and emptied in our times by a friar of Como, which thing the Romans never could do». In August 1516, Leonardo would have still made some measurements of the basilica of San Paolo Fuori le Mura (CA, f. 172 *ra-vb* [471 *r*]), but before the arrival of winter, being dead by now his benefactor, patron and friend Giuliano, escorted by the royal emissaries and accompanied by the faithful Francesco Melzi and by domestic servant Batista de Villanis of Milan, he started his travel to France. And so, surpassed the Alps through the pass of the Monginevro, he goes up along the river Arve through the Savoy, then Saint-Gervais and in the end the Valley of the Loire, where his new dwelling of Clos-Lucé is waiting for him, at a short distance from the refined world of the royal court of Amboise: «Coast of Arna near Geneva, ¼ of mile in Savoy, where they make the fair, it tolls in San Giovanni in the village of San Cervagio» (CA, f. 87 *vb* [237 *v*]).

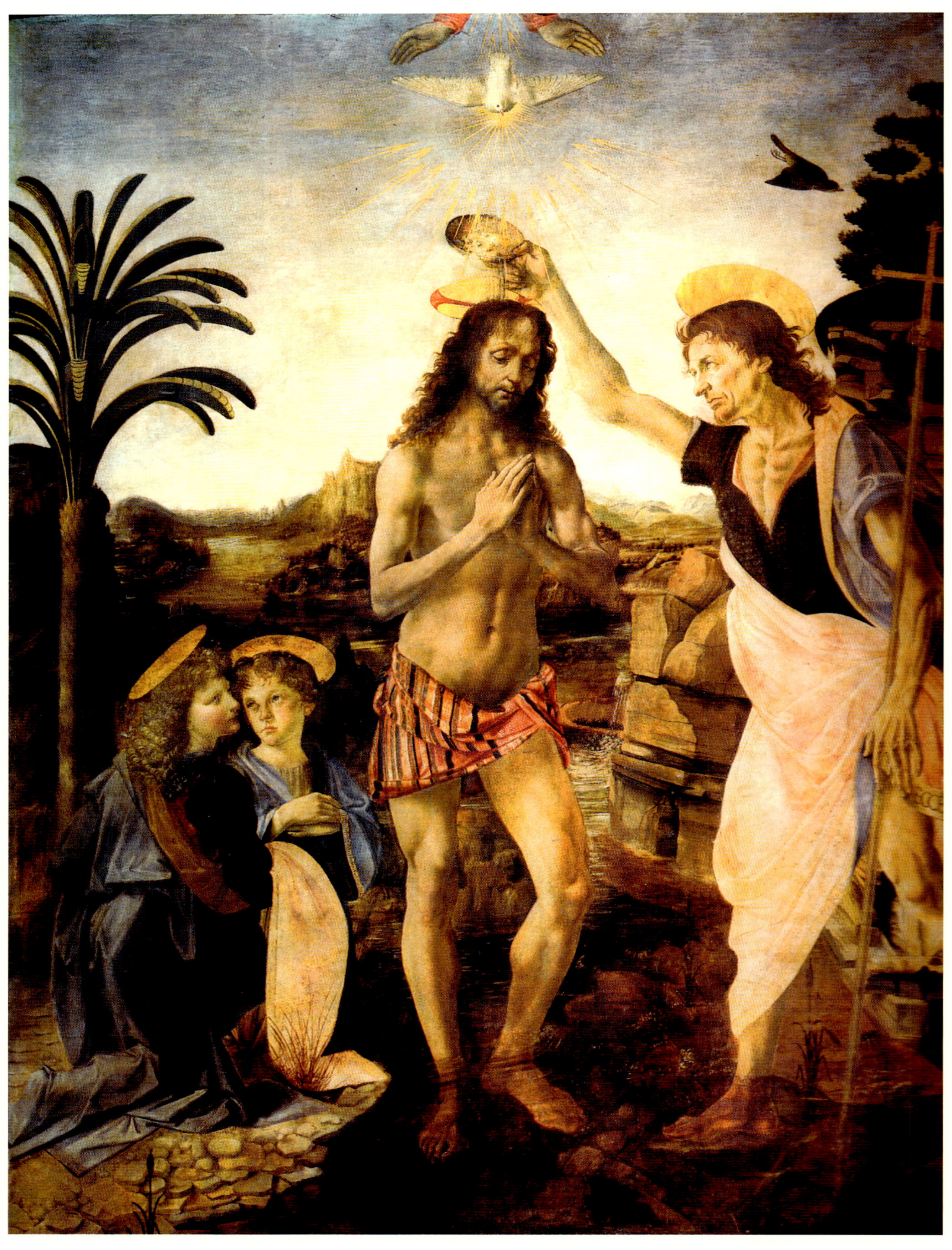

Andrea del Verrocchio and Leonardo, *Baptism of Christ*, *c.* 1473-75. Oil and tempera on table, 177 x 152 cm. Florence, Galleria degli Uffizi

Leonardo
and the *Baptism* of Donatello
in the Dome of Arezzo

ACCORDING TO Vasari, Donatello would have addressed his studies on cameos, coins, masks, Roman ornaments, let alone on the sealed ceramics of Arezzo with the passion and the delight that, in full Humanism, were reserved to the world of the antiquities. And the «stiacciato» or «flattened relief», a kind of drawing and superficial engraving, derived for certain aspects from the analyses of those documents, would have been particularly appreciated by Leonardo. Paolo Giovio, who knew the vincian artist better than any other biographer, stated that he «preferred the plastic to the paint-brush, as a model of the images to represent in relief on the plane».

In fact Leonardo considered the «stiacciato» in close proximity to painting, for its intrinsic qualities and for the investigation that it involved about the effects of light, of perspective and of volume, that is to say about those theoretical requirements already postulated by Alberti in his *Della Pittura* (1436):[1]

But the bas-relief is of more speculation without comparison to the all-relief, and in greatness of speculation it approaches somewhat to painting, because it is obliged to perspective and the all-relief is not bothered for nothing in such recognition, since it uses the simple measures as it has found them true to life; […] But to return to the theme of what has been said about the bas-relief, I say that that one is of lesser corporal hard work than the all-relief, but of much greater investigation, notwithstanding that in that one it has to be considered the proportion that have the interposed distances between the first parts of the bodies and the second ones, and from the second ones

to the third ones subsequently; which if will be considered by you in perspective, you will not find any work in bas-relief that is not full of errors in the cases of the greater and lesser relief that is required to the parts of the bodies that are more or less near to the eye (*Libro di Pittura*, f. 21 *v*, *cap.* 37).

Since the first appearance of his artistic and intellectual formation in the workshop of Verrocchio, Leonardo had directly experienced the art of sculpture, receiving and intensifying its visual, plastic and spatial possibilities, subordinated to a stringent comparison with painting:

Since I make use not less of sculpture than of painting and I am exercising the one and the other in a same degree, it seems to me that with small imputation I am able to give a sentence about it, which is of greater talent and difficulty and perfection, about the one and the other (*Libro di Pittura*, f. 23, *cap.* 38).

Therefore, exalting the characterizing aspects of the bas-relief, Leonardo came to indicate also its artistic limits, to highlight, in a vision that was diametrically opposite to the one of Michelangelo, the superiority of painting in comparison to sculpture, since,

sculpture lacks the beauty of colours, lacks the perspective of colours, lacks the perspective and confusion of terms of the things far-off from the eye; therefore it will make known the terms of the things that are near as well as of those that are far-off: it will not make the interposed air between the remote object and the eye occupy that object more than the closest object; it will not make the bodies polished and transparent as the veiled figures which show the naked flesh under the veils placed on them; it will not make the small jar of various colours under the surface of transparent waters (*Libro di Pittura*, f. 25 *v*, *cap.* 41).

---

[1] See C. GRAYSON, *Leon Battista Alberti, On Painting and On Sculpture*, edited and translated by C. Grayson II, London, Phaidon, 1972; ID., *Studi su Leon Battista Alberti*, a cura di P. Claut e con premessa di A. Tenenti, Centro Studi Leon Battista Alberti di Mantova, Firenze, Olschki, 1998.

The painter in fact, with the «two perspectives» and «the light and shade of the shadows and of the lights» manages «to make to relieve that which is not in relief» (*Libro di Pittura*, f. 22, *cap.* 37), that is to say, by controlling light he confers corporeity and threedimensionality to the figures, while the sculptor shows his vulnerability in the same research of the effects of depth, so that, forced to make a deformation of the relief, he obtains a scenography produced not by the volume of the full relief, but by a flattening in perspective that deforms the proportional regularity of the single figures.

If the mastery of the «stiacciato» had pushed Donatello to partially recuperate in the bas-relief the advantages of painting, Leonardo saw in painting, the only art capable of improving itself, exceeding the defects of the bas-relief, with which he had established since his first experiences a preferential direct relationship for the expressive force that it had reached.[2]

Mario Salmi defined the *Baptism of Christ*, in the hexagonal baptismal font of the Dome of Arezzo, together with two other narrations from the life of Saint Donatus (the other three on the back brought the coats of arms of the people of Arezzo, of the Municipality and of the Labourers of the Dome), realized with fresh naturalism by Bernardo Rossellino (*Baptism of St. Donatus* and *Saint Donatus that baptizes Syrianne*), certainly work of Donatello: interpretation confirmed by John Pope-Hennessy, that granted singular attention to the relief.[3]

A composition devised from the artist and «spatially defined» perhaps around 1440, after the circular paintings of the Old Sacristy of San Lorenzo in Florence, where the facial typology of Saint John the Evangelist is correlated in an obvious way to the one belonging to Saint John the Baptist of the bas-relief of Arezzo: a small marble 63,6 cm high and 40,5 cm wide.

Here, the series of trees and the groups of the personages-spectators, distributed along a water course, are aimed to tie, with novelistic effectiveness and in a new physical and ideal relationship, the human and the divine plane to the naturalistic one, so that the landscape, pervaded with a diffused sense of cosmic energy, becomes an integral part of the celebration of man.

This singular work, today almost completely unknown, undoubtedly had a great resonance at half the fifteenth century for its originality, so as to constitute reason of recall and of study from life, with its precise textual basis, for Piero della Francesca as well as for Verrocchio and Leonardo.[4]

[2] See J. POPE-HENNESSY, *Italian Renaissance Sculpture*, London, Phaidon, 1958; ID., *Interaction of Painting and Sculpture in Florence in the Fifteenth Century*, «Journal of the Royal Society of Arts», 117, 1969; L. GRASSI, *Tutta la scultura di Donatello*, Milano, 1963; U. SCHLEGEL, *Zu Donatello und Desiderio da Settignano*, «Jahrbuch der Berliner Museen», 1967; L. Berti, A. Cecchi, A. Natali, Donatello, «Art Dossier», 3, Firenze, Giunti, 1986; C. Pedretti, A Proem to Sculpture, «Achademia Leonardi Vinci. Journal of Leonardo Studies and Bibliography of Vinciana», II, Firenze, Giunti, 1989; M. KEMP, M. WALKER, *Leonardo on Painting* (a cura di), New Haven/London, 1989; A. PARRONCHI, *Nuove proposte per Leonardo scultore*, «Achademia Leonardi Vinci. Journal of Leonardo Studies and Bibliography of Vinciana», II, Firenze, Giunti, 1989; ID., *L'Arpia svela: è Donatello*, «La Nazione», 4 gennaio 1991; ID., *Donatello: saggi e studi 1962-1997*, Vicenza, Neri Pozza, 1998; K. WEIL-GARRIS BRANDT, *Leonardo e la scultura*, «Lettura Vinciana», XXXVIII, Firenze, Giunti, 1999.

[3] See M. SALMI, *Civiltà artistica della terra aretina*, Novara, De Agostini, 1971; ID., *La pittura di Piero della Francesca*, Novara, De Agostini, 1979; J. POPE-HENNESSY, *Donatello scultore*, Milano, Motta, 1993. According to Pope-Hennessy the attribution that Vasari does of the bas-relief to an «imaginary brother of Donatello named Simone» is depending on the lesser perfection of the work in comparison with the relieves of his maturity. For that reason Pope-Hennessy included it between his juvenile works, with a dating that could go back to around 1415, while for Salmi it was datable to the «fourth decade of the Fifteenth century».

[4] See P. ADORNO, *Il Verrocchio. Nuove proposte nella civiltà artistica del tempo di Lorenzo il Magnifico*, Firenze, EDAM, 1992; A. NATALI, *Lo sguardo degli angeli. Verrocchio,*

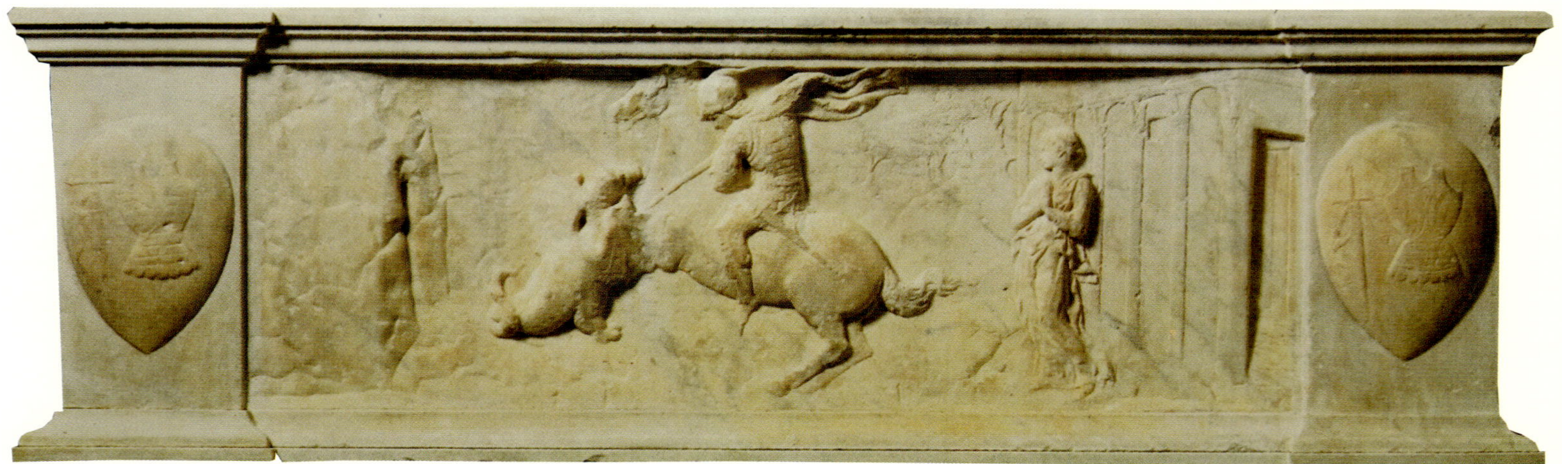

DONATELLO, *St. George and the Dragon*. Marble, 40 x 120 cm. Florence, Museo Nazionale del Bargello

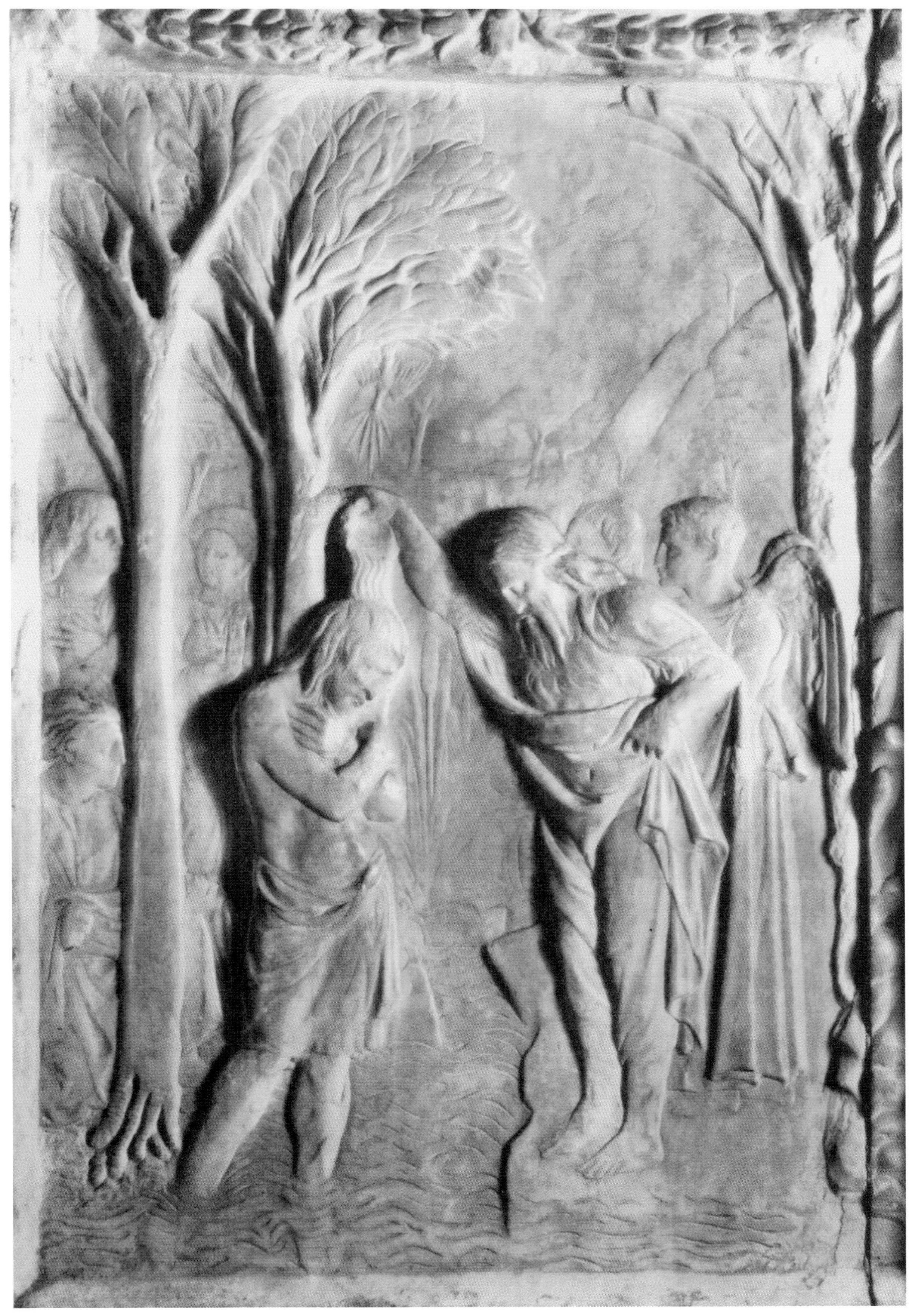

Donatello, *Baptism of Christ*. Marble, 63,6 x 40,5 cm. Arezzo, Dome, Christening Font

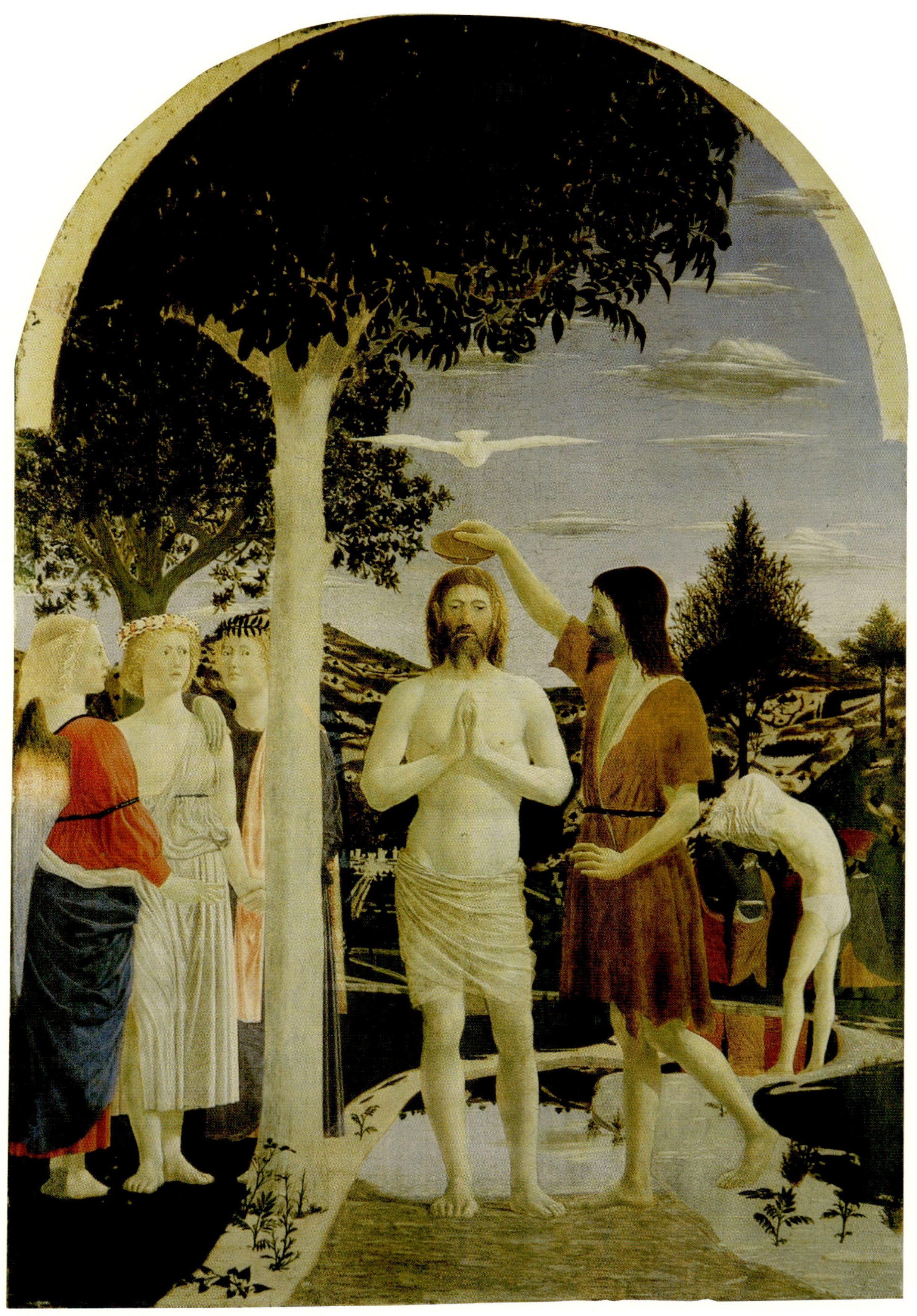

Piero della Francesca, *Baptism of Christ*, c. 1450. Table, 167 x 116 cm. London, National Gallery

The «practice» of drawing, as exercise of copy from a sculpture, will be prescribed from Leonardo among his prescriptions in his *Libro di Pittura* (f. 39 *v*, *cap.* 82):

Depict at first drawings of a good master, made on the art from the natural and not of practice; and then of a relief, in company of the drawing [taken] from that same relief; and then of the natural, which you have to put in use.

Precepts that were part of the multiple activities of the workshop and inherent, in the artistic itinerary of every apprentice, to know how to better carry out a painting, studying the perspective, making portrays of the natural, imitating and following the style and the indications of the «first painters», that are so rare and the only ones that «with truth will be able to evaluate you» (*Libro di Pittura*, f. 33 *v*, *cap.* 59). And Donatello was a consecrated author, that had exercised a great fascination on the young Leonardo, so much that in maturity he would have recommended him even to Baccio Bandinelli, numbering him among the «good masters» on which practicing and having «to accustom first the hand» (*Libro di Pittura*, f. 34, *cap.* 63),[5] in order then to draw progressively and in a directed way from nature, as Giotto and Masaccio made, to whom the rebirth of painting was due, for their wisdom in distributing light on the surface of things and for the invention of the play of volumes on tangible bodies, a reason of inspiration also for Piero della Francesca: «he largely praised the works of Donato, telling him that he should make some marble thing, like heads or bas-relief».[6] Donatello had, for the first time, immersed the sacred event of the *Baptism of Christ* in nature, in a landscape that by Piero would have shaped with the geomorphological characteristics of the high Valley of the Tiber, for its view in the distance of Borgo San Sepolcro (London, National Gallery) and by Leonardo with those of the Valley of the Arno, already observed from Monte Albano in the direction of Fucecchio in the first autograph draw of the Uffizi (Gabinetto dei Disegni, n. 8 Pr), made the «day of Saint Mary of the Snow, the day 5 of August 1473».[7]

The *Baptism of Christ*, already existing as an iconographical motive in the mosaics of Ravenna, but with the landscape cancelled by the polished sparkle of the golden background,[8] it is from now on conceived and represented with respect to the theological contents of the Trinitarian doctrine, reaffirmed by the Church of Rome during the Council of 1439 in Florence, with the representation of the three Persons of the Holy Trinity.[9] There was the intention to reconfirm, be-

Uffizi a Firenze, Firenze, Giunti, 1985; M. CLAYTON, *Leonardo da Vinci. A curious vision*, London, Merrel Holberton, 1996; A. FARA, *Leonardo nel «dì di Santa Maria della neve / addì 5 d'aghossto 1473». Paesaggio e cultura militare*, «Dialoghi di Storia dell'Arte», 3, 1996; ID., *Leonardo e l'architettura militare*, «Lettura Vinciana», XXXVI, Firenze, Giunti, 1997; R. NANNI, *Osservazione, convenzione, ricomposizione nel paesaggio leonardiano del 1473*, «Raccolta Vinciana», XXVIII, 1999.

[8] LORENZO GHIBERTI represents the *Baptism of Christ* in one panel in golden bronze of the second door of the Baptistry of Florence (1403-24). Jesus is still dipped in water to his hips, like in the Byzantine representations, and the background plane offers certain naturalistic motives of plants, derived from late-gothic botanical models, that are still inclined towards a stylized representation of reality. In the Chapel of the Seminary of Arezzo, coming from the near Church of San Marco al Murello, there is a beautiful Romanesque bas-relief with the topic of the *Baptism of Christ*, a work of great modernity, attributed to the School of Antelami. In the *Baptism* by Piero della Francesca we look in its place at an iconographical variation in comparison with the tradition, since Christ is not dipped in water, but he lays down his feet as well as the Baptist on a dry land and he has a frontality that remembers «Byzantine precedents passed through Tuscany, especially in the world of Siena of which an example remains close to Sansepolcro, in the Picture Gallery of Città di Castello, in an unpublished work by Sano di Giovanni da Siena (1356), ordinary for his style but iconographically remarkable», see M. SALMI, *La pittura di Piero della Francesca*, 1979, *op. cit.*

[9] In the Council of Ferrara-Florence (1438-39), the Christian world tried to come up to an effective agreement of unitary re-composition between the Eastern Church and the Western one in face of the Turkish threat. The presence of the Eastern Emperor John VIII Paleologus, with the dignitaries of his court, and of the Patriarch of Constantinople, Joseph II, with his bishops and theologians, confirmed this sincere will of pacification. In 1439, Paleologus and the Patriarch were received in Florence with liberality by Cosimo de' Medici and the chancellor of the Republic, Leonardo Bruni. Personages of eminence were also the great humanist Ambrogio Traversari, that carried out an intense activity of mediation for the Latins, due to his deep knowledge of the patristics, of Greek and of Latin (for this reason he was instructed to write the dual text of the Bull *Laetentur coeli*, with which the reached union of the Churches was certified), while the other courageous defender of the union, for the Greeks, was the bishop of Nicaea, Bessarion, subsequently named cardinal, for his acquired merits, by Pope Eugene IV. On 11 of April 1438, the Traversari wrote from Ferrara to the monk Michele to prepare him the works of Cyril and Athanasios, considered absolutely necessary for the future theological arguments. In fact, moved the Council to Florence for will of the Pope, the disputes on the Holy Spirit broke out again and the Traversari refuted with such ability the objections of the Greeks, to make them accept the following conciliar dogmatic definition: «The Holy Spirit is ab aeterno from the Father and from the Son according to the essence, and from the one and from the other he proceeds like from a single origin». The agreement had been reached, considering that the problem of the «Filioque» was not an adding to the *Creed*, but a clarification of already implicit truths. And the *Creed* is the faith action that is still today at foundation of the liturgy of the «Baptism». Many artists wanted to recognize the importance of the counciliary event in their works. Antonio Averlino known as Filarete (*c.* 1400-post 1466) described its main vicissitudes on a panel of the door in bronze of the Basilica of Saint Peter's, while John VIII Paleologus, already represented in a medal by Pisanello, and the Patriarch appear, together with Piero de' Medici, Lorenzo the Magnificent and Giuliano, in the fresco of the *Travel of the Magi* by Benozzo Gozzoli (1459-62), in the Chapel of the Medici-Riccardi Palace in Florence. The traits of John VIII Paleologus then are represented by Piero della Francesca in the face and the hat of Constantine, in his *Battle of Ponte Milvio* (1452-59), in San Francesco's at Arezzo, where the art-

Leonardo e il «Battesimo di Cristo» (a cura di), Cinisello Balsamo, Silvana Editoriale, 1998; D. A. BROWN, *Leonardo da Vinci. Origini di un Genio*, Milano, Rizzoli, 1999.

[5] BACCIO BANDINELLI certainly followed the piece of advice of Leonardo in imitating the art of Donatello; in fact, for the influence of the flattened relief, it is sufficient to compare the *Madonna of the Clouds* of Boston (Museum of Fine Arts) by Donatello with the famous *Madonna with the Child* of Baccio in a private collection of Florence or, for the general style, with the drawing already in the Heseltine collection and now at the Victoria and Albert Museum of London.

[6] See G. VASARI, *Vita di Baccio Bandinelli*, in *Le Vite*, a cura di L. e C. L. Ragghianti, Milano, Rizzoli, 1976.

[7] See C. G. ARGAN, *5 d'aghossto 1473*, in ID., *Classico anticlassico. Il Rinascimento da Brunelleschi a Bruegel*, Milano, Feltrinelli, 1984; A. VEZZOSI, *Toscana di Leonardo*, Firenze, Becocci, 1984; C. PEDRETTI, *Introduzione* a G. DALLI REGOLI, *I disegni di Leonardo da Vinci e della sua cerchia nel Gabinetto Disegni e Stampe della Galleria degli*

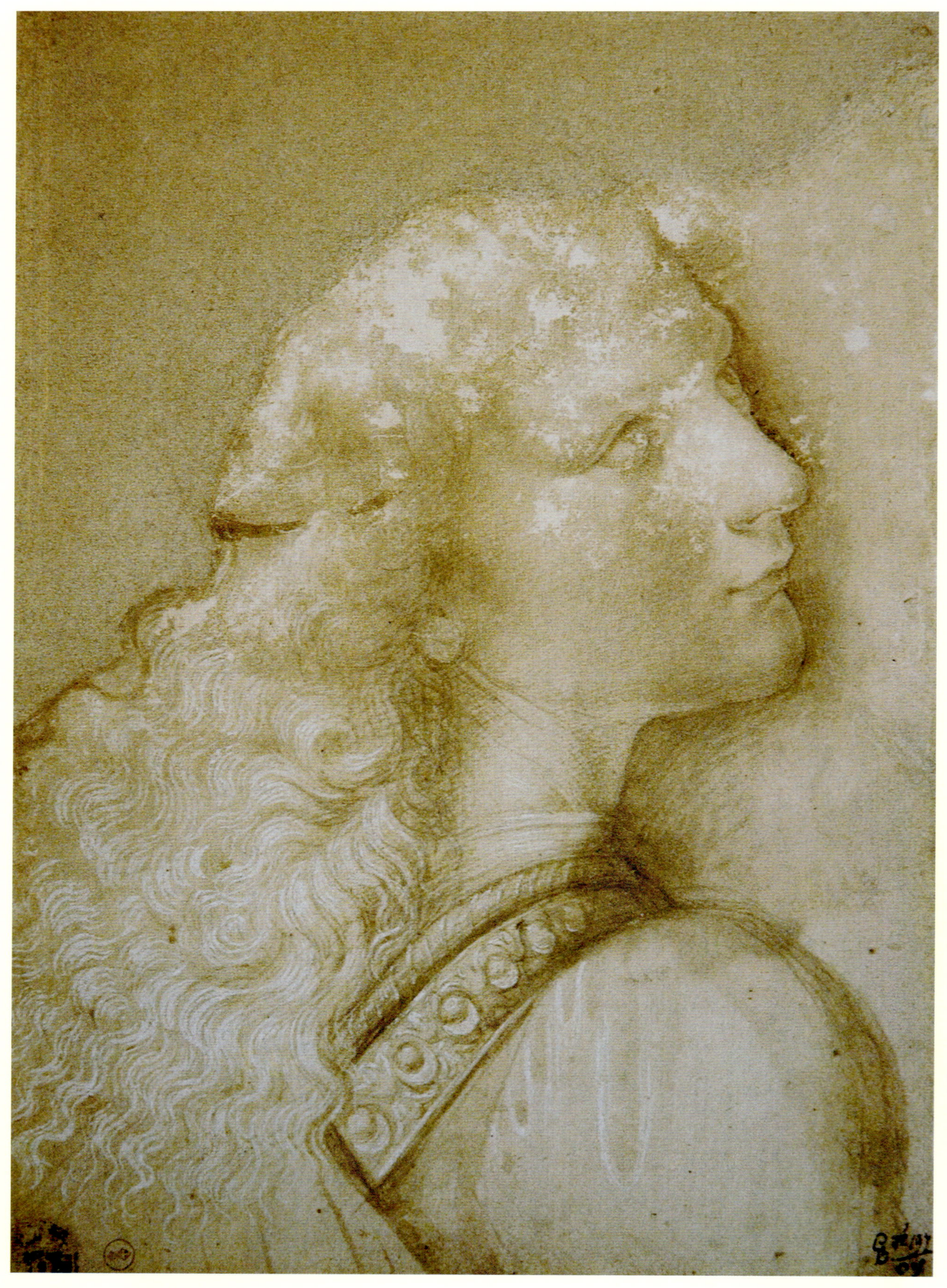

Leonardo da Vinci, *Study for the Angel of the «Baptism of Christ» of Verrocchio, c.* 1475. Turin, Biblioteca Reale, n. 15635

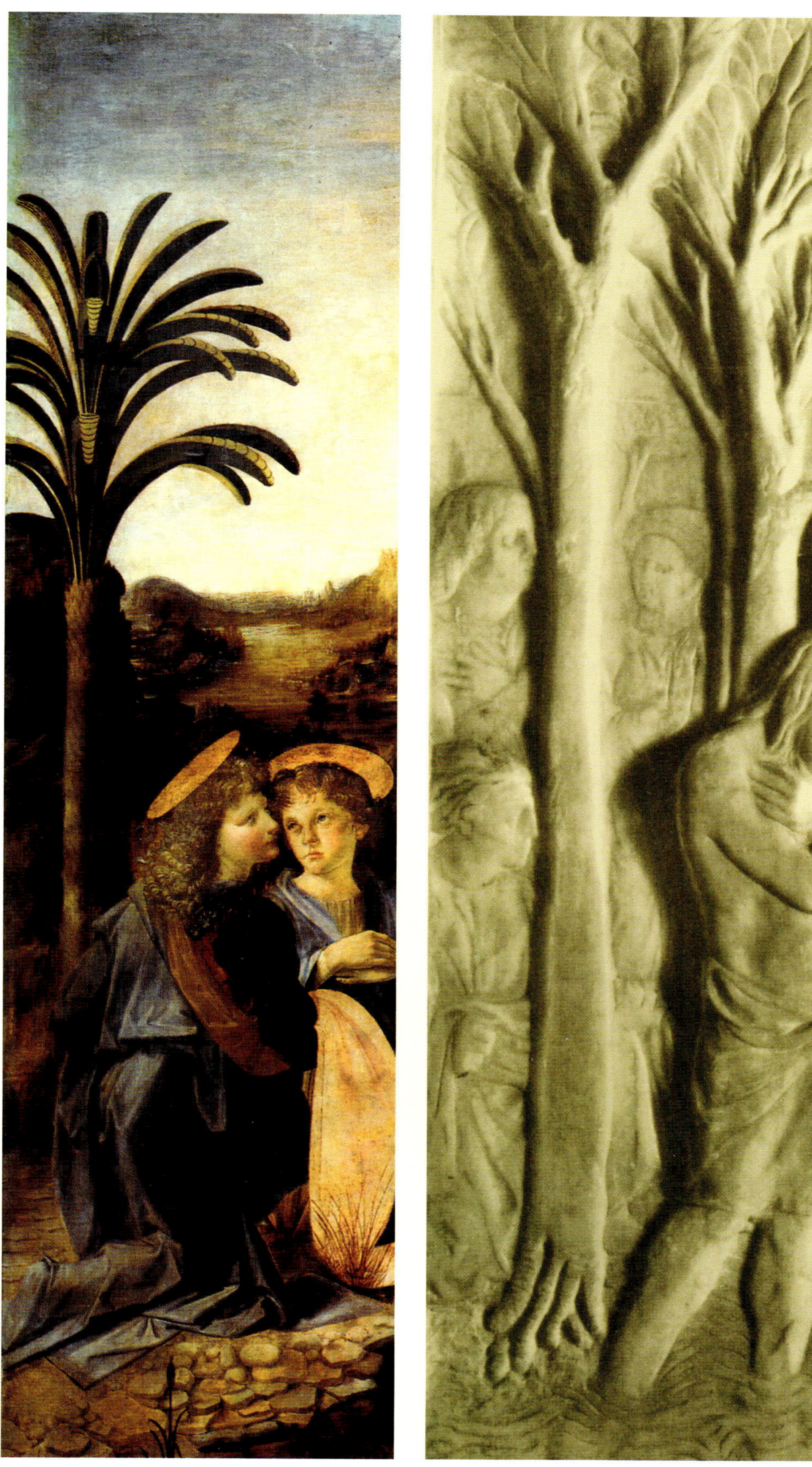

Comparison between the *Baptism of Christ* by Verrocchio and Leonardo with that by Donatello in the Christening Font of the Dome of Arezzo

tween the foundations of the mysteries of faith, not only the creed of God as one and trine, but also the human and divine nature of Christ, so it was transcribed on the figurative plane what had been made explicit by the Gospels: «the skies opened and John saw the spirit of God coming down in the shape of a dove, and come over him. And here: a voice came from the skies and said: This is my preferred Son, of which I pleased» (Matthew, 3, 16-17; John, 1, 31-34). The epiphany of the Trinity with the combined presence of the three persons seems to be caught up in the *Baptism of Christ* realized, between 1473 and 1478, by Verrocchio and Leonardo for the monastery of San Salvi, today at the Galleria degli Uffizi, while in Piero della Francesca the revealing figuration is resolved with the two persons, Jesus and the dove of the Holy Spirit that, if in Donatello and Verrocchio arrives headlong from the sky, in Piero it is gliding down suspended in perfect axis over the head of Christ. But the original paging up of the sacred fact, made by Donatello, reveals how much profoundly Piero, as well as Verrocchio and Leonardo, have to be considered as his debtors. In the bas-relief of the baptismal font of the Dome of Arezzo there is in fact a real and suspended atmosphere about the mystery of the event, entirely constructed on the solid centrality and athletic robustness of the body of Jesus who, in the unveiling of all his inner largeness, bends the head while crossing his arms on his chest as a sign of adoration and as a supreme act of royal humility and obedience to his Father, while the plants slightly degrading with their cylindrical and straight trunk, similar to lateral columns, serve as an umbrella with their wide foliage to the Man-Messiah, that turns out to be inserted in an architectural structure, allusive to a central nave with cross arches. Also Leonardo, in the *Baptism* of San Salvi, as a new figurative typology places the Angel on his kneels on the extreme left with the garment of Jesus on his arms and, like in Donatello, the Christ is immersed well beyond his feet in the current of the Jordan, which is actually a view of the Arno, while, with soft and sinuous movement, water overflows the proscenium and rippling seems to bundle up itself around his right ankle. Vasari, in 1550, attributed to Leonardo the realization of «one angel, that held some clothes» in the painting made by his master for San Salvi, confirming what reported by Francesco Albertini in his *Memoriale*, who indicated to be represented in that table «one angel by Leonardo da Vinci».[10] And precisely the introduction in the painting of that *Angel* from the back who, with torsion of his head, addresses his eyes on Jesus, in the subsequent anecdotage of Vasari, bent to the mythicizing of the extraordinary virtues of the young Leonardo, would have induced Verrocchio to come to an end with painting forever:

> *Making a table, where Saint John baptized Christ, Lionardo worked out an angel who held some garments; and though he was young, he made it in such a way, that the angel of Lionardo was much better than the figures of Andrea; that was the reason why Andrea did not want to touch colours any more, offended that an adolescent knew more than he did.*

And certainly the image of the first Angel kneeling, with the tunic of Christ on his arms, is an indisputable citation, to which Leonardo inspired himself without restraint, transforming it in an intellectual and creative occasion for new composing solutions, where the delicacy of the realization of the face, in a perfect equilibrium between reality and ideality, shines with grace and vitality as direct expression of a physical and mental motion.

Developing the sculptural model of Donatello, Leonardo had transformed the convex profile of the Angel's face, in order to represent its movement of progression in space, after the fast torsion of shoulders and face in the directrix of Christ, suggesting consequently the three-dimensional reality of painting. Therefore the study in profile of the *Angel* of the *Baptism of Christ* of Turin (Biblioteca Reale, n. 15635), seen from the back in the instantaneous turning of the eyes upwards, it is certainly a leonardian invention, but derived from the initial suggestion of a specific sculptural idea of Donatello. We shall observe a similar attitude of formal experimentation, about 1503-06, when Leonardo will represent in black pencil a seated young man (Windsor, RL 12540), having as inspiration source the famous «Diomedes»: a figure carved in a gem belonged to Niccolò Niccoli, then to Pope Paul II and to Lorenzo de' Medici, and represented in a roundel of marble of the Palace Medici-Riccardi right by Donatello.[11] A rather spontaneous attitude, practiced by

---

ist, with open reference to the bridge of pacification constructed between the East and the West in the Council of Florence, represented the Queen of Sheba that, in visit to Salomon, kneels down in front of the bridge of wood, obtained from the tree that was born from the body of Adam. Piero could follow closely all the conciliar vicissitudes, being at that time in Florence in the workshop of Domenico Veneziano. The memorable event of the Council was then celebrated also by Lorenzo Ghiberti, in the plate in golden bronze of the *Encounter of the Queen of Sheba with Salomon* in the *Door of Paradise* of the Baptistry of Florence (1425-1452).

[10] See F. ALBERTINI, *Memoriale di molte statue et picture sono nella inclyta ciptà di Florentia per mano di sculptori et pictori excellenti moderni et antiqui*, Firenze, Tubini, 1510.
[11] See M. CLAYTON, *Leonardo da Vinci. One hundred drawings from the collection of Her Majesty the Queen*, London, Merrell Holberton, 1997. The adherence of Leonardo to the ancient world is recognizable also for the dedication contained in the small poem in triplets *Antiquarie prospetiche romane composte per prospectivo Melanese Depintore*, of which Bramante would be the author, which calls him «cordial pleasant beloved associate / Vinci my beloved».

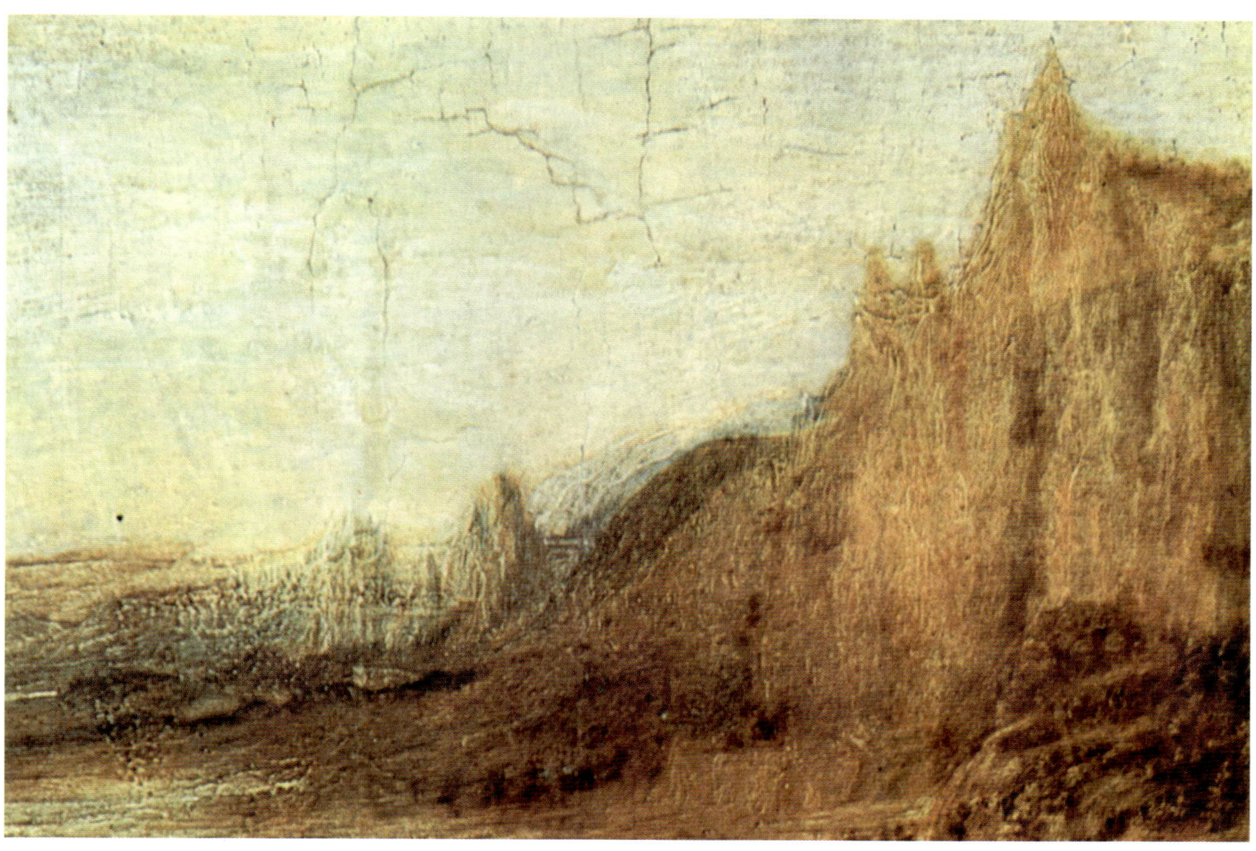

Andrea del Verrocchio and Leonardo, *Baptism of Christ*, *c.* 1473-75. Oil and tempera on table, 177 x 152 cm. Florence, Galleria degli Uffizi. Particular of the landscape

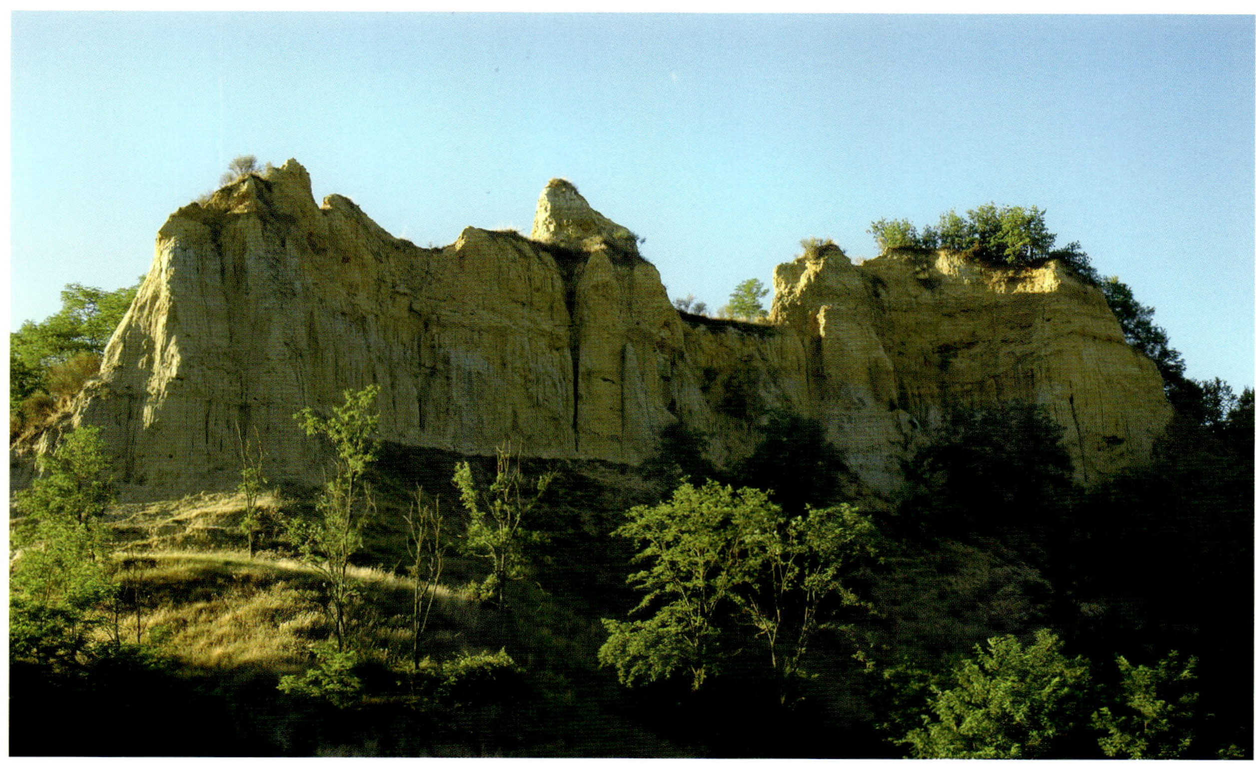

The landscape of the upper Valdarno, characterized on a geo-morphological plan by laminar pinnacles and crests, reveals close analogies to the *Baptism of Christ* of Verrocchio

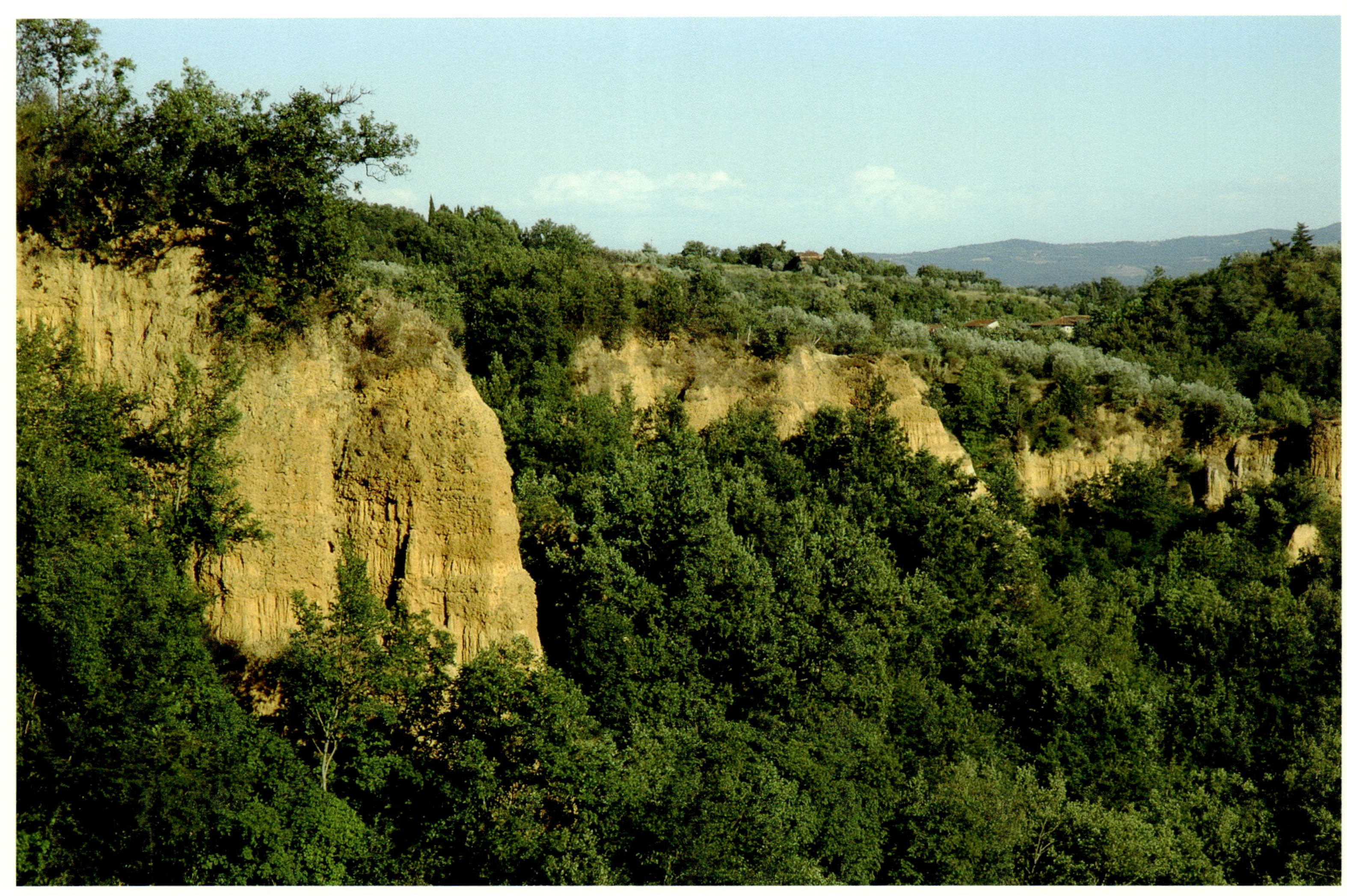

Comparison between a drawing of Leonardo (Windsor, RL 12395) and a part of the *Balze* of the Upper Valdarno: an example of the erosive force of meteoric water and of the vertical lithologic variation

Leonardo as a strategy in his relationship towards examples of previous sculptures, considered as a rich source of inventions and variations, that he will even renew in his full and direct adhesion to the world of the ancients, «the imitation of the ancient things is commendable more than that of the modern ones» (CA., f. 147 *rb* [399 *r*]), considered therefore an incentive for emulation as much as «the natural things», as the statuary models consulted for the complex gestation of the *Leda* and of the *Saint Anne* or the antiquarian models, derived from sarcophagi and coins, for garments, horses and heads, can document (Windsor, RL 12315; 12556; 12553):

Do observe the honour with which you clothe the figures according to their degrees and their ages; and over all, that the clothes do not occupy the movement, that is the limbs, and that the aforesaid limbs are not cut by the folds, neither by the shadows of the clothes, and do imitate as much as you can the Greeks and the Latin with the way to discover the limbs, when the wind leans on them their clothes. And do few folds; just do much of them in the old men wearing a gown and of authority (Libro di Pittura, f. 168, cap. 533).

Now Verrocchio, taking part in the *Baptism* of San Salvi, for whose conception he was the responsible, was going to invert the twisted legs of the Jesus of Donatello, representing him with the head faintly slanted and the hands united, in a sign of maximum concentration and absorption,[12] while the Baptist, subordinated to a careful research of interaction be-

---

[12] According to A. CHASTEL the traditional gesture of the worshipper with his opened arms, was replaced during the thirteenth century, in the pontificate of Gregory IX, with the prayer «manibus junctis» [«with hands joined» Tr.N.]. That was rigorously recommended in the Franciscan liturgy of the Mass, since the «junctio manuum», at the moment of the Offertory, favoured the necessary attention, to offer to God the body of Jesus. See A. CHASTEL, *Il gesto nell'arte*, Roma-Bari, Laterza, 2002.

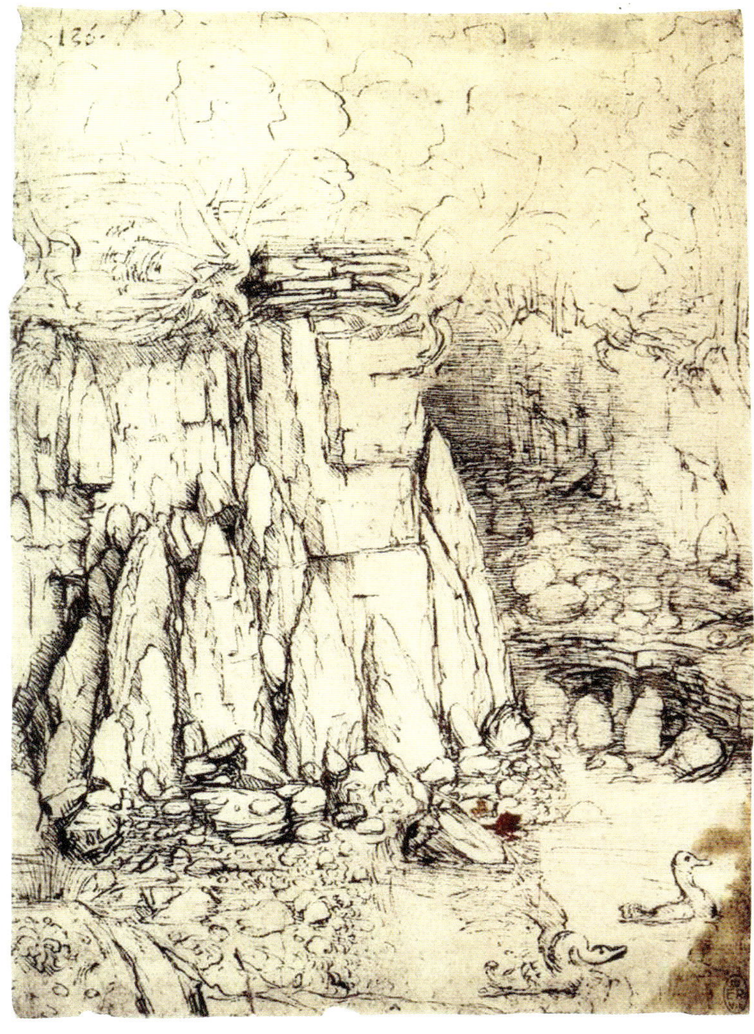

This is the theory of the «motions» and the «mental accidents», that will be subsequently developed by Leonardo in the study of the hands and of the glances of his personages, from the *Virgin of the Rocks* to the *Last Supper*, from the *Battle of Anghiari* to the *Saint Anne* and to the *Saint John the Baptist*, where the deep intensity of feelings would have been made clear in a direct relation between physiognomy and psychology, to grant farther «philosophical» dignity to painting (*Libro di Pittura*, f. 109 v, cap. 294):

You will make the figures in such action, that is sufficient to demonstrate what the figure has in its mind; otherwise your art will not be praiseworthy.

The naturalism of Donatello, farther deepened by Leonardo, can be grasped in the same landscape in the background («the first realistic landscape of the Renaissance, in conjunction to the one of *Saint George and the Dragon*»), so far away from the small run of water in the foreground, garnished with swamp bulrushes and cattails or reed maces (preferred by Leonardo, as a botanical study, in sheet 12430 of Windsor, and connected, as a phallic symbol, to the concept of «natura naturans», for the *Leda kneeling*; Rotterdam, Boijmans Van Beuningen Museum), and therefore enlarged in spatial depth, in the perspective distance of a bending sky, in the varied rapid succession of steep slopes that, from the lateral rises, fall steeply in terraces towards the centre. Vinci could grasp the excellence of certain results caught up by bas-relief sculpture, able to transmit of itself, for the relief extremely low and limited by a line that makes it a drawing on marble, «some appreciation to the one who contemplates it, like does painting, that in a flat surface by force of knowledge displays the widest countries with their remote horizons» (*Libro di Pittura*, f. 20, cap. 35). An observation that is quite suitable to his first works in the workshop of Verrocchio, where it can be noticed the co-presence of the linear perspective and of the natural effects of the atmosphere, already experienced by Donatello in the spatiality of his landscape views. Therefore Leonardo, reached a conscious artistic maturity, would have resolved the landscape background of the *Baptism*, where already the fascination of a certain Flemish influence can be perceived, by entrusting himself for the first time to the detailed pictorial transcription of the unusual morphologies of the erosion furrows of the Superior Valdarno, placed under a physical and at the same time divine source of light, which exalts its values and natural characteristics. A vision of nature much in close proximity, in its suggestions, to the following developments tuned up in the landscape of the *Mona Lisa* and of the *Saint Anne* and anyhow meant to give prominence to the interest for the specific figurative element, where the recourse

tween light and relief for a greater anatomical representation of nerves and muscles, made reference to him with a tangible analogy of movements. This latter one, animated from inner vigour, raises the right arm pouring water from the small basin on the head of the Messiah, while with his left arm he withholds the garment on his flank, detached from earth and water, with the identical gesturing and posture, with which Donatello had amazingly animated the entire scene of his *Baptism*, employing a masterly dosage of lights and shadows, in order to confer naturalness and volume to the figures, farther on defined by the incisiveness of the draperies. An interpretation of gestures and attitudes, that turned out to be correspondent to the albertian pictorial dictates, founded on the concept that the «movements of the limbs show the movements of the soul» (*Della Pittura*, II, 43), so that the mimic and gesture function of the figures communicated the multiplicity of their «affections».

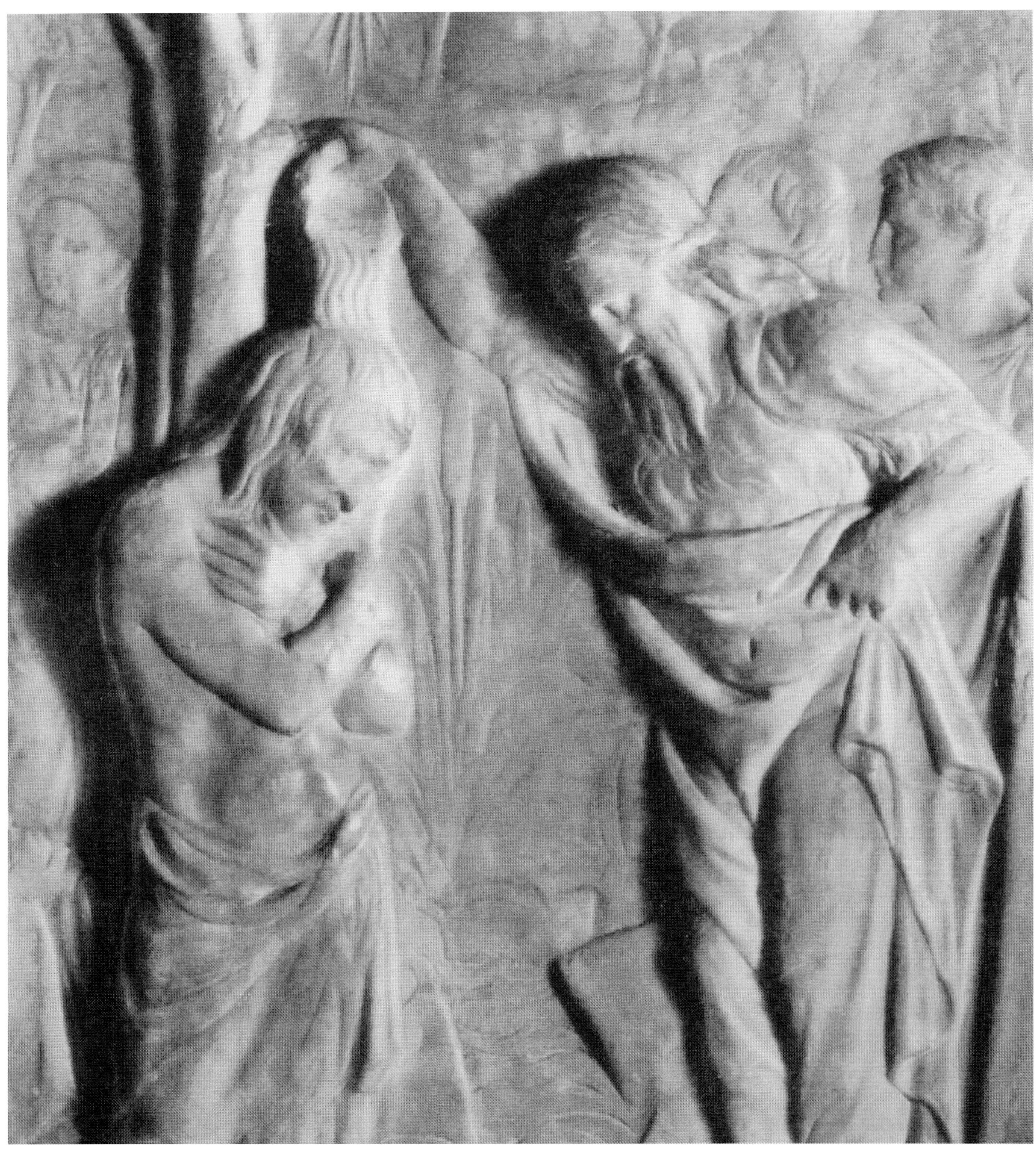

The «corkscrew rush» is a symbol of secret cosmic vitality both in the *Baptism* by Donatello and in the *Leda* by Leonardo kept at the Boymans-van Beuningen Museum of Rotterdam (on the right)

 CARLO STARNAZZI

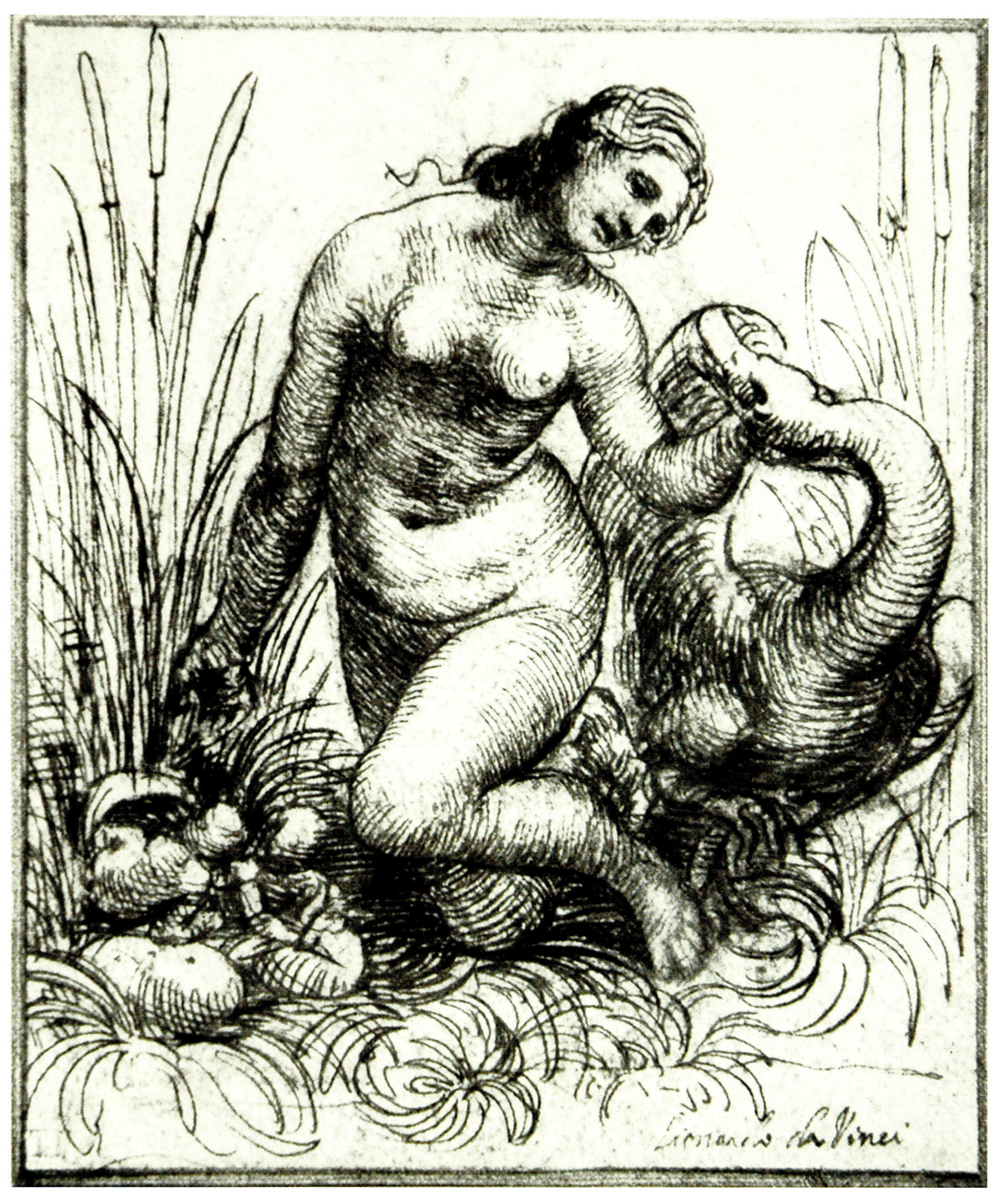

Leonardo and the *Baptism* of Donatello in the Dome of Arezzo

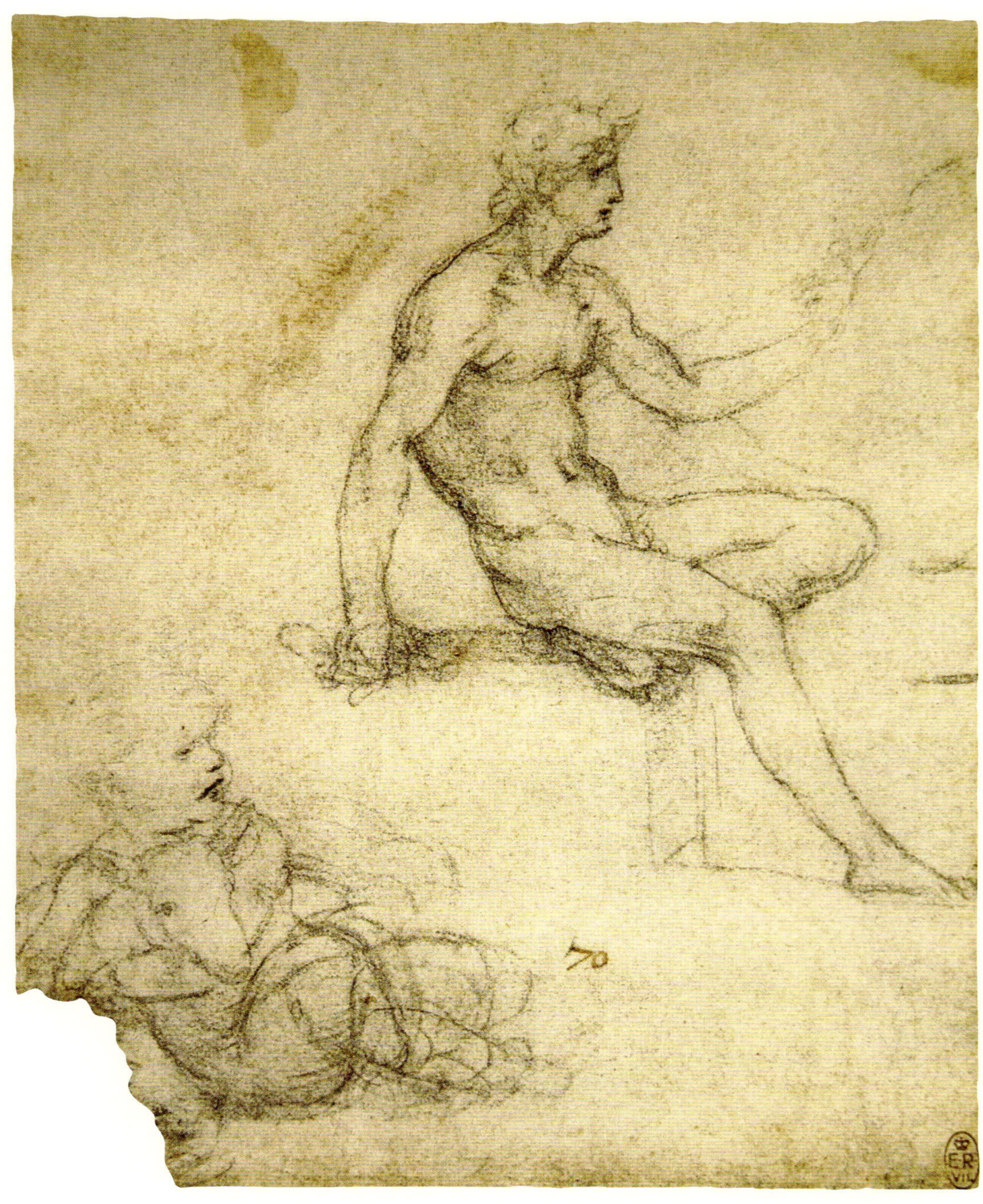

LEONARDO DA VINCI, *Sitting young man and child with a lamb*, *c.* 1503-06. Charcoal, 173 x 140 mm. Windsor, RL 12540

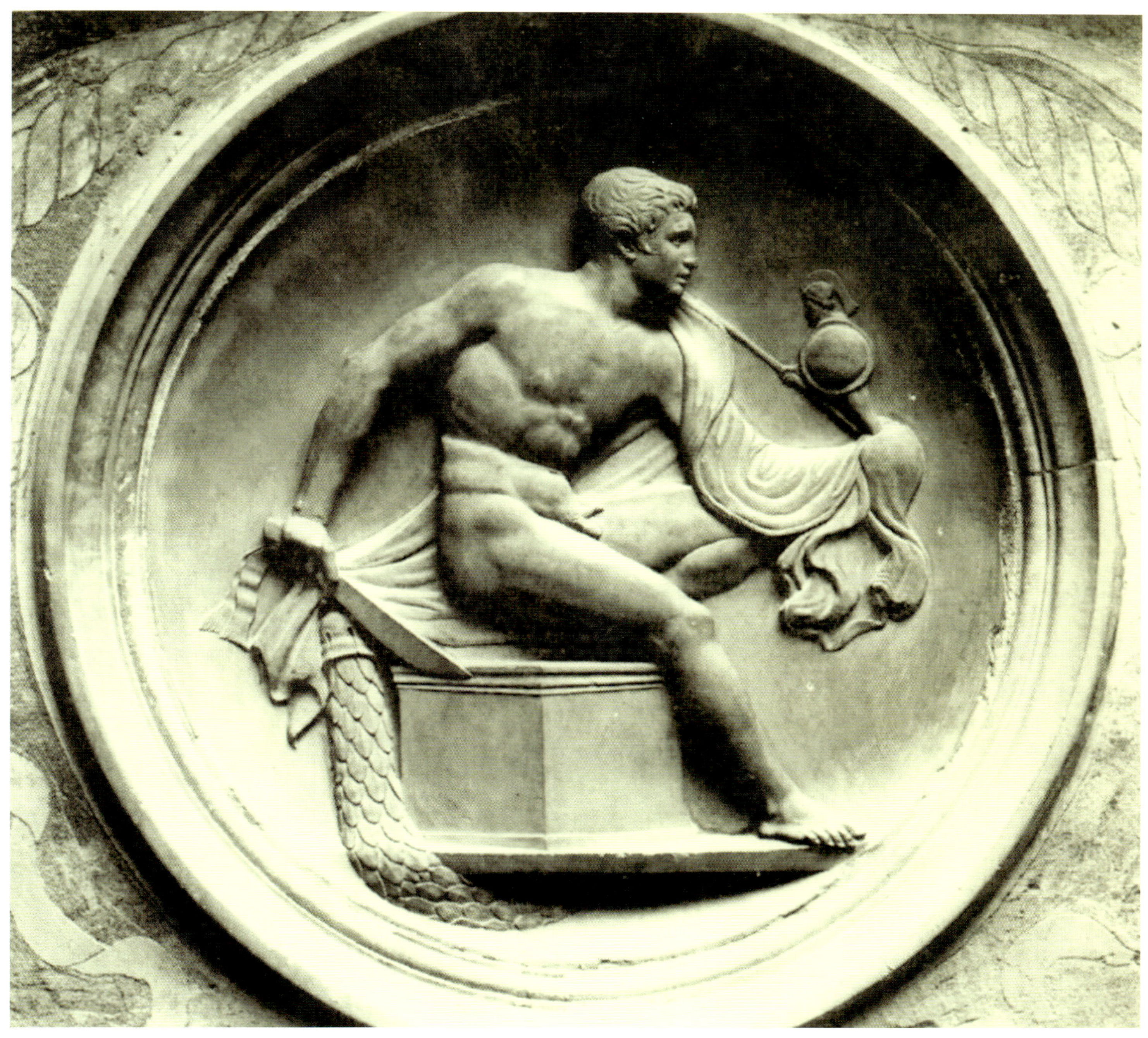

Donatello's workshop, *Diomedes*. Marble. Florence, Palazzo Medici-Riccardi

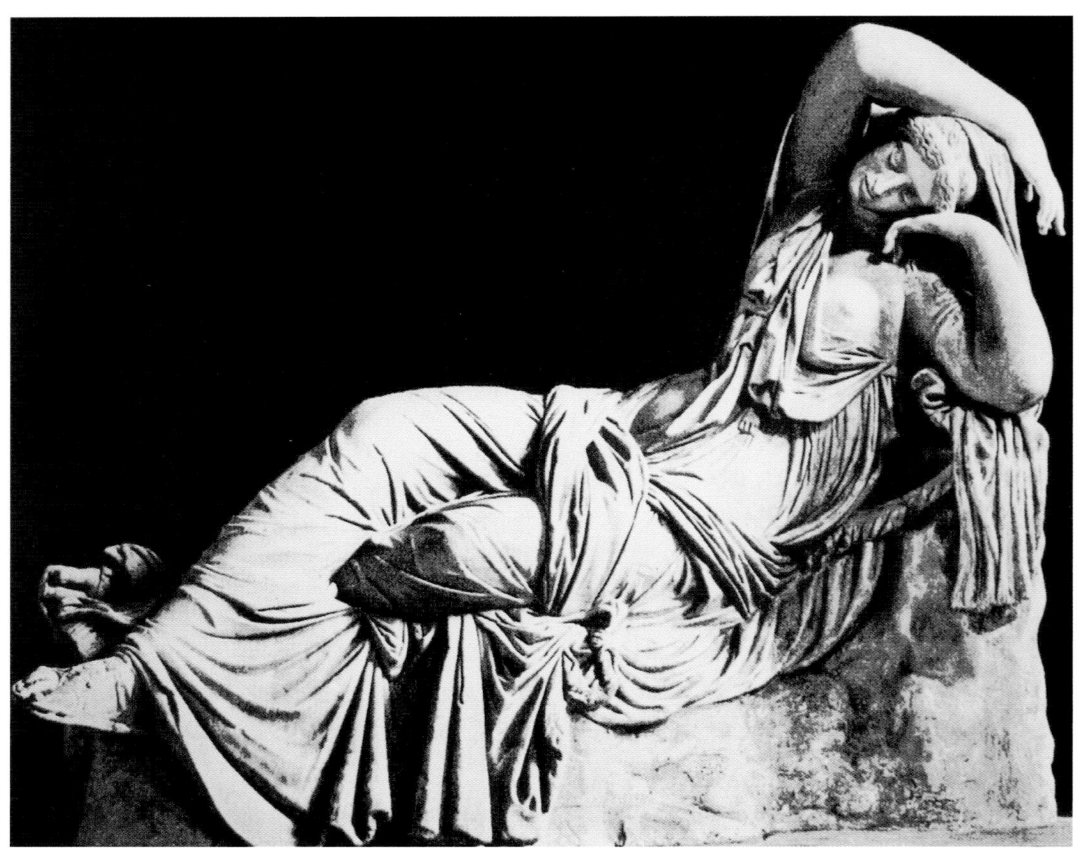

Ariadne, II sec. d. C. Vatican City, Museo Pio-Clementino

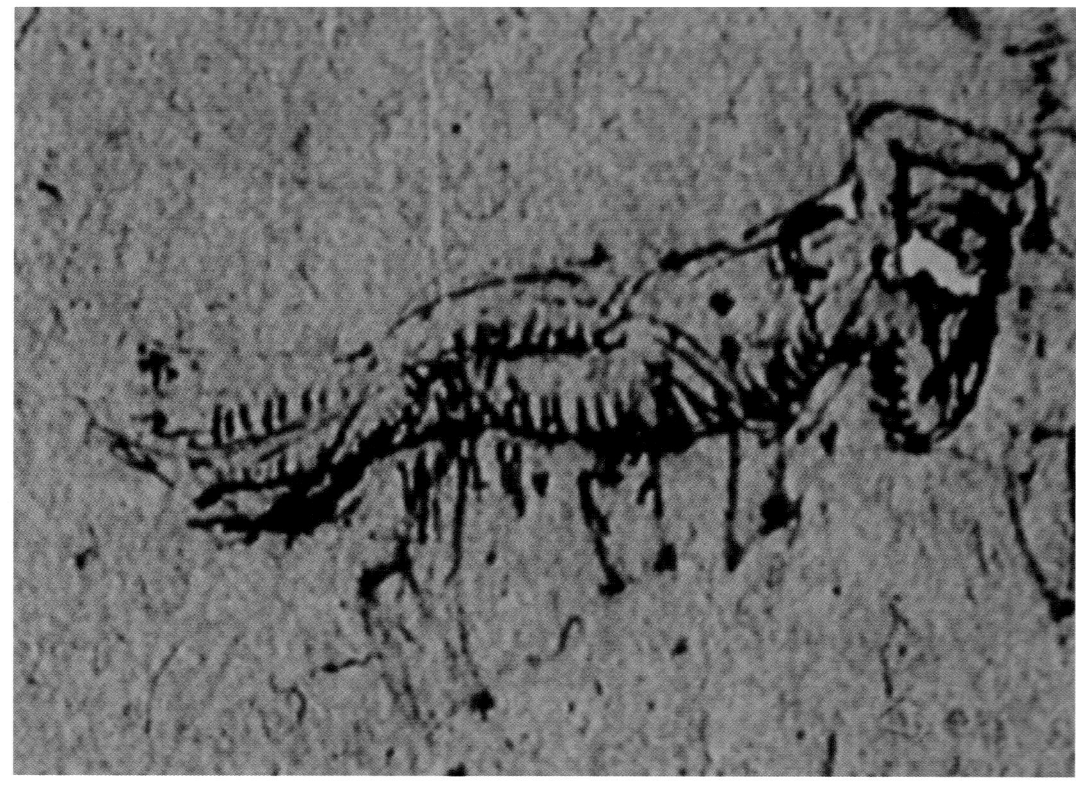

Leonardo da Vinci, *Ariadne*, c. 1513-15. Codex Atlanticus, f. 770 *v*. Pen and ink, 192 x 250 mm. Milan, Biblioteca Ambrosiana

to a process of veiling inclines to confer anatomical smoothness to figures. Many times Verrocchio has been considered as a disciple of Donatello, but it would have been exactly Leonardo to make himself the heir of his figurative culture, not only for the psychological introspection, but also for the singular effects of chiaroscuro, to which sends back the subsequent tracing over of the head, of the hair and of the body of Christ in oils,[13] a technique by now correctly acquired, but also for the attention given to the phenomenal reality, where he would have become an incomparable interpreter in the representation of the atmospheric shading off and of the kinds of erosion produced by water, «carrier of nature» and regenerating ritual symbol of the entire cosmic life. This extraordinary encounter with Donatello would strengthen the acquaintance that Leonardo had with the city and the land of Arezzo, since the years of his long apprenticeship in the workshop of Verrocchio (1469-76). For that reason the drawings related to the «cliffs» of Valdarno of the Windsor collection (RL 12395), datable to this period, together with the representation of the *Forked Siren* by Bayonne (*c.* 1480), that was made having as an example the one of the pulpit of Gropina, would come to confirm what some historians have farther sustained on the definite Florentine nature of the *Virgin of the Rocks* (Paris, Louvre Museum), whose general structure of composition should have been defined by Leonardo still before going to the court of Ludovico the Moor (1482), with a direct connection to the great artistic tradition of Tuscany, from Antonio Rossellino to Desiderio da Settignano,[14] and with particular landscapes of the territory of Arezzo, subdued to the re-examination of an articulated and complex «mental speech» that, transforming reality from the starting element, though bound topographically to it, it creates yet, according to the pictorial tradition of Tuscany, a very tight relationship of proportions and of harmony between the figures and the neighbouring space, between the feature and the contents of the work.[15]

[13] See P. C. Marani, *Leonardo. Catalogo completo dei dipinti*, Firenze, Cantini, 1989; Id., *Il problema della «bottega» di Leonardo: la «praticha» e la trasmissione delle idee di Leonardo sull'arte e la pittura*, in *I leonardeschi. L'eredità di Leonardo in Lombardia*, Milano, Skira, 1998.
[14] See S. Reinach, *Répertoire de Peintures du Moyen Age et de la Renaissance (1280-1580)*, III, Paris, Leroux, 1905; K. Clark, *Leonardo da Vinci…*, 1939, op. cit.; M. Davies, *The Virgin of the Rocks*, London, Balding/Mansell, 1947.
[15] See C. Starnazzi, *La Gioconda nella Valle dell'Arno*, «Archeologia Viva», Firenze, Giunti, 1996; Id., *Leonardo da Vinci: la rappresentazione cartografica e pittorica del paesaggio Toscano*, «L'Universo», LXXVI, 5, Settembre-Ottobre, Firenze, I. G. M., 1996; Id., *Leonardo e la Terra di Arezzo*, 2005, *op. cit.* To such purpose, I transcribe here the judgment of M. Kemp, sent to me on 25 August 1997: «Very many thanks sending the various items relating to the landscape in the Mona Lisa. The anchoring of Leonardo's landscape in his concrete experience of the landscape around the Arno makes a good deal of sense […] As always, Leonardo strives to combine the most scrupulous detailed observations with the general sense of the causes behind the effect». Instead, C. Vecce, on 25 September 1995, had intervened with the following observation: «There are not many annotations of mine to your writing, that illustrates with precision the possible relationship of Leonardo with Arezzo and the Valdichiana: a land that certainly, for its orogenetic and hydrogeological characters, must have made a deep impression on Leonardo in the course of his travels, particularly between 1502 and 1503». The study, set up on the relationship between Leonardo and the land of Arezzo, provoked a deep suggestion also in E. Garin, that in examining it, on 13 December 1996, added a note of personal enthusiasm: «many many thanks for your so interesting and so elegant pages. I love Leonardo very much, but sure not less the Superior Valdarno. I explored it when I was young with my bicycle and later I returned to it with my car, to see again the cliffs of Castelfranco di Sopra». The same A. Paolucci, on 5 November 1997, took part to the discussion with a judgment of positive merit: «Your reflections on the landscape of Arezzo in the background of the *Mona Lisa* seemed to me acute and probable», while F. Zeri, on 12 October 1997, put an end to the question of the identification of the vincian landscapes with a Caesarean judgment, almost definitive: «Thank you for your leonardian contributions. I have read them with factual interest, and I believe that the identification of the background of the 'Mona Lisa' with elements drawn from the territory of Arezzo is right». In the end, D. A. Brown, on 12 May 1999, wanted to underline the analytical and innovative aspect of my research, subtended to point out the mixture of art and science in the paintings of Leonardo: «The comparisons you make are certainly striking, in any case, and they point up the fact that, however abstract Leonardo's aqueous, mountainous landscapes may seem, they are based on an infinitude of concrete observations of the kind that you discuss».

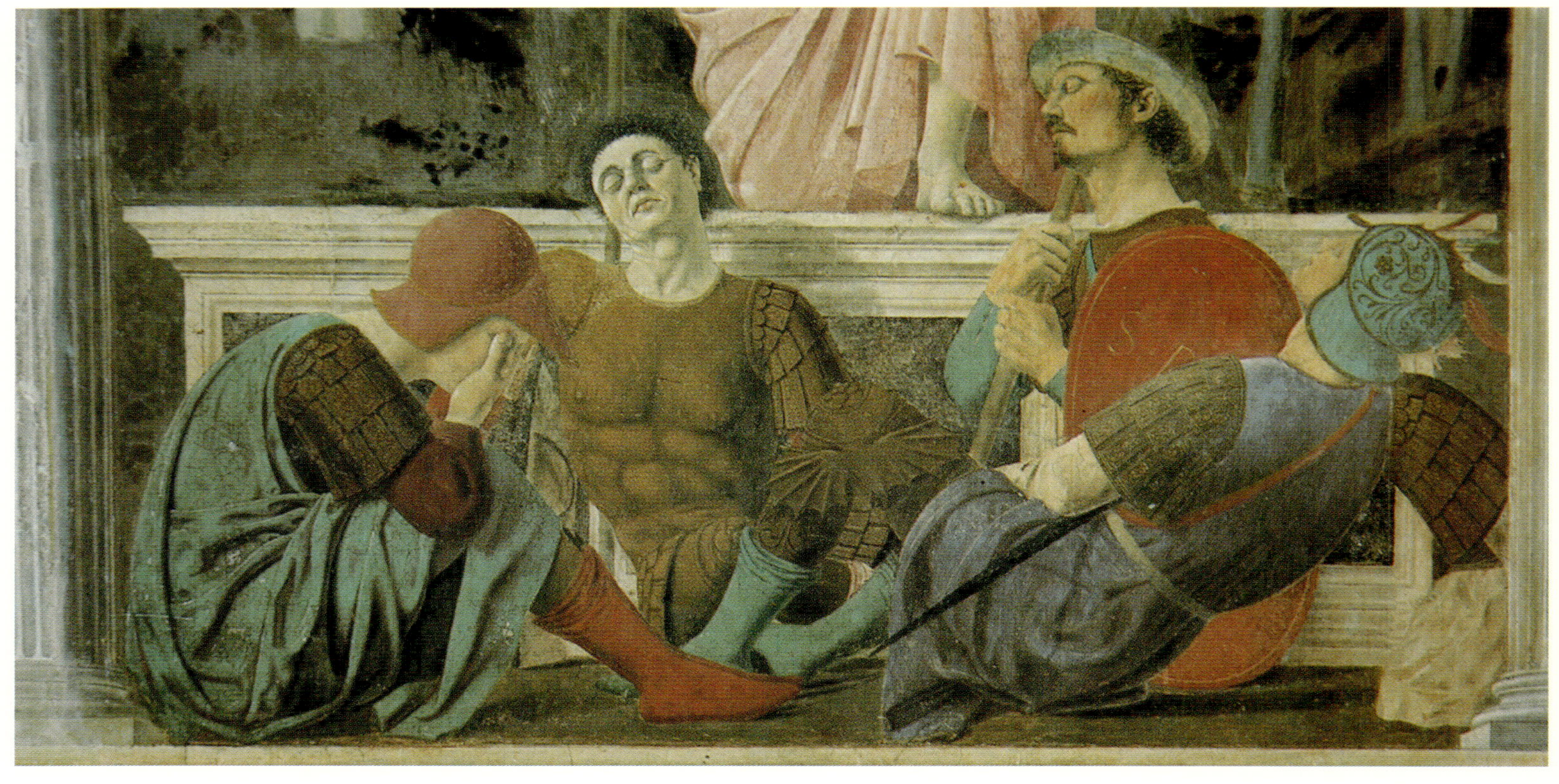

PIERO DELLA FRANCESCA, *Resurrection of Christ*, c. 1450. Fresco, 225 x 200 cm. Sansepolcro, Pinacoteca Comunale. Particular

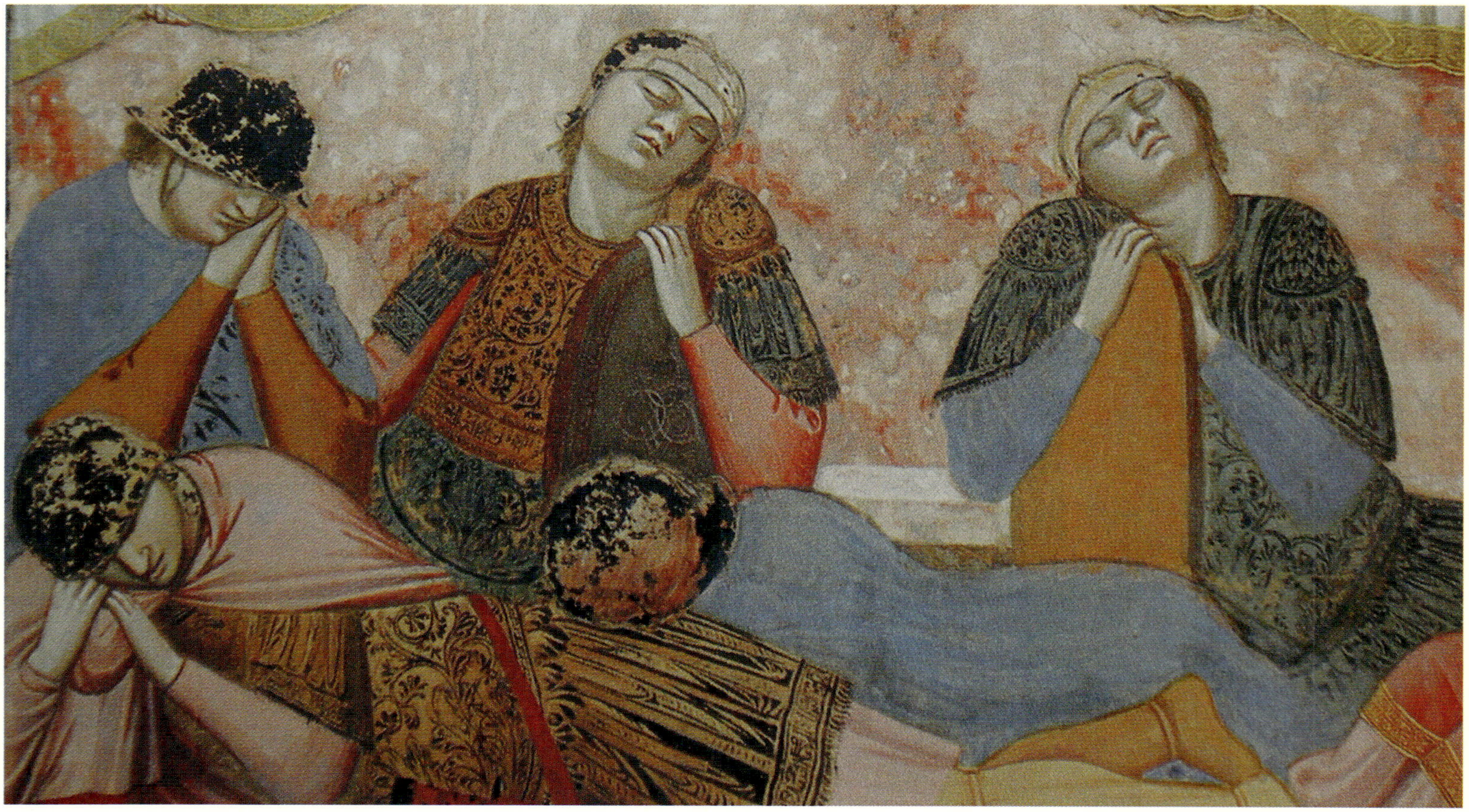

GIOTTO, *Jesus appears to Magdalen*, 1303-06. Fresco. Padua, Cappella degli Scrovegni. Particular

Francesco di Giorgio and Leonardo
A shared architecture

Francesco di Giorgio was a painter and a sculptor, but above all an inventor and an architect among the most brilliant of the Fifteenth century, active in Siena, in the Marches, in Umbria and also in the territory of Arezzo. The «Register of deaths» of the convent of Saint Bernardine of Siena records his passing away in date 29 November 1501.[1]

Right in Siena, Martini had been also responsible, from 1469 to 1492, for the operation of the «bottini», that is of the underground aqueduct that, with 25 Km of galleries, supplied of water the entire city, always encouraged by the hope «to find the Diana» (Dante, *Pg* XIII 153).

Inventor and «mechanic» he belonged to the group of those artist-engineers who, like Mariano di Jacopo known as Taccola and Filippo Brunelleschi, out of the eloquence of the liberal arts, had distinguished themselves for a solid polytechnic knowledge, founded on the close examination of experience, through the scientific knowledge borrowed from antiquity (Archimedes, Vitruvius, Frontinus, Vegetius) and bent, also through the construction and with the help of new machines (winches and rotating cranes on circular railroads), to the planning and realization of original architectural structures.

In 1477, Federico da Montefeltro, a munificent prince also celebrated by Piero della Francesca in a portrait with a landscape background all considered from above, was the first to choose him as his architect, after the departure of Laurana from Urbino, in order to finish that Ducal Palace, that would have become one of the highest expressions of the Italian Renaissance.

For the Duke of Urbino, Martini would have also constructed, with absolutely modern criteria, revealing all his professional attitude in the field of military architecture, the fortresses of San Leo (1475), of Sassocorvaro (1476-78),[2] of Cagli (1481) and of Mondavio (1488-1501),[3] dedicating him his *Opusculum de Architectura* (1477), rich in those blueprints of fortified structures that he was then realizing in the Montefeltro territory and where it can be noticed, in the outlining of the work, an obvious influence as well as its derivation from the Cod. Lat. Monacensis *197* (BSBM) by Mariano di Jacopo known as Taccola.

But his masterpiece or at least the higher example of his religious architecture was the church of Santa Maria delle Grazie at the Calcinaio (1485-1513),[4] on the slopes of Cortona, that would have then inspired, for its particular blueprint, the sanctuary of the SS. Annunziata or Madonna of the Tears of Arezzo, that saw to take part, in the various moments of its constructive story, at first the painter and architect Bar-

---

[1] See Francesco di Giorgio Martini, *Trattati di architettura, ingegneria e arte militare*, a cura di C. Maltese, Trascrizione di L. Maltese Degrassi, 2 voll., Milano, Il Polifilo, 1967; A. Venturi, *Francesco di Giorgio*, Architetti dal XV al XVIII secolo, «Biblioteca d'arte illustrata», II, 2, Roma, 1925; R. Papini, *Francesco di Giorgio architetto*, Firenze, Electa, 1946; M. Tafuri, F. P. Fiore, *Francesco di Giorgio architetto*, Milano, Electa, 1985; P. Torriti, *Francesco di Giorgio Martini*, Milano, Electa, 1985; G. Scaglia, *Francesco di Giorgio, autore*, in *Prima di Leonardo, Cultura delle macchine a Siena nel Rinascimento*, catalogo della mostra a cura di P. Galluzzi, Milano, Electa, 1991.

[2] During the Second World War, Pasquale Rotondi (1909-1991), supervisor of the Cultural Assets at Urbino, since 1939, beginning the «Operation Rescue» authorized that more than ten thousand works of art coming from all Italy (Milan, Venice, Rome) were hidden and therefore saved in the Rocca di Sassocorvaro and in the Palace of the Princes of Carpegna, localities far from military targets. See P. Rotondi, *Contributi urbinati a Francesco di Giorgio*, «Studi Artistici Urbinati», I, Urbino, 1949.

[3] See M. Stoppini, *Le Rocche di Sassocorvaro, Cagli, Sassofeltrio e Mondavio: nella concezione e nello stile di Francesco di Giorgio Martini*, Milano, Liocorno, 1960; G. Miletti, *La rocca di Sassocorvaro*, Facoltà di Architettura, Università di Roma, «Quaderni dell'Istituto di Storia dell'Architettura dell'Università di Roma», 55-60, 1963.

[4] The toponym «Calcinaio» derives from the presence of basins of lime (in Italian "calce", Tr. N.) at the slopes of Cortona, where the Guild of the Shoemakers dipped the skins for the tanning. See A. Tafi, *Immagine di Cortona*, Cortona, Calosci, 1989.

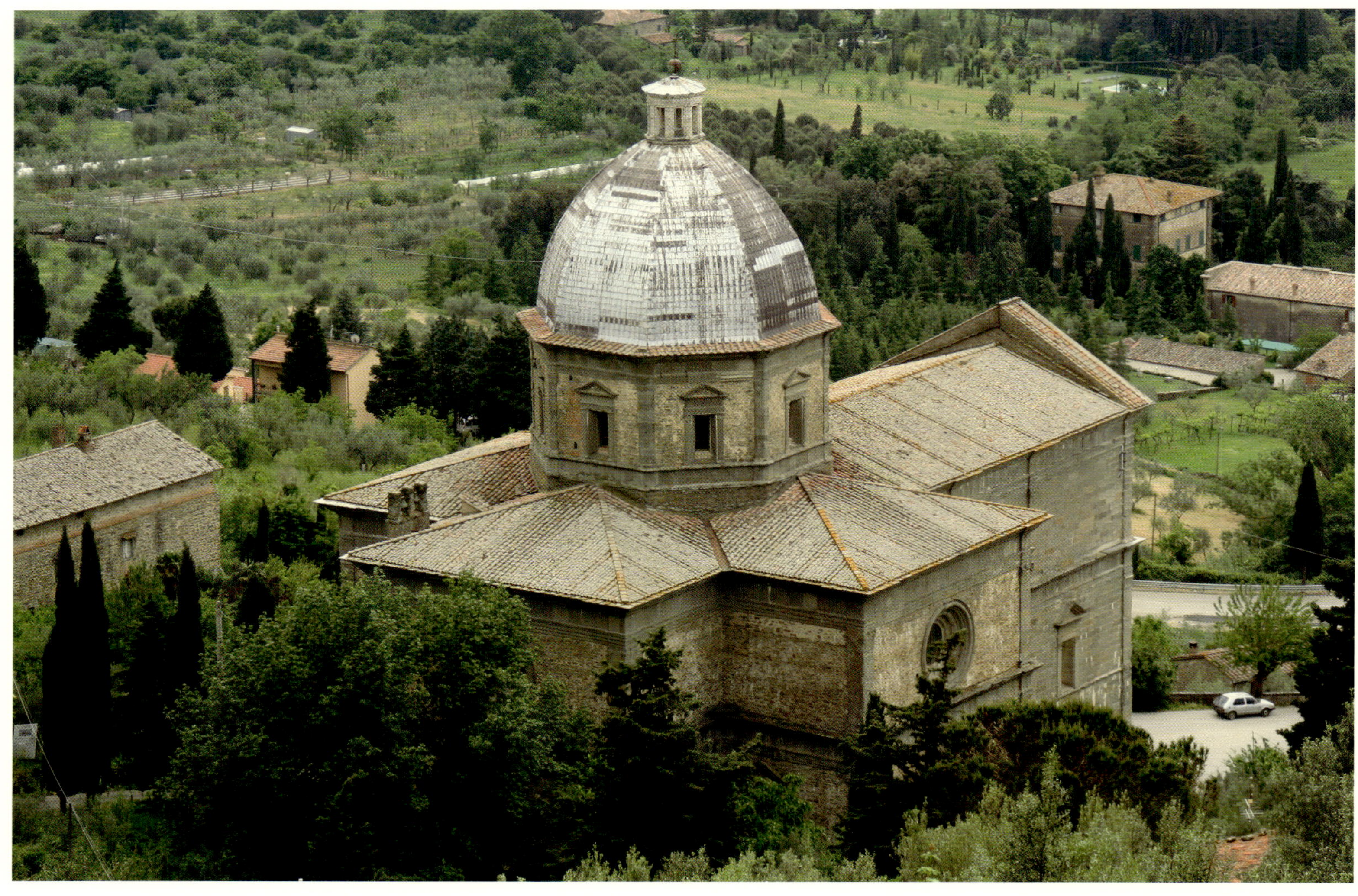

View of the Church of Santa Maria delle Grazie at the Calcinaio of Cortona, seen from North-West

tolomeo della Gatta, following the indication of Vasari, not bear out with other documents, and in the second phase (1504-05) Antonio da Sangallo the Elder, which consolidated its foundations and redefined in its formal aspect a part of the building.[5]

It had been the same Luca Signorelli (*c.* 1450-1523) to impose over the decisions of the government of the city of Cortona, so as to order the plan of the work to «Franciscus de Senis singularis architector»[6], then at the service of Guidobaldo Duke of Urbino, that a short time before had replaced his father Federico da Montefeltro († 1482), and, he in person, on 17 June 1484, went to Gubbio to meet his friend, there responsible of the construction sites for the Ducal Palace, that had to rise as a replica, but in a smaller tone, of the one of Urbino.

The foundation stone was laid on 6 June 1485 by Silvestro di Giuliano Ciaffini, captain of Cortona, and the construction went on in the following years until the drum, in order then to be stopped, to be continued again, after 1508, by the Florentine architect Pietro di Domenico di Norbo, that, eight years after the death of Martini, tied his name to the completion of the cupola, crowned with the lantern.

The building of Santa Maria delle Grazie, among the most perfect space organisms of the Renaissance, comprises some assonances with the Sant'Andrea by Alberti in Mantua and, for the imposingness of its structures, with several churches of Lombardy by Bramante. It is covered outside with pilaster strips corresponding to the inner partition and with two architectural orders placed one on top of the other, while on the cross-centre the octagonal cupola raises, resting on the high drum.

[5] See M. SALMI, *Civiltà artistica…*, 1971, *op. cit.*; R. PACCIANI, *La Chiesa della SS. Annunziata in Arezzo*, in *La chiesa della SS. Annunziata di Arezzo nel 500° della sua costruzione*, «Atti del convegno di Studi», 14 settembre 1990, Arezzo-Casa del Petrarca, Città di Castello, Tibergraph, 1993.
[6] «excellent architect Francesco from Siena» Tr. N.

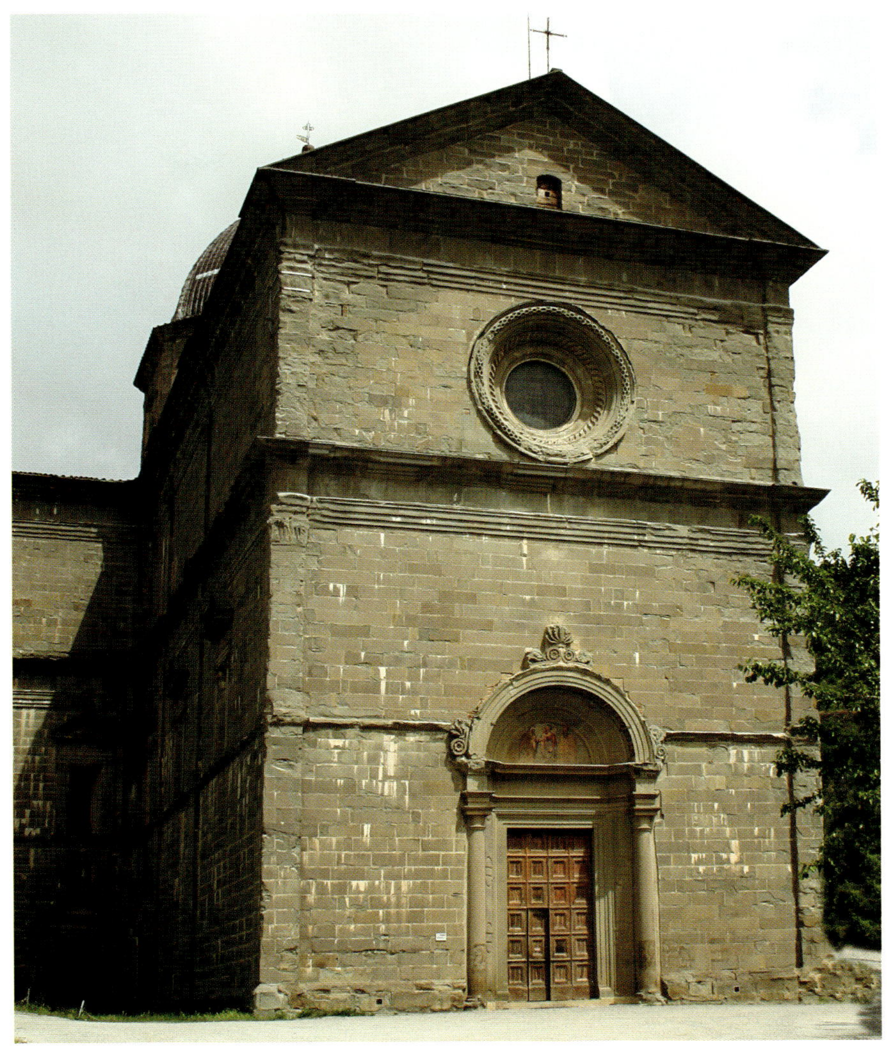

View of the Church of Santa Maria delle Grazie at the Calcinaio of Cortona, seen from South–West

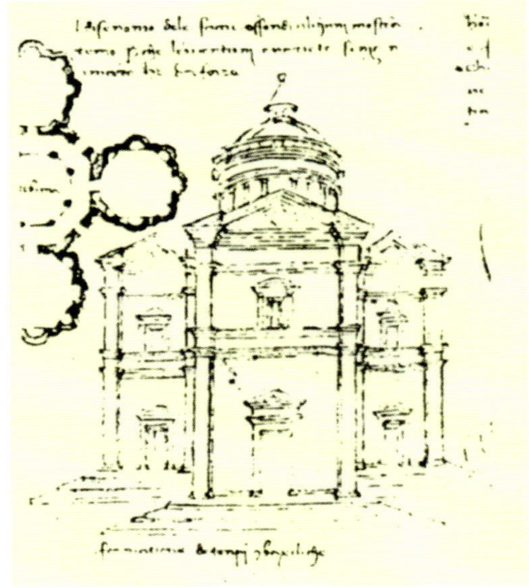

FRANCESCO DI GIORGIO, *Drawing of a church with a dome at the center of the cross*. Codex of Saluzzo, c. 14. Turin, Biblioteca Reale

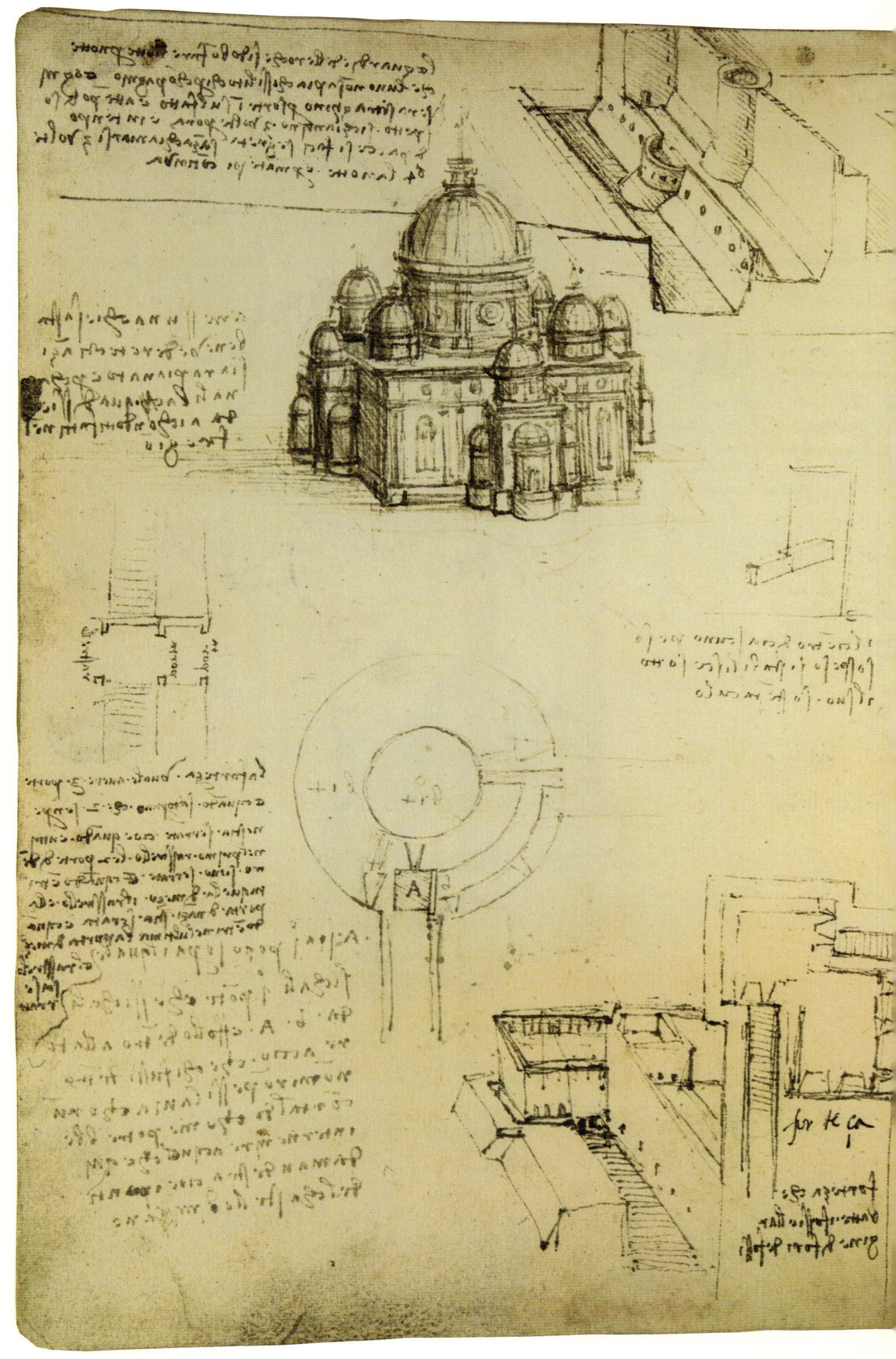

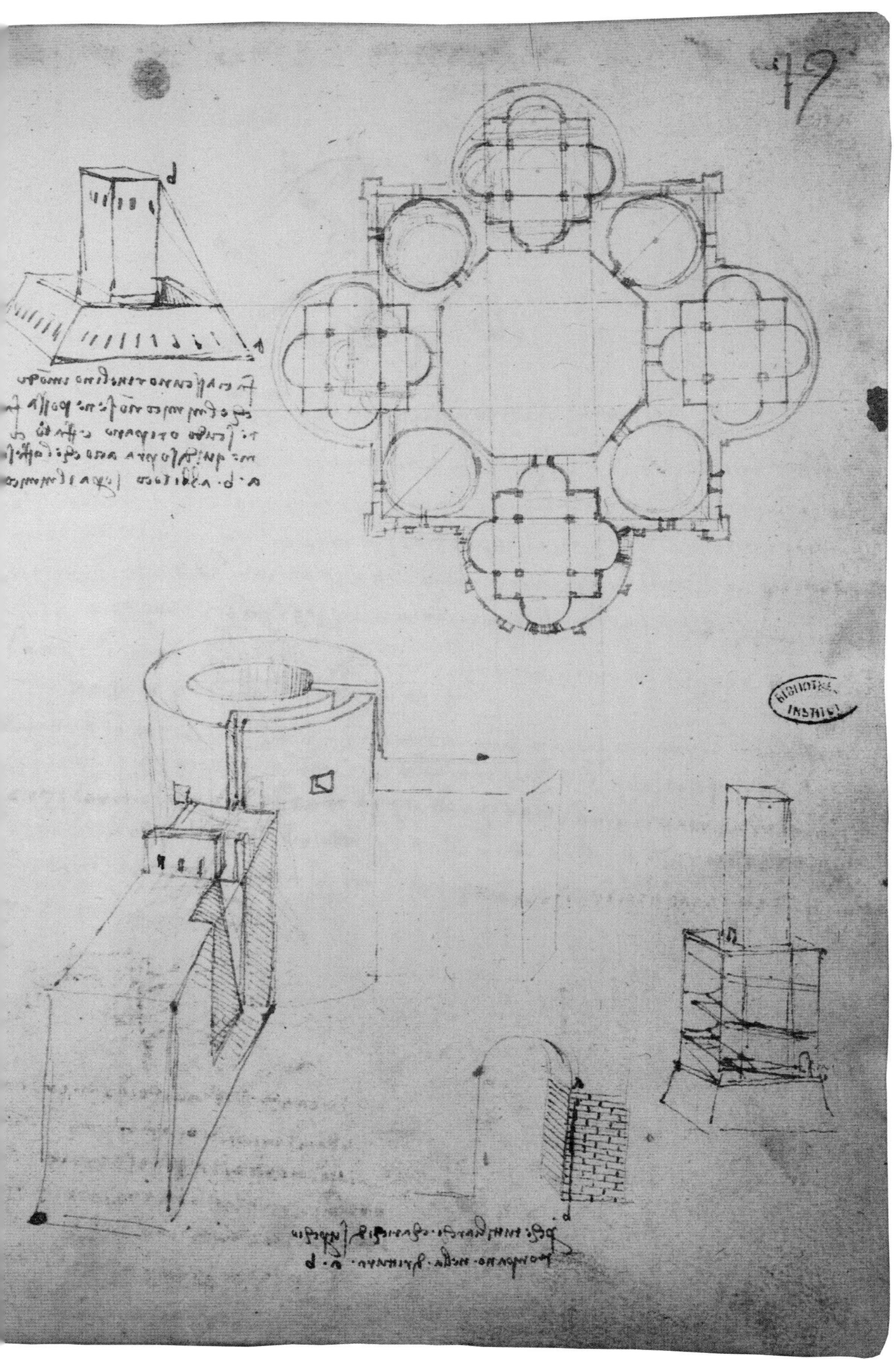

Leonardo da Vinci, *Projects of churches with central plan and drawings of military architectures*, c. 1487-90. Pen and ink, 231 x 167 mm. Ms. B, ff. 18 *v*-19 *r*. Paris, Institut de France

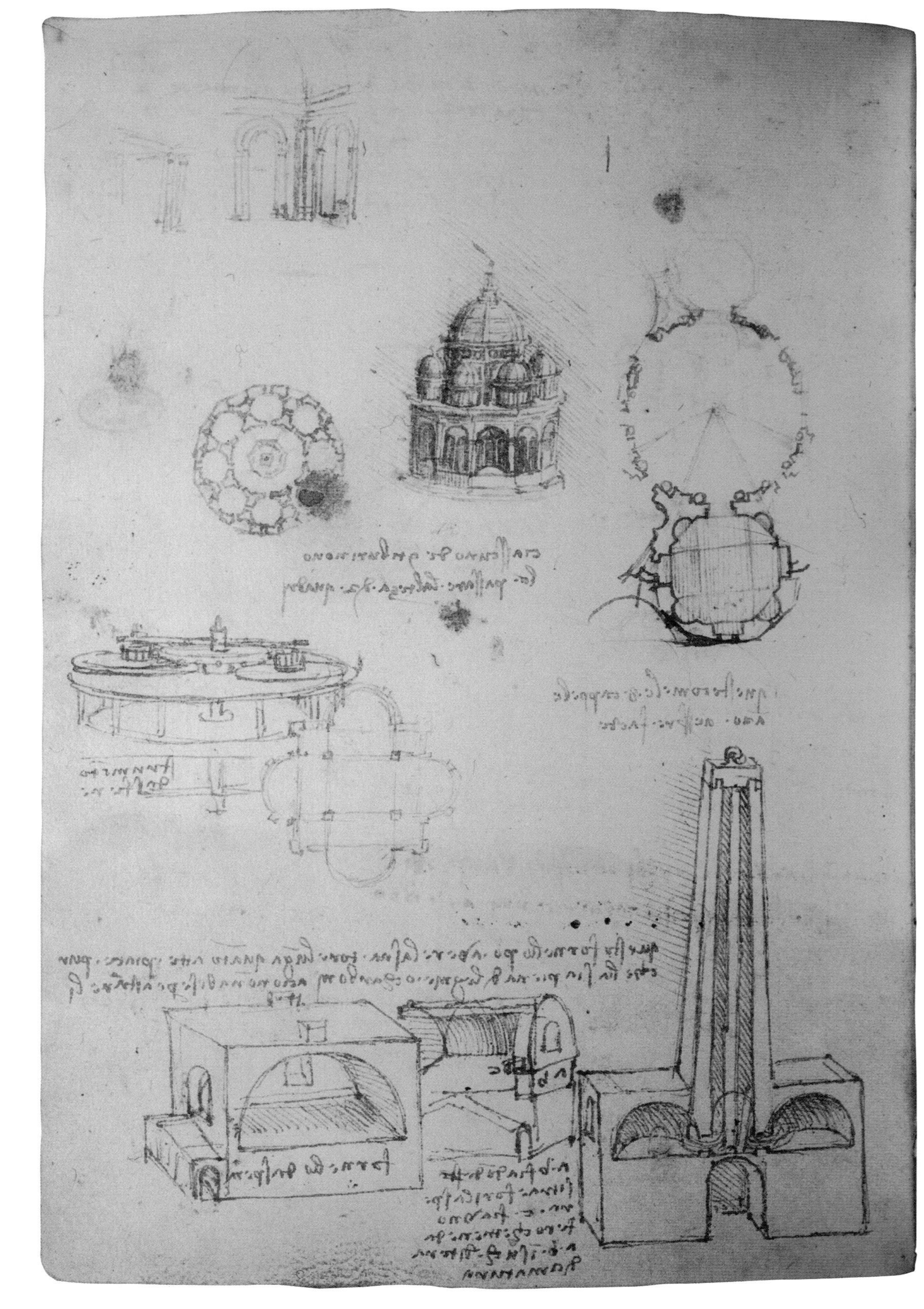

Leonardo da Vinci, *Studies of churches with central plan*, c. 1487-90. Pen and ink, 231 x 167 mm. Ms. B, ff. 21 *v*. Paris, Institut de France

Considered the singular curvature of the cupola, many times in the course of the years, it has been tried to supply an interpreting answer to the question of the curve of the arch that, according to Giuseppe Rocchi, after a recent much reliable measure, «turns out to be a pointed arch following a not less illustrious Florentine constructive tradition, from the cupola of the Baptistry of San Giovanni to the one of Santa Maria del Fiore»,[7] as well as the Tabernacle by Orcagna.

In fact, the pointed directrix of the cupola of the Calcinaio made more difficult the comprehension, for the art historians, of the co-existence in the edifice of such different styles, so as to induce one of them, Mario Salmi, to assume that there was in Francesco di Giorgio a certain indulgence not to scorn «some archaistic solutions».[8]

Already in 1946, Roberto Papini, in his renowned monographic work, had been of the opinion that the model in wood, constructed by Norbo, had betrayed the original inspiration of Francesco di Giorgio Martini, since, in conformity with the style of the building, its cupola should have been hemispheric, «as it is demonstrated in a drawing of Francesco di Giorgio in the Codex Laurenziano 361 (at the f. 12 *v*), in which it is not difficult to recognize a first idea for the church of the Calcinaio».[9]

Of opposite opinion it remained Salmi, that, examined the subject over and over, did not think that the drawing of the Codex Laurenziano might constitute «a first idea for the Calcinaio», while he indicated as amazing the solution of the proceeding of the cupola so slender, since it conferred to it an aesthetic result by far «superior and perfectly unitary as regards the whole body».[10]

After all, such unusual and original configuration of the cupola of the Calcinaio, and for certain aspects, so anchored to the Florentine tradition,[11] has recently induced the same Pietro Matracchi to admit that «if it can be attributed with certainty to Pietro di Norbo at least the solution of the problems of statical and constructive nature connected to the realization of the drum and of the cupola, from the facts currently available it is not possible instead to determine with the same certainty who is also the author of the planning of these structures».[12]

The interior of the church, that has the body in Latin cross, where the three smaller wings correspond in strict interdependence to a third part of the greater one, following accurate proportional and harmonic relations contained in the *De re aedificatoria* by Alberti, published in 1485 with a presentation by Politian and dedicated to Lorenzo the Magnificent,[13] it is articulated in two wide luminous rooms with barrel vaults, as a type of modern architecture. The walls in fact exclude mural paintings and emphasize the new taste for shrine-shaped compositions, with regular cornices, one within the other, niches and openings that reproduce the modular character of the structure. The whole is therefore orchestrated on precise mathematic-spatial interactions, where the inheritance of Brunelleschi and of Piero della Francesca is perceived without any doubt. But Francesco di Giorgio was also a friend of Leonardo.[14]

---

[7] See G. Rocchi, *Contrassegni di lapicidi sulle pietre dei palazzi rinascimentali di Firenze*, «Ricerche di Storia dell'Arte», 27, 1986; Id., *La diffusione dei modi Rinascimentali a Milano: esemplificazioni*, «Arte Lombarda», 86-87, 1988; Id., *Presentazione*, in P. Matracchi, *La Chiesa di S. Maria delle Grazie al Calcinaio presso Cortona e l'opera di Francesco di Giorgio*, Cortona, Calosci, 1992.

[8] See M. Salmi, *Il Palazzo Ducale di Urbino e Francesco di Giorgio*, «Studi Artistici Urbinati», I, Urbino, 1949; Id., *Civiltà artistica…*, 1971, op. cit.

[9] See R. Papini, *Francesco di Giorgio…*, 1946, op. cit.; P. Matracchi, *La Chiesa di S. Maria delle Grazie al Calcinaio…*, 1992, op. cit.

[10] See M. Salmi, *Il Palazzo Ducale di Urbino…*, 1949, op. cit.; Id., *Civiltà artistica…*, 1971, op. cit. We must add that, in 1956, Fehring attributed to Pietro di Norbo not only the realization of the cupola, but also that of the drum, see G. F. Fehring, *Studien über die kirchenbauten des Francesco di Giorgio*, Würzburg, 1956.

[11] See G. Scaglia, *Drawings of Brunelleschi's Mechanical Inventions for the Construction of the Cupola*, «Marsyas», 10, 1960-61; Id., *Drawings of Machines for Architecture from the Early Quattrocento in Italy*, «Journal of the Society of Architectural Historians», XXV, 2, New York, 1966; L. Reti, *Tracce dei progetti perduti di Filippo Brunelleschi nel Codice Atlantico*, IV, «Lettura Vinciana», Firenze, Giunti Barbèra, 1964; P. Sanpaolesi, *Strutture a cupola autoportanti*, «Palladio», 1971; Id., *La cupola di Santa Maria del Fiore*, Firenze, EDAM, 1977.

[12] See P. Matracchi, *La Chiesa di S. Maria delle Grazie…*, 1992, op. cit.

[13] In the Renaissance the concept of beauty was based on the proportional interaction of the single parts among them and with the entirety, according to the analytical-comparative method of the precepts of Vitruvius, so that «nothing can be added or removed or changed if not for the worse», (L. B. Alberti, *De Re Aedificatoria*, VI, II). Moreover, Alberti added that beauty is agreement and harmony of the parts in relation to a whole to which they are tied following a certain number («numerus»), marking out («finitio») and positioning («collocatio»), as demands the *concinnitas*, that is the fundamental and more exact law of nature (*De re aedificatoria*, IX, V). For the concept of «symmetry», on the basis of the relation established between geometry and anthropometry, it was made recourse to the figures of the circle, of the square and of the equilateral triangle. Examining the relation that exists between music and the plastic arts, Alberti asserted that the more harmonic relations are 1/2, 2/3, 3/4, that is «diàpason», «diapènte» and «diatèssaron», corresponding to the areas called double, sesquialter and sesquithird. Precisely on a sheet of the Codex of Madrid II, ff. 2 *v*-3 *r*, datable about 1504, Leonardo reveals of being in possession of a copy both of the *Trattato* by Alberti, «Batista Alberti in architecture» as well as of that by Francesco di Giorgio, «Francesco from Siena». The *Trattato* by Alberti, for whom, as a theorist, the work of the architect begins and ends in the drawing, was decisive also for the second writing up of the *Trattato* by Francesco di Giorgio. See Cfr. L. B. Alberti, *De Re Aedificatoria*. Introduzione e note di P. Portoghesi, Trascrizione e traduzione di G. Orlandi, Milano, Il Polifilo, 1966; L. Reti, *The Leonardo da Vinci Codices in the Biblioteca Nacional of Madrid*, «Tecnology and Culture», VIII, 1967; C. Maccagni, *Riconsiderando il problema delle fonti di Leonardo: l'elenco dei libri ai fogli 2verso-3recto del Codice 8936 della Biblioteca Nacional di Madrid*, X, «Lettura Vinciana», Firenze, Giunti Barbèra, 1970.

[14] For the rapport of Leonardo with Francesco di Giorgio, see: F. Malaguzzi-Valeri, *Leonardo da Vinci e il tiburio del Duomo di Milano*, «Il Marzocco», 44, 1903; T. Arkin, *Le idee di un grande architetto*, «Rassegna Sovietica», III, Roma, 1952; L. H. Heydenreich, *Leonardo architetto*, «Lettura Vinciana», II, Firenze, Giunti Barbèra, 1962; Id., *Leonardo architetto*, Firenze, Bemporad, 1963; A. M. Brizio, *Leonardo e Bramante alla corte di Ludovico il Moro*, in *Atti del Congresso Internazionale di Studi Bramanteschi*, Milano-Urbino-Roma, 1970, Roma, 1974; L. Firpo, *Leonardo architetto e urbanista*, Torino, UTET, 1971; Id., *Leonardo architetto militare e civile*, «Lettura Vinciana», XVI, Firenze, Giunti Barbèra, 1976; A. C. Carpiceci, *L'architettura di Leonardo: indagine e ipotesi su tutta l'opera di Leonardo architetto*, Firenze, Bonechi,

The two architects had met for the first time in June 1490 in Milan and in Pavia, in order to intervene with their technical competence at a projecting level on the two most important religious buildings of the respective cities. Moreover, already in 1482, just appealing to his ability as machine-maker and architect, Leonardo, in his letter to Ludovico the Moor, had illustrated with ambitious attitude his multiple technical competences, ready to give demonstrative evidence in any time to the Duke: « […] In time of peace I believe to satisfy very well in comparison to any other in architecture, in composition of buildings both public and private», (CA, f. 391 *ra* [1082 *r*]).

At the beginning of 1487, Leonardo, already celebrated by the court poet Bernardo Bellincioni for his excellent pictorial qualities («from Florence an Apelles here is brought», *c.* 1485-87), received the assignment from the Board of Trustees of the Dome of Milan, being considered also one of the best engineers of that time and numbered among the «Ingeniarii Ducales»,[15] to construct a model in wood for the lantern of the Cathedral, for whose solution had operated with his team, from 1483 until 1486, the German John Nexemperger. «German in Dome», Leonardo had annotated, next to one of the eight sketches on the way to give a vault to a cupola, in the Ms. B, f. 10 *v*, with reference to the collaborator of the Master of Graz, the Dominican Giovanni Mayer, author as well of a wood model, that was rejected and paid from the Fabric in 1488.

The employment of models in wood was becoming more and more important among the engineers of the end of the Fifteenth century, which became authentic specialists in their production, since these latter allowed them to codify their ideas and, in the internal vertical sections, to observe, before the execution of the works, the relations among the various elements of a construction, with the consequent possibility

to intervene, so that the walls and the main bodies preserved the necessary harmonic rapport.

In this period, the architect Luca Fancelli, in the letter sent on 12 August 1487 to Lorenzo the Magnificent, reported that the Dome of Milan needed for its cupola immediate and difficult interventions of restoration: «The principal reason is that the cupola of the Dome here seemed to ruin, wherefore it has been demolished and they are considering to rebuild it. And since this building is without framework and without measure, not without difficulty it will be done».

Facing this new assignment that had precise building responsibilities and a great scientific commitment,[16] involving calculations and geometries, Leonardo answered with a famous letter, enclosed in a sheet of the Codex Atlanticus (f. 270 *rc* [730 *r*]). Here, taking the distances from the «practicals», in order to wear with boast the garments of the artist-professional and of the technocrat, he emphasized the fundamental importance of the theoretical knowledge, to plan then, in an anthropomorphic vision of the building, where the cupola had, in a direct relationship with his contemporary studies of anatomy, the function of top of the skull and of seat of the intellect for the entire organism, the way following which a «medical architect» can supply the solution of the various structural problems. Besides, Sabba da Castiglione, in his *Ricordi ovvero ammaestramenti* […] (1549), and Gerolamo Cardano, in his *De subtilitate libri XXI* (1550), will praise the passion with which Leonardo, neglecting painting, concentrated on the study of geometry, of architecture and of anatomy: «a few other works can be found of his hand, because when he had to apply himself to painting, in which with no doubt would have become a new Apelles, he dedicated all himself to Geometry, to Architecture and Natomy»:

Fathers of the Board, as the doctors, the tutors, those who heal the ill people, must have in mind what is man, what is life, what is health, and in which way a parity, an agreement of elements maintains it, and consequently a disagreement of those can ruin and demolish it, and, having studied well the aforementioned natures, he will be able to better repair those who have been deprived of it. You know that the medicines, being well used, restore health to the sick ones […]. The sick Dome needs the same thing, that is a doctor architect, that has well in mind what building is, and from which rules the right building up derives, and whence the mentioned rules are drawn, and in how many parts they are divided, and which are the causes that hold the construction together, and that make it permanent, and which nature it is that of the weight, and which is the objective of

1978; A. Bruschi, *Pareri sul tiburio del Duomo di Milano. Leonardo, Bramante, Francesco di Giorgio*, in *Scritti rinascimentali di architettura*, Milano, Il Polifilo, 1978; C. Pedretti, *Leonardo architetto*, Milano, Electa, 1978; P. C. Marani, *Il Codice Ashburnham 361 della Biblioteca Medicea Laurenziana di Firenze. Trattato di Architettura di Francesco di Giorgio* Martini (a cura di), 2 voll., Firenze, Giunti Barbèra, 1979; Id., *Leonardo, Francesco di Giorgio e il tiburio del Duomo di Milano*, «Arte Lombarda», 62, 1982; Id., *Leonardo e l'architettura fortificata: connessioni e sviluppi*, in *Leonardo e l'età della ragione*, a cura di E. Bellone, P. Rossi, Milano, Scientia, 1982; G. Scaglia, *Leonardo e Francesco di Giorgio a Milano*, in *Leonardo e l'età della ragione*, a cura di E. Bellone, P. Rossi, Milano, Scientia, 1982; J. Guillaume, K. De Jonge, *De l'esquisse au modèle: comment "construire" une église de Léonard*, «Achademia Leonardi Vinci. Journal of Leonardo Studies and Bibliography of Vinciana», I, Firenze, Giunti, 1988; R. V. Schofield, *Amadeo, Bramante and Leonardo and the tiburio of Milan Cathedral*, «Achademia Leonardi Vinci. Journal of Leonardo Studies and Bibliography of Vinciana», II, Firenze, Giunti, 1989.

[15] In his *Ricordi*, Sabba da Castiglione would have annotated that the artist, «when he had to apply himself to painting, in which with no doubt would have become a new Apelles, he dedicated all himself to Geometry, to Architecture and Natomy». See S. Castiglione, *Ricordi*, Venezia, Gherardo, 1555.

[16] The undertaking of precise responsibilities in building, in the last fifteen years of the Fifteenth century, is present in Leonardo much more than it can be generally supposed. See C. Pedretti, *A Chronology of Leonardo da Vinci's…*, 1962, *op. cit.*

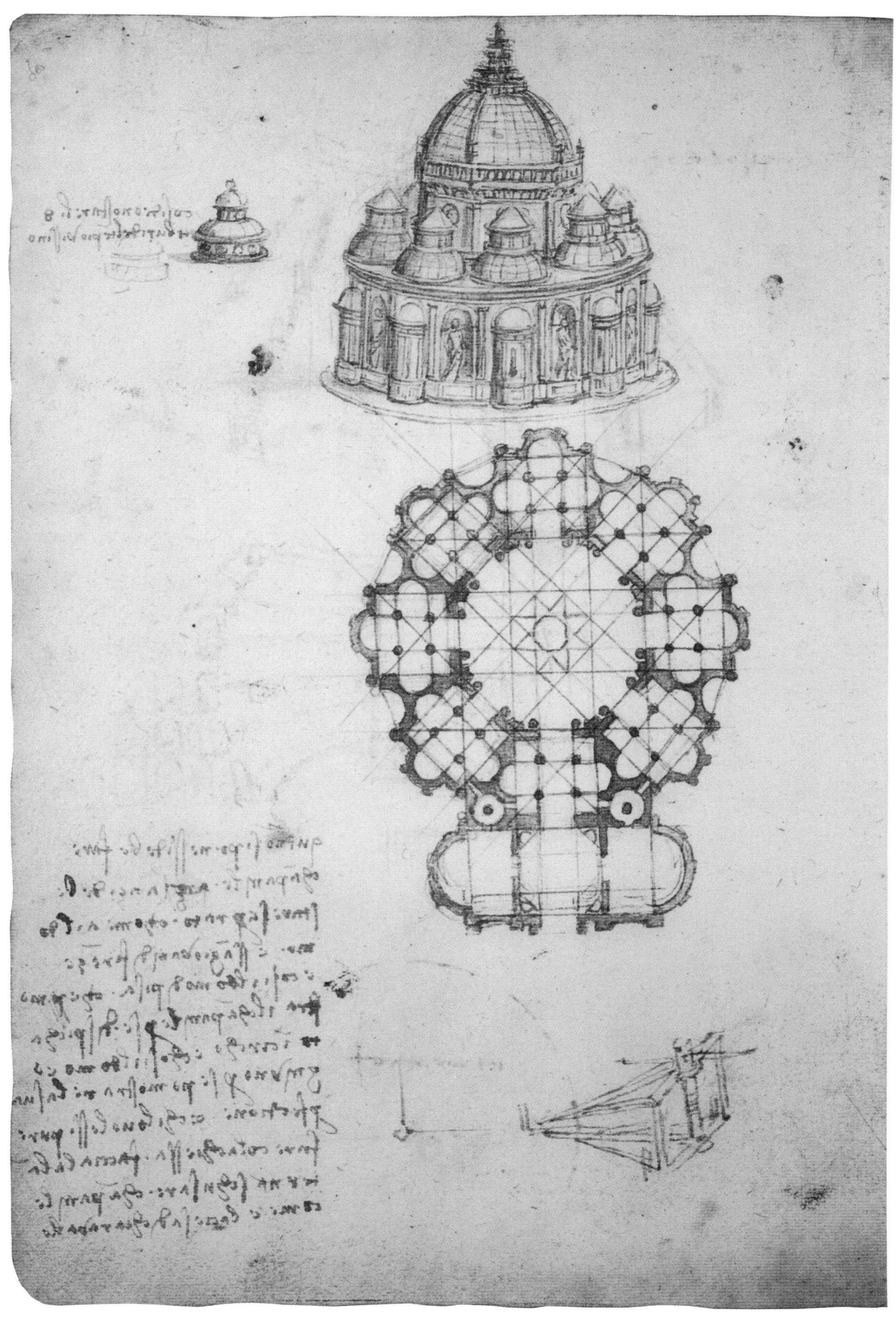

LEONARDO DA VINCI, *Study of a church with central plan*, *c.* 1487-90. Ms. Ashburnham, f. 5 *v.* Paris, Institut de France

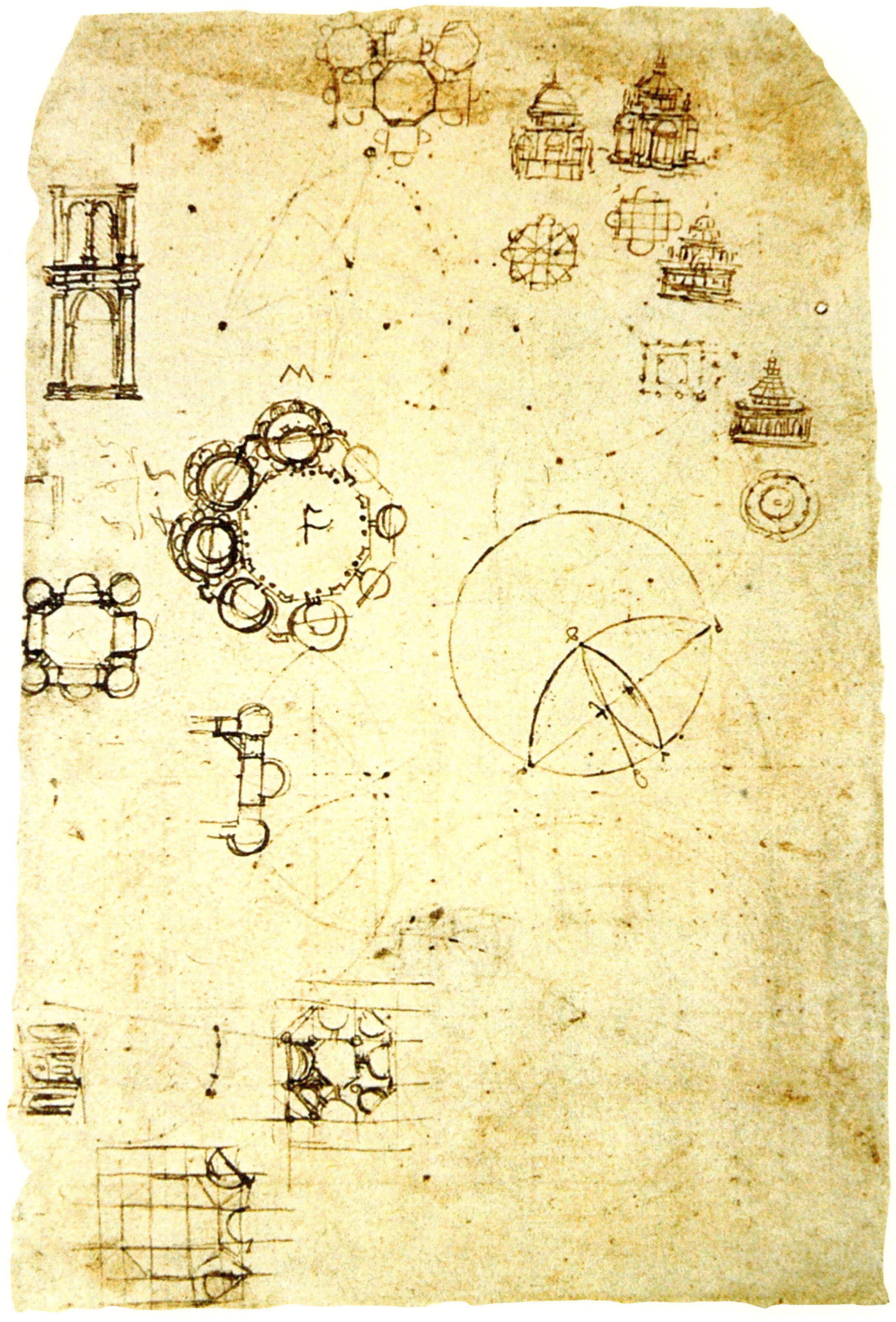

Leonardo da Vinci, *Studies of architecture for the Cathedral of Pavia*, c. 1487-90. Pen and ink, 186 x 273 mm. Codex Atlanticus, f. 1010 *v*. Milan, Biblioteca Ambrosiana

the force, and in which way they must be interwoven and connected together, and being combined which effect they generate. Whoever of these aforementioned things will have a true knowledge, he will let you satisfied of his reason and work. Whence for this motive I will try, not distracting, not dishonouring anybody, to satisfy in part with reasons and in part with works, now demonstrating the effects through the causes, now stating the reasons with the experiences, to these arranging some height of the ancient architects, the demonstrations of the buildings made, and which are the causes of their ruin and their permanence etc. And with those to demonstrate which [is] before the load, and which and how many are the causes that bring buildings to ruin, and which is the way to make them steady and permanent. But in order not to be verbose to Your Excellences, I will say first the invention of the first architect of the Dome, and I will demonstrate you clearly which was his intention, asserting that by means of the commenced building; and making you comprehend this, clearly you will be able to know that the model I made has in itself the symmetry, the correspondence, the conformity, which belongs to the commenced building. What building is and whence the rules of the aforementioned building up draw their origin, and how many and which are the parts belonging to those. Or me, or any other one that demonstrates it better than me, just put aside every passion.

Leonardo revealed the systematic intensity of his theoretical and doctrinal researches («from which rules the right building up derives and whence the aforementioned rules are drawn»), emphasizing his interest for problems of a more general kind and related to dynamics («which is the objective of the force») and to statics or *de ponderibus* («which nature it is that of the weight»),[17] that is to the science of the distribution of weights in architectural structures, in conformity with the perspective and the proportions («symmetry»), in order to confer the requirement of «lightness» and «beauty» to the entire composition.

For Leonardo architecture was not only addressed towards the study of the optical effect and of the beauty of a structure as a simple expression of a closely theoretical elaboration, but, having this to obey in a rigorous way to mathematical principles, it came to shape itself like a problem that involved aspects of technical and architectural character related to the praxis of planning and constructing, with an analysis of forces, resistance of materials and equilibriums of masses. Among these studies that he made, it can be picked the intention to privilege and to increase in a total way the value of the role carried out by the cupola in its complex correlation with the constructive unit, since «for the volumes that, seen from outside, it creates, and for the new articulation that it imposes inside, it indeed becomes the key element of architecture».[18] Besides, the fundamental subjects and the scientific and technological solutions connected to the construction of a cupola were all well known to Leonardo who, since he was an apprentice in the workshop of Verrocchio, where it was cultivated, according to what was reported by Vasari, also the architectural and technological drawing, he showed an «intellect so much divine and wonderful that being he an excellent Geometrician he not only operated in sculpture […], but in architecture», where «he made many drawings as well of plants as of other buildings». And, in 1471, he had been a witness of the execution, the raising and the placing, after the advice of the great mathematician Paolo dal Pozzo Toscanelli,[19] of the enormous ball of copper on the lantern of the cupola of Santa Maria del Fiore, to completion of the grandiose engineeristic work of Brunelleschi, of which Leonardo outlines the architectural characteristics also in a sketch that can be dated to the end of the eighties (CA, f. 17 *va* [57 *v*]).[20] «Do remember the weldings with which the ball of Santa Maria del Fiore was welded […] of copper made similar to stone, as the triangles of such ball», he would have recorded, in 1515, in a note of the Roman years (Ms. G, f. 84 *v*), when he was dealing, for a project with textile industrial purposes, with parabolic mirrors, made of wedges welded together and employed, taking advantage of solar energy, to make the boilers of the Medicean dye-houses bubble (CA, f. 279 *ra* [750 *r*]). Moreover, and made by Brunelleschi, Leonardo would have then admired also the unfinished Round of Santa Maria degli Angeli (1434-37), and even so much as to make it a modular paradigm in the structural and of composition conception of some of his architectural inventions (Ms. B, ff. 11 *v*-12 *r*). But the drawings of Leonardo, together with those of Buonaccorso Ghiberti (Zibaldone, Ms. BR 228, ff. 105 *r*; 106 *r*), even document the knowledge that he had of the machines employed by Brunelleschi in his

---

[17] In a memorandum, datable about 1489, Leonardo reveals how his research in the most varied fields of investigation is, in that moment, subordinated to the studies in depth on the science of weights (statics) and on the principles of dynamics, that is the cause or force that provokes movement: «Let them show you at the Friar of Brera de ponderibus», CA, f. 225 rb [611 ar]). The *de ponderibus* contained all the theoretical teachings of the medieval scientific tradition, which had allowed also the construction of the great cathedrals, and had reached the Renaissance through the work of Biagio Pelacani: «the heirs of Master Giovan Ghiringhello have works by the Pelacano» (Codex Forster III, f. 86 r).

[18] See A. CHASTEL, *La chiesa: facciata e pianta centrale*, in ID., *La grande officina. Arte italiana, 1460-1500*, Milano, Feltrinelli, 1966.
[19] PAOLO DAL POZZO TOSCANELLI (1397-1482), returned to Florence from the University of Padua, had introduced to the study of Euclid and of the mathematics, not only Cusano (*c.* 1401-1464), but also Brunelleschi, celebrated by the contemporary humanists as the «second Archimedes». Leonardo, following his teachings in his juvenile years, mentions him in a memorandum of his as «Master Pagolo, doctor», (CA, f. 12 *va* [42 *v*]).
[20] See C. PEDRETTI, *Progetti brunelleschiani a Milano nei ricordi di Leonardo*, in *Atti del Convegno internazionale di Studi Brunelleschiani…*, 1977, Firenze, 1978.

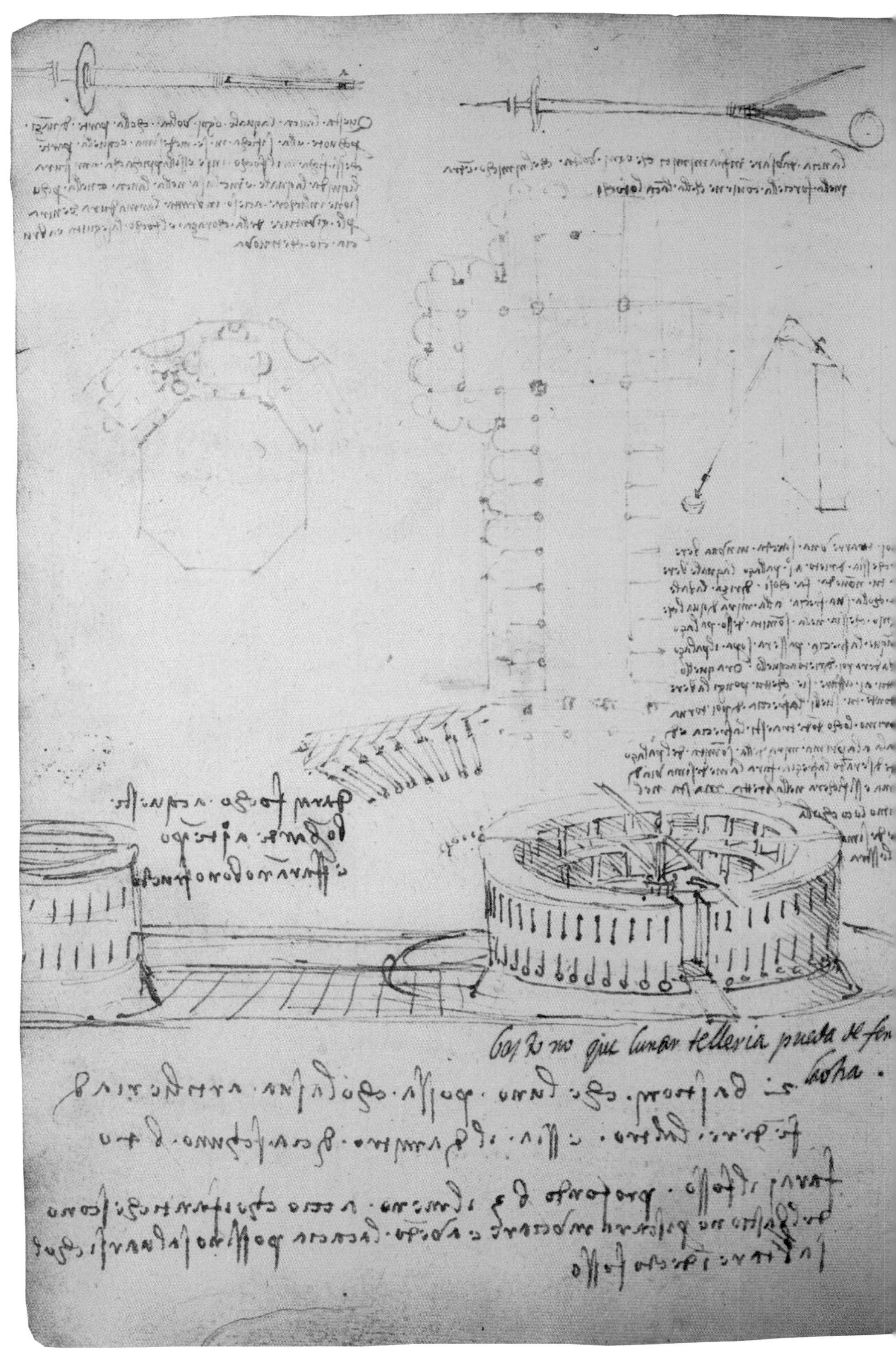

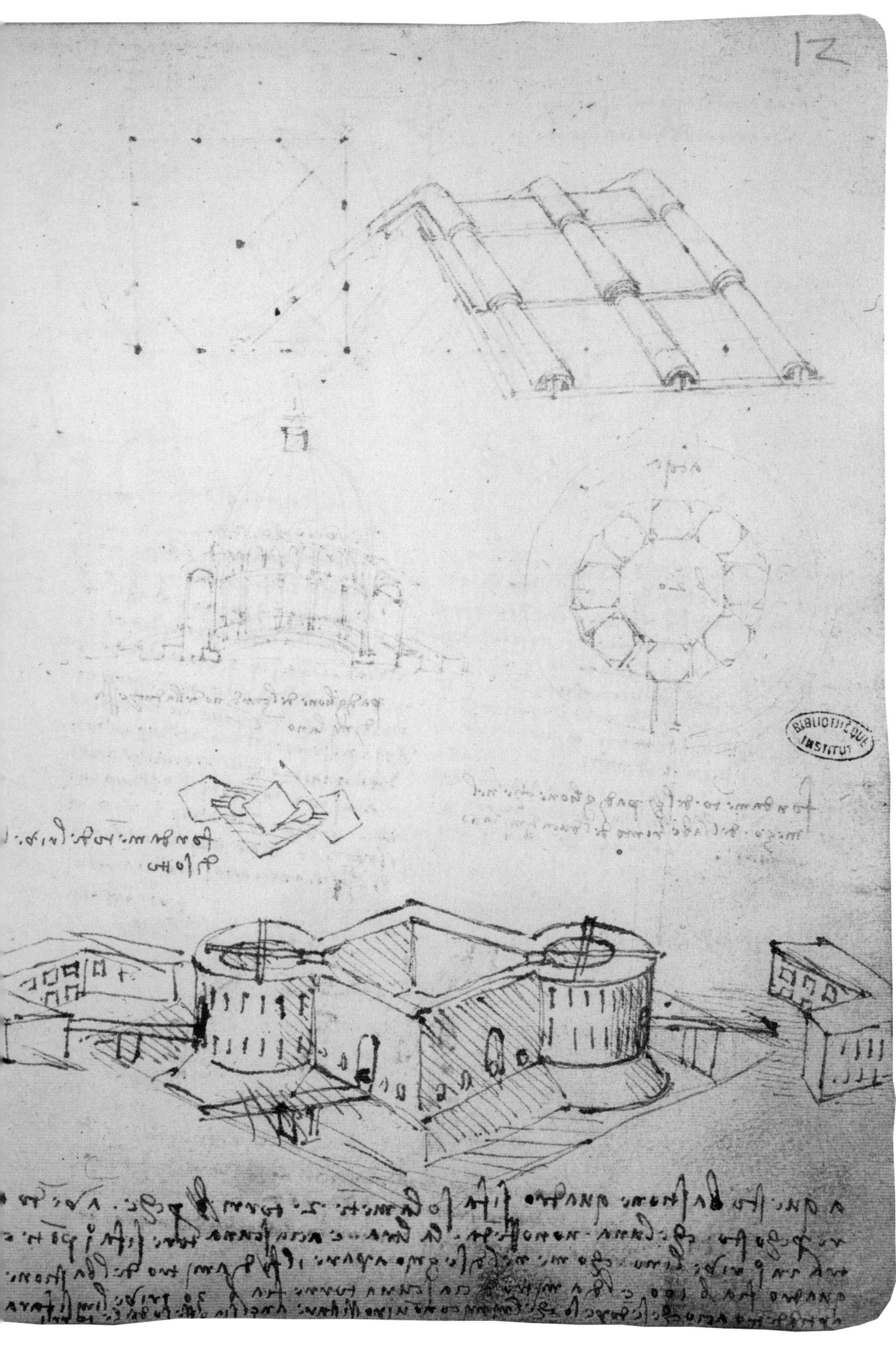

Leonardo da Vinci,
*Reminiscences of buildings by
Brunelleschi in Florence and of the
pavillion in the Castle of Milan,*
c. 1487–90. Ms B, ff. 11 *v*–12 *r*.
Paris, Institut de France

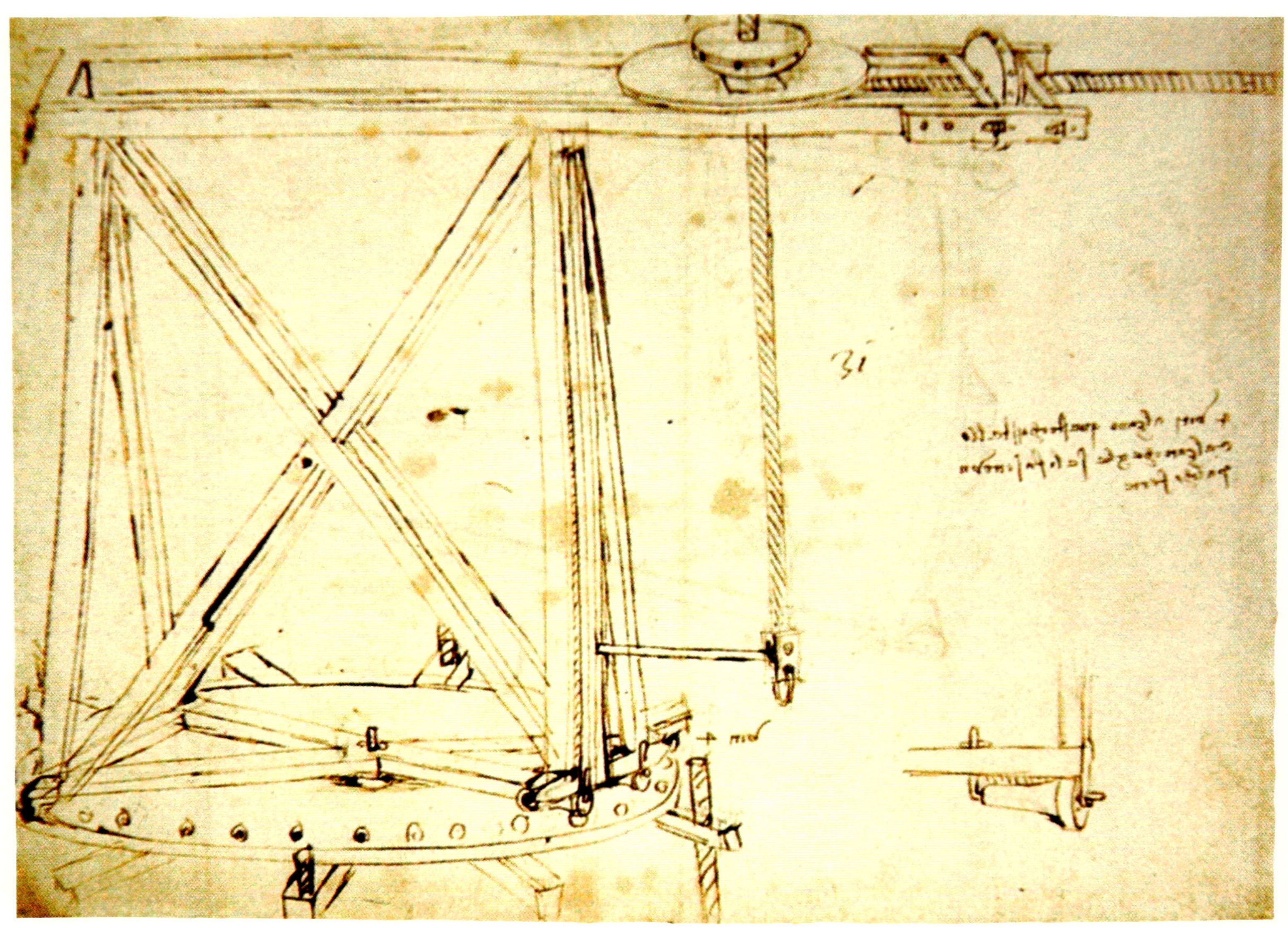

Leonardo da Vinci, *Revolving crane for the lantern*, *c.* 1487. Pen and ink, 208 x 283 mm. Codex Atlanticus, f. 808 *v.* Milan, Biblioteca Ambrosiana

extraordinary enterprise, as the great winches able to realize a continuous cycle motion (CA, f. 391 *vb* [1083 *v*]) and the counterweighted cranes (CA, ff. 295 *rb* [808 *r*]; 349 *ra* [965 *r*]; 37 *vb* [105 *bv*]), that multiplying, by means of devices made in shape of screws, the force of raising and transport of enormous weights to great heights, allowed to place with perfect precision the marble blocks: «there is the need to prepare one of the 3 iron screws of the works of Santa Liberata; shape a mould and cast wax» (CA, f. 333 *va* [909 *v*]). Reflections of a practical character that seem to echo what Vasari will assert in his outline of the activity of Da Vinci as an engineer, always turned towards research and experimentation: «And every day he made models and drawings to be able to easily unload mountains and drill them in order to pass from a plane to another and by means of levers and winches and screws he showed that great weights could be raised and pulled and [showed] ways to empty harbours and pumps to take low waters away of places, because that brain never ceased dreaming up».

But Leonardo knew very well also the system of covering in bricks of a vault made according to the method of Brunelleschi, the one of the «herring-bone», with which the stability of the segments of the cupola was guaranteed, by predisposing courses of bricks placed flat, intercalated to spirals of bricks laid on edge. A technique of construction that Leonardo demonstrates to know well just in a sketch of the nineties, made in a sheet of the Codex Atlanticus (CA, f. 341 *va* [933 *v*]), to which can be placed side by side his studies of wood technology dedicated to architectural coverings (CA, f. 190 *ra* [518 *r*]), to the composite beams and to the way to bend them (CA, f. 33 *vb* [91 *v*]), to scaffoldings (CA, f. 93 *rb* [255 *br*]), to the construction of the centering and to the trusses for the

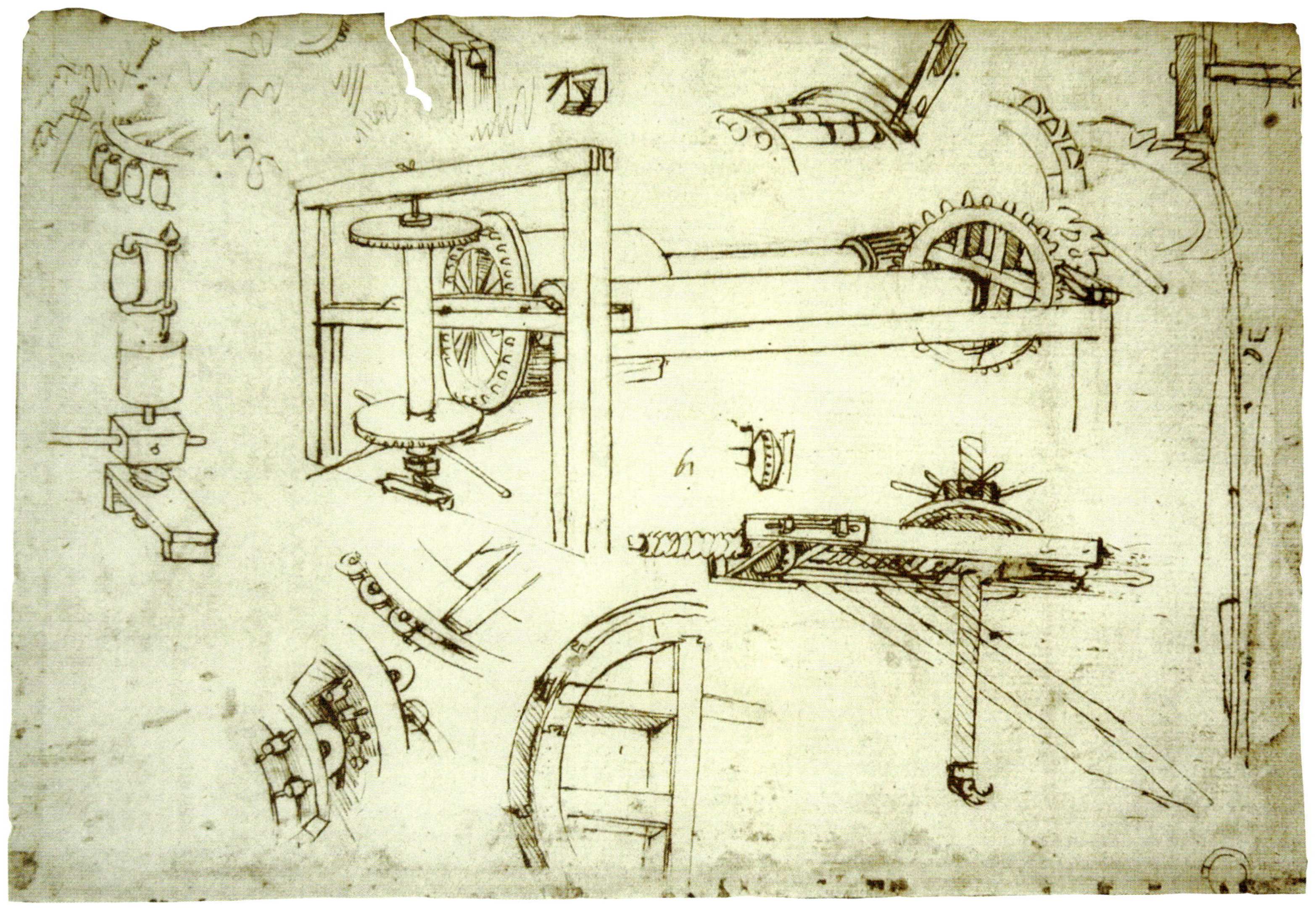

LEONARDO DA VINCI, *Winch with many speeds*, c. 1478. Pen and ink, 190 x 278 mm. Codex Atlanticus, f. 1083 *v*. Milan, Biblioteca Ambrosiana

arches (CA, f. 200 *ra* [537 *r*]) or to the wood cages on which to lean the masonries of the cupolas (CA, f. 266 *r a-b* [719 *r*], to reach then the invention of the trellises with «geodetic» covering (CA, f. 328 *va* [899 *v*]), prelude, as Carlo Pedretti has well illustrated, of the ingenious constructions of the North American engineer Richard Buckminster Fuller (1895-1983), inventor of the «geodetic» cupola, which he equipped with a structure with supporting elements connected in a triangular shape and such as to revolutionize the technology of covering, inspiring himself precisely to Leonardo.[21]

In the Milan period, perhaps following proposals and reflections exchanged with his friend Donato Bramante («groups of Bramante», CA, f. 225 *r* [611 *a*]), passionate admirer of ancient things, bloomed also studies for a system of «arches very strong and light» (Ms. B, f. 78 *v*) and elaborated plans for churches with cupola and central plan, with variations of geometric outlines and the original creation of secondary volumes and spaces around the central body (Ms. Ashb., f. 5 *v*), corresponding to the humanistic ideal and destined to the writing up of a «treatise on architecture».

Bramante in fact had participated in the great architectural enterprise of arrangement of the church of Santa Maria near San Satiro in Milan (1482-84), where he had managed to achieve a proportional and organic equilibrium of the structural masses with the invention of a fictitious chorus, example of «architectural perspective» with singular pictorial

[21] See C. PEDRETTI, *Leonardo architetto*, 1978, *op. cit.*; ID., *Leonardo: dalla pianta centrale allo spazio sferico*, in *La chiesa a pianta centrale, tempio civico del rinascimento*, a cura di B. Adorni, Milano, Electa, 2002. The American engineer Buckminster Fuller, dedicating in 1957 some of his drawings to Carlo Pedretti, announced him, as it has then in fact happened, that his geodetic cupola would have been adopted by the parks and the museums all over the world.

effects for a careful correlation between real space and illusory space. "On 30 July and on 28 September 1487, Leonardo received the first payments from the Fabric of the Dome for his model in wood, constructed with the collaboration of the carpenter Bernardino de Madiis de Abbiate, an account that, after a subsequent payment of 40 Liras carried out on 11 January 1488, was definitively paid off on 17 May 1490 (12 Liras),[22] when Leonardo, after a series of controversies with the local workers and following an advice of Bramante,[23] with which he will collaborate in 1494 for the rearrangement of the ducal residence of Vigevano, studying its «walls», the «garland», the «hall» and the «stairs» (Ms. H, f. 65 *v*),[24] and, around 1497, for the transformation and the cupola of S. Maria delle Grazie, «arches of the Grazie» (Cod. Madrid I, f. 113 *v*),[25] abandoned the plan, after having re-entered into possession of the model (10 May), after agreement or promise to give it back in case of any possible demand.[26]

It was under these circumstances that, on 31 May 1490, arrived to Milan from Siena Francesco di Giorgio Martini, after he had received there an invitation, on 19 April 1490, from the hands of Caradosso (Cristoforo Foppa, known as), goldsmith and maker of medals at the court of the Sforza House.

After an agreement of the engineer arrived from Siena with Antonio Amadeo and Giangiacomo Dolcebuono («in order to find some shape in a perfect way»), on 27 June 1490, it was rapidly proposed the definitive model, quite probably, considered the celerity of the execution, the same one by Leonardo, slightly modified and that Martini made to turn out to be his. In fact, Carlo Pedretti underlines why nobody «has ever wondered how Francesco di Giorgio, that had arrived to Milan at the end of May, could prepare a model in a few days, when he even had to leave Milan and reach Pavia – in the company of Leonardo - for a consultation on the works of that cathedral».[27] Sharing the solutions devised by Leonardo, Martini would not have strayed from his model and, proposing the project to the commission, he would have met the approval of the other engineers, with the exception of Amadeo. In fact, on 8 June 1490, Ludovico the Moor had ordered to Bartolomeo Calco,[28] upon request of the members of the Board of Trustees of the Dome of Pavia and according to the wishes of the local ecclesiastical authorities, included the brother of the Duke, the Cardinal Ascanio Sforza, Bishop of the city, so that Francesco di Giorgio, accompanied by Amadeo and Leonardo (considered of identical professional dignity), would go to Pavia, in order to express a technical opinion about the foundations of the new cathedral that was to be erected:

> *Master Bartholomeo. These deputies of the Board over the Fabric of the greater church of this City have required it and have made a great urgency that we want to be pleased to offer them that engineer from Siena, which those deputies of the Board over the Fabric of the Dome of Milan use, to make him see that church: and since we wish to please them for being their demand the most honest, we tell you that you must meet with the mentioned Deputies, speaking also to the mentioned engineer, and do act as to make him come here to see this fabric here. Dat. Papie 8 junij 1490. Ludovicus Maria Sfortia etc. Postscripta. Requiring also Master Leonardo from Florence and master Io. Antonio Amadeo, you will operate also so that they too will come. Dat. ut in litteris. Idem Ludovicus Maria Sfortia etc.*

The answer of Bartolomeo Calco to the Duke was rapid and, on 10 June, the ducal Secretary assured that the departure of Francesco di Giorgio and of Leonardo for Pavia would have taken place in the space of a week, while Amadeo would not have been there, because occupied on the lake of Como, but actually in professional bad terms with the two rival en-

---

[22] See L. Beltrami, *Documenti*, n° 31-33.
[23] In the famous *Opinio* by Bramante on the various models displayed, the proposals of Leonardo and of Francesco di Giorgio Martini would seem to be included in the considerations expressed on the octagon lantern with square support.
[24] See E. Solmi, *Leonardo da Vinci nel castello e nella Sforzesca di Vigevano*, «Viglevanum», V, 1911; L. Barni, *Ricerche intorno all'opera di Leonardo e del Bramante in Vigevano*, «Annuario della R. Scuola Complementare G. Ribecchi in Vigevano», Vigevano, 1928; R. Schofield, *Ludovico il Moro and Vigevano*, «Arte Lombarda», 62, 1982.
[25] See P. Murray, *Leonardo and Bramante. Leonardo's approach to anatomy and architecture, and its effect on Bramante*, «Architectural Review», CXXXIV, 1963; L. H. Heydenreich, *Leonardo and Bramante: Genius in Architecture*, in *Leonardo's Legacy*, a cura di C. D. O'Malley, Berkeley e Los Angeles, 1969; C. Pedretti, *The original projet for S. Maria delle Grazie*, «Journal of the Society of Architectural Historians», XXXII, 1973; Id., *Il progetto originario per Santa Maria delle Grazie e altri aspetti inediti del rapporto Leonardo-Bramante*, in *Studi Bramanteschi. Atti del Congresso internazionale*, 1970, Roma, 1974; Id., *Leonardo architetto*, 1978, *op. cit*. Pedretti puts forward with precaution also the hypothesis that the dome of Santa Maria delle Grazie has been devised by Leonardo, considered the friendship and the exchange of ideas elapsed with Bramante. Besides, an anonymous writer of the seventeenth century, perhaps Father Sebastiano Resta, defined Leonardo «architect of the dome of the Grazie in Milan». Some hints of this evocative hypothesis turn out from the plan of the apse of S. Maria delle Grazie (Ms. I, ff. 69 *v*-70 *r*) and from the schematic sketches of a vault in shape of a cupola in a sheet of the Codex of Madrid I (f. 113 *v*), where it is discussed about a principle of mechanics applicable to the dome of St. Maria delle Grazie: «That part of the disjointed weight more presses which is closer to the centre of its heaviness. A clear thing it is that the part that is within an arc or lantern in the places *b c* presses more than out of it in *a d*. The more resists the perpendicular *g p* than the curved *f g*, for the fifth of the ninth». The persistent collaboration of Leonardo with Bramante is demonstrated also by a note written in this period, on a side of a sketch of a drawbridge, where we can read: «that Donnino showed me», (Ms. M, f. 53 *v*) and, in the Ms. L, once abandoned Milan, among the works that were left unfinished for Ludovico the Moor, Leonardo will still remember the «buildings of Bramante».
[26] See C. Pedretti, *Leonardo architetto*, 1978, *op. cit*.

[27] See C. Pedretti, *Leonardo architetto*, 1978, *op. cit*.; C. Vecce, *Leonardo*, Roma, Salerno, 1998.
[28] See L. Beltrami, *Documenti*, n° 48-49; G. C. Sciolla, *Leonardo e Pavia*, «Lettura Vinciana», XXXV, Firenze, Giunti, 1996.

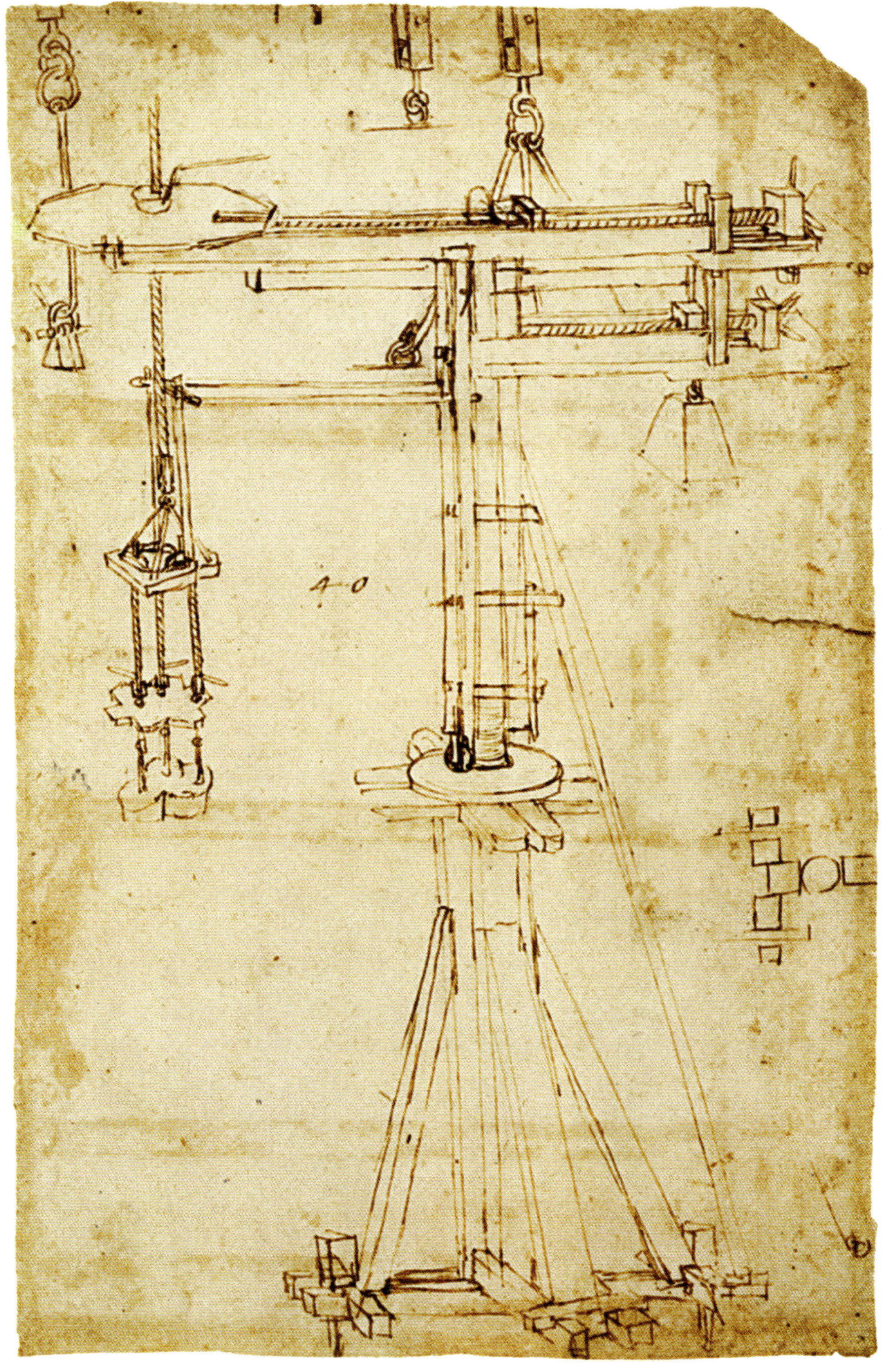

Leonardo da Vinci, *Revolving crane, c.* 1480. Pen and ink, 315 x 200 mm. Codex Atlanticus, f. 965 *r.* Milan, Biblioteca Ambrosiana

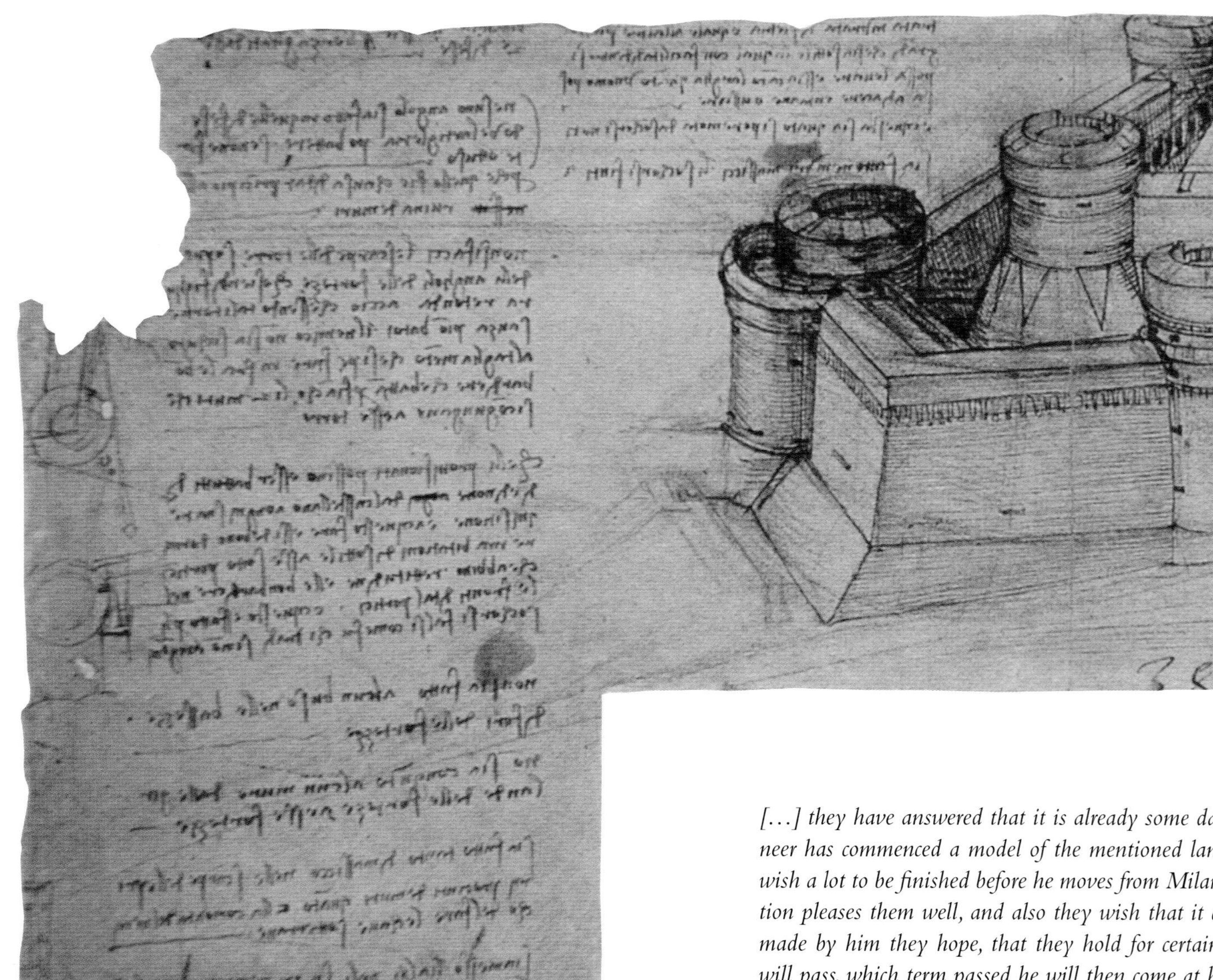

Leonardo da Vinci, *Project of a great fortress*, c. 1502-07. Pen and ink, 422 x 131-202 mm. Codex Atlanticus, f. 117 *r*. Milan, Biblioteca Ambrosiana

[…] they have answered that it is already some days that the engineer has commenced a model of the mentioned lantern, which they wish a lot to be finished before he moves from Milan, that the invention pleases them well, and also they wish that it can soon be seen, made by him they hope, that they hold for certain that eight days will pass, which term passed he will then come at his pleasure: having communicated the same thing to the engineer, he has answered me in conformity to what have said the aforementioned monsignor and members of the Board of Trustees: nevertheless that he at every hour is ready to execute the will of Your Lordship - Master Leonardo from Florence told me he will always be ready whenever requested: so that, as the engineer from Siena will be sent, he too will follow. I doubt that Master Jo. Antonio Amadeo will be able to be there, because he is on the lake of Como, for an enterprise of not small importance: nevertheless when Your Excellence will want in any case that he were there, it will be possible to write him to come. Continuously commending myself to those. Mediolani X junij 1490. Ser.or Bartholomeus Chalcus.

gineers from Tuscany, that with all their servitude and the horses will relocate, on 21 June, to Pavia, where they will lodge at the tavern of the Moor («ad signum Saracini Papie»), as a payment of 20 pounds to Giovanni Agostino de Berneriis documents,[29] («pro expensis sibi factis per dominos Franciscum Senensem et Leonardum Florentinum ingeniarios cum sociis et famulis suis et cum equis»):[30]

Francesco di Giorgio and Leonardo will begin immediately a relationship based on admiration and friendship. Mar-

---

[29] See L. Beltrami, *Documenti*, n° 50; R. V. Schofield, J. Shell, G. Sironi, *Giovanni Antonio Amadeo. I documenti*, Como, 1989.

[30] «for the expenses made for themselves by masters Francesco of Siena and Leonardo of Florence engineers with their attendants and servants and their horses» (Latin; Tr. N.)

 Carlo Starnazzi

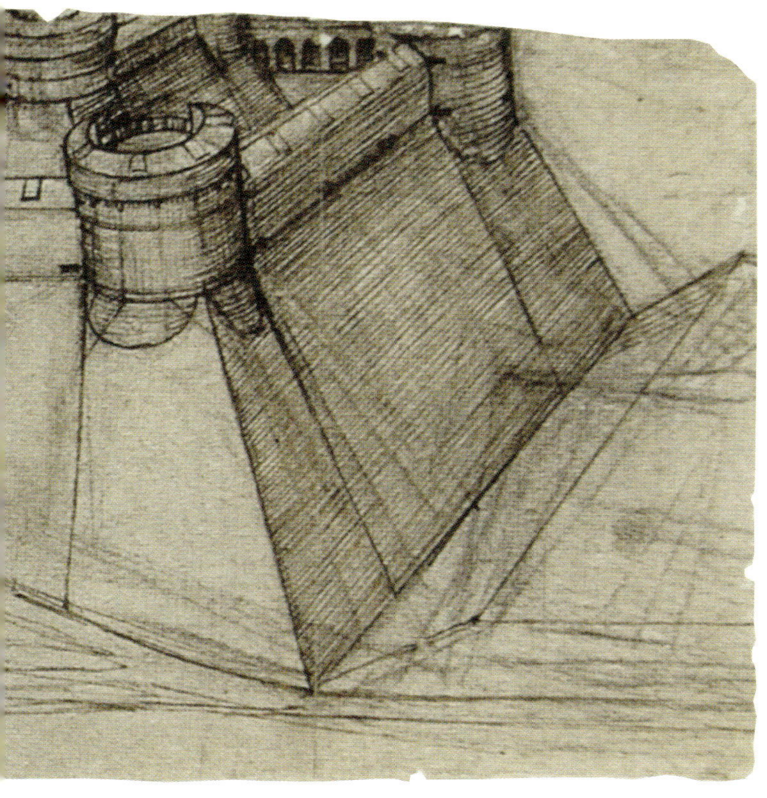

esis that such generosity might have been generated by the moral debt of Martini ahead of the magnanimity and liberality of Leonardo for the model of the lantern and for having submitted to his attention the «treatise of architecture» that he was compiling. Besides, every encounter with Leonardo left always an indelible mark in those who met with the fascination of his inexhaustible inventiveness and creativity. And certainly Martini admired his solutions in architecture, precisely as Raphael, Perugino, Giorgione, Dürer and many others would have made for painting.

It is a matter of fact that Leonardo will record in his possession the *Trattato* by Francesco di Giorgio still around 1504, annotating it with 12 autograph comments (*Laurenziano Ashburnham 361* - Biblioteca Medicea Laurenziana, n. 282),[32] after that for the Duke Valentino he had carried out studies of fortifications in Romagna and for Jacopo IV Appiani in Piombino, a system of towers and casemates, analyzing the degree of resistance of the circular fortresses in bearing the impact of the fire-balls in front of the progress of the technical-scientific knowledge in the ballistics field (Ms. L, f. 43 *v*; cod. di Madrid II, f. 25 *r*).

Precisely on a sheet of the Codex Atlanticus (CA, f. 41 *vb* [117 *r*]), there is a fortress designed with the characters of traditional defence of the style of Martini, that, started perhaps in 1502, will subsequently be modified by the artist with new shapes, aimed to a multiplication of external and internal defences. The plan of this powerful military structure will be completed by Leonardo, around 1507, when, at the service of Charles d' Amboise (1507-10), he will strive to realize a prototype of fortress suitable to a mountain military strategy, with high escarpment and cylindrical large towers with parapets tilted towards the outside, more appropriate to divert the projectiles of the enemy artillery. In fact, the reinforcement of the military work in a uneven ground, to whose characteristics the entire structure is bending, makes him record the memory of the bloody episode of Simone Arrigoni, rewarded by Louis XII for the murder of Antonio Landriani (1499), treasurer of the Moor, and then betrayed from a captain of his, Gerolamo Poggio, that had convinced him to let a contingent of enemy troops penetrate at night in his Castle of Valsassina with fraudulent intentions:

No angle has to be made in those defences, where the artillery can strike, if it is not strongly obtuse; because that might be cause to give principle to the ruin of the walls. Do not make the escarpments of the towers over the angles of the fortresses, that are of round figure,

tini had constituted a valid point of reference for Leonardo both for the formation of his culture and his architectural language, since the drawings of fortified architecture of the Ms. B of the Institut de France, but above all after having received as a gift from the master from Siena, on the basis of what was traditionally accepted, copy of the second writing of the *Trattato di architettura militare e civile*, constituted of the Codices Senese (S.IV.4) and Magliabechiano (II.I.141),[31] written between 1487 and 1489, which were followed by various copies between 1489 and 1492. A writing that, compared with the previous one of the Codex Torinese Saluzziano *148* (1481-84), was characterized for the new and more original literary organization of the subjects, in the deliberate and conscious staying apart of the artist-intellectual from the «practical» world of the workshops. This manifestation of courtesy between the two Tuscan artist-scientists, theoretical princes of architecture in the difficult and competitive atmosphere of the Lombard world, developed, in a climate of collaboration and of maximum mutual esteem, without neglecting the fascinating hypoth-

---

[31] See Francesco di Giorgio Martini, *Trattati di architettura…*, 1967, op. cit.; C. Maltese, *L'attività di Francesco di Giorgio Martini architetto militare nelle Marche attraverso il suo «Trattato»*, in Atti dell'XI Congresso di Storia dell'Architettura, Roma, Centro Studi per la Storia dell'Architettura, 1965.

[32] The chronological definition of the annotations by Leonardo on the *Trattato* by Francesco di Giorgio do not certify with certainty the year in which he has entered in possession of them.

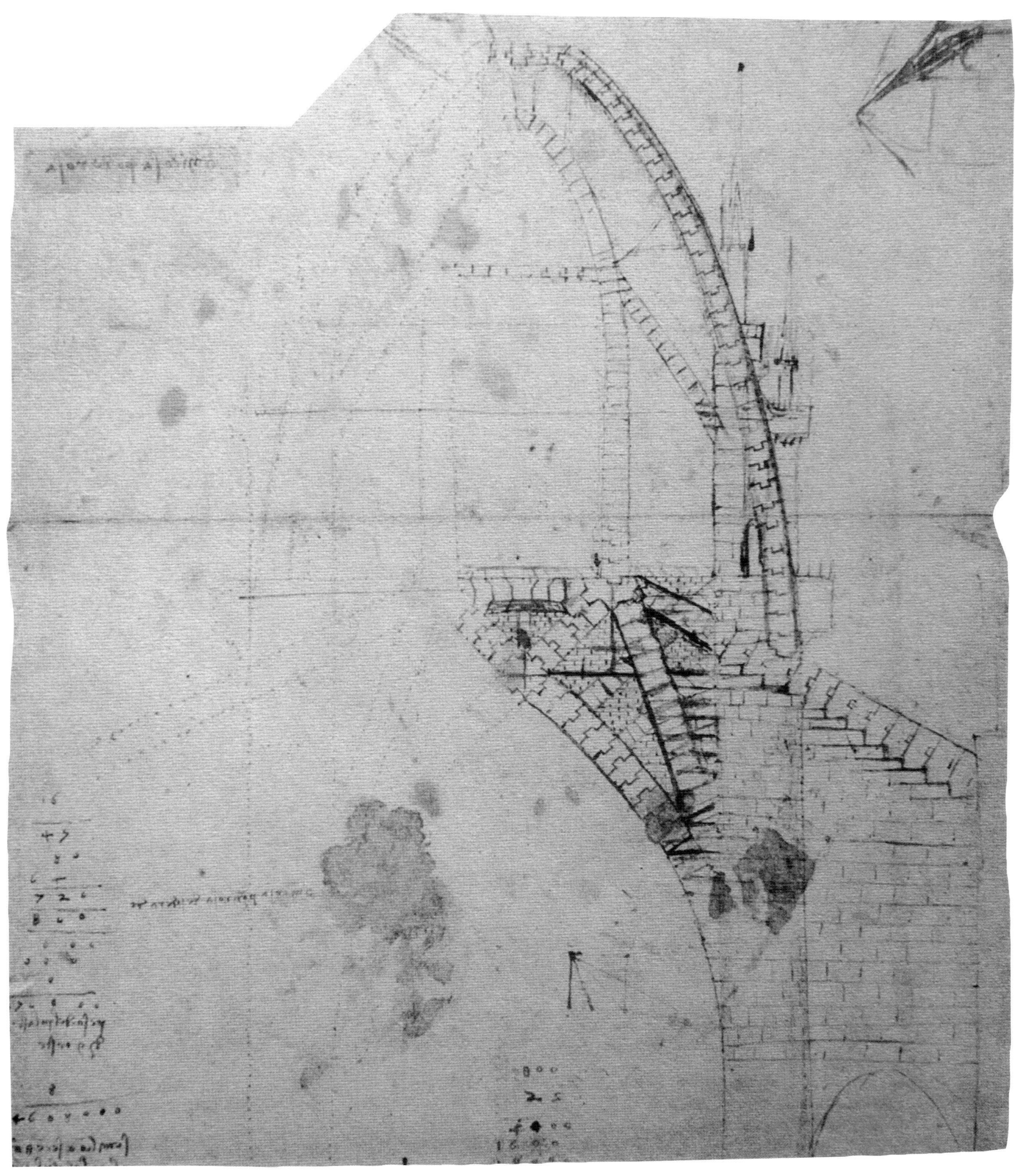

LEONARDO DA VINCI, *Study on the thrust of the arches for the lantern of the Dome of Milan*, c. 1487-90. Pen and sepia ink on black chalk, 330 x 290 mm. Codex Atlanticus, f. 850 *r*. Milan, Biblioteca Ambrosiana

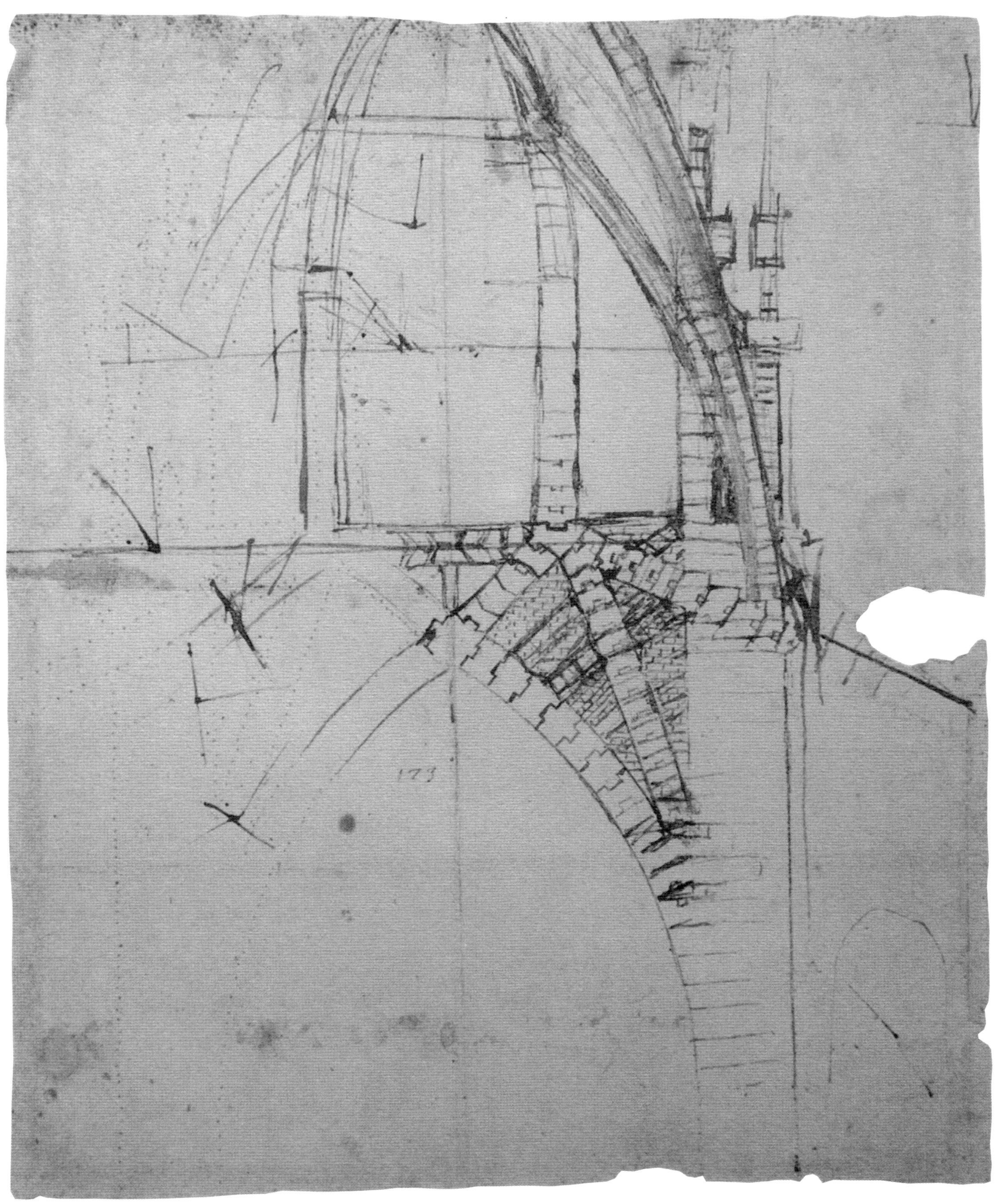

LEONARDO DA VINCI, *Study for the lantern of the Dome of Milan*, c. 1487-90. Pen and sepia ink, 282 x 237 mm. Codex Atlanticus, f. 851 *r*. Milan, Biblioteca Ambrosiana

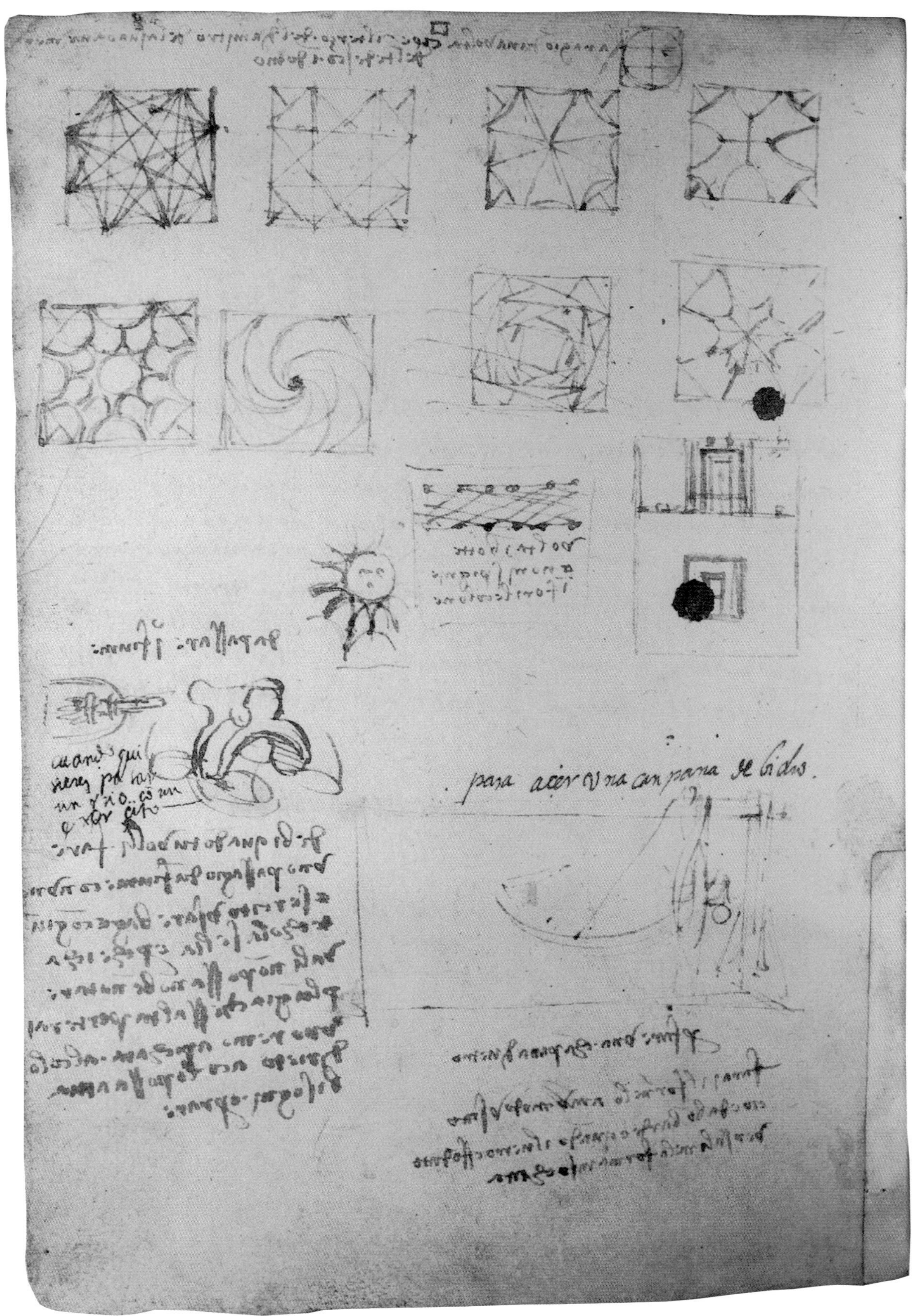

Leonardo da Vinci, *Scheme of a dome on a squared base, c.* 1487-90. Pen and ink, 231 x 167 mm. Ms B, f. 10 *v*. Paris, Institut de France

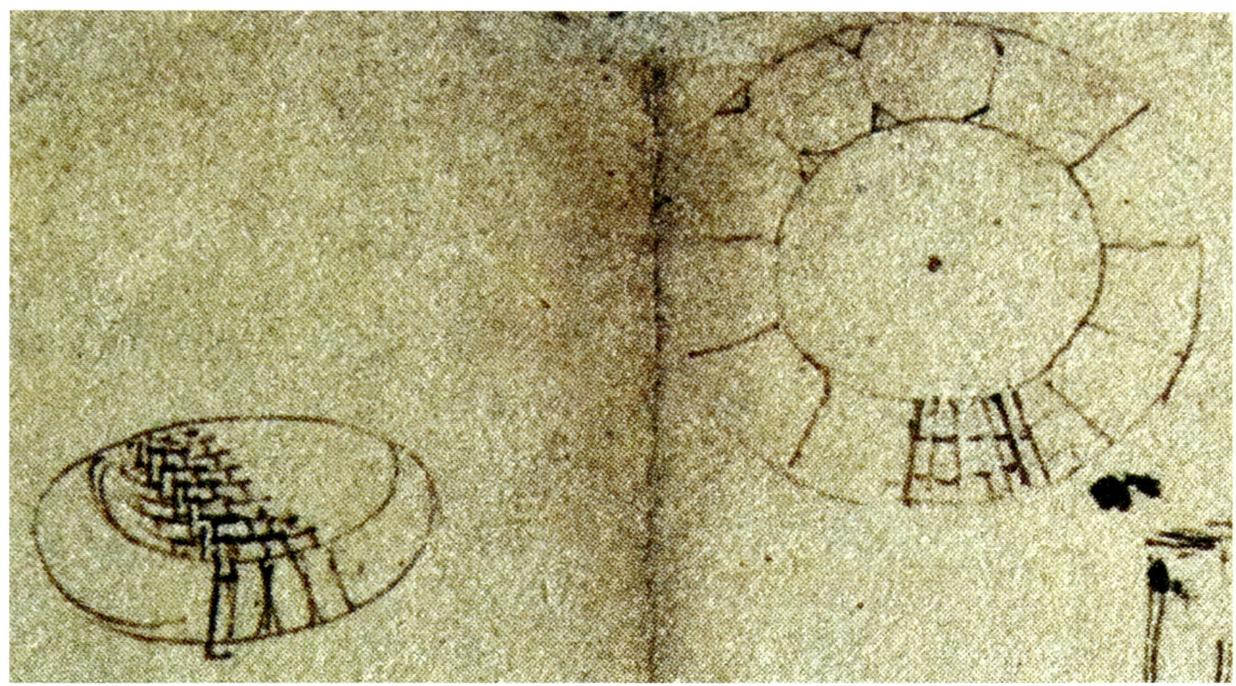

so that being such towers without machicolations, the enemy is not sure of the cutting off that can be done amid the embrasures that hit on flank the 2 walls that join to these towers. [Act so] that the mercenary soldiers may be mustered day and night by the commander of the Castle at any his request. And to do this, they must sleep in lodgings of thin boards, under open galleries that must be straight, and the embrasures in the front of such open galleries. And that is done against the false aid, as it was who betrayed Simon Arrigoni. It has not to be made any hole in the low parts outside the fortresses. It has not to be joined any wall by the garlands of the fortresses to the fortresses themselves. It has to be done as much stone ballast in the foundations of the first circles of the walls, as much is the comfort of the enemy to dig underground galleries. It has to be planted trees in the spurs of the walls, so that such spurs are not separated from the surface of the walls.

Leonardo will succeed in perfecting the studies of Francesco di Giorgio and in bringing innovations, precisely where Martini had concluded his own research, like the realization of convex and absconding surfaces with long and narrow embrasures, and the new conception of the defilade in circular fortresses, dealt with in the sheets of the Codex Atlanticus (CA, ff. 43 *vb* [121 *v*] and 48 *ra* [132 *r*]), anticipating of years the same Antonio da Sangallo the Younger in person.

He had gone beyond the uncertainties of Francesco di Giorgio, as well as those of Antonio Averlino known as Filarete, also in the adoption of an orthogonal or radial road network in the plan of a modern town-planning system, the only one that might allow, unlike the city structure of the late-medieval cities of the new Florentine lands, fruit of a planning of the territory of the excellent engineer-architect Arnolfo di Cambio (as San Giovanni Valdarno, Castelfranco and Terranova), to facilitate a rapid action of the defenders, from a front to the other, in case of enemy attack (Ms. B, f. 48 *r*).[33]

On the consultation for the Fabric of the Dome of Pavia there remained but some sketches related to the technical opinions formulated (CA, f. 362 *vb* [1010 *v*]),[34] while remain more articulated studies (CA, ff. 148 *ra*-148 *rb* [400 *r*]; Cod. Trivulziano, ff. 8 *r*; 22 *v*) and the splendid drawings by Leon-

[33] See D. FRIEDMAN, *Terre nuove. La creazione delle città fiorentine nel tardo medioevo*, Torino, Einaudi, 1996; A. FARA, *Leonardo e l'architettura militare*, 1996, *op. cit.*

[34] In Pavia Leonardo, taking advantage of the presence of Francesco di Giorgio Martini, interested with passion to the evidences of the ancient art, lingering particularly to examine the equestrian statue of the *Regisole* (I cent. b.C.), of which he admired the movement in amble: «Of that of Pavia the movement is praised more than any other thing. The imitation of the ancient things is more praiseworthy than that of the modern things. It cannot exist beauty and usefulness like appears in fortresses and in men. The trot is nearly the quality of a free horse. Where a natural vivacity lacks, we must make an accidental one», (CA, f. 147 *rb* [399 *r*]). Cfr. E. MOTTA, *Leonardo da Vinci e la cattedrale di Pavia*, «Bollettino storico della Svizzera italiana», VI, 1884; L. POZZI, *Leonardo da Vinci e il disegno del duomo di Pavia*, «Bollettino della Società pavese di storia patria», III, 1903; E. SOLMI, *Leonardo da Vinci, il duomo, il castello e l'università di Pavia*, «Bollettino della Società pavese di storia patria», XI, 1911; C. SALETTI, *Il Regisole di Pavia: storia di un nome*, «Bollettino della Società pavese di storia patria», 46, 1994; ID., *Il Regisole e la pittura pavese del primo Cinquecento*, in *Minuscola varia. Miscellanea di studi archeologici offerti ad Antonio Frova*, Roma, 1995; G. C. SCIOLLA, *Leonardo e Pavia*, 1996, *op. cit.*

ardo on the lantern of the Dome of Milan (CA, ff. 310 *v-b* [850 *r*]; 310 *r-b* [851 *r*]), where the artist, focusing in his research on the language of images, in which the architectural particulars are inserted and are represented in detail, even if without axonometric views, makes drawing become an instrument of theoretical activity, an expression of a constant interaction between art and science.

For the realization of the lantern, Leonardo planned to insert an architectural body with central plan on a structure in gothic style. It was not a matter therefore to intervene on the linearity of a fifteenth century building, but to invent a structural innovation by foreseeing the force ratios that could come out of an architectural anomaly, due to the presence of elements both Gothic and of the Renaissance.

The originality of the theoretical studies of Leonardo, carried out for the completion of the lantern (CA, ff. 310 *v-b* [850 *r*]; 310 *r-b* [851 *r*]), like insisting on one of the four pylons of the half-pointed double cap structure with ribbings in stone, the cupola with eight segments, with octagonal base enclosed within a square, the vertical wall of the drum, on which to set up the cupola following the tradition of Brunelleschi (CA, f. 17 *va* [57 *v*]), found in Francesco di Giorgio their higher interpreter, able to translate into reality and to reply what enunciated on a theoretical ground and planned with precise and admired drawings by Leonardo, who well knew that the cathedral of Florence had a cupola with a double structure with the inner and external profiles equivalent to a fifth and to a quarter of a pointed arch. This hypothesis finds its confirm in the same correspondence of the chronological interaction related to the collaboration between the two artist-scientists in Milan and constructive phases of the church of the Calcinaio, where the works had been interrupted, right in 1490, at the moment of the realization of the vaults, in order to start again, in 1491, and to go along with the definition of the nave well after 1508, when the construction of the cupola started. Therefore, we can conveniently conclude that Martini, departed from Milan and returned to Siena, transferred the innovation of the leonardian architectural inventions to the plan of the still-to-be-built Church of Santa Maria al Calcinaio of Cortona,[35] where the cupola is set up on a drum with a strong vertical development and with walls with tabernacle windows, composed of two pilaster strips, a lintel and a triangular tympanum, framed between vertical bands of angular false-strips, on their turn dominated by a thin frame and in the second level by a high trabeation. These architectural solutions are represented up to the minimum details in the sketch of a plan for a church with central plan elaborated by Leonardo (CA, f. 205 *va* [547 *v*]),[36] always wary in his plans of ecclesiastical buildings to dispense and irradiate a diffused atmospheric light in the independent space of the presbytery area. Moreover the cupola of the Calcinaio does not have a lowered structure with hemispheric cap with arches at half sixth, as in the drawing of the Codex Laurenziano *361* (f. 12 *v*), but has an octagonal plan and it is concluded with a curving to fifth of a pointed arch quite slender, like to conciliate those two worlds, the gothic one and that of the Renaissance, on whose co-existence the exchange of ideas concerning the projects of the two friends, the «engineer from Siena» and the «Master Leonardo from Florence» had prolonged. And the obvious influence of Leonardo on Francesco di Giorgio went on till the possible involvement of Martini with an original vincian concept, matured right during the experience of Pavia and on the basis of which it was clear the intention to suggest that, to emphasize in a work of art the dynamic visual feeling of movement in the space, where «a natural vivacity» lacked, there was the need «to make one accidental», (CA, f. 147 *rb* [399 *r*]). Therefore the necessity of a «special effect» was thus discovered, reached up in a completely new way in Santa Maria delle Grazie al Calcinaio, where the building, because of the elegance and the peculiarity of the drum and the vertical development of the leonardian cupola, that ends up in the alternation of empty and full spaces in the lantern, broke its strict solidity and classic monumentality, hovering in the space with much greater energy and structural continuity.

---

[35] The assessments about the dating of the several phases and vicissitudes of the building construction make the realization of the western wing of the transversal body go back to 30 September 1485; while the construction of the apse would go back to October 1486 and the eastern wing, together with the span of the nave at the entrance of the transept, to a period subsequent to 1488. Moreover, the definition of the nave would have been started about the end of the century and completed in 1508. See Cfr. P. MATRACCHI, *La Chiesa di S. Maria delle Grazie al Calcinaio…*, 1992, *op. cit.*

[36] This study of a church with central plan, even if datable around 1505, and therefore preceding the construction of the drum and of the cupola of Cortona, but not the death of Martini, that had already passed away in 1501, sends back conceptually to the architectural variations that Leonardo, with extraordinary projecting creativity, was devising since the contest for the lantern of Milan (1487-90), when he was about to prepare also a treatise on cupolas and on sacred buildings with central plan.

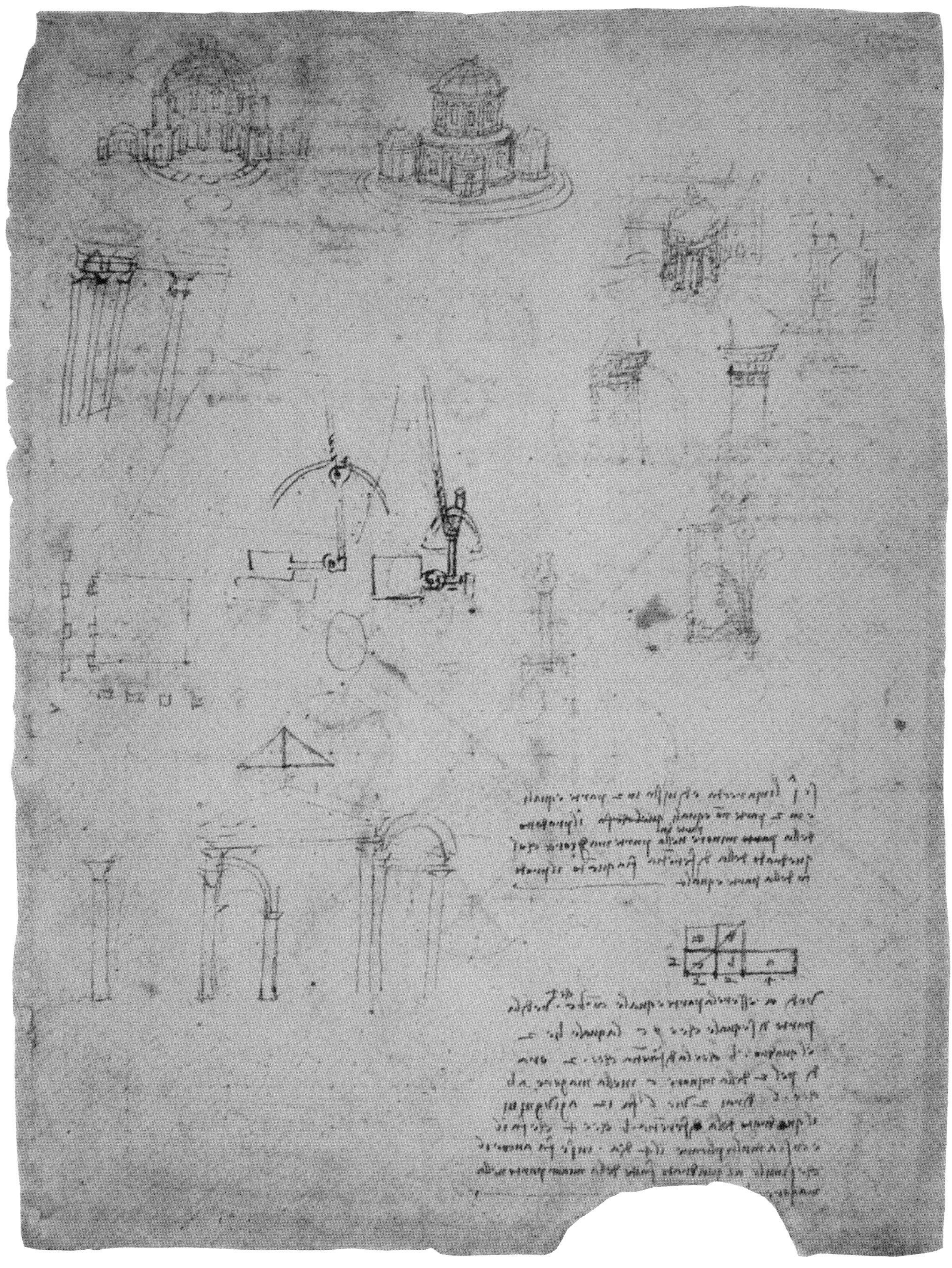

Leonardo da Vinci, *Study of a small temple*, c. 1505. Pen and reddish ink, 280 x 215 mm. Codex Atlanticus, f. 547 *v*. Milan, Biblioteca Ambrosiana

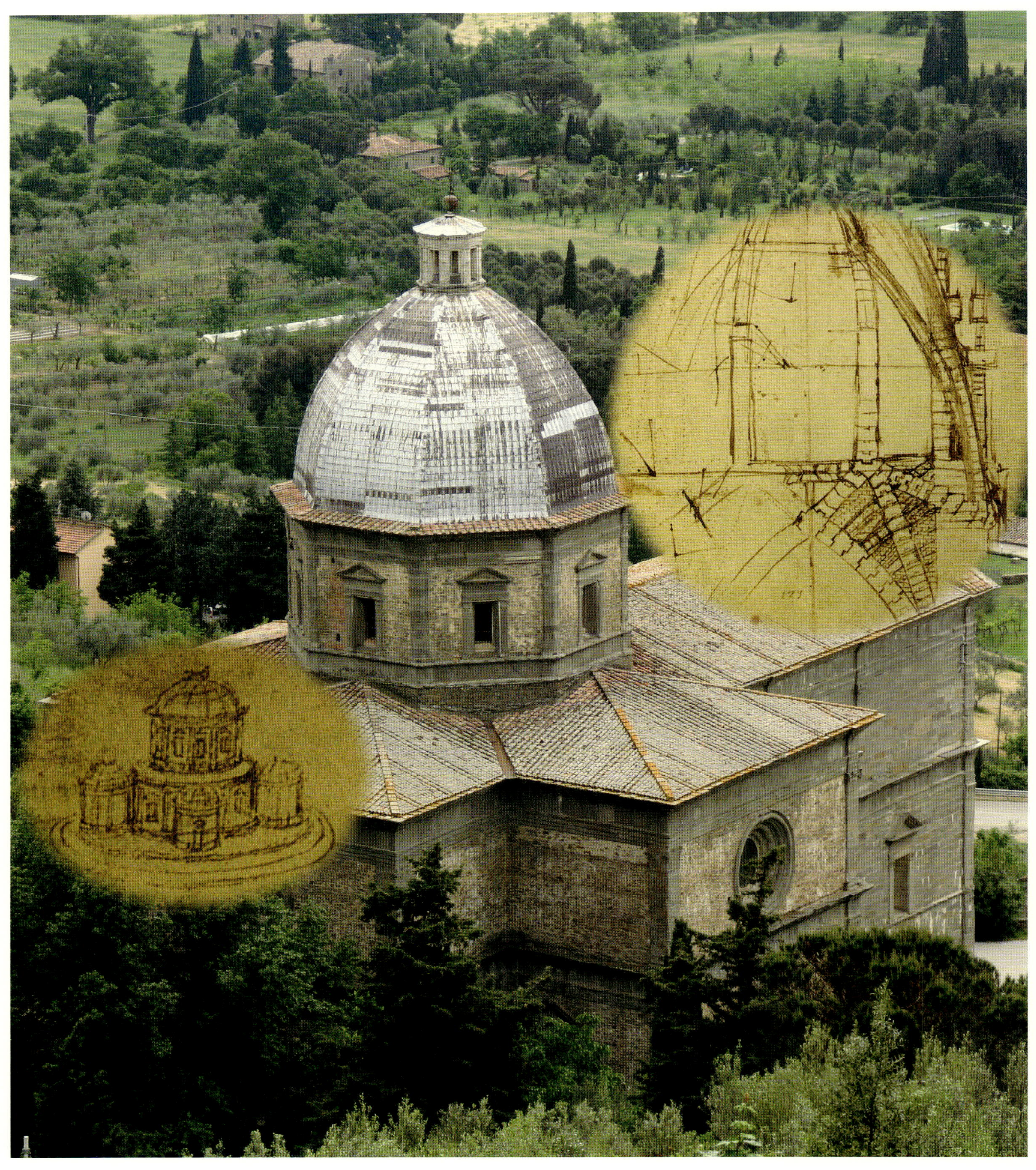

Correspondence between the architectural ideas of Leonardo and the dome of Santa Maria delle Grazie at the Calcinaio of Cortona

Leonardo and the Etruscans
An original central plan architecture

A RUTHLESS dispute between Leonardo and his brothers determined the occasion for the artist that would
have put him in relation, with singular enthusiasm and curi-
osity, to the world of the Etruscans.

It was in fact on summer 1507, at the death of Francesco da
Vinci, the uncle of Leonardo, that it was opened and read
that will, in which the bastard son of master Piero had to appear as the only universal heir of his assets. The brothers, in
front of a will that they reputed as unjust, appealed the will,
delegating as representative of the common interests master
Giuliano, he too experienced notary public,[1] as it had been
his father master Piero da Vinci, died on 9 July 1504 («Today
9 of July 1504 on Wednesday at 7 hours died Master Piero da
Vinci, notary public at the palace of the chief magistrate. My
father, at 7 hours. He was 80 years old. He left 10 sons and 2
daughters», Cod. Arundel, f. 272 *r* = P 79).[2]

Leonardo, saddened and offended, invoked the help of King
Louis XII, which, in the attempt to support him in his cause,
sent a letter to the Florentine Seigniory, countersigned by his
powerful Secretary of State, Florimond Robertet, recognizing to his protect for the first time the title of «notre paintre
et ingénieur ordinaire».[3] For that reason, on 18 September,
Leonardo moved from Milan to Florence and availing himself of old acquaintances like Agostino Vespucci, former secretary of Machiavelli, he sent a letter, turned out not to be
an autograph though with his seal stamped on sealing-wax
on its back,[4] to the Cardinal Ippolito d'Este, so that with his
influence he could intervene in his favour. In the meantime,
in a sheet of the Codex Atlanticus, where there is a first
draft of a letter, maybe preliminary to a testimony in court,[5]
he poured out all his resentment and his contempt for the
blameworthy behaviour of his brothers:

> *You hated strongly Francesco and you let him enjoy what was yours*
> *while still alive; you bear me a huge ill-will to <…>*
> *Who were you fond of most, of Francesco or of me? Of you this one*
> *was fond of, and mine gives me after, so that I cannot do my will,*
> *and he knows that I cannot alienate my heir. I want then to ask*
> *my heirs, and not as a brother, but as an absolute extraneous; and I*
> *as an absolute extraneous will receive him and his. Have you given*
> *such money to Lionardo? No. Because he will be able to say that you*

---

[1] Master Giuliano da Vinci, step-brother of Leonardo, was in 1516 notary public of the Seigniory and, in 1518, orator at the Helvetian Alloy. In the argument
for the inheritance of his uncle Francesco, he revealed himself as the fiercest
opponent of Leonardo, but in time their relationship appeased again, if in 1515
Leonardo helped him to get easily into the entangled bureaucratic world of the
Vatican chancery. He married a certain Alessandra («Lesandra»: CA, 287 *va* [780
v]) and died in 1525. See G. UZIELLI, *Ricerche intorno a Leonardo da Vinci. Serie prima*,
Firenze, Pellas, 1872; ID., *Ricerche intorno a Leonardo da Vinci. Serie Seconda*, Roma,
Salviucci, 1884; S. MONTI, *Albero ossia discendenza della famiglia Da Vinci*, Como,
Società Storica Comense, 1909; E. MÖLLER, *Ser Giuliano di ser Piero da Vinci e le
sue relazioni con Leonardo*, «Rivista d'Arte», XVI, 1934; R. CIANCHI, *Vinci, Leonardo
e la sua famiglia (con appendice di documenti inediti)*, Milano, Museo Nazionale della
Scienza e della Tecnica, 1953; C.VECCE, *Leonardo*, 1998, *op. cit.*

[2] The date of death of Master Piero da Vinci is quickly recorded by Leonardo also in a sheet of the Codex Atlanticus (f. 71 *vb* [196 *v*]): «Wednesday at 7
hours died Master Piero da Vinci, in the day 9 of July 1504, Wednesday close to
7 hours».

[3] «our official painter and engineer». (Tr. N.)

[4] See G. CAMPORI, *Lettere artistiche inedite*, Modena, Soliani, 1866; L. BELTRAMI,
Documenti, n° 193, 1919, *op. cit.*; C. PEDRETTI, *Documenti e memorie…*, 1953, *op. cit.*

[5] See C. PEDRETTI, in J. P. RICHTER, *The Literary Work of Leonardo da Vinci Compiled
and Edited from the Original Manuscripts* (edited by), 2 vols, London, Low-Marston-
Searle and Rivington, 1883, *Commentary* by C. PEDRETTI, Oxford, Phaidon, 1977,
that reproduces the entire passage and intervenes to correct its reading, supplying
towards the end his interpretation, since to the phrase «want you then give back
the money lent on yours to the heirs», he replaces «yours» («votro») with «botro», that is Botro, a farm in the territory of Vinci mentioned also elsewhere, for
example in the Codex Arundel, f. 191 *r*, in a list of things to do: «the evaluation
of the Botro». In this interpretation, PEDRETTI was immediately followed by A.
MARINONI, in the Vol.VII (1978) of his transcriptions. On the contrary C.VECCE,
in *Leonardo* (1998), does not seem to receive such correction and has maintained
the traditional interpretation of «yours».

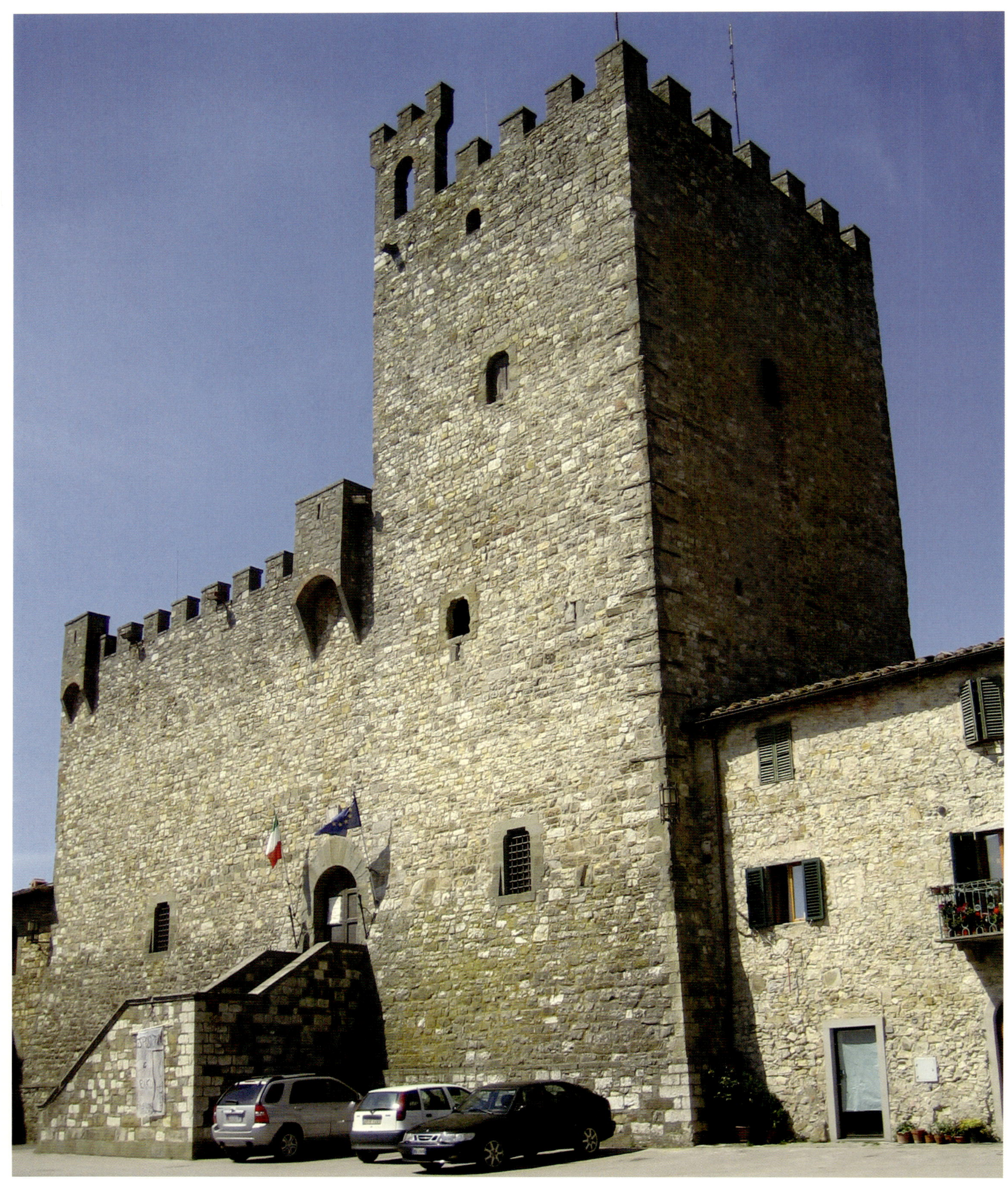

The City Fortress of Castellina in Chianti (15th Century)

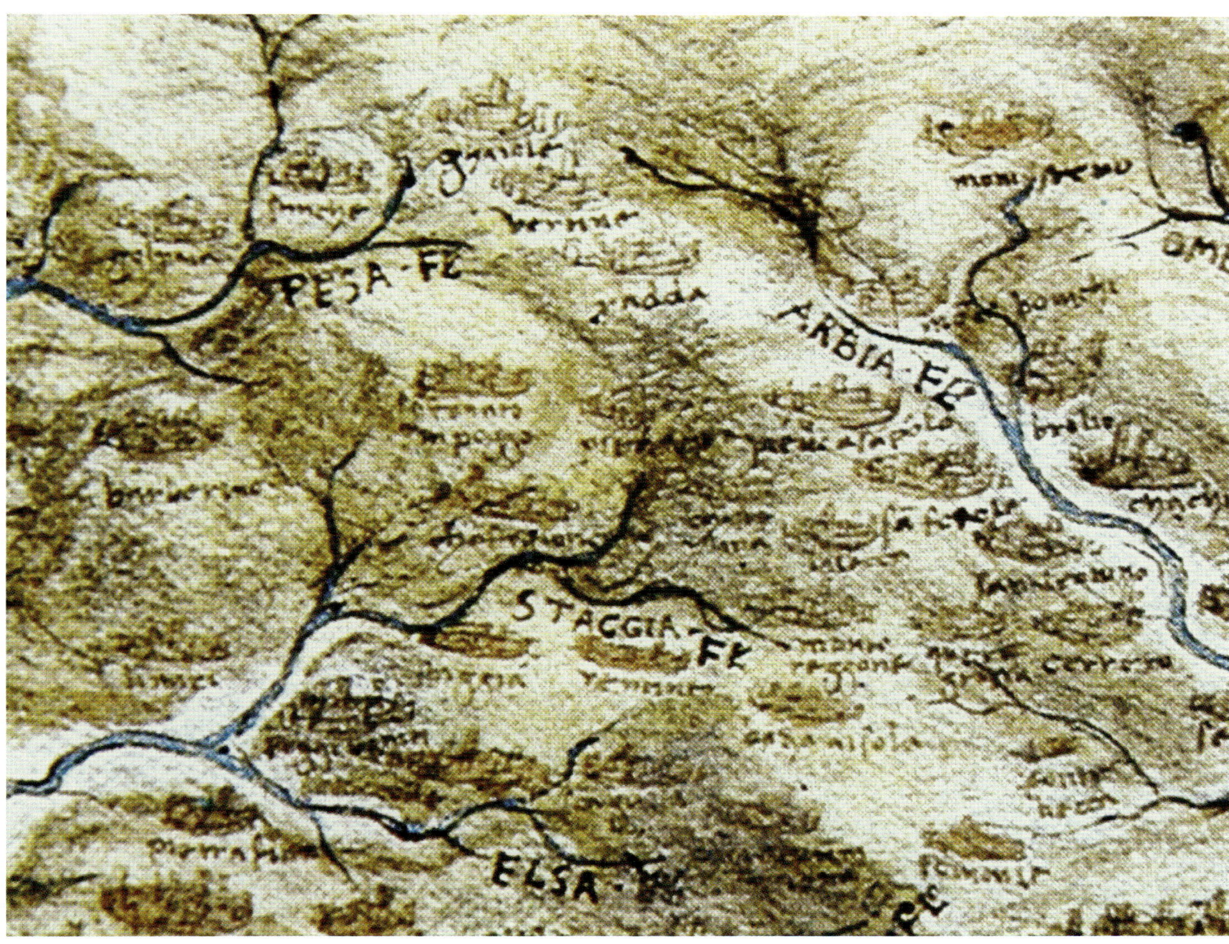

Leonardo da Vinci, *The hills of the Chianti region between Arbia, Pesa and Staggia*, c. 1503. Pen and ink, watercolour and charcoal, 33,8 x 48,8 cm. Windsor, RL 12278. Particular

have drawn him in this trap, true or false that it is, just for taking his money, I will not say anything to him while he lives. Moreover then, you do not want to give back the money lent on the yours ('botro') to the heirs, but you want that he pays the earnings that he has of such property.

Did not you let him enjoy it while he was still alive, provided that then we returned them to your children? Now, could not he still live for many years? Yes. Now, imagine that I am that one. You wanted that I were heir, so that I could not ask you specifically, as heir, the money that I must have from Francesco (CA, f. 214 va [571 av]).

For that reason, it will be during his stay in Florence that Leonardo, while he was facing the trial requests related to the inheritance of his uncle, will be informed of the piece of news, since some months widely diffused in Florentine cultured and erudite environments, of the extraordinary finding of various Etruscan tombs, on 29 January 1507, in a tumulus, constituted of backfill earth and stones, at Montecalvario (so called in medieval age, because of a station-apex of a Way

of the Cross) near Castellina in Chianti,[6] then integral part of the Florentine Republic, at the centre of the valleys of Arbia, Elsa and Pesa, and joined with the valley of the Arno and with the cities of Cortona, Chiusi and Volterra through natural routes.[7]

[6]   See L. A. Milani, *Montecalvario-Ipogeo paleoetrusco di Montecalvario presso Castellina in Chianti*, «Notizie degli Scavi», Roma, Tipografia della R. Accademia dei Lincei, 1905; L. Pernier, *Castellina in Chianti-Grande tumulo con ipogei paleoetruschi sul poggio di Montecalvario*, «Notizie degli Scavi», Roma, Tipografia della R. Accademia dei Lincei, 1916; M. Martelli, *Un disegno attribuito a Leonardo e una scoperta archeologica degli inizi del Cinquecento*, «Prospettiva», 10, 1977.
[7]   Not far away from Castellina in Chianti there is the ancient fortified medieval village of Volpaia or Golpaia, native land of Lorenzo and of Benvenuto della Golpaia. Lorenzo della Volpaia (1446-1512) was inventor and most skilful constructor of clocks as well as of a planetarium. In 1500, he was called to replace Carlo Marmocchi, mentioned by the same Leonardo for his quadrant (CA, f. 12 va [42 v]), with the assignment of regulating the clock of Palazzo Vecchio and, in 1504, he was among the thirty artists and scientists, consulted to define the right location to assign to the David by Michelangelo. Its connection with Leonardo is also confirmed by the notes and by the technological drawings, transcribed by his son Benvenuto, after 1520, in the Codex Marciano it. IV 41 = 5363, where, repeatedly, the name of the artist is made with regard to a method of disassem-

The site was placed on one of the main routes of trade and of communication of northern Etruria, that allowed the development of mercantile traffic with the more economically advanced cities and communities of the Tyrrhenian coast and of the fertile inner alluvial territories, like those of Quinto Fiorentino, Artimino or Murlo.[8]

The literature written in the manner of a chronicle of the time, much careful to all that concerned the antique things, if we think that the first systematic census of the classic statuary, *Le antichità della città di Roma* by Ulisse Aldrovandi (1558) goes back to this period and the newly born Vitruvian Academy of Rome (1545), just for a little time subsequent to the institution of the Florentine Academy (1541), continued over and over to deal with the singular archaeological finding. Pierfrancesco Giambullari, in his *Il Gello*, a work printed in Florence, in 1546, and dedicated to Cosimo I, in which the intention was to exalt the ideology of the Medicean princedom and to consolidate the politic of expansion, recovering the topic of the origins of Florence, in order to make the «Florentine» language and history derive from the Etruscans and their glorious past (ID., «Origini della lingua fiorentina», 1549),[9] reported that «in 1507, on 29 of January, next to the Castellina, uprooting a vine, it was discovered a room all under the ground, that was long 20 arms, high five, and wide three, with some projecting parts aside, where there were found statues, ashes, ornaments and Etruscan letters, of which I will show you copy at your pleasure, as to me showed and gave me the most scholar and similarly most human Pierro Vettori, most diligent investigator of the ancient things, together with the Etruscan alphabet that at the time was not outside».

Always in the first half of the fifteenth century, between 1541 and 1545, in a manuscript of the Dominican Santi Marmocchini of San Casciano Val di Pesa, the *Dialogo in defensione della lingua Toschana*, kept at the Biblioteca Nazionale of Florence,[10] it was replicated with greater ampleness and abundance of detail the same information about the sensational finding, brought back here in the transcription of the archaeologist Filippo Buonarroti (1661-1733):[11]

> *Directly in front to this [cistern] there is a small hill, where in the year of the Lord 1507, the day 29 of January at 18 hours, planting those [inhabitants] of Lando a vine, and making a hole with an iron rod in order to plant a grapevine, the rod fell in an ancient entombment of the Etruscans, and came out from the hole a stench of musty smell, and they found in the direction of the road a door, closed with limestone marble slabs, and the room was in cross. In its length, that it was 20 arms, there was one way three arms wide, where there was nothing, and the height was 5 arms. To the left hand there was a warehouse, wide, long and high 5 arms, where there were pots of earth, full of ashes of dead people of low class, and certain pots, where the bodies were burnt, and to the right part were buried the nobles, and there were there [...] an altar, the ornaments of a Queen, that is a silver mirror, in the shape of a clog of a donkey, a wide-toothed comb of silver, handles of silver, and in a vase of ash a cicada of gold, and four cicadas of gold, one for each side of the vase, a woman till the bust in alabaster, with a thread of gold diagonally across the shoulders, a vase of copper with the lid over in the shape of a brazier as for a barber, where there were cassettes full of rings. They found there precious stones, and much foliage of silver in quantity, that was sold in Siena, and I spoke to the goldsmith who bought it. I saw an interment where there was a carved woman, who had in one hand a bowl, [...] there was there the name of that one in Etruscan characters: and many stone and marble urns, with ash inside, were found there. It was vaulted without lime mortar, that is to say with large and heavily built slabs, that from one side to the other little by little one over the other approached to the middle, and here joined themselves [...].*

And then, the humanist Sigismondo Tizio (1458-1528), in his *Historiarum Senensium tomi X*, lingering on some Etruscan inscriptions coming from «urna atque sepulchra cum litteris», discovered inside of a circular hillock «apud Castellinam»,[12] transcribed its texts, analyzing also its ceramic objects, the tools and the feminine ornaments, that had been there recovered, subsequently by and large dispersed or stolen.[13] But

<hr>

bling of one line in equal parts (f. 39 *r*), to the use of compasses (f. 43 *v*) and to a hydraulic wheel: «an instrument that sent Lionardo to Bernardo Rucellai from France made there from a peasant from Dom Dassoli which here drawn can be seen» (f. 7 *v*). See Cfr. G. GAYE, *Carteggio inedito d'artisti*, Firenze, Molini, 1839-40; C. PEDRETTI, *Documenti e memorie…*, 1953, *op. cit.*; C. VECCE, *Leonardo*, 1998, *op. cit.*

[8]   See W. HELBIG, *Antica tomba a cupola scoperta presso Quinto Fiorentino*, «Bullettino dell'Instituto di Corrispondenza Archeologica», 1885; E. PETERSEN, *La Mula*, «Römische Mitteilungen», 19, 1904; G. CAPUTO, *La Montagnola di Quinto Fiorentino, l'orientalizzante e le tholoi dell'Arno*, «Bollettino d'arte», 47, 1962; F. NICOSIA, *Schedario topografico dell'archeologia dell'agro fiorentino e zone limitrofe*, «Studi Etruschi», 35, 1967.

[9]   See G. CIPRIANI, *Il mito etrusco nella Firenze repubblicana e medicea nei secoli XV e XVI*, «Ricerche storiche», 5, 1975; A. D'ALESSANDRO, *Il «Gello» di Pierfrancesco Giambullari*, in *La nascita della Toscana*, Convegno di Studi per il IV centenario della morte di Cosimo I de' Medici, Firenze, Olschki, 1980.

[10]   See Fondo Magliabechiano, classe XXVIII, cod. 20.

[11]   See PH. BONAROTI, *Ad monumenta etrusca operi Dempsteriano addita explicationes et conjecturae*, in THOMAE DEMPSTERI, *De Etruria regali Libri VII*, II, Florentiae, 1723. This work, written up by the Scot Thomas Dempster between 1616 and 1619 and published with an appendix of *Explicationes et conjecturae* only in 1723 by the Florentine printer Tartini, with dedication to the royal height of Cosimo III Great Duke of Etruria, made him to be considered the true initiator of the studies of Etruscology, since his investigation was based not only on the news reported in the literary texts, but also on the archaeological documents, outlining a new historical perspective of research.

[12]   «cinerary urns and sepulchres with letters» [...] «next to Castellina» (Tr. N.)

[13]   See P. PICCOLOMINI, *La vita e le opere di Sigismondo Tizio (1458-1528)*, Siena, 1903; G. BUONAMICI, *Rivista di epigrafia etrusca 1941-1942*, «Studi Etruschi», 17, 1943.

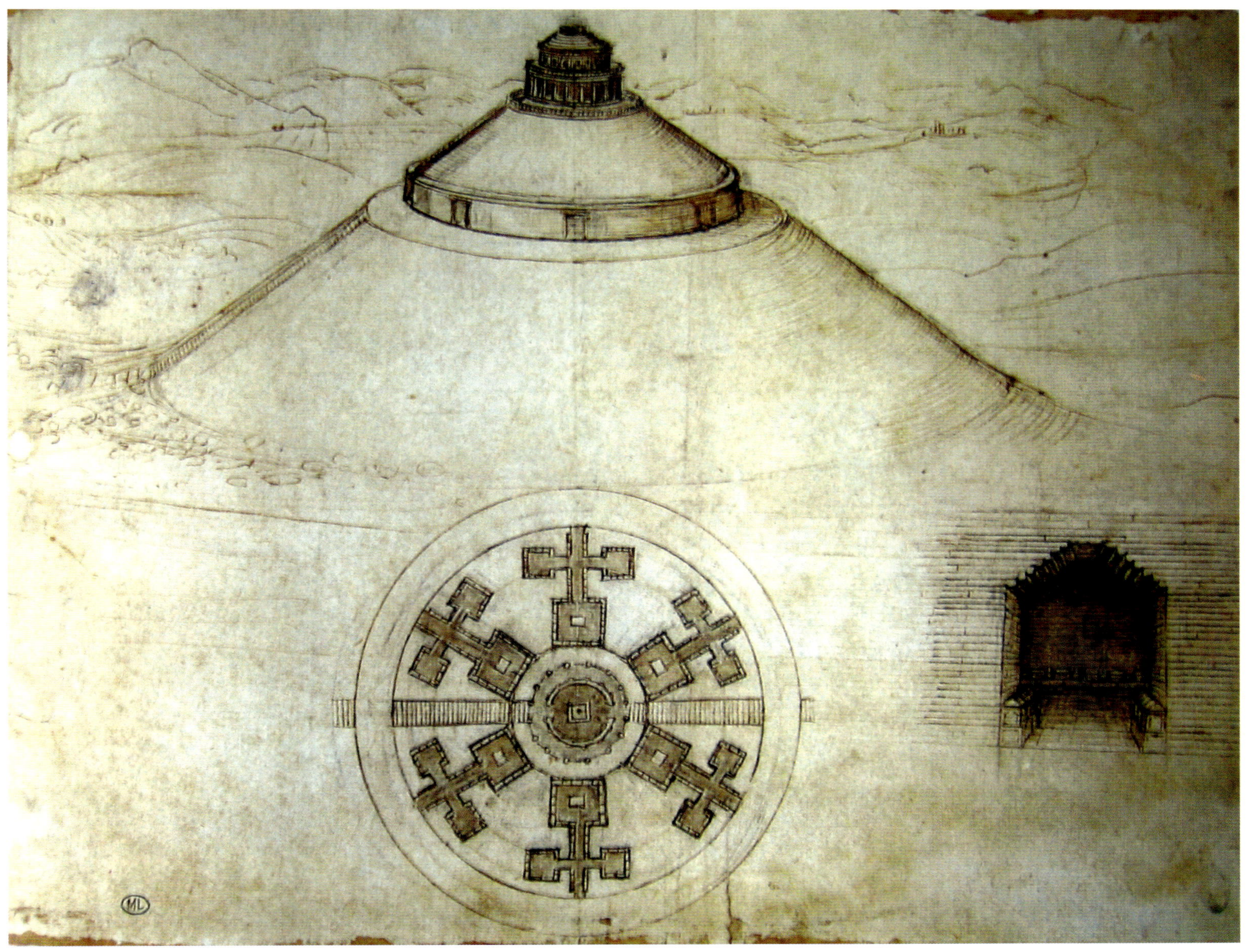

LEONARDO DA VINCI, *The Etruscan Mausoleum*, *c.* 1507. Pen and ink, watercolour and charcoal, 195 x 268 mm. Paris, Musée du Louvre, Département des Arts graphiques, inv. 2386

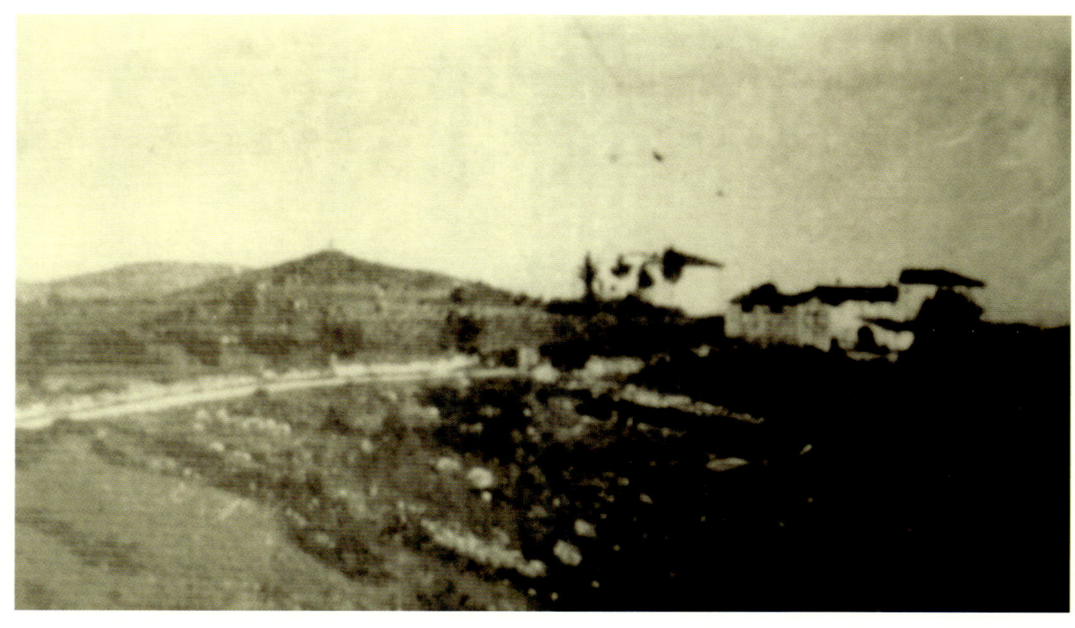

The tumulus of Montecalvario in a picture of the early 20th Century: view from West

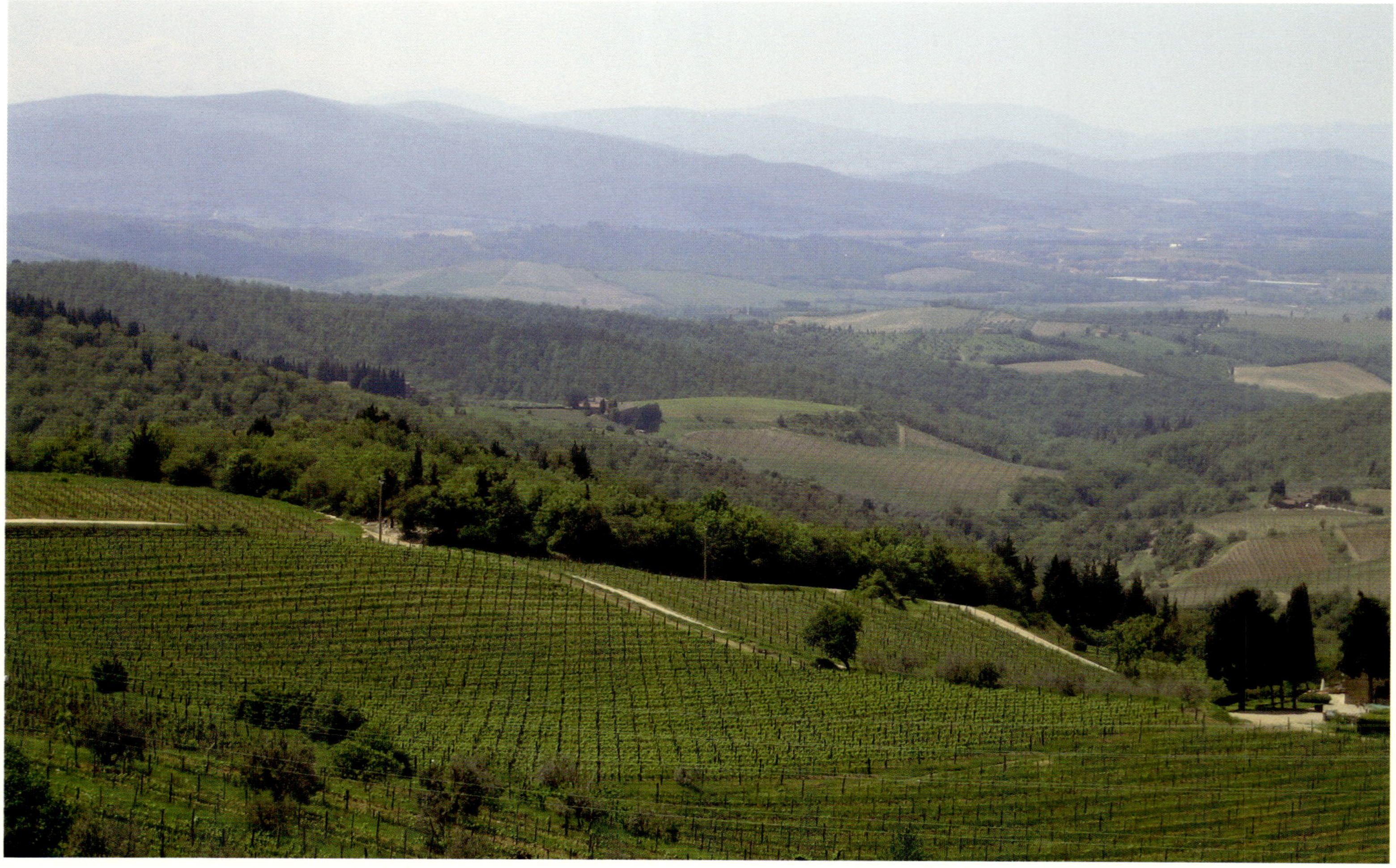

The landscape of the Chianti region as seen from Montecalvario, marked by the wavy sequence of its hilly profiles

the attention of the chronicles had above all lingered to illustrate the building technique employed in the construction of the hypogeum of Montecalvario, whose vault was made out of large blocks of limestone marble, in courses progressively jutting out until the top.

The plan of the imposing tumulus, that has a diameter of approximately 53 meters, comprised four underground tombs, with cover to false vault, oriented both in structures and in entrances almost according to the four cardinal points and preceded by an axial vestibule, on which there were set up on the side cells of adequate amplitude. The tombs to east and to west had an identical structure with three cells (two lesser lateral ones and a rectangular main room), which could be entered through a long *dromos*, while the tomb to north lacked the final room. In a cell of the south tomb was recovered a valuable and archaic head of a lion with jaws opened wide in serene stone (end of VII cent. b. C.), probably derived from the decoration of a jamb of a door, with a symbolic value of vigilance and defence of the sacred against any possible profanation (Luigi Pernier, 1916). If the material recovered in various tombs of the environs, since the sixteenth century, and described by the scholars has turned out to be attributable to a late-classic and Hellenistic age, the structural and decorative elements of the precious fragmentary burial equipment («iron sheets embossed with animals advancing and underlying embroidered lace, angular harpoons, fragments of rims of the wheels in wrought iron of a chariot, coverings of the wooden skeleton of the chariot in concave rod and tubular iron, bronze spiral with six turns, lance points in shape of leaves» etc…, Luigi A. Milani, 1905) and a sufficient amount of deteriorated material and of fragments recovered in this gigantic hypogeum, certainly of scarce market value, but of great technical and artistic interest, they have instead allowed to date these depositions to a late-orientalizing and archaic age, when new groups of nobles, emerging in the Etruscan society, between the VIII and the VII century b. C., flaunted power and wealth by constructing huge barrows, destined to be transformed in a monumental sanctuary for the deceased ones of the entire family.

Therefore the tomb of Castellina in Chianti and what is left of its funeral equipment, let us suppose that it belonged to a family of elevated social rank or even to a family of «principes», permitting to presume, because of the analogous archaeological situation, a tightened correlation between the imposing interment architecture of Montecalvario and the barrows of Sodo of Cortona and of Camucia (the «Melon»), aligned along precise guiding routes between the bottom of the valley and the zone at the foot of the hills and of the mounts near Cortona, where the Etruscan leading class of the VII and VI century b. C. was determined to assert its own ideology and culture, but also to emphasize its own political and economic power, derived from commerce and from a flourishing and agricultural production of great virtue, founded on the cultivation of grapevines and of olive trees: therefore huge tombs for a rich and cultured land aristocracy.[14]

The singular archaeological finding of 1507, that offered an interesting example of funeral architectural organization for the celebration of a powerful noble family, renewed in Leonardo the passion for the ancient things and for those structures with central plan, that could have «in themselves the figure of the world», in a cosmological vision, already present in the *Timaeus* (VII, 33 b) by Plato, being the Earth «a sphere equally distant in every its point from the centre to the extremities» and «the circular globe the most perfect of all the figures», then recalled in its meaning of absolute perfection also by Vitruvius in his *De Architectura*.

A sublime idea, therefore, that of the temple set up on a central space, that will be recovered and celebrated by Palladium in person, to be in the end considered among the most divine examples of the architecture of the Renaissance (Villa Almerico-Capra, «*La Rotonda*», Vicenza, 1550-51; Church of San Giorgio Maggiore, Venice, 1556-1610).[15]

For that reason, Leonardo, captured by the mysterious and poetic appeal of a disappeared civilization, went to Castellina, in order to examine with his own eyes the monument, that he reproduced up to minimum details in a drawing, inserting it in the immensity of a landscape, taken in aerial perspective to flight of bird and punctuated with cottages, that well recalls with high topographical definition the geographic

<hr>

[14] See D. MIRRI, *I procedimenti costruttivi dell'architettura a Cortona dall'origine della città fino ai nostri tempi*, Cortona, Stabilimento Tipografico Sociale, 1923; A. NEPPI MODONA, *Cortona etrusca e romana nella storia e nell'arte*, Firenze, 1925; L. PERNIER, *Tumulo con tomba monumentale al Sodo presso Cortona*, «Monumenti antichi dei Lincei», XXX, 1925; A. MINTO, *Cortona. Il secondo Melone del Sodo*, «Notizie degli scavi», VII, 1929; ID., *La Tanella Angori di Cortona. Problemi di architettura funeraria etrusca*, «Palladio», I, 1951; M. CRISTOFANI, *Dizionario della civiltà etrusca* (a cura di), Firenze, Giunti Martello, 1985; G. CAMPOREALE, *La cultura dei «principi»*, in *Civiltà degli etruschi*, a cura di M. Cristofani, Milano, Electa, 1985; P. BRUSCHETTI, *Cortona. Guida archeologica*, Roma, Vision, 1985; P. BRUSCHETTI, P. ZAMARCHI GRASSI, *Cortona etrusca. Esempi di architettura funeraria*, Cortona, Calosci, 1999; P. ZAMARCHI GRASSI, *La Cortona dei Principes* (a cura di), Cortona, Calosci, 1992; ID., *Un edificio per il culto funerario. Nuovi dati sul tumulo II del Sodo a Cortona*, «Rivista di Archeologia», 22, I, 1999.

[15] See A. PALLADIO, *Quattro libri dell'architettura. Ne' quali, dopo un breve trattato de' cinque ordini, et di quelli avvertimenti, che sono più necessarij nel fabricare; si tratta delle case private, delle Vie, de i Ponti, delle Piazze, de i Xisti, et de i Tempij. Con privilegi*, In Venetia, Appresso Dominico de' Franceschi, 1570. The Church of San Giorgio Maggiore, although it has a great longitudinal extension, for anyone who is at the crossing of the central nave with the transept, he cannot but to perceive to be not in a basilica, but in a building with central plan. The Venetian Daniele Barbaro, in his comment to *I dieci libri dell'Architettura di Vitruvio tradotti e commentati* (Venezia, 1556), will make use of the collaboration of Palladium (1508-1580), transforming his comment in an authentic encyclopaedia, since the inheritance of the ancient world and the representation of the classic architecture had become so important.

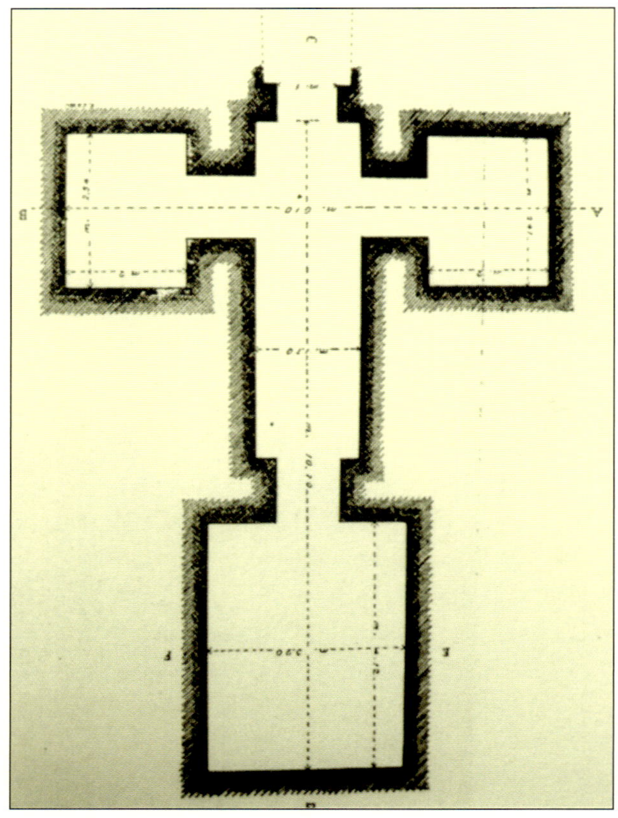

Plan of the hypogeum of Montecalvario. Castellina in Chianti

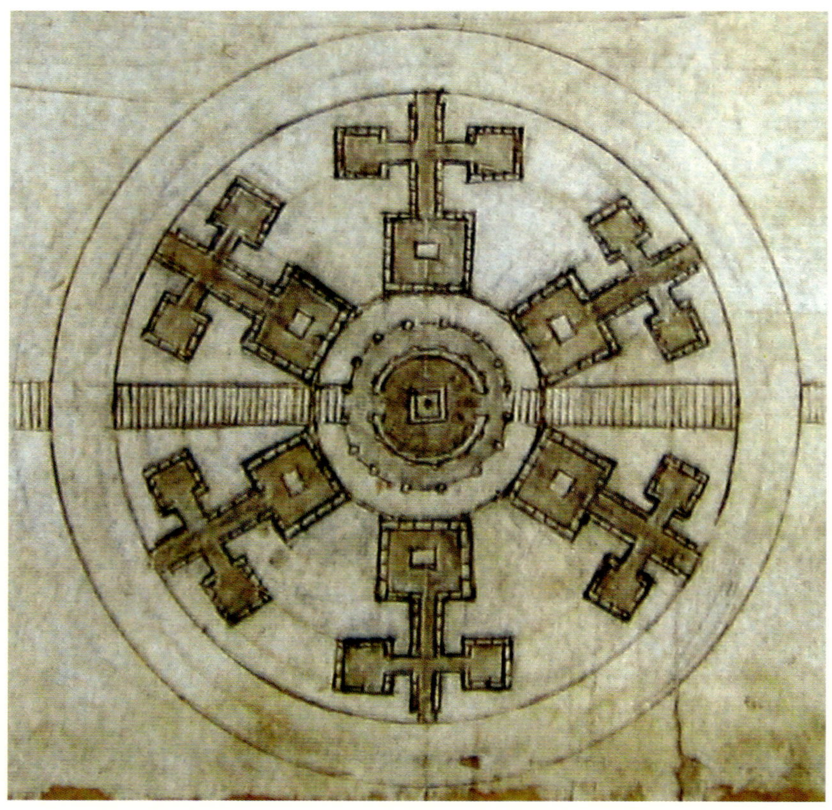

Leonardo da Vinci, *Planimetry of the Mausoleum, c.* 1507. Pen and ink, watercolour and charcoal, Paris, Musée du Louvre, Département des Arts graphiques, inv. 2386. Particular

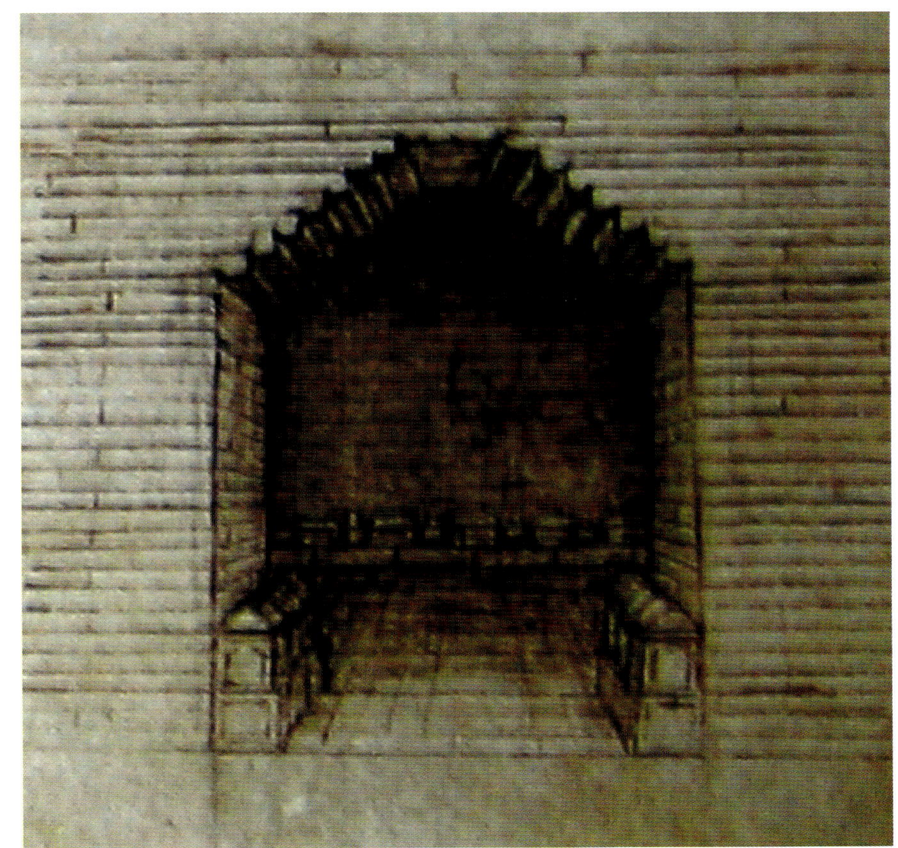

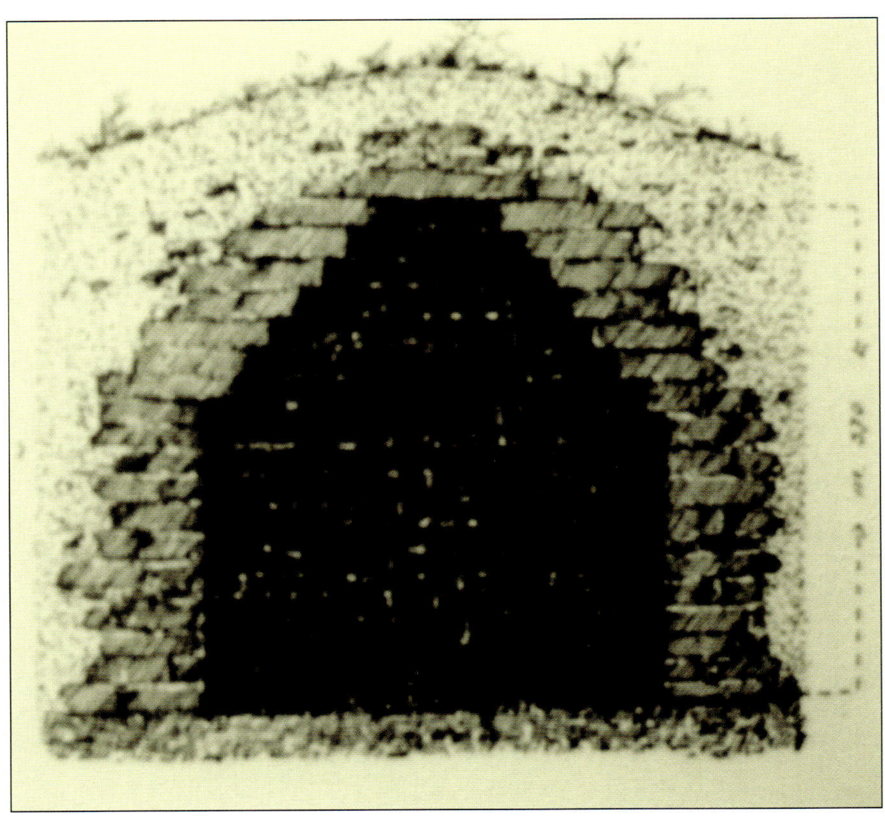

Analogy between the transversal section of the entrance door of one of the corridors sketched by Leonardo and that of the tumulus of Montecalvario

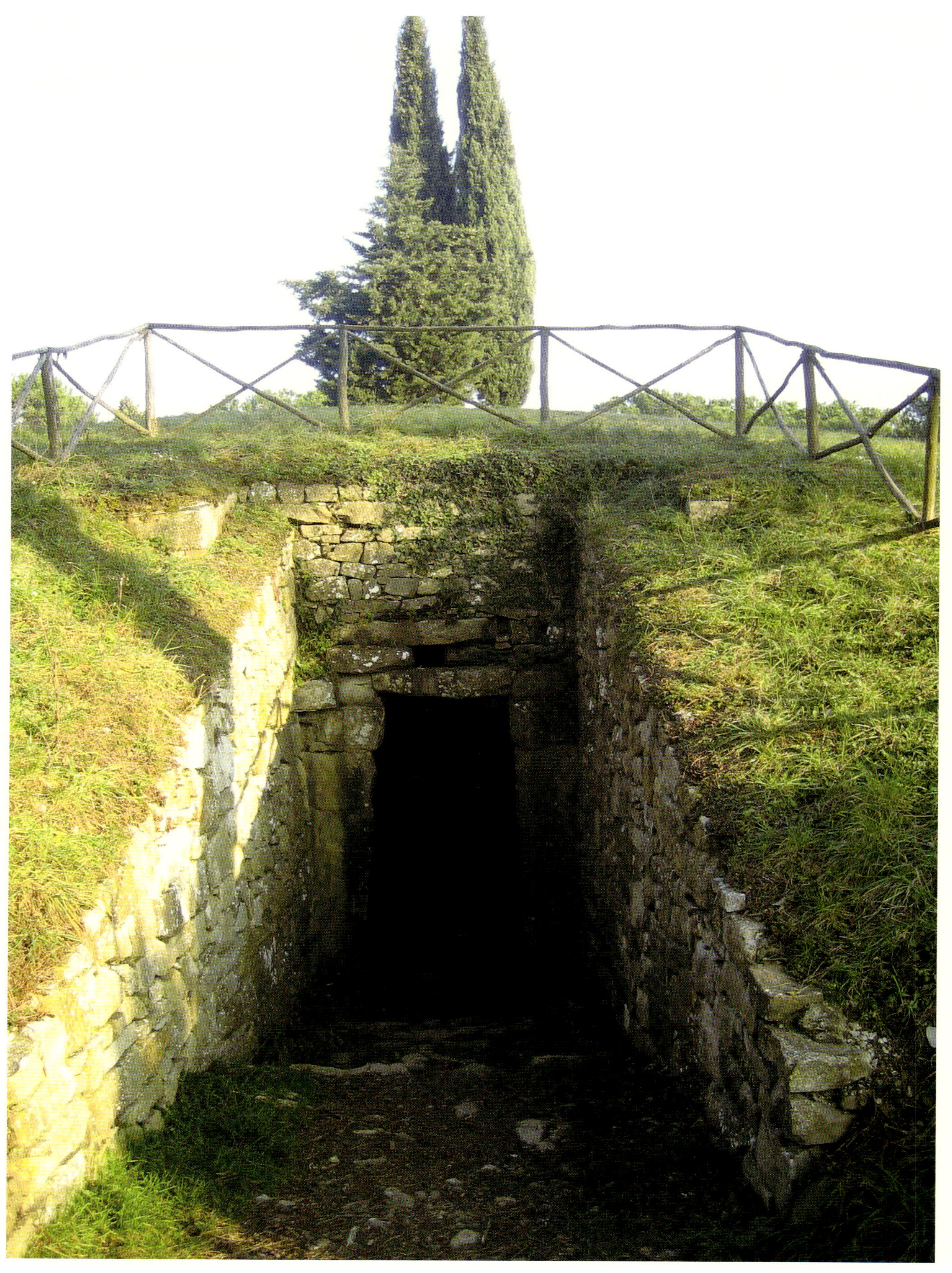

Hypogeum of Montecalvario. External and internal view of the western tomb. Castellina in Chianti

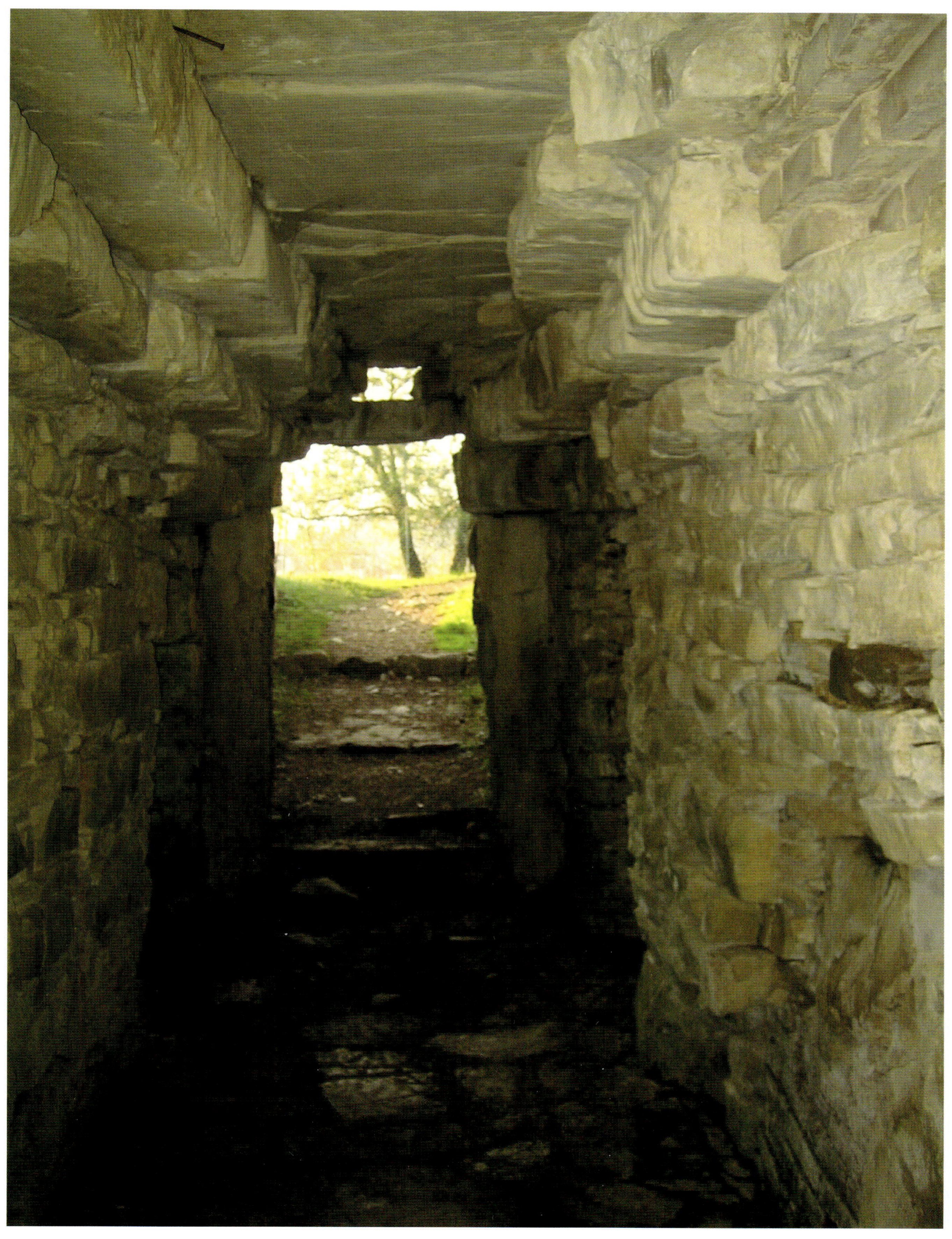

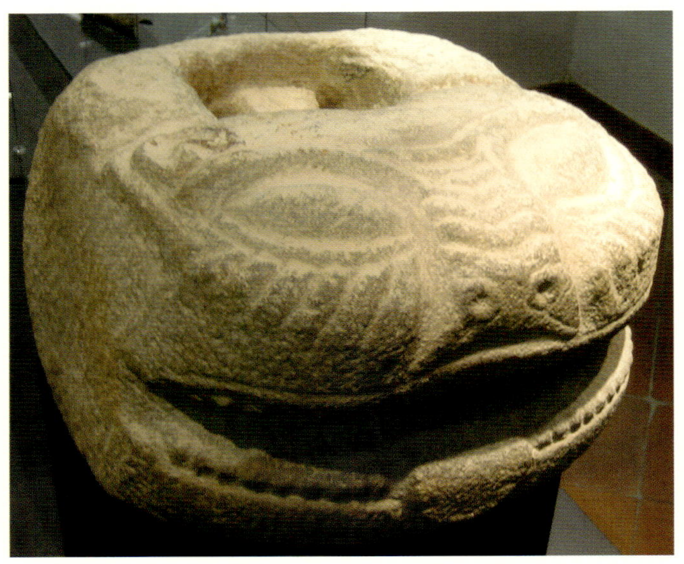

Lion-shaped head made in serene stone (VII cent. B. C.), Museo Archeologico del Chianti Senese. Castellina in Chianti

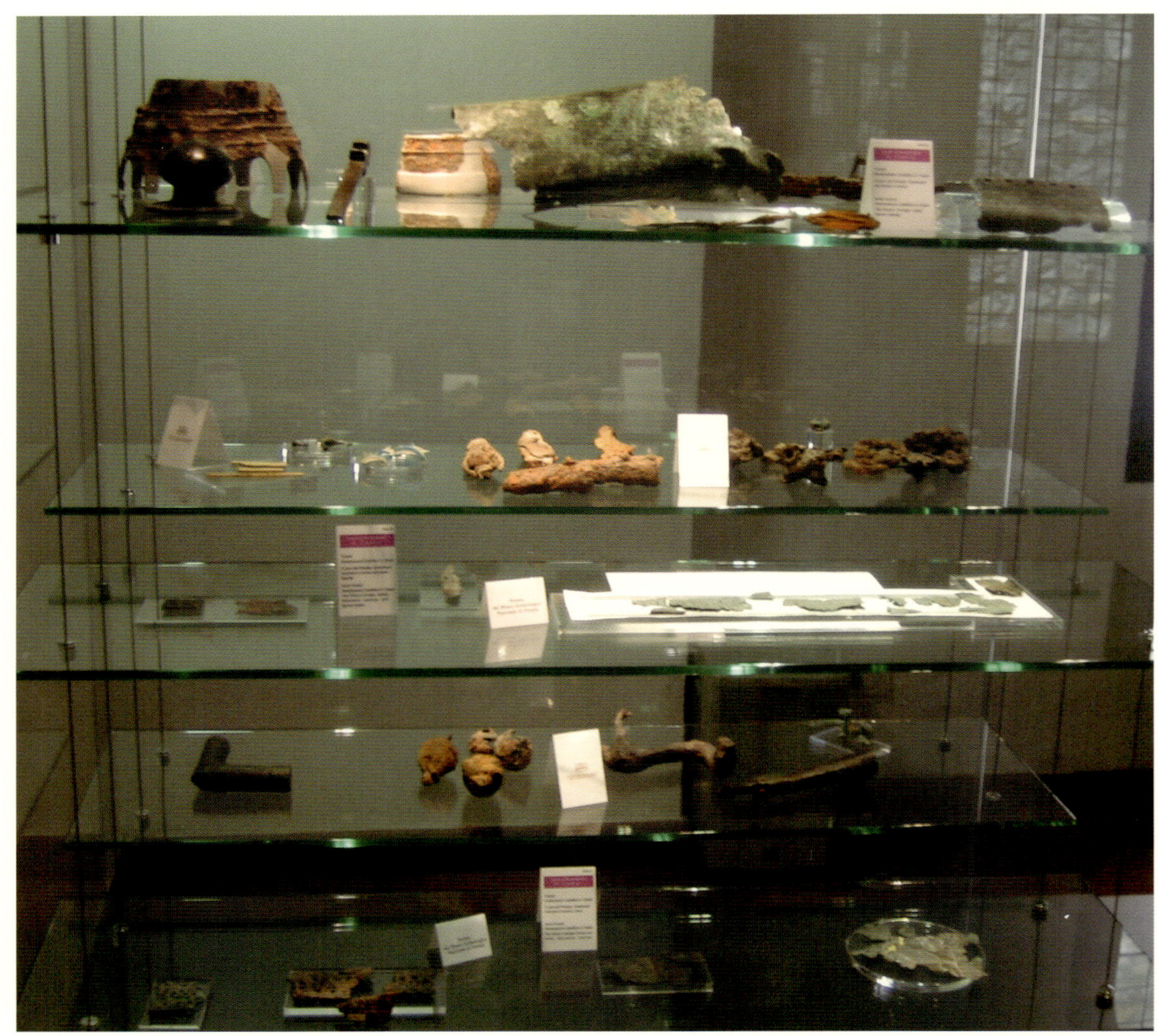

*Remains from the tumulus of Montecalvario.*Castellina in Chianti, Museo Archeologico del Chianti Senese.

environment of the Mounts of the Chianti, with the profiles of the hills that chase each other and overlap on the horizon in an animated and undulated way, similar to those realized, around 1503, along the valley of the Arno (Cod. of Madrid, ff. 17 *r*; 17 *v*; 19 *r*, 20 *v*).[16]

The drawing to pen and ink, watercolour and charcoal, currently kept at the department of Graphical Arts of the Musée du Louvre (inv. n. 2386), at the half of the nineteenth century it was property of the collector Giuseppe Vallardi (1794-1863),[17] which illustrated its content like the «project of a colossal burial monument of jonic order that raises over an artificial hill of conical shape, which is approached through lateral stairs; the back of the country is mountainous with a small lake». And certainly the similarities between the drawing and the planimetry of the tomb, as well as the sections of the hypogean rooms and the shape itself of the tumulus are amazing, so much to confirm the hypothesis that Leonardo has truly drawn from here the inspiration for the ideal construction of his «mausoleum», undoubted expression of an evident learning. But this building, for an innumerable series of elements that recall the Etruscan funeral architecture, it is also the result of a meditated project that has produced an original and complex architectural vision. In Leonardo, the naturalistic and symbolic elements interpenetrate dynamically, nearly to outline a constant in his artistic production, like the plain observation of an archaeological data, in the spreading passion for the ancient things of that time, by itself apparently insignificant, but that could generate in his fervent mind, the creation of new shapes, that he submitted, in a continuous process of research, to experimental reconsideration and to a kinetic and spatial variation. The example of the ancients, could therefore supply the prompt for new inventions and in considering them as good teachers, Leonardo sustained on the theoretical plan that their imitation, faced not as a simple erudite game, was unavoidable for whichever modern artist (CA, f. 147 *rb* [399 *r*]), since such adhesion would have favoured also a careful investigation on Nature. And, how much had been influential in him the study of the ancient things will be remembered, around 1560, also in the letter sent from Guglielmo Della Porta to Bartolomeo Ammannati: «Leonardo da Vinci was used to say, being he in Milan, that Rome is the true teacher of that art, that goes under the name of drawing».[18]

Therefore, the large Etruscan hill tumulus of Montecalvario could send back, for the subtle correspondences and analogies that there were in the heart of the Renaissance between what is nature and artifice, also to the architectures with cylindrical structure of the classic period, that Leonardo, at the beginning of the sixteenth century, after having visited Villa Adriana at Tivoli (CA, f. 227 *va* [618 *v*]), could have admired in Rome, like the *Temple of Vesta* (III cent. b. C.), the *Mausoleum of Augustus* (27 b. C), the *Pantheon* (118-128 a. C.) with the same fascination with which Bramante, revisiting the ancient things, well documented in the pamphlet *Antiquarie prospetiche romane* composed for a «perspective painter from Milan» (*c.* 1500), had translated their shapes, with poetic interpenetration between architecture and atmosphere, in the admirable *Pavilion of Saint Peter in Montorio* (1503).[19]

This *Pavilion* with ring-like colonnade and cylindrical structure, that rose, according to the tradition, where Saint Peter had been crucified, is currently situated in a courtyard and circumscribed in an artificial way by anonymous walls, quite the reverse to what planned in his first idea by Bramante that, adhering to the canons of «renovatio» of the treatise by

---

[16]   The attribution of the drawing to Leonardo and the approach of its content to the Etruscan barrows was carried out for the first time by J. P. RICHTER, that found an analogy with the structure of the famous tomb Regolini Galassi of Cerveteri (650 b. C.). But the recall to the tomb of Cerveteri turned out to be of little pertinence, since it had been discovered only in 1836. Also A. CHASTEL, not convinced of the leonardian autography of the drawing, and more inclined to attribute it to Francesco di Giorgio, returned on the Etruscan subject of the content, observing that only the tomb of the Mula (province of Florence) could be taken into consideration, since it was the only tomb discovered between 1481 and 1494 and of which Leonardo could at least be informed. But also in this case the chronological reference did not corroborate the suggested hypothesis, because the inner structure of the tomb was to tholos and therefore architecturally different from the one of the drawing. It was only with L. H. HEYDENREICH that his autography was recognized and the «plan» was included between the leonardian drawings related to his interest for architecture. An interpretation that was subsequently resumed and supported also by C. PEDRETTI and D. ARASSE. See J. P. RICHTER, *The Literary Work of Leonardo da Vinci…*, 1977, *op. cit.*; C. LAURETI, *Progetto pel monumento a Dante Alighieri in Roma da un disegno di Leonardo da Vinci,* Venezia, Norsa, 1911; A. CHASTEL, *Arte e umanesimo a Firenze…*, [Paris, 1959], 1964, *op. cit.*; HEYDENREICH L. H., *Leonardo architetto*, «Lettura Vinciana», II, Firenze, Giunti Barbèra, 1962; PEDRETTI C., *A Chronology of Leonardo da Vinci's…*, 1962, *op. cit.*; ID., *Leonardo architetto*, 1978, *op. cit.*; ID., *Leonardo: dalla pianta centrale allo spazio sferico*, 2002, *op. cit.*; S. VALTIERI, *Il 'revival' etrusco nel Rinascimento toscano*, «L'architettura», 17, 1971; D. ARASSE, *Léonard de Vinci. Le rytme du monde*, Paris, Hazan, 1997.

[17]   See G. VALLARDI, *Disegni di Leonardo da Vinci posseduti da G. Vallardi*, Milano, Vallardi, 1855.

[18]   See C. PEDRETTI, *'Le Magne opere Romane'*, in *Leonardo e il leonardismo a Napoli e a Roma*, a cura di A. Vezzosi, Firenze, Giunti Barbèra, 1983; B. M. PATTISON, *A Letter from Guglielmo Della Porta to Bartolommeo Ammannati*, Los Angeles, University of California, 1981; P. C. MARANI, *The 'Hammer Lecture' (1994): Tivoli, Hadrian and Antinoüs. New Evidence of Leonardo's Relation to the Antique*, «Journal of Leonardo Studies & Bibliography of Vinciana», VIII, Firenze, Giunti, 1995.

[19]   In the letter to the Ammannati, with reference to the relationship between Bramante and the ancient things, Guglielmo Della Porta reported: «Bramante the architect asserted that to all those who come to Rome already masters in this profession, it was necessary that they undressed themselves in the way of the snakes of all that they had elsewhere learned, and that he in person demonstrated it with the example of himself, saying that before having seen this city, he really believed to be a painter and an excellent Architect, but that after he had frequented it for many years, he noticed his error, which was the cause, that having he commenced to draw a great part of the ancient buildings of Rome, of Tivoli, of Praeneste, and of many other places, studying, noticing and learning some new thing every day, he opened the way to the ancient good and regulated Architecture».

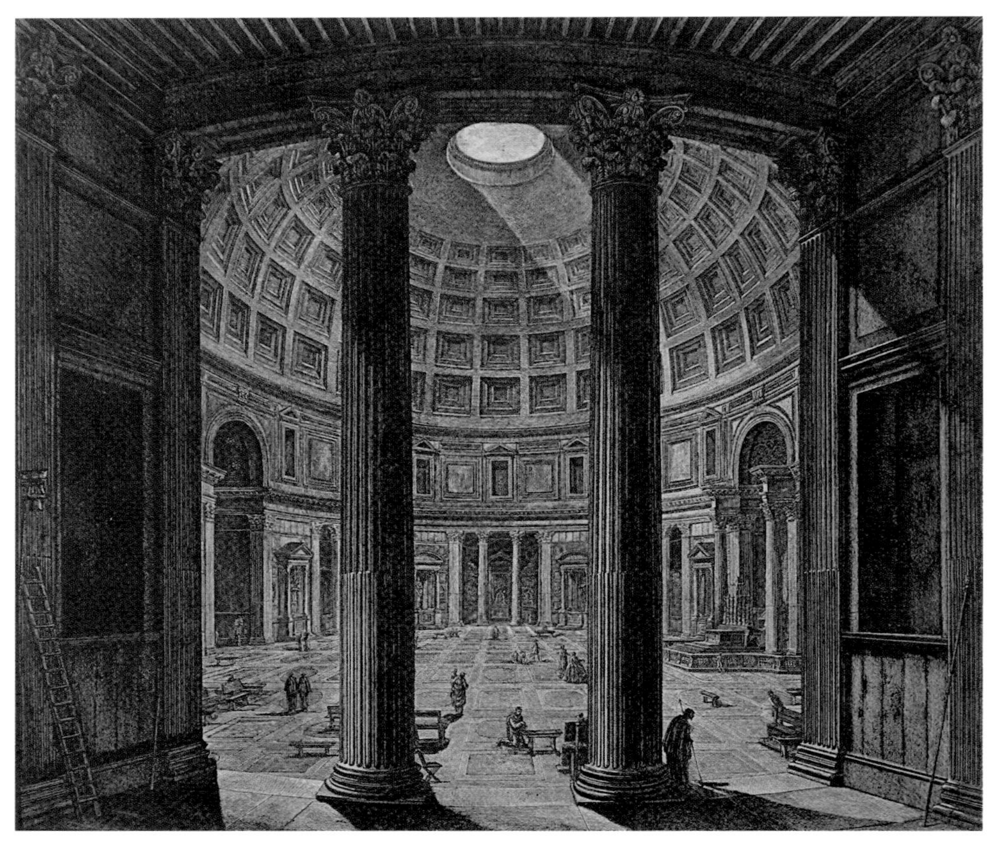

Giovan Battista Piranesi, *Internal view of the Pantheon*, in «Vedute di Roma», 1748-75

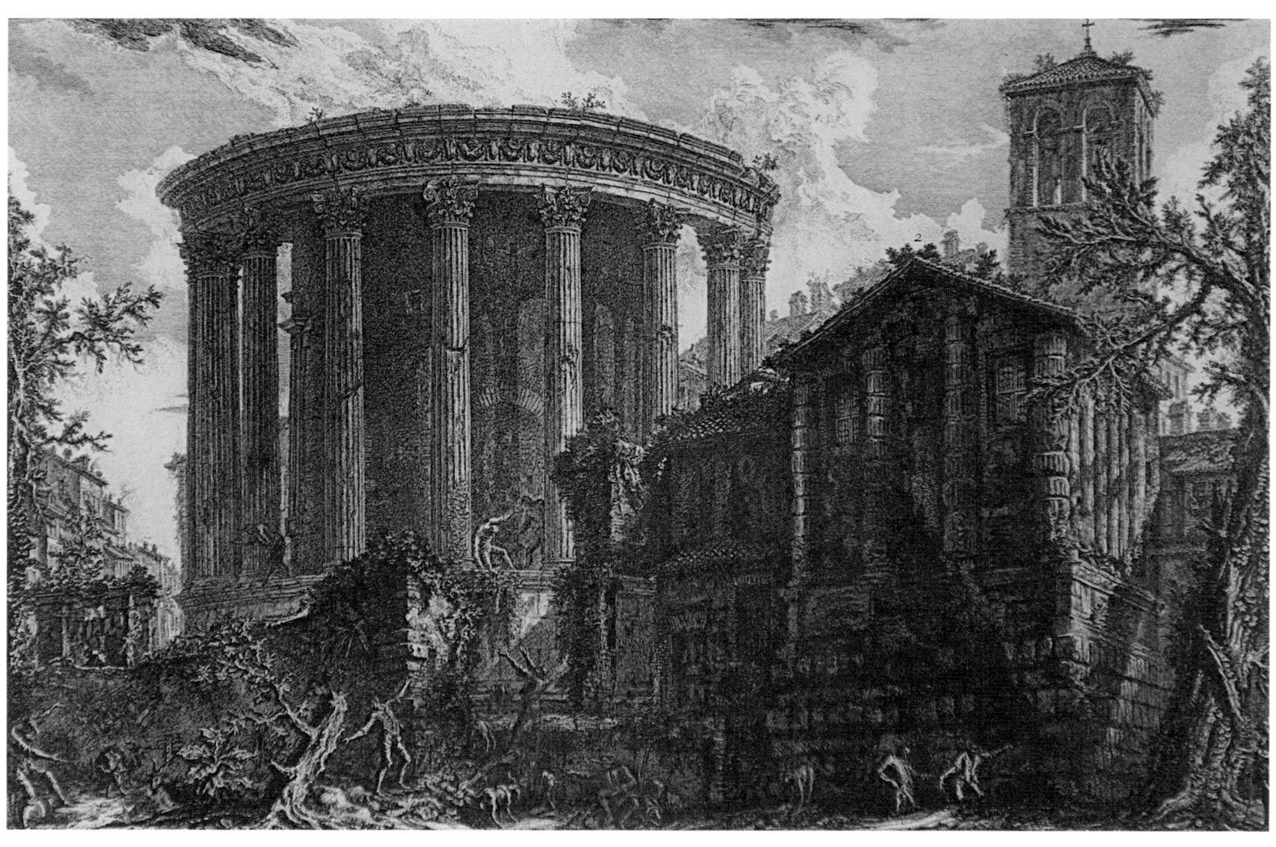

Giovan Battista Piranesi, *View of the Temple of the Sybil in Tivoli*, in «Vedute di Roma», 1748-75

Leon Battista Alberti (*De Re Aedificatoria*, 1452),[20] exemplified on the classic one by Vitruvius, but surpassed in the rigid technicality and widened with a vast knowledge of the art of constructing and the ideal of beauty of the ancient world, planned its inclusion in a courtyard with a circular porch and a squared plan, in a play of convergences between closed and empty spaces rotating around it. This vision, that will constitute a paradigmatic model and a principle of beauty, received in the lexicon of the architecture of Renaissance, is already present in the drawing of the *Vitruvian Man* by Leonardo (Venice, Gallerie dell'Accademia, n. 228), where the circle and the square, beyond to the metaphoric and esoteric value of «universal structure», will acquire volume and will be changed into a plastic and structural element right with Bramante, after the convergence of ideas and experiences between the two artists, connected to their collaboration during the Milan stay at the court of the Moor.

Also in Raphael, the ideal positioning of a temple, with sixteen sides and therefore next to a circular shape, was proposed in the centre of a public square (*Nuptials of the Virgin*, 1504. Milan, Pinacoteca di Brera), with chequered paving and towards which we converge with geometric exactness, commending us to a perspective, that unveils beyond the building an atmospheric and landscape opening, distant from the centrality of men.

In Leonardo on the contrary we take part in an architectural operation supported by the opposite philosophical conception, that one of «an opened architecture, where the wall does not have to be but a development of spaces» to pass by and to live,[21] since every building, church or palace, plays a part «in the rhythm of nature, following and expressing its laws».[22] The mausoleum in fact is included inside the naturalistic component, where the artist, developing the Etruscan monumental invention, sets up on a highest artificial hill with the shape of a truncated cone, because interrupted to two thirds by a terrace, the base of the building with the wall of containment, split up by the entrance doors of the corridors (*dromos*) of the six interment rooms, replied according to the model of the Etruscan tomb of Montecalvario, to which the same description of the entrance door sends back, made in detail on its right side. Along the perimeter of the walls of the cells it is indicated the occurrence of numerous cinerary urns, an archaeological data documented by all the sources of the period, that in the review of the finds describe also urns with a lid with double slope. Then, along the flanks of the second hill formation with truncated cone shape, Leonardo draws two staircases of admittance to the small temple, placed in natural continuity on the top and characterized by a central plan, with peristyle and a hemispheric cupola in steps and with oculus, that recall with great immediacy the architectural structure of the *Pantheon*, able to represent in itself the symbolic perfection of the celestial vault and of the creation. This type of architecture with central plan, geometrically well coordinated, but mobile both in the space and in the environment, in which its inclusion was planned, would have been for certain aspects renewed by Leonardo as main body, shortly after (1508-10), also in the studies for the grandiose equestrian statue in honour of marshal Gian Giacomo Trivulzio, whose placing had been considered at the entrance of the basilica of San Nazaro in Milan. Leonardo, for the base of the equestrian statue, beyond having devised its aspect similar to a triumphal arc (Windsor, RL 12355), had planned there a high stand in marble with a circular structure supported by columns, an echo of the *Pavilion* by Bramante and of the Roman *Temple of the Sibyl* of «old Tivoli», as the sketch of Windsor, RL 12353, indeed reveals.

---

[20]   The «editio princeps» of the *De Re Aedificatoria* was realized for will of Lorenzo the Magnificent, in 1486. Since that date, the treatise would have met an extraordinary fortune. We must in addition remember that the architectural plans of Alberti for *San Sebastiano* (1460-70) and *Sant'Andrea* (1470) in Mantua, subsequently realized by the Tuscan Luca Fancelli (1430-1495), turn out to be among the first examples of central plant churches of the Renaissance.

[21]   See D. ARASSE, *Léonard de Vinci. Le rythme du monde*, 1997, *op. cit.*

[22]   See E. GARIN, *La città in Leonardo*, «Lettura Vinciana», XI, Firenze, Giunti Barbèra, 1972.

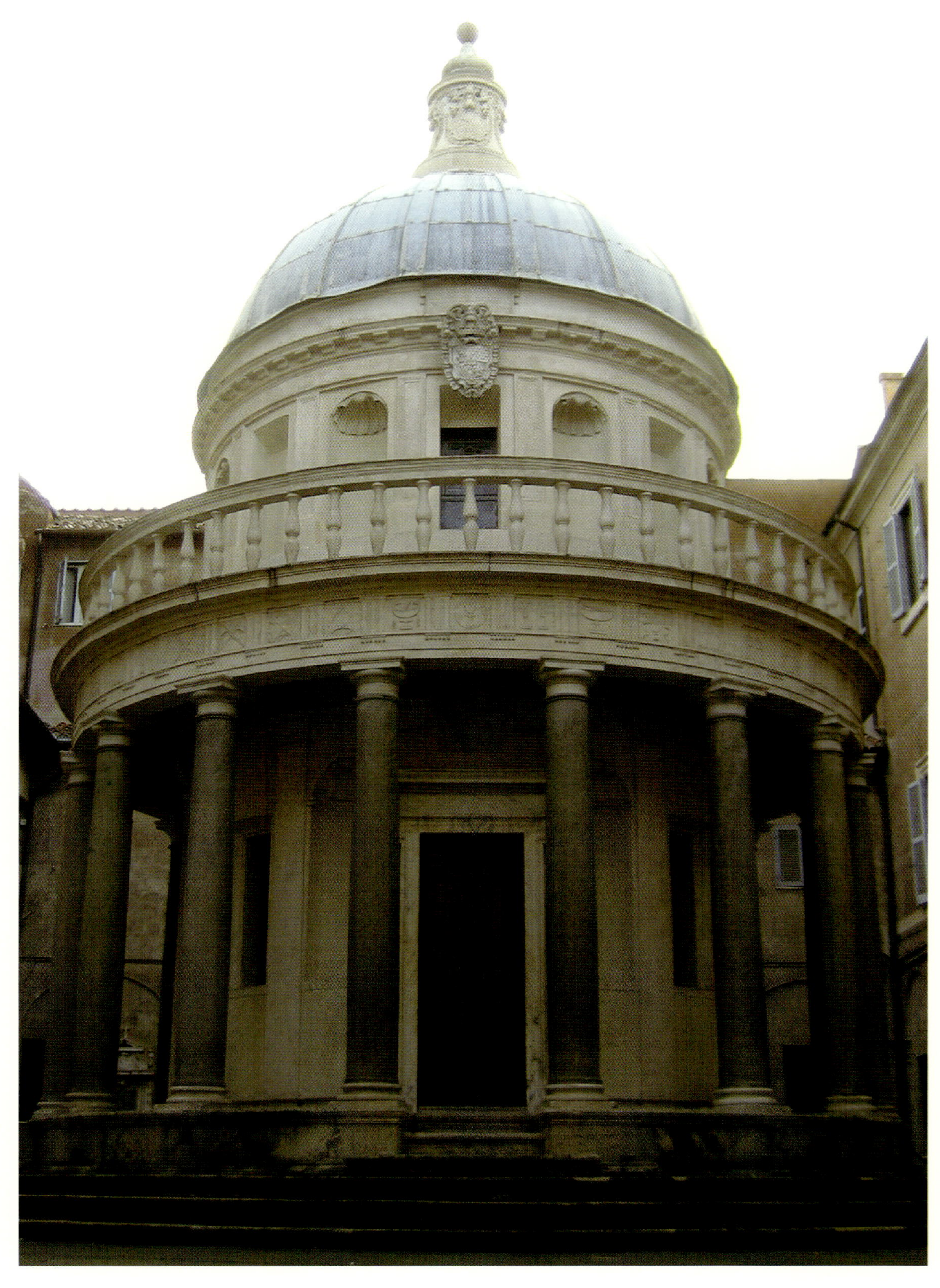

Donato Bramante, *Tempietto of Saint Peter in Montorio*, 1503. Rome, Church of Saint Peter in Montorio

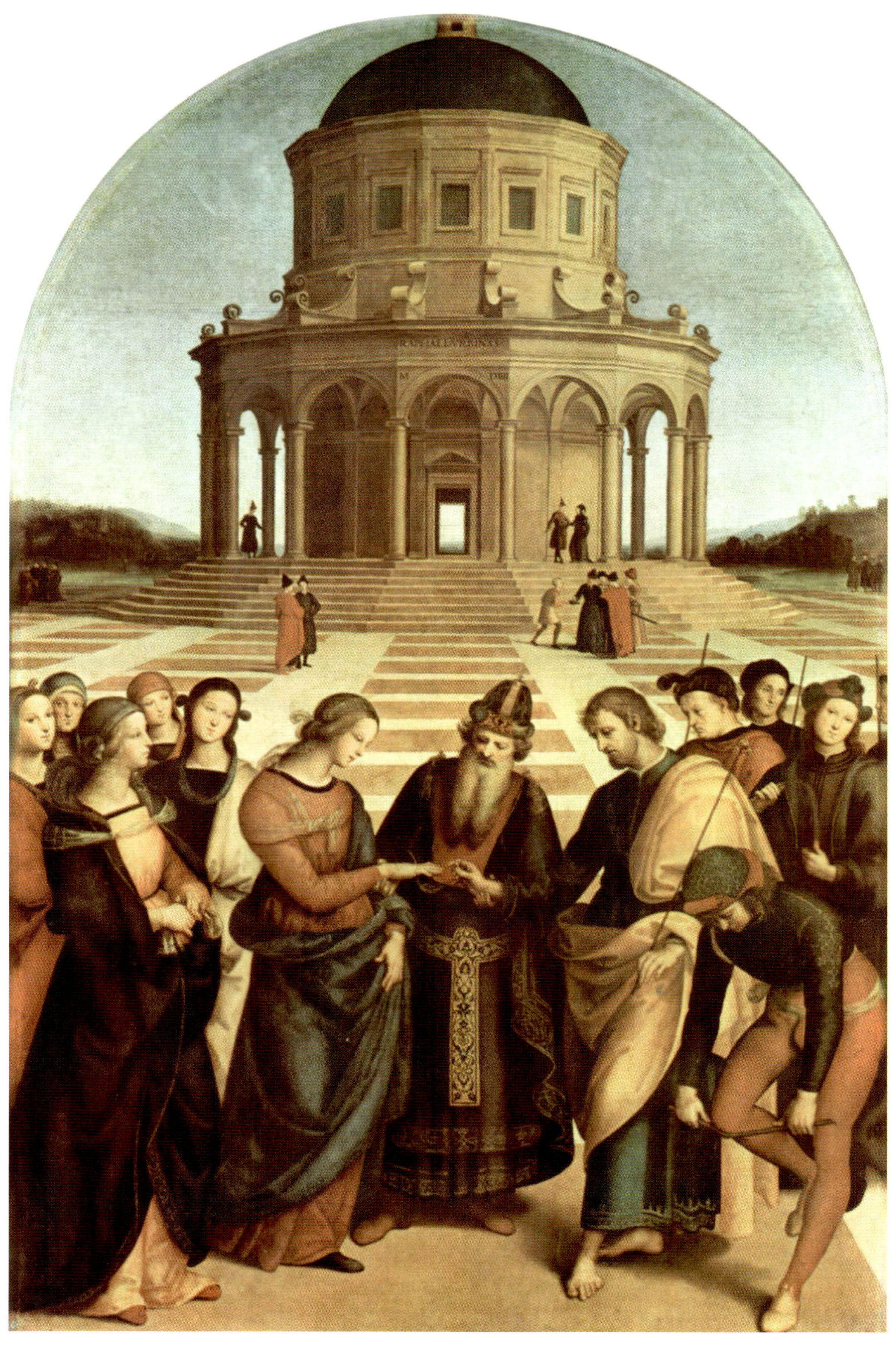

RAPHAEL, *The marriage of the Virgin*, 1504. Oil on table, 1,70 x 1,17 m. Milan, Pinacoteca di Brera

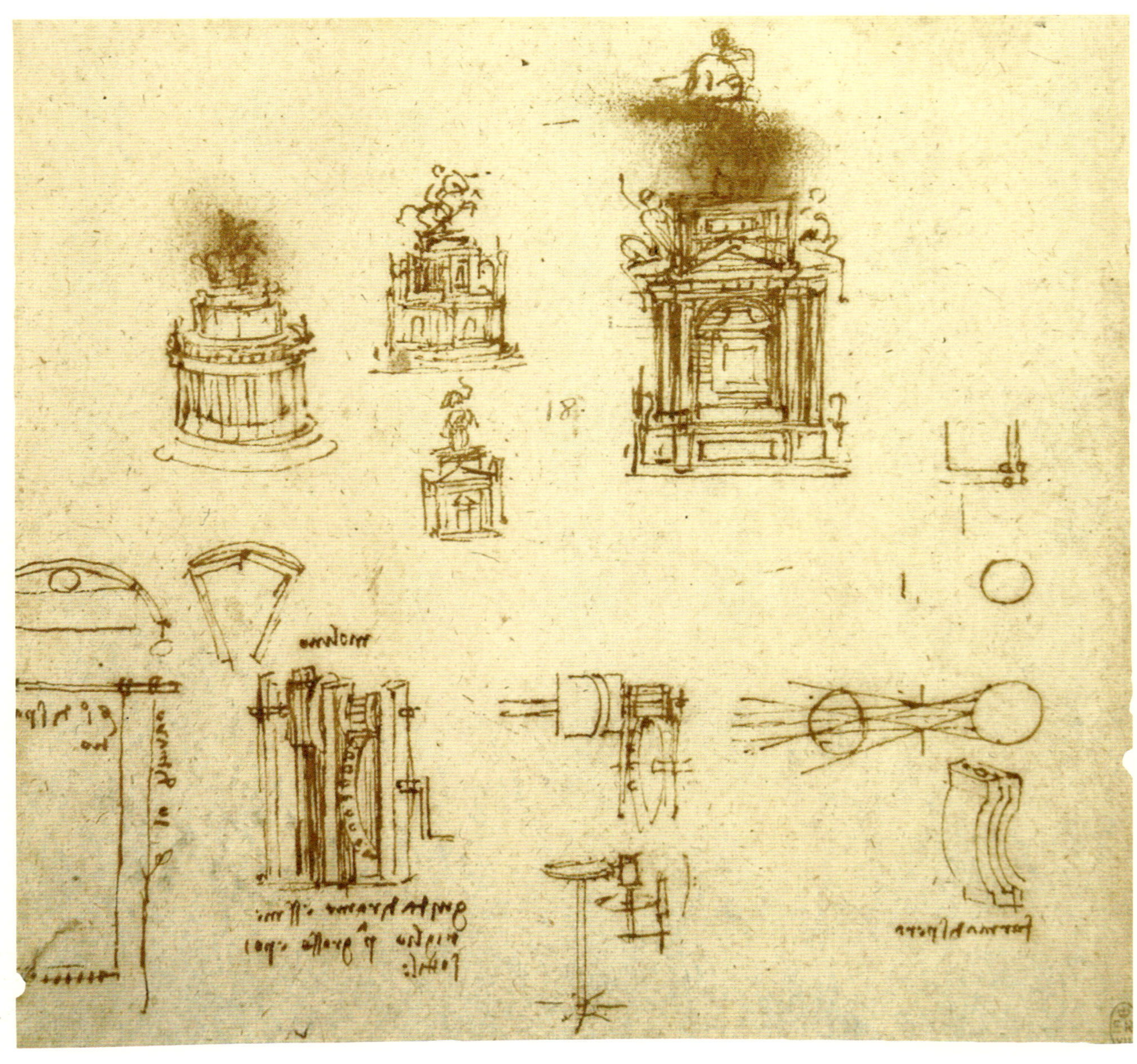

Leonardo da Vinci, *Sketches for the monument of Gian Giacomo Trivulzio, c.* 1508–10. Pen and ink, 278 x 196 mm. Windsor, RL 12353

Leonardo and Perugino
on the shores of the Lake Trasimeno

T HE RHYMES of a triplet of the *Cronica rimata* (*c.* 1488), composed by Giovanni Santi, father of Raphael, and meant to evoke his encounter with the artists of Florence, so declaimed on Leonardo and Pietro Perugino: «Two young men of the same age and of the same love / Leonardo da Vinci and the Perusino / Pier of the Pieve divine painter». It was the first historical acknowledgment attributed to the two great protagonists of the painting of the Renaissance, that Santi had met when, already enrolled in the company of San Luca (1472), they exercised their collaboration and their apprenticeship in the workshop of Andrea del Verrocchio, at the corner between Via Ghibellina and Via dei Macci.[1]
The creative understanding between these two exceptional contemporary young people is offered to us since the realization in the workshop of Verrocchio, where there was a systematic operation in a concur of collaboration between many artists, of the splendid *Virgin with the Child and Angels* (London, National Gallery).[2] If the grace and the softness of the faces recall here the Perugino art, «which was liked so much at his time, that many came of France, of Spain, of Alemannia and other provinces in order to study it» (Vasari,

1568), the precise botanical definition of the lily, analogous to the one of Gabriel in the *Annunciation* (Florence, Galleria degli Uffizi) and the geologic rendering of the cliff, much near to the one defined in the first autograph *Landscape* of 1473 (Florence, Uffizi), undoubtedly seem to prove the direct participation of Leonardo, that gives immediately a demonstration of his deep passion and knowledge of the natural world.[3]
Perugino, like Botticelli, had had the occasion to admire, in the experimentations of the workshop, the extraordinary graphical mastery of Leonardo, those bundles of lines curved «fan-shaped», those outlines in a zigzag, that in their hatching succeeded to evoke the whisper of trees and to confer volumetric consistency to figures, the lines in semicircle («a line that goes around the limbs of which the human beauty is generated», *Libro di Pittura, cap.* 29), appropriate to produce the double effect of relief and of shading. Those effects produced by the game of light and shadow that considered as necessary the curving of their shapes, for their continuous overlapping as in the uninterrupted flow of a wavy motion («the greater or smaller dusks of shadows are generated in the more curved parts of the limbs, and the less dark will be found in the broader parts», *Libro di Pittura,* f. 192 *v, cap.* 648). The singular importance attributed to the outline of a figure, by the employment of a line that curves, had been illustrated also by Pliny (*Naturalis historia,* XXXV, X), in celebrating the pictorial technique of Parrasius:

> *[…] To paint a figure in relief is already, without any doubt, a remarkable result, although there are many up to now who have made it. They are but a few those who have managed to find a way to*

[1] See F. CANUTI, *Il Perugino*, 2 voll., Siena, La Diana, 1931; E. CAMESASCA, *Tutta la pittura del Perugino*, Milano, Rizzoli, 1959; P. SCARPELLINI, *Perugino. L'opera completa*, Milano, Electa, 1984; J. M. WOOD, *The early paintings of Perugino*, University of Virginia, Ann Arbor, 1985; B. TOSCANO, *Il Trasimeno scoperto dal Perugino*, in *Trasimeno Lago d'arte, paesaggio dipinto e paesaggio reale* (a cura di A. Mariotti, B. Bernardi), Torino, Seat, 1994; A. NATALI, *Perugino, Rosso, Pontormo, Pagani. Quattro restauri agli Uffizi*, «Gli Uffizi. Studi e Ricerche», 25, 1995; V. GARIBALDI, *Gli affreschi del Cambio a Perugia. Un Perugino in Collegio*, «Art Dossier», 101, Firenze, Giunti, 1995; ID., *Perugino. Catalogo completo*, Firenze, Octavo, 1999; ID., *Perugino*, «Art Dossier», 197, Firenze, Giunti, 2004; R. H. VON GAERTRINGEN, *L'uso del cartone nell'opera di Perugino*, in *Perugino il divin pittore*, a cura di V. Garibaldi e F. F. Mancini, Cinisello Balsamo, Silvana Editoriale, 2004; T. MOZZATI, *Produzioni in serie, derivazioni e modelli: Perugino e la bottega di Andrea del Verrocchio*, in *Perugino il divin pittore*, a cura di V. Garibaldi e F. F. Mancini, Cinisello Balsamo, Silvana Editoriale, 2004.
[2] See P. C. MARANI, *Leonardo. Una carriera di pittore*, Milano, Motta, 1999.

[3] See D. A. BROWN, *Leonardo da Vinci. Origini di un Genio*, Milano, Rizzoli, 1999.

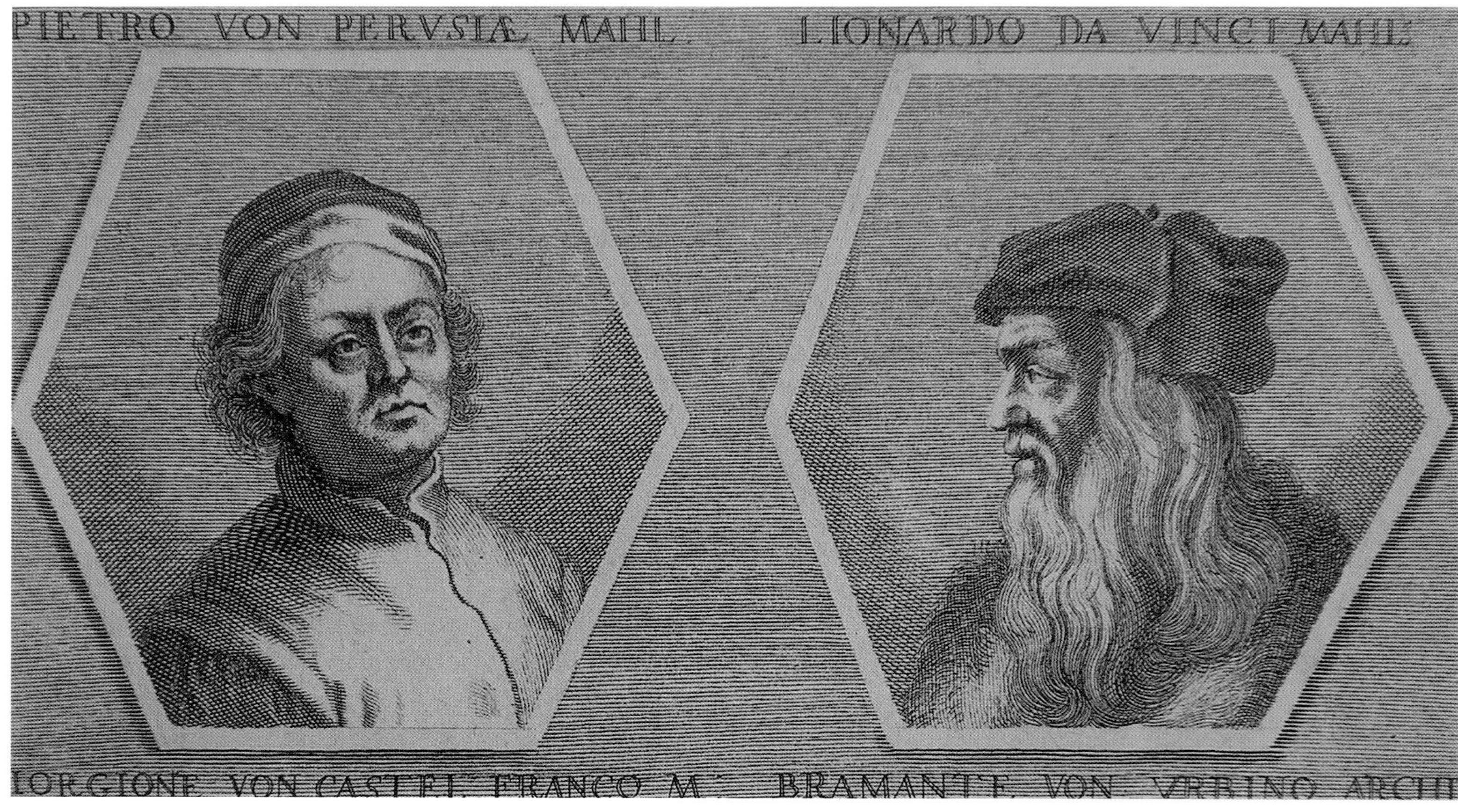

Joachim von Sandrart, *Perugino and Leonardo*, 1675. Engraving. Nürnberg, Deutsche Academie

contour figures with lines in order to produce the effect of the three dimensions. Because the contour lines must curve as to turn around the shape and even suggest what is not seen.

For such reason the permanence of Leonardo inside the workshop of Verrocchio had been so long, and he had indeed largely admired his excellent good quality as a drawer, the delicacy and the precision of touch demonstrated in the accurate representation of nature, as in the rendering of faces, bodies, hands and draperies, using earth models covered with clothes «dirtied with earth». Also Giovan Paolo Lomazzo (1563), in describing the way of painting of Perugino will remember, speaking through Leonardo, nearly suggesting mutual influences, the way he had to drive «the paintbrush in circles, making, in the way of semicircles his figures admirably united, as it can be seen, beyond to the other works and the portrait of Pope Sixtus, in the table that is now in the temple of the Carthusian friars in the town of Pavia».[4]

Lines of outline bent with deliberated sluggishness, in order to confer roundness and a direction to shapes, used then also by Giorgione, Michelangelo and by Raphael, of which Perugino was admired master in sharing out those teachings that would have made him become a star of the new and great modern manner. But Leonardo and Perugino were also «of same love», the same «feminine» sensibility, the same grace and sweetness, the same inclinations, in a city like Florence considered the «native land of sodomy», since it is the same Leonardo, in the *Libro dei sogni* by Giovan Paolo Lomazzo, a manuscript exemplified on the model of the *Dialogue of the dead* by Lucian and published only in 1973, to reclaim the primacy alluding with subtle irony right to Perugino, during

---

[4]   See C. Pedretti, *Leonardo e Perugino in Lombardia. Quelle figure «a semicircoli»*, «Art Dossier», 170, Firenze, Giunti, 2001; Id., *L'anatomia della «bellezza umana»*, in *Leonardo. L'anatomia*, a cura di C. Pedretti, D. Laurenza, P. Salvi, «Art Dossier», 207, Firenze, Giunti, 2005; Id., *La 'linea circonferenziale' generatrice della «bellezza umana»*, in *L'anatomia di Leonardo da Vinci fra Mondino e Berengario*, Firenze, Cartei e Becagli, 2005. E. Delacroix, in his *Journal, precédé d'une étude sur le maître*, [*Diary, preceded by a study on the master, Tr.N.*] remembers of having seen in the house of Mr. Détrimont a drawing by Leonardo and of having been hit by the way to draw with rounding lines that followed the figure, as to suggest its three-dimensionality: «What has hit me most in his collection of autographs is a writing by Leonardo da Vinci accompanied with sketches where it is explained the system of the ancients to draw rounding. He has discovered all. The writing of his manuscripts is reversed».

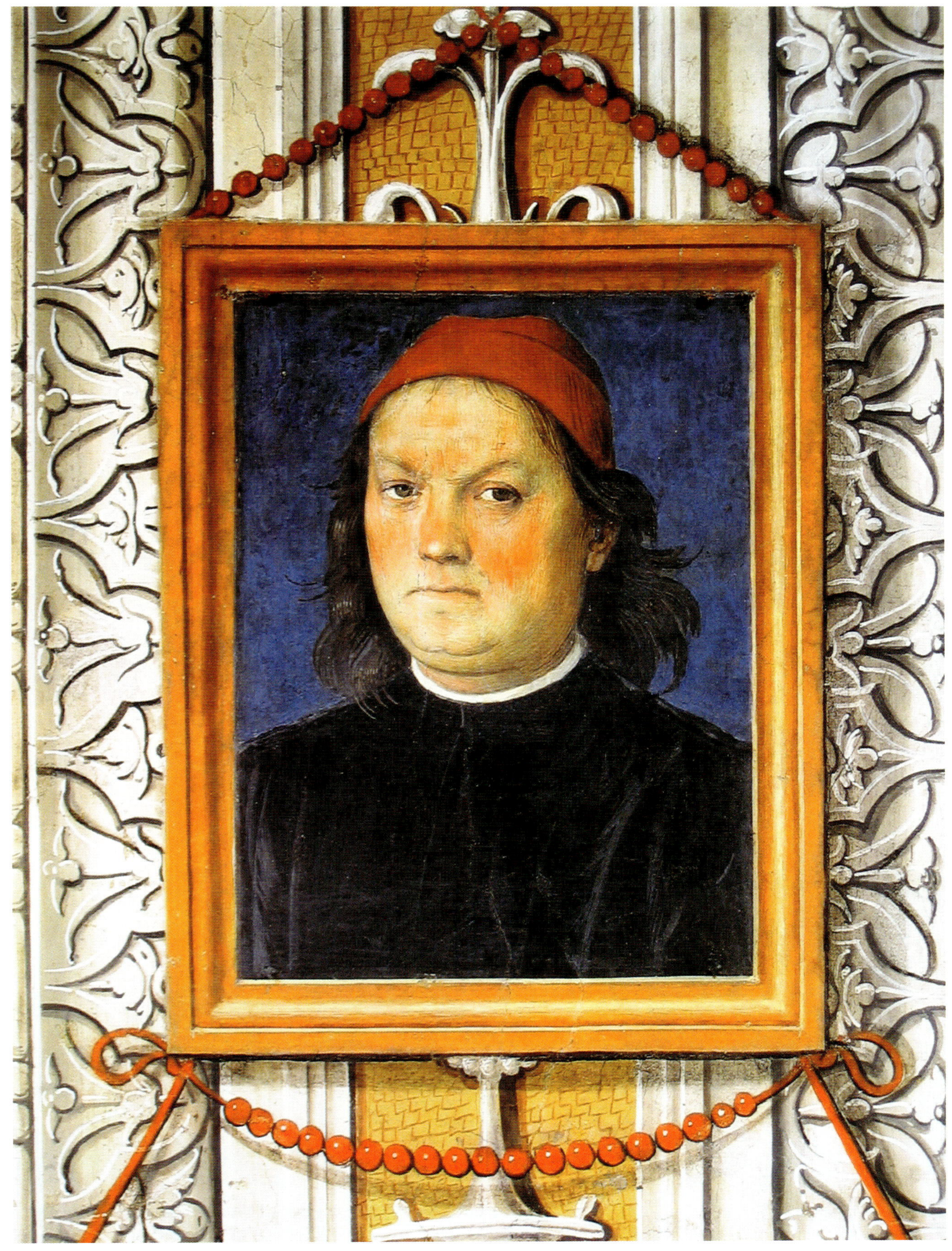

PIETRO VANNUCCI KNOWN AS PERUGINO, *Self-portrait*, c. 1500. Fresco, 40 x 30,5 cm. Perugia, Collegio del Cambio

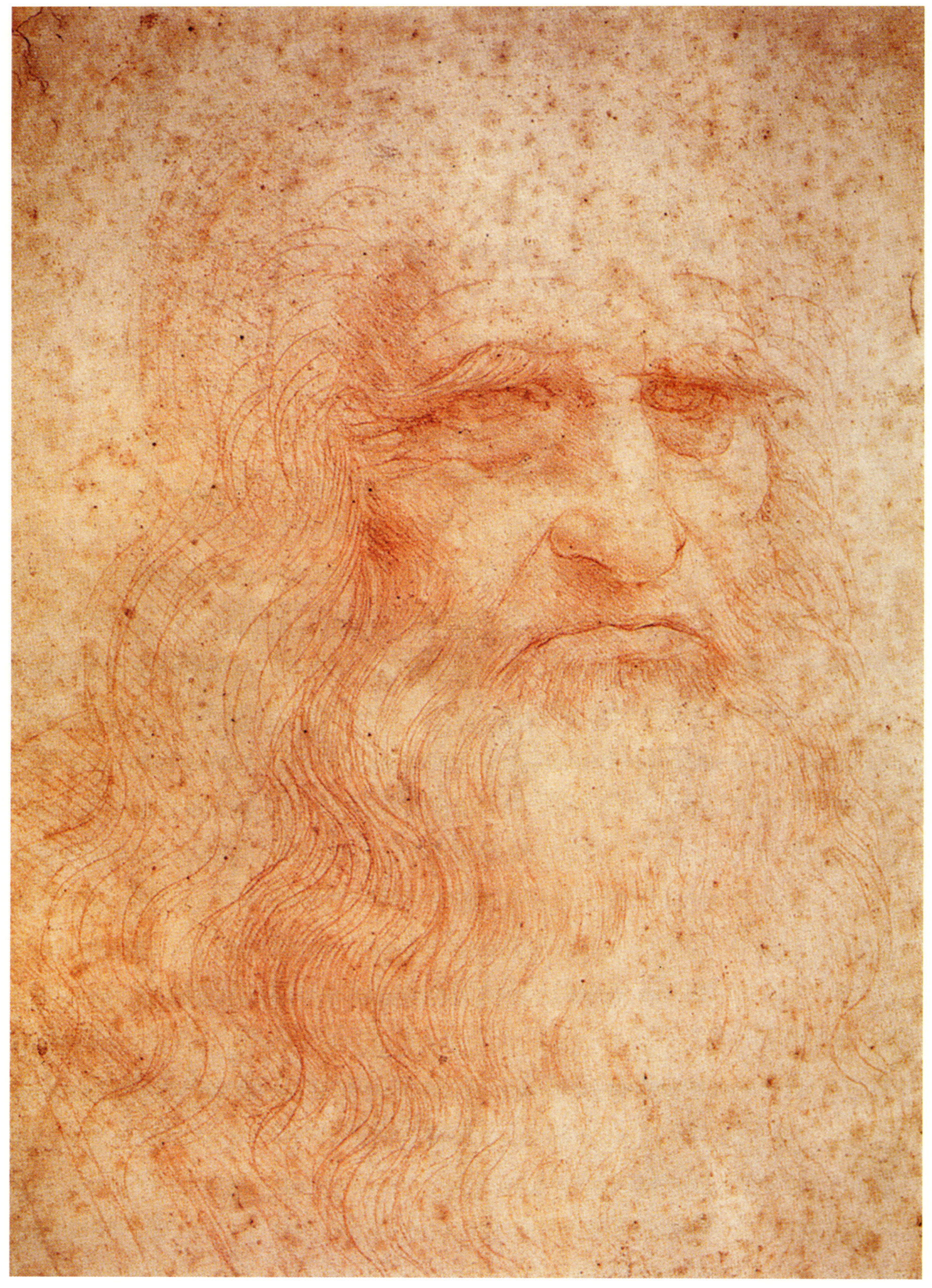

Leonardo da Vinci, *Self-portrait*, *c.* 1515. Sanguine, 333 x 213 mm. Turin, Biblioteca Reale

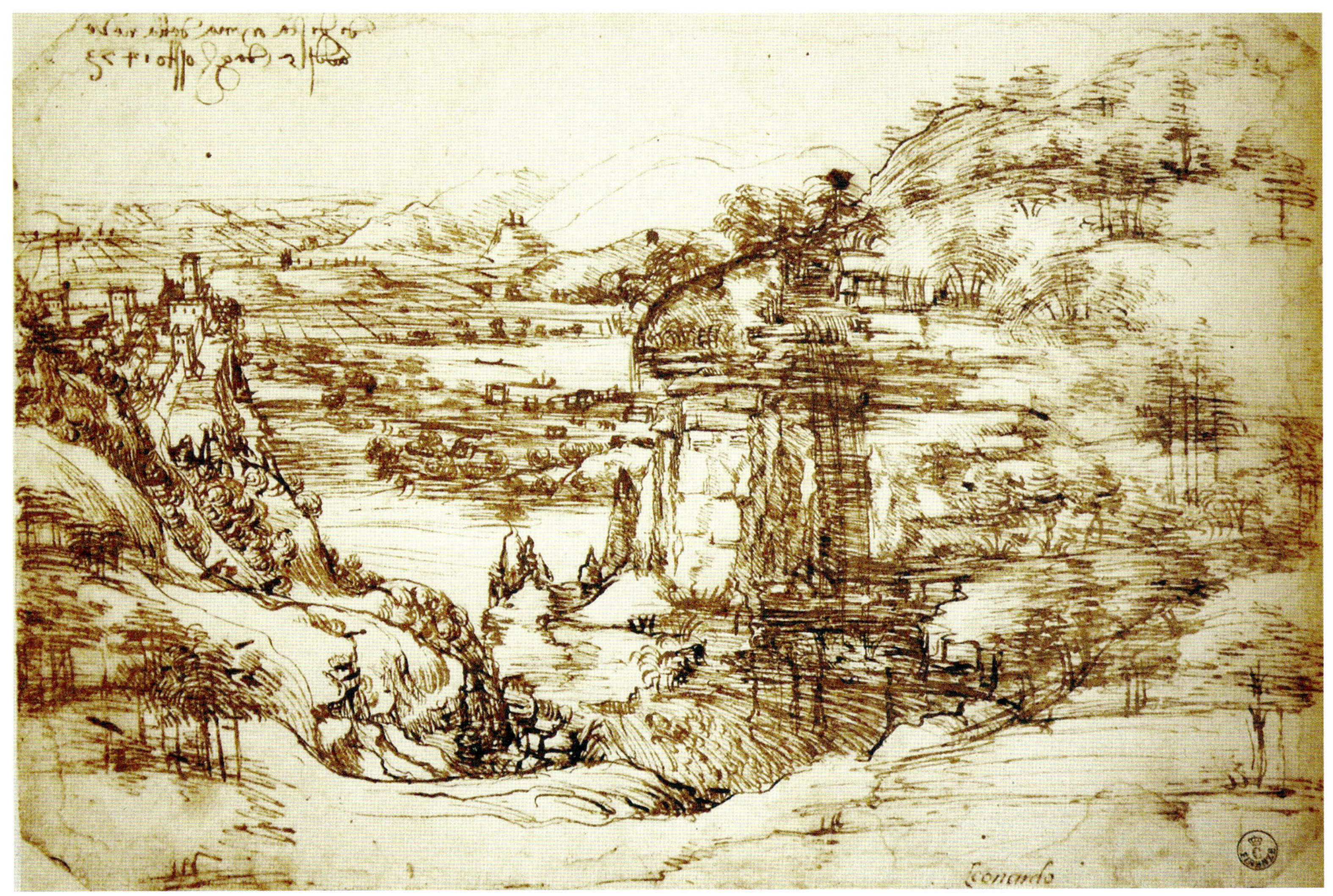

LEONARDO DA VINCI, *Landscape, «on the day 5 of August 1473»*. Pen and watercoloured ink on paper, 196 x 287 mm. Florence, Uffizi, Gabinetto dei Disegni e delle Stampe, n. 8P

their permanence in the workshop of Verrocchio and today reaffirmed by the study of Michael J. Rocke, according to which in Florence, in the turn of a few decades, more than ten thousand people were accused and placed under process for sodomy.[5] Leonardo loved to represent, in analogy to the movement of water and the bending curves of cosmic life, the curly cascade of his beautiful Salaì, «the motion of the surface of water, which does in the same way of hair» (Windsor, RL 12579 *r*),[6] while Perugino delighted in comb-

ing with his fingers along the «graceful» hair of his wife and to arrange it with loving grace, translated in the images of his celebrated and imitated Virgins. He had married, in 1493, in the presbytery of Fiesole, Chiara, the beautiful daughter of Luca Fancelli from Settignano, the famous architect assistant of Alberti in Mantua[7] and that met Leonardo at the court of the Moor, where he remained nine months, while, in 1487, he was adviser of the Fabric of the Dome, in order to examine the wood models of the various concurring engineers, among which those made by Bramante and by Leonardo. With Fancelli, examining the contents of the letter that the latter one on 12 August 1487 sent to the Magnificent, Leonardo certainly had a fruitful exchange of ideas also in relation

[5] See K. CLARK, *Leonardo da Vinci. An Account of His Development as an Artist*, Cambridge, Cambridge Univ. Press, 1939; M. J. ROCKE, *Il Controllo dell'omosessualità a Firenze nel XV secolo*, Gli Ufficiali di Notte, «Quaderni storici», 66, XXII, 3, 1987; C. PEDRETTI, *Paolo di Leonardo*, «Achademia Leonardi Vinci. Journal of Leonardo Studies and Bibliography of Vinciana», V, Firenze, Giunti, 1992. According to K. CLARK (1939) the homosexual tendencies of Leonardo are implicit in the androgynous character of many works.

[6] See K. CLARK, *Leonardo da Vinci…*, 1939, *op. cit.*; ID., *Leonardo e le curve della vita*,

«Lettura Vinciana», XVII, Firenze, Giunti Barbèra, 1979.
[7] See A. M. BRIZIO, *Bramante e Leonardo alla corte di Ludovico il Moro*, «Studi Bramanteschi», Roma, De Luca, 1974.

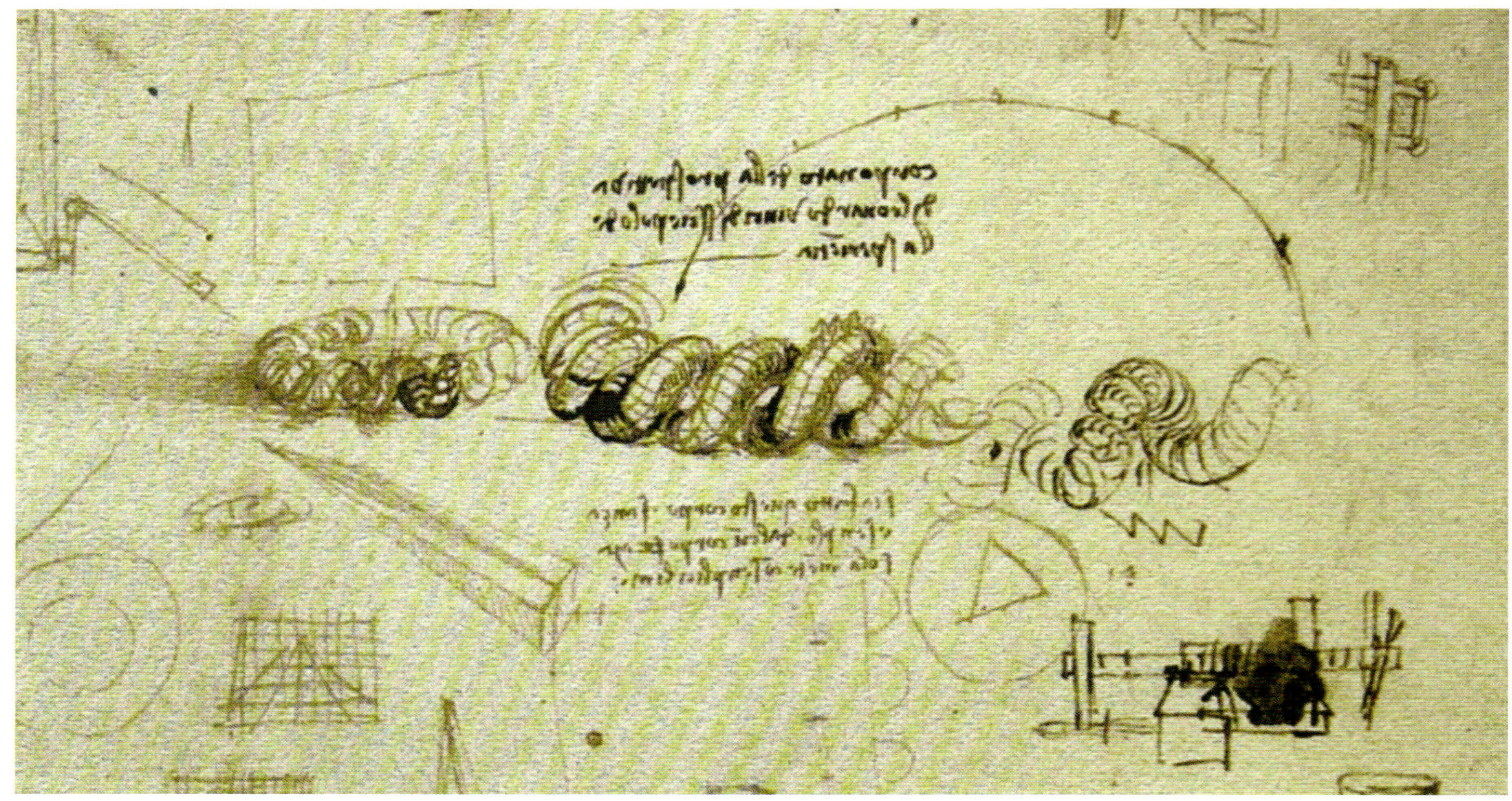

Leonardo da Vinci, *Studies on a body in perspective, c.* 1490. Pen and sepia ink and watercolour, 283 x 207 mm. Codex Atlanticus, f. 520 *r*. Milan, Biblioteca Ambrosiana. Particular

to the project of canalization of the Arno, since both of them considered the necessary diversion of its course, from Prato to Signa, so that in such a way it could turn out to be «easily navigable». In 1496, also Perugino would have been contacted by Ludovico the Moor, in order to realize some works or perhaps, being recognized as a valuable «master» in fresco, in order to carry to an end the *Last Supper*, in the Refectory of Santa Maria delle Grazie, or the Small rooms of the Castle. Precisely an agent of the Moor, around 1490, in an «informative» sent from Florence to the Duke about the main painters that could be found and contacted in their availability for possible works (Canuti, 1931; Baxandal, 1974),[8] had already exalted the singular artistic qualities of Perugino in executing frescoes and his admirable mastery in representing faces with a much angelic and sweet air, even if «air» has to be meant in an extensive sense that might be referred even to «things», like already asserted by the same Leonardo, in the Codex Ashburnham, «It seems to me that it is not a small grace the one of that painter which makes good airs to his figures»:

Sandro de Botticello, excellent painter in table and in wall: his things have a vigorous air and are with excellent reason and full proportion. Philippino di Frati Philippo, very good: Disciple of the aforesaid and son of the most excellent master of his times: his things have a sweeter air: I do not believe they have much art. Perusino, an excellent master: and most of all in wall: his things have an angelic air, and very sweet. Dominico de Girlandaio, a good master in table and even more in wall: his things have good air and he is an expeditious man, and that works a lot: All these aforesaid masters have given testimony of them in the chapel of Pope Sixtus except Philippino. But all then at the Hospital of the M.nt Laur.o and the palm is almost doubtful.

A similar praise, directed towards those painters considered «famous and supreme» in perspective, had been traced also by Luca Pacioli in the introductory *Epistle* of his *Summa Arithmetica*, published in Venice in 1494, and addressed «to the most illustrious prince Guidobaldo Duke of Urbino»:

In the mentioned art [...] in Florence Alessandro Boticelli, Filippino and Domenico Ghirlandaio; [...] and in Perosia Pietro known as Perusino [...]; which always with level and compasses dividing their works, they educate to an admirable perfection. In a way that it is

---

[8] See F. Canuti, *Il Perugino*, 1931, *op. cit.*; M. Baxandal, *Painting and Experience in Fifteenth Century Italy*, Oxford, Oxford Univ. Press, 1974.

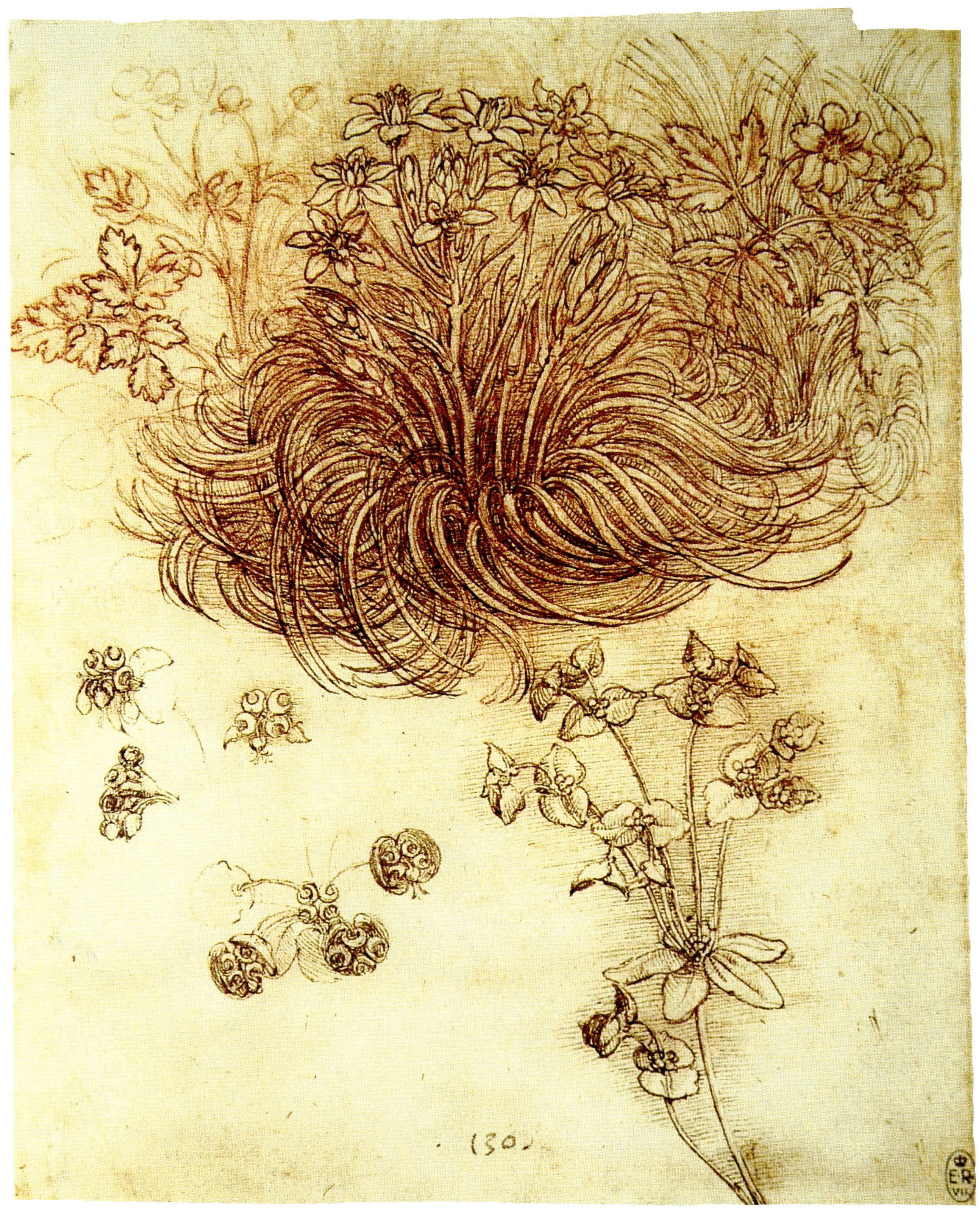

Leonardo da Vinci, *Star of Bethlehem*, *c.* 1505–07. Red pencil, pen and ink, 198 x 160 mm. Windsor, RL 12424

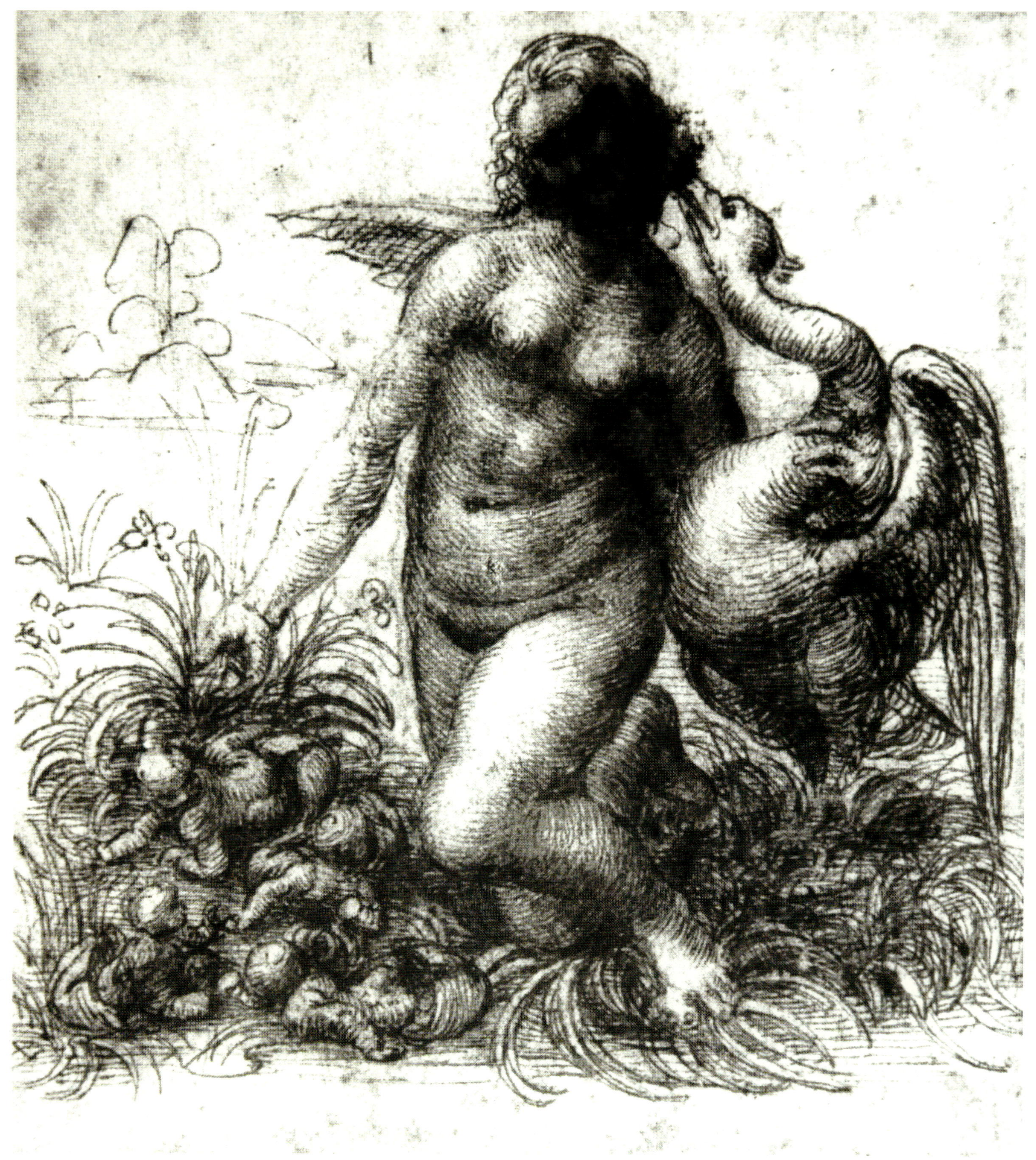

LEONARDO DA VINCI, *Leda genuflecting and the Swan*, *c.* 1504. Black pencil, pen and tawny ink, 160 x 139 mm. Chatsworth, Collection of the Duke of Devonshire, inv. n. 717

CARLO STARNAZZI

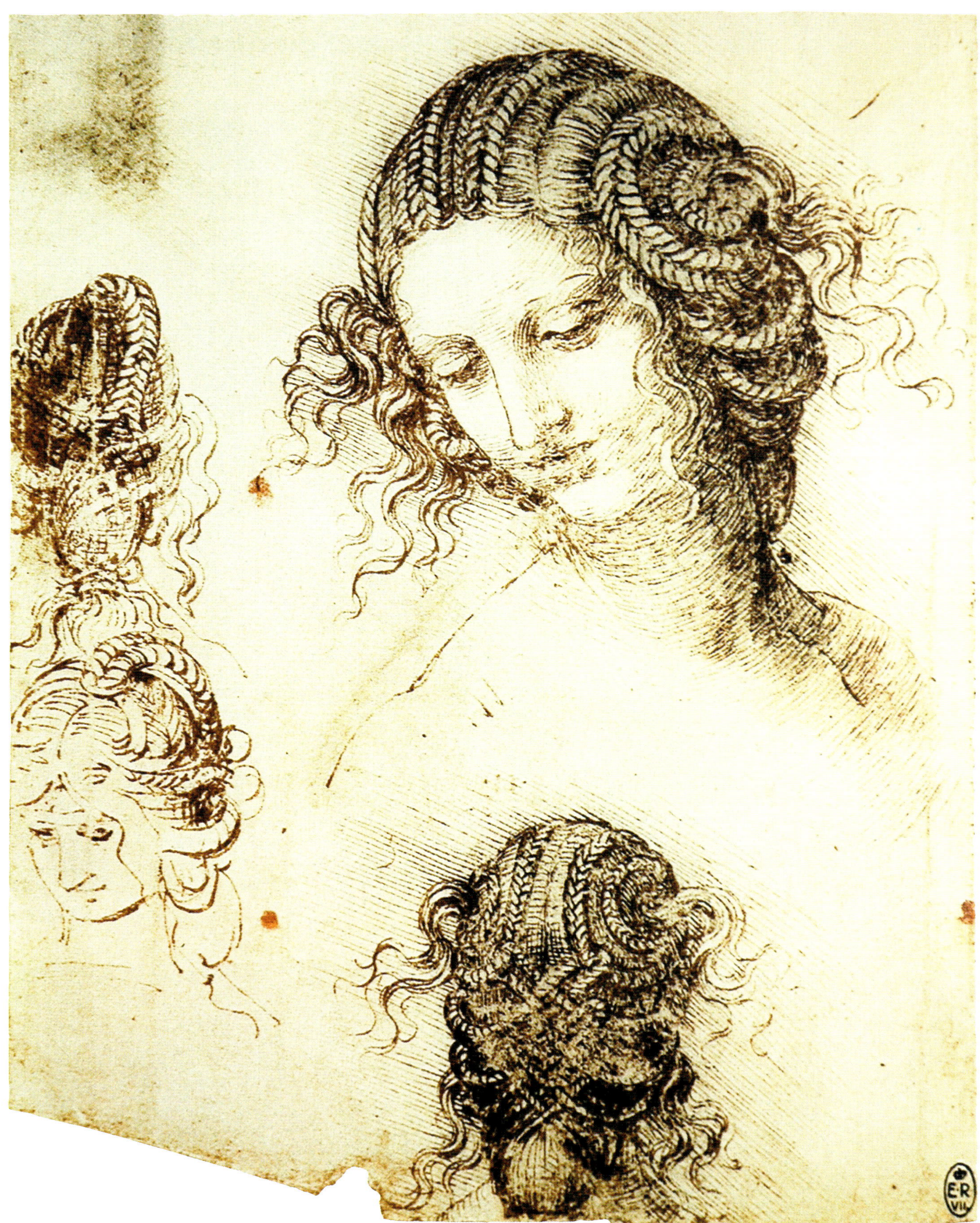

Leonardo da Vinci, *Studies of Leda's hairstyle, c.* 1506–08. Charcoal, pen and ink, 177 x 147 mm. Windsor, RL 12516

Therefore, already at the end of the fifteenth century the reputation of Perugino had extended from central to northern Italy.

Leonardo instead, that will be celebrated in the *Antiquarie prospetiche romane* as the sculptor that had exceeded the ancients, was then working to the Small rooms of the Castle and the Moor, complaining of his unexpected absence from Milan, on 8 June 1496, wrote to the bishop of Milan, Guidantonio Arcimboldi, then in Venice, that «that painter which painted the Small rooms today has made a certain scandal since he has stayed away».[9]

Therefore, knowing that Perugino was in Venice, he asked his Bishop to verify the availability of the Umbrian artist to reach Milan. Asked the Doge, Arcimboldi answered that the painter was not any more in Veneto.[10] The Duke in fact was exasperated by the extreme slowness with which Leonardo proceeded, that, forced to long pauses for the employment of the technique with tempera mixed to oil and for his obsessive research of perfection, risked again to be substituted also for the *Last Supper*, like in 1478, when, not carrying out the engagements taken on for the altar-piece with the Florentine Seigniory, had seen the commission pass in the hands of Filippino Lippi.[11] [11] In the prologue of one of his *Novelle* (I, 58), Matteo Bandello has described in «close view» the singular method of working, with which the artist proceeded:

> *Early in the morning he climbed on the scaffolding, because the Last Supper is somewhat high from the ground: he was used (I say), from the dawning sun until the evening had got dark, never to take the paintbrush off his hand, but forgot eating and drinking, to paint continuously. Then there would have been two, three and four days, that he would not have worked at it, and however he stopped sometimes*

one or two hours a day and he merely stayed contemplating, he considered examining [them] on his own, he judged his figures.

And it is the same Leonardo who, in his *Libro di Pittura* (f. 32 v, cap. 58 b), nearly to justify this behaviour he had, caused by his obsession for perfection and artistic excellence, recommended to the painter the necessity of «being as a hermit and to consider what he sees and to speak with himself selecting the most excellent among the parts of the sort of any thing he sees».

An attitude that the Vasari discovered also in Giovan Francesco Rustici, that had taken advantage of the collaboration of Leonardo for the statues of the door of the Baptistry of Florence: «you must think before it, then make the sketches, and after that the drawings and after having made them, let them stay for weeks and months without looking at them, and, then chosen the best ones, put them to work». But, on 29 June 1497, the Moor, with no more delay, wrote to Marchesino Stanga, so that Leonardo carried to an end the painting: «In the same way, to urge the Florentine Leonardo so that he ends the work of the Refectory of the Grazie he had already begun».[12] The intolerance of the Moor for the method of work of Leonardo had been made manifest also in the letter that the Duke had made to send, on 22 July 1489,[13] from Pietro Alamanni to Lorenzo the Magnificent:

> *Lord Ludovico has a good mind to make an appropriate burial to his father and already has ordered that Leonardo da Vinci makes the model of it, that is a greatest bronze horse, with over the Duke Francesco equipped for war: and since His Excellence would like to make something in a superlative degree, he told me that on his behalf I wrote you that he would like that you sent him a master or two, good at such work: and that although he had given commission of this thing to Leonardo da Vinci, it does not seem to me he is much convinced he knows how to carry it out.*

At the beginnings of 1500, Perugino was still forced to divide himself between the engagements taken on in Perugia for the decoration of the Hall of the Audience in the Collegio del Cambio (1496-1500) and where he will inaugurate a workshop of his own in 1501, and the city of Florence, nevertheless considered a favourite place, a second native land according to the testimony of the *Memoriale* by Francesco Albertini: « […] he can be said a Florentine, that has been grown up here». In Florence, the Umbrian artist in fact had opened a workshop in total independence, since 1486, in the

---

9 See L. BELTRAMI, *Documenti*, n° 70.
10 See L. BELTRAMI, *Documenti*, n° 71.
11 LUCA PACIOLI, in the dedicatory epistle to Ludovico the Moor, contained in the *De divina proportione*, concluded saying that the work had already been finished, on 8 February 1498. But right in the *Supper* of Santa Maria delle Grazie, Leonardo, according to LOMAZZO (*Trattato*, II, 2), would have more than elsewhere reflected the science of the «motions», that is the correspondence between the motions of the spirit and those of the body: «among all his other things, it is a very clear test of it the wonderful supper of Christ with his Apostles that is seen painted in the refectory of Santa Maria delle Grazie in Milan, in which he expressed in such a way the motions of the passions of minds of those Apostles, in the faces and in all the rest of their body, that it can well be said that the true was not different in anything from this representation, and that that work has been one of the wonderful painting works that in any time was ever made by any painter, how excellent he could be. Therefore, in those Apostles there can distinctly be perceived admiration, fright, dolour, suspicion, love and similar passions and affections which they all then felt: and finally in Judas, betrayal conceived in his mind, with an appearance in all similar to a traitor».

12 See L. BELTRAMI, *Documenti*, n° 76.
13 See L. BELTRAMI, *Documenti*, n° 36.

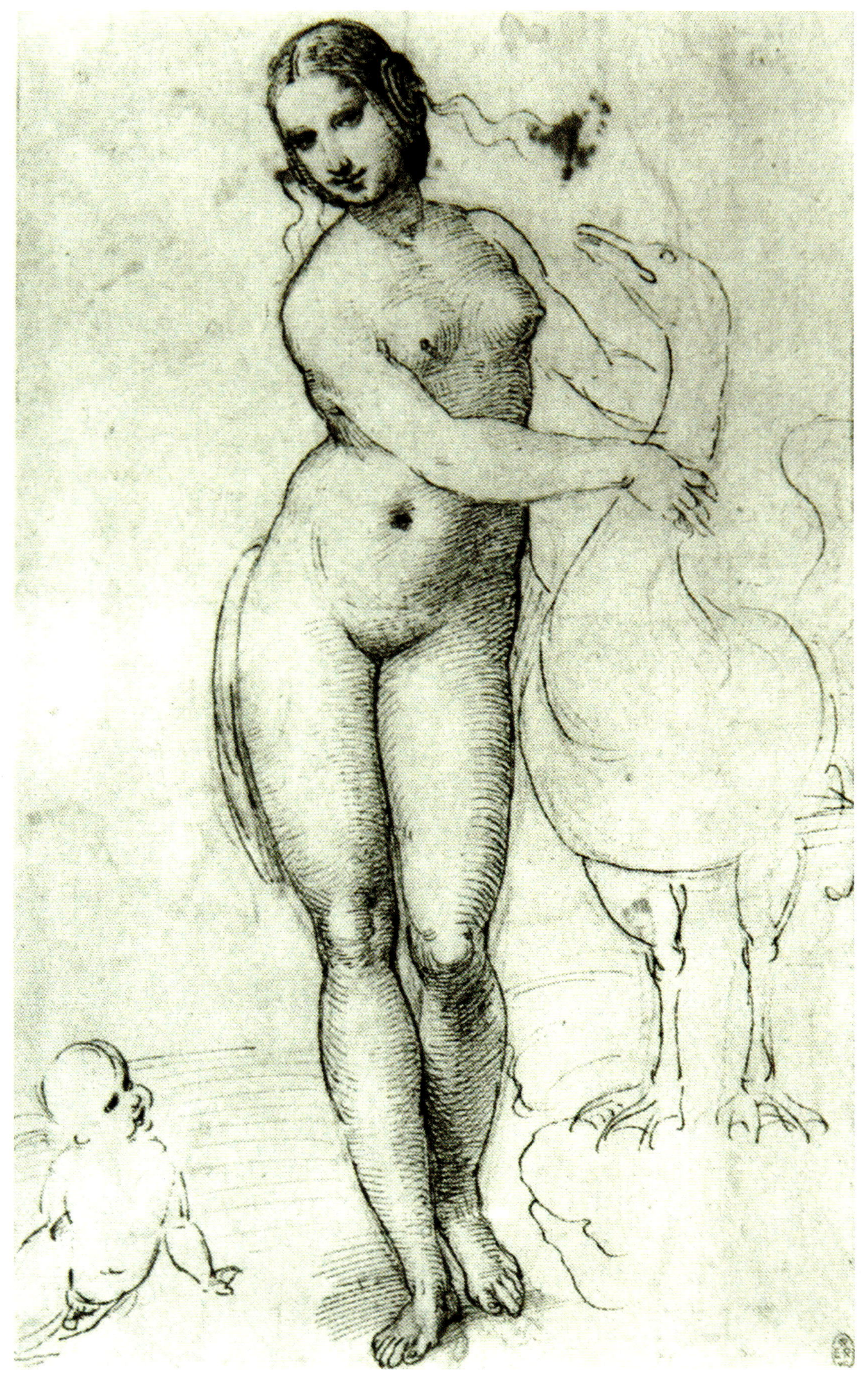

RAPHAEL, *Leda and the Swan*, c. 1504–08. Stylus, pen and ink, 308 x 192 mm. Windsor, RL 12759

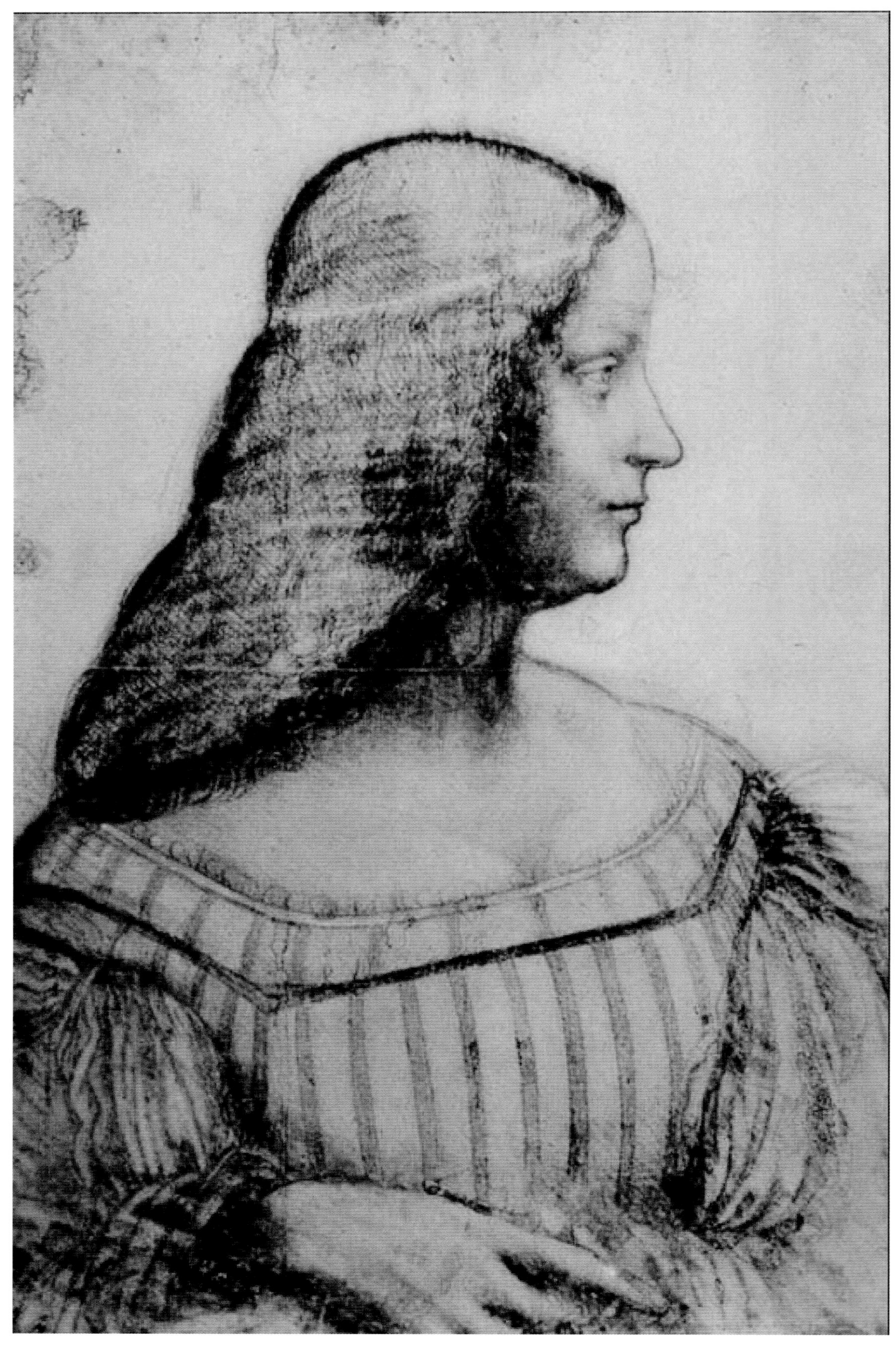

Leonardo da Vinci, *Portrait of Isabella d'Este, c.* 1499-1500. Charcoal, pastel with touches of red on the hair and of yellow on the dress. Pierced for pouncing, 63 x 46 cm. Paris, Musée du Louvre

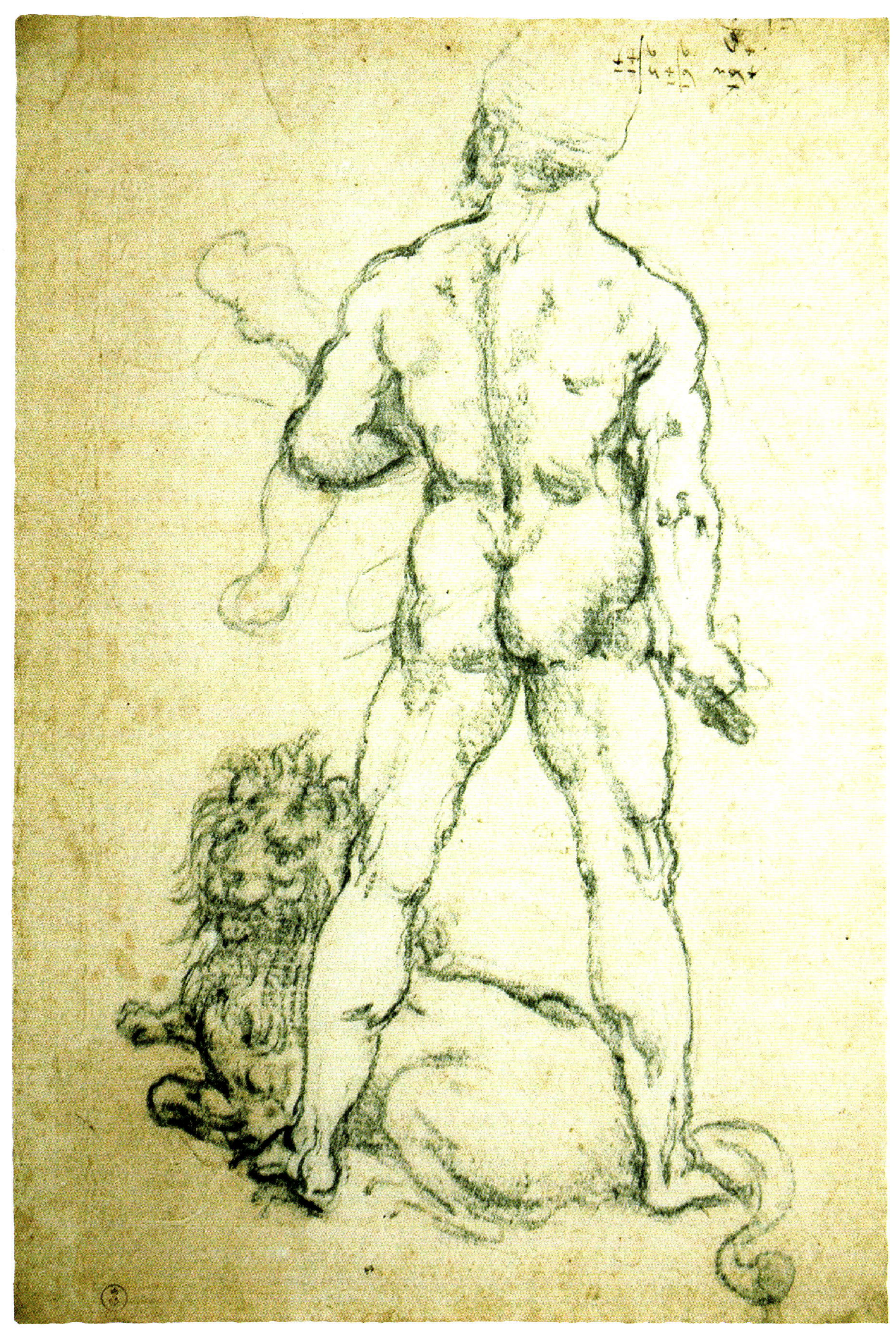

Leonardo da Vinci, *Study for a Hercules with the Nemean Lion*, *c.* 1508. Turin, Biblioteca Reale, n. 15630

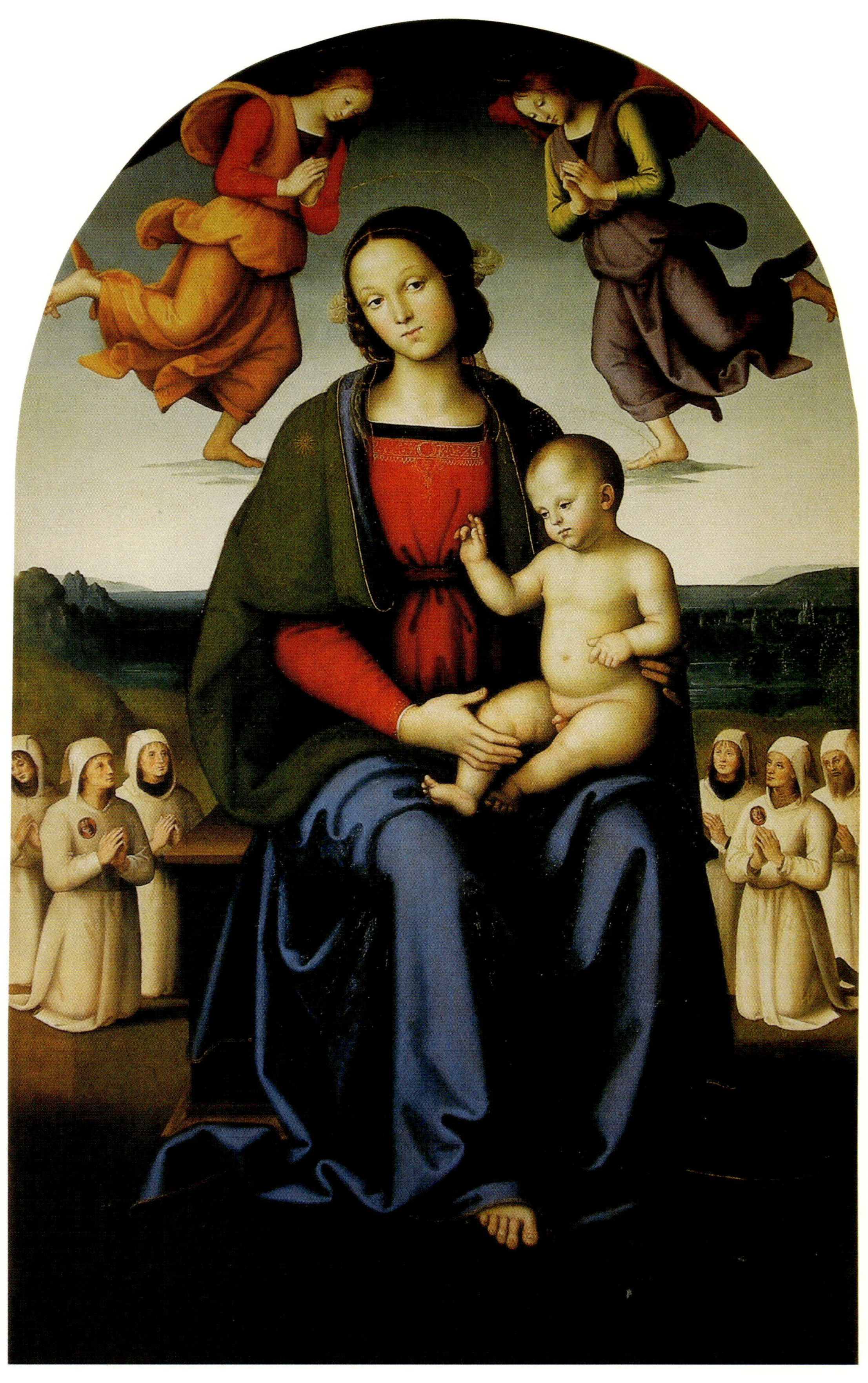

Pietro Vannucci known as Perugino, *Virgin of the Archconfraternity of Our Lady of the Consolation,* c. 1496–98. Tempera on table, 146 x 104 cm. Perugia, Galleria Nazionale dell'Umbria.

street of San Gilio near the hospital of Santa Maria Nuova, after Verrocchio had moved to Venice and after the celebrated success obtained in the participation, with Sandro Botticelli, Domenico Ghirlandaio, Cosimo Rosselli and the assistants of the respective workshops (1481-82), to the decoration of the great cycle of frescoes on the wall of the Sistine Chapel (*Delivery of the keys; Travel of Moses to Egypt; Baptism of Christ*), ordered by the Sovereign Pontiff Sixtus IV.

Therefore, animated by the desire to realize good transactions, Perugino would have organized in time his plentiful artistic production for rich and demanding customers, that he meant to satisfy in any case also regardless of art, so as to compromise shortly after the great notoriety of those soft shapes, that, as said by Vasari, publicly Michelangelo, in 1503-04, will denounce as expression of a «clumsy» painting:

> *The doctrine of his art was so reduced to manner, that he gave to all the figures the same air [...]. And for this he deserved, beyond some ugliness made him by the makers, that Michelangelo in public said to him, that he was clumsy in the art.*

But in Florence, as Vasari remembers as well, Perugino had discovered a city that naturally seemed to cultivate excellence, freedom and a feeling of largeness for the talents longing «by means of virtue to reach some level»:

> *To Florence more than elsewhere came men that were perfect in all of the arts, and especially in painting, since in that city men are incited by three things: the first one, by the blaming that they make so many and so much, to make that air the naturally free talents, and that they are not satisfied universally of works, as mediocre as they can be, but more and more they take into consideration them to honour of goodness and of beauty, more than with respect to the maker; the second one, that if you want to live there you must be industrious, which does not mean other than to use incessantly talent and judgment and to be shrewd and fast in your things, and finally to earn, not having Florence any wide and abundant country, of such a way that he who stays here can spend little, so as, where there is some good, [can spend] much; the third one, that perhaps is not less important than the other ones, it is the cupidity of glory and honour, that that air generates largest in those that have every perfection, which, in all the persons who have spirit, does not allow that they want to be compared, nor to remain behind to those ones whom they see to be as men as they are, even though they recognize them to be masters. [...] Moved by these warnings therefore and by the persuasions of many others, came Pietro to Florence with the intention to become excellent.*

And, right in Florence he would have met again his friend Leonardo, that Isabella d'Este Gonzaga, was with insistence contacting through Friar Pietro da Novellara, in order to obtain a portrait or a devotional picture, to the point that on 29 March 1501, she invited the Carmelite to inquire into the activity of the artist:

> *If he has begun any work as it has been reported he has done, and which work it is that one: and if you believe that he has to stay there for some time, asking him then you if he would accept the appointment to make a picture in our study, that when he would be pleased to do it we would let the creation and the time to his decision.*

In a subsequent exchange of letters with Francesco Malatesta, between 3 and 12 May 1502, Isabella d'Este asked again the «painter» Leonardo, making him ask a consultation for the purchase of four vases in semi-precious stones, to her offered at the price of 940 ducatoes and that belonged to the art collection of Lorenzo the Magnificent, that «she held for things much beloved» and that was dispersed after the driving away of the Medici from Florence (1494). The proposal had arrived on 27 April through the same Malatesta that informed Francesco II Gonzaga about the possible purchase of those vases «of hard stones, that is: jasper, crystal and amethyst» and one in agate. Leonardo expressed his judgment of evaluation on those works of art, shifting all his interest of expert on the piece «of amethyst or jasper», since it was characterized by «various mixtures of colours and it is transparent, it has the basis of solid gold, and it has many pearls and rubies around that are indicated to have the price of 150 ducatoes. Leonardo likes this thing a lot, for being it a new thing and for the admirable diversity of colours. All have carved in the body of the vase capital letters that display the name of Laurenzo de' Medici». But for the price considered to be too much high, the negotiations did not lead to the purchase of the vases, destined to appear again in the Medicean collections with Cosimo I.[14]

On 25 January 1504, the Seigniory would have consulted Leonardo and Perugino in order to decide, together with thirty artists among which Botticelli, Lorenzo di Credi, Cosimo Rosselli, Filippino Lippi, Giuliano and Antonio da Sangallo, Francesco Granacci and Andrea della Robbia, supported side by side by technicians and craftsmen of remarkable ability as Lorenzo della Golpaia, the more appropriate setting to assign to the statue of the *David* by Michelangelo, considered, as the illustrious ones previously realized by Donatello (*c.* 1435) and

---

[14] See L. Beltrami, *Documenti*, n° 115-116; G. M., Brown, *Little Known and Unpublished Documents concerning Andrea Mantegna, Bernardino Parentino, Pietro Lombardo, Leonardo da Vinci and Filippo Benintendi*, «L'arte», VII-VIII, 1969; Id., *Lorenzo de' Medici and the Dispersal of Antiquarian Collections of Cardinal Francesco Gonzaga*, «Arte Lombarda», XC-XCI, 1989.

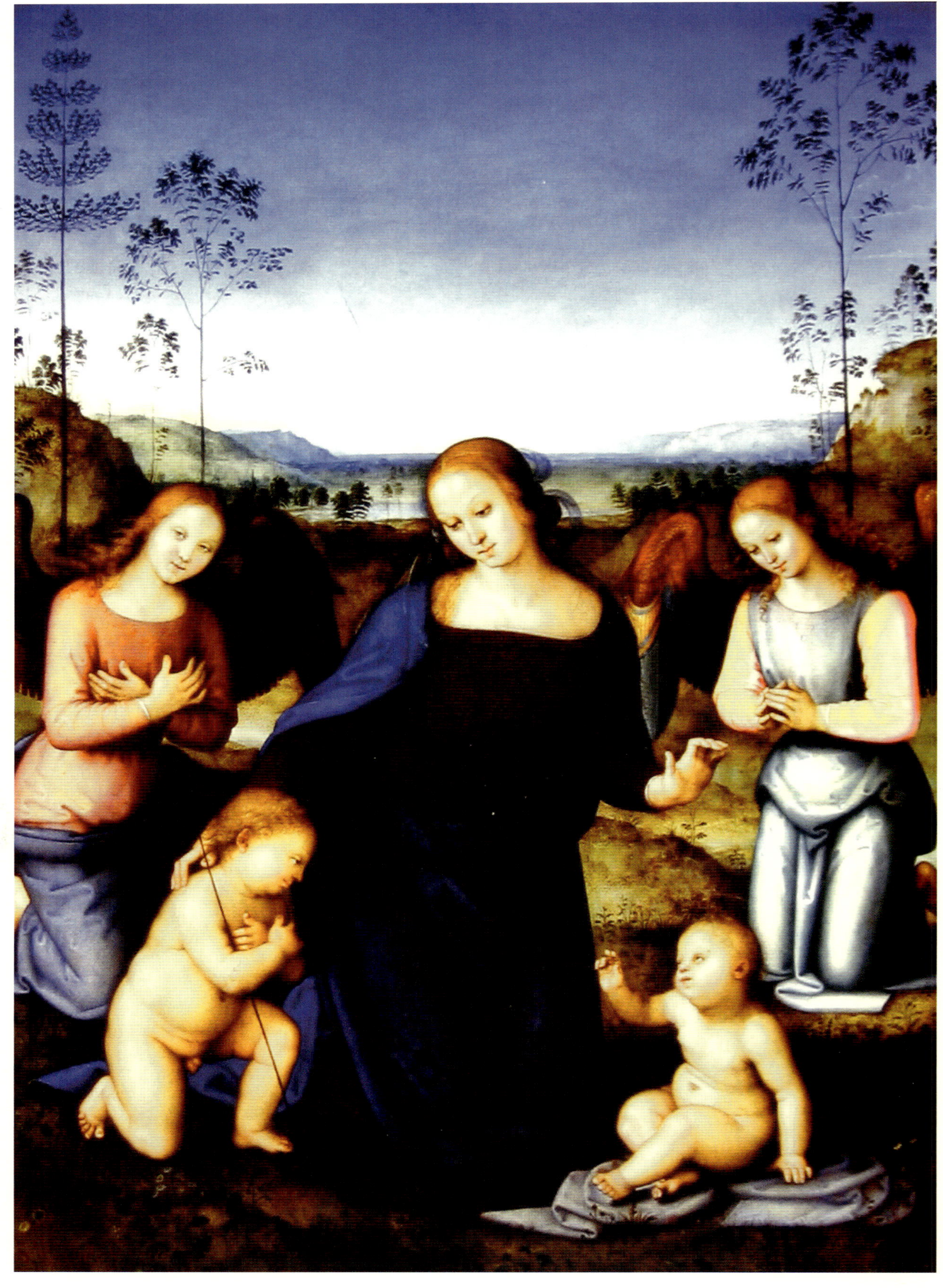

PIETRO VANNUCCI KNOWN AS PERUGINO, *Madonna with infant Saint John and two Angels adoring the Child*, *c.* 1504-05. Table, 162 x 118 cm. Nancy, Musée des Beaux-Arts

CARLO STARNAZZI

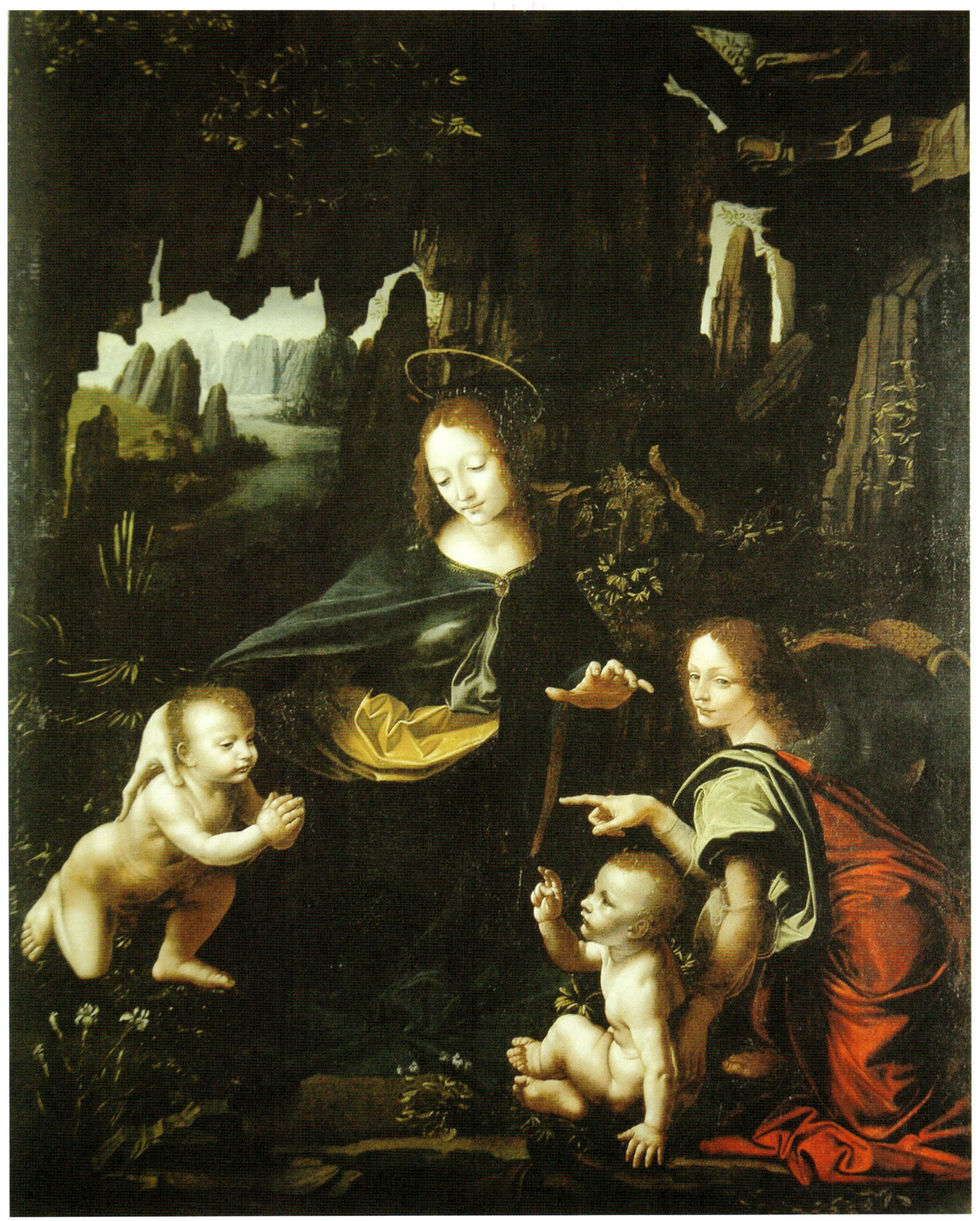

Leonardo da Vinci, *Virgin of the Rocks*, 1483–86. Oil on table, 199 x 122 cm. Paris, Musée du Louvre

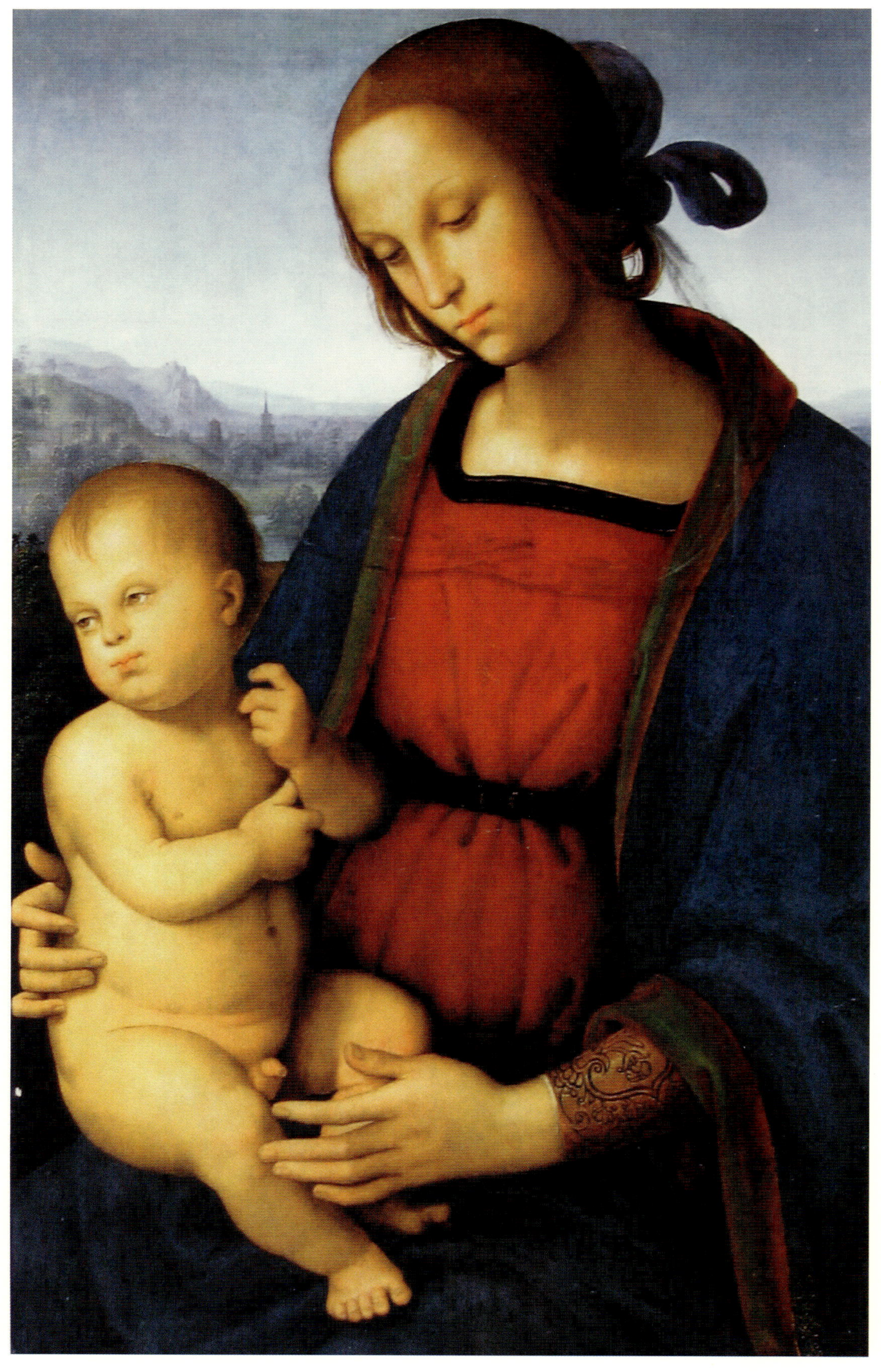

PIETRO VANNUCCI known as PERUGINO, *Madonna with the Child*, *c.* 1495-1505. Oil on table, 70 x 51 cm. Washington, National Gallery

by Verrocchio (1469-76), an emblem of the civic freedom of Florence.[15] A statue, that of the *David*, whose realization the Gonfalonier Pier Soderini had thought to assign at first to Leonardo, that, after the setting of the masterpiece at the entrance of Palazzo Vecchio, was devising to associate as a twin statue, that of an Hercules, with the features of a muscular wrestler, that one too expression of the Florentine civic virtues (Windsor, RL 12593; 12594; 12596).[16]

On the following 14 May, still the Marchioness of Mantua had recommended by letter to her agent and correspondent, Angelo del Tovaglia,[17] the names of Leonardo and that one of Perugino, which was «among the other excellent painters that exist at present», in order to obtain something of important, with which to embellish her small Study, following a precise iconographic program, together with the works by Mantegna. To Perugino she made a clear demand to add to the painting, as a separate trial, also a landscape, «one, placed far away, that is a river or a sea» (Verheien, 1971),[18] and, with an attached letter, she also invited Leonardo to make for her a juvenile and graceful Christ:

> *A figure of a Christ young boy approximately twelve years old, that would be of that age that he was when he disputed in the temple, and made with that sweetness and delicacy of air that you have for peculiar art in excellence.*

Recommendation that Isabella would have renewed to Leonardo, on 31 October, so that, once diverted his attention «from the Florentine history» of the *Battle of Anghiari*, he wanted «for recreation» to put himself to make that «small figure». The Tovaglia, who knew both the engagements and nature of the two artists, would have sent a discouraging answer:[19]

> *Therefore I strongly doubt that they do not have to compete together in sluggishness: I do not know who in this will surpass the other one: I hold for sure that Lionardo has to be the winner.*

On 22 January 1505, Alvise Ciocca, after having verified with the Abbot of Fiesole the state of advancing of the engagements taken on by Perugino and considered the hesitations of Leonardo, had involved, for a consultation on the painting of Vannucci the shrewd and ambitious Salaì (Giangiacomo Caprotti),[20] that introduced himself as a reliable connoisseur of art works: «disciple of Leonardo da Vinci, young for his age, very valuable». And, in the letter that Ciocca sent to the Marchioness, that had made demand of the opinion of «a painter much expert and of good talent» (Canuti, 1931), it was promptly transmitted also what he had expressed: «he has praised the fantasy much and he has corrected a lot some small things that the aforementioned Reverend and I had told to Perusino […]. The said Salaì would have a great desire to make something gallant for Your Excellence. And nonetheless having you that desire of some small picture or other thing, you can give me notice of it, and for the price I shall try to have them at will». Vannucci had been appointed to make a profane allegorical painting on the topic of «virtus» and of «voluptas», meant to a celebration of the Marchioness, one of the more illuminated and generous noblewomen of the Renaissance, that had advanced in such sense some precise requests, with the attempt to tie up «in scriptis» as much as possible to her desires the program and the work of the artist, which did not have to go too far away from the suggested literary indications:

---

[15]   The majestic statue of *David*, according to the opinion of Giuliano da Sangallo and of Leonardo, so that it did not hinder the course of public ceremonies, should have been placed under the loggia, while for Michelangelo, that in the end prevailed, revealing once again all his hostility towards his traditional competitor, it had to be arranged well in sight and in a privileged place, beside the main entrance of the Palace of the Seigniory (L. BELTRAMI, *Documenti*, n° 135).

[16]   See K. WEIL GARRIS POSNER, *Leonardo and Central Italian Art: 1500-1515*, New York, 1974; C. BAMBACH, *A Leonardo drawings for the Metropolitan Museum of Art. Studies for a statue of Hercules*, in «Apollo», CLIII, 469, March 2001.

[17]   The rich merchant Angelo del Tovaglia had housed the Marquis of Mantua, Giovan Francesco Gonzaga, in his splendid villa, placed in the south on the Florentine hills, from which a superb panorama could be enjoyed. Villa Tovaglia had the facade placed on the way to St. Maria at Montici and was turned towards Florence, with its terraces and garden degrading in opposite sense towards the Val d'Ema. The Gonzaga was so enthusiastic about it to send a letter to Leonardo, through his correspondent Francesco Malatesta, so that he replicated for him such a beauty in the outskirts of Mantua, where later would have been built the fabulous villa of Marmirolo, of which no trace is left any more. On 11 August 1500, Malatesta sent to the Marquis the drawing by Leonardo, perhaps the one included in the sheet of Windsor (RL 12689), reporting also what expressed with subtle irony by the artist: «the abovementioned Leonardo says that to make a perfect thing there would be the need to carry the site which is here, there where Your Lordship wants to build, and that only then Your Lordship would be satisfied». The drawing was again sent back to Leonardo, so that he completed it with terraces, colonnades and gardens, according to his architectural and naturalistic conception, marked by a harmonic integration between man and environment (L. BELTRAMI, *Documenti*, n° 105). Also Alberti in his treatise *Della Famiglia*, among the «fixed principles» for the ideal house, recommended including the villa in a natural environment and in a well high place, exposed to the sun and placed between woods and fields.

[18]   See E. VERHEIEN, *The Paintings in the Studiolo of Isabella d'Este at Mantua*, New York, 1971.

[19]   See L. BELTRAMI, *Documenti*, n° 143.

[20]   SALAÌ is a demonic name, that Leonardo assigned to his disciple, drawing it from *Morgante* (XXI, 47, 7) by Luigi Pulci and, as he in person noted down in the Ms. C (f. 15 *v*), the Caprotti from Oreno was hired as boy of workshop, on 22 July 1490: «Iacomo came to stay with me the day of the Magdalene in 1490, 10 years old». For the singular beauty of his face and his long curly hair, «charming for grace and beauty, having beautiful curly and in ringlets hair», he posed many times for the master. But the attribution of that infernal nickname very soon came to designate the restless character of the boy: «The second day I made to cut for him 2 shirts, a pair of stockings and a jacket, and when I placed the money beside in order to pay the aforesaid things, he stole me the aforesaid money of the purse, and never was it possible to make him confess it, even though I had true certainty of it - Liras 4», and after that on the margin of the same sheet he added: «thief, liar, obstinate, greedy».

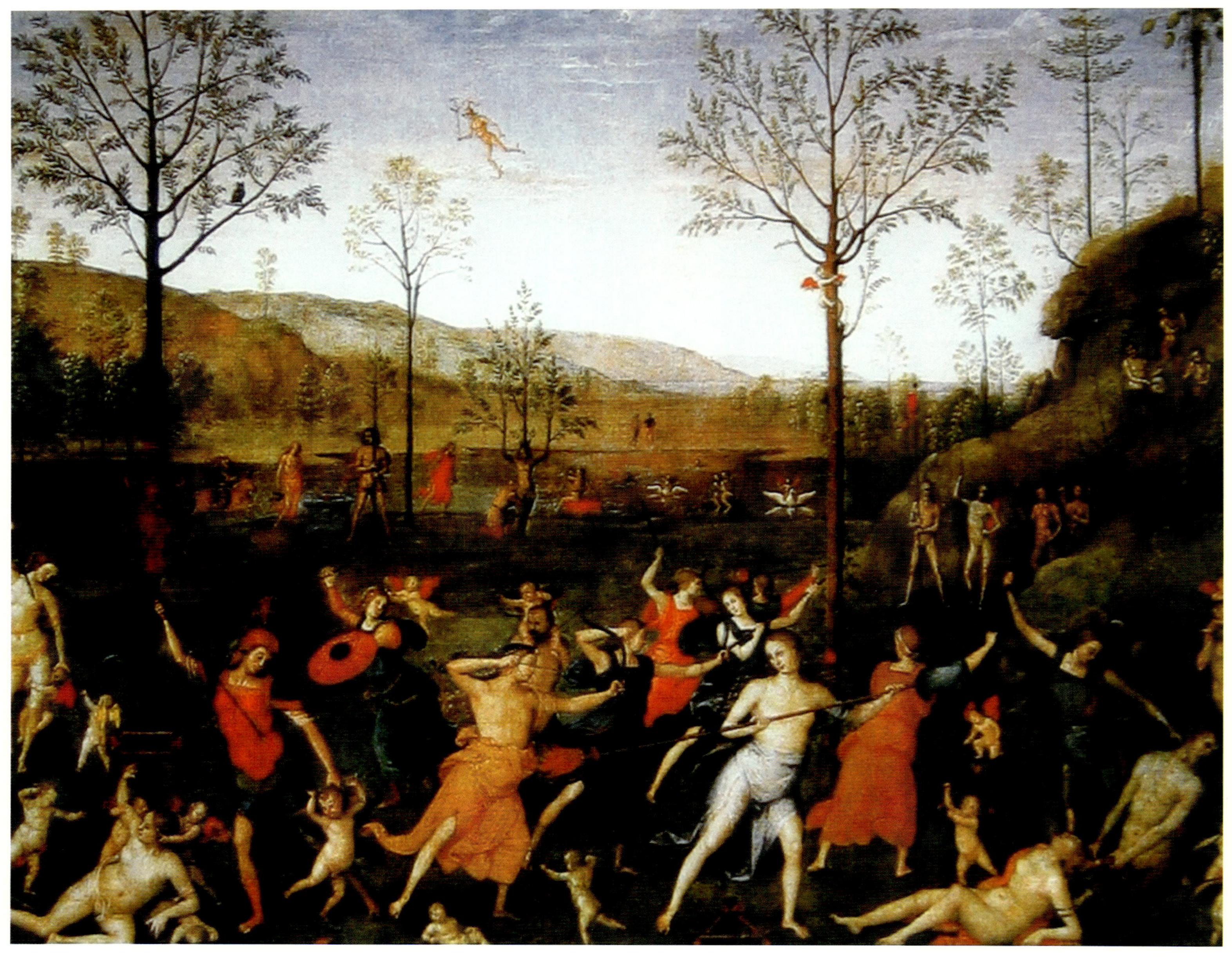

Our poetic invention, which largely I wish from you […] it is a battle of Chastity against Lust, that is Pallas Athena and Diana fighting strongly against Venus and Love. And Pallas Athena wants to seem to have nearly won Love, having broken his golden dart and silver bow placed under her feet, holding him with one hand for the veil that the blind has in front of the eyes, with the other raising the spear that is positioned so as to hurt him. And Diana in the contrast with Venus have to be portrayed the same in the victory; and that only in the extrinsic part of the body, as in the mitre and the garland, or in some light veil that has around, she Venus is darted; and Diana has a part of her clothes burnt by the flame of Venus, and in no other part they must be beaten among them. After these four gods, the most chaste follower nymphs of Pallas Athena and Diana have to

fight harshly with various ways and actions, as you will like it most, against a lusty multitude of fauns, satyrs and thousands of various loves: and these loves, in comparison to the first, must be smaller, with bow not of silver, neither with darts of gold, but of more base matter, like of wood or of iron or of other matter that you will like: and for more expression and ornament of the painting, beside of Pallas Athena it is needed to be the olive, a tree dedicated to her, where it is replaced with the head of Medusa, making to settle down among those branches an owl, which is a bird typical of Pallas Athena; beside of Venus it must be made the myrtle, the most pleasing tree to her. But, for greater embellishment, there should be the need of an ample fountain, that is of a river, or a sea, where there could be seen to pass in succour of Love fauns, satyrs, and other loves, and some of

CARLO STARNAZZI

In February, Leonardo had already finished the cardboard for
the *Battle of Anghiari*, revealing the great innovative energy of
his expressive style, while arrived unexpectedly to Perugino
the bitterness and the disappointment of the cold acceptance
that Isabella d'Este had reserved to the picture sent her on
30 June, that of the *Combat between Love and Chastity* (Paris,
Musée du Louvre):

> *The picture has been brought to us safe and sound, which we please,
> since it is well drawn and well coloured: but if it had been finished
> with greater diligence, having to be placed nearby those by Mantinea,
> that are extremely defined, it would have been a greater yours hon-
> our and a greater our satisfaction, and dislikes us that Lorenzo of
> Mantua dissuaded you from colouring it in oils: because we wished
> it, knowing that your profession was great and of greater adornment.*

The artist, on 10 August, would have answered full of con-
sternation, justifying himself to have learned too late the desire of the Marchioness of a work in oils, but that however he
would have demonstrated to her all his talent very soon with
«some other thing, which will prove to be highly detailed»
(Canuti, 1931).
But in this period, the Umbrian painter would be fascinated
by the revolutionary composition of the *Virgin of the Rocks*
of his friend Leonardo, that in the setting of the scene, in the
twist of the bust, in the reproduction and in the adjustment
of the posture of the personages, with manifest references
to ancient iconography, had revealed the most original experimentations and solutions. Therefore Perugino, while his
«doctrine of art was reduced so much that he made to all
his figures a similar air» (Vasari, 1568),[21] keeping a few facial

stereotypes, between 1500 and 1505, exemplified on the vincian masterpiece the composition and the pose of the central
characters of the *Virgin with the infant John, the Child and two
adoring Angels* (Nancy, Musée des Beaux Arts).
Vannucci adhered with his style to the leonardian prototype,
without carrying out any significant modification to the
iconographic context, even if the Virgin, picked in unstable
equilibrium, reveals in her face a more serene air and the angel, which assists Jesus, is replaced by two angels adoring the
Child, intent on giving his blessing to his favourite.
If Leonardo, with a radical naturalism, had distinctly singled
out the complex and dramatic luminous magic of the Valley
of the Arno, Perugino included, in the immense perspective space of the background, the crystal-clear mirror of the
beautiful «lake of Perugia», resolved in the embrace of sweet
hilly profiles that revealed that love, with which he meant
to recall, between halos and reverberations, the most inti-
mate suggestions of his land. In more than one occasion his
landscapes, marked by a rhythmic scansion of space, make
perceive their Flemish derivation,[22] but in the construction of the environment and of the perspective of this work,
as in the same *Combat between Love and Chastity*, Perugino
unquestionably makes recourse with a different artistic representation to a depiction of true and familiar places, where
thin small trees stand out definite and delicate between the
marine blue of the sky and the slimy green of the hills, reflected in lacustrine bays. Landscapes with topographically
realistic recalls and typical partial views of the Umbrian territory, well ordered and deprive of precipitous cliffs, but that,
though unveiling, with their soft light and the silence in the
background, the psychology of the personages, in the end
proposed themselves in a repetitive formula of limited sig-
nificance, since the artist had not grasped the variety of nature and of life, like instead can be evicted in the repertoire
of the leonardian landscape geomorphologies, in any case
subtended to express a philosophical concept and to make
painting a science.
And the Trasimeno turned out to be a territory on which
Leonardo right in those years (1502-03) was unfolding his
scientific interest and his high technical-hydraulic competence, involved in a global plan of reclamation, where drawing would have allowed him to visualize and dominate the
real hydro-geological problems of the entire region (Windsor, RL 12278 *r*), devising for the Lake a grandiose plan that
would have made it communicating with the swamp of the
Chiane, the Arno and the Tiber in order to eliminate over-

---

[21]   Vasari recalls, among the episodes that embittered the life of Perugino, the
realization of an *Ascension* for the greater altar of the Annunziata, carried out after
the abandonment of Leonardo and the premature death of Filippino Lippi. The
work, once completed (4 November 1507), was immediately criticized by all the
artists for the repeated proposition of figurative formulas already seen and completely «ordinary», becoming thus a subject of common jesting so as to provoke
the twilight of his Florentine fame: «They say that when the above said work
was unveiled, then it was blamed much by all the new artists. Pietro had made
use of those figures which other times he was used to put in effect, about which
tempting him, his friends said that he did not get tired and that he had omitted
the good way of operating and for avarice and in order not to lose time he had
incurred in such an error. To which Pietro answered: «I have put in effect the
figures that other times they praised, and that they infinitely liked; if now they
dislike them and they do not praise them, what can I do?». But those people un-
pleasantly with sonnets and public insolences teased him». Pietro Vannucci, born
around 1448-1450 at Castel della Pieve (that, since 1601, took the denomination of

Città della Pieve), died of plague in Fontignano di Perugia, in February 1523.
[22]   See M. Friedländer, *From Van Eyck to Bruegel*, London, 1965.

flowing, epidemics and to favour trade activities with navigation. Holding in consideration these aspects, Paolo Giovio, in his *Dialogi de viris et foeminis aetate nostra florentibus* (1528), where classic and humanistic motives cohabit, intended to describe through the intervention of Giovanni Antonio Muscettola, in the invention of a conversation set and held in Ischia with Alfonso d'Avalos, the long artistic route of Perugino, shining now of its own light, now wrapped with dense penumbra, in front of the pictorial excellence and the fresh and varied communicative inventions, in the ways and in the solutions, created by Leonardo, Michelangelo and the same Raphael:

Who in fact has ever exercised painting, in his valid years, with more success and fame than Perugino, which although eighty years old continues to paint with enough firm hand, but with no glory anymore? Nevertheless, for much time, and ostentatiously, all the Italian princes paid tribute to him, when he spread outstanding - as then they seemed to be - documents of his art. Nobody in fact represented with more sweetness and seduction than he did the face and the expression of the saints and above all of the angels, and the same Pope Sixtus gave testimony of it, that gave him the palm when the artists harshly competed in decorating his private chapel. But after that those stars of a perfect art called Vinci, Michelangelo and Raphael, risen all of a sudden from the darkness of that age, submerged both his reputation and his name with their wonderful works, to no avail Perugino, emulating and imitating better things, strained to keep the grade reached, because the running dry of his imagination forced him to always return to those affected faces on which he had fixed when he was young, so that his mind resisted with difficulty to shame, while they depicted with wonderful variety in every kind of subjects the naked limbs of majestic figures and the pressing forces of nature.

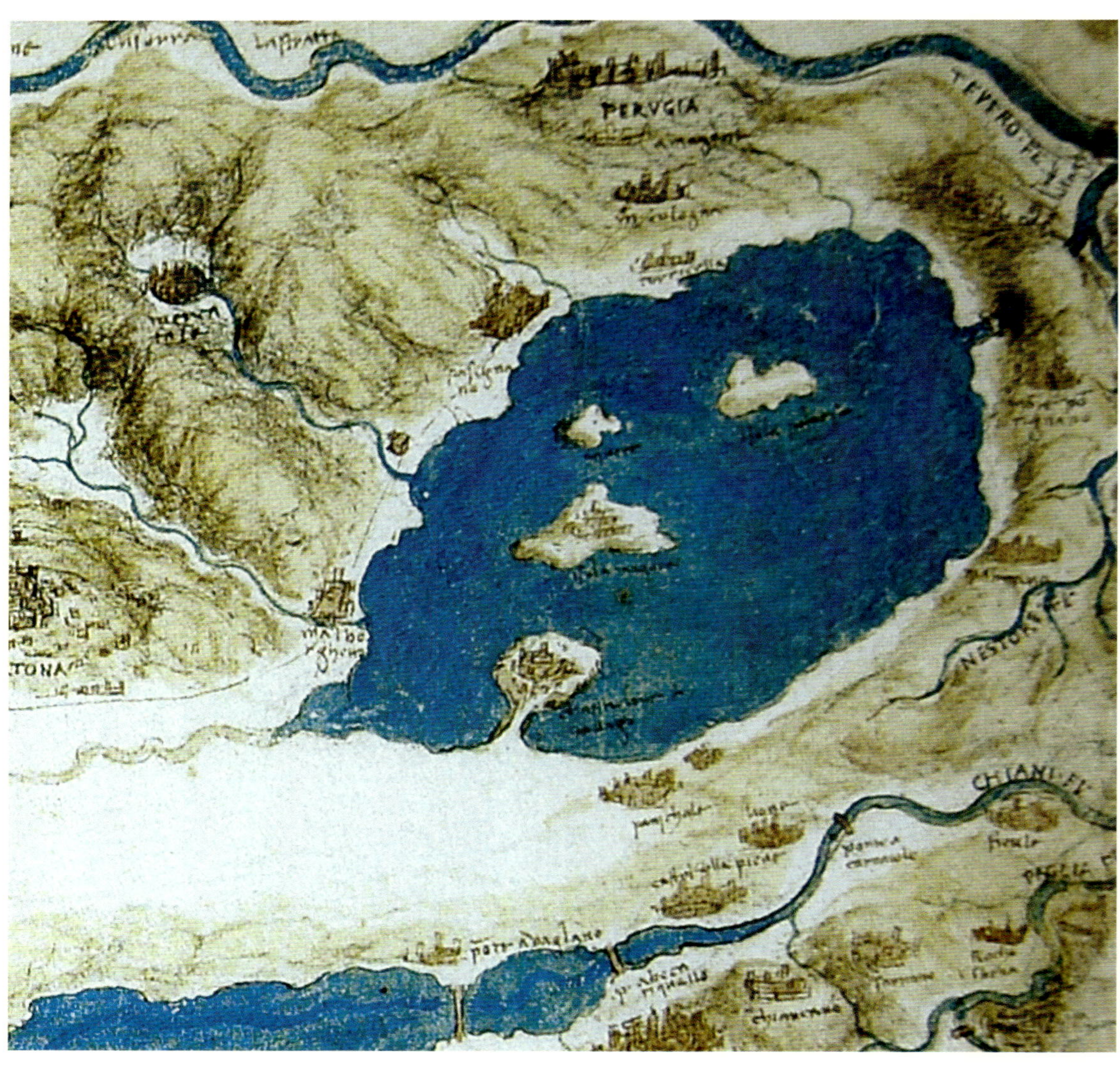

LEONARDO DA VINCI, *The Val di Chiana, the Trasimeno Lake and the surrounding regions, c.* 1503. Charcoal, pen and ink and watercolour, 338 x 488 mm. Windsor, RL 12278 *r.* Particular

Leonardo and the flight over the Lake Trasimeno

AMONG THE plates that make the base of the Bell tower of Giotto in Florence even more precious, in the representation of the mechanical and liberal arts, Andrea Pisano decided to reproduce the flight of Daedalus, the man «faber», inventor and technologist, that first desired to glide in the air, challenging gravity laws.[1]

And the dream of Icarus would have fascinated Leonardo since his juvenile years, when he realized, with a series of technical–anatomical illustrations (CA, ff. 341 *rc* [934 *r*]; 308 *r-a* [844 *r*]), defined by the perfection of the drawing, meant as a scientific demonstration, the first visual representation of his flying machines with flapping wings, in analogy with the movement of birds. And right from the analytic observation of their flight, with the fast disassembling of the movements for bending, distension, rotation and raising of the mechanical wing and with the study of the various positions of the head, of the tail and of the centre of gravity of birds, he would have worked out in the course of years his own theory about the flight.

The same archetypical similarity between the human arms and the wings of flying creatures would have corroborated in his mind the possibility of this extraordinary event (Windsor, RL 12656 *r*; RL 19000 *v*).

Studying and reproducing faithfully the shape and the various articulations of the wings, included the examination of the *alula* considered as determining for its function of rudder and for the permanence in the air of a bird, Leonardo would have reached the certainty to grant to his attempt of flight the necessary safety also in order to face the force of the wind (Codex on the Flight of Birds, ff. 7 *v* and 8 *v*): «because the wings have to row downwards and backwards so as to sustain the instrument and so that it goes ahead» (Codex on the Flight of Birds, ff. 16 *v*-17 *r*).

The human flight in fact constituted for his mind the higher experience of the mechanical utopia, the conquest of space, a sublime wonder, the projecting of a dream that was on the way to realize itself, the oneiric pleasure of the immensity and of absolute freedom.

From here his careful observation on the flight of the dove and of the swallow (CA, f. 369 *r-a* [1030 *r*]),[2] of the skylark and of the crane (CA, f. 220 *v-a* [220 *v-c*]),[3] of the bat (CA, f. 311 *v.b-c-d* [854 *r*]) and of the kite (Codex on the Flight of Birds, f. 6 *v*),[4] that would have lead him, the last one, to the reconstruction of an obsessive nightmare, with a strongly erotic content, suffered in his early childhood.

In a powerful oneiric vision, the kite would have come down,

---

[1] See A. PAOLUCCI, *I rilievi del campanile: una teologia del lavoro,* in *Alla scoperta di piazza del Duomo in Firenze, 2: La Cattedrale di Santa Maria del Fiore,* a cura di T. Verdon, Firenze, Centro DI, 1993.

[2] Leonardo, in his studies for the construction of a mechanical wing, lingers on the description of the swallow's wing: «The swallow has its wings very different from those of the kite, because it is very short of arms and long of hand. Its flying is beaten in two directions, that is the hand is rowed towards the tail and the arm towards the ground; and in this way the first motion pushes it ahead and the other maintains it in its height and at its will it leads both of them on one direction», (CA, f. 1030 *v*).

[3] Studying the relationship of gravity and resistance of the air, Leonardo examines the flight of cranes and reports that the alternation of the gliding flight, with wavy resumptions or short circular evolutions, extends the distance covered by the bird: «Descending of bird without wind or beating of wings […] If the bird that does not beat the wings, does not want to go down soon, it will do as to go up again, after some slanting descent, by means of reflected motion and to turn round, rising to similarity of the cranes, when they disband the ordered lines of their flight, and they concentrate in a horde, and go up with many turns like in a screw, and then, returned to the first line, they follow again their first motion, which falls down with sweet slope, and then concentrate again in a horde, and turning round again they move up», (CA, f. 591 *v*).

[4] See LEONARDO DA VINCI, *Codice sul Volo degli Uccelli, c.* 1505. Torino, Biblioteca Reale; *Codice sul Volo degli Uccelli e varie altre materie,* a cura di G. Piumati e T. Sabachnikoff, Paris, Rouveyre, 1893; *Il Codice sul Volo degli Uccelli nella Biblioteca Reale di Torino,* a cura di A. Marinoni, Firenze, Giunti, 1976.

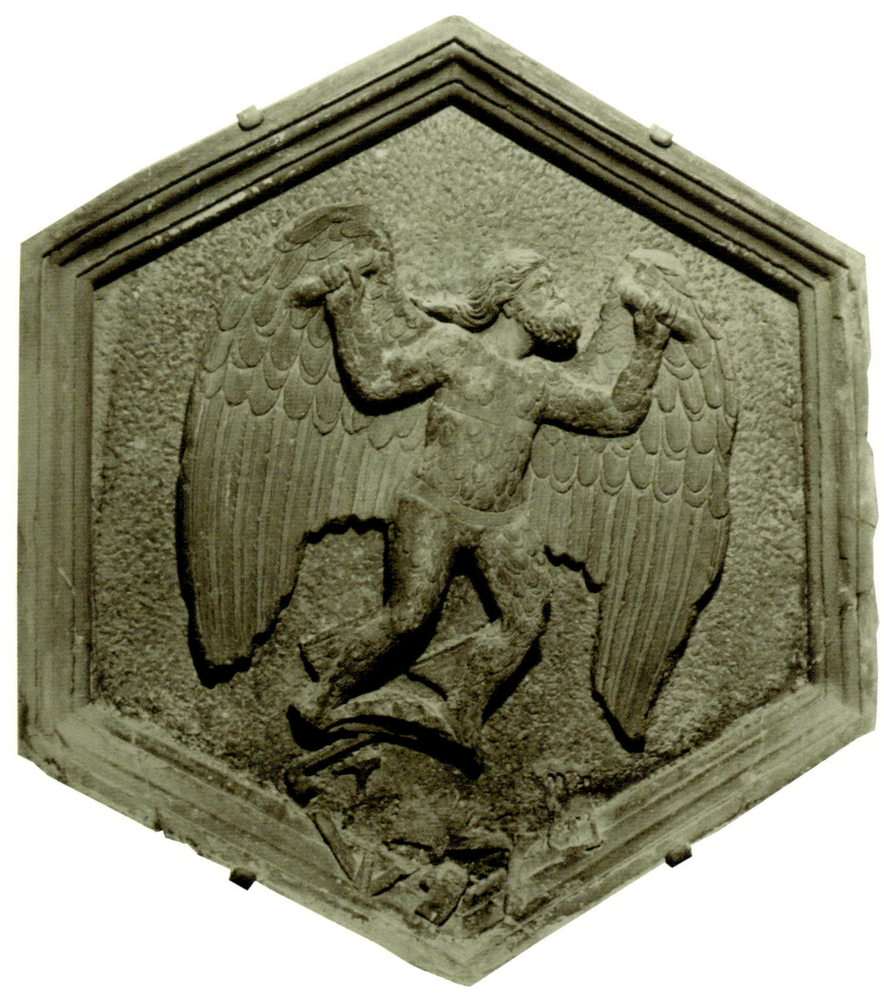

penetrating his lips with its tail, a symbol according to Freud of the androgynous figure of his mother, primary origin of his homosexuality:[5]

This writing so distinctively about the kite seems to be my destiny, because in the first remembrance of my infancy it seemed to me that while I was in the cradle, that a kite came to me and opened me my mouth with its tail, and many times hit me with such tail within the lips, (CA, f. 66 vb [186 v]).

[5] Such remembrance-daydream would have determined, among the psycho-analysts of the past century, the rising of an interpretation crowded with contro-versies. See S. Freud, *Eine Kindheitserinnerung des Leonardo da Vinci*, Leipzig und Wien, Denticke, 1910; E. Maclagan, *Leonardo in the consulting room*, «Burlington Magazine», XLII, 1923; M. Shapiro, *Leonardo and Freud: an Art-historical Study*, «Journal of the History of Hideas», XVII, 2, 1956; K. R. Eissler, *Leonardo da Vinci. Psychoanalytic Notes on the Enigma*, New York, Int. Univ. Press, 1961; S. Viderman, *La construction de l'éspace analitique*, Paris, Denoël, 1970; Id., *Le céleste et le sublunaire*, Paris, PUF, 1977. On the flight of the kite in presence or absence of wind, Leon-ardo would have added: «The kite and the other birds that beat little their wings look after the course of the wind, and when the wind reigns up, then they can be seen flying in great height, and if it reigns low, so they are low. When the wind does not reign in the air, then the kite beats more and more times its wings in its flight, in such a way so that it rises up and it acquires force, with which force it then declining to some extent, it goes for a long space without beating its wings, and when it has lowered, it again does the same, and so it follows afterwards, and this lowering without beating wings offers them a way to rest through the air after the fatigue of the aforesaid beating of wings», (Codex on the Flight of Birds, f. 6 v).

Instead, the studies on the wing of the bat, as expression of an experimental and fantastic elaboration, had appeared since the first leonardian devising of a flying machine with flapping wing, destined, in juvenile years (c. 1480), to the show of a sacred representation (Florence, Gabinetto Disegni e Stampe degli Uffizi, n. 447E v). But this type of wing is present also in several works of the contemporary Florentine art and above all in those that came out from the workshop of Verrocchio, like the Harpies of the marble *Lavabo* of the Old Sacristy of San Lorenzo, the relief of *Alexander the Great* in Washington, the *Bust of a commander of troops* at the British Museum, or in the same drawings by Leonardo reserved to the description of *winged dragons* (Windsor, RL 12370 r).

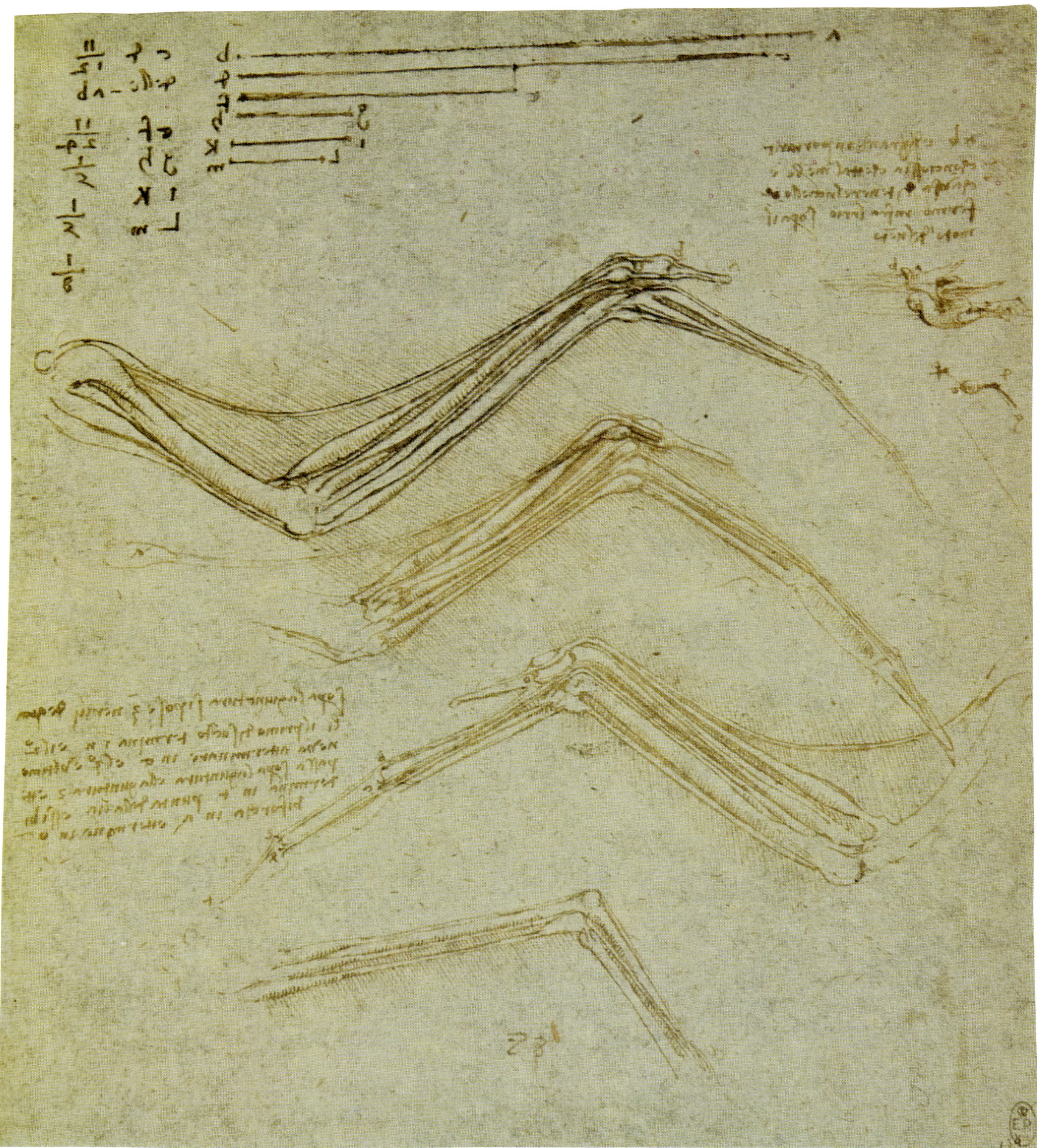

Leonardo da Vinci, *Anatomy of the wing of a bird*, c. 1513. Pen and ink, 225 x 205 mm. Windsor, RL 12656 *r*

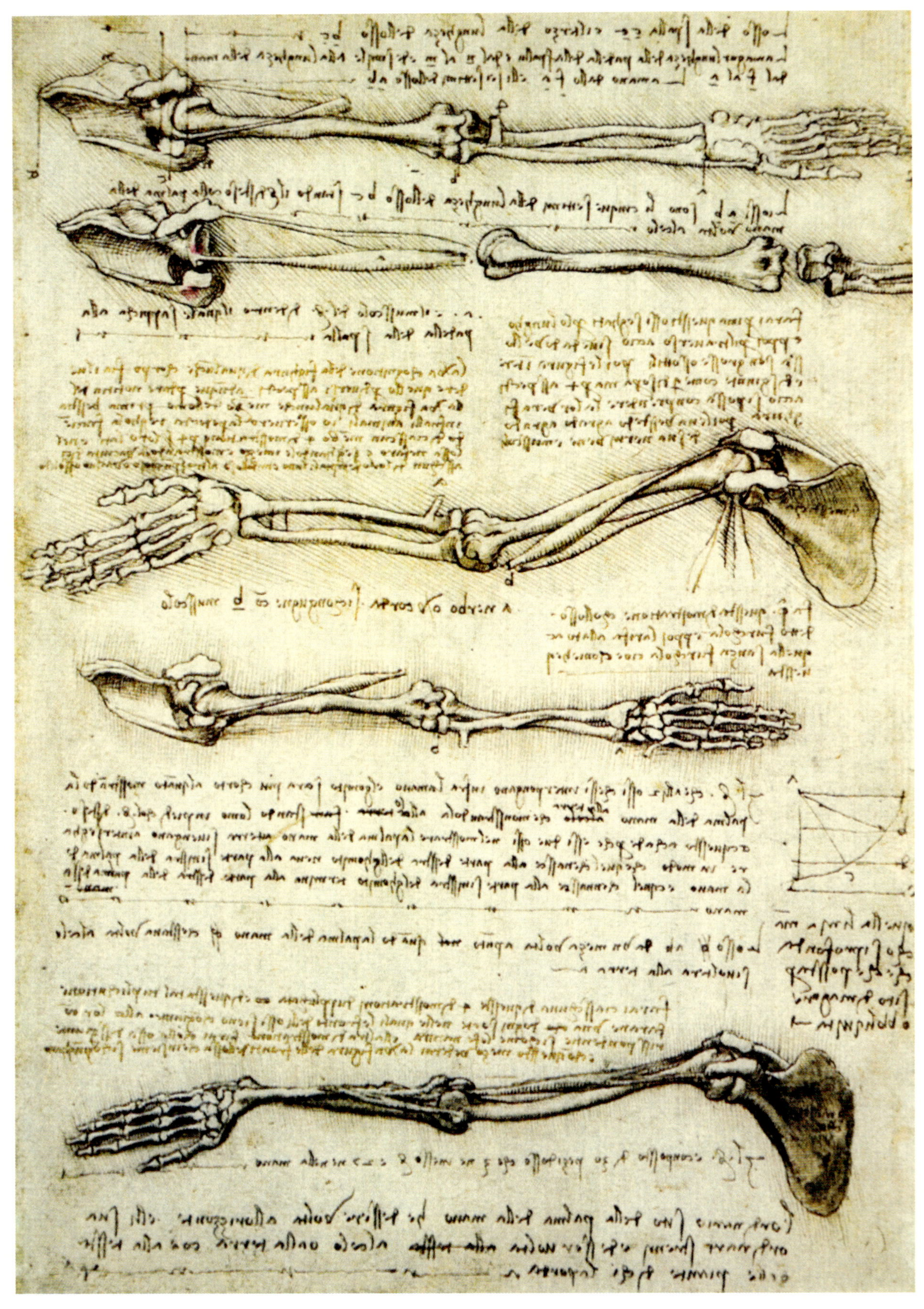

Leonardo da Vinci, *Anatomy of a human arm*, c. 1509-10. Pen and tawny ink, watercoloured on traces of charcoal, 219 x 200 mm. Windsor, RL 19000 *v*

After the experimentation of the flapping wing (Ms. B, f. 88 *v*), devised in order to verify the capability of the human strength in beating it during the flight and in order to study its resistance, the first plan of a true flying machine was the ornithopter (Ms. B, f. 74 *v*; CA, f. 302 *ra* [824 *v*]). This one, aspiring to imitate nature, in order then to triumph over it, following the wing beating of birds, would have moved using the muscular force of the man-pilot who, lying prone (Ms. B, f. 79 *r*) or with the body in vertical position (Ms. B, f. 80 *r*) and engaging at the same time his arms and feet, would have set in action a series of devices. The ensemble of these mechanisms, made of pulleys, winches, ropes, cranks, pedals (CA, ff. 307 *va* [843 *r*]), was destined, still on an experimental plane, to provide motion to the particular device of the wings, that beyond to the rotating motion were bent towards the inside for the sustentation and the advancing of the machine (CA, ff. 308 *va* [844 *v*]; 313 *ra* [858 *r*]).

Moreover, in order to favour even more the affirmation of the flight, these should have had to be covered with a membrane similar to that which covers the wings of a bat or the fins of the flying gurnard (CA, f. 308 *r-a* [844 *r*]). Such investigations arose from the concomitance of his researches committed to the world of zoology and ethology, of anatomy and of mechanics, where statics, dynamics and kinematics converged on the analysis of human motions in the most varied postures, in order then to pick and choose their different potentialities.

Considering, furthermore, the air as a compressible fluid and therefore capable of material thickness, Leonardo will carry out also studies in order to realize the upward motion inventing his «aerial screw» or «helicopter» (Ms. B, f. 83 *v*). It was a device with shovels, with which to penetrate and screw in the fluid, and the positive result of the experiment would have been depending on the speed with which the operator would have made rotate the device spiral-shaped and of which the artist devised to supply precise technological indications:

> *The outer extremity of the screw must be of iron thread as large as a rope, and from the circle to the centre it must be 8 arms. I am sure, if this instrument made in shape of a screw will be well made, that is to say of linen cloth, closed every pore with starch, and turned with promptness, that the aforesaid screw will be female in the air and it will climb up. Take example from one line wide and thin, and shaken with fury in the air: you will see your arm to be guided by the cutting line of the aforesaid axis. It must be the structure of the aforesaid cloth made of long and large cane. You can do a small model of it made of paper, whose style is of a thin slab of iron, and it is twisted by force, in returning to free condition it makes the screw turn around.*

As a result, the aerial navigation, from a simple literary fantasy, that had animated the creative mind of other scientists, from the naturalist philosopher Ruggero Bacone (*c.* 1214-1294)[6] to the engineer of Siena Mariano di Jacopo known as Taccola (1382-1458),[7] was transformed in his analytic mind in an experimental event, to be lived in the thrilling prophetic vision of the first flight in history.

Therefore, considered insufficient the muscular force of man in relation to his weight and to the largeness of the machine,[8] analyzed the resistance of the air, the ascending currents of dynamic origin, the delicate mechanisms of equilibrium of the body, the position of the barycentre and the trim of the wings, Leonardo, in the years between 1496 and 1505, passed from the study of the machine for the flapping flight, set in action with the muscular force, to that one for the gliding flight, where the wings offered a greater surface to the currents and the pilot, with light movements, could modify the centre of gravity of his own body and perform the ma-

[6] See D. Laurenza, *Gli studi leonardiani sul volo. Spunti per una riconsiderazione*, in *Tutte le opere non son per istancarmi. Raccolta di scritti per i settant'anni di Carlo Pedretti*, a cura di F. Frosini, Roma, Edizioni Associate, 1998; Id., *Leonardo. Il volo*, Firenze, Giunti, 2004; See *Epistola Fratris Rogeri Baconis de Secretis Operibus Artis et Naturae, et de Nullitate Magiae*, cap. IV; J. S. Brewer, London, 1859: «Nam instrumenta navigandi possunt fieri sine hominibus remigantibus, ut naves maximae, fluviales et marinae. Item currus possunt fieri ut sine animali moveantur cum impetu inaestimabili; ut aestimamus currus falcati fuisse, quibus antiquitus pugnabatur. Item possunt fieri instrumenta volandi, ut homo sedeat in medio instrumenti revolvens aliquod ingenium, per quod alae artificialiter compositae aerem verberent, ad modum avi volantis […] Possunt etiam instrumenta fieri ambulandi in mari, vel fluminibus, usque ad fundum absque periculo corporali […] Et infinita quasi talia fieri possunt; ut pontes ultra flumina sine columna, vel aliquod sustentaculo et machinationes et ingenia inaudita». [«In fact the instruments to navigate can exist without men rowing, as huge ships made for rivers and seas. In the same way carts that can move without animals with immeasurable force can exist; as we think they were the scythed chariots, with which in ancient times they fought. In the same way instruments to fly can exist, that a man sits in the middle of the instrument turning some sort of device, by means of which artificially made wings can beat the air, in the way of the flying birds (…) Can furthermore exist instruments to walk in the sea, or in rivers, to the bottom without danger for the body (…) And such things can be almost infinite; as bridges across rivers without pylons, or any sustentation and machines and devices never heard before». From Latin. Tr. N.]

[7] See A. Chastel, *Les limites du savoir scientifique chez Leonardo*, in *Leonardo e l'Età della Ragione*, a cura di E. Bellone e P. Rossi, Milano, Scientia, 1982; P. Galluzzi, *Leonardo da Vinci: dalle tecniche alla tecnologia*, in *Gli ingegneri del Rinascimento da Brunelleschi a Leonardo da Vinci*, Firenze, Giunti, 1996.

[8] See L. Beltrami, *L'aeroplano di Leonardo*, in *Leonardo da Vinci. Conferenze fiorentine*, Milano, Treves, 1910; G. Boffito, *Il volo in Italia: storia documentata e aneddotica dell'aeronautica e dell'aviazione in Italia*, Firenze, Barbèra, 1921; R. Giacomelli, *Gli scritti di Leonardo da Vinci sul volo*, Roma, Bardi, 1936; Id., *Leonardo da Vinci aerodinamico, aerologo, aerotecnico ed osservatore del volo degli uccelli*, «Atti del Convegno di Studi Vinciani», Firenze, Olschki, 1953; A. Uccelli, C. Zammattio, *I libri del volo di Leonardo da Vinci*, Milano, Hoepli, 1952; C. Pedretti, *Studi Vinciani*, Genève, Droz, 1957; L. Reti, *Helicopters and Whirligigs*, «Raccolta Vinciana», XX, Milano, 1964; C. H. Gibbs-Smith, *Aviation. An Historical Survey from its Origins to the End of World War II*, London, HMSO, 1985; G. P. Galdi, *Leonardo's Helicopter and Archimedes Screw: The Principle of Action and Reaction*, «Achademia Leonardi Vinci. Journal of Leonardo Studies and Bibliography of Vinciana», IV, Firenze, Giunti, 1991; M. Pidcock, *The Hang Glider*, «Achademia Leonardi Vinci. Journal of Leonardo Studies and Bibliography of Vinciana», VI, Firenze, Giunti, 1993.

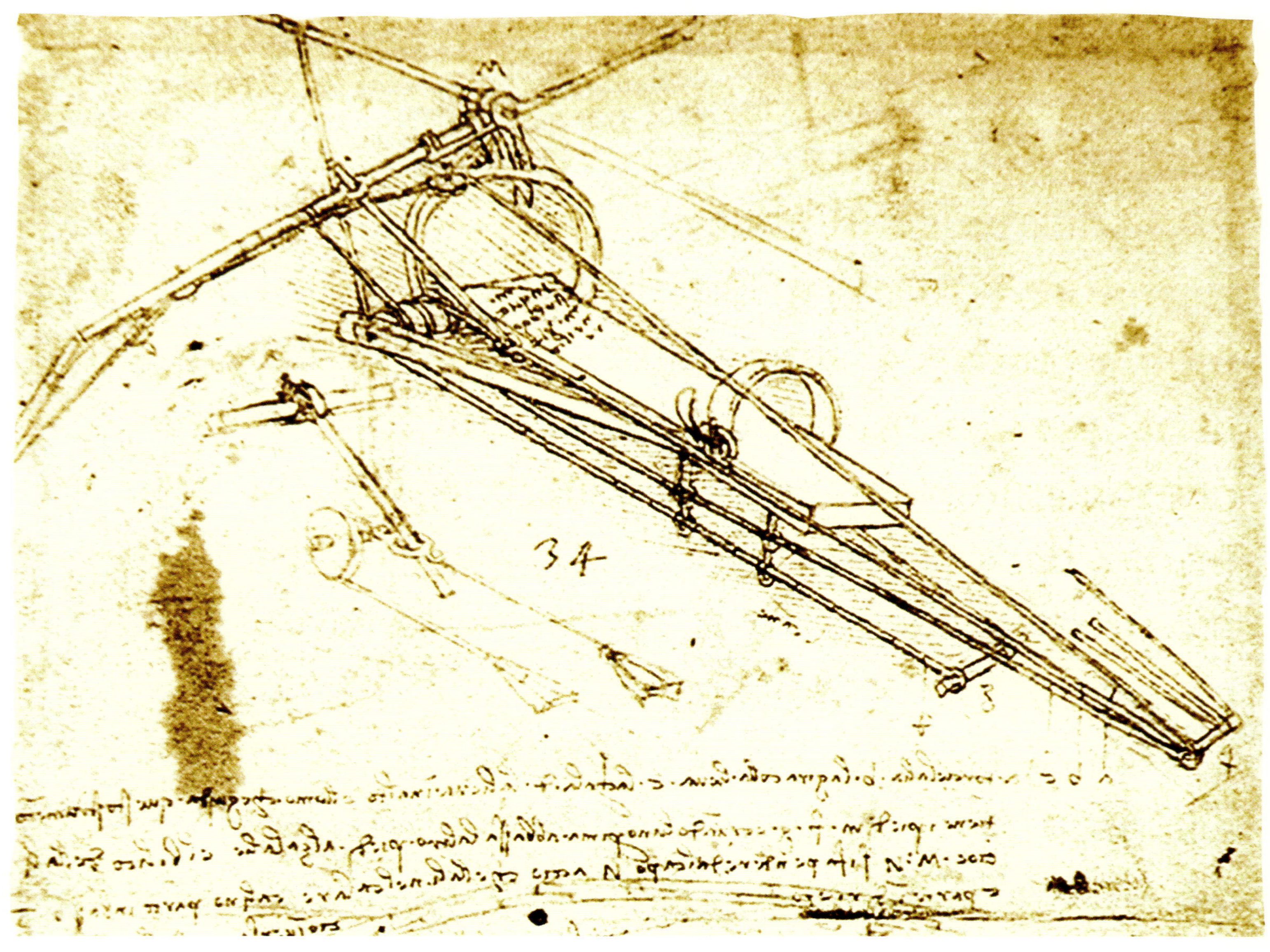

LEONARDO DA VINCI, *Flying machine*, c. 1485-87. Pen and ink, 282 x 193 mm. Codex Atlanticus, f. 824 *v*. Milan, Biblioteca Ambrosiana

noeuvres of equilibrium and direction on the aerial currents. It was around 1505 that Leonardo, under the constant impulse to realize his flying machine, continued to deepen in a meticulous way his studies on the flight of birds (Codex on the Flight of Birds, f. 8 *r*), with aesthetic and scientific annotations on the disposition of wings and their influence on the rapidity of the descendent flight in presence of wind, as on the fall of bodies in vertical and in oblique, according to their weight, to their shape, to their homogeneity and to the aerodynamic reaction or resistance of the air, generally considered of uniform density (CA, ff. 66 *ra-va-rb* [185 *r-v*; 186 *r*]). He did not lack to avail himself, in the verification of certain principles necessary to gliding, of the direct observation of the behaviour in presence of wind of kites, also of great dimensions, able to raise a man and already employed in military activities and operations, as can be deduced by the notes written, around 1497, on sheet 64 *r* of the Codex of Madrid I.

From the study of the dynamics of fluids in fact he would have developed his investigations about the discontinuous, circular and whirling motion of the wind (the «science of the winds», Ms. E, f. 54 *r*),[9] the importance to avoid with skill,

---

[9] Leonardo, between 1513 and 1516, in a stringent parallelism, combining the study, for him more than familiar by now, of the water currents with that of the science of the winds, diffusely deals with the subject of the aerial currents, where birds are precisely destined to move: «To give true knowledge of the motion of birds in between the air it is necessary to give first knowledge of the winds, which we shall demonstrate by means of the motions of water in itself and this such perceptive knowledge will transform itself into a stairway to make us reach the cognition of the winged creatures between the air and the wind», (Ms. E, f. 54 *r*).

CARLO STARNAZZI

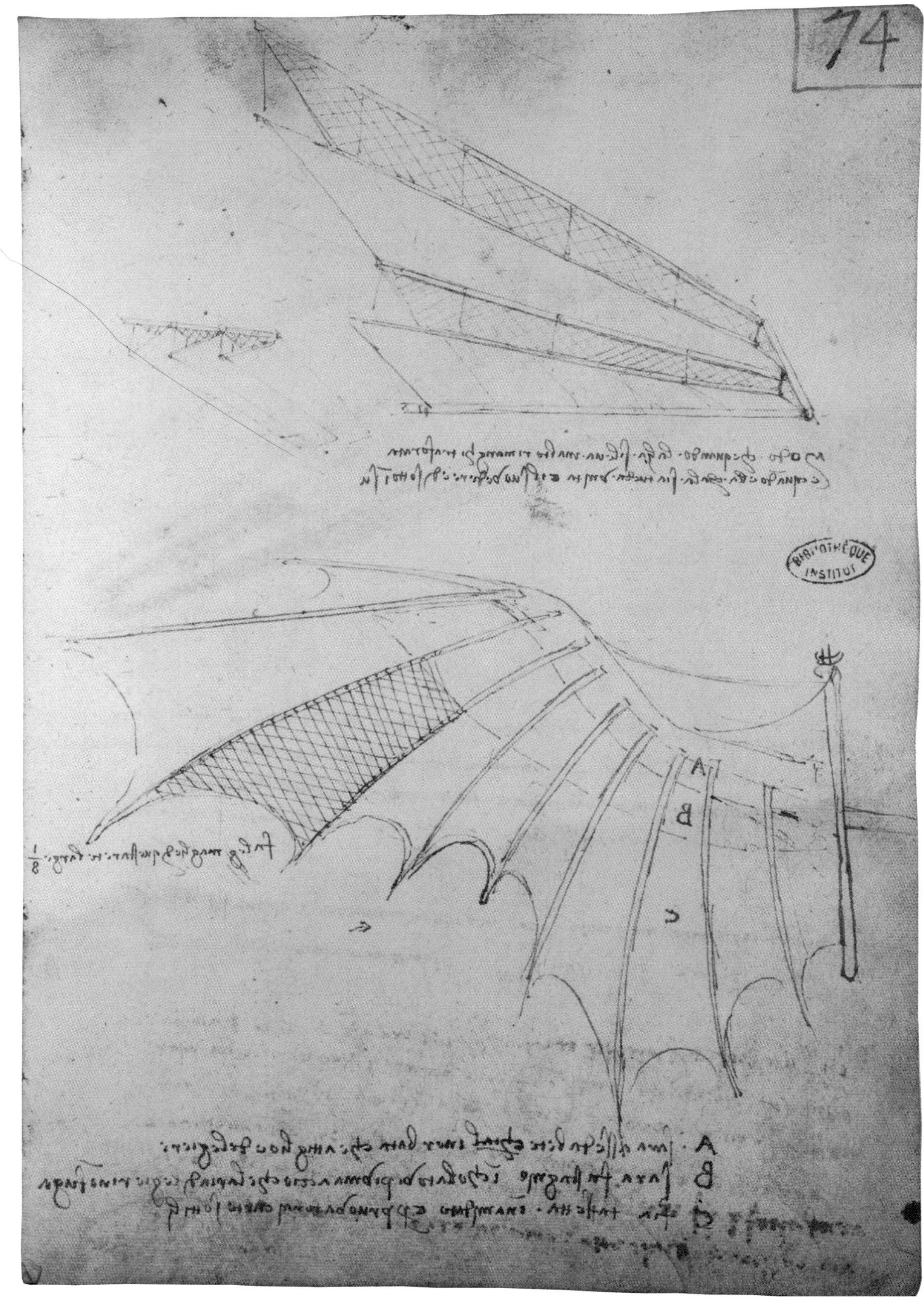

LEONARDO DA VINCI, *Study of the wing's structure of a flying machine, c.* 1485–87. Pen and ink, 231 x 167 mm. Ms. B, f. 74 r. Paris, Institut de France

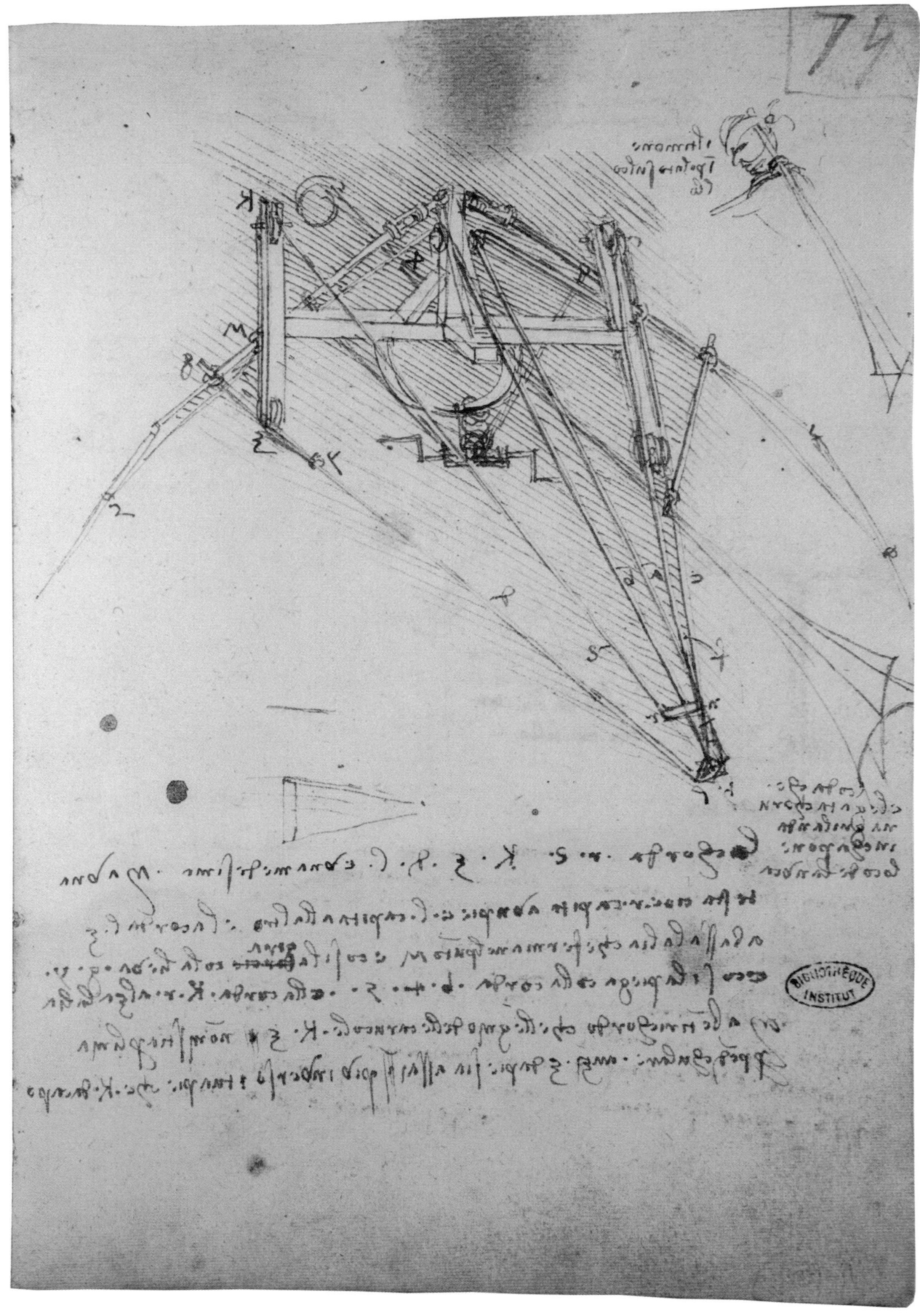

Leonardo da Vinci, *Flying machine with pilot in horizontal position*, c. 1485–87. Pen and ink, 231 x 167 mm. Ms. B, f. 75 *r*. Paris, Institut de France

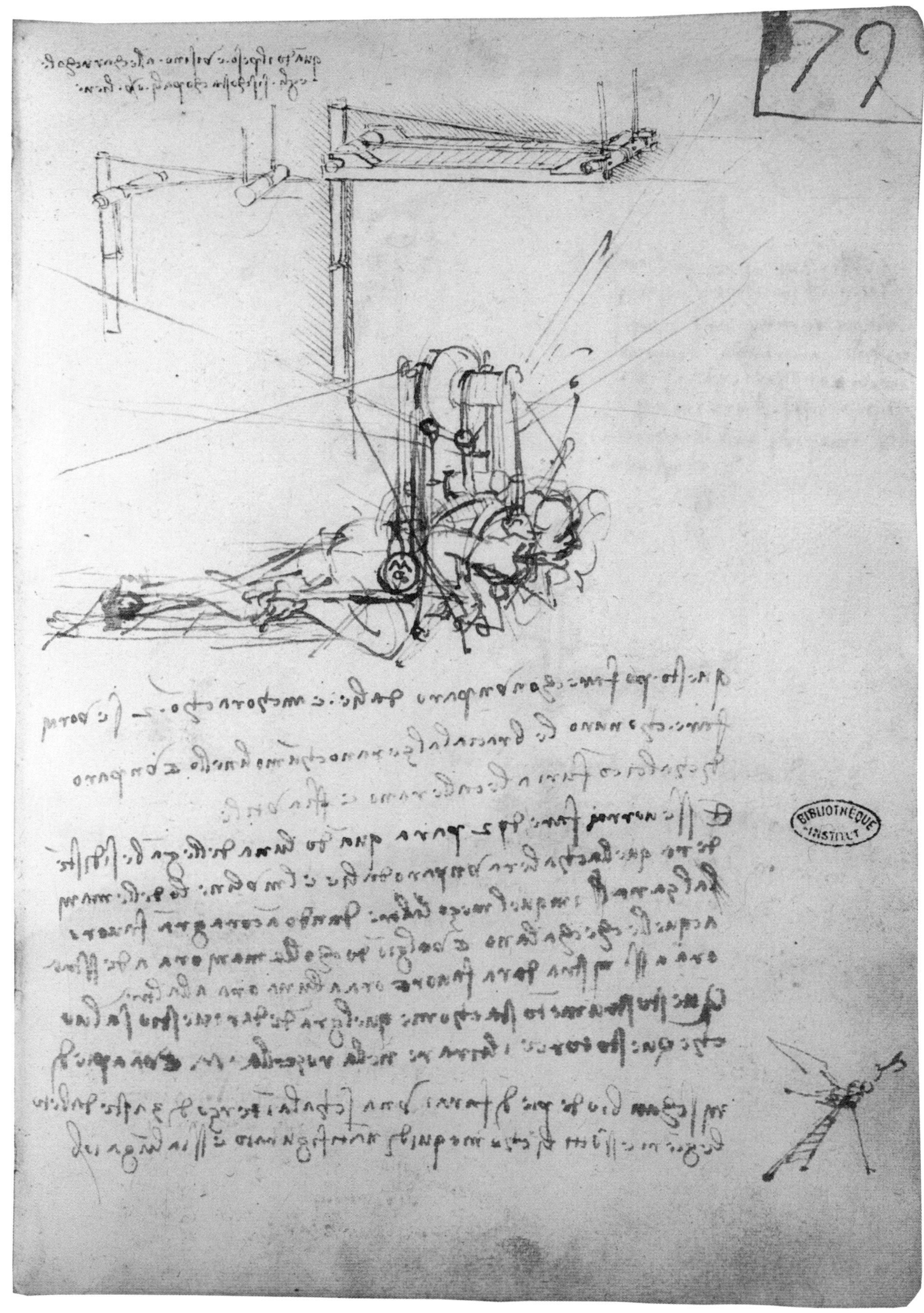

Leonardo da Vinci, *Ornithopter with pilot in prone position*, c. 1487-90. Pen and ink, 231 x 167 mm. Ms B, f. 79 *r*. Paris, Institut de France

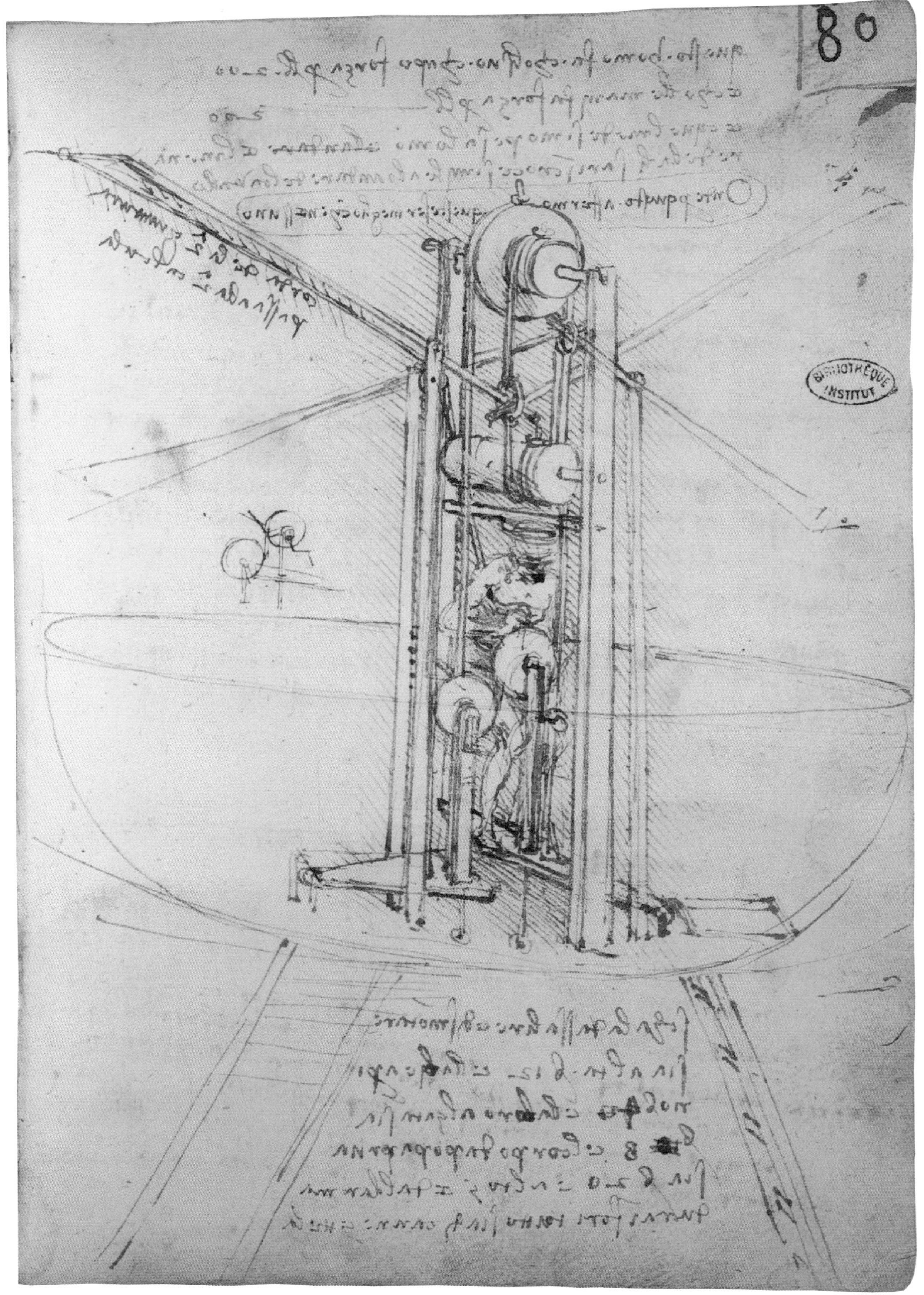

LEONARDO DA VINCI, *Flying vessel*, *c.* 1485–87. Pen and ink, 231 x 167 mm. Ms. B, f. 80 *r*. Paris, Institut de France

as for his cognition, the zones of turbulence at the «mouths of the mountains»,[10] the attention to deserve to the exploitation of the aerial currents (Codex on the Flight of Birds, f. 8 *r*; Ms. E, f. 42 *v*). He wished to rise himself in the air and slide like birds do over plains and over mountains, to «discover more countries», the valleys, the rivers, the lakes and to observe them in that richness of particulars, with which he had represented, in aerial perspective at bird flight and in a constant relationship between science and art, the Valdichiana and the Tyrrhenian coast, from the mouth of the Serchio to Civitavecchia, Central-Northern Italy, from the Adriatic to the Appennines, the course of the Sieve and of the Arno (Windsor, RL 12277 *r*; 12278 *r*). As a result, to widen and to close the wings, to spread the tail, to come down in oblique, to decline, to decrease, to turn, to go around and to rise, will be the movements carefully studied about the flight of birds, observed and inquired up to the smallest detail, but also lived over again in the representation of his mind.

Moved from Peretola with Zoroastro, his collaborator in the *Battle of Anghiari*, to the real space of Monte Ceceri, a hill near Fiesole after the quarries of Maiano, he experimented, in a fantastic and prophetic tension, where man for the first time became spirit of the instrumental bird, the functional capabilities of his flying machine, a sort of glider or hang-glider with light great wings (Codex on the Flight of Birds, II cop.*v*):

> *The great bird will take the first flight over the elevation of the great Cecero, and filling up with astonishment the universe, filling up with its reputation all the writings, and eternal glory to the nest where it was born.*

The disaster happened, the machine fell right after the take-off, ruining to earth and demonstrating the impossibility to realize a technological dream. But Leonardo, animated by the knowledge of the laws of nature and of the «admirable» secrets of technique, as a tireless machine-maker devised to experiment the flight again, turning his attention to the shores of the lake Trasimeno, for a long time subject of his hydraulic and cartographic studies (Windsor, RL 12278),[11] where to formulate his last challenge for the overcoming of human limits.

He meant to take wing from above a tower, perhaps that so singular of Castiglion del Lago, dominion of Giampaolo Baglioni, known in the months of the uprising of Arezzo against Florence, in Summer 1502.

It had been perhaps Baglioni to introduce him the figure and the cases of Giovan Battista Danti, nicknamed the «Daedalus of Perugia», crash-landed on the roofs of the city for the detachment of one joint of his wings. It was a matter then to safeguard the pilot, protecting him from the risks of a possible fall in water or on the mainland. Therefore, after having for a long time carried out studies on the parachute and the slow descent to the ground («If a man has a pavilion made of impregnated linen cloth that is 12 arms in its face and high 12, he will be able to launch himself from any great height without damage for himself, CA, f. 381 *va* [1058 *v*], *c.* 1480), between 1503 and 1505, equipped the navigator wrapping him in a life-jacket, constituted from a series of swollen wineskins, so that, on the first impact, nearly anticipating the principle of the «air-bag»,[12] it swelled itself «as a paternoster» (Codex on the Flight of Birds, f. 16 *r*) and protected all the body. An experience already devised since his first years of stay in Milan (1487-90), when he was deepening with enthusiasm his theoretical studies on the flight and planned to experiment the functionality of his flying machine, assuming also its possible fall on the surface of a lake: «you will wear attached encircled to your belt a long leather bag, so that in falling you are not drowned» (Ms. B, f. 74 *v*).

To navigate in the sky will be the dream also of Otto Lilienthal (1848-1896) that, as it appears in his book *The Flight of Birds as a Basis of the Art of Flying* (1889), would have tried to resolve the problems of the mechanical flight, on the basis of the natural flight and of its laws, that is by imitating the flight of birds. In 1896, having read the manuscript of Leonardo, he will try many times the glided flight down from an artificial hill in the outskirts of Berlin with an apparatus with wings made of oilcloth. But, on 9 August of the same year, losing control of the apparatus, governed only with the movements

---

[10] Examining, around 1505, the course of the wind along the slope of the hills, on the top of the mountains or in the outlet of the valleys, Leonardo observed: «In the top of the mountains the wind is made of great density and in the mouths of the valleys, when the mountains that close them are of great height [...] The whirls or vortices of the winds are born in the winds that open in the embrace of mountains or of some building, and then in rejoining, they strike each other with strength; and their reflected motions are not following a straight line, because it is blocked in its own sphere, where it moves, by a matter similar to itself, which has the force to stop the direct force and to bend it; whence such wind, not being able to stretch itself, is consuming its strength with mo<tion>», (CA, f. 493 *v*) and, in the Codex Arundel (f. 276 *r*), he continued: «The wind condenses itself over the native places of its percussion, and more on the top of the mountains than on the beaches, by it beaten, because here come all the reflected winds, that is on the top of the directness of the sides of the mountains, where the winds beat, which then do not continue all transversal ones to follow the shape of the top of the mountain, but many of them go up along a straight line and most of all those who beat nearer to the bases of the mountains, so that, after that they are over the top of the mountain, they start bending and, after such incurving, they go along the course of the other wind that had beaten them and that before had incurved them».

[11] See S. ALBERTI DE MAZZERI, *Leonardo. L'uomo e il suo tempo*, Milano, Rusconi, 1983; M. KEMP, *Leonardo da Vinci. Le mirabili operazioni della natura e dell'uomo*, Milano, Mondadori 1982; ID., *Les inventions de la nature et la nature de l'invention*, in *Léonard de Vinci ingénieur et architecte*, catalogo della mostra di Montreal, Montreal Museum of Fine Arts, 1987; C. VECCE, *Leonardo*, 1998, op. cit.

[12] See C. PEDRETTI, *Leonardo. Le macchine*, Firenze, Giunti, 2000.

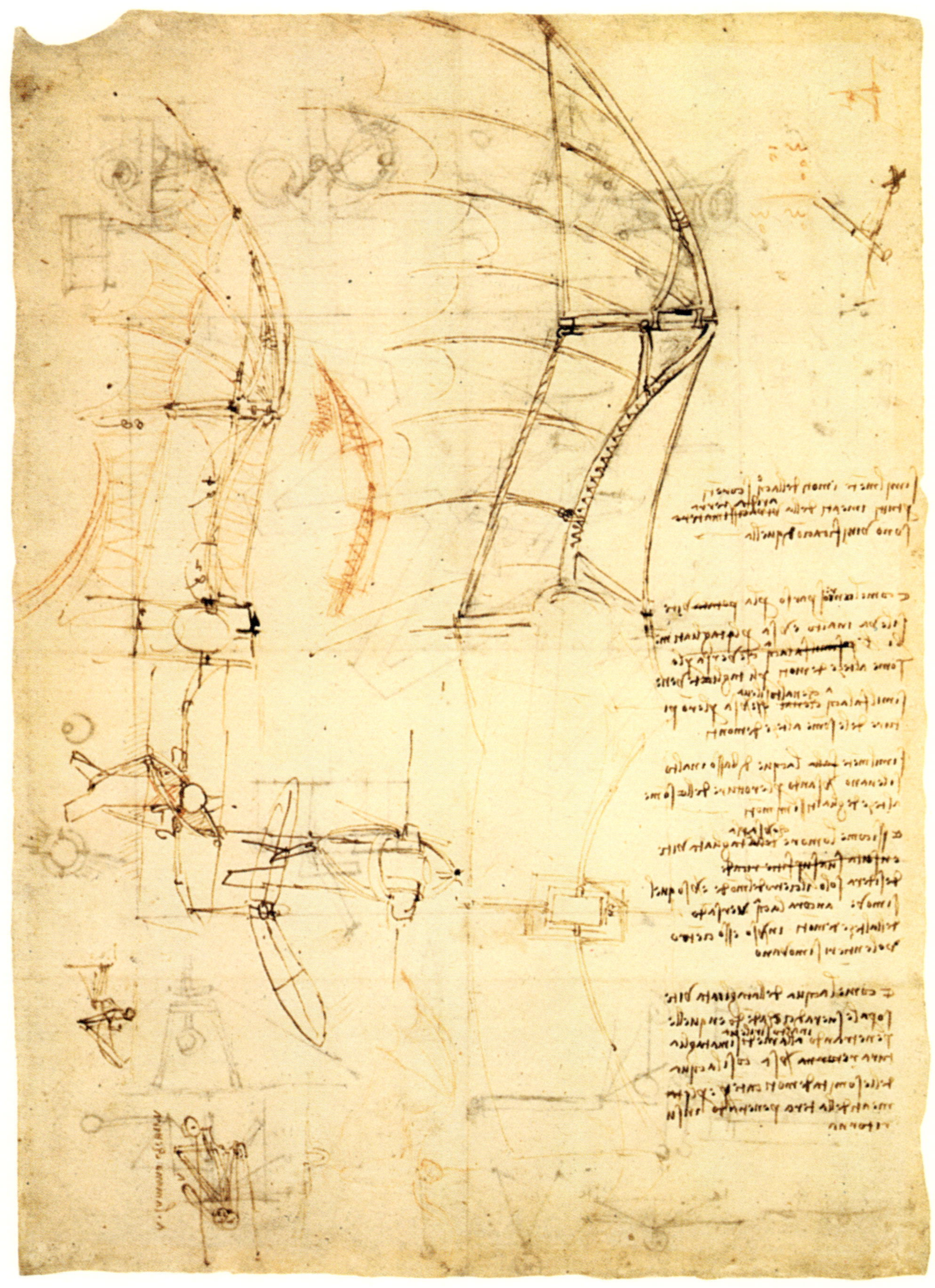

LEONARDO DA VINCI, *Studies for the flying machine*, *c.* 1493-95. Pen and ink, 289 x 205 mm. Codex Atlanticus, f. 846 *v.* Milan, Biblioteca Ambrosiana

of the body, he fell from a height of more than twenty meters and died. Only the brothers Wilbur and Orville Wright (1867-1912 and 1871-1948), constructors of bicycles of Dayton, Ohio, will be the first to fly with a biplane, abandoning the natural imitative flight, along the sandy dunes of Kitty Hawk, in North Carolina. On 17 December 1903, these dunes would have been theatre of the extraordinary realization of a dream that would have set off the modern history of aeronautics.

To the Wright brothers, four years of attempts had been necessary with kites and gliders, in order to try the system of twisting of wings and the construction of a 12 HP gasoline engine for the biplane that, as a sign of good wishes, they had christened with the name of *The Flyer*. They had become excited by the ideas of Leonardo, reading his studies about the flight in the *Aeronautical Annual* (I, 1899) of Boston. But only Allen Bryan, in 1977, making use of muscular force, according to the vincian rules, will succeed to cross with his flying machine the straits of the Channel, [13] while Angelo D'Arrigo, in 2005, making use of the results achieved by the engineers of the Fiat Research Centre together with the Federico II University in the studies of aerodynamics for the reproduction of the wing of a condor in relation to the human flight, according to the most traditional vincian spirit, making the most of the upward dynamic currents with the slightest waste of energy, like the birds of prey, as «the eagles and the vultures» (Ms. E, f. 43 *v*), he managed to fly for 4 hours over the Andean Cordilleras, at a speed of 180 Km per hour, reaching, under prohibitive conditions (50° C below zero), an altitude of 9100 meters. D'Arrigo, in 2003, had made another singular experience, piloting with success the model of a light hang-glider reconstructed faithfully according to the drawings of Leonardo (Codex of Madrid I, f. 64 *r*), by the Ideal Museum Leonardo da Vinci, in collaboration with the Municipality of Sigillo (in the Province of Perugia), the Association «Progetto Insieme» and «Icaro 2000»,

thus demonstrating the validity of the vincian gliding and aerostatic flight, where the pilot of the hang-glider, whose devices contemplated the coupling with a deformable or cardan mechanical joint, entrusted himself to the course of the winds, as the artist-scientist had proposed with his glider around 1495, once abandoned the idea for a long time longed for of the flight with a flapping wing.

To reach the highest peaks, to fly from continent to continent, to communicate to other people universal values, this one too a prophetic vision and the auspice of a long-lasting peace founded on dialogue: «men will speak each other from the most remote countries, and they will answer each other» (CA, f. 370 *va* [1033 *v*]).

It is not surprising then that NASA, following a suggestion of some of my friends entrepreneurs in Arezzo, passionate of Leonardo and involved in the idea of his privileged relationship with the Territory of Arezzo, has shared the singular plan to send to space a miniature of the «Bridge of the Mona Lisa» that is of the Bridge of Buriano.[14]

The American Space Agency was not new to similar ideas. A young engineer of theirs, Mark Elling Rosheim,[15] after having reconstructed the «automaton of Leonardo», had made to place it inside a space probe. The courage of utopia is sometimes rewarding and it is often ready to transmute itself into a beautiful story, able to make man bet on the common potentialities to build a more definite and better future, «Because the eye sees the thing more definite in dreams, than it does with imagination when it is awaken» (Codex Arundel, f. 278 *v*).

---

[13]   See C. Pedretti, *Prefazione*, in *Il codice sul Volo degli Uccelli*, a cura di A. Marinoni, ed. inglese, New York, Harcourt Brace Jovanovich, 1982.

[14]   See Cfr. A. Pierini, *A scuola dagli astronauti*, «La Nazione», 18 aprile 2002. The Shuttle had taken off with NASA flight STS 104, on 12 July 2001, and Janet Kavandi, the only woman of the mission with three flights on her credit, had carried in a pocket of her space-suit a model in miniature of the Bridge of Buriano. Because of the attack on 11 September 2001 to the Twin Towers of New York, for emergency reasons it was possible to carry out with them only a television live show from Cape Canaveral in November 2001. On that day the astronauts attended the inaugural ceremony in Arezzo of the goldsmith centre «Megastore» (R. Salvi, *La città dell'oro nello spazio*, «Corriere di Arezzo», novembre, 2001), but in order to celebrate the event it was allowed them to reach the city only on 17 April 2002.

[15]   See M. E. Rosheim, *L'automa programmabile di Leonardo*, «Lettura Vinciana», XL, Firenze, Giunti, 2001.

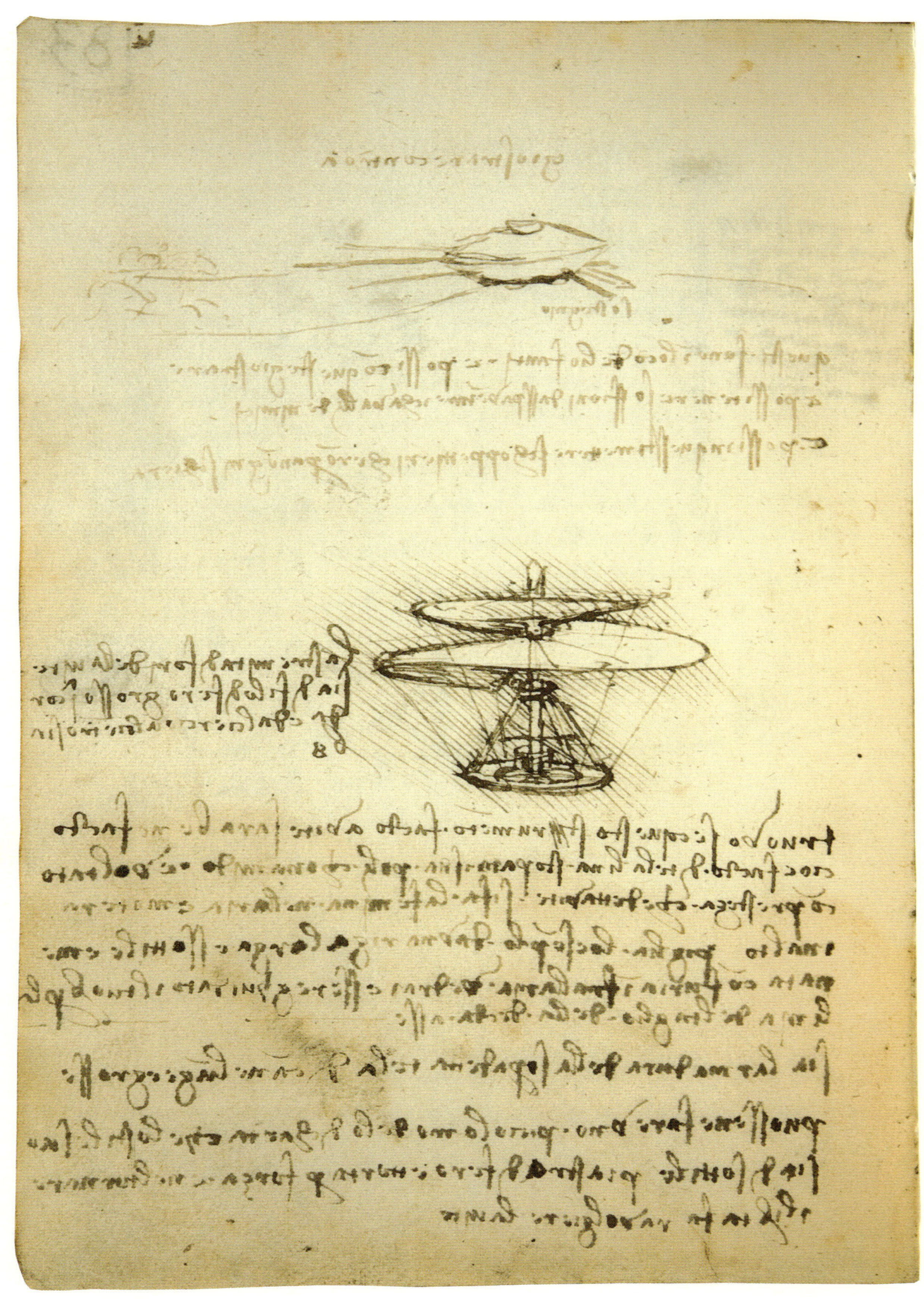

Leonardo da Vinci, *Aerial screw or «helicopter»*, c. 1487-90. Pen and ink, 231 x 167 mm. Ms. B, f. 83 *v*. Paris, Institut de France

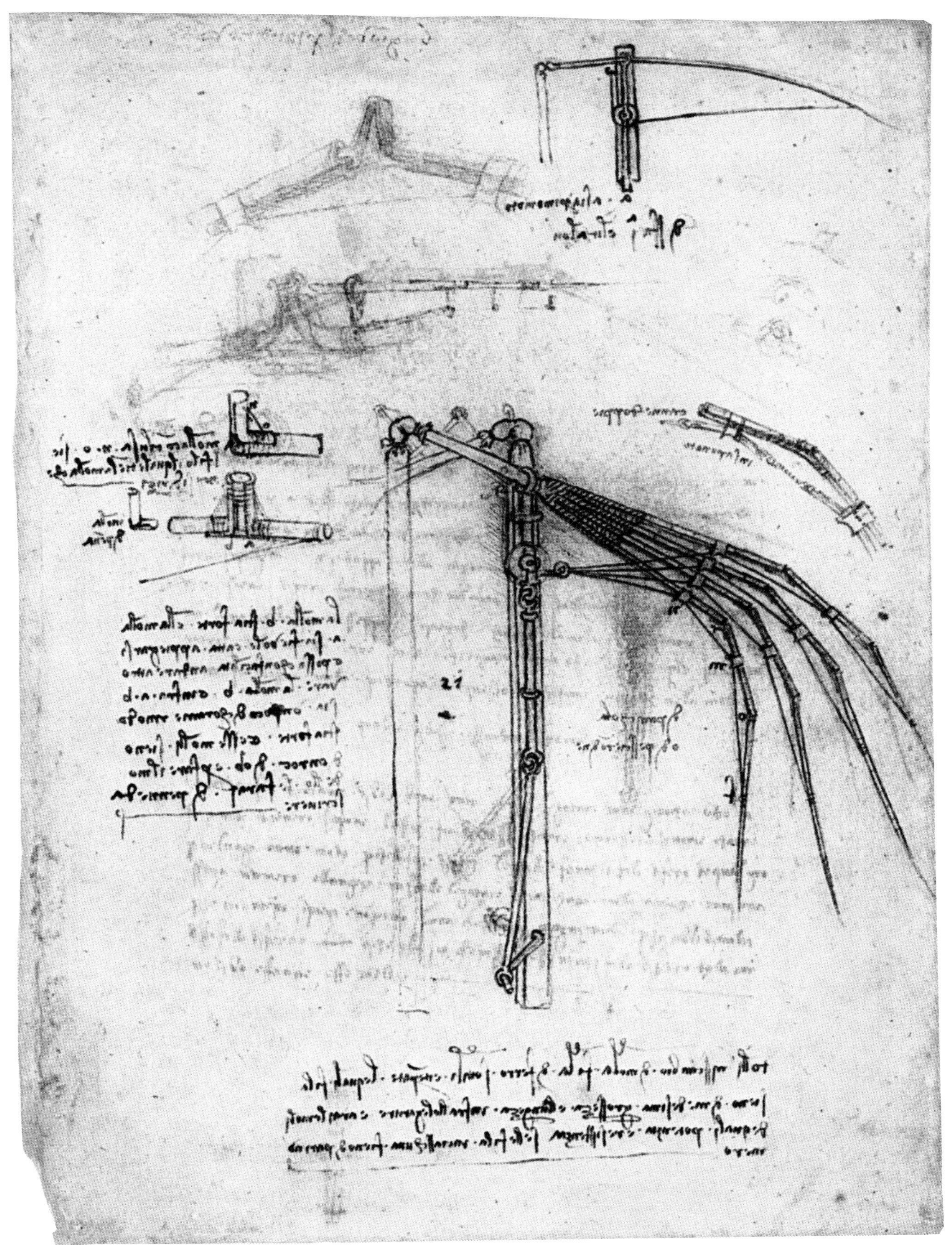

Leonardo da Vinci, *Study of a mechanical wing*, c. 1493-95. Pen and ink. Codex Atlanticus, f. 844 *r*. Milan, Biblioteca Ambrosiana

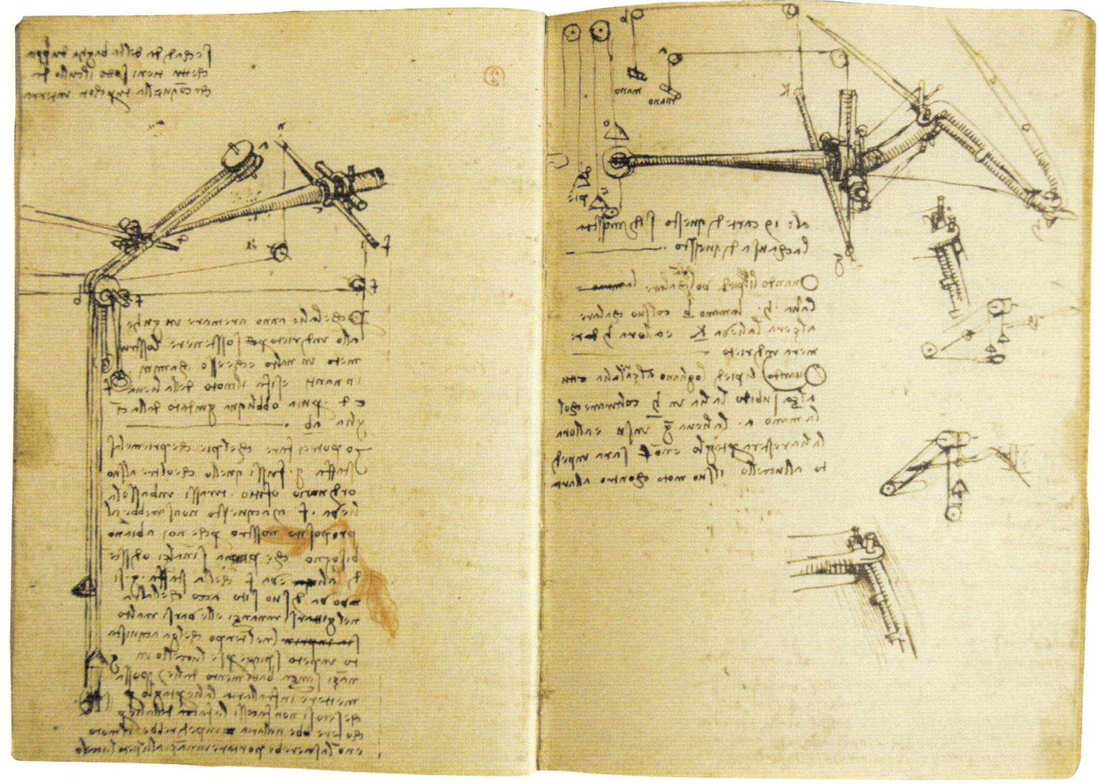

Leonardo da Vinci, *Drawings of a device for the wing rotation*, c. 1505. Pen and ink, 213 x 158 mm. Codex on the Flight of Birds, ff. 16 *v* – 17 *r*. Turin, Biblioteca Reale.

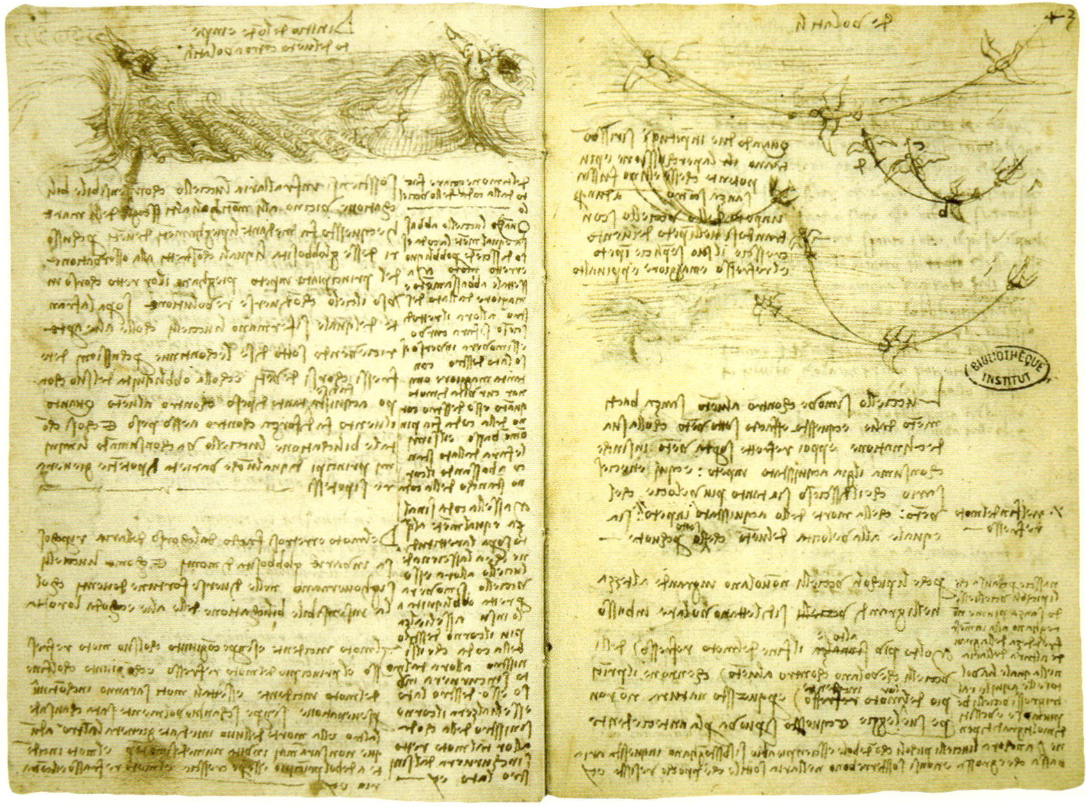

Leonardo da Vinci, *Study of the flight of birds related to the wind*, c. 1513-14. Pen and ink, 150 x 105 mm. Ms. E, ff. 42 *v* – 43 *r*. Paris, Institut de France

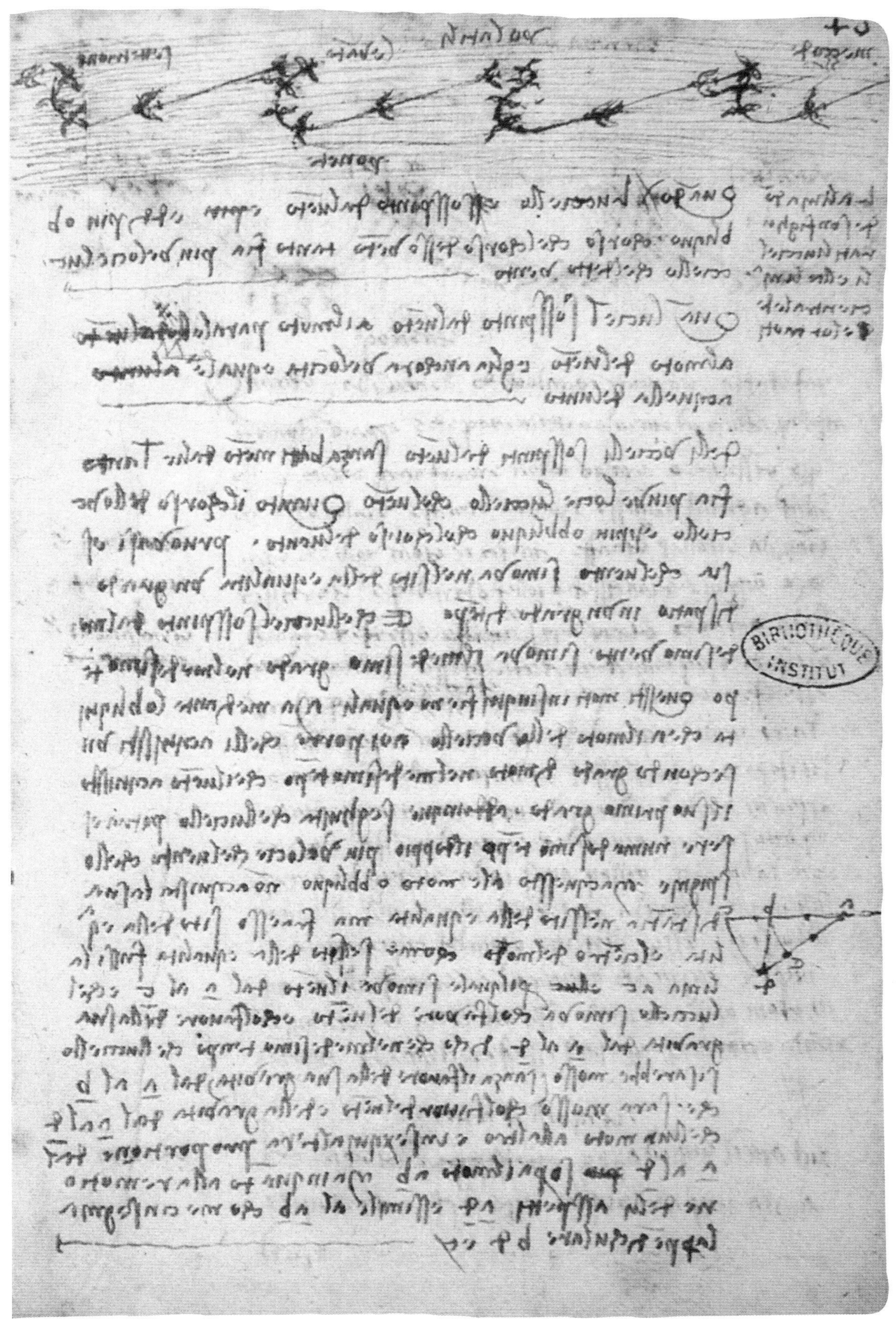

LEONARDO DA VINCI, *Study on the various trajectories of flight related to the direction of the wind*, c. 1513-14. Pen and ink, 150 x 105 mm. Ms. E, f. 40 *r*. Paris, Institut de France

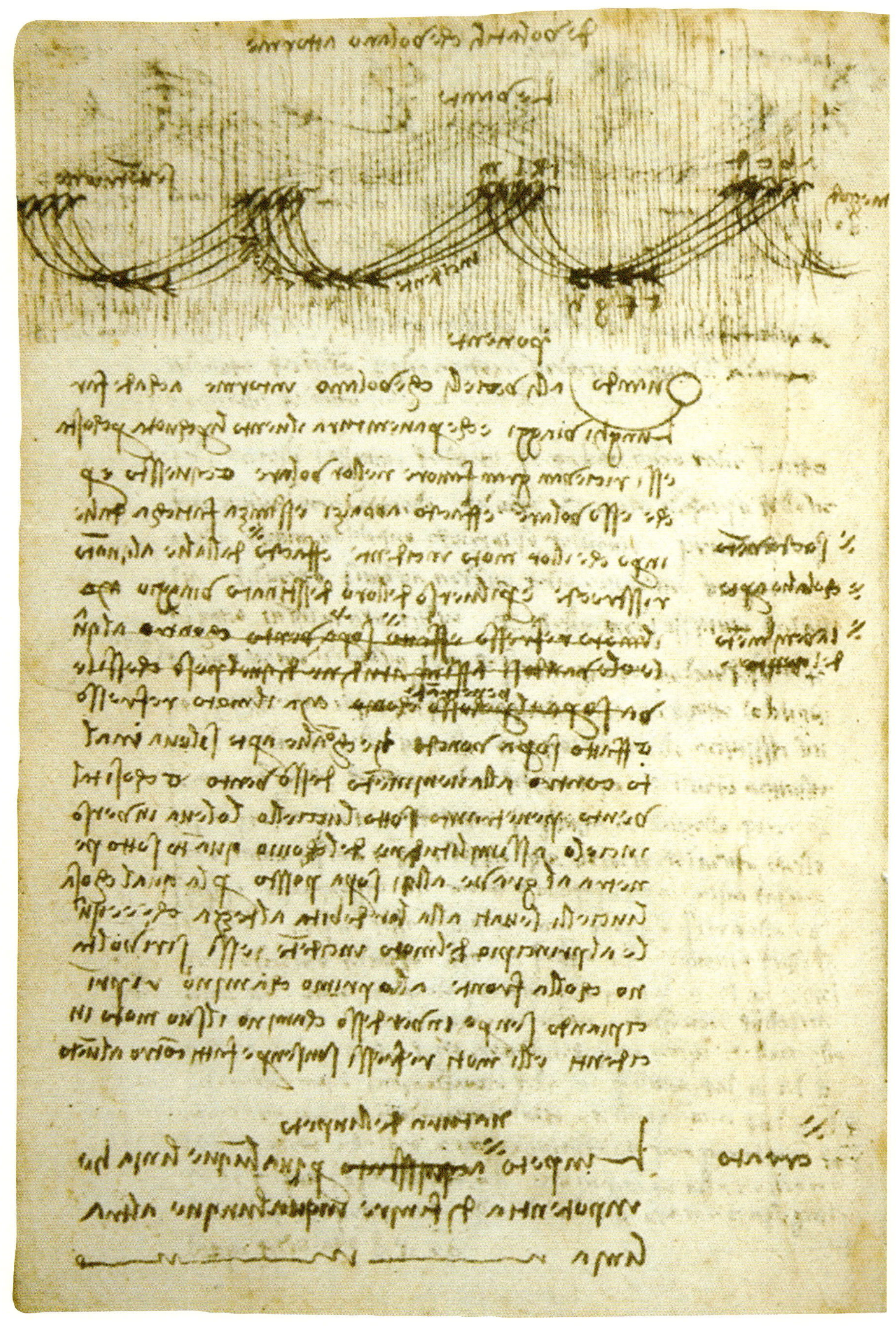

Leonardo da Vinci, *Study on the changing of trajectories related to the direction of the wind*, c. 1513–14. Pen and ink, 150 x 105 mm. Ms. E, f. 40 *v*. Paris, Institut de France

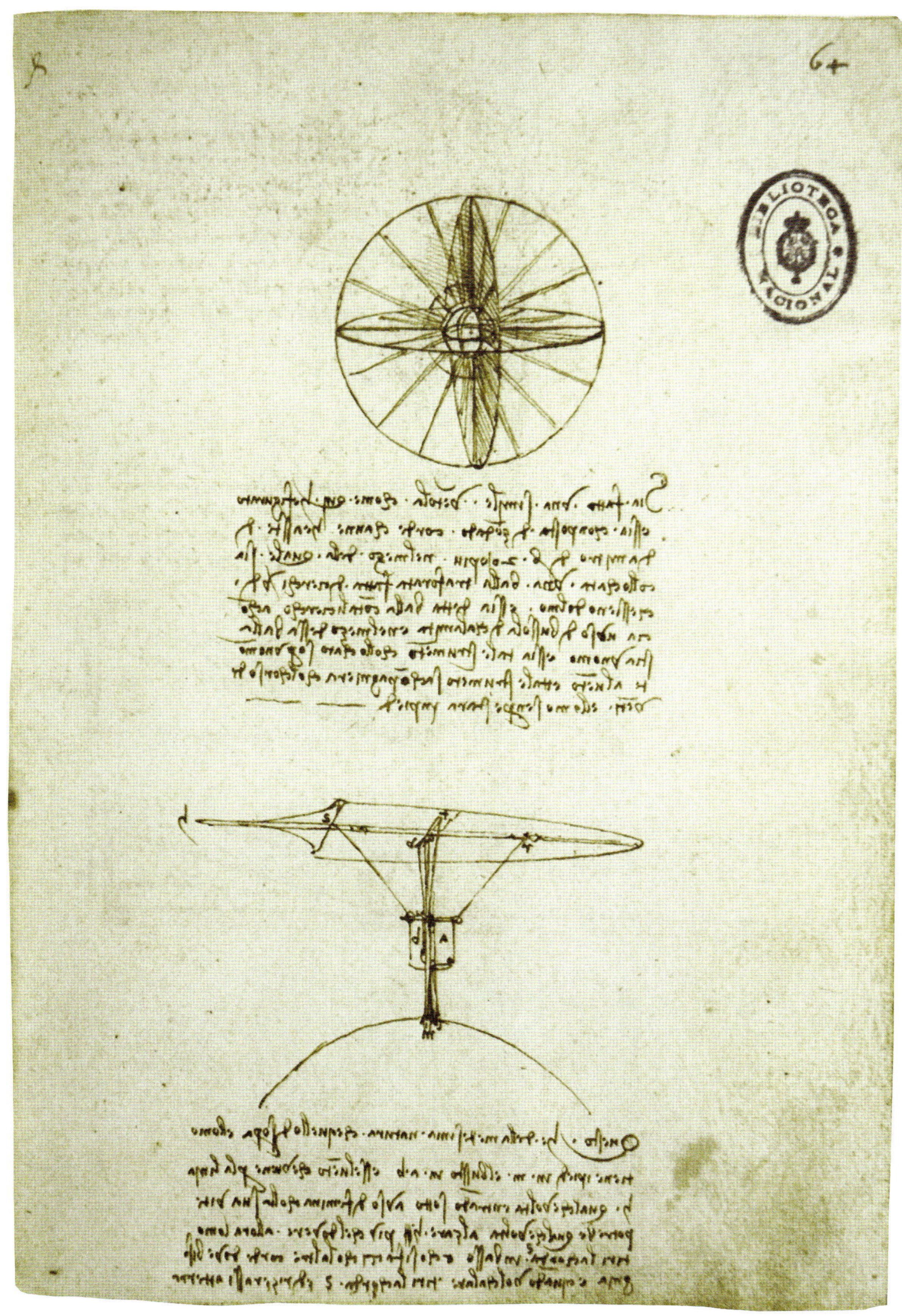

Leonardo da Vinci, *Study of kites for hang-gliding, c* 1497. Codex of Madrid I, f. 64 *r.* Madrid, Biblioteca Nacional

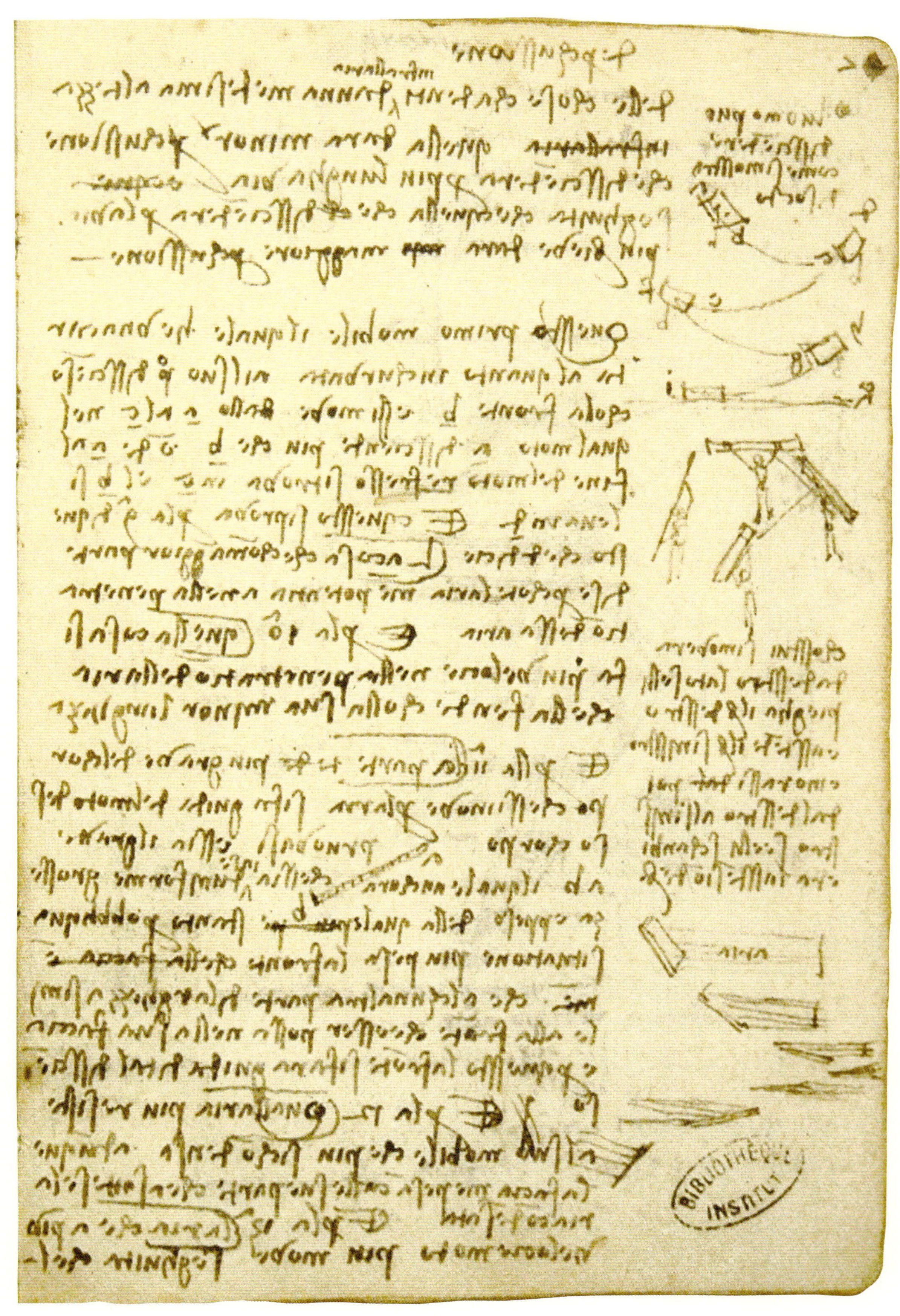

LEONARDO DA VINCI, *Studies of aerostatics with a man descending in the air hung to a board. c.* 1512. Pen and ink, 139 x 97 mm. Ms. G, f. 74 *r.* Paris, Institut de France

Leonardo and Domenico da Cortona
From Amboise to Chambord

IN 1494, Charles VIII, reclaiming his rights of inheritance over the kingdom of Naples, supported also by Pope Innocent VIII and Ludovico the Moor, descended to Italy, where, after the death of Lorenzo the Magnificent (1492), considered the architect of the equilibrium among the five Italian princedoms, such a political and diplomatic crisis had opened, that it would have started a long series of wars and of invasions.

If Florence, after the impulse of the Magnificent, had consolidated its intellectual leadership, Naples, ruled by the Angevins and the Aragonese, had not exercised in culture a prominent role, but it had distinguished, as a consequence of its relationship with Provence and with Sicily, as a significant centre of Flemish art, for a breeding ground of artists like Colantonio, that admired Jan van Eyck, Rogier van der Weiden and their school, in order then to become, around 1490, capital centre of architecture.[1]

As a result, Charles VIII, concluded quickly his campaign of Italy (1495),[2] beyond to works of art, books, clothes and carpets, in his return to France, carried away to his service painters like Guido Mazzoni, stone-cutters, smiths, upholsterers, goldsmiths, cabinet-makers, an organ-maker, a perfumer, humanists as the Byzantine Giano Lascaris (that would have celebrated in his *Epigrammi* the *Saint Anne* of Leonardo),[3] engineers as Friar Giocondo, celebrated philologist and scholar of Vitruvius,[4] and Domenico Bernabei († 1549), known as «Becalor» or «Boccadoro», for the red-yellowish colour of his beard.[5]

---

[1] See A. CHASTEL, *I centri del Rinascimento. Arte Italiana 1460-1500*, Milano, Rizzoli, 1965.

[2] The descent of Charles VIII and his quick conquest of Italy brought up again to the heart of the debate the traditional structure of fortifications, which had not been capable to resist to the blows of the French cannons. From this moment on, military engineers will begin to take more and more into consideration regular polygonal shapes.

[3] According to LASCARIS the *Saint Anne* of Leonardo, at the moment of his death, had not been completed yet: «In divae Annae imaginem inchoatam, / Ne veterum celebres vincas exacta tabellas / Anna, tuus pictor Vincius ille obijt. / At mage quam Venerem, quam non absolvit Apelles, / Te mirata celer sedula posteritas» [In the commenced image of Saint Anne, so that the perfect Anne does not surpass the famous tables of the ancients, your painter Vinci passed away. But more than Venus, which Apelles did not finish, the diligent posterity [is] quick fond of you. Tr.N.] See G. LASCARIS, *Epigrammata*, Basilea, Lasio e Platter, 1537; M. GOUKOVSKY, *Du nouveau sur Léonard de Vinci. Léonard et Janus Lascaris*, «Bibliothèque d'Humanisme et Renaissance», XIX, 1957.

[4] Friar GIOCONDO, one of the most famous hydraulic engineers of his time and, since 1488, famous for his controversy on the works about the diversion of the course of the Brenta, operated in France, from 1495 to 1505, most of all at the service of Louis XII. We will find him again among the humanists and the scholars who, like Paolo Biringuccio and Alessandro Benedetti, will attend the lessons on Euclid given, in August 1508, by the Franciscan confrère Luca Pacioli in the church of Saint Bartholomew in Venice. In 1509, he will realize in Treviso a system of regulation of waters under the «bridge of Pria» that closely recalls the one devised by Leonardo along the Ticino and the Adda (Ms B, ff. 37 *v*; 38 *r*), with the intention to defend the city, making water flow down into the external ditch and improving the economic-environmental conditions by means of a greater operation concerning the flour mills. Here he put to work also a concept of defence, destined to have a great success and related to the construction of the first masonry bastions, sustained by a rampart in the back. In 1513, he will be in Rome among the most expert architects and engineers, among which the same Leonardo, that had gathered around Giuliano de' Medici, patron and passionate of art and literature. Here he will supervise, together with Raphael and Giuliano da Sangallo, to the Fabric of the new basilica of Saint Peter's. And it is symptomatic that Friar Giocondo dedicates precisely to Giuliano de' Medici the edition of Caesar published by Aldo Manuzio in 1513. But the name of Friar Giocondo is also tied to a writing, begun in 1489 and now lost, of the *Trattato* «of master Francesco of Siena (Francesco di Giorgio Martini) in paper of papyrus», for which he made 126 drawings.

[5] See J. BERNIER, *Histoire de Blois*, Paris, Muguet, 1682; A. DE MONTAIGLON, *Etat des gages des ouvriers italiens employés par Charles VIII…*, «Archives de l'art française», I, 1851-52; E. MÜNTZ, *La Renaissance en Italie et en France à l'époque de Charles VIII*, Paris, 1885; J. DE CROŸ, *Nouveaux documents pour l'histoire de la création des résidences royales des bords de la Loire*, Paris et Blois, 1894; P. LESUEUR, *Dominique de Cortone, dit le Boccador*, Paris, 1928; ID., *Les Italiens à Amboise au début de la Renaissance,* «Bulletin de la Societé de l'histoire de l'art française», I, 1929; ID., *Nouveau document sur Dominique de Cortone (1510)*, «Bulletin de la Societé de l'histoire de l'art française», I, 1936; L. HAUTECOEUR, *Histoire de l'architecture classique en France*, I, I, Paris, Picard, 1943; P. ROSEMBERG, J. FOUCART, *Bernabei Domenico*, in *Dizionario Biografico degli Italiani*, Roma, Istituto della Enciclopedia Italiana, 1967.

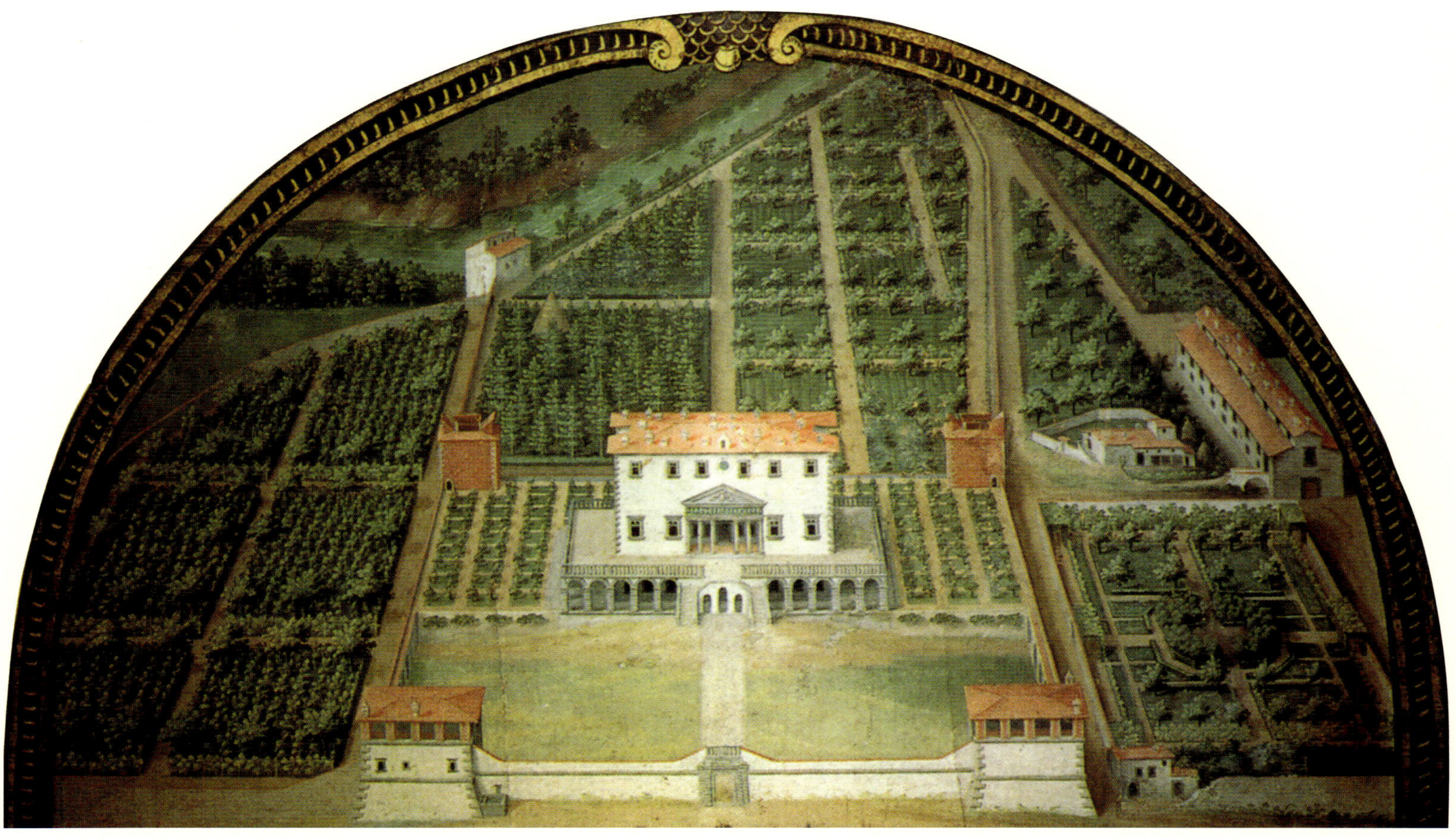

GIUSTO UTENS, *View of the Villa at Poggio a Caiano, c.* 1598-99. Particular of the frescoed lunette from the medicean villa of Artimino. Florence, Museum of 'Florence as it was'

The latter one was born in Cortona around 1470, since, when he became a naturalized French in 1510, he was 40 years old, and he would have been, according to the tradition, a student of Giuliano da Sangallo, one of the greatest architects of the Renaissance, that, beyond to the original creation of the Medicean Villa of Poggio a Caiano, had executed, in 1488, on explicit consent of the Magnificent,[6] the project of a complex and great Palace-Castle in the city of Naples for Ferrante of Aragon, never later realized.

Although he did not realize any work in Italy, that had made him famous or that at least in some way had made to remember his name, Bernabei appears among the 22 «ouvriers et gens de métiers» carried to his service by the King of France to Amboise. The name of Domenico da Cortona in fact is mentioned in the contracts stipulated, in 1498, between the same artists and the royal house, with the title of «faiseur de chasteaulx et menuisier», therefore a specialist in the construction of models in wood for buildings and artist-craftsman for the equipment of festivities, commitment for which it was assigned to him the sum of 180 pounds.

Charles VIII was born and grown in Amboise and there, since 1489, he had transformed the old medieval Castle, erected on a hill spur on a side of the Loire, in a royal palace where the royal apartments, constituted of two angular building units, had received a sumptuous aspect never seen before, with the rooms overflowing with carpets and furniture, and the walls painted in the preferred colours of the King, purple and gold, while on the fireplaces and on the fine dividing columns there had been represented the coats of arms of France and of Bretagne and the royal emblems of lily and of ermine.

The *parterres* had been designed by the most famous architect of gardens of the time, the Neapolitan Pacello da Mercogliano († 1534), employed later also by Louis XII in order to embellish with terraced flower-beds the Castle of Blois, where Friar Giocondo had carried out hydraulic works of canalization and irrigation (Ms. K, f. 100 *r*), while through the best Flemish workers, it was built up the northern wing

---

[6]   See E. PONTIERI, *Per la storia di Ferrante I d'Aragona re di Napoli*, Napoli, Morano, 1946; V. JUREN, *Le projet de Giuliano da Sangallo pour le palais du roi de Naples*, «Revue de l'Art», XXV, 1974; S. BORSI, *Giuliano da Sangallo. I disegni dell'architettura e dell'antico*, Roma, Officina, 1985; ID., *Il progetto del Palazzo per il re di Napoli di Giuliano da Sangallo (1488)*, Bollettino Storico di Salerno e Principato Citra, 1-2, 1985; F. QUINTERIO, *Napoli*, in *'Per bellezza, per studio, per piacere'. Lorenzo il Magnifico e gli spazi dell'Arte*, a cura di F. Borsi, Firenze, Giunti, 1991.

                                                                CARLO STARNAZZI

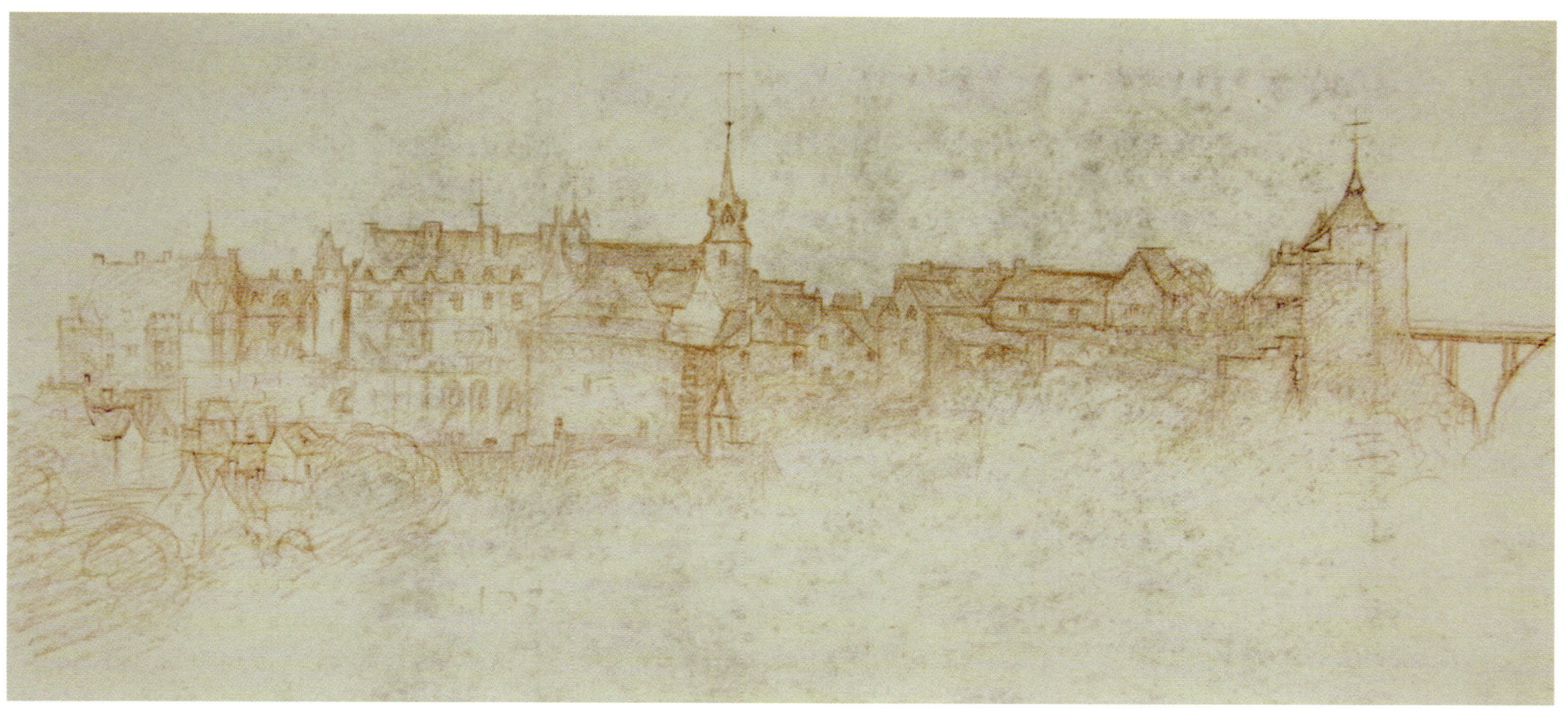

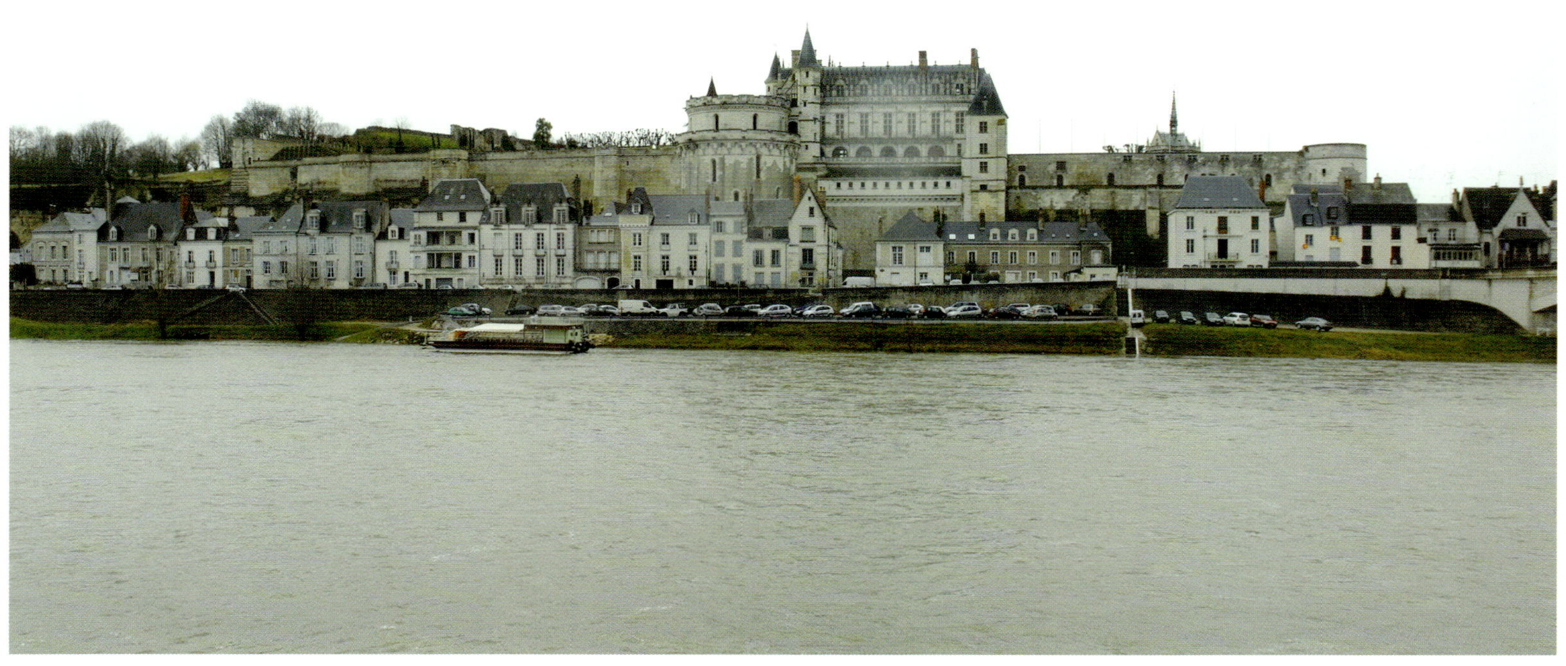

The Castle of Amboise

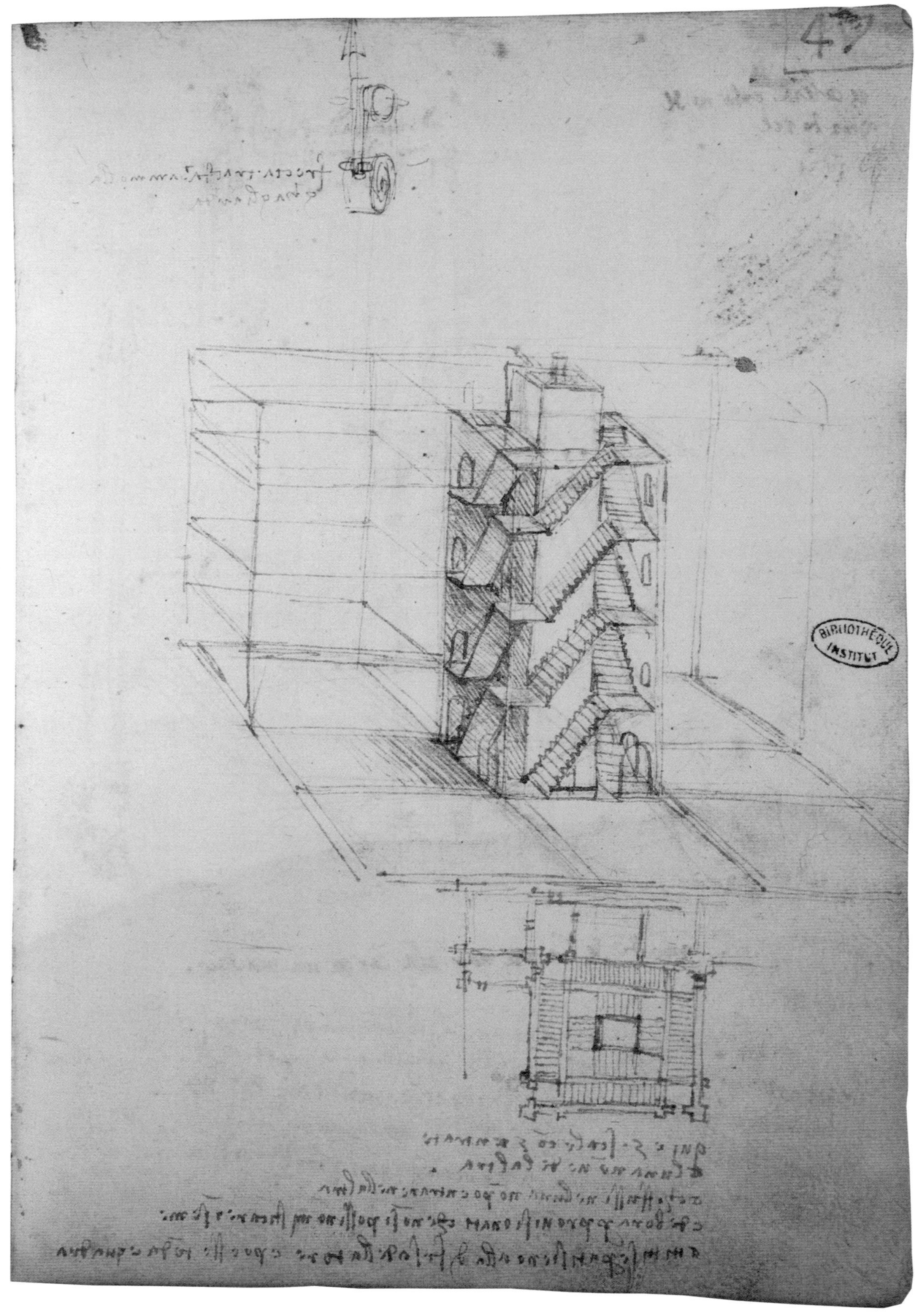

Leonardo da Vinci, *Study of staircases*, c. 1487-90. Pen and ink, 231 x 165 mm. Codex B, f. 47 *r*. Paris, Institut de France

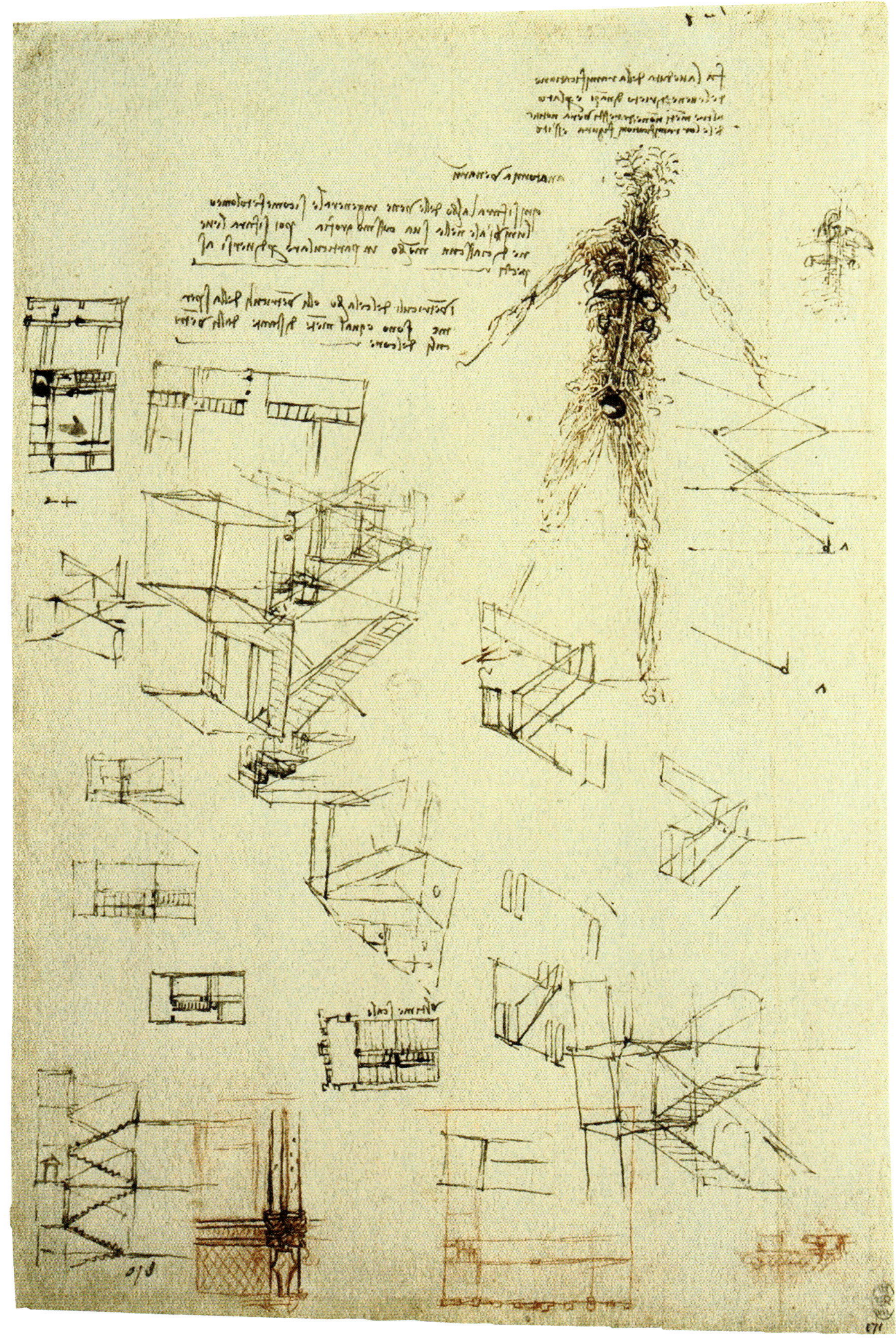

Leonardo da Vinci, *Studies of staircases*, c. 1508-10. Pen and ink, with touches of sepia and sanguine, 292 x 197 mm. Windsor, RL 12592 *r*

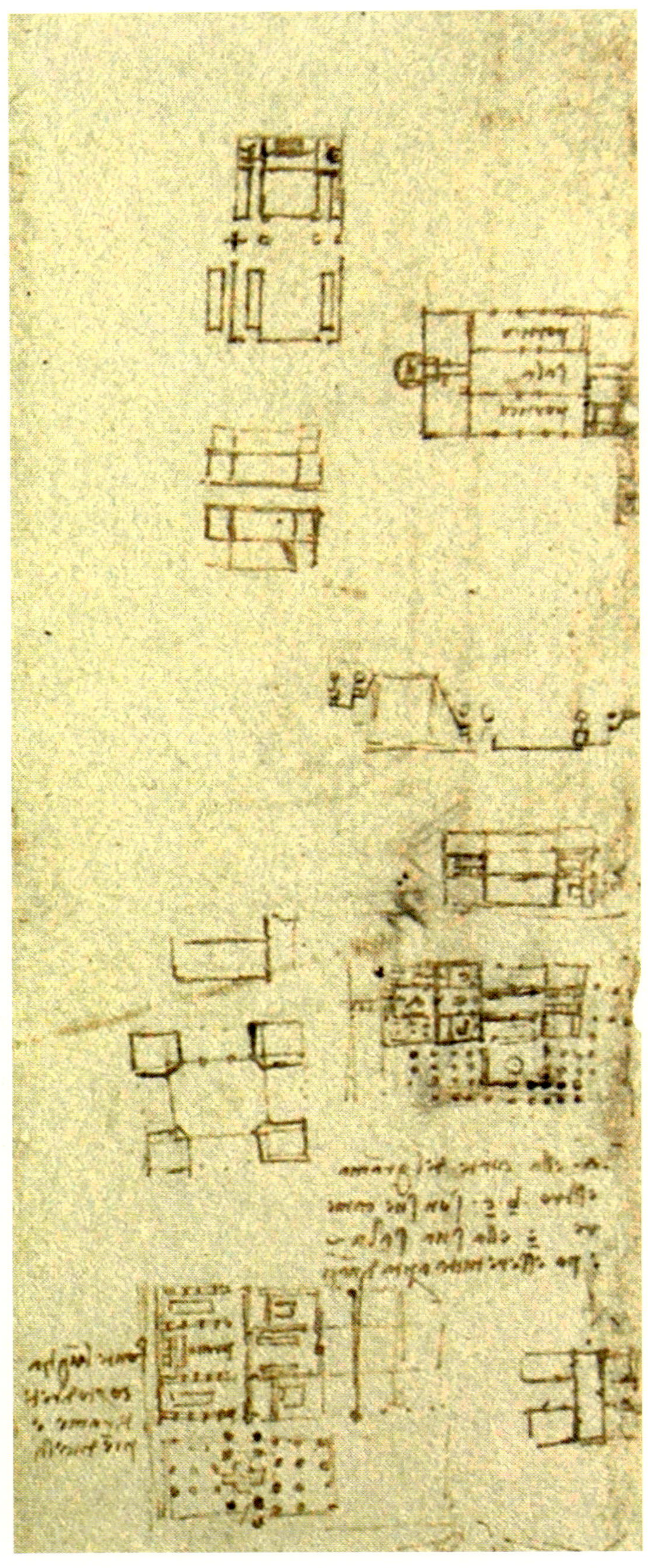

in flamboyant gothic style, with one large grafted tower (*Tour des Minimes*), and with a facade, facing towards the river, with balustrades and with mansard windows. At the same time it was being constructed the chapel of Saint Hubert (1491), today keeper of the presumed remains of Leonardo and marked by a multiplication of the sections of the vaults and by its spires decorated in an extremely refined way.

In 1507, Domenico da Cortona was housed in Tours and a lease contract defined him «varlet de chambre et menuysier de la Reine», that is of Anne of Bretagne, for which Charles VIII had made to build, at the end of the fifteenth century, far away from the clamours of the Court, a Chapel in the small Castle of Clos-Lucé, erected by a minister of Louis XI, Etienne Le Loup, in 1472.

The latter one had been acquired by the King for 3500 scudoes of gold, on 2 July 1490, at a short distance from Amboise, and had become usual residence of the Queen, after the mourning of four sons died in their tender years and buried in the Cathedral of Tours, historical capital city of Touraine.

Clos-Lucé will constitute a good shelter also for Louise of Savoy and her sons, Marguerite, the future Queen of Navarre and the Duke of Angoulême, the future Francis I, that here spent their youth.

Queen Anne, still seventeen years old, for a clause of the marriage contract, stipulated with the celebration of the wedding in the imposing Castle of Langeais, on 16 December 1491, and with the aim of definitively annexing Bretagne to France, would have been forced to marry, on 7 January 1499, nine months after the death of Charles VIII, the heir to the throne, the Duke of Orléans.

The latter one, become King with the name of Louis XII, considered as his privileged residence the Castle of Blois, inherited from his father Charles d' Orléans († 1465), where Anne of Bretagne moved with all her retinue, staying there until her death, occurred in 1514.

On 10 October 1517, Antonio De Beatis, Secretary of the cardinal Louis of Aragon, a passionate traveller and relative to Lucrezia Borgia and Isabella d' Este,[7] would have described, in his travel diary, the different residential choices of the French Court, in these first decades of the sixteenth century:

From Tours, where we dwelled for all the ninth day of the month, after lunch we went to Amboise, distant VII leagues, which though it is a little villa, it is glad and well placed; it is in plane, but there is a Castle in a project, that though it is not a fortress, of rooms, it

7   See A. Chastel, *Luigi d'Aragona un cardinale del Rinascimento in viaggio per l'Europa*, Bari, Laterza, 1987.

     Carlo Starnazzi

*is comfortable and it has a very beautiful perspective. Here the Roy
Charles who was in Naples stayed a lot willingly: Roy Louis, the
father, in Tours, and the Roy Ludovico, the successor, in Blois.*

Precisely in Blois, in the course of 1510, Domenico Bernabei,
being carpenter and inlayer, will realize for his Queen works
of carpentry well documented, (six «chalits»), and, in October in the same year, he will complete some works for the
scenographies and the decorations for the ceremony of the
baptism of the young Renée of France.

From this moment his activity in the Court's employ reveals
assignments of engineering and of architecture more and
more important, that were correlated to his ability in the art
of wood, which allowed him to be appreciated and preferred
for the preparation of fictitious arches of triumph and wood-
en facades. Therefore in 1512, he will be engaged in Paris in
the construction of an imposing triumphal arch, erected on
occasion of the arrival of Queen Mary of England at the city,
for which he will receive a remuneration of 400 pounds and
the flattering acknowledgment of being officially designated
as «maître des oeuvres de maçonnerie du Roi».

This prestigious assignment of *maître maçon*, that combined
the offices of planner and executor of the works, was associated to the recurring one of «menuysier de la feu Reine»,
with reference to Anne of Bretagne, passed away in 1514. A
distinguishing assignment, the last one, that will follow him
also on the occurrence of the rites for the funerals of Louis
XII,[8] that had soon got married again with young Mary of
England, sister of Henry VIII. In the day of the death of Louis XII, on 9 January 1515, as Leonardo annotated (Ms. G, cop.
v), Giuliano de' Medici, appointed Duke of Nemour since
a short time, had left Rome in order to marry Philiberte of
Savoy, while Francis of Valois was preparing to ascend the
throne of France and to descend to Italy, in order to face
victoriously the Swiss infantry and the Imperial soldiers, in
the battle of Marignano. It will be during the summit of Leo
X with Francis I, organized in Bologna for a new Concordat
between the Church and France, from 7 to 17 December
1515, that Leonardo will be able to meet directly the King and
various dignitaries of the Court, prompted by the hope of
being portrayed by the artist. But the relationship of Leonardo with the French Court was not new, indeed it had established since October 1499, when the King of France made

his triumphal entrance in Milan. In 1501, cardinal Georges
d' Amboise, the most powerful prelate of France, bishop of
Rouen and plenipotentiary of the King, that would have
proposed him as successor of Alexander VI to the papal seat
(Machiavelli mentions him in his *Il Principe* as the «Roano»),
had been involved in the negotiations with Ercole d' Este,
Duke of Ferrara, in order to define the destination of the
«mould» for the fusion of the horse, realized by Leonardo
for the equestrian statue in honour of Francesco Sforza and
still remained in the workshop in Corte Vecchia beside the
Dome. To the cardinal it would have been promised, in 1505,
also the leonardian painting of a Bacchus. And the same
Louis XII, as Paolo Giovio reports, perhaps on suggestion
of his artistic counsellor Jean Perréal,[9] would have wished to
carry with him back to France the best works of Leonardo,
included the *Last Supper* of Santa Maria delle Grazie, detach-
ing it from the bearing wall:

> *It can be admired however in Milan, painted on a wall, the Supper
> of Christ with his disciples, a work that the king Louis – as far as
> they say - wished to have so passionately to ask with insistence to
> those who were next to him while he was contemplating it, if it was
> not possible to remove it cutting the wall all around, so as to transfer
> it to France also to the cost of destroying that famous Refectory.*[10]

Still, in 1501, some assignments arrived at the artist from his
French clients, in particular from the Baron of Alluye, Bury and
Brou, the powerful Secretary of State Florimond Robertet,
that in the end, in 1507, could receive in Blois the *Madonna of
the yarn winder* or *of the reel*, in order to show it with boast to
the entire Court and exhibit it privately in his Hôtel d' Alluye.
The King would have appreciated it so much, to reveal to
the Florentine ambassador Francesco Pandolfini his intention to make to paint to Leonardo «certain tablets of our
Lady and other, according to what it will be in my desire,
and perhaps also I will make him portray myself». In fact
Leonardo, for the «most Christian» King of France, of which

---

[8] On this circumstance, Domenico da Cortona realized a platform («protonère»),
endowed with three bars of 20 feet and others arranged transversally, in order to
lay on it, like in a litter («litière»), the simulacrum of the defunct King, protected
with a canopy, constituted of 12 long rods of fir-wood and adorned with clothes
and fringes in gold, interspersed with azure silk. Louis XII was carried in procession until Notre-Dame of Paris for the funeral honours, in order then to be
entombed in the abbey of Saint-Denis.

[9] See P. Durrieu, *Les relations de Léonard de Vinci avec le peintre français Jean Perréal*,
«Études Italiennes», I, 1919; L. Dorez, *Léonard de Vinci et Jean Perréal (Conjectures)*,
in *Léonard de Vinci 1519-1919*, «Nouvelle Revue d'Italie», Roma, 1919; C. Vecce,
«Piglia da Gian di Paris», «Achademia Leonardi Vinci. Journal of Leonardo Studies
and Bibliography of Vinciana», X, Firenze, Giunti, 1997.

[10] The first document, that reports about the premature conditions of precari-
ousness of the *Last Supper*, made in temper and oil, is the travel diary of Antonio
de' Beatis, where, on date 20-30 December 1517, the Secretary of the cardinal
Louis of Aragon annotated: «In the monastery of Santa Maria delle Grazie, which
was made by Mr. Ludovico Sforza, very beautiful and well kept, we saw in the
refectory of the friars, who are of the order of Saint Dominic *de observantia*, a
supper painted on the wall by master Lunardo Vinci, which we found in Amboys,
that is the most excellent one, although it begins to ruin, I do not know if for
the humidity that the wall gives back or for other inadvertence. The personages
of that one are of the natural portrayals of many persons of the court and of the
people from the city of Milan of that time, of true stature»

he had become «notre paintre et ingénieur ordinaire»,[11] beyond realizing new «instruments and things» (CA, ff. 317 *rb* [872 *r*]; 372 *va* [1037 *v*]), according to father Sebastiano Resta, he would have begun the famous Burlington Cardboard of the *Saint Anne* (London, National Gallery). Leonardo was therefore much admired in France and when unexpectedly his friend and patron Giuliano de' Medici died, on 17 March 1516, he decided to go, before winter, to the court of Francis I, that provided lodgings for him in the Castle of Clos-Lucé, receiving an annual wage of 2000 scudoes. Here Leonardo, according to the precious testimony of De Beatis, settled also the masterpieces that he had carried with him, the *Mona Lisa*, the *Saint Anne* and the *Saint John*:

> *In one of the villages the Lord together with us went to see master Lunardo Vinci of Florence, that was more than seventy years old, painter in our age most excellent, which showed to his Most Illustrious Lordship three paintings, one of a certain Florentine woman, depicted of the natural, on request of the once magnificent Iuliano de' Medici, the other a young John the Baptist, and one of the Holy Virgin and of the child who are placed on the lap of Saint Anne, all are the most perfect.*

The first date that the artist transcribed, in this his last dwelling, was 21 May 1517: «day of the Ascension in Anbosa [Amboise] 1517 of May in the Clu [Clois]» (CA, f. 103 *rb* [284 *r*]). Francis I appointed him as his «Premier paintre & ingénieur & architecte du Roy, méschanicien d' État, & c. »,[12] revealing an unconditioned esteem for his value and his versatile personality, shared with Benvenuto Cellini («which I do not believe that a greater man was ever born into this world than he»),[13] that well knew how to translate and testify with enthusiasm the importance of that consideration in his speech *Della architettura*:

> *And because he was abundant of such a supreme talent, having he some cognition of Latin and Greek letters, the King Francis, being in the strongest way fond of those great virtues he had, he took so much pleasure in hearing him reasoning, that he detached from him only a few days of the year; which was the cause not to give him the possibility to put into work those admirable studies he had made with such discipline. I do not want to refrain from repeating the words, that I heard the King say about him, which he said to me, while the cardinal of Ferrara and the cardinal of Lorena and the king of*

[11]   See L. BELTRAMI, *Documenti*, n° 189.
[12]   See L. BELTRAMI, *Documenti*, n° 246.
[13]   See B. CELLINI, *Della architettura*, in J. MORELLI, *I codici manoscritti della Libreria Naniana*, Venezia, Biblioteca Nazionale Marciana, 1776, reprinted in B. CELLINI, *I Trattati dell'oreficeria e della scultura*, per cura di C. Milanesi, Firenze, Le Monnier, 1857.

> *Navarre were present; he said that he did not believe that any other man was ever born in this world, that knew as much as Lionardo, not as much as of sculpture, painting and architecture, but that he was a very great philosopher.*

A similar assignment, beyond recognizing the supreme dignity of his painting, defined its unquestionable technical and technological competence also in his activity as a mechanic and a royal architect, with the unconditioned authority to coordinate and to control the various experts that collaborated to the execution of every work, as it had already been cleared in the dictation of the «Ducal Permit», to him granted by Cesare Borgia, in 1502, where it was ordered that «Any Engineer is compelled to confer with him and to comply with his judgment». Just on the inferior margin of a sheet of the Codex Atlanticus (f. 174 *va* [475 *v*]), datable to the French period and with geometric drawings related to the subject of the double angles, it is unexpectedly mentioned, not by leonardian hand, and in a completely familiar way, Domenico da Cortona: «memory to us master domenico», with the customary title recognized to him in the contracts of work by the Court of France. It is a singular fact that this citation has not been transcribed by Giovanni Piumati, in 1894, neither that it has been put under any investigation in the essay about *Onomastica vinciana* of Nando de Toni in 1934, while it will appear only in the studies reserved to the palace of Romorantin by Carlo Pedretti, in 1970 and 1972, in order then to be reconsidered in its importance also by Augusto Marinoni, in 1977.[14] Leonardo was certainly famous as a «preparer» of feasts, since his first Milan stay (1482-99),

[14]   C. PEDRETTI, in the catalogue of his Codex Atlanticus (Vol. I), returned on the subject and, asserting that the memorandum could have been transcribed precisely by Domenico Bernabei da Cortona, he specified: «But the *ductus* it is somewhat similar to the one of that Anonymous author of a book of drawings from the antique published by A. Schmitt in *Münchner Jahrbuch der bildenden Kunst*, XXI, 1970 (see. fig. 2 that reproduces f. 10 *v*)». This observation was meant to suggest a systematic search that began right from the finding of examples of the writing of Domenico da Cortona, in order to ascertain if it corresponded closely enough to that of the note in the sheet of Leonardo, in which case it invited to control the several booklets from the antique of anonymous or not better identified authors, like the already well-known one by a not better known architect «Menicantonio». Pedretti would interpret it as an abbreviation for «Domenico Antonio» and wonders whether Antonio can be a second name of Domenico Bernabei. See G. PIUMATI, *Il codice Atlantico di Leonardo da Vinci nella Biblioteca Ambrosiana di Milano, riprodotto e pubblicato dalla Regia Accademia dei Lincei. Trascrizione diplomatica e critica di G. Piumati*, Milano, Hoepli, 1894-1903; E. SOLMI, G. B. DE TONI, *Intorno all'andata di Leonardo da Vinci in Francia*, «Atti del Reale Istituto Veneto di Scienze, Lettere e Arti», LXIV, 1904-05; N. DE TONI, *Saggio di onomastica vinciana*, «Raccolta Vinciana», XIV, 1930-34; C. PEDRETTI, *Leonardo da Vinci, Manuscripts and Drawings of the French Period 1517-1518*, «Gazette des Beaux-Arts», s. VI, LXXVI, 1970; ID., *Leonardo da Vinci. The Royal Palace at Romorantin*, Cambridge (Mass.), Harvard Univ. Press, 1972; ID., *The Codex Atlanticus of Leonardo da Vinci. A Catalogue of Its Newly Restored Sheets*, 2 vols, New York, Johnson Reprint Corporation, Harcourt Brace Jovanovich, 1978; A. MARINONI, *Codice Atlantico*, trascrizione diplomatica e critica 12 voll. (a cura di), Firenze, Giunti, 1975-80.

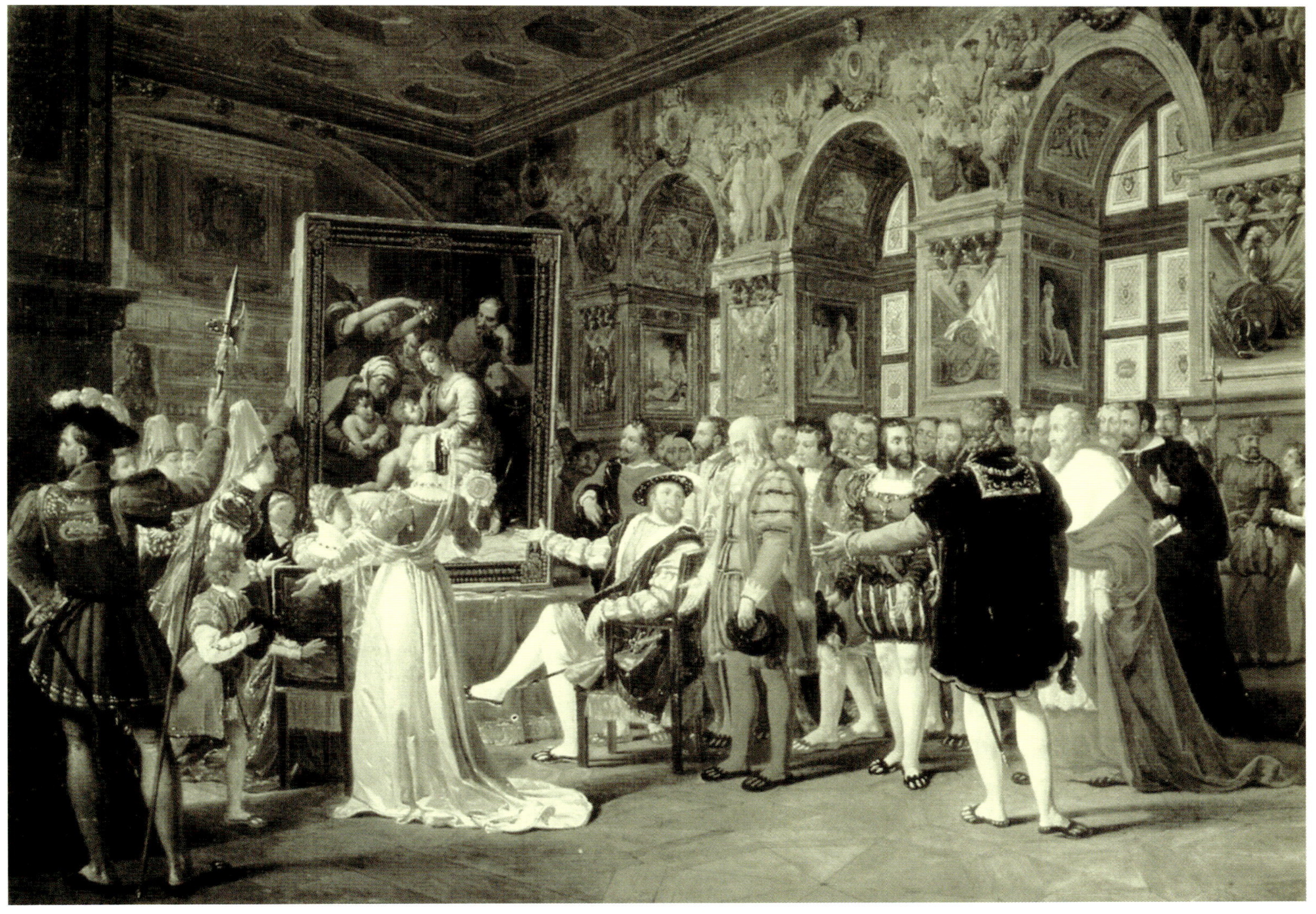

when he was as a ducal engineer at the court of Ludovico the Moor. And already in Lyon, the community of the rich Florentine merchants and bankers had honoured the triumphal entrance of the new King in town, offering him, on 12 July 1515, a sumptuous banquet with the show of a «mechanical lion», that, after some pace, would have revealed out of his chest numerous lilies. A celebration financed by Lorenzo di Piero de' Medici, governor of Florence, hope of his family and of the same Machiavelli that dedicated to him *Il Principe*, and made spectacular, although its director was distant, by the inventiveness of Leonardo, as it would have remembered, in 1600, even Michelangelo Buonarroti the Younger in his *Descrizione delle felicissime nozze della Cristianissima Maestà di Madama Maria Medici: Regina di Francia e di Navarra* with Henry IV, where the grandson of the great Michelangelo mentioned a mechanical lion that, after some

paces, reared itself up opening its chest full of *fleurs de lis*, as a remembrance of those granted to ratify an alliance between the two peoples in the fifteenth century, from Louis XI to the Florentine Republic:

> *With this work it was embellished the royal table, and of the similar that one of the ladies in proportion. At the head of the table in the middle of those, to fill up the wonder, there was a Lion with fierce aspect, resting up on four feet, that when those ones sat down at the table, taking motion, and raising itself on the rear legs, it was seen to open its breast, and show it full of lilies: a concept similar to that one which Lionardo da Vinci in the City of Lyon, at the arrival of King Francis, put to work for the Florentine nation.*

and that the same Vasari (1568), although reporting it to another circumstance, would have so described:

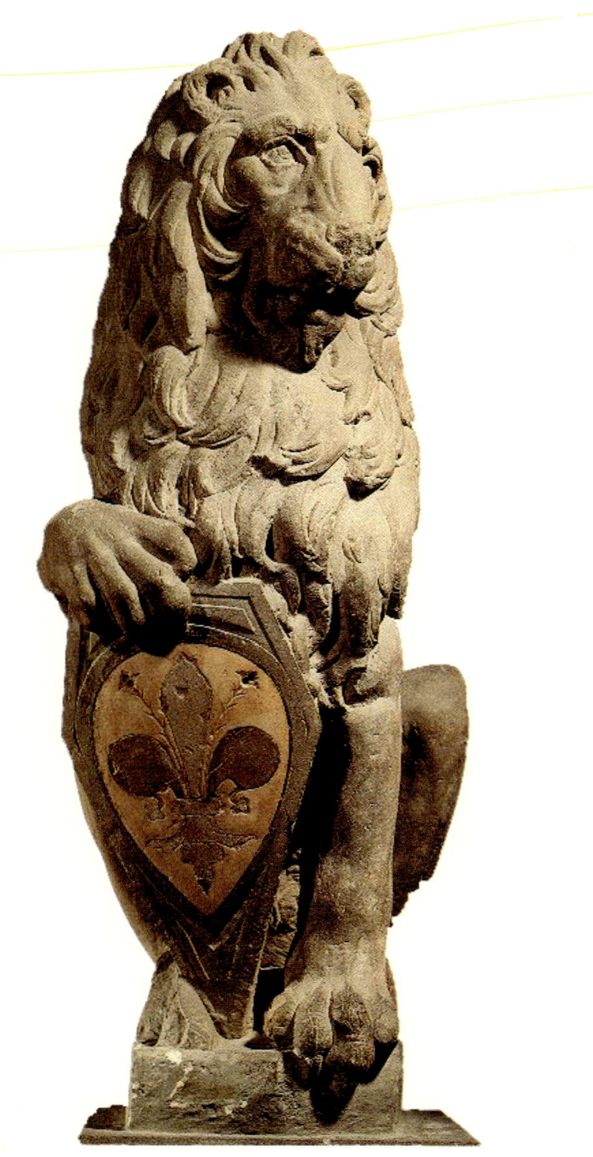

DONATELLO, *«Marzocco»*, c. 1420. Sandstone, 135,5 x 38 x 60 cm. Florence, Museo Nazionale del Bargello

Therefore, asked Lionardo to make some bizarre thing, he made a lion, that walked several paces, and then it opened its chest and showed it all full of lilies.

An ingenious good idea, this mobile automaton of the «Marzocco» or «Florentine lion», a political allegory of the alliance of Florence with France, that had a true success, so much to be proposed again, on 1 October 1517, for the arrival at Argentan, in low Normandy, of Francis I with his aunt Philiberte of Savoy, widow of Giuliano de' Medici: «[His Majesty] carried her where it was the Lion, stroke it with a stick, that had given him the aforesaid hermit, and this Lion opened itself and inside it was all azure, which thing meant

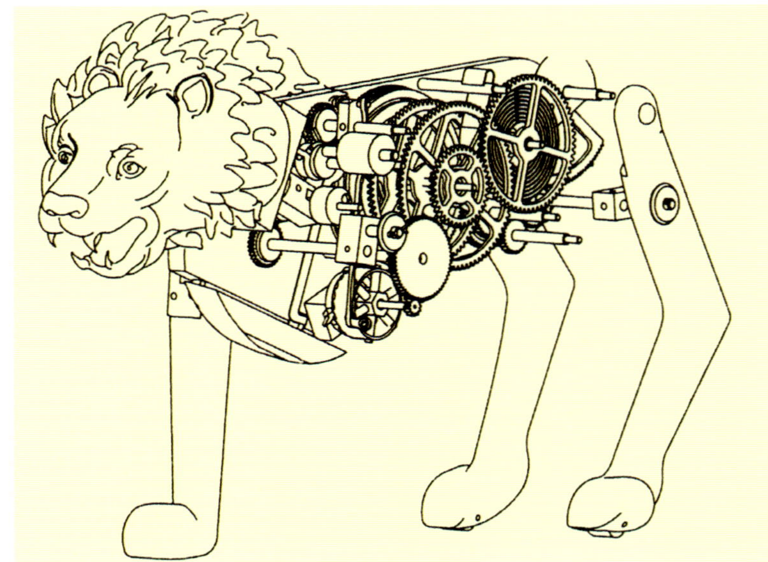

The mechanical Lion of Leonardo in the interpretation of Luca Garai

love, according to the customs here».[15] Moreover, it is during this French period that Leonardo, next to the drawing of a planimetry, will write «Room of the lions of Florence» (CA, f. 249 *ra* [673 *r*]), alluding to the menagerie of the lions that was behind Palazzo Vecchio, as a remembrance of the *Marzocco* by Donatello (*c.* 1420, Florence, Museo del Bargello), symbol of the civic virtues of Florence.

In this particular moment, Bernabei was employed by Francis I for choreographic compositions on the occurrence of theatre shows, of dances or of important diplomatic and political events. And precisely to Domenico da Cortona, for his singular practical culture and his rich embellishing repertoire, the King would have made recourse, also in the following years, in 1531, for the entrance of Queen Eleanor into Paris, and in 1532, for his meeting in Boulogne with the King of England.

As a reward for this long activity of expert artist-craftsman carried out, since 1518, for a period of 15 years, «master» Domenico would have received from Francis I a compensation of 900 pounds.

---

[15] Letter written by Rinaldo Ariosto to Federico Gonzaga, kept in the Gonzaga Archives of Mantua, *Esterni* (Francia), XV, 3, 634. Also G. P. LOMAZZO narrates that «once in front of Francis I King of France, [Leonardo] made to walk from its stand in a hall, a Lion, made with admirable artifice, and then made it stop opening its chest, all full of lilies and various flowers». See E. SOLMI, *Le fonti dei Manoscritti di Leonardo* (1908), e *Nuovi contributi alle fonti dei manoscritti di Leonardo* (1911), in ID., *Scritti vinciani. Le fonti dei Manoscritti e altri studi*, presentazione di E. Garin, Firenze, La Nuova Italia, 1976; C. PEDRETTI, *Leonardo at Lyon*, «Raccolta Vinciana», XIX, 1962; ID., *Leonardo architetto*, 1978, *op. cit.*; ID., *Presentazione*, in *L'Europa del Cinquecento* (a cura di H. G. Koenigsberger, G. L. Mosse, G. Q. Bowler), Storia Universale, 12, Bergamo, Nuovo Istituto d'Arti Grafiche, 2004.

CARLO STARNAZZI

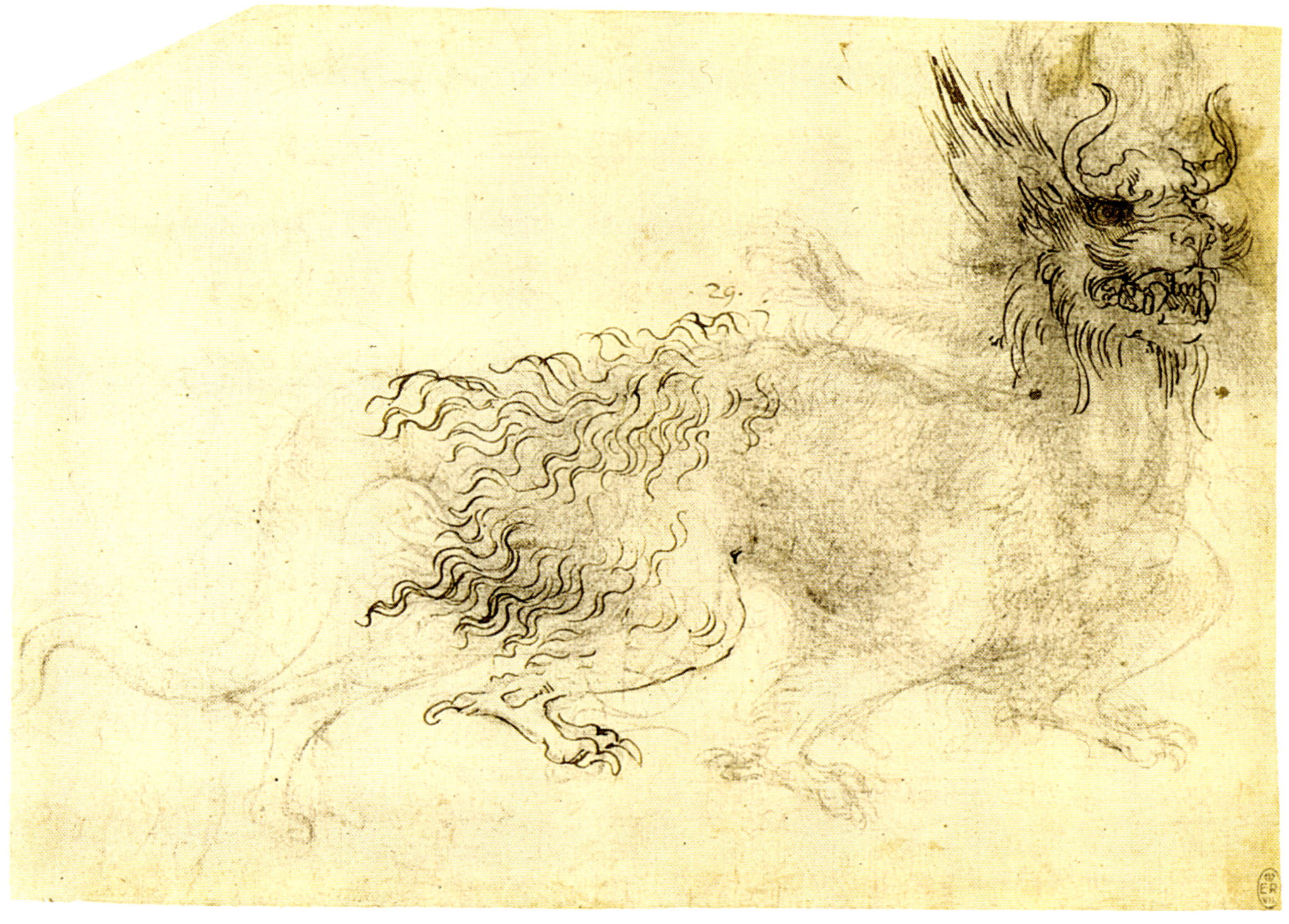

Leonardo da Vinci, *Study of a fantastic animal for an automaton*, c. 1516. Charcoal, pen and ink, 188 x 270 mm. Windsor, RL 12369

Therefore, considered the amazing technical-practical ability of Bernabei and his prestige at Court, he could not do other than to work together with Leonardo on the occurrence of the splendid celebrations that took place, on 25 April 1518, at Amboise for the baptism of the Dolphin († 1536), so long awaited by the King, and also, the following 3 May, for the wedding of Lorenzo de' Medici, Duke of Urbino and grandson of Leo X,[16] that took place in Boulogne, with Madeleine de la Tour d' Auvergne, grand-daughter of Francis I and future mother of Caterina de' Medici († 1589). The event had been so important, also for the new pro-French papal policy, that Leo X, not being able to attend to the ceremony, had sent his portrait with cardinals Giulio de' Medici and Luigi de' Rossi, painted on purpose by Raphael (Florence, Galleria degli Uffizi), so that it was placed in the room of the nuptial banquet. At Amboise in fact, among dances, jousts and tournaments, the resounding feasts of Leonardo, for which he designed most elegant dresses and costumes and complex mechanical scenographies with sonorous and luminous ef-

---

[16] Lorenzo di Piero de' Medici, Duke of Urbino (1492-1519), and Giuliano de' Medici, Duke of Nemours (1479-1516), both hope of the House of Medici, but prematurely passed away, will be portrayed by Michelangelo in the famous statues of the New Sacristy of San Lorenzo in Florence (1520-34). But the portrays, today lost, of Lorenzo di Piero and of Giuliano de' Medici had been as well made in the years 1514-16, as Vasari recalls, also by Raphael: «He similarly made the Duke Lorenzo and the Duke Giuliano with perfection, painted by him no better than by any other as for the grace of the colouring; which are near to the heirs of Ottaviano de' Medici in Florence».

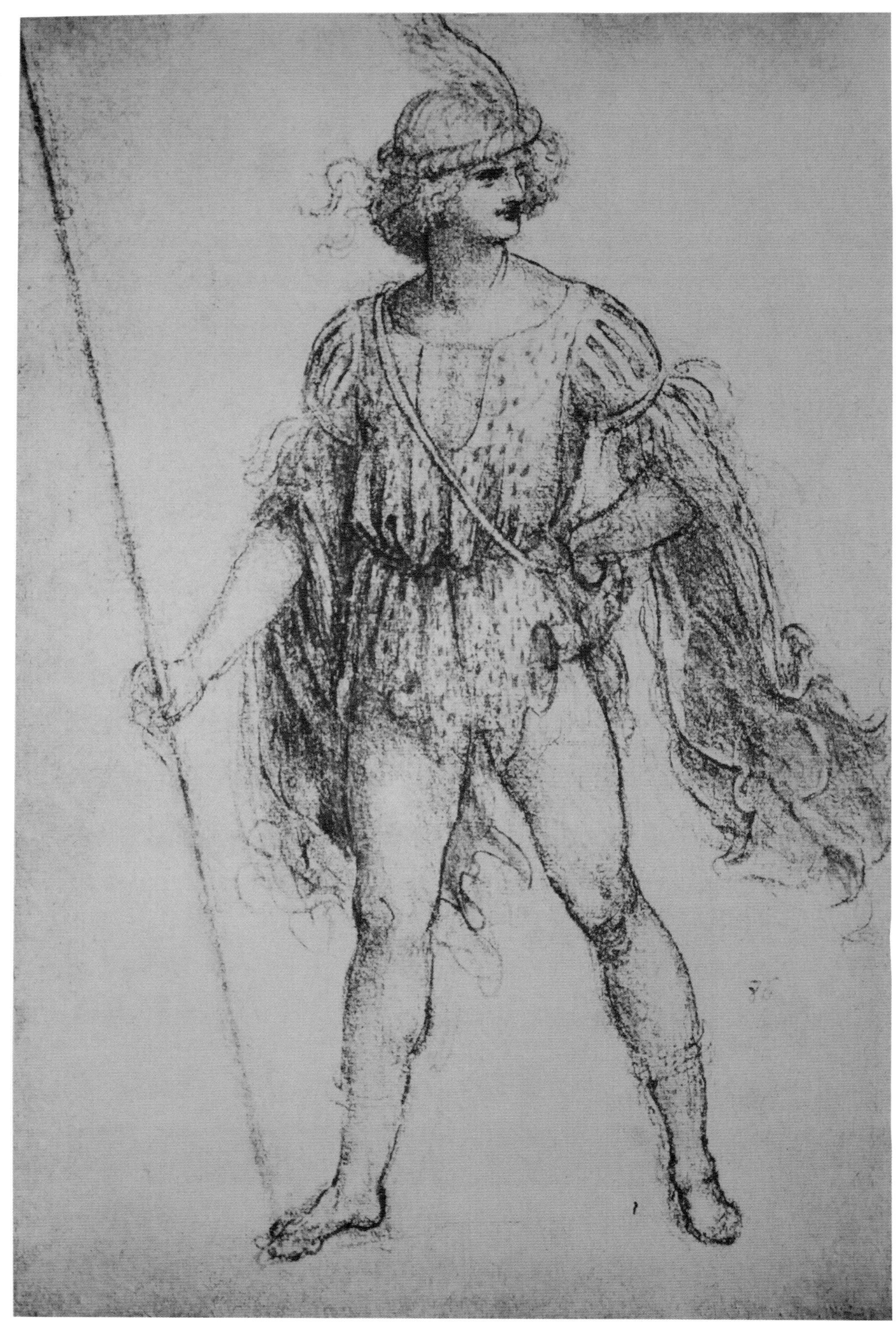

Leonardo da Vinci, *Costume for a court feast, c.* 1517-18. Pen and ink and watercolour on charcoal, 273 x 183 mm. Windsor, RL 12575

Carlo Starnazzi

fects, that knew how to capture the attention of the audience, they would have been admired also by the King of France and by his refined Court. And everyone then could have admired the triumphal arch, where at the centre a naked figure showed a flag with lilies in the right hand and a dolphin in the left one, while, at the top of the arch, a salamander, bringing the motto of Francis I «nutrisco et exstinguo», was opposed to the figure of the ermine, symbol of purity, that boasted the motto «potius mori quam foedari»,[17] remote remembrance of the Milan period at the court of the Moor, awarded of the Order of Saint Michael or of the Ermine by Ferrante of Aragon.[18] And so, even on 19 June, at the presence of the King and of Luigi Gonzaga, Leonardo would have proposed again, in the gardens of Clos-Lucé, the Feast of Paradise held in Milan, on 13 January 1490,[19] in order to celebrate the wedding of Isabella and Giangaleazzo Sforza. But in that circumstance, since the feast would have been carried out at night in open air inside the gardens of the Castle, so appropriate for their scenographical character to theatre and to a typically courtesan setting belonging to the aristocratic-chivalrous tradition, he would have simulated there, with games of light and dramatic coup de theatre, the vault of heaven and the motion of the stars:

First the court was all covered with clothes in azure with stars of gold to similarity of the sky, then there were the main planets, the sun on one side and the moon on the opposite one, that it made an

admirable view, Mars, Jupiter and Saturn were placed according to their order, with the 12 zodiacal signs. Around the court, upstairs and downstairs, there was a circle of columns, which similarly was adorned with clothes and with stars, and among their architraves there were circles of ivy with their festoons in the middle. The soil was covered with boards and covered with clothes with the arms of the Most Christian on one side, but out of the square of the court which was wide about 30 arms and long 60 arms, there was the court of women, adorned as I said with clothes and stars, and certainly there were 400 two-branched candlesticks illuminated so much that it seemed that the night had been driven away.

Apart from the feasts, Leonardo continued to work without pause: he outlined planimetries of roads along the route from Romorantin to Orléans (Cod. Arundel, ff. 263 *v*; 270 *r*), helped by Melzi that drew also one view of Amboise (Windsor, RL 12727), studied the currents of the Loire and the canalization of the Sologne for the drying of the swamps, submitting to Francis I a program of grandiose urbanistic plans, that give evidence of the evolution of his thoughts about architecture. And so, at the end of 1517, received appropriate horse riding mounts, he headed out with his retinue from Amboise in the direction of Romorantin: «A mons.r le contrerolleur des chevaucher de l'escuyerie du Roy en court pour les bailler faytement ou envoyer a M.r Lyonard florentin paintre du Roy pour les affers du dit seigneur. A Amboyse» (CA, f. 174 *rb-vc* [476 *r*]).

The artist met in the palace of Romorantin with the King, and there remained until 16 January, making inspections in the swampy environs for an hydraulic rearrangement of the zone, calculating the length of the courses of water and their difference in level and illustrating to Francis I the project to build an immense royal palace: «Eve of Saint Anthony I returned from Romorontin to Amboise and the king left two days before from Romorontin», and on the left of the sheet he adds: «You will make a test of the level of that channel that has to be carried from the Era to Remolontin with a channel wide an arm and deep an arm» and below: «Era river - Scier river - Villafrancho - Sodro Bridge - Sodro river – Barco», to conclude with the localities of the region transcribed on the right, «Mon Ricardo (Montrichard) - Remorantin - Tors (Tours) - Ambosa (Amboise) - Bres (Blois)» (CA, f. 336 *vb* [920 *r*]).[20]

Once again Leonardo proposed another time his conception of an ideal city, where the Palace-Castle had the feature of a complex organism, rich in architectural solutions for its

---

[17]   The description of the Festivities for the wedding ceremony of Lorenzo de' Medici is narrated by Stazio Gadio and kept in the Gonzaga Archives, *Esteri* (Francia), XV, 3, 634. See E. SOLMI, op. cit.

[18]   In the first one of the three small notebooks of the Ms. H, written up in 1494, Leonardo, dealing with the allegorical-moral value of the animals, on provision of the indications supplied by the *Acerba* of Cecco d' Ascoli, adduced as an illustrious example of virtue and purity the figure of the salamander and that of the ermine. To the salamander corresponded the element of fire, and the flames released from its mouth sent back to love: «the salamander in the fire refines its skin. It does not have passive limbs and does not care of other food than of fire and often in that one it renews its skin. For the virtue» (Ms. H, f. 13 *r*); while for the figure of the ermine, emblem of moderation, pushed from purity to prefer death rather than to get dirty, Leonardo wrote: «The ermine, for its moderation, it does not eat if not but a single time a day, and it lets the hunters to take it rather than to escape in the muddy earth, not to maculate its decorum» (Ms. H, f. 12 *r*); «Moderation holds all the vices. The ermine prefers to die than to stain itself» (Ms. H, f. 101 *r*). There is an open comparison between the candour of the mantle of the ermine and the nobility of mind of the female personage to which it refers. The ermine constituted also a clear reference to the Moor, as it turns out from a sonnet, written by Bernardo Bellincioni, where the Duke was defined, in a researched chromatic contrast, «the italic dark horse, white ermine».

[19]   In that feast Leonardo wanted to give proof of his extraordinary ability in the «inventions of motion». Bellincioni remembers that «the Feast was called of the Paradise because it had been manufactured there with great talent and art by Master Leonardo Vinci of Florence the Paradise with all the seven planets that turned round». See E. SOLMI, *«La festa del Paradiso» di Leonardo da Vinci e Bernardo Bellincioni (13 gennaio 1490)*, «Archivio Storico Lombardo», XXXI, 1904; K. T. STEINITZ, *Leonardo architetto teatrale e organizzatore di feste*, «Lettura Vinciana», IX, Firenze, Giunti Barbèra, 1969.

[20]   See J. MARTIN-DEZÉMIL, *Léonard de Vinci et les astuces de la construction solognote*, «Revue de l'Art», 87, 1990.

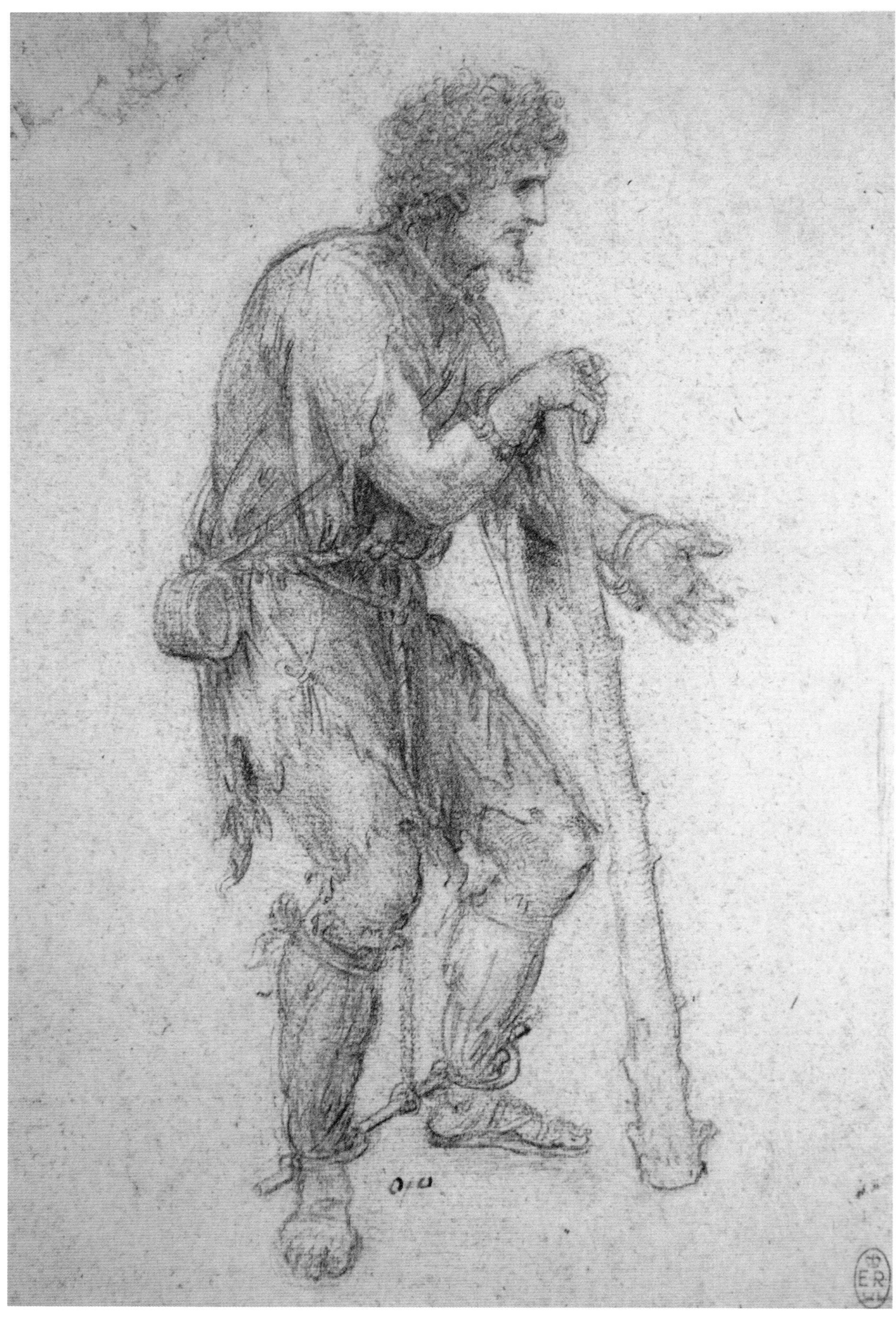

Leonardo da Vinci, *Study of a costume for a masquerade, in the manner of a prisoner, c. 1517–18.* Charcoal, with some shading of red pencil, 184 x 127 mm. Windsor, RL 12573

Carlo Starnazzi

inhabited structures, made more pleasant through gardens and gladdened, also for practical uses, by a dense orthogonal net of waterways and water courses (CA, ff. 217 *vc* [582 *r*]). The employment of technical devices would have produced a definite regularity to the flow of water to full advantage of the healthiness of the air and the hygiene of the entire city system, including the economic benefits derived from a greater work of the mills of the region:

> *The course of water does not have to pass through the ditches that are within the earth, so that when the river becomes turbid it does not unload the earth at the bottom of the aforesaid ditches. And for this reason these ditches will have to be refilled by means of cataracts and therefore they will remain always clear; but it is necessary to change it every month with the water of the river, when it is clear, and so it will make the air purified and healthy, and in this way the water that will move along the river, will be useful to the mills and to clean up often the mud of the earth and the other rubbish (CA, ff. 217 vb [583 r]).*

To the urbanistic plan it was tied the idea of the development of other channels, destined to irrigation and to navigation, taking steps to rectify the course of the rivers Sauldre and Cher and to install some sluices, in order to regulate them and to go beyond the differences of level with the Loire, as he had already realized along the Isonzo (Cod. Arundel, f. 270 *v*), in March 1500, to hold back the feared invasion of the Turks of Bajazet II from the eastern border of the Venetian Republic. For a better scenography with which to exalt the centrality of this palace destined to accommodate also the mother of the King, Louise d'Angoulême countess of Savoy and a prelude in its monumental definition in elevation to the structure of the Louvre (Windsor RL, 12292 *v*),[21] Leonardo had planned to realize, beyond to fountains, bridges and stables,[22] an immense rectangular lake, along one of the flanks of the building, where to represent, for amusement reasons, «jousts» and scenes of «naval battles» (CA, ff. 76 *vb* [209 *r*]; 217 *v* [583 *r*]). On the front of the palace, as in a dream of foundation of a new Rome («Romolontino»), along the shores of the

Sauldre,[23] he had planned, perhaps with symbolic-religious intentions, the presence of an immense public square with a great cathedral on one side, «The palace of the prince must have in front of it a public square», an observation cancelled by the artist, but that was referred clearly to the ideas of ancient plans for an ideal city (1490) and to what had been expressed by Francesco di Giorgio in his *Trattato*: «The houses of the princes and of the great gentlemen it is preferable that they are made in their first façade with beautiful and pleasing aspect, situated with an ample public square in front of them, near to the cathedral temple» (Cod. Ashburnham 361, f. 16 *v*). But, for the beginning of an epidemic of malaria, the works, already started, were abruptly interrupted and the interest for the construction of the new dwelling moved from Romorantin to the royal forest of Chambord, an immense park rich in game and much adapted to satisfy the passion of Francis I for the hunting parties.[24]

The grandiose and graceful construction of Chambord (156 m of facade and 56 m of height), although begun some months after the death of Leonardo (1519), shows in its volumetric development certain structural innovations and a variety and fineness of particulars, that anticipate, for the splendour of the whole, the originality of the palaces of the *grand siècle*, so that since those could not be attributed, for obvious cultural reasons, to the master builders (François de Pontbriand, Jacques Sourdeau and Pierre Trinqueau, that did not know neither to read neither to write nor to count), they implicate the joint action of Leonardo and of Domenico da Cortona. Furthermore, still at the end of the nineteenth century, Joseph De Croy (1894) and Girolamo Mancini (1897) would have wondered about which important encounter or which extraordinary circumstances had transformed Boccadoro from woodworker and inlayer into an architect, that is when «he started to execute the other people's concepts, were they suggested by the king, or by artists remained unknown».[25] In fact it had been the same Leon Battista Alberti, in his treatise *De Re Aedificatoria* (1452), to distinguish with polemic tones the activity and the wisdom of the artist-architect from that of the architect-inlayer, that is of the artist craftsman closely tied to the world of the mechanical arts: «the work of the woodworker, in fact, it is nothing but instrumental as regards

---

[21]   See C. Pedretti, *Leonardo da Vinci. The Royal Palace…*, 1972, *op. cit.*

[22]   In this period at Amboise was present, with the assignment of supervisor to the royal stables, Giangaleazzo Sanseverino, in honour of which Leonardo, in 1491 in Milan, had taken care of the decorations of the tournament with the triumphal float and had created the costumes of the knights and the music with bagpipes and drums. The tournament was celebrated by Bellincioni, that for the occasion thought himself to be an emulator of Politian. See G. Porro, *Nozze di Beatrice d'Este e di Anna Sforza. Documenti copiati dagli originali esistenti nell'Archivio di Stato di Milano*, «Archivio Storico Lombardo», IX, 1882; G. Fumagalli, *Gli «omini salvatichi» di Leonardo*, «Raccolta Vinciana», XVIII, 1960; G. Lopez, *Festa di nozze per Ludovico il Moro*, Milano, De Carlo, 1976; C. Vecce, *Leonardo e il gioco*, in *Passare il tempo. La letteratura del gioco e dell'intrattenimento dal XII al XVI secolo*, Roma, Salerno, 1993.

[23]   See C. Pedretti, Leonardo da Vinci. The Royal Palace…, 1972, op. cit.

[24]   See M. Reymond, *Léonard de Vinci, architecte du château de Chambord*, «Gazette des Beaux-Arts », I, 1913; L. H. Heydenreich, *Leonardo da Vinci Architect of Francis I*, «Burlington Magazine», X, 1952.

[25]   See J. De Croy, *Nouveaux documents…*,1894, *op. cit.*; Id., *Quelques reinsegnements inédits sur les maîtres maçons des chateaux de Chambord et d'Amboise*, «Mémoires de la société archéologique et historique de l'orléanais», XXVIII, Orléans, 1902; G. Mancini, *Cortona nel Medio Evo*, [1897], Ristampa anastatica, Cortona, Editrice Grafica L'Etruria, 1992.

the one of the architect. I will call Architect he who with certain method knows how to plan rationally and to realize practically through the motion of weights and by means of the composition of bodies, works that in the better way adapt to the most important needs of man». Therefore, the correctness of this hypothesis about the professional profiles is found also on what reported by the same André Félibien, that in his *Mémoires* testifies to have seen in Blois, describing and drawing its characteristics, in the seventeenth century, the model in wood of the central donjon of Chambord, built up by «Boccadoro».[26] At the same time, Leonardo continued to associate studies of hydraulics and of geometry, of topography and of technology, as the indication of the handrail for the winding staircase (Cod. Arundel, f. 269 *rv*)[27] and to influence with his extraordinary inventiveness, also in the subject of residential architecture, all the environment of the Court, to which his ideas on such purpose were well known, since the project for the villa of Charles d'Amboise (*c.* 1506-08), gentleman of Chaumont and governor of Milan (CA, f. 231 *rb* [629 *br*]).[28] Precisely the Amboise, in a letter of 16 December 1506 to the Seigniory of Florence, had recognized, first among his clients, the greatness and the universality of the genius of Leonardo, exalting him more as an architect, than as a painter:[29]

The outstanding works, which has left in Italy, and most of all in this city, Master Leonardo da Vinci, your citizen, have brought the tendency to all that have seen them, to love him in particular, even though they had not ever seen him. And we want to admit we are in that number of people that we loved him before that we ever knew him in person. But after that we have dealt with him here, and with experience we have demonstrated his various virtues, we see, to tell the truth, that his name, famous for painting, it is obscure as regards what it should deserve to be praised for other qualities, which are in him of the greatest good value; and we want to admit that in the proofs made by him of some thing that we had asked him, of drawings and architecture and other things pertaining to our condition, he has given satisfaction in such a way, that not only we remained of him satisfied, but we remained of him admired […].

In the villa for the Amboise, placed between what today is via Monte Napoleone and Corso Venezia, where the «Neron from Sancto Andrea» at that time flew in «Fonte Lunga», the artist had planned a stairway with two parallel flights, leading, like at Chambord, from the entrance through a corridor to the «court of the Great Master» (CA, f. 231 *rb* [629 *br*]) placed for a greater protection on the first floor. This latter one, flanked by a garden of delights, «covered with a net of copper and full of birds» and with perennial «spring water» (CA, f. 271 *va* [732 *v*]), resulted to be «all open in front», to approach to the room of the feasts, while the stairs should have had to be wide and bright, because the «dark ones» generate melancholy.

The attention reserved to the improvement of every practical aspect in the court life is registered also in the studies made for the palace of Romorantin, where to the realization of «comfortable stairs in a way that they are spacious», so «that the people do not need to hit the masked ones and put out of order their shapes, if ever should come out […] a multitude of people […] with such masked ones», it was even combined the attempt to search solutions to guarantee an appropriate aeration of the rooms neighbouring the «latrines», «so that the stench does not blow through the rooms» (CA, f. 76 *vb* [209 *r*]).

Also a sheet with drawings of anatomical studies, kept at Windsor (RL 12592 *r*) and datable around 1508-10, is full of outlines of stairways. Beside the straight stairways of traditional shape, studies of double staircases can be singled out: divergent stairways on one part and on the other of the entrance, staircases with two crossed opposite flights, in the end (in the middle of the sheet) stairways with two parallel flights leading to a floor, whence leaves in inverse sense, like at Chambord, a third flight placed between the first two and leading to an upper floor.[30]

The Castle of Chambord, with the purpose to celebrate the splendour of the Court, was correlated in perspective to the immensity of the surrounding landscape, while symmetries developed around the central donjon with square plant, flanked by four angular towers, in their turn divided in four identical parts by two wide corridors, according to a Greek cross planimetry, already present, but in a less perfect way, in the famous Medicean residence of Poggio a Caiano.[31]

---

[26]   See A. FÉLIBIEN, *Mémoires pour servir à l'histoire des maisons royalles et bastimens de France*, Paris, De Montaiglon, 1874; ID., *Vues des châteaux du Blésois au XVII siècle*, Paris, Lasueur, 1911.

[27]   See M. REYMOND, *Léonard de Vinci, architecte du château de Chambord*, «Gazette des Beaux-Arts », I, 1913.

[28]   See C. PEDRETTI, *Il «Neron da Sancto Andrea»*, «Raccolta Vinciana», XVIII, Milano, 1960.

[29]   See L. BELTRAMI, Documenti, n° 181.

[30]   See Cfr. C. PEDRETTI, *A Chronology of Leonardo da Vinci Architectural Studies after 1500*, Genève, Droz, 1962. But the interest of Leonardo for stairways is documented since 1487-90 in sheets 47 *r* and 68 *v* of the Ms. B of the Institut de France, where there are drawings of double stairs with flights between them independent and systems of stairways with four flights each independent from the others for a military building.

[31]   See F. LESUEUR, *Léonard de Vinci et Chambord*, «Etudes d'Arts», 8-10, 1953-54; J. GUILLAUME, *Léonard de Vinci, Dominique de Cortone et l'escalier du modèle en bois de Chambord*, «Gazette des Beaux-Arts», VI, LXXI, 1968; ID., *Léonard de Vinci et l'architecture française. II. La villa de Charles d'Amboise et le château de Romorantin: Reflexion sur un livre de Carlo Pedretti*, «Revue de l'Art», 25, 1974.

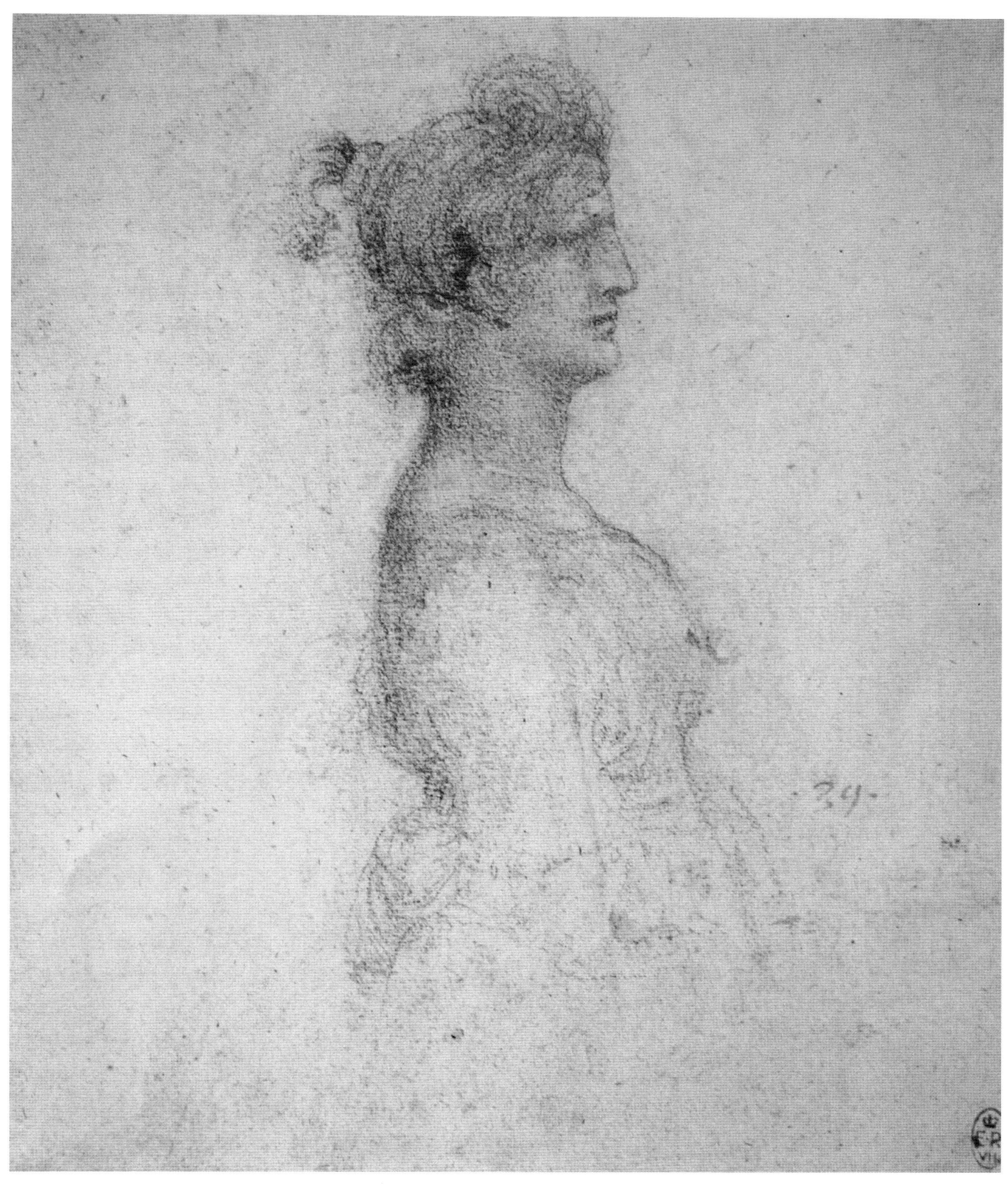

Leonardo da Vinci, *Study of a costume for a masquerade, in profile, c.* 1517–18. Charcoal, with some shading of red pencil, 170 x 146 mm. Windsor, RL 12508

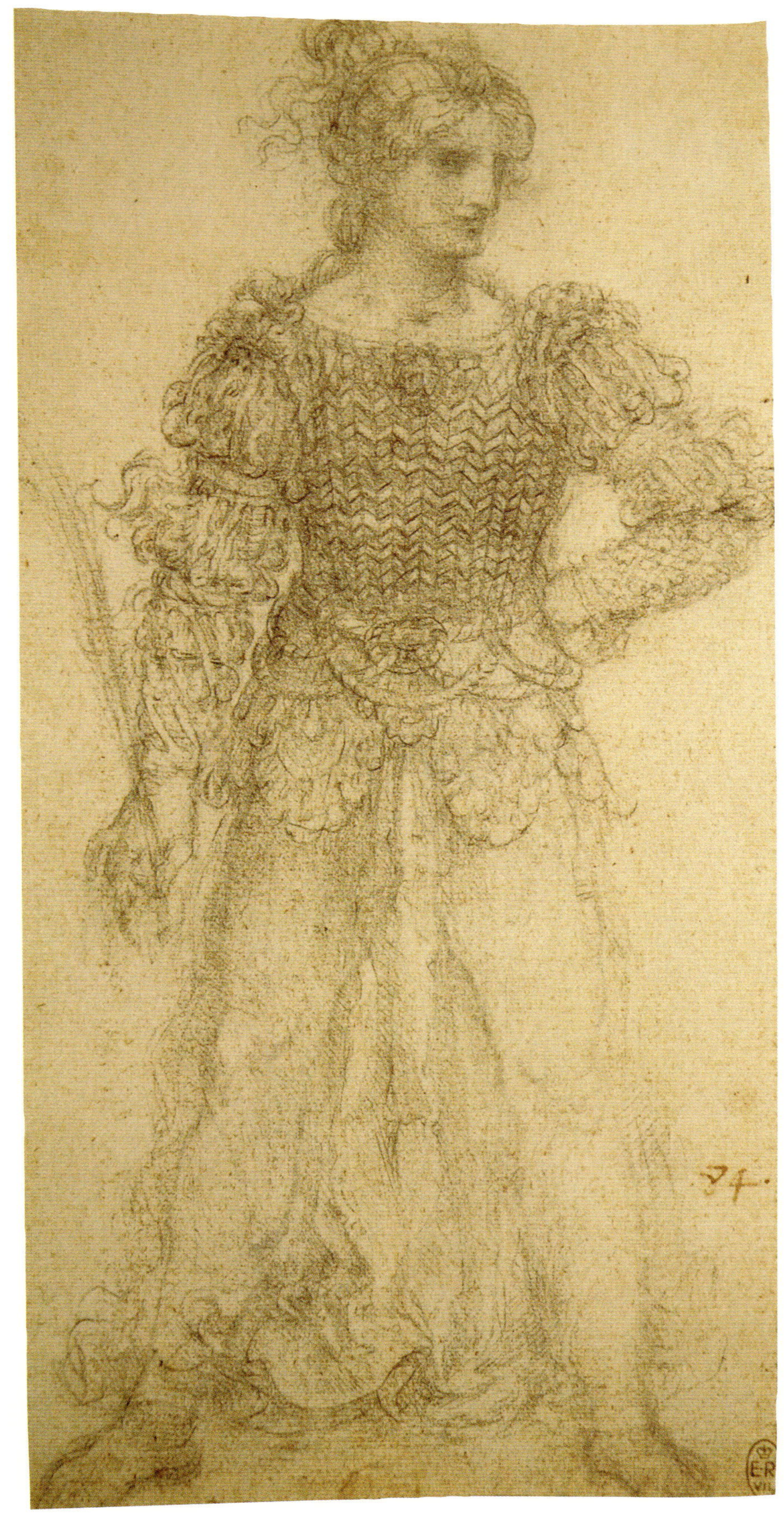

Leonardo da Vinci, *Study of a costume for a court feast, c.* 1517-18. Charcoal, 215 x 112 mm. Windsor, RL 12576

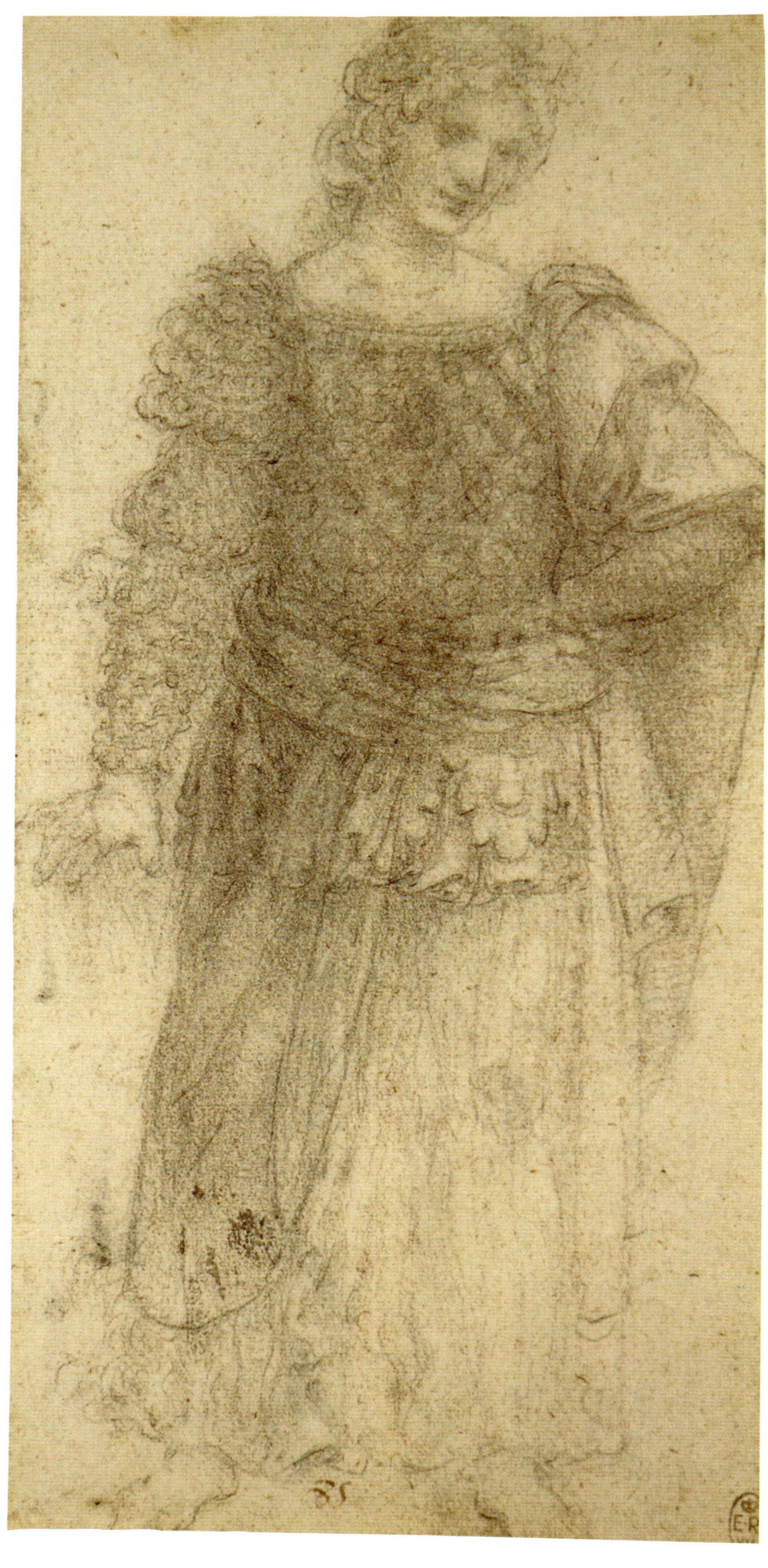

LEONARDO DA VINCI, *Study of a costume for a court feast, c.* 1517-18. Charcoal, 214 x 107 mm. Windsor, RL 12577

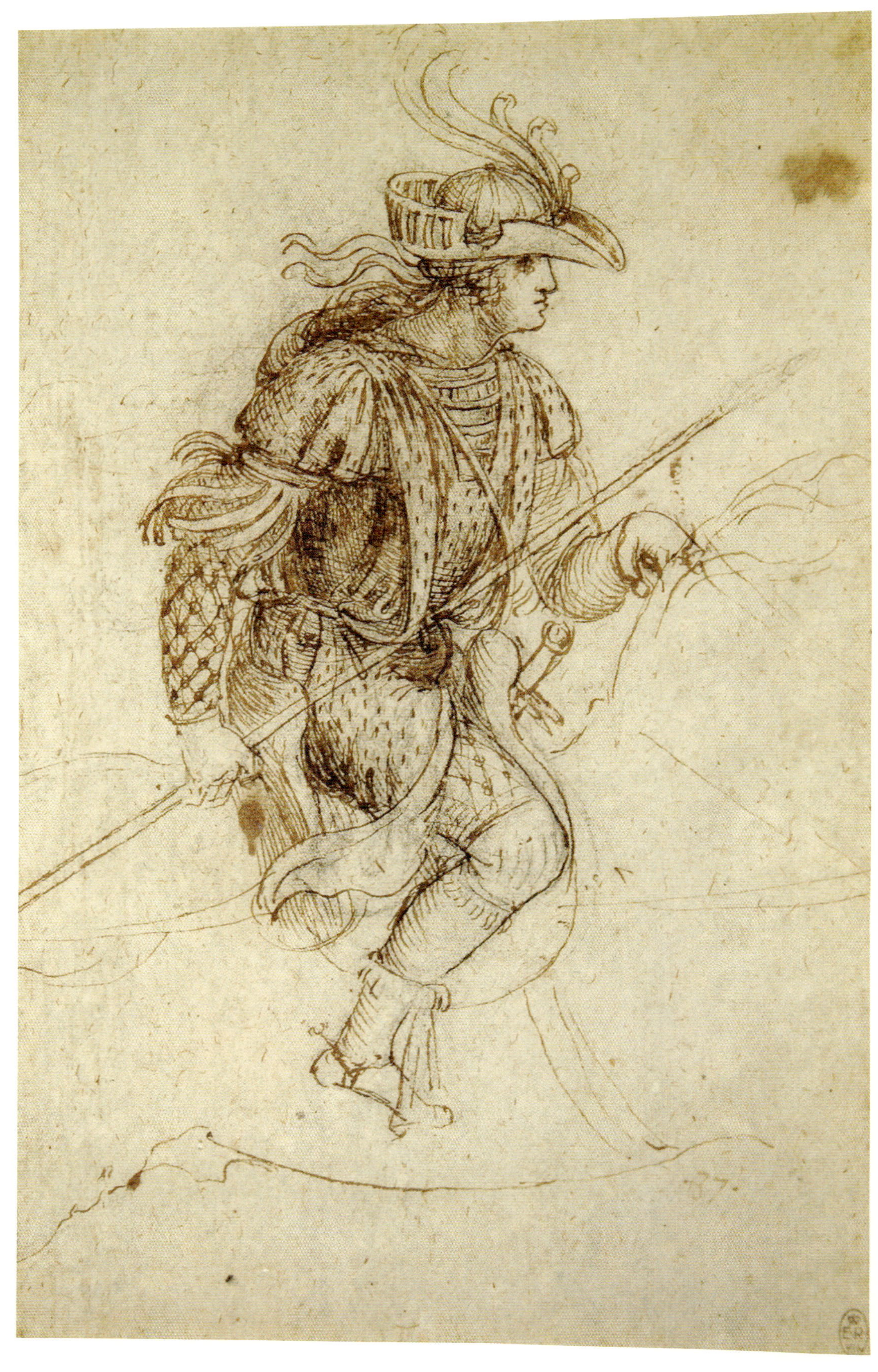

LEONARDO DA VINCI, *Study of a costume for a court feast, with a horse, c.* 1517-18. Charcoal, pen and ink, 240 x 152 mm. Windsor, RL 12574

CARLO STARNAZZI

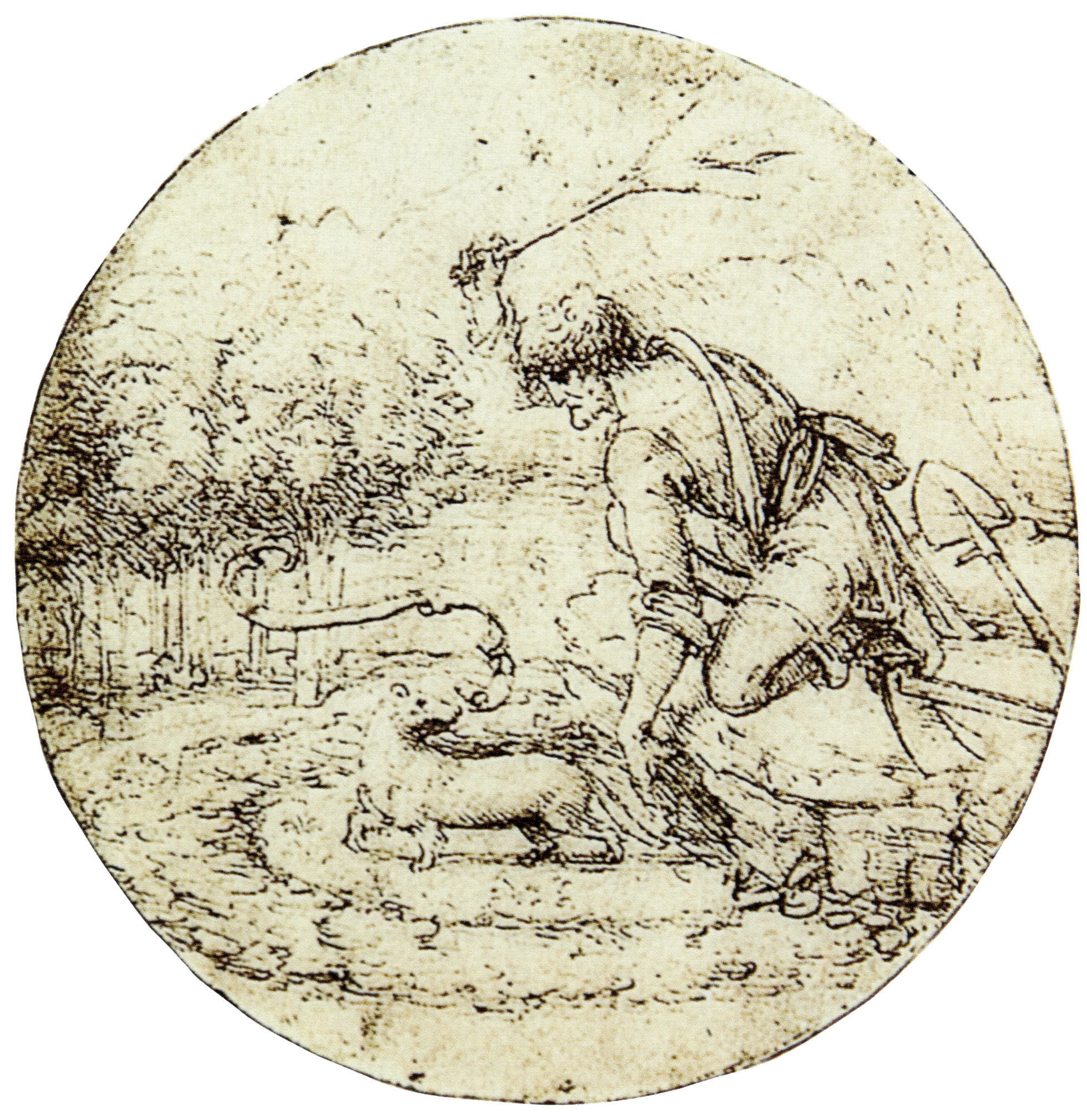

Leonardo da Vinci, Allegory of the ermine, c. 1490. Cambridge, Fitzwilliam Museum, n. PD. 120-1961

However, this type of architecture, a great palace with angle towers, had been designed little years before from the same Leonardo, in 1515, on the occurrence of the new residence to build in Florence for the governor of the city, Lorenzo di Piero de' Medici (CA, f. 315 *r–b* [865 *r*]), grandson of the Pope. But it is at Chambord that finds its development an admirable grand staircase, made up of two distinguished stairways that wind themselves round in a double spiral, constituting one of the most original contributions given by Italy to French architecture for high-class residences. In fact, going beyond the classic Italian outline of the great staircase with parallel and straight flights, present with evident variations first at Azay-le Rideau and then at Chenonceaux, these two flights, that allow two people to come down and to go up without meeting, turn out to be separated by an empty space equal to their width, while the communication is guaranteed by a single flight situated between the two that come from the ground floor, permitting with great solemnity the communication between the first and the second floor. To such purpose Félibien offers a detailed description of the model, adding to it the following observations:

This staircase is double until the first floor, that is there are two flights one on the right and the other on the left, and, because one

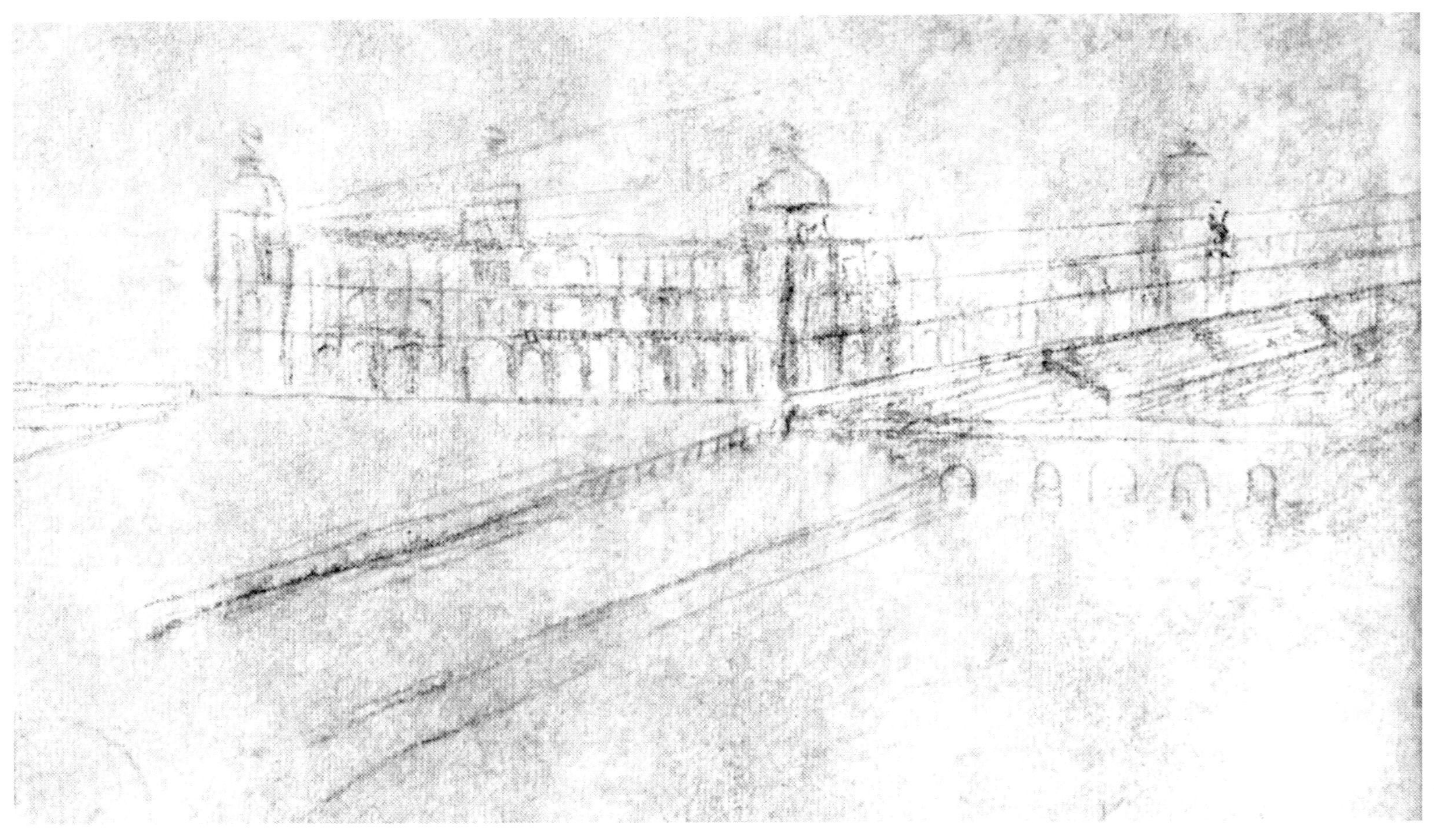

Leonardo da Vinci, *Project for the Castle of Romorantin, c. 1517-18. Windsor, RL 12292 v*

enters in the vestibule from three doors, the one in the middle and the two others between the sides and the centre, that are used as passage for the low lodgings. At the upper floor there is a similar lodging, but to go up from the second floor to the third one the staircase has but a flight, that rises in the middle of the two passages, that are used for the communication of the lodgings that are on the front facade.

Therefore the staircase with multiple spiral of the wood model of «Boccadoro» is a deeply original work and it is the first example that appears in France of a symmetrical staircase, where two parallel flights frame a third one, testifying the passage from the gothic style to an Italianizing Renaissance. Now, also as an idea, a volume or a structure that rises on itself in a wrapping way, turns out to be coherent with the artistic vision of Leonardo, that to confer the spirit and the movement to his figures continuously creates spiral shapes in a complex equilibrium of opposing impulses.
In fact, the idea of overcoming the Euclidean geometry is pursued by Leonardo in all of his works, obsessed as he was with images with a spiral shape, from the screw of Archimedes to the vortices of water, from the *Battle of Anghiari* to the *Leda*, from the *Saint Anne* to the *Saint John*, to favour their dynamic hovering in space. The amazing creation of this grand staircase that soars upwards at the centre of the donjon could not do but to call back into play Leonardo, already author of similar devices, conceived in a way completely functional to the requirements of court life, since they favoured a greater disengagement for the ladies in their descent from the apartments towards the hall below, on the occurrence of the splendid masquerades. To such purpose, Leonardo had annotated with shrewdness that «the rooms where one has to dance in» have to be placed at ground floor, «because I have already seen them to fall into ruin, with the death of many». Therefore, in favouring the enthusiasm of Francis I, that had the intention to realize a magnificent and sumptuous palace at Chambord, symbol of the splendour of the crown of France, Domenico da Cortona, adhering to the graphical and oral indications of Leonardo, would have put in elevation the masterpiece of French architecture of Renaissance. And one evening, while the master of Vinci followed the advice of the insistent voice of the maid-servant Mathurine

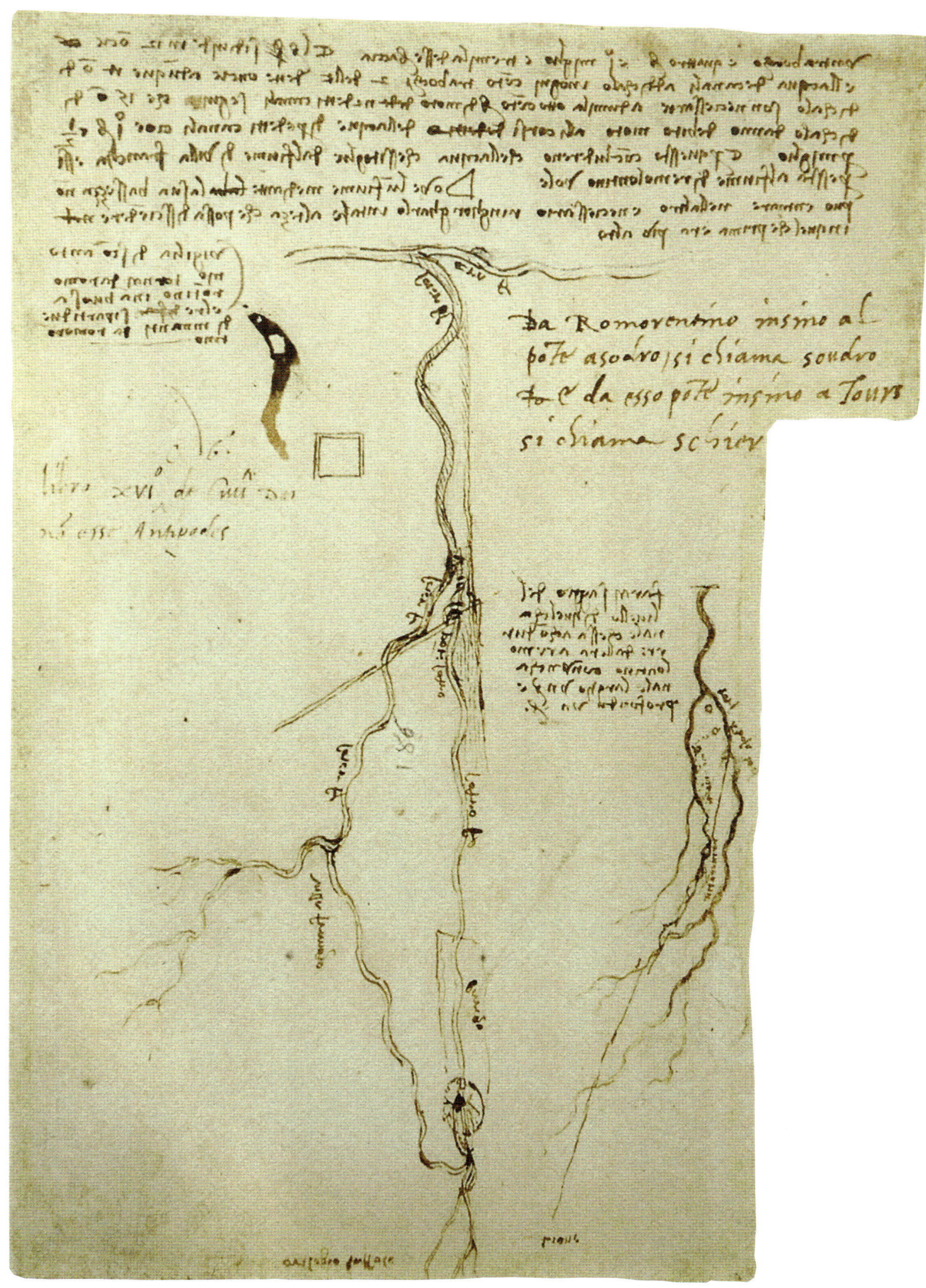

Leonardo da Vinci, *Study for the canalization of the Sologne, c.* 1517. Pen and ink, 86-285 x 172-210 mm. Codex Atlanticus, f. 920 *r.* Milan, Biblioteca Ambrosiana

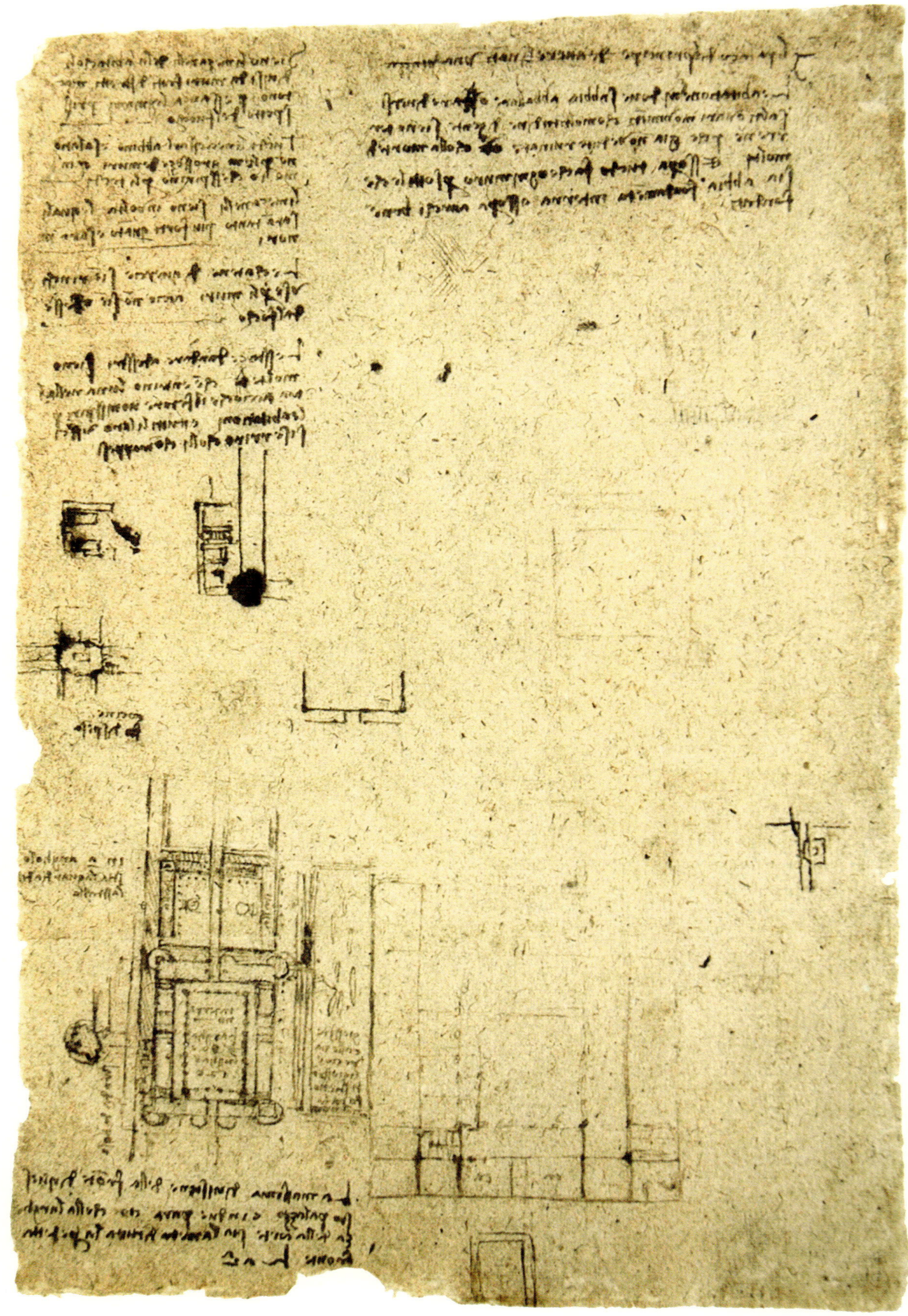

Leonardo da Vinci, *Studies for the royal Palace of Romorantin*, c. 1517–18. Pencil, pen and ink, 287 x 197 mm. Codex Atlanticus, f. 209 *r*. Milan, Biblioteca Ambrosiana

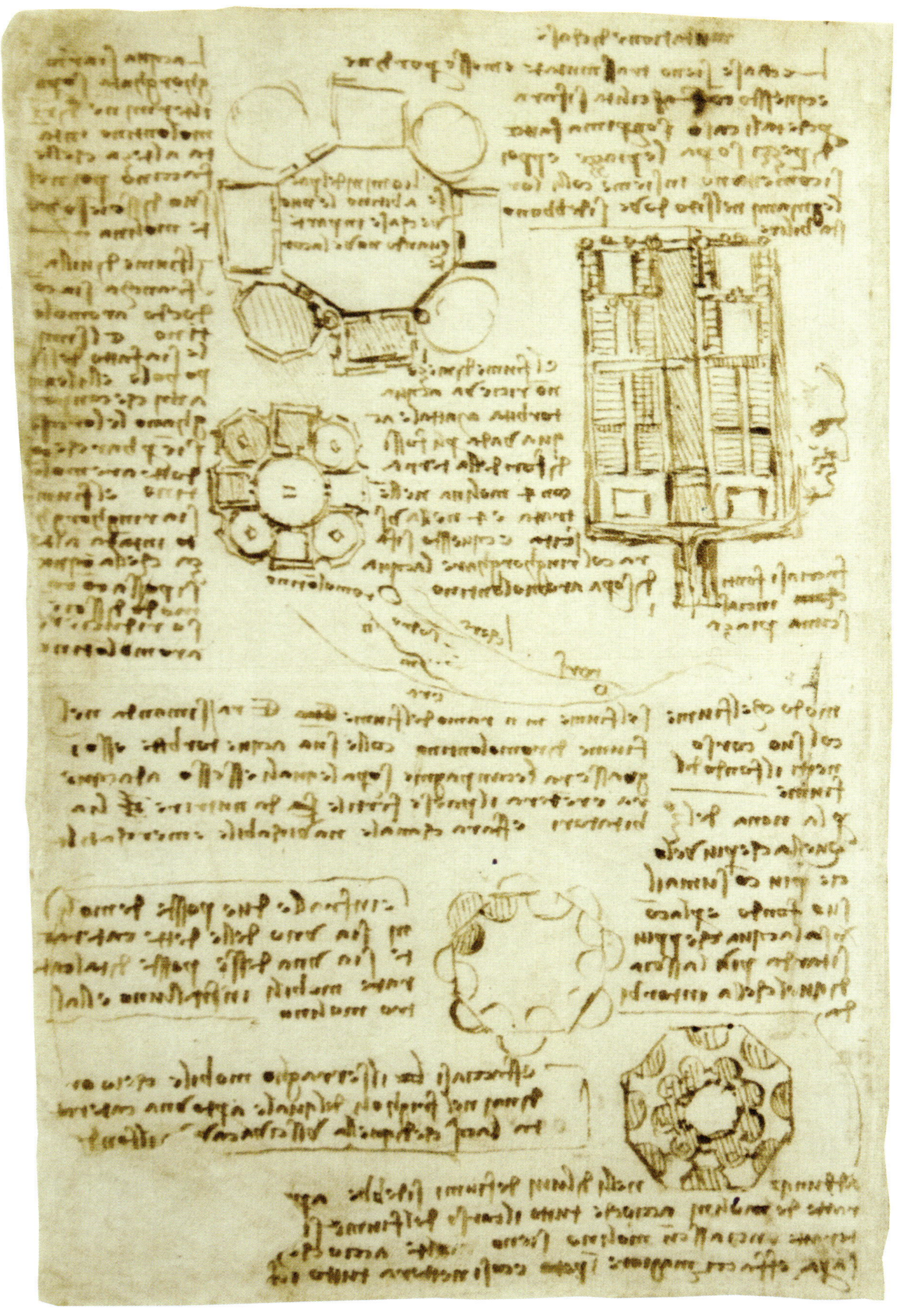

Leonardo da Vinci, *Studies for the royal Palace of Romorantin and of a pavilion with central plan, c. 1517-18.* Codex Arundel, f. 270 *v.* London, British Library

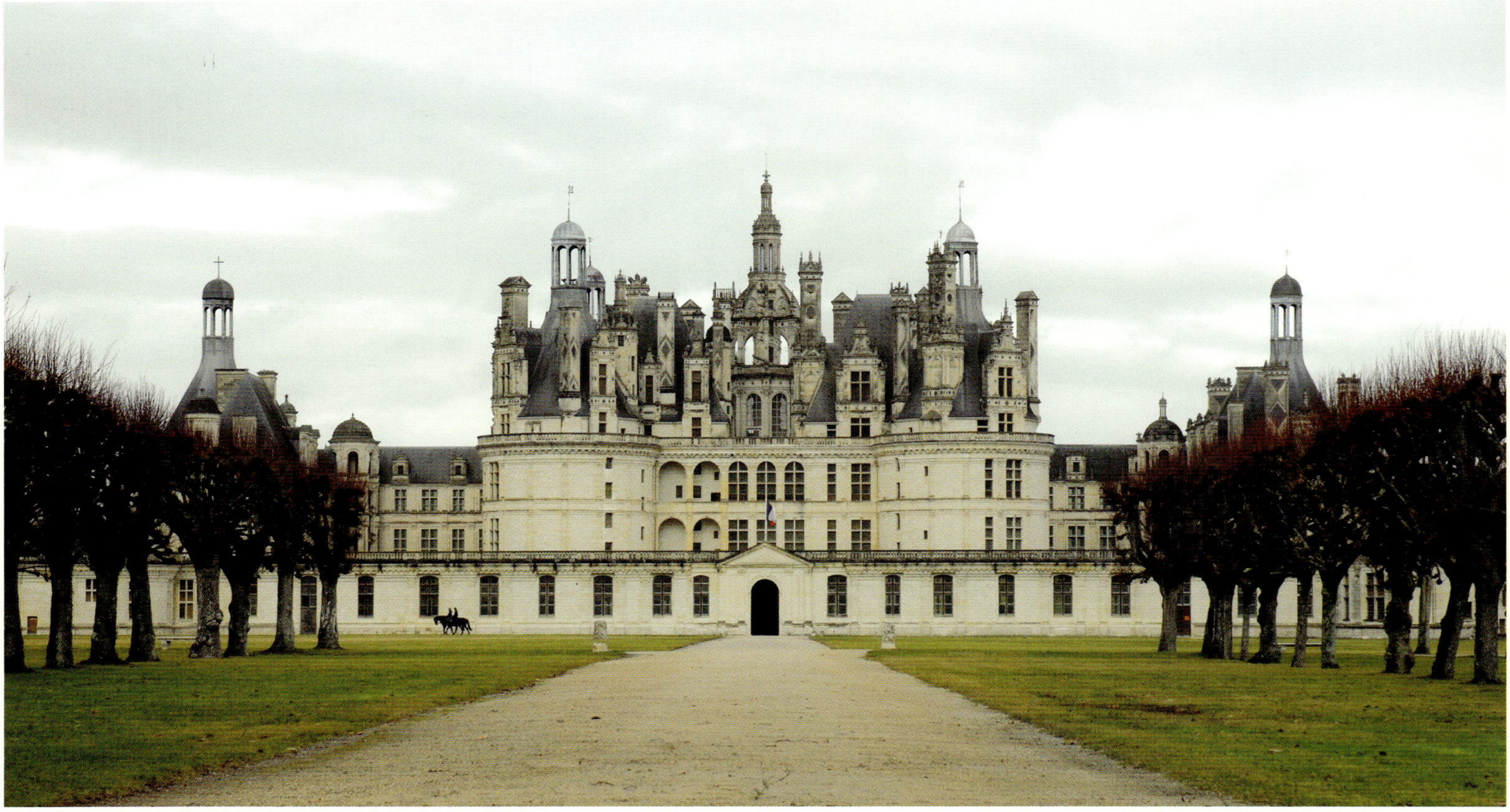

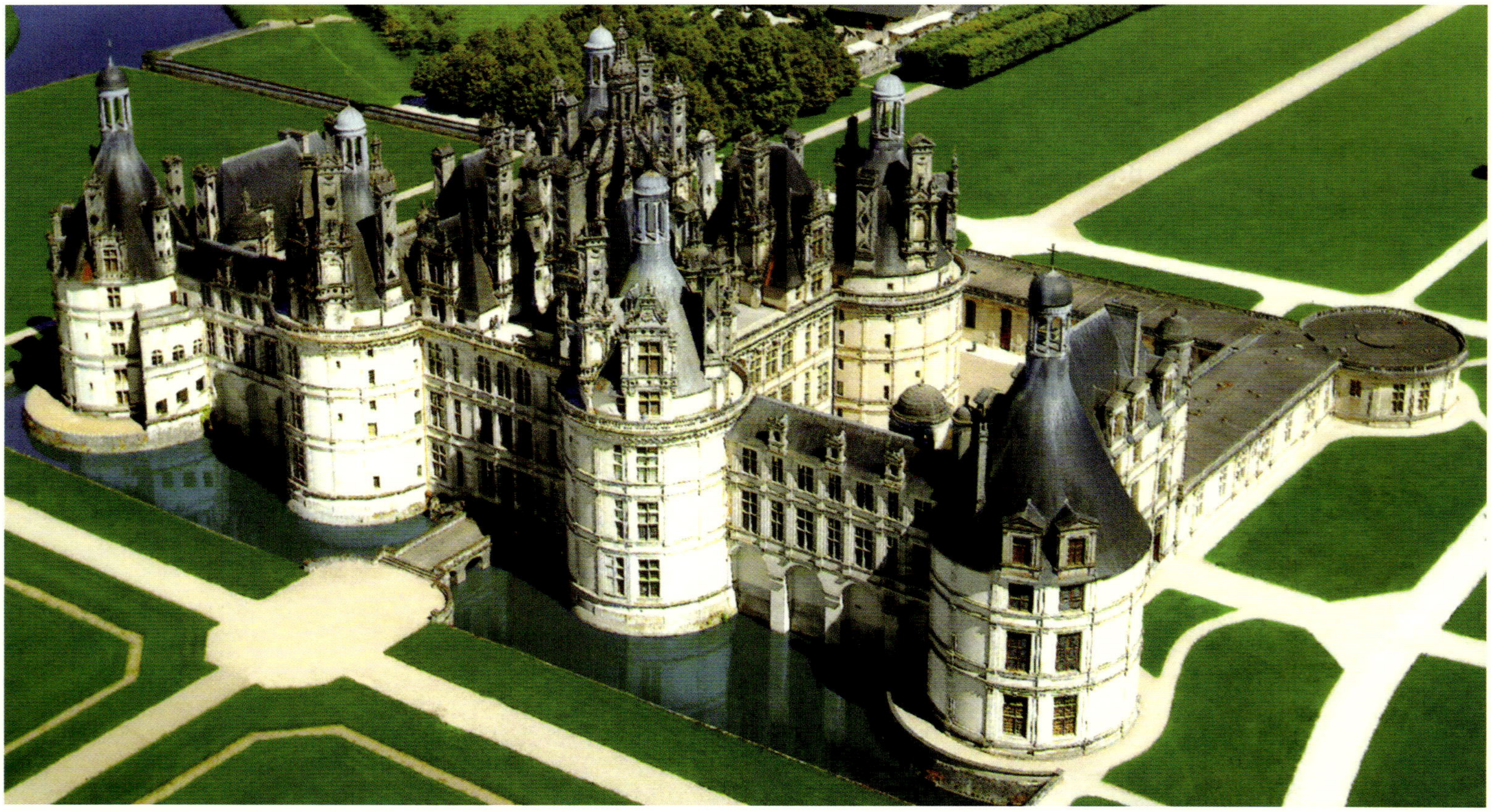

Two views of the Castle of Chambord

and suspended his geometry studies, registering in the sheet the truly human note: «etcetera because the soup gets cold» (Cod. Arundel, f. 245),[32] master «Boccadoro», following Francis I and his Court to Paris, would have defined with success, mindful of those remote teachings, the new planimetry and the reconstruction of the southern side of the Hôtel de Ville (1533), still today a prestigious administrative centre of the city.[33]

[32] See C. PEDRETTI, *Eccetera: perché la minestra si fredda,* «Lettura Vinciana», XV, Firenze, Giunti Barbèra, 1975.
[33] See L. BELTRAMI, *L'Hôtel de Ville di Parigi e l'architetto Domenico da Cortona,* Roma, 1882; B. PROST, *Le véritable architecte de l'ancien Hôtel de ville de Paris,* «Gazette des Beaux-Arts», 3, VI, 1891; H. STEIN, *Boccador et l'Hôtel de ville de Paris,* «Bulletin de la Societé de l'histoire de Paris», XXXI, 1904; L. DOREZ, *Dominique de Cortone et Pierre Chambiges,* «Bulletin de la Societé de l'histoire de Paris», XXXI, 1904. The foundation stone for the construction of the Hôtel de Ville was laid on July 1533 and in September the memorial stone was engraved, which brought the following inscription, with the memory of Domenico da Cortona as architect: «Senatui, populo, equiti / busque Parisien. Pie de / se meritis, Franciscus / primus Francorum rex po / tentissimus has aedes / fundamentis extruendas / mandavit ac curavit / cogendisque publice con / siliis et administrandae / reipublicae dicavit An / no a salute condita MD / XXXIII idibus julii / incisum MDXXXIII / idibus septemb. Petro Viola praefecto / decurionum, Claudio Dani / ele, Joanne Bartholomeo / Martino Bragelonio Joan / ne Curtino Decurionibus. Dominico Cortonensi Architectante». [«To the Senate, the people and the chevaliers of Paris. Piously of his merits, Francis The First of the French most powerful king ordered these buildings to be constructed from their foundations and he took care of the councils that publicly collected and dedicated to the administration of the republic In the year 1533 at the ides of July, engraved 1533 at the ides of September, Prefect of the decurions Petrus Viola, Decurions Claudio Daniele, Joanne Bartholomeo, Martino Bragelonio, Joanne Curtino. Domenico of Cortona architect». Tr.N.] Also in the *Antiquités de la ville de Paris* (tome II), Sauval reports that «Dominique Bocador, dit de Cortone, qui en fit le dessin et conduisit l'édifice, avait 250 livres de gages»; consideration repeated in many other documents of the *Histoire de l'Hôtel de Ville.* In 1789, Louis XVI received in the Hôtel de Ville the three-coloured cockade from the hands of Bailly and, in 1794, Robespierre was there arrested, to be then led to the guillotine. On 26 March 1871, the Commune took there office and on 26 May 1871, there flared up a fire that destroyed the entire building. From 1872, the Hôtel de Ville was reconstructed with identical shape in Renaissance style.

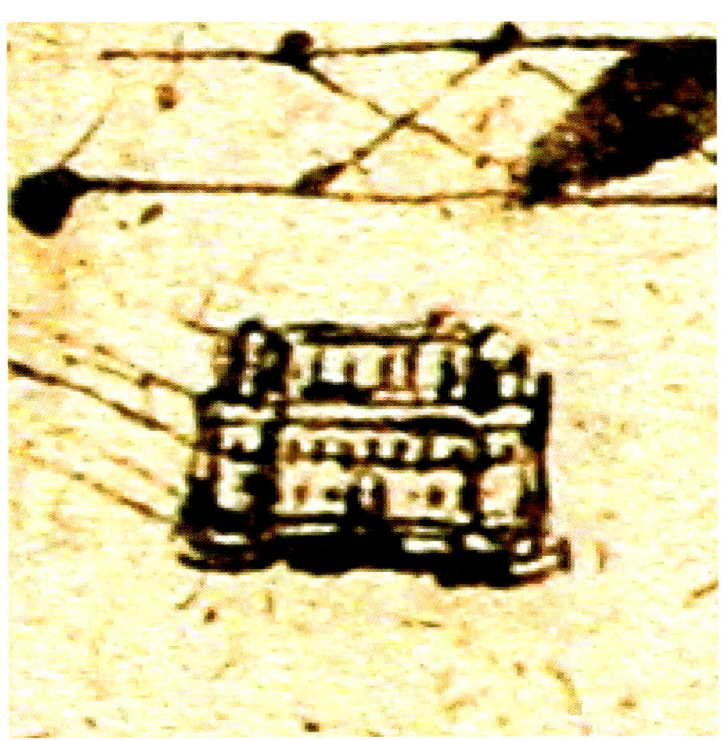

LEONARDO DA VINCI, *Palace for the Governor of Florence Lorenzo di Piero de' Medici, c.* 1515. Codex Atlanticus, f. 865 r. Milan, Biblioteca Ambrosiana. Particular

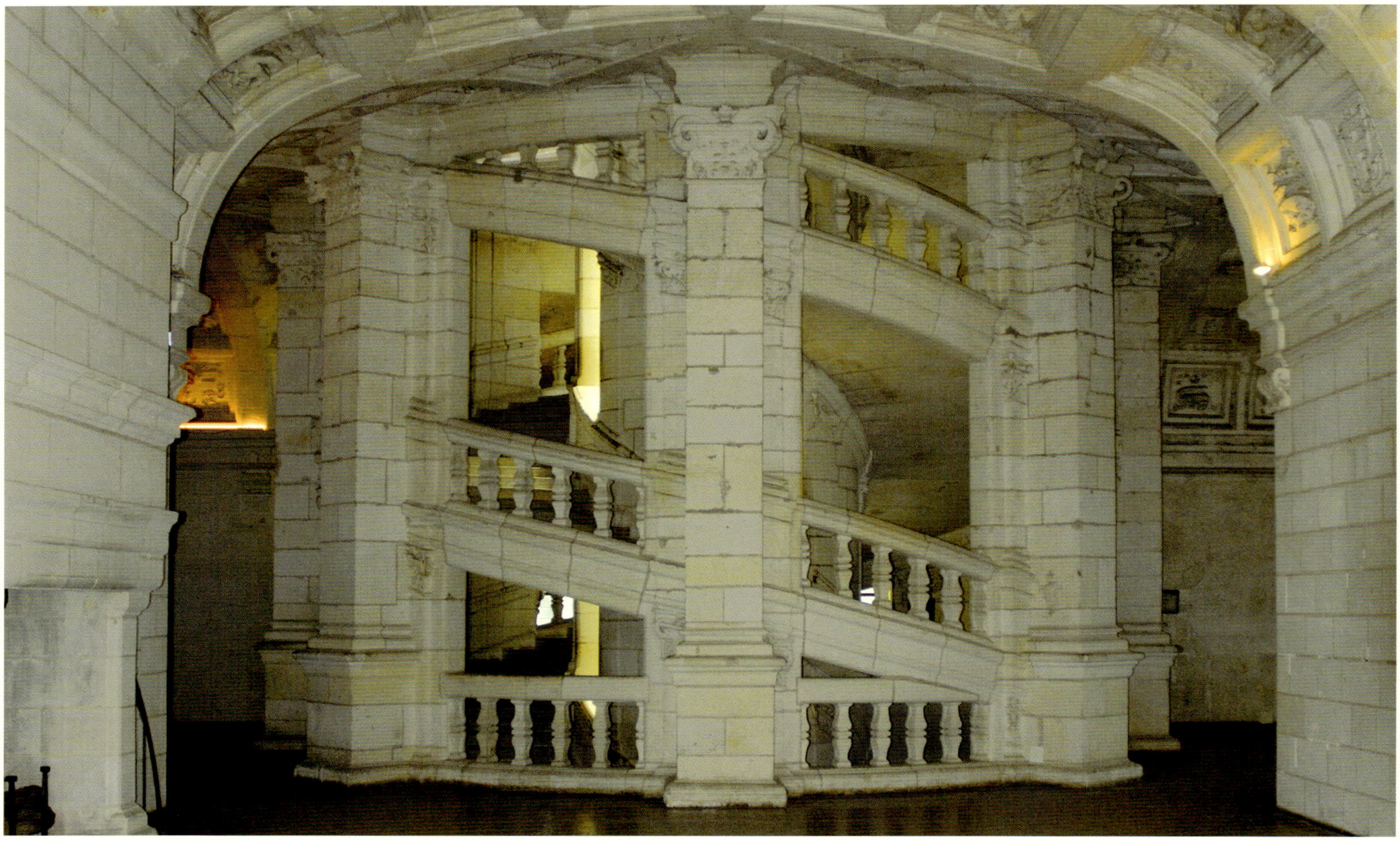

Double spiral grand staircases at the centre of the Donjon of the Castle of Chambord

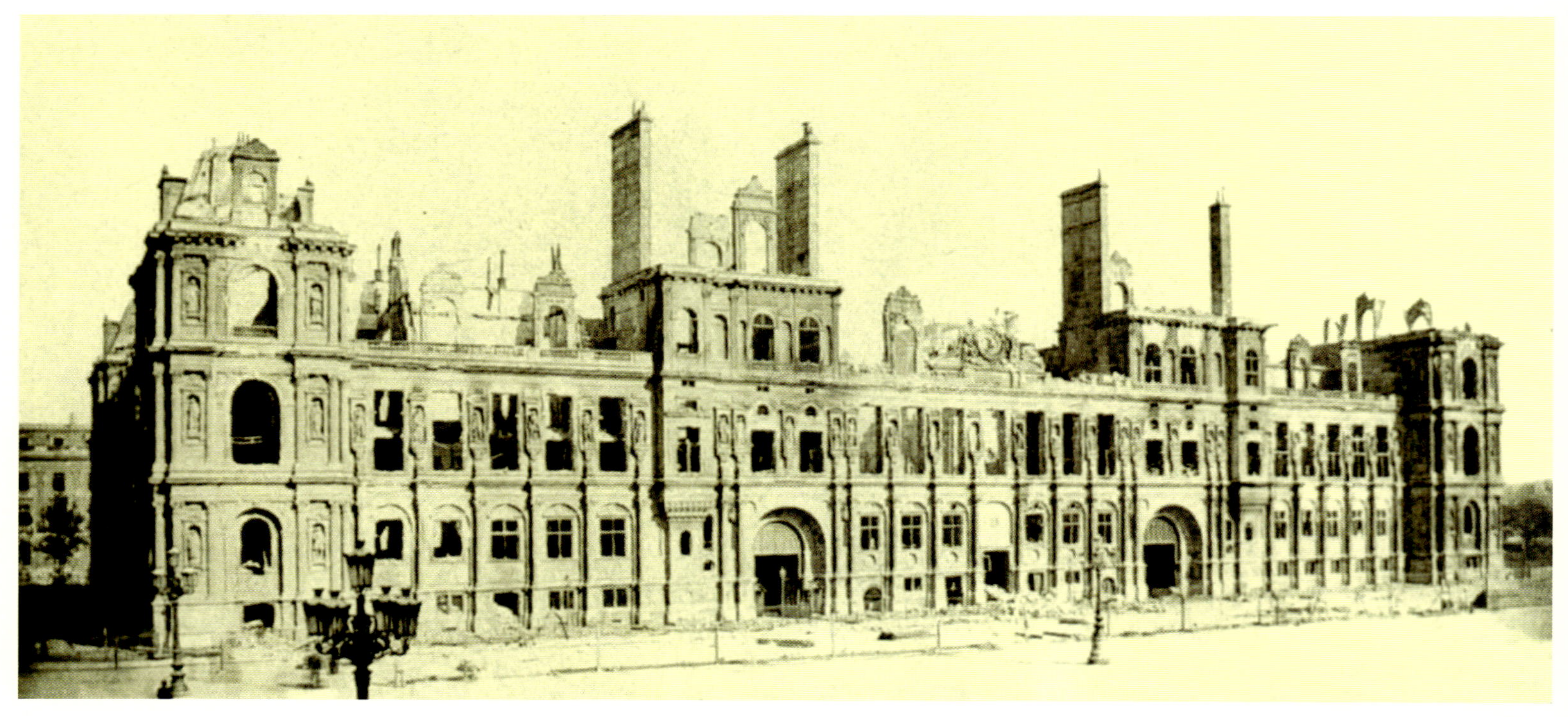

Domenico da Cortona, *Hôtel de Ville*, 1533. Paris

The will of Leonardo

ON 23 April 1519, Leonardo dictates his last will to the royal notary public Guillaume Boreau (or Boureau)[1] and on 2 May he dies, being 67 years old, in the Castle of Clos-Lucé, not far from the royal Palace of Amboise, while Francis I,[2] on the contrary of what sustained in the vasarian narration, revised and published in full Counter-Reformation climate in 1568, is well far away, perhaps in the residence of Saint-Germain-en-Laye, where the Court in those days celebrated with Queen Claudia the birth of the second born, the future Henry II:

Arrived then there the king who often and lovingly was used to visit him; for which thing he for reverence got up sitting on the bed, talking about his illness and the accidents of that one, showed

however how much he had offended God and the men of the world, not having operated in art as it becomes. Whence, it came to him a paroxysm messenger of death. For the which thing, got up the king and holding his head to help and make him a favour, so that the evil be lightened, his spirit, that was a most divine one, knowing not to be able to have a greater honour, died in the arms of that king, being he of age 75 years old.

In the period of the Restoration, marked by the alliance between throne and altar, Jean Auguste Dominique Ingres (1780-1867) would have interpreted the story of the death of Leonardo embracing the vasarian thesis of the conversion[3] and, in his *Francis I receives the last breath of Leonardo da Vinci* (1818), focused the dramatization of the scene on the faces of the King and of the dying artist, while Francesco Melzi with a declamatory gesture justified his pain in front of the cardinal and the friar confessor.[4]

The celebration of the death of Leonardo in the arms of Francis I, in this beginning period of romanticism of catholic mark, seemed to move also in opposition to the figure of Raphael, that, initially pervaded with divine and with noble greatness, shining in him «all the rarest virtues of the mind», he had got lost amid the flesh pleasures in front of the pagan beauty of the *Fornarina* (Rome, Galleria Nazionale).[5]

---

[1]   The BOUREAU family was in Amboise a notarial dynasty until the nineteenth century. A. HOUSSAYE (*Histoire de Léonard de Vinci*, Paris, Didier, 1869), during his search for vincian documents, with the assent of one of the Boureau notary public, tried to single out in his archives the original document of the will of Leonardo (G. UZIELLI, *Ricerche intorno a Leonardo da Vinci*. Serie prima, Firenze, Pellas, 1872). A copy of the notarial deed in French was recovered at Romorantin in 1893. See E. MÜNTZ, *Léonard de Vinci*, Paris, Hachette, 1899.

[2]   Benvenuto Cellini, in his *Life*, would have given evidence of the great admiration that the king Francis I had for Leonardo: «And because he was abundant of such a supreme talent, having he some cognition of Latin and Greek letters, the King Francis, being in the strongest way fond of those great virtues he had, he took so much pleasure in hearing him reasoning, that he detached from him only a few days of the year; which was the cause not to give him the possibility to put into work those admirable studies he had made with such discipline. I do not want to refrain from repeating the words, that I heard the King say about him, which he said to me, while the cardinal of Ferrara and the cardinal of Lorena and the king of Navarre were present; he said that he did not believe that any other man was ever born in this world, that knew as much as Lionardo, not as much as of sculpture, painting and architecture, but that he was a very great philosopher». And precisely the apograph of a treatise of Leonardo «on the three great arts, sculpture, painting and architecture», would have been purchased in 1542 by Cellini, for 15 scudoes. See B. CELLINI, *Discorso dell'architettura*, in *Due trattati di Benvenuto Cellini uno dell'oreficeria l'altro della scultura coll'aggiunta di alcune operette del medesimo*, Milano, Società de' Classici Italiani, 1811; C. PEDRETTI, *Libro di Pittura*, 1995, *op. cit.*

[3]   This vasarian interpretation, that places Francis I at the bedside of Leonardo, while he dies in his arms, will be followed also by G.P. LOMAZZO both in his *Gli sogni e raggionamenti* (*Scritti*, I) and in his *Idea* (ivi). An «equivocal and faustian image», which Garin invited the critic to get rid of. See E. GARIN, *Universalità di Leonardo*, in *Scienza civile nel Rinascimento italiano*, Roma-Bari, Laterza, 1965.

[4]   See R. P. CIARDI, *Leonardo illustrato: genio e morigeratezza*, in *L'immagine di Leonardo. Testimonianze figurative dal XVI al XIX secolo* (a cura di R. P. Ciardi e C. Sisi), Firenze, Giunti, 1997.

[5]   The Raphaelesque model of the *Fornarina*, portrayed from life and whose identity has been approached to that of the *Veiled girl*, will represent a constant factor in the ideal of feminine beauty for Ingres, that will propose her even un-

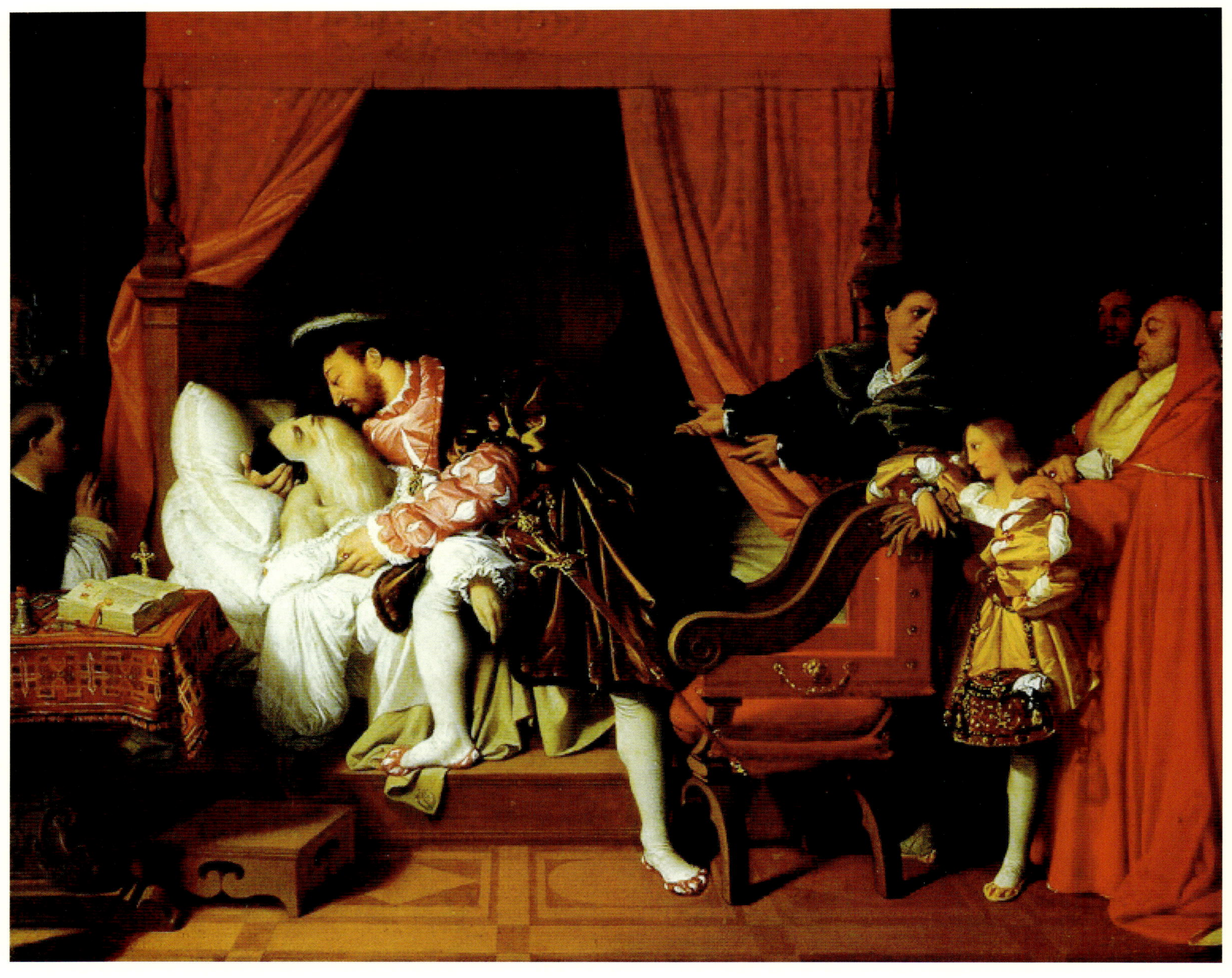

JEAN AUGUSTE DOMINIQUE INGRES, *Francis I receives the last breath of Leonardo da Vinci*, 1818. Paris, Musée du Petit Palais

Leonardo instead, while still alive unreligious and anticlerical, and become for certain aspects an icon of the libertarian thought, recovered on his death-bed, as a conclusive balance of his existence, the faith in God:

Seeing himself to be near his death, he wanted diligently to be informed of the catholic things and of our good and Saint Christian religion, and then with many moaning confessed and penitent, although he could not stand on his feet, supporting himself on the arms of his friends and servants, he wanted devoutly to receive the Saintest Sacrament out of his bed.

Francesco Melzi («Master Francesco de Melzo, gentleman from Milan»), son of Girolamo, captain of the Milan militia at the time of Louis XII, had been the executor and had become heir «for remuneration of the services to him made for the past», of the books «that the aforesaid Testator has at the moment, and other instruments and Portraits about his art and the industry of the Painters».

The body of Leonardo was buried in the church of Saint-Florentin (1477-84) at Amboise, but, for the reason that it had been devastated during the pillages and the bloody wars of religion, that involved also the Castle in the ferocious slaughter of the Huguenots (1560), revealing a cruelty not inferior to that of the terrible night of Saint Bartholomew (23-24 August 1572), it was demolished in 1808, for order of Roger Ducos.

On 23 June 1863, Arsène Houssaye, a passionate admirer of Leonardo and director of the magazine «L'artiste», to which Théophile Gautier contributed, with the intention to create a place of pilgrimage to render homage to his genius, began to dig in an unsystematic way all around the church, recovering three fragments of stone, on which it was engraved «LEO… INC…/… EO… DUS VINC», and numerous bones and skulls, of which he chose one, asserting that, for its singular anatomical conformation, it had to belong to Leonardo.

Therefore, the presumed remains of the artist were transferred to the crypt of the chapel of Saint Hubert, constructed in flamboyant gothic, in 1491, by Charles VIII in the Castle of Amboise, and where, still today, a slab of granite is covering his supposed entombment.

On 1 June 1519, Melzi would have sent a sorrowful letter to Giuliano da Vinci and to the brothers of Leonardo («As long as these limbs will sustain themselves together, I will have a perpetual unhappiness»), informing them of his death, that happened, with his assent, in a Christian way according to the modalities prescribed by the Holy Mother Church:

I believe you received official information about the death of master Lionardo your brother and my excellent almost father, for whose death it would be impossible that I could express the pain that I have: and as long as these limbs will sustain themselves together, I will have a perpetual unhappiness, and deservedly, because passionate and most burning love he gave to me every day. It has upset everyone the loss of such a man, which is no more in power of nature. Now, may the omnipotent Lord grant him eternal quiet. He passed away from the present life on the 2 of May with all the orders of the Holy Mother Church and in good disposition.

With this testimony, Melzi would have contradicted and darkened what later reported by Vasari in the torrentinian edition of the life of Leonardo (1550), where he made to fall on the artist the charge, for certain aspects inconvenient, of an agnostic and irreligious philosophical creed, setting off a passionate controversy, never appeased in time, between the supporters of the one or of the other thesis. In 1855, Alexis Rio, in his *Léonard de Vinci et son école*, and, in 1861, Charles Clément,[6] vice-keeper of the Louvre, would have claimed the death of Leonardo like that of a good catholic, that gave rigorously directions for a religious funeral. Stendhal said that he was sure that Leonardo «had too much intelligence to admit the religion of his century»[7] and likewise Gabriel Séailles, assertor of the free thought and one of the first biographers of the artist (1892), would have manifested all his embarrassment in front of those last wishes, wondering whether to consider them dictated by precaution or motivated by religious sincerity.[8] The same Walter Pater, on the conclusion of his famous essay on Leonardo,[9] had lingered on the evaluation of the religiosity of the artist, sustaining that it had indeed a limited importance to comprehend his genius:

Two questions remain, after much busy antiquarianism, concerning Leonardo's death – the question of the exact form of his religion, and the question whether Francis the First was present at the time. They are of about equally little importance in the estimate of Leonardo's genius. The directions in his will concerning the thirty masses and the

---

dressed on a sofa in his *Odalisque with the slave* of 1839. See D. FARABULINI, *Raffaello e la Fornarina*, «Il Raffaello», IX, 1879; A. ANSELMI, *La vera Fornarina di Raffaello*, «Nuova Rivista Misena», V, 1882; E. CAMESASCA, *Tutta la pittura di Raffaello*, Milano, Rizzoli, 1956; D. A. BROWN, K. OBERHUBER, *Monna Vanna and Fornarina, Leonardo and Raphael in Rome*, in *Essays presented to M. P. Gilmore*, a cura di S. Bertelli, Firenze, La Nuova Italia, 1978.

6   See C. CLÉMENT, *Michel-Ange, Léonard de Vinci, Raphael*, Paris, Michel Lévy Frères, 1861.
7   See STENDHAL, *Histoire de la peinture en Italie*, [1814], a cura di P. Arbelet, Paris, Champion, 1969.
8   See G. SÉAILLES, *Léonard de Vinci: L'artiste et le savant: Essai de biographie psychologique*, Paris, Perrin, 1892.
9   See W. PATER, *Il Rinascimento. Studi d'arte e di poesia*, [1873], traduzione di A. De Rinaldis, Napoli, Ricciardi, 1925.

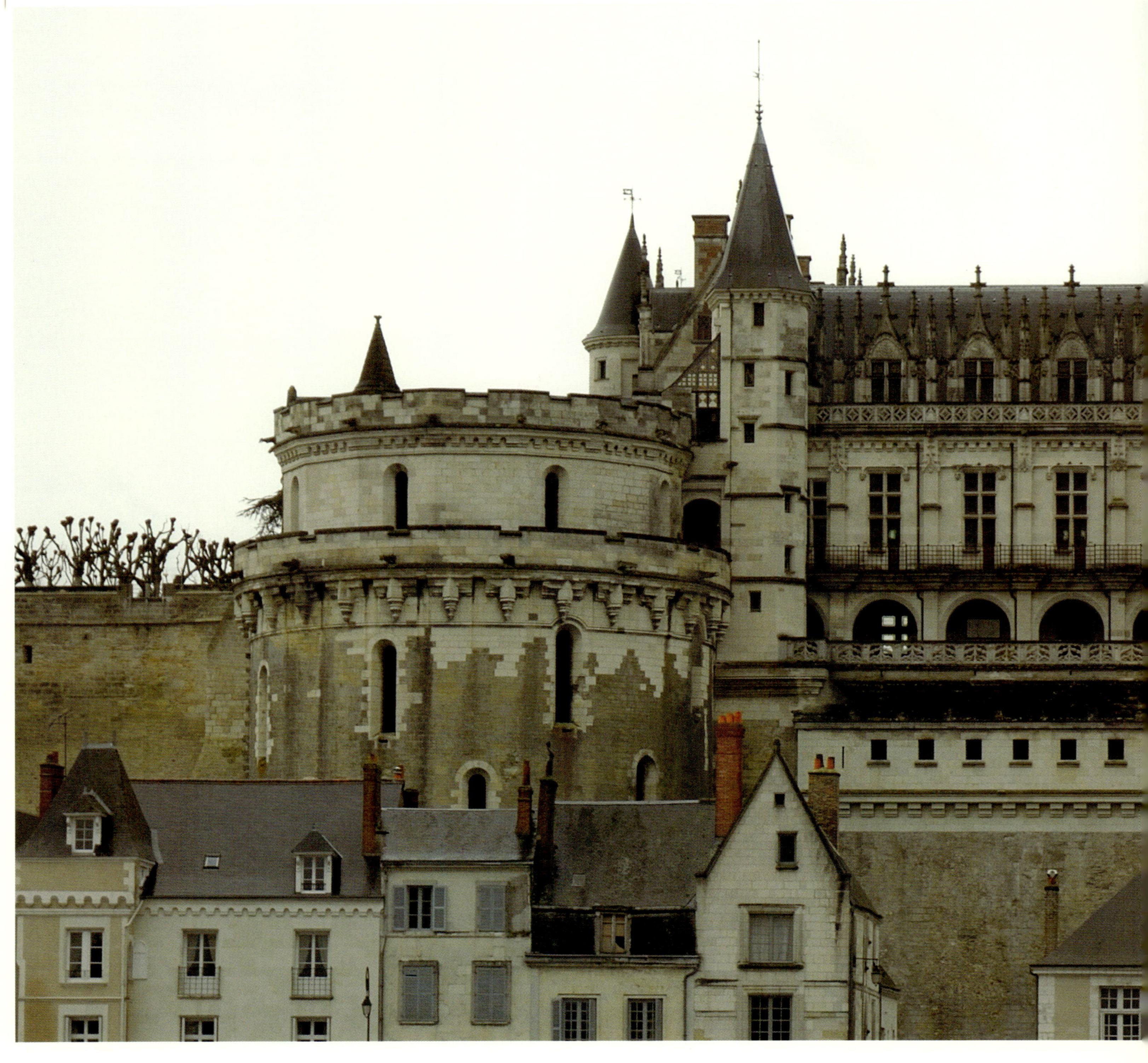

The Castle of Amboise

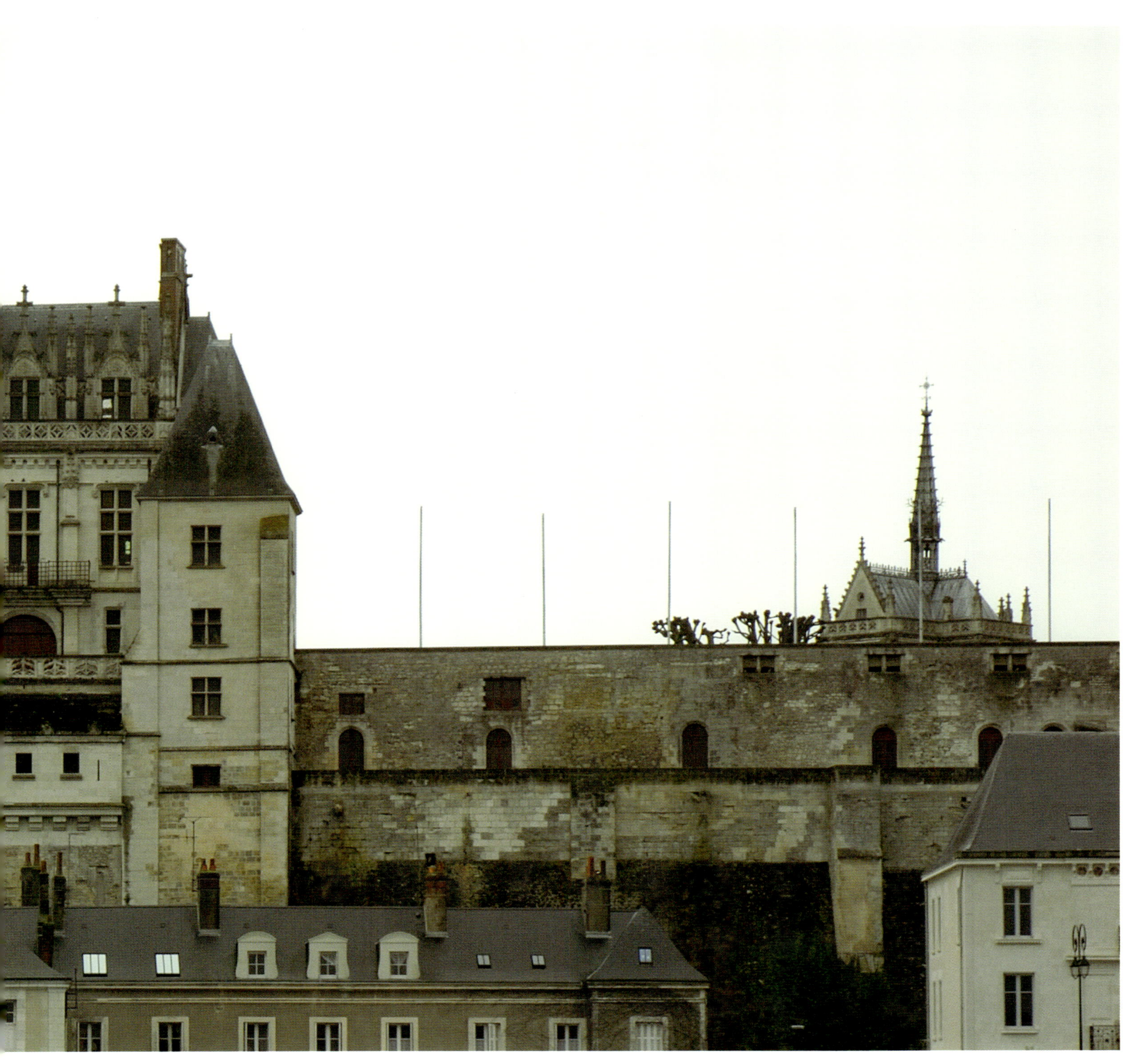

The stakes of the two formations were high, since the matter was not only to make clear the features of a titanic personality, extraordinary for wisdom, and while still alive already compared for his magical and intellectual qualities to Hermes Trismegistus and Prometheus,[10] but to make the probative reasoning to have a weigh in a sense or in the other, in that dialectic relationship between science and faith that, set off at the time of Humanism and of the Renaissance, would have continued between flaming controversies until the Enlightenment, to the positivism and the contemporary age, where it was arranged to make of Leonardo the great master of a secret society:[11]

And so many were his whims, that reasoning of the natural things, he attended to understand the properties of the herbs, continuing and observing the motion of the sky, the course of the moon and the courses of the sun. For which thing he made in his mind such a heretical concept, that he did not come near to any whatever religion, estimating, by chance, much more to be a philosopher than a Christian.

In the second edition of the *Lives* (1568), published when there was a full reformist climate, Vasari would have taken off the last phrase, narrating how Leonardo, «had offended God and the men of this world, not having operated in art as it becomes», that is to say never believing in the saints and never representing the «crucifix», symbol and fundamental theological assumption of Christian faith in the mystery of the history of salvation.[12] The biographer of Arezzo, moreover, availing as an informer of Paolo Giovio (1483-1552), em-

phasized in an exemplary and insisting way the singularity and the peculiarity of those his inventions, devised in the study created for him by the Magnificent Giuliano in Belvedere (CA, f. 90 *va* [244 *v*]):

He made animals very thin and full of wind, blowing in which, he made them fly through the air; but when the wind stopped, they fell to the ground. On a green lizard, found by the vine-dresser of Belvedere, which was the most bizarre, with a mixture of quick-silver he fixed wings, made of scales skinned from other green lizards, that moving when it walked, they shook; and made to it eyes, horns and beard, domesticated it and keeping it in a box, he made to escape for fear all the friends to whom he showed it. He often used to make meticulously remove fat from the bowels of a wether and purge them and to make them to come so thin, that they would have been kept in just one hand; and he had put in another room a pair of blacksmith bellows, to which he put an end of the mentioned bowels, and by inflating them, he filled up with them the room, which was very large.

Also Baldassar Castiglione, the first man of letters to consider the value of painting as superior to mechanical arts (*Cortegiano*, I XLIX) and to exalt Leonardo among the «most excellent» painters (I XXXVII), had remained so strongly impressed by the fascinating peculiarity of his bizarre reasoning, that he annotated:

Another of the first painters of the world disdains that art where he is the most rare, and he has started to learn philosophy, in which he has such strange concepts and new chimeras, that he with all his painting would not know how to depict them (II, XXXIX).

In the same drafts of letter that Leonardo transcribed for his friend and patron Giuliano de' Medici, which, according to Vasari, «attended much to philosophical things and most of all to alchemy», it can be perceived his worry for the malevolence of Giovanni degli Specchi that was prone to arouse suspicions, misrepresenting the truth of things («they eavesdrop the speech for the contrary», Windsor, RL 19128 *r*), and to divulge insidious accusations of magic («the old scandals»), or worse of heresy, at the papal Court, to make forbid him anatomy, that is the dissection of corpses, that being carried out in this case in the rooms of the Hospital of Santo Spirito, it can be presumed that it was an experience officially tolerated: «This other one has prevented me from anatomy blaming it with the Pope, and so at the hospital» (CA, ff. 182 *vc* [500 *r*]; 247 *vb* [671 *r*]).[13]

---

[10] See S. MIGLIORE, *Tra Hermes e Prometeo: il mito di Leonardo nel decadentismo europeo*, Firenze, Olschki, 1994.

[11] This mystification, according to which Leonardo, initiated into secret and esoteric doctrines, would have been the great master of the «Priory of Zion», a society keeper of the mystery of the «Holy Grail» and that would have continued to be led until our days by illustrious personages like V. Hugo, C. Debussy, J. Cocteau, it has indeed widely favoured the success of the novel by D. Brown, *The Da Vinci Code* (2003). All subjects already well known in literature. See X. Pasquini, *Léonard, grand maître d'une société secrète*, «Historia», 440, juillet, 1983.

[12] Leonardo, in a sheet of the Codex Atlanticus (f. 252 *r-a* [680 *r*]), formulates a reflection that is strongly allusive to certain his religious interpretations in an esoteric key, that were considered as heretical by the Church, and such as to make him undergo a sentence of detention in jail: «When I made Our Lord as a child, you put me in prison; now, if I do him <g>reat, you will make me even worse».

[13] On 8 October 1515, Leonardo, as a result of the presentation of a certain doctor Gaiaco, was accepted in the brotherhood of Saint John of the Florentines, which was not far from the Vatican. The brotherhood, to those who had paid regularly

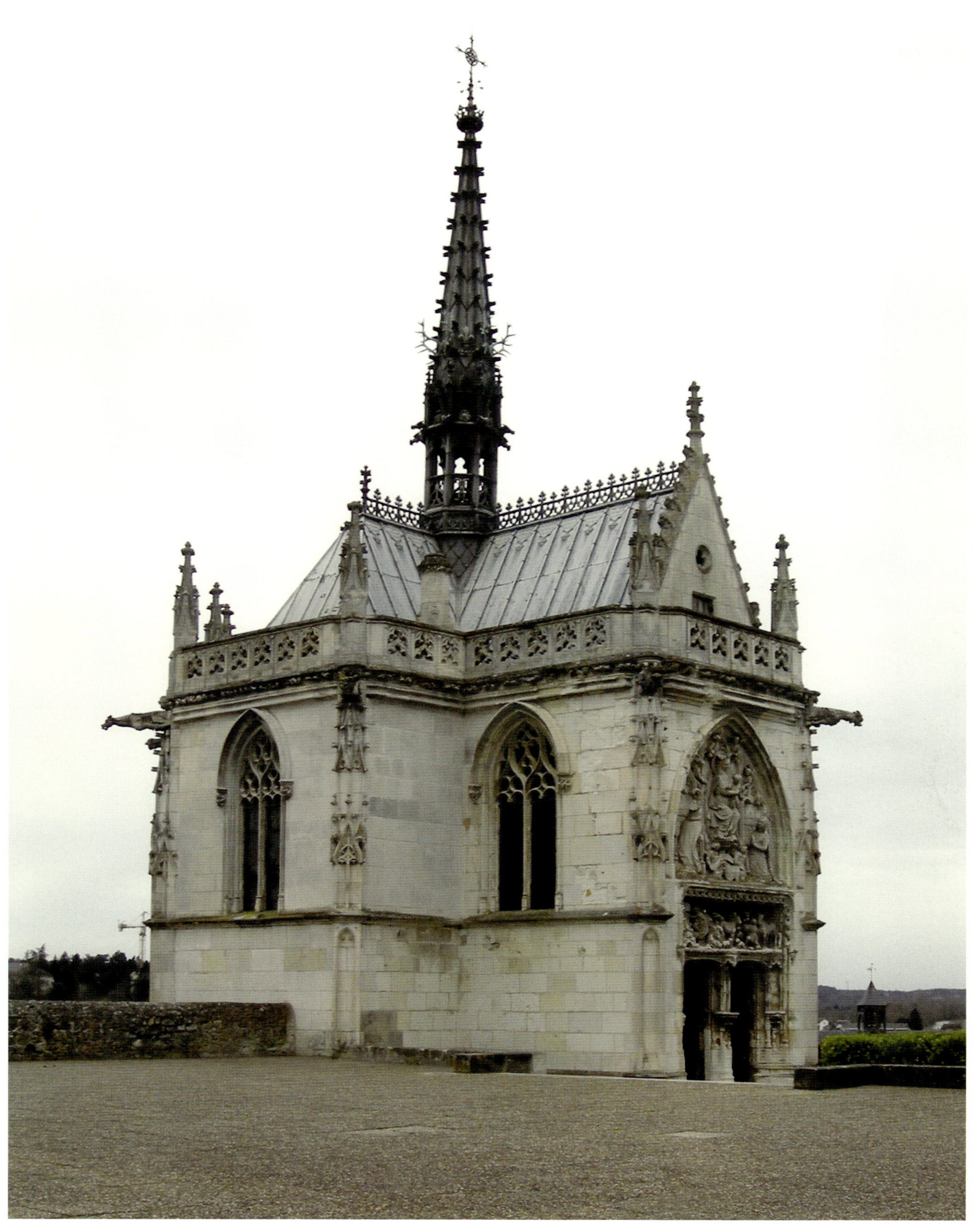

The Chapel of Saint-Hubert in the Château of Amboise

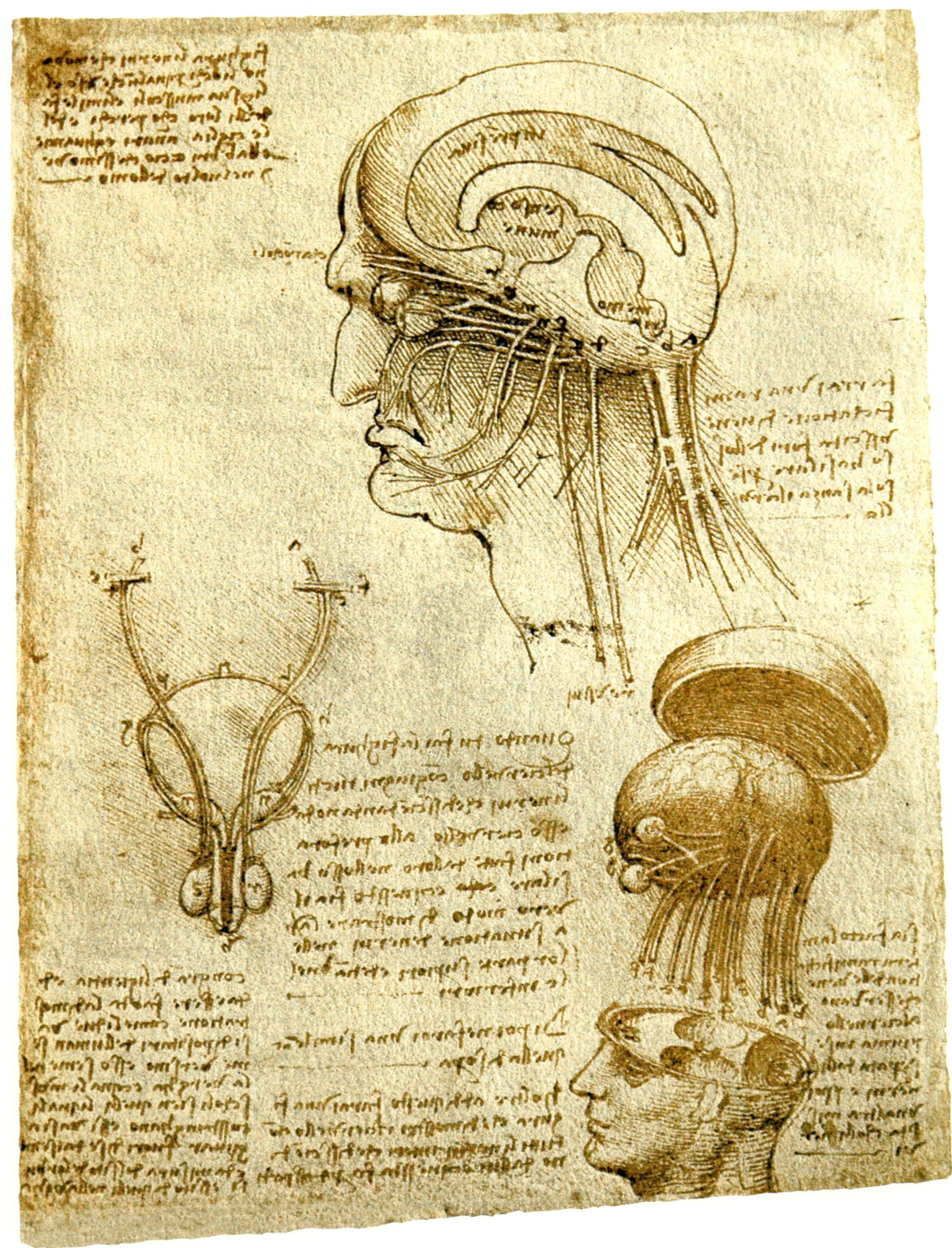

Leonardo da Vinci, *Study of the brain with the cranial nerves and of the male genitourinary apparatus, c. 1506–08, KK 6287. Weimar, Schlossmuseum*

Precisely Giovio, covering a place of great importance in the papal Court, being a familiar of Leo X and a reader of moral philosophy at the roman university of the Arch-Gymnasium, had been direct witness of Leonardo's studies of anatomy, embryology and natural philosophy. And therefore, around 1540, in his *Vita di Leonardo da Vinci*, he just praised the passion with which Leonardo had carried out in those roman years his studies of anatomy, when one of the most debated subjects was all about the immortality or not of the soul (1514-16):

> *In addition, he had learned, in medicine schools, to dissect, with inhuman and repugnant effort, the corpses of the criminals, in order to succeed in painting the various curving and tensions of the limbs by force of nerves and joints, following faithfully the order of nature. Therefore he represented in tables, with admirable attention, the shape of all the small organs, until the thinner veins and the most secret parts of the skeleton, so that from that long-lasting effort there could be drawn, by means of copper engraving, infinite copies as a profit of the art.*

Consequently, to the problems of anatomy it was connected the issue of the nature of the soul, that in that moment in time had provoked the fury of the theologians about the Aristotelian philosophy. The supporters of its mortality had been considered, during the Fifth Lateran Council (1513), «heretical and infidel», for which reason the *De immortalitate animae* of Pietro Pomponazzi, once published (1516), met the opposition of the same Leo X that made it to be publicly burnt, ordering to Pomponazzi to recant what he had sustained.[14] For Leonardo, since the writings with an anti-ficinian flavour and since the reading of the *De imortalità*

d'anima of Iacopo Canfora, in consonance with his friend Luigi Pulci the soul was tied to the activities of the body and could be accepted only through faith and not because of scientifical reasons. Thus, in a passage by now become famous, with sarcastic «guicciardinian» irony he gave himself up, around 1493, to argue with the «Pharisee» friars, devoted to «cheat the foolish multitude», for the presumption to read in the mind of God: «And the rest of the definition of the soul, I leave it in the mind of the friars, fathers of the people, which for inspiration know all the secrets. Do leave apart the crowned letters [that is theology], because they are prime truth», (Windsor, RL 19115 *r*).

Although adhering to the outline of the *Of the Soul* of Aristotle, where the three degrees of the soul jointly determine and characterize the vitality of Nature, Leonardo will consider this subject also in the light of his investigations of anatomy, assuming the co-existence in the second ventricle of the brain of the «common sense», of the imaginative, intellective and critical activity (Windsor, RL 19019 *r*; 12603 *r*), whose interaction was to foundation of the same artistic activity.[15] But, in 1510, when he collaborated for the anatomical experimentations with Marcantonio Della Torre in Pavia («book of waters to master Marcantonio», Ms. K, f. 48 *v*), Leonardo would have also offered a different definition of the soul,[16] considering it a divine sparkle, superior to the admirable architecture of the machine of the body:

> *And you man, that are considering in this my effort the admirable works of nature, if you will judge it a nefarious thing to destroy it, well do think as the most nefarious thing to take the life of a man, of which, if this his composition seems to you a wonderful artifice, do think that this is nothing as regards the soul that in such architecture lives; and truly, whichever it is, it is a divine thing, for which reason leave it live in his work as it likes, and act so that your wrath or malevolence does not destroy one such life (Windsor, RL 19001).*

Therefore, up to the present day, precisely as it is impossible to refer to an iconography that knows how to faithfully document the features and the true aspect of Leonardo, so the subject of his relationship with the faith and with how much conviction he joined to the sublime artistic creations of his Christian «stories», still remains dipped in mystery and in the «unfinished». This entire world turns out to be in fact like transferred into the legendary dimension of that myth

the registration fee, would have granted the funeral honours. The admission of Leonardo took place through the vote of the various members and a confrère in that circumstance so annotated: «Novice / Leonardo da Vinci painter and sculptor went to vote in assembly and he won for 3 black broad beans, and then he went in the body of the company and he won for 41 black broad beans and 2 white ones, for he was led from master Gaiacqo doctor, and for him he promised the entrance». But Leonardo was not so precise in the payment of the fee, and therefore he was turned out: «And still in the above-mentioned our governing father and his advisors proposed to put Lonardo da Vinci painter in the good morning because he had not paid the entrance in the said time, and sent him to vote in assembly, and he won for three black broad bean». See C. L. FROMMEL, *Leonardo fratello della Confraternita della Pietà dei Fiorentini a Roma*, Raccolta Vinciana, XX (1964).

[14] See E. SOLMI, *Per gli studi anatomici di Leonardo da Vinci, in Miscellanea di studi critici pubblicati in onore di Guido Mazzoni*, Firenze, 1907; V. ROCCHI, *Leonardo da Vinci e i suoi studi nell'Ospedale di Santo Spirito*, «Giornale di Medicina e Chirurgia», Roma, 1912; G. FAVARO, *Gli studi anatomici di Leonardo nei Regesti vinciani*, «Atti e Memorie della Reale Accademia di Scienze, Lettere e Arti di Venezia», V, III, 1938; G. DI NAPOLI, *L'immortalità dell'anima nel Rinascimento*, Torino, 1963; M. KEMP, *Dissection and Divinity in Leonardo's Late Anatomies*, «Journal of the Warburg and Courtauld Institutes», XXXV, 1972; K. KEELE, C. PEDRETTI, *Disegni anatomici dalla Biblioteca Reale di Windsor* (a cura di), catalogo mostra, Firenze, Giunti Barbèra, 1979; D. LAURENZA, *Leonardo nella Roma di Leone X…*, 2003, *op. cit.*

[15] See D. LAURENZA, *De figura umana. Fisiognomica, anatomia e arte in Leonardo*, Firenze, Olschki, 2001; C. STARNAZZI, *La razionalità del cosmo*, in ID., *Leonardo. Acque e terre*, 2002, *op. cit.*

[16] See C. PEDRETTI, *Leonardo e l'arte sacra*, «L'Osservatore Romano», Domenica 12 Settembre 2004; ID., *Introduzione*, in S. CREMANTE, *Leonardo da Vinci*, Firenze, Giunti, 2005.

that he in person, while still alive, contributed to construct, so that his same contemporaries might give a superhuman connotation to his image and to his thought.

On 23 April 1519, feeling his death arrive, Leonardo made to write up in Italian his will by the French notary public Boreau at the presence of Melzi («in his presence, accepting and consenting») and at the presence of the witnesses Spirito Fleri vicar of Saint-Denis, the curate Guillaume Croysant, Cipriane Fulchin, friar Francisco da Cortona (maybe a relative of Domenico Bernabei known as «Boccadoro») and friar Francesco da Milano, of the Franciscan convent of Amboise. Melzi sent, immediately after, a copy of the notarial deed to the brothers of Leonardo, while, to take care of the various offices and to calm down the impetuous Salaì, he would have availed of the participation of father Girolamo, requesting urgently his departure from Milan. Also the Gaddian Anonymous, informed by one of the brothers of Leonardo, would have transcribed in a sufficiently detailed and precise way the modalities and the contents of it (88 *r*):

He left for will to master Francesco da Melzio, kind man from Milan, all the money with all the clothes, books, writings, drawings and instruments and portraits about the painting and art and industry which was here, and they made him executor of his will. And he left to Batista da Villani his servant the half of one garden, that he had outside of Milan, and the other half to Salaì his disciple. And left to his brothers 400 ducatoes, which he had in an account in Florence in the Spedale of Santa Maria Nuova, where after his death they did not found more than 300 ducatoes.

The testamentary deed reappeared in 1700 during the researches of Giambattista Dei about the documents of the family of Leonardo, until, after a series of passages, it reached the hands of Venanzio De Pagave, that would have assigned Carlo Goldoni, in 1775, during his stay in France as a poet of the «Comédiens du Roi de la Troupe italienne», to make researches on Leonardo at Fontainebleau.

Then, the original of the will disappeared, but a copy reproduced from the manuscript by De Pagave, was for the first time published in Milan, in 1804, by Carlo Amoretti in *Memorie storiche su la vita, gli studi e le opere di Leonardo da Vinci*, at the Society of the Italian classics.

The diffusion of the testamentary content, which informs on the last will of the artist, would not have favoured any reconsideration about the merit, leaving every modern reader of the vincian thought, in a silent and personal search for truth. The first dispositions given by Leonardo were of a religious character, with the recommendation of the soul to God, to the glorious Virgin Mary, Saint Michael Archangel and to all the angels and the saints of Paradise. The obsequies and the funeral procession were described with the same detachment and attention for detail, that Leonardo was used to reserve to the scenographic apparatuses in the preparation of the feasts for the Court: he would have liked to be buried in the church of Saint-Florentin («The aforesaid Testator wants to be buried inside the church of Saint Florentin of Amboise, and his body to be carried there by the curates of that chapel») and that there were celebrated three High Masses with deacon and vice-deacon and thirty Low Masses in Saint Gregory, Saint-Denis and Saint Francis. Moreover, that sixty poor people were benefited, at discretion of Melzi, so that they accompanied with torches the coffin, transported by the chaplains of Saint-Florentin and followed by the college (or chapter) of the said church, by Rector or Prior, or by the vicars and chaplains of the church of Saint-Denis, as by the Minorite friars of the city. Thirty pounds of wax in candles had to be offered to the three mentioned churches, while to the poor people of the Hôtel de Dieu and of Saint-Lazarus of Amboise, had to be given seventy tournois pieces.

Then, returning with the mind to his most precious assets as the manuscripts, the books and the drawings, he decided to leave them, together with the instruments concerning his art and his profession of painter, to who had loved him as a father, Francesco Melzi. He would have kept them with great zeal, dedicating himself also to select those writings with which to compile the *Libro di Pittura*, so that, on 6 March 1523, Alberto Bendidio,[17] correspondent of the Duke of Ferrara, would have written about him to Alfonso d' Este:

And because I have made mention of the house of Melzi, I inform Your Excellence that a brother of that which has jousted, was created by Leonardo da Vinci as his heir, and he has many of his secrets, and all of his opinions, and he paints very well as far as I can understand, and in his reasoning he shows to have judgement and he is a very kind young man. I have prayed him many times to come to Ferrara, promising him that Your Seigniory will see him with good will, and after that I came, I have replied it to a relative of his, a gentleman much honest and honoured, that I have not been able to say it to him, because he is in villa because of the quartan fever. If it will please to Your Excellence, I will make of it a still greater instance. I believe that he has those booklets of Leonardo of the anatomy, and of many other beautiful things.

But Leonardo did not lack to donate also to the persons who had reserved their affection to him in the daily services, as the maid-servant Mathurine and the waiter Batista de Vil-

---

17 See G. GAYE, *Carteggio inedito…*, 1839-40, *op. cit.*; E. SOLMI, *La resurrezione dell'opera di Leonardo*, in *Leonardo da Vinci. Conferenze fiorentine*, Milano, Treves, 1910.

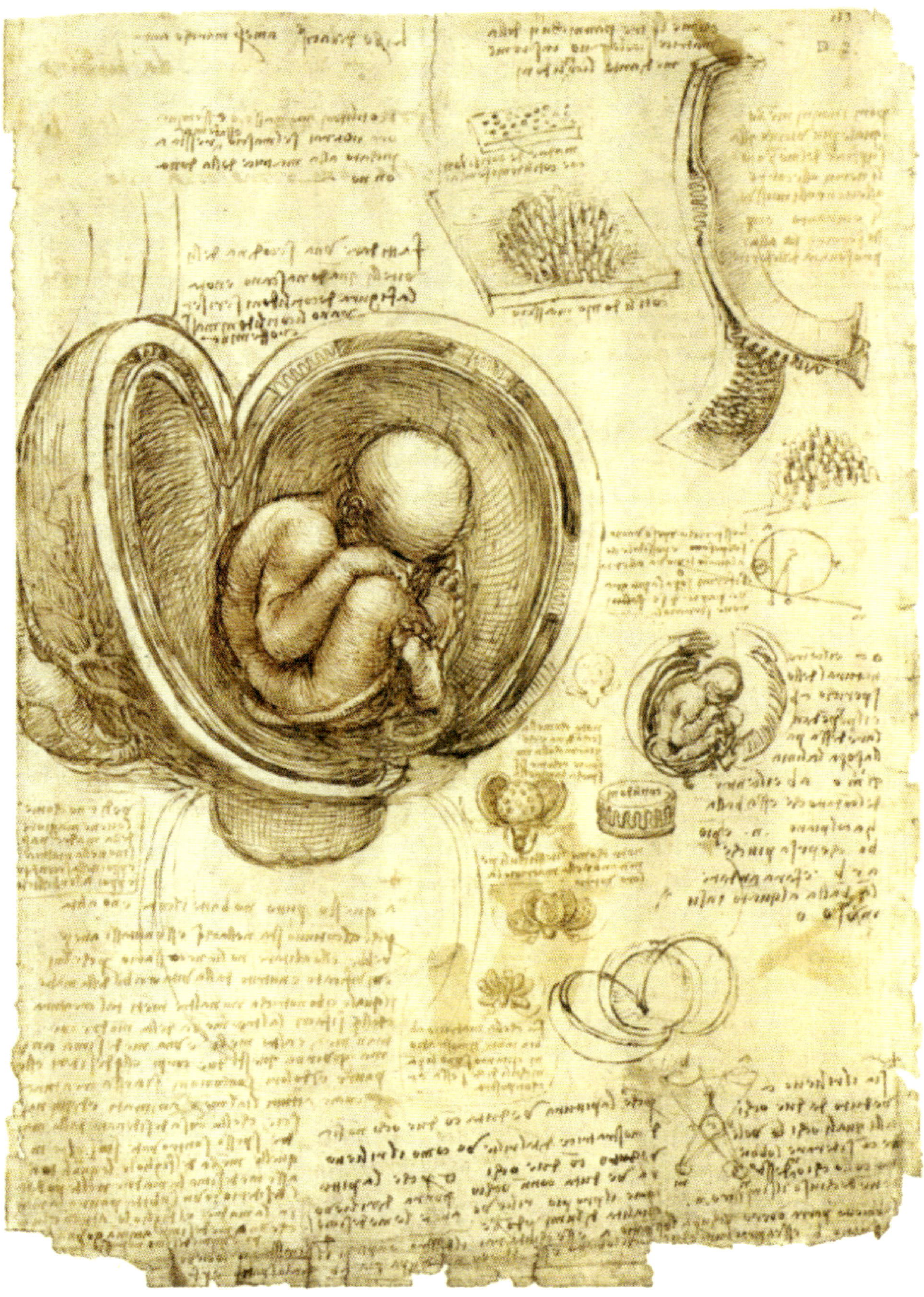

Leonardo da Vinci, *Studies of embryology, c.* 1510-15. Pen and tawny ink, watercoloured on traces of charcoal and sanguine, 305 x 220 mm. Windsor, RL 19102 *r*

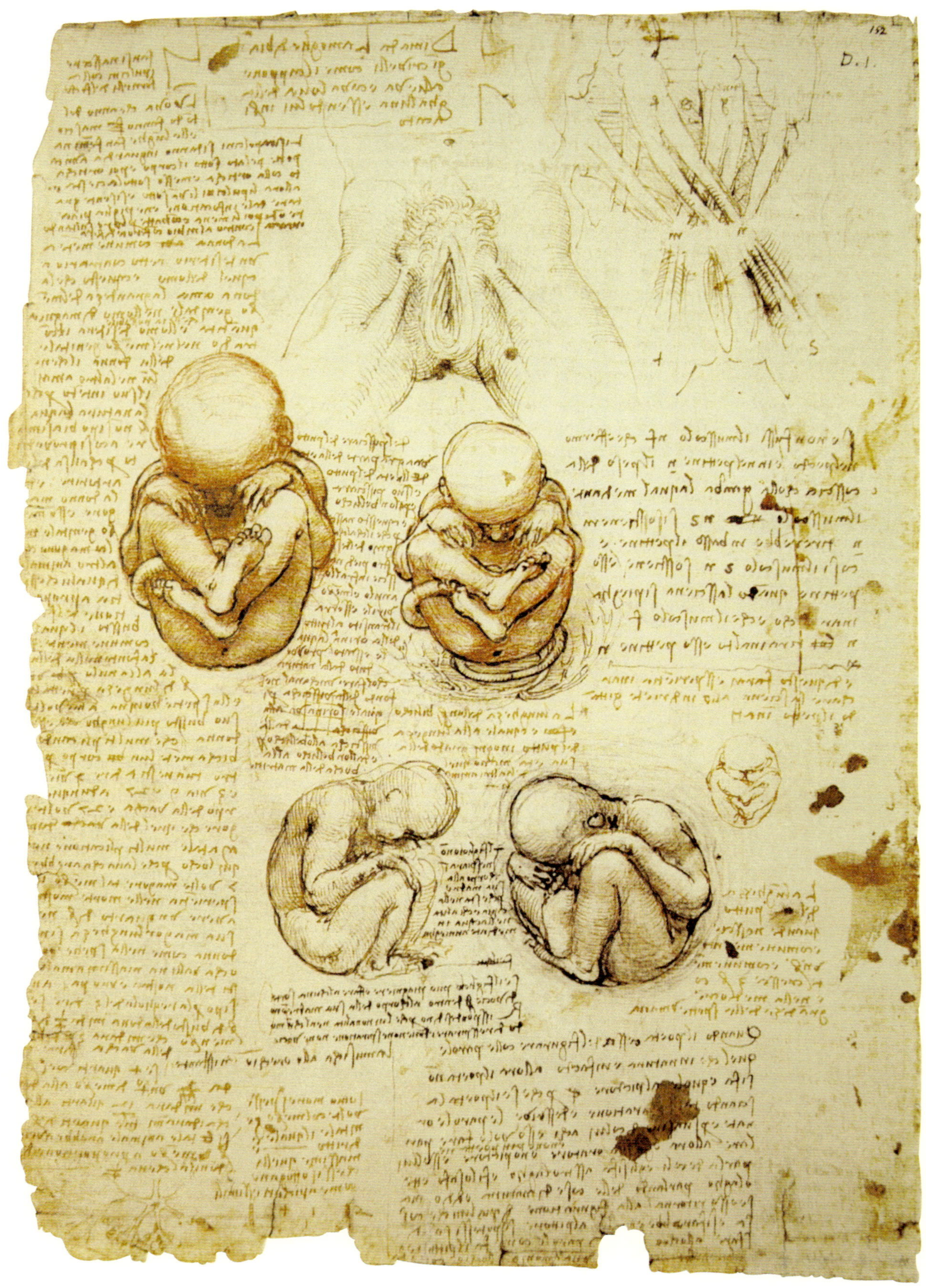

Leonardo da Vinci, *Studies of embryology*, c. 1511-16. Pen and tawny ink, with charcoal and sanguine, 303 x 220 mm. Windsor, RL 19101 *r*

lanis. To the maid-servant he donated «a garment of good black cloth, lined with skin, a cassock of cloth and two ducatoes, once only paid, and that in remuneration similarly of the good services to him made by the said Mathurine from now on».

To De Villanis he granted for his fidelity all the furniture and the tools of the house, the income of the twelve ounces of water of the Naviglio of San Cristoforo in Milan, a «donation» that had been made to him by Louis XII, and the vine donated to him by the Moor on 2 October 1498, in the area of Porta Vercellina out of the city walls, between the convent of the Grazie and the monastery of San Vittore. This latter had to be divided in two in its land value with the ardent Giangiacomo Caprotti known as Salaì or Salaino, that had already constructed a house there and to which he had moved without any hesitation with his family.[18] That the rest of the due pension, paid by the general treasurer of the king of France, Jean Sapin,[19] was granted with his wardrobe to Melzi, while to his stepbrothers, even though they, in July 1507, had taken legal action against him for the inheritance of their uncle Francesco, he left four hundred ducatoes, deposited in Santa Maria Nuova in Florence, included his farm on the hill of Fiesole, not mentioned in the will.[20]

The works, that Antonio De Beatis, Secretary of the cardinal Louis of Aragon, on 10 October 1517, had seen in the study of Clos-Lucé, «three paintings, one of a certain Florentine woman, depicted of the natural, on request of the once magnificent Iuliano de' Medici, the other a young John the Baptist, and one of the Holy Virgin and of the Child who are placed on the lap of Saint Anne, all are the most perfect»,[21] do not receive any mention.

The *Mona Lisa*, the *Saint Anne* and the *Saint John the Baptist*, the masterpieces that Leonardo had carried to France from Italy and that today are placed together in one same room of the Louvre, had become property of the King Francis I. Leonardo, although plagued by a paresis to his right arm («It is true that from him since it has come to him a certain paralysis on the right, we cannot anymore wait a good thing», De Beatis then wrote), would have continued to work on his pictures, included the *Mona Lisa*, on which he spread more than 40 coatings.

And, in the first inventory of the paintings kept at Fontainebleau, *Le Trésor des merveilles de la Maison Royale de Fontainebleau*, written up in 1642 by Pierre Dan, advanced father of the contiguous convent, it was remembered that Francis I had acquired precisely the *Mona Lisa*, «a wonder of painting», for the colossal sum of 12000 francs (4000 scudoes of gold).[22] Between the vapours and the scents of the *Salle des*

---

18 DE VILLANIS, at variance with SALAÌ over the property of the vine, will find an agreement on 25 January 1521, according to which 8 perches of land will remain in his property, subsequently sold to the monks of Saint Jerome for 280 Liras. Married with Bianca de' Coldiroli, Salaì would have passed away in obscure circumstances, for violent death «ex scopleto», on 19 January 1524, leaving to his heirs significant assets and a great number of pictures, much probably copies of the masterpieces of Leonardo, among which: one *Leda*, one *Saint Anne*, one *Mona Lisa*, one *Saint Jerome*, one *Saint John*, one *Virgin with the Child*, a *Christ to the column*, one *Half undressed woman*, to identify perhaps as the *Mona Lisa undressed* or the *Colombina*. See J. SCHELL, G. SIRONI, *Salaì and the Inventory of his Estate*, «Raccolta Vinciana» XXIV, 1992.

19 JEAN SAPIN had even paid two thousand six hundred and four tournois Liras to Salaì for the pictures sold to the King. See *Estat fait a maistre Jehan Grolier, conseiller du Roy notre sire, tresorier et receveur general de ses finances en ses pays et duché de Milan, conté d'Asti et seigneurie de Gennes [...]*, a. 1517-18; Paris, Archives Nationales, J 910, fasc. 6.

20 The brothers of Leonardo will soon draw from the open account of the bank deposit of Santa Maria Nuova, where with great disappointment they will not find 400 ducatoes, but 300 florins, (f. 193 *v*): «Lionardo of master Piero da Vinci countersigned has to give on the day 11 of May 1520 twenty-five florins of wide gold to master Giuliano of master Piero da Vinci his blood brother, he carried in cash 25 florins and on 18 July seventy-five florins of gold in all to Lorenzo and Antonio brothers and sons of master Piero, Lorenzo carried for himself and like deputy of Antonio his brother notarized by Bartolomeo of master Ma [...] from Bibiena on the day 22 of June 1520 75 florins and on the mentioned day 37 florins and 10 pieces of gold in all to master Giuliano his brother he carried cash for his part 37 florins and 10 pieces. And on the mentioned day one hundred and fifty florins of gold in all for Benedetto, Guglielmo and Bartolomeo and Giovanni brothers and sons of master Piero da Vinci [that] are for many facts creditors in our red book marked G in sheet 302 for their part that reaches in the countersigned sum 150 florins And on the day 7 of December 1520 seventeen florins wide and 10 pieces he to Domeniche of master Piero da Vinci he carried cash for his part 17 florins 10 pieces And on the day 4 of January twenty florins of gold in all he to Domeniche of master Piero aforesaid and he to master Giuliano his brother he carried cash for the rest 20 florins»; f. 194 *r*: «Lionardo of master Piero d'Anto-

nio da Vinci painter has to have on the day ten of October three hundred florins of gold in all, deposited to the said in cash to have back to its place 300 florins And on the day 18 of July 1520 twenty-five florins of gold from master Giuliano of master Piero da Vinci he carried in cash». See G. UZIELLI, *Ricerche intorno a Leonardo da Vinci…*, 1872, *op. cit.*; L. BELTRAMI, *Documenti*, n° 248-50; G. CALVI, *Vita di Leonardo*, Brescia, Morcelliana, 1936; C. VECCE, *Leonardo*, 1998, *op. cit.*

21 *Resoconto del segretario del cardinale Luigi d'Aragona, Antonio de Beatis, del 10 ottobre 1517, a seguito della visita a Leonardo nel castello di Cloux presso Amboise*; Napoli, Biblioteca Nazionale Vittorio Emanuele II, Ms. X, F 28. See E. VILLATA, *Leonardo da Vinci. I documenti e le testimonianze contemporanee*, Milano, Ente Raccolta Vinciana, 1999.

22 The *Mona Lisa* was not much liked by the successors of Francis I, to the point that Louis XIII tried to sell it to Charles I of England and, only for the intervention of Pieter Paul Rubens, he replaced it with the *Saint John* in exchange of a Titian and of a Holbein. The portrait of this unknown and foreign woman did not interest neither the king neither his court. In 1665 the picture was transferred to the Louvre together with the royal collection, but with Louis XIV it was moved to Versailles and the Roy Soleil wanted it to be placed in his private gallery, the Petite Galerie du Roy. After the nationalization of the assets of the monarchy, in 1797, the *Mona Lisa* made return to the Louvre where, remained for a long time in a desolate corridor, the following year was exposed in the Salon Carré facing the general indifference of the time. In 1801, Napoleon would have made transfer it to the Tuileries, in the bedroom of Joséphine, to make it then return to the Louvre, after his crowning as emperor. But the fame of the *Mona Lisa* turns out to be conquered, as if by magic, by her strict relationship with the cultural and political vicissitudes of the last one hundred and fifty years. Addressing to her, in 1850, in «Revue des deux mondes», Gustave Planche spoke about a Medusa, a lunar and silent divinity that petrifies who contemplates it, while, in 1858, in «L'artiste» and in 1864 in *Les Dieux et demi-dieux de la peinture*, Théophile Gautier, the most estimated critic of art of the time, picking out in it the fascination of the eternal feminine, defined it as a sort of Isis, a goddess that knows all and that sweetly rejects the disrespectful vulgarities, considering the painting as

the Renaissance portrait par excellence. The decadent Walter Pater, emphasizing the passional aspect of every age, perceived in it the animality of Greece and the lust of Rome, the mysticism of the Middle Ages and all the sins of the Borgia (*Studies in the History of the Renaissance*, London, Macmillan, 1873). According to Sigmund Freud, behind the charge of sodomy uphold against Leonardo, during the trial against Iacopo Saltarelli, the smile was not that of a sphinx, but the Oedipus-maternal one, lost and found again by the artist. On 20 August 1911, the picture was in a clamorous way stolen from the Louvre and the French newspapers commented the fact as an irreparable loss, a crime against humankind. France felt orphan, deprived of the masterpiece of the masterpieces. Wilhelm II was accused to be a deceitful tactician that tried to humiliate France in his attempt to obtain Morocco. The same Guillaume Apollinaire was imprisoned, since he was suspected to protect his futurist friends, which had declared war to the museums-cemeteries. When, on 13 December 1913, it was found again in Florence, the *Mona Lisa* received the honours reserved to a great statesman: Italy celebrated the picture, and its kidnapper, Vincenzo Peruggia, was made to appear even by his lawyers as a patriot, indeed a national hero, but in the end he spent more than a year in jail. Hence, the work was given back to France and it returned to its place, on 4 January 1914, in a European state of affairs by now next to the First World War. From then on, the most famous picture of the world entered with force in the history of men and all the Chiefs of state have revealed their ambition in making themselves represented between the folds of the garments and the ambiguity of its smile, from De Gaulle to Mitterrand, from Mao to Mrs. Thatcher, to become then, in 1993, the symbol of freedom killed in the public square of Tien-An-Men. See J. SUYEUX, *Le Testament de Léonard*, «Le Gnomon: Revue internationale d'histoire du notariat», 88 (1993); S. MIGLIORE, *Tra Hermes e Prometeo. Il mito di Leonardo nel Decadentismo europeo*, Firenze, Olschki, 1994; C. STARNAZZI, *La Gioconda nella Valle dell'Arno*, 1996, *op. cit.*; D. SASSOON, *La Gioconda. L'avventurosa storia del quadro più famoso del mondo*, Roma, Carocci, 2002.

Bains of Fontainebleau, in 1625, during his travel to Paris with the cardinal Francesco Barberini, also Cassiano Del Pozzo would have seen it, that, although considering it compromised in the garments, but admiring its pictorial qualities, defined it as «the most perfect work that of this author can be looked at, because except for speech it does not lack any other thing».[23]

[23]   See CASSIANO DEL POZZO, Ms. Barberini, 1625. Roma, Biblioteca Barberini, LX, n. 64, foll. 192 *v*-194 *v*: «A portrait, made in life-size, in table framed of carved walnut wood, it is a half figure and it is the portrait of a certain Jocund. This is the most perfect work that of this author can be looked at, because except for speech it does not lack any other thing. The figure depicts a woman from 24 to 26 years old, in face not at all in the manner of the Greek statues of woman, but somewhat wide with a certain tenderness in the cheeks and around the lips and the eyes, that we cannot hope to reach that exquisiteness. The head is adorned with a very simple hairstyle, but equally well refined; the dress showed to be or black or dark lemon, but it has been damaged by a certain varnish given to it to such an extent that it can not be distinguished very well. The hands are very beautiful and in conclusion, with all the misfortunes that this picture has endured, the face and the hands appear so much beautiful, that they capture who admires them. We notice that this woman, on the other hand a beautiful one, lacked a little in her brow, that the painter has not made it appear a lot, the same way as she should not have it».

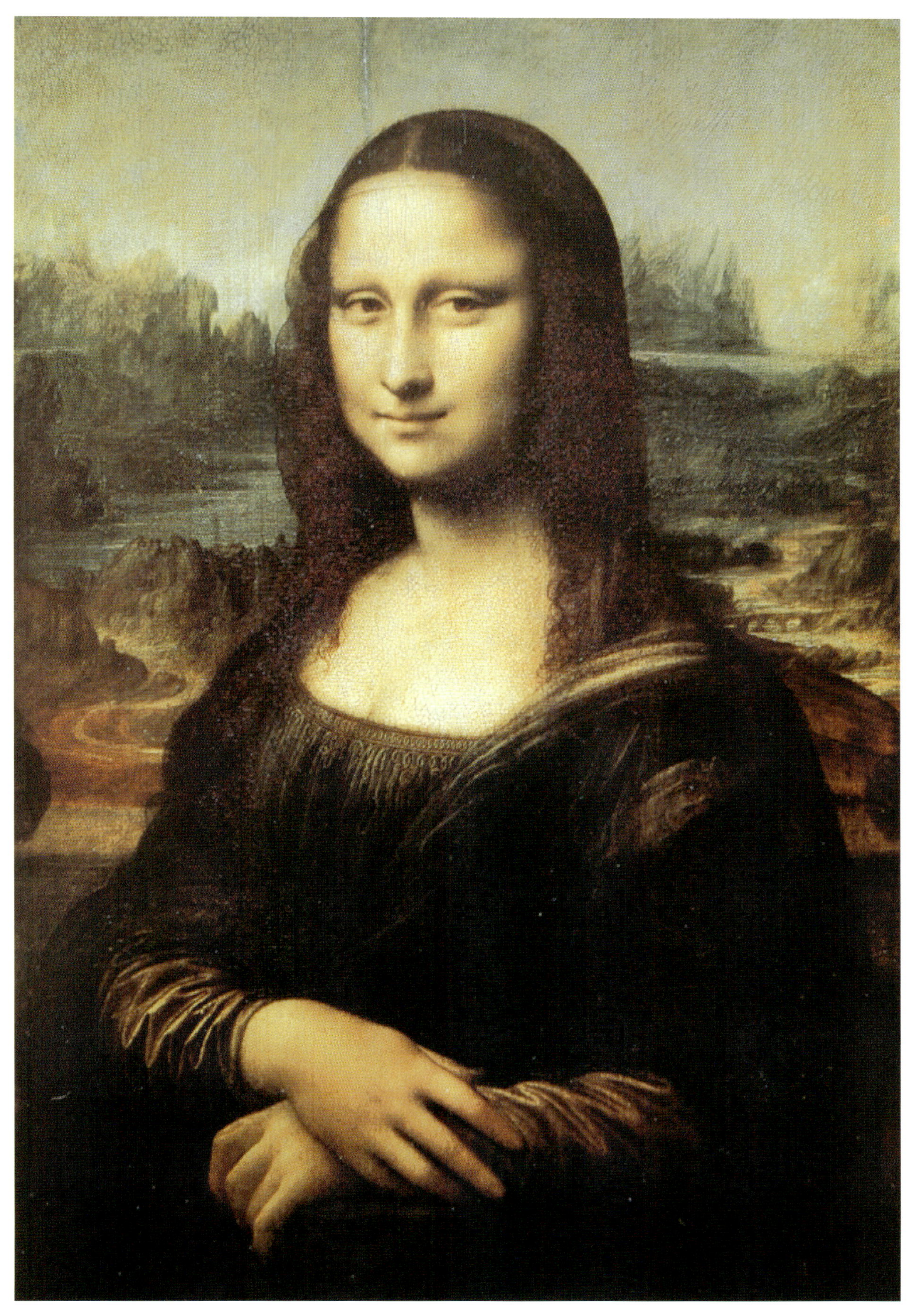

Leonardo da Vinci, *Mona Lisa*, 1503-1506. Oil on table, 77 x 53 cm. Paris, Musée du Louvre

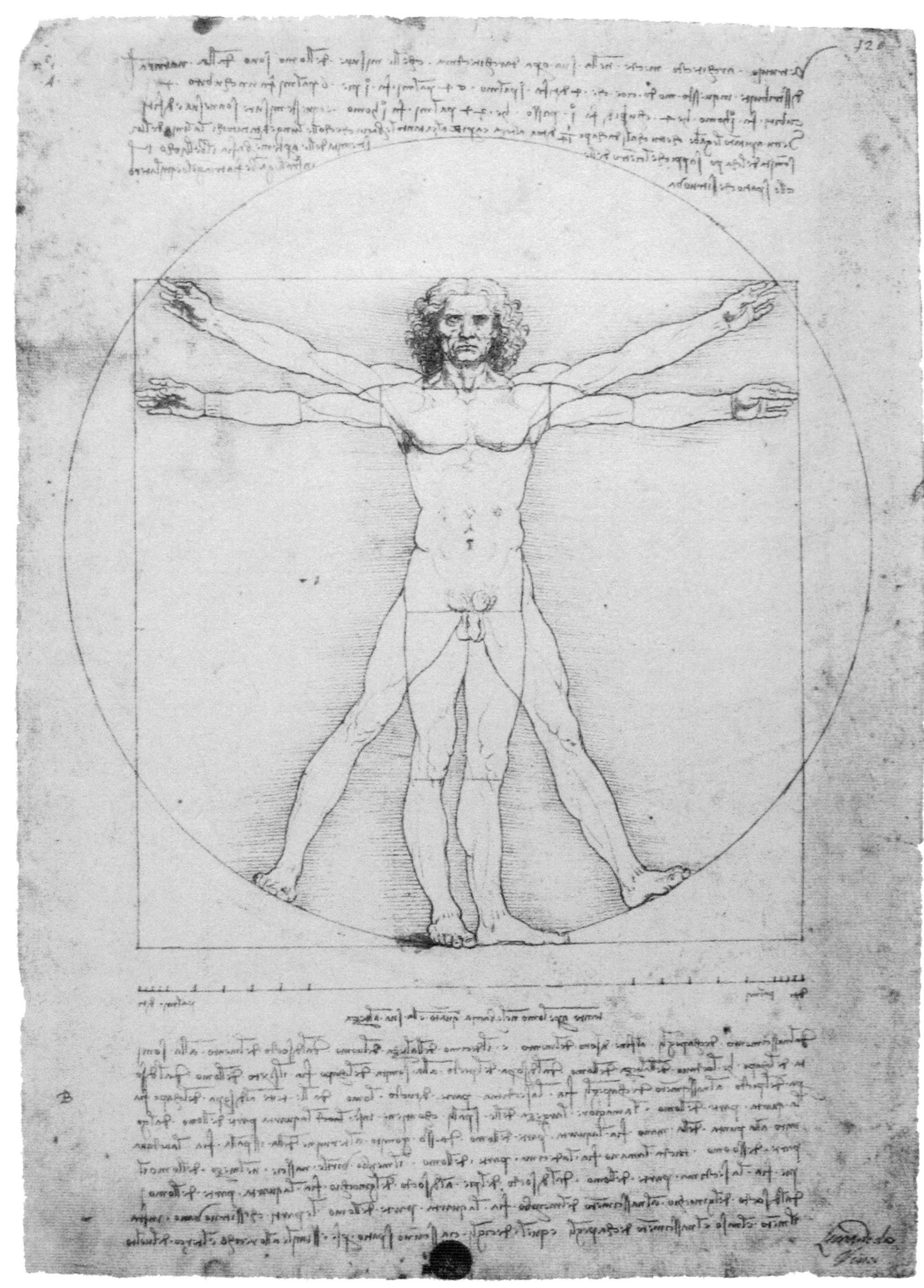

Leonardo da Vinci, *Vitruvian Man*, *c.* 1490. Metallic point, pen and ink and watercolour, 344 x 245 mm. Venice, Gallerie dell'Accademia, n. 228

Leonardo and the physiognomy
From Vasari to Mariette

ARISTOTLE, DEALING in his *Poetics* with the artistic definition of moral and intellectual qualities that single out an individual as a personality, insists on the description of his «character», remembering that this, though turning out to be an expression of an abstract process of idealization, must however concentrate on the likelihood: «It must be that the poets follow the example of good portraitists, which, though reproducing the peculiar features of a model, depict a portrait that, without failing in likeness, it is however more beautiful of its origin» (*cap. XV*, «Of the character of the personages»). Aristotle, with this theoretical consideration, meaning to make the principles of proportion of the *Canon* of Polycletus,[1] contained in the statue of the *Doriphoros* (450-440 b. C.),[2] fit the naturalistic requirements of Hellenistic art, in *Rhetoric* (III, 7), dealt with the problem of the types, defined in its general lines and closely connected to the one of the characters: «every class of men, every type of nature will have its appropriate way to demonstrate its true appearance. In 'class' I include differences in age like child, man, old; in sex, like man or woman; in nationality, like Spartan or Thessalian». But it would have been Theophrastus, author of the *Charac-*

ters and his disciple and collaborator, to carry out a first negative and systematic review of the several character typologies, of the inclinations of the mind and of the various temperaments, with which the individual reacts and is inclined to get in touch with the outside. It gushes out a review of human types, of which the comic aspect is showed with irony, exaggerating their defects and imperfections, in order to intentionally rouse the smile, compared with a series of treatises that meant to celebrate the character of the beautiful one and of the honest one.

In the artistic work, the ideal of beauty, as virtuous imitation of nature, had to correspond to and to come true through symmetry and harmony, the unit and the proportion, while the ugliness, as an exception of the rule, was reproduced «instantaneously if by chance there is something less or something more».[3]

Since 423 b. C., with the *Clouds* of Aristophanes, Socrates was represented in parodical terms in his difficult relationship with truth, while he observed the Sun from an aerial thinking place, arousing that comicality that the new comedy of Menander, Plautus and Terentius would have renewed and transmitted to the Renaissance in Italy, France and England. The comic aspect of truth, therefore, was produced by the fracture of an artistic ideal category, founded on the convenient and the beautiful one, with the exaggeration of an use of gestures and of a precise attitude, antagonist to them. The derision of a defect aroused hilarity, and the laughter the awareness of exorcising the defects of an individual, in order to exalt his opposite virtues. Art began to not identify itself only with the traditional concept of beautiful, founded on the principle of an equilibrium and a harmony expressed in

---

[1] PLINY THE ELDER, remembering the great phases of sculpture, annotated that «Polycletus of Sycion, disciple of Ageladas, made the *Diadumenos* [Crowned], effeminate figure of young man, famous for its price of one hundred talents and in the same way also the *Doriphoros* [Spearman], a figure of a boy already man in aspect. He composed moreover what the artists call as «canon», looking after in it, as in a law, the rules of art, and he is thought to be the only one to have theorized art by means of an art work […] It is common opinion that he has carried this art to its apogee and that if Phidias has been the initiator of bronze sculpture, it was him that brought it to perfection». See PLINY THE ELDER, *Naturalis historia*, 55, 56.

[2] See L. STEFANINI, *Ispirazione pitagorica del «canone» di Policleto*, «Giornale critico della filosofia italiana», 28, 1949; E. LA ROCCA, *Policleto e la sua scuola*, in *Storia e civiltà dei Greci, 4, La Grecia nell'età di Pericle. Le arti figurative*, a cura di Ranuccio Bianchi Bandinelli, Milano, Bompiani, 1979; A. LAMI, *I presocratici. Testimonianze e frammenti da Talete a Empedocle*, Milano, Rizzoli, 1991; G. PUCCI, *L'antichità greca e romana*, in *Estetica della Scultura*, a cura di Luigi Russo, Palermo, Luxograph, 2003.

[3] See PLUTARCO, *Sul giusto modo di ascoltare*, 45 c-d.

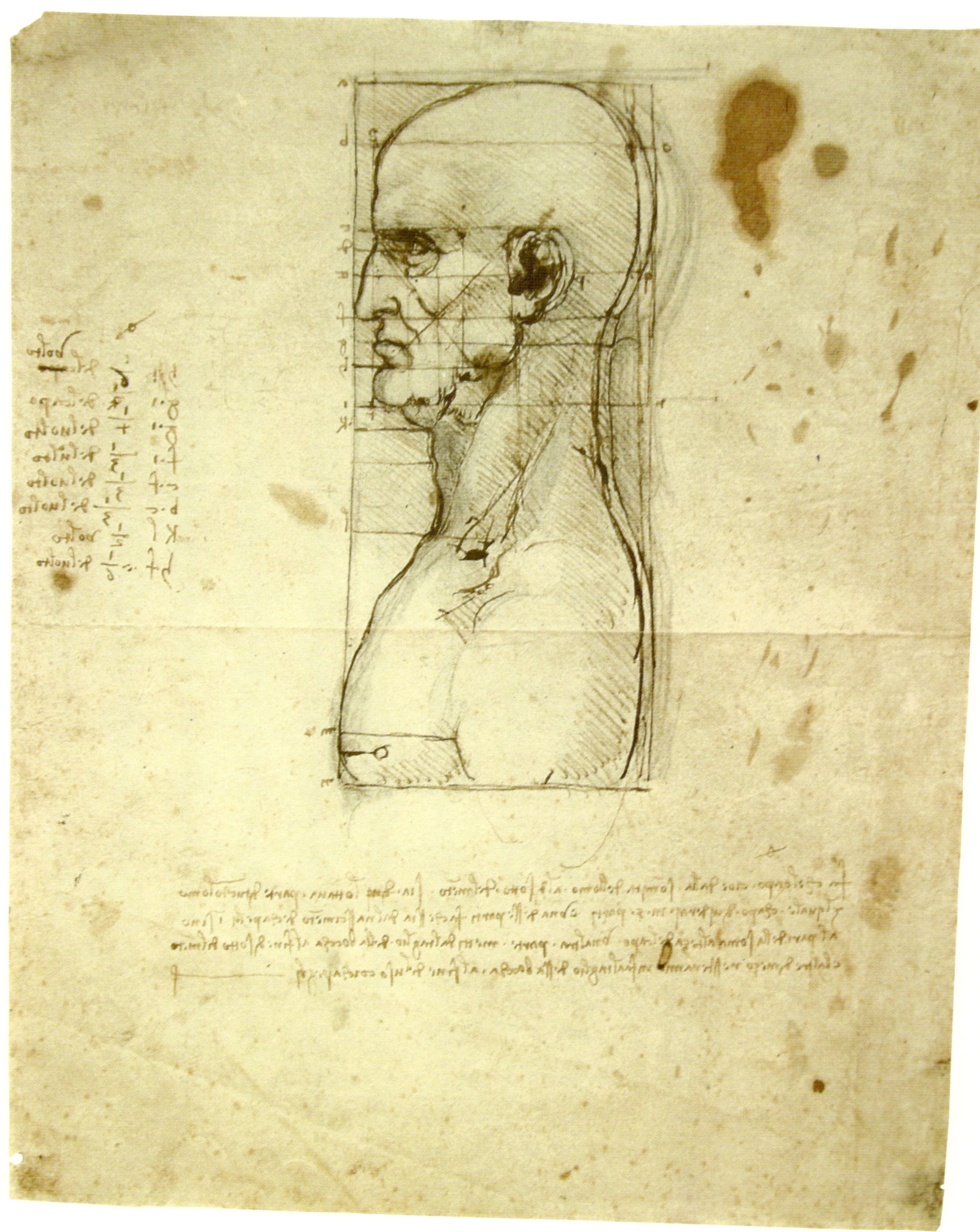

Leonardo da Vinci, *Study on the proportions of the head*, c. 1490. Pen, 280 x 222 mm. Venice, Gallerie dell'Accademia, n. 236 *v*

a mathematical language, neither to be rigidly bound to it, in order to make the «not beautiful», in its pejorative meaning, a parallel artistic style.

Since the first humanistic experiences, with the writing up in Latin and vulgar Italian of the first treatise on perspective, the *De Pictura* (1435) or *Della Pittura* (1436) by Leon Battista Alberti, and with the *De Prospectiva Pingendi* (c. 1475) by Piero della Francesca, the objects and the body of man would have been again represented in a space, according to a rigorous relationship of proportion, in a mathematical and geometric sense. Therefore such an intent to follow the laws of the convenient measure would have made the artist to achieve and to represent beauty and the perfection of things also in a perspective key, beginning, as for man, from the face, considered as a starting point to build the right proportions of the entire body (*De Prospectiva Pingendi*, Ms. Reggiano A 41/2, ff. 63v–64r). To such purpose Alberti had avowed the necessity to turn upside down the Vitruvian canon, set up on the measure of the foot («Vitruvius architect measured the length of man with his feet»), in order to privilege an anthropometry founded on the measure of the head: «To me it seems worthier that the other limbs refer to the head, although I have noticed that it is nearly common in all men that the foot is long as much as from the chin to the summit of the head», (II, 36).

In Vitruvius (*De Architectura*, III, 1, 2), what had to turn out pleasant to sight was subordinate to the relations that had to elapse between the total height of the figure and the single parts of it. Such concept had given origin to the notion of «symmetry», that is to the fundamental principle of aesthetic perfection, based on the relationship of proportionality not only of two or more measures among them, but between the single parts with the whole, as it appears in the *homo bene figuratus*[4] and in the most varied interpretive outcomes that it would have received during the Renaissance and the successive ages.

In 1490, Leonardo da Vinci would have translated it in the most famous drawing, made in pen, metallic point, ink and watercolour, now in the Gallerie dell'Accademia of Venice (n. 228), where, to correct the Vitruvian errors, he would have empirically reproduced, after anthropometric studies (Windsor, RL 12304; 12601, c. 1489; Venice, Gallerie dell'Accademia, 236 v, c. 1490), a right dimension for all the limbs, making to touch, with the extremities of the arms and of the opened legs, the angles of the square inscribed in the circle, whose centre coincided with the navel only in the *homo ad circulum*[5], while

in the *homo ad quadratum*[6] it was under the pubic region.[7] In short, for Leonardo, the navel divided man in a golden way:

> *Vetruvius architect puts in his work of architecture that the measures of a man are from nature distributed in this way. That is, that 4 fingers makes a palm and 4 palms make a foot; 6 palms make one cubit, 4 cubits make a man, and 4 cubits make a step, and 24 palms make a man; and these measures are in his buildings. If you open your legs so much that you drop off from your head 1/14 of your height, and open and raise your arms so much that with the extended fingers you touch the line of the top of the head, you must know that the centre of the extremities of the opened limbs will be*

<hr>

[6] «man in the square», Tr. N.

[7] See F. ZÖLLNER, *Vitruvs Proportionsfigur. Quellenkritische Studien zur Kunstliteratur im 15. Und 16. Jahrhundert,* Worms, Werner, 1987; ID., *Die Bedeutung von Codex Huygens und Codex Urbinas fur die Proportions-und Bewegungsstudien Leonardos da Vinci*, in «Zeitschrift fur Kunstgeschichte», 52, 1989, 3; G. BERRA, *La storia dei canoni proporzionali del corpo umano*, «Raccolta Vinciana», 25, 1993. In the leonardian sheet of the study on the Vitruvian Man, in which there are illustrated the measures of the body, it can be read: «Man opens his arms as much as it is his height […] The member of man is originated in the middle of man. A foot is the seventh part of man. From under the foot to under the knee it is a fourth part of man. From under the knee to the origin of the member it is a fourth part of man. The parts that are placed between the chin and the nose and the origin of hair and of the eyebrows, each space for itself is similar to the ear, it is a third of the face». In his *De Architectura* (cap. 3, III), Vitruvius reported that «the centre of the human body is by nature the navel. If in fact a man laid on its back, with hands and feet extended, and you pointed a compass on the navel, you would touch tangentially, describing a circumference, the extremities of the fingers of the hands and of the toes of the feet. Moreover, measuring the distance from the end of the feet to the summit of the head and comparing it with the one between the two opened hands, you would find that height and width coincide, as in a square area». As for the numerical data related to the proportions of the human body, Vitruvius reported in a normative way that the face, from the origin of hair to the chin, had a relationship of 1/10 of the total length; the head of 1/8 from the apex to the chin; the hand, from the wrist to the tip of the middle finger, 1/10; the length of the foot 1/6 and the width of the chest 1/4. Always around 1490, Leonardo, in his indications of measure for the human head, that accompany the drawing of a man seen in profile (Venice, Gallerie dell'Accademia), annotated: «Do so that the head, that is from the top of man to under the chin, is the eighth part of the whole man, which head you will divide in 5 parts; and one of these parts do so that it is from the origin of hair till the same maximum height of the head; put another part from the cut of the mouth to the inferior end of the chin, and the others in the middle will be between the cut of the mouth to the end of the face with hair». But, the passions and the symmetry of the human body in painting and sculpture were subjects on which also ALBRECHT DÜRER took part, whose work was translated from Latin and published in Venice, in 1591, at Domenico Nicolini, by GIOVAN PAUL GALLUCCI: *Di Alberto Durero Pittore, e Geometra chiarissimo. Della simmetria dei corpi humani, Libri Quattro. [Of Albert Durer Painter and most clear geometrician. Of the Symmetry of the Human Bodies, Books Four].* Newly translated from the Latin language into Italian, by M. Gio. Paolo Gallucci Salmodiano. Increased also of the fifth book, in which the matter is, with which ways can Painters, and Sculptors demonstrate the diversity of nature of men, and women, and with which the passions, that they feel for the various accidents, that happen to them. Now printed again. Work to Painters, and Sculptors not only useful, but necessary, and to every other one, that of such matter wishes to acquire a perfect opinion: «This is that prudent Painter, which has not only considered in the particular bodies all the beautiful parts to produce precepts out of them, but all that Pliny, Vitruvius and others that have reasoned about it have written of it, and has reduced all this to perfection: such that it can not in any way be improved. So that he has not only given the precepts to the bodies well proportioned; but he has given rules to it, and taught the precepts, and found again proportion in bodies in all uneven» (G. P. Gallucci, in A. Dürer, *Della simmetria de i corpi umani*).

<hr>

[4] «man well represented», Tr. N.

[5] «man in the circle», Tr. N.

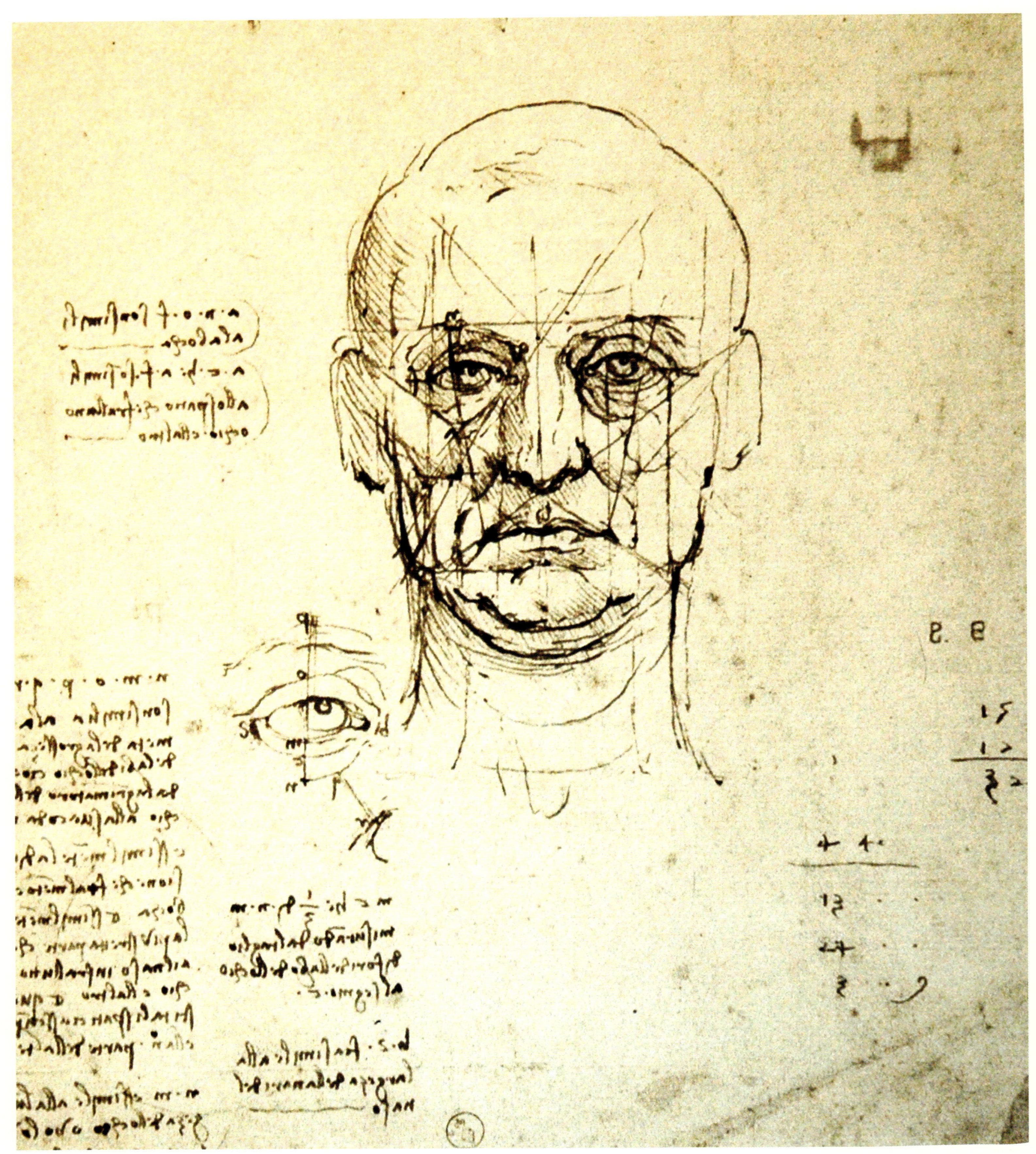

Leonardo da Vinci, *Study on the proportions of the face, c.* 1489–90. Pen and tawny ink on yellowish paper, 196 x 159 mm. Turin, Biblioteca Reale, n. 15576 r

the navel and the space that there is between the legs will be an equi-
lateral triangle, (Venice, Gallerie dell'Accademia, n. 228).

On the contrary, Cesare Cesariano, disciple of Bramante and admirer of Leonardo whom he considered his «preceptor»,[8] would have forced, in 1521, the figure of the naked man to a completely frontal posture and inserted in a single square, where not respecting the canons of the proportional quantitative theory he caused disharmony in the excessive extension of feet and of hands. The addition of «something more» in comparison with the model, as the phallus in strong erection and the bushy hair adorned of vine leaves, loaded his *Vitruvian Man* with a curious sensationalism, fluctuating between obscene and Dionysian and in a disguised opposition to the ideal of an absolute beauty.

Pliny the Elder, known by Leonardo in the popularization of the *Naturalis historia* made by Cristoforo Landino,[9] remembered that, with the plastic and pictorial art of the Hellenistic period (Scopas), it was exceeded the symmetry and the movement in power typical of the works by Myron («more varied in rhythms compared to Polycletus», *N.H.*, XXXIV, 58),[10] for a better reproduction of feelings and of emotions

(«pathos»), since there was a greater ability to translate the qualities of a character with more effectiveness («ethos»). These aspects will enter in the artistic theory of the Renaissance and will be defined by Alberti (*De pictura*, II, 41) and by Leonardo as «accidents» or «mental motions» (*Libro di Pittura*, f. 107, *cap.* 285), like emotional valences that become visible in the individual, independently of his nature. The individualization of passions, of ages and of sexes involved in the Renaissance also the search for the physiognomic expressions of the single types, from which derived the necessity of a correspondent and exhaustive study of anatomy: «then describe the adult man and the female and his measures and nature of complexion colour and filosomy» (Windsor, RL 19037 *v*), Leonardo will write.

Claudius Galen (II cent. a. C.), for his extensive researches about the human body and his accurate study of passions, appeared at the time of the Renaissance as the continuer of the Hippocratic medicine, for having tried to re-establish the equilibrium of the forces operating in the individual; such purpose justified his widespread researches about the human body and his accurate study of passions.[11]

So that it was possible a diagnostic, Galen had also delineated a combination of principles, of clinical pictures and of causes within which ordering the theory of the four types of temperament (anger, blood, phlegm, melancholy), that were inside the organism, where the structure of the great cosmos with the four elements of fire, air, water, earth was repeated, and whose qualities were warmness, coldness, humidity and drought. Following the same outline, the vital element of blood would have had in its circle the four humours, from whose equilibrium or according to whose predominance, the different temperaments of human nature were determined: irascible, sanguine, phlegmatic and melancholic.[12]

---

[8]   See CESARE CESARIANO, *Volgarizzamento dei libri IX di Vitruvio, De Architectura, secondo il manoscritto 9/2790 Secciòn de Cortes della Real Academia de la Historia,* Madrid, a cura di Barbara Agosti, Pisa, 1996; C. PEDRETTI, *Cesare Cesariano (1483-1543), Di Lucio Vitruvio Pollione de Architettura Libri Dece traducti de latino in Vulgare Affigurati,* in *Leonardo in Casentino. L''Angelo incarnato' tra archeologia e leggenda,* mostra ideata e curata da Carlo Starnazzi, Catalogo a cura di Carlo Pedretti, Stia 1 luglio-28 ottobre 2001, Firenze, Grantour, 2001. The model of the represented «Vitruvian Man» represented by CESARIANO is accompanied by the following heading: «A pariqvadrata svperficie hvmani corporis perdistincta eo naturali centro vmbilici circvlvm excipere: et in eo qvadratvm minorem inscribere» [«Extract from a squared surface of a human body defined by the natural centre of the navel a circle: and draw inside of it a smaller square» Tr.N.]. Studies on the definition of the objective proportions of human figure were completed also by Galen, that, in his *Placita Hippocratis et Platonis* (V, 3), so reported: «Chrysippus […] affirms that beauty does not reside in the single elements but in the harmonious proportion of the parts, in the proportion of a finger regarding the other, of all the fingers regarding the rest of the hand, of the rest of the hand regarding the wrist, of this regarding the forearm, of the forearm regarding the entire arm, in the end of all the parts regarding all the others, as it is written in the canon of Polycletus».

[9]   See *Historia naturale di C. Plinio secondo tradocto di lingua latina in fiorentino per Christophoro Landino fiorentino,* Venezia, Janson, 1476.

[10]   PLINY THE ELDER, in a famous passage of his *Naturalis Historia* (XXXV, 98), adds that « [Aristides of Thebes] was the first among all the painters to depict the mind, both the human feelings, that the Greeks call ethe, and the emotional perturbations», favouring in this way the beginning of a long artistic-theoretical tradition in the representation of human face, in which naturally affections and passions of the mind shine through. With the same intention to put in evidence 'the motions of the mind' Alberti participated in *Della Pittura* (II, 41), recalling again the painter Aristides: «They say that Aristides of Thebes equal to Apelles well knew these motions, which certainly we too will know when we shall put study and diligence to know them». With relation to the «affections», GIOVAN PAOLO LOMAZZO, in the I chapter of his *Trattato dell'arte della pittura, scoltura, et architettura* (Milano, Paolo Gottardo Ponzio, 1584), would have repeated that «painting […] not only represents in plane the greatness and relief of the bodies, but also their motion, and it visibly demonstrates to our eyes many affections and passions of the Man».

[11]   For this reason, Leonardo will sustain that «medicine is a re-balancing of unequal elements» (Codex Trivulzianus, f. 4 *r*). In 1487, from these considerations came to his mind also the idea that only the «doctor architect» could have supplied the reorganization of the «sick dome» (CA, 270 *rc* [730 *r*]), in order then to intervene on the lantern with a project able to adequately harmonize the shape of the single parts with the entire complex.

[12]   Of the many works by CLAUDIUS GALEN there must be considered, for the subjects dealt with, *Of his own books; The medical art; The customs of the mind follow the temperaments of the body; Diagnosis and cure of the passions and defects of everybody; Comments on the nature of man; On the temperaments; On the temperaments and the faculties of simple medications; On the concatenation of causes; Anatomical investigations.* See C. GALEN, *Opera omnia,* Leipzig, Kühn, 1821-33 (reprint Hildesheim, 1964-65). The expression «man-microcosmos» was made up by Democritus (Diels-Kranz, 68 B 34) and was resumed by Aristotle, that employed it jointly to the complementary expression «macrocosmos» (*Phis.*, VIII, 2, 252 b, 26-27). The two terms were transmitted to the Latin middle-age by Isidore of Seville (PL, 83, col. 978). Also Bernard of Tour will compose a poem *De mundi universitate sive megacosmus et microcosmus,* while Ugo and Goffredo of San Vittore will entitle their treatises *Microcosmus* and Thomas Aquinas will remember this definition of man in the *Summa Theologica* (I, q. 91, a. 1): «Homo dicitur minor mundus, quia omnes creaturae mundi quodammodo inveniuntur in eo». [«Man is said to be a small world,

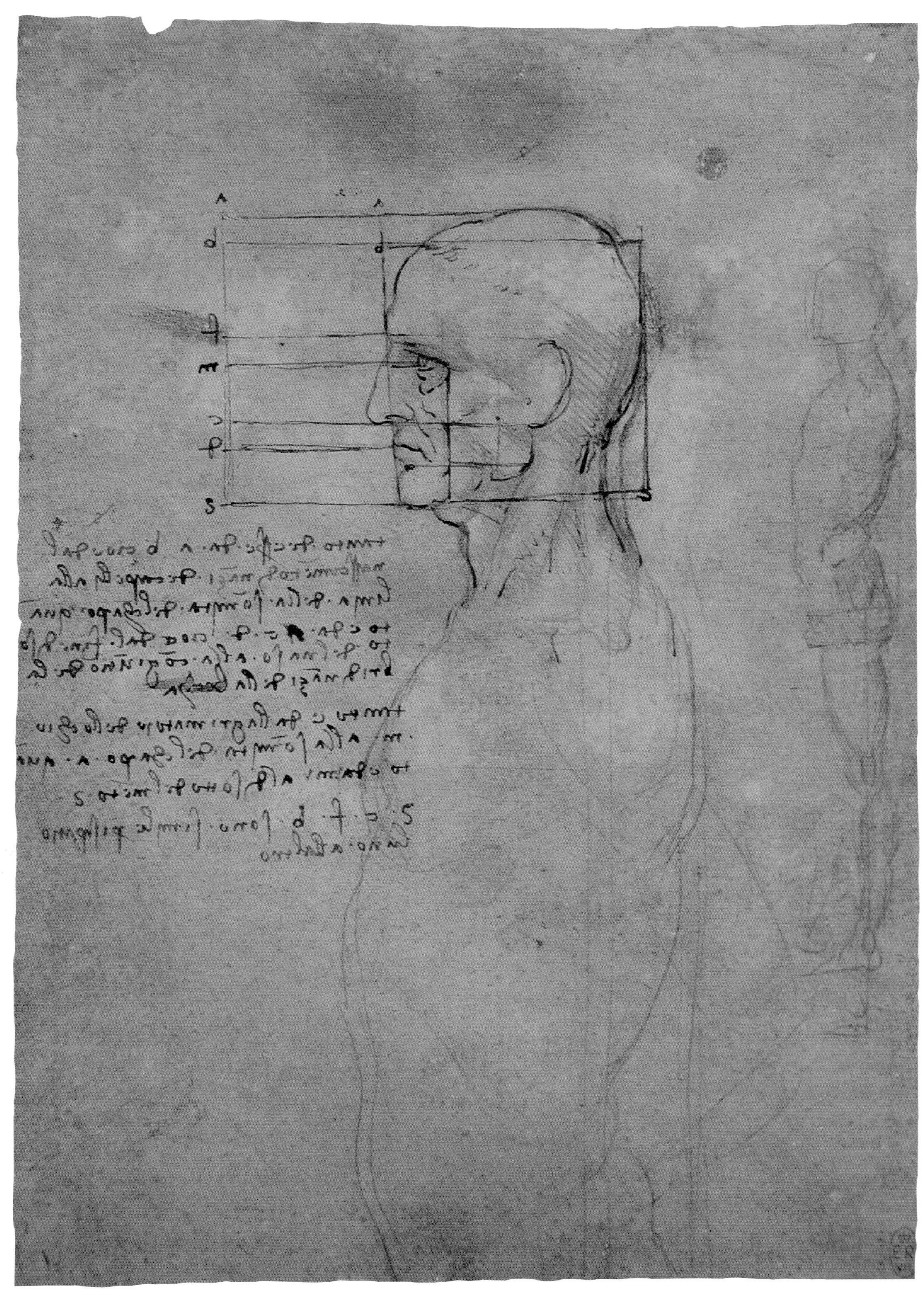

Leonardo da Vinci, *Study on the proportions of the head*, c. 1488-89. Pen and ink on prepared blue paper, 213 x 153 mm. Windsor, RL 12601

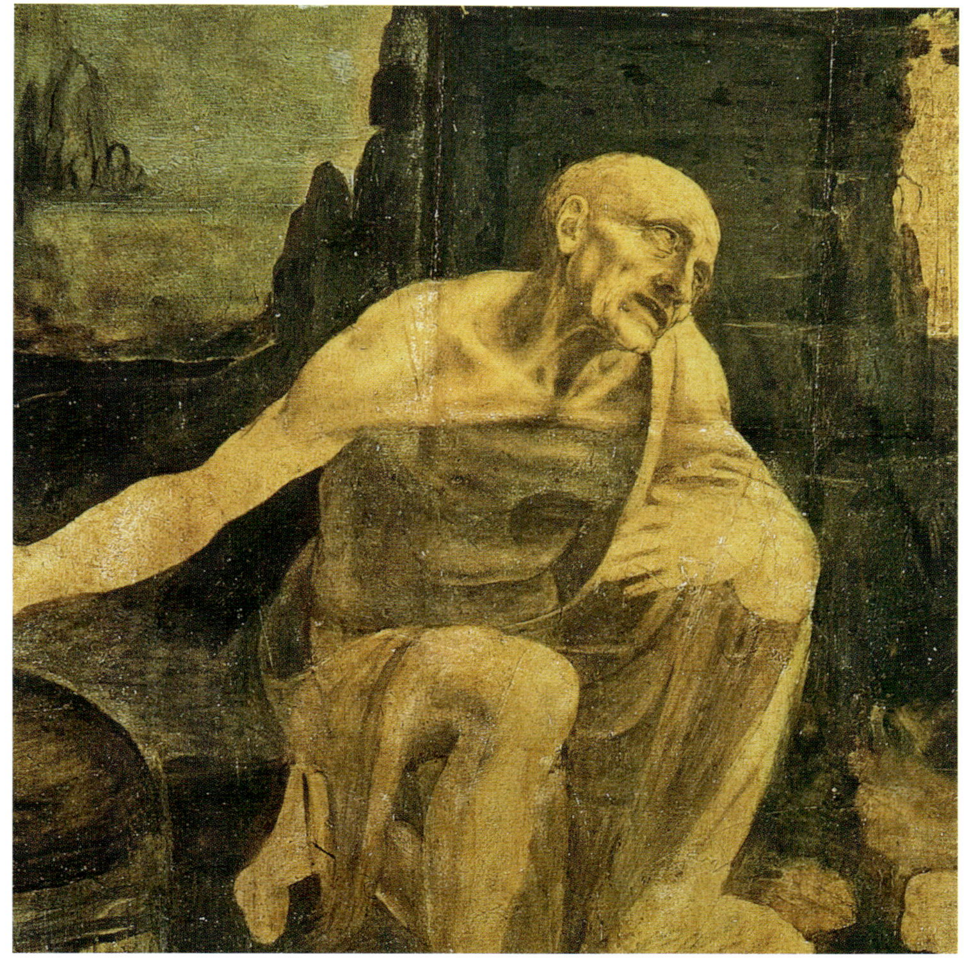

LEONARDO DA VINCI, *Saint Jerome*, *c.* 1480–82. Oil on table, 103 x 75 cm. Vatican City, Pinacoteca Vaticana. Particular

Leonardo, borrowing from the medical science of Galen, from the *Canon Medicinae* of Avicenna, from the *Philosophia naturalis* of Albertus Magnus, from the *Liber phisionomiae* of Miche Scoto and from the *Anathomia* of Mondino de' Liuzzi contained in the *Fasciculus medicinae* of Johannes de Ketham (popularized and published in Venice by Sebastiano Manilio, in 1493), his physiological conception, according to which to every organ corresponded a specific emotional function, he thought that a direct relationship between the character and the human physiognomy indeed existed. A certainty that he had already expressed in his *Saint Jerome* (Rome, Vatican Museum) where, in a burning focus, the anatomy of the body and the careful physiognomic analysis, reserved to the hollows of the face and the furrows of the throat, dramatically reflected the tension of his spirit.

because in any way all the creatures of the world can be found in him» Tr. N.]. Leonardo, as already Ristoro d'Arezzo in his *Composizione del mondo*, remembers that «man is said by the ancients a smaller world» (Ms A, f. 55 *v*).

Therefore, between 1487 and 1493, he would have started, in a more organic way, a first phase of studies of physiognomy and anatomy, opening his researches to the representation of the motions of the mind, through the study of the movements of the body and of the expression of faces. An artistic intention evidenced also in the precepts of Alberti: «it is convenient that the movements of the body are well known to painters, which they will learn from nature, since it is very difficult to imitate the many motions of the mind», (*Della Pittura*, II, 42). And precisely the study of the motion of the bodies makes painting a sort of natural philosophy, an intellectual discipline that, since Leonardo was a «good member-maker», would have allowed him to exceed the conventional manner inherited from the workshops of Verrocchio and Pollaiolo.

The two Florentine workshops had insisted on the psychological characterization of the personages, now resolved in the vigour of the male features of the face of Bartolomeo Colleoni, that showed a severe and frowning self-confidence,

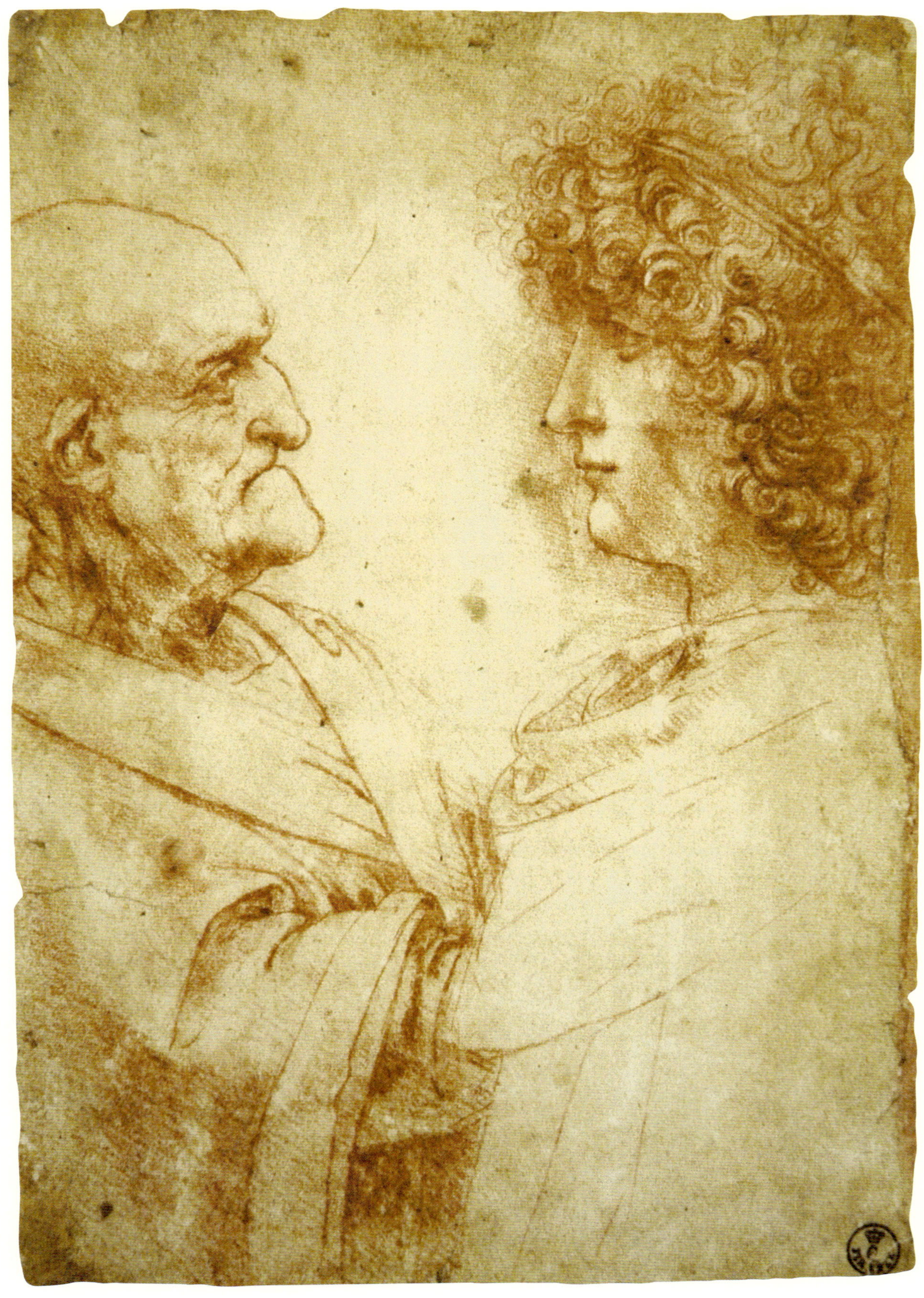

Leonardo da Vinci, *Facing busts of an old man and of an adolescent*, c. 1495. Sanguine on yellowed white paper, 208 x 150 mm. Florence, Gabinetto Disegni e Stampe degli Uffizi, n. 423 E

now in the faces of the famous engraving of the *Battle of the Nudes* (Florence, Uffizi, Gabinetto dei Disegni e delle Stampe) or of the *Male nude in front view* (Paris, Louvre, Cabinet des Dessins) by Antonio del Pollaiolo, among the first to study human anatomy.

Therefore, in Leonardo, the will to be «interpreter between nature and art» (Libro di Pittura, f. 24, cap. 40 *v*) motivated his investigation in the direction of a more scientific context and forced him to take into consideration a complex system of mechanisms, made up of nerves, bones and muscles «firmly tied», dismountable and answering to precise stimuli. To put in relation anatomy and physiognomy was for the artist a constant interest, that, on several occasions, after 1487-89, repeatedly indicated in his scientific program their descriptive categories of galenic origin: «This work has to be started at the conception of man […]

Then describe the adult man and the female, and his measures, and nature of complexion, colour and filosomy» (Windsor, RL 19037). And to this end was destined his survey on facial muscles (Windsor, RL 19012 *v*), on the movements of the mouth and of lips (Windsor, RL 19055 *v*), the study of skulls (Windsor, RL 19057 *r*), of optical nerves, of the «common sense» (centre of the organic spirit) and even of the direct relationship between the male genital organ, defined «minister of the human species», with the spinal cord and the brain (Windsor, RL 19097 *v*), from which the intellectual qualities would derive.

In the sheet of Weimar in fact, despising those that are not «sons of love», he would have emphasized the tight relation between the organic and psychical elements in the determination of the natural character, observing that «the son generated by the annoying lust of a woman, and not of the will of the husband, will be worthless, vile and of rough mind. The man that uses the coitus with containment and uneasiness, makes quick-tempered and quarrelsome sons».

From here took its origin the attempt to indicate, since his juvenile drawings, without to fix any typological taxonomy, as Giovan Paolo Lomazzo will do in his *Trattato* (1584),[13] the way to represent, in a gradual scientific research, the expressions and the «attitudes» of the various masculine and feminine subjects, from the vagueness of the beautiful one to the tension of the grotesque one, from the recreation of the awkward one to the fever of the quick-tempered one. Exalting the creative ability and the divine mind of the artist (*Libro di Pittura*, f. 36, *cap.* 68), Leonardo sustained that it was

in his power, as for magic, to be the master to represent, with all his knowledge and imagination, every type of person:

> *If the painter wants to see beauties that make him fall in love, he is master to generate them, and if he wants to see monstrous things that scare, or that are clownish and ludicrous, or truly pitiful, he is Lord and God of them, (Libro di Pittura, f. 5, cap. 13).*

The representation of the sweetness of the faces was accompanied to the study of shadows and lights, of the imperceptible vibration of the penumbrae and of the different tonalities with which the reality appears in the different hours of the day, better at the beginning of the twilight («perfect air»), when it seems to unveil every secret and intimacy. In that moment the painter will know how to conjugate style and psychological exploration, and how to stretch on the faces of men and women, with the finest outlines of light and shade and highlighting, a rare grace and vagueness, in perfect affinity with the one of the mind:

> *Turn your mind on the roads at nightfall to the faces of men and of women, when the weather is bad, how much grace and sweetness can be seen in them, (Libro di Pittura, f. 51, cap. 138).*

To this artistic style, subtended towards a process of idealization, belong the drawings of heads of young men or women corresponding to a figurative typifying with a sweet and regular forehead, and a soft and melancholic expression. The observation of reality favoured the activity of the «mental motions» and allowed to go beyond the appearance of things in order to pick off their essence, every secret aspect of nature in its aesthetic and physical shape. In 1492, in the effort to arouse the talent of the artist, the following invite appears among the precepts of Leonardo:

> *To see in the spots on the walls, or in the ash of the fire, or clouds, or mud, or other similar places, which, if they will be well considered by you, you will find inside them most admirable inventions, that the talent of the painter is aroused to new inventions both of compositions of battles, animals and men, and of various compositions of countries and monstrous things, as of devils, and similar things, because they will be motive to appreciate you; because in confused things the talent is aroused to new inventions, (Libro di Pittura, f. 35 v, cap. 66).*

The shadows on the walls, with their accidental shapes and their bizarre doodles, constituted the starting point and could have favoured the emerging of new ideas for the creation of landscapes, the invention of grotesque images as if they were alive creatures and quite verisimilar facial expressions, almost

---

[13]   See R. P. CIARDI, *Gian Paolo Lomazzo, Scritti sulle arti* (a cura di), Firenze, Marchi e Bertolli, Centro DI, 1973-75 [includes the following works: *Gli sogni e raggionamenti*, 1563; *Trattato dell'arte della pittura*, Milano, Ponzio, 1584; *Idea del tempio della pittura*, ivi, ID., 1590].

to recognize the superiority of imagination on imitation, the innovative character of the «deity» of the knowledge of the painter.[14] This evocative effect produced in the mind of the artist would again appear around 1510, when he was about to a program of review and collection of notes on painting, adding that the painter must «know to make well all the limbs of those things that he wants to figure», in order to define, with the expressive clarity of his drawing, the anatomical complexity of the «confused things» and to animate them with an inner causality.

Art, in short, with its inventions, following the dictates of the Aristotelian *Poetics*, probably consulted in a popularized text of the «poetics of Horace» (Ms. G, f. 8 *r*) or nonetheless present in the *De Pictura* of Alberti, had to know how to affect, to influence and to provoke the spectator («animos deinde historia spectantium movebit»)[15] with all that managed to invent and to produce as animated body, both with beautiful and with «clownish and ludicrous» images:

> *You will see that who is melancholic has the forehead pressed, the neck is faint, in all every his member falls down nearly exhausted and neglected. True, to whom is angry, because anger stimulates the mind, for that reason full of temper in the eyes and in the face, and inflames with colour, and every his member, as much the fury, so much fearless he throws himself. Joyful and happy men have movements that are free and with certain pleasant inflection,* (II, 41).

Leonardo, achieved the dominion of the physiognomic expression, recommended to the artist that intended to make portraits of young or old persons, to represent them according to the ages: «Of the conveniences of the limbs. And I recall you, still, that you pay great attention in giving the limbs to your figures, so that they appear, after being concordant with the largeness of the body, still in the same way to their age; that is, the young people with few muscles in their limbs, and veins and of a delicate surface, and round limbs of pleasant colour. Men must have them vigorous and full of muscles. The old people must have them with wrinkled, rough and venous surface, and nerves much evident» (*Libro di Pittura*, f. 127, *cap.* 383).

Subordinate to a constant investigation turns out to be the study of the profile of the old people, now exalted in their humanity and wisdom, with the representation of the psychological depth of their look, other times observed and represented, in a more analytical way, in the anatomical aspects of the skull and of the face, with a grotesque tension of the artistic whole.[16]

Precisely Giorgio Vasari tells us that Leonardo went along the roads in search of characteristic faces to fix in his memory,[17] in order to employ their facial representations in caricature portraits: «He liked it so much when he saw certain bizarre heads, natural men or with beards or with hair, that he would have followed that one, that he liked, for an entire day and he put him so much in his mind, that later, arrived at home, he portrayed him as if he had him there present». And also Lomazzo, in his *Trattato* (II, 2), sustaining that an artist in order to make a good portrait must concentrate on the study of the expression of the facial «motions», mentioned Leonardo as a model who «did not make any motion in a figure that before he did not want, accompanied with his study, to see a feature in the living one, if it were only for taking from it a certain natural vivacity with which then, adding his art, he made to see the portrayed men better than the living ones». Other times, the analysis of the faces and of the old age, often represented by means of light and shadow contrasts, led him to more thoughtful reflections about the somatic transformations caused by time (Windsor, RL 12276 *r, c.*

---

[14] Also Justinus Kerner (1786-1862) would have made recourse to the ink spots, on sheets of folded paper, in order to stimulate his fantasy, while Alexander Cozens (1717-1786) would have taken advantage of the vincian method of the spots on the walls to theorize the realization of landscapes in his *Nouvelle méthode pour secourir l'invention dans le dessin des compositions originales de paysages*, published in 1785. This method that he had and that leaves space to imagination would have turned out to be a prefiguration of the spots of Victor Hugo and the astounding surrealist decalcomanias of André Breton that, in his theoretical notions, declared to attain from the method of Leonardo. See E. H. Gombrich, *Arte e illusione. Studio sulla psicologia della rappresentazione pittorica*, Torino, Einaudi, 1965; C. Pedretti, *Le macchie di Leonardo*, «Lettura Vinciana», XLIV, Firenze, Giunti, 2004. The topic of the shapeless spots on the walls would have been reason of controversy also between Leonardo and Botticelli about the realization of landscapes, that according to Vinci had to be further reason of investigation in a direct relationship between science and art: «if one does not like the countries, he thinks that they are a thing of short and simple investigation, as our Botticella said, that such study was vain, because with the simple throwing of a sponge full of various colours against a wall, it left in that wall a spot, where it could be seen a beautiful country. It is absolutely true that in such spot it can be looked at itself in various inventions what man wants to look for in that one, that is heads of men, various animals, battles, cliffs, seas, clouds and forests and other similar things; and does as the sound of the bells, in which you can understand them to say what you like. But still if these spots give you any invention, they do not teach you to finish any particular. And this such painter made the saddest countries» (*Libro di Pittura*, ff. 33 *v*-34, *cap.* 60). Here, for certain aspects, found its origin in Leonardo also the taste for the «unfinished», for the indefinite, a sort of revenge, even if controlled, of the imagination over the accuracy of art, that can involve the risk of paralyzing the «mental motion».

[15] «the history then will move the souls of the viewers» (Tr. N.)

[16] See L. Cogliati Arano, *Leonardo e la rappresentazione della terza età*, «Lettura Vinciana», XXXI, Firenze, Giunti, 1992.

[17] In his *Libro di Pittura* (f. 109, *cap.* 290) describing the «Way to hold the shape of a face in mind», Leonardo recommends: «If you want be at ease in keeping to mind the air of a face, do keep first in mind many heads, eyes, noses, mouths, minds and throats and necks and shoulders […] when you have given a glance to the face of the person you want to portray, you will watch then in part which nose or mouth, if it is similar to it, and do a small sign in order to recognize it, then at home put it together. Of monstrous faces I do not speak, because without hard work they are kept to mind».

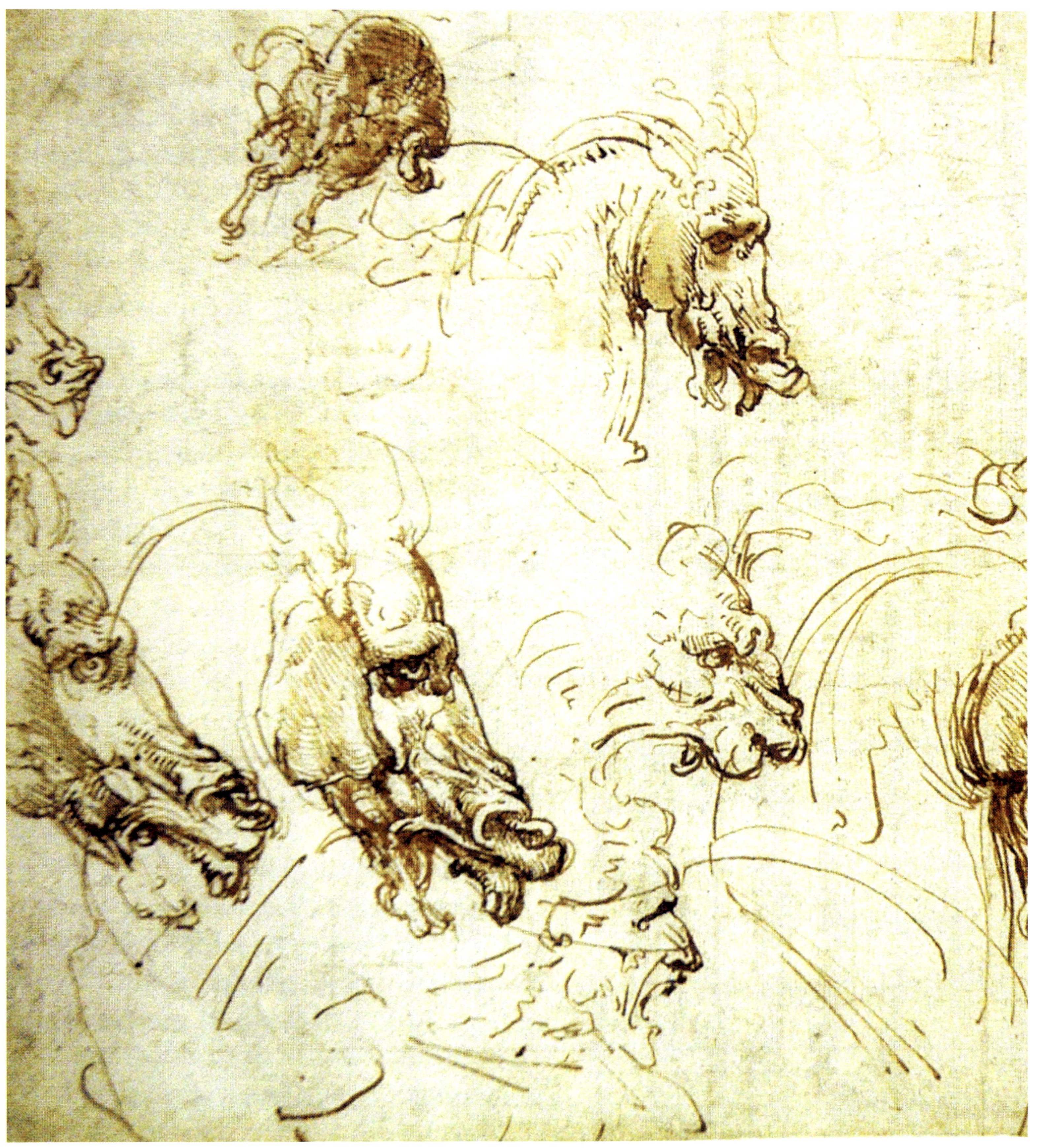

LEONARDO DA VINCI, *Comparative study of the emotive expressions of man and beast*, c. 1503–05. Pen, ink, watercolour and sanguine, 196 x 308 mm. Windsor, RL 12326

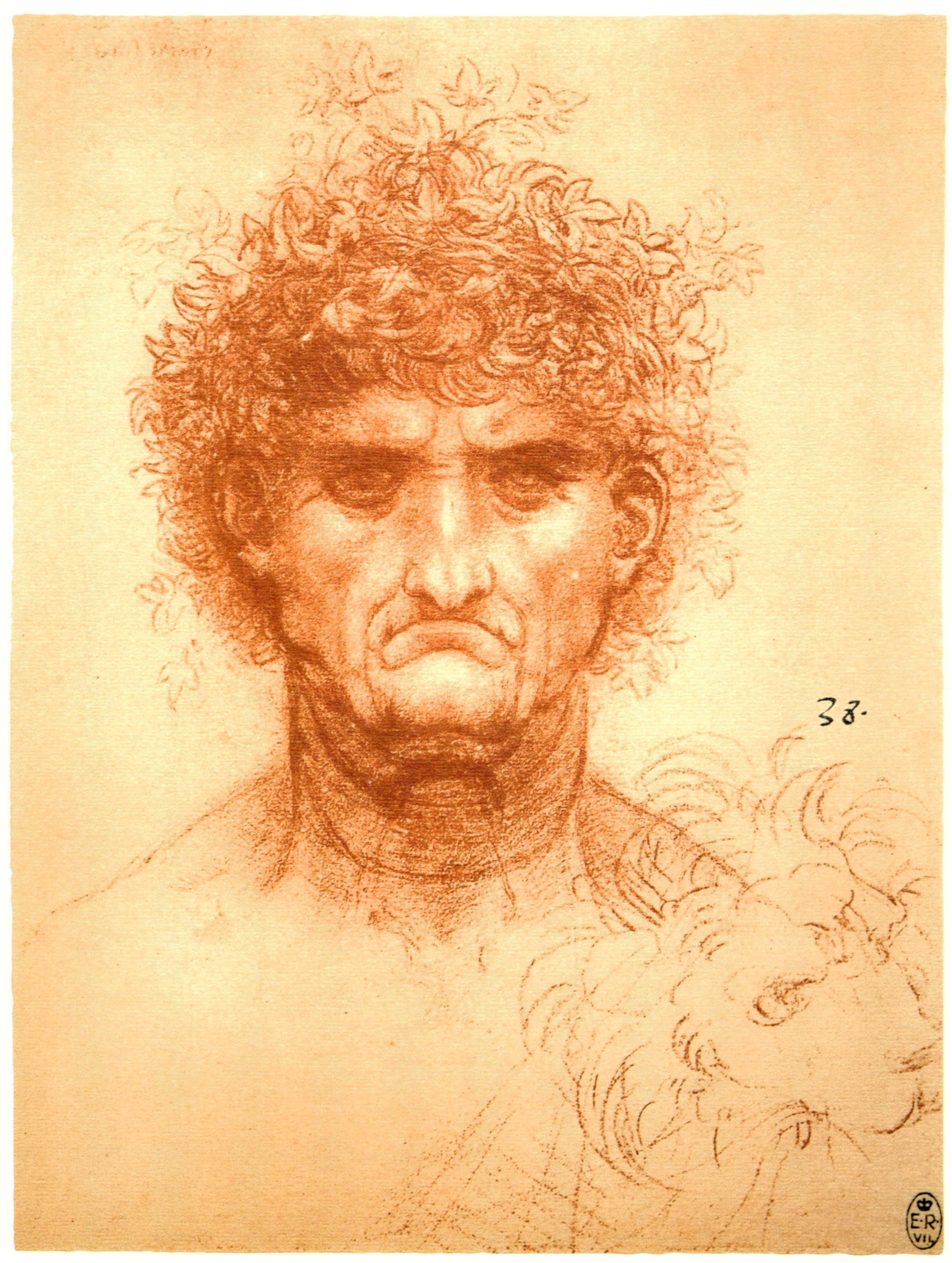

Leonardo da Vinci, *Study of a leonine subject*, *c.* 1503–05. Sanguine, pen and ink, 183 x 136 mm. Windsor, RL 12502

Carlo Starnazzi

1478) interpreted, according to the *Metamorphoses* of Ovid,[18] as consumer and predator of all beautiful things (CA, f. 195 *r* [71 *ra*], *c.* 1480):

Oh, time, consumer of things, and oh, envious antiquity, you destroy all the things, and [have] consumed all the things by the rigid teeth of the old age, little by little, with slow death. Helen, when looked at herself in the mirror, seeing the withered wrinkles of her face, caused by the old age, weeps and thinks in her heart to the reason why she was kidnapped twice.

To such end Leonardo, recommending to every artist to train his own visual memory, in order to better fix in mind what nature could offer to who was about to work on somatic morphologies, he in person advised to make use of a system with which to classify the elements of the face, after having studied the variety of their shapes. Therefore he invited to acquire a great ability in drawing eyes, noses, mouths, chins and foreheads, illustrating the most various categories, to portray a face in front or in profile, after a single glance (*Libro di Pittura*, f. 108 *v*, *cap.* 289):

We will first say of the noses, which are of three kinds, straight, concave and convex. Of the straight ones there is not but four varieties, that is to say long, short, high with the tip, and low. The concave noses are of three kinds, of which some of them have the concavity in the upper part, some in the middle and others in the inferior part. The convex noses still are varied in three ways, that is to say some have a hump in their upper part, some in the middle and others in the inferior part. And then: if you want to have capability in keeping to mind the air of a face, do learn first by heart many heads, eyes, noses, mouths, chins, and throats and necks and shoulders. […] carry with you a small booklet where must be noticed such parts and when you have given a glance to the face of the person you want to portray, you will watch then in part which nose or mouth, if it is similar to it, and make to it a little sign in order to recognize it, then at home put it together, (f. 109, cap. 290).

In such way the artist became an authentic creator of physiognomic portraits, by paying attention to favour as much as possible the variety of the physiognomic subjects, once surpassed the first impression.

Recovering what sustained by Alberti, that is, how it is difficult for the painter to distinguish the shadings and to represent the subtle variations of a face that laughs or that cries, Leonardo, after having highlighted the similarity of expression created by laughter and by crying («they are quite similar in the mouth and in the cheeks and locking of the eyes, but only they vary in the eyelashes and their interval», *Libro di Pittura*, f. 107, *cap.* 285) he recommended, in a direct way and by means of analysis, to obviate to the difficulty to reproduce the muscular contractions of the face with some stratagems: «From the one that laughs to the one that cries they do not vary neither the eyes, neither the mouth, neither his cheeks, but only the rigidity of the eyelash that join up in the one who cries, and go up in the one who laughs», (*Libro di Pittura,* f. 127, *cap.* 384).

The smile was for Leonardo one of the universal aspects characterizing human nature, a specific feature that distinguished man from animals, also on the basis of the Aristotelian tradition and of what asserted by Isidore of Seville in his *Etymologies* (II, XXV, 2-3; 7-8): «man is a rational animal, mortal, earthly, with two feet, able to laugh», and then after that «man is an animal that laughs, and this manifestation does not exist in no other animal but in man».[19] The smile had achieved a precise «physiognomic» value, since beyond to be an element of sweetness diffused on the face, it translated the motion of an inner life.

Therefore Leonardo will insist on the «various actions of laughing» and on figuring «the cause of laughter» (Windsor, RL 19037 *v*), that, in the paintings of the *Mona Lisa* and of the *Saint John the Baptist*, it would have transmuted itself in a allusive expression of the unfathomable mystery that covers cosmic life.

Leonardo granted space to the physiognomy, and in order to consolidate its objective value he opposed with force to the «fallacious» and «judicial» astrology, that expected to influence human life since birth, as well as to chiromancy that, boasting the ability to interpret this influence from the lines marked on the palm of the hand, had acquired among the contemporary naturalist philosophers, above all in the environment of the culture of the court, where prognostics of every kind were made, a divining power.[20]

---

[18]   «Ovid Metamorphoseos», records Leonardo in the directory of his books (Codex of Madrid II, ff. 2*v*-3*v*).

[19]   The *Etymologies* by Isidore of Seville are remembered by Leonardo as «Chronicle of Esidero» (CA, f. 210 *ra* [559*r*]) or «Chlonic of Saint Esidero» (Codex of Madrid II, ff. 2*v*-3*v*). Isidore of Seville, *Etymologiarum sive Originum libri XX*, edited by W.M. Lindsay, Oxford, Oxford Univ. Press, 1911.

[20]   See E. Garin, *Lo zodiaco della vita*, Bari, Laterza, 1982; C. Vasoli, *Note su Leonardo e l'alchimia*, in *Leonardo e l'età della ragione*, a cura di Enrico Bellone e Paolo Rossi, Milano, Scientia, 1982; S. Caroti, *L'astrologia in Italia*, Roma, Newton Compton, 1983; E. H. Gombrich, *Leonardo e i maghi: polemiche e rivalità*, «Lettura Vinciana», XXIII, Firenze, Giunti Barbèra, 1984; G. Federici Vescovini, *Su un trattatello anonimo di fisiognomica astrologica*, in *Uomo e Natura nella letteratura e nell'arte italiana del Tre-Quattrocento*, Quaderni dell'Accademia delle Arti del Disegno, 3, 1991; Id., *Pietro d'Abano e la medicina astrologica dello Speculum physionomiae di Michele Savonarola*, «Musagetes, Festschrift fur Wolfram Prinz», Berlin, Mann, 1992; M. W. Kwakkelstein, *Leonardo da Vinci as a physiognomist. Theory and drawing practise*, Leiden, Primavera Pers, 1994; P. Zambelli, *L'apprendista stregone. Astrologia, cabala e arte lulliana in Pico e seguaci*, Venezia, Marsilio, 1995; Id., *L'ambigua natura*

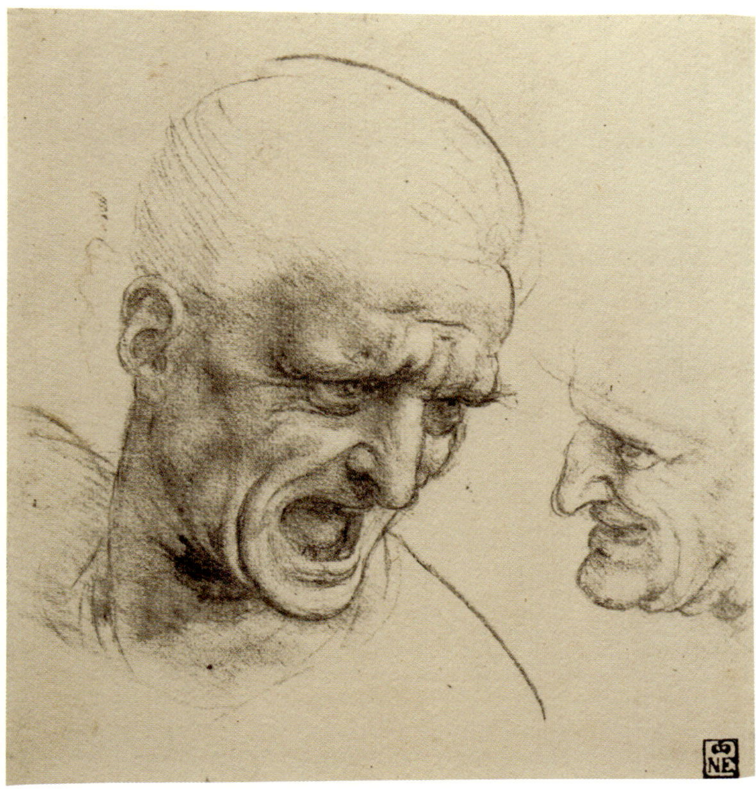

Leonardo da Vinci, *Study of two heads of warriors for the Battle of Anghiari, c.* 1504-05. Sanguine, 227 x 166 mm. Budapest, Szépmüvészeti Múseum, n. 1775

In the f. 109 *v* of the *cap.* 292 of his *Libro di Pittura* whose subject was «About physiognomy and chiromancy», Leonardo thus wrote: «About the fallacious physiognomy and chiromancy I will not keep me away, because in them there is not truth; and this is manifest, because such chimeras do not have scientific foundations».

The subjects of astrology were interlaced and melted with those of chiromancy that, for their lack of scientific foundations, as the other occult sciences (necromancy «does not give origin to any thing if not similar to itself, that is lies»; RL 19048), were practiced with a view to profit by interested swindlers, always ready to trick «the foolish multitude» (Ms. F, f. 5 *v*).

Leonardo is inclined to ridicule the fraudulence of this practice and to reveal its absurdities and its groundlessness, adding that on the basis of the reading of the lines «of the hand you will find that huge armies were dead at the same hour of a knife, that no sign of the hand is similar to any other, and the same in a shipwreck». In this same paragraph he lingered also

to enunciate on a theoretical plan some reflections of patho-gnomonic character on temperament and the signs of the face,[21] on which his investigation mainly insists, not going afar from the traditional psychosomatic theory of Aristotle and of the galenic medicine,[22] according to which to physical anomalies («parts of the face of great relief») correspond psychical defects («beastly» and «with little reason») and that body and spirit are naturally and mutually connected:

It is true that the signs of the faces in part show the nature of men, of their vices and complexions; if in the face the signs that separate the cheeks from the lips of the mouth, and the nostrils of the nose and the cavities of the eyes are evident, they are men cheerful and often laughing; and those that little mark them are men operating with the thought; and those which have the parts of the face of great relief and depth are beastly men and irascible with little reason; and those who have the lines interposed between the eyelashes strongly evident are irascible, and those who have the transversal lines of their forehead aligned are men abundant in hidden or evident lamentations.

According to Leonardo, the signs of the faces showed in part the nature of men, their vices, that is they turned out to be effect of an emotion able to alter temporarily the equilibrium or to manifest itself in a repetitive way during the organic process of the various ages of life, modifying gradually, but in a permanent way, the aspect of an individual (Windsor, RL 12596; 12631).[23]

In the previous passage, following the indications of a static physiognomy,[24] Leonardo seems to be interested to fix for types the psychosomatic relations between the outer phys-

---

della magia. Filosofi, streghe, riti nel Rinascimento, Venezia, Marsilio, 1996; R. Nanni, *Astrologia e Prospettiva. Per lo studio dell'immagine della scienza nel 'Paragone' delle arti di Leonardo*, «Raccolta Vinciana», XXVII, 1997.

[21]   During the eighteenth century, Georg Christoph Lichtenberg, as Leonardo had thought, defined patho-gnomic the study which is made about the expression derived from the customary passions and its durable effects on the face in the various circumstances of life, opposing the determinist conception of the thought of Johann Kaspar Lavater, that, in his *Physionomische Fragmente* (1775), dedicated to the study of physiognomy, sustained the strict connection between character and shape of the skull (forehead, nose, mouth): a theory that was appreciated also by Honoré de Balzac. See E. H. Gombrich, *Le teste grottesche…*, 1986, *op. cit.*; D. Laurenza, *De figura umana. Fisiognomica, anatomia e arte in Leonardo*, Firenze, Olschki, 2001.

[22]   See D. Laurenza, *De figura umana…*, 2001, *op. cit.*

[23]   In *Analitici Primi* (II, 27, 70b, 10), Aristotle carries out the following considerations: «It is possible to physiognomize if one admits that body and spirit change together in all the natural affections. I mean affections as outbursts of temper or desires». See P. Meller, *Physiognomical Theory in Renaissance Heroic Portraits*, «The Renaissance and Mannerism. Studies in Western Art, Acts of the Twentieth International Congress of the History of Art», Princeton, Princeton Univ. Press, 1963; E. H. Gombrich, *La maschera e la faccia: la percezione della fisionomia nella vita e nell'arte*, in *Arte, Percezione e Realtà*, a cura di E. H. Gombrich, J. Hochenberg, M. Black, Torino, Einaudi, 1978.

[24]   In pseudo-Aristotelian *Physiognomy* (I, 805 *a*, 25-30; 812 *a*, 1) are contained the following observations: «being corrugated [in the forehead] indicates audacity and being smooth propension to flattery […]. Who has a gloomy forehead is of a sad nature: this sends back to the state of mind». See Pseudo Aristotele, *Fisiognomica*, a cura di Giampiera Raina, Milano, Rizzoli, 1993.

                                                                     Carlo Starnazzi

ical shape and its affections. The individuals that have the lines that separate their cheeks from the lips and from the nose well marked «they are men cheerful and often laughing», those that have deep furrows in the «lines interposed between the eyelashes» are irascible and stupid, when then, for their age, they are more inclined to sad thoughts, they reveal a phlegmatic temperament, and being «men abundant in hidden or evident lamentations» they have a face more marked by the «transversal lines of their forehead».[25]

Since his juvenile period, the representation of the irascible type had, as a distinguishing symbol of his temperament, a protruding forehead. This prominence, corresponding to the frontal sinus (Windsor, RL 19057),[26] would have been subsequently correlated, for an analogy of scholastic derivation, to the head of a roaring lion, in the attempt to associate men and animals as creatures moved from one same sensitive and passionate spirit.[27]

The fury was an anatomic-physiognomic aspect that united the living beings, men and beasts («all the terrestrial animals have similarity of limbs, that is muscles, nerves and bones»), therefore the comparative study of the facial expression of a shouting man that had the features of a lion with a horse and a lion with the mouth opened renewed the conceptual adhesion to the connection among contingent emotions and physiognomic aspects, both without motion and in motion (Windsor, RL 12326 r, c. 1503-04).

The approach man-lion (Windsor, RL 12502, c. 1505-10), recovered from the traditional literature, favoured also a type of physiognomic portrait, the variation from the typology of the quick-tempered man to that one of the heroic and courageous man (Turin, Biblioteca Reale, 15575), opposite to the phlegmatic one, to be proposed again in the course of his artistic activity after nearly thirty years, at the time of his iconographic studies of the heads of warriors in the drawings for the *Battle of Anghiari* (Windsor, RL 12326 r; Budapest, Szépmuvészeti Muzeum).

The inclination to repeat an iconography for fixed types, although his sensibility in considering the human body as subordinate to continuous and infinite metamorphoses, was emphasized by Kenneth Clark,[28] that, in the study of the heads, recognized two complementary aspects in his continuous research for beauty: «the virile and the effeminate one», both symbols of the contrast existing in the personality of Leonardo, exampled on the gracefulness of the *David* and parallel to the martial proud of *Darius* and of the *Colleoni* by Verrocchio:

> *These are, in fact, the two hieroglyphs of Leonardo's unconscious mind, the two images his hand created when his attention was wandering […] both types go back to his earliest Florentine years, were indeed taken from Verrocchio: the elegant youth from such a head as the David, the warrior from the lost Darius relief […] these two images reflect deep and fixed necessities in Leonardo's nature. Even in his most conscious creations, even in the Last Supper, they remain, as it were, the armature round which his types are created.*

Therefore, around 1478, they would have made their first appearance, approached in opposition, the profile of the old bald man, with hooked nose and prominent chin, and the one melancholic and absent-minded of the ephebic young boy (Windsor, RL 12276 v). Aspects of a particular somatic morphology, of which, according to Ernst H. Gombrich, the artist, although his repeated attempts to broaden his own repertoire, never would have got rid.[29] In those grotesque heads, Leonardo revealed a passion for all that in nature showed itself as singular and anomalous, nevertheless to put in relation and to approach to his «ideal types».

Grotesque images that, for Arthur E. Popham, turned out to be «the link of conjunction between the normal and the abnormal, between the sublime and the ridicule», a mock-

---

[25]   Also Giovan Battista Della Porta, that realized a synthesis of the classic-medieval thought on Physiognomy (*Humana Physiognomonia*), including chiromancy and astrology, sustained that it was to be considered «a science that learns from the signs that are fixed in the body» (I, XXX). See G. B. Della Porta, *Humana Physiognomonia*, Vici Equensis apud Iosephum Cacchium, 1586; C. Caputo, *Un manuale di semiotica del Cinquecento: il «De humana Phisiognomonia» di Giovan Battista della Porta*, in *Giovan Battista della Porta nell'Europa del suo tempo*, atti del convegno (a cura di M. Torrini), Vico Equense, Napoli, Guida, 1990; P. Castelli, *«Viso cruccioso e con gli occhi turbati». Espressione e fisionomica nella trattatistica d'arte del primo Rinascimento*, in *L'ideale classico a Ferrara e in Italia nel Rinascimento*, a cura di P. Castelli, Firenze, Olschki, 1998.

[26]   According to Kenneth Keele, the frontal sinus is one of the most original discoveries of Leonardo. See K. Keele, *Leonardo da Vinci. Disegni anatomici dalla Biblioteca Reale di Windsor*, introduzione di Anthony Blunt, Prefazione di Carlo Pedretti, Firenze, Giunti Barbèra, 1979. Also Alberti in his *De Pictura* had described the tension of the faces when they redden inflamed with temper: «and the face, and the eyes swell, and they become red; and the motions of all the limbs for the fury of the anger are in them very vigorous and much irritated».

[27]   Della Porta will continue this visual equation between man and beast, abandoning anthropometry and the theory of proportions, to stop himself in an ingenuous and nearly popular way to emphasize the psychophysical characters. Such doctrine of Aristotelian tradition would have favoured the development of a type of caricature that, in the attempt to know the character of a man, it thought sufficient to single out in his physiognomy the features of the animal which most resembled. Therefore the profile of a man with an aquiline nose was approached to the profile of a sheep, to unveil his mild mind; a man with a gaze as fixed as that of a fish was considered cold and taciturn; a man with its face similar to a mastiff revealed an obstinate character.

[28]   See K. Clark, *Leonardo da Vinci*, Milano, Mondadori, 1983.

[29]   See Cfr. E. H. Gombrich, *Leonardo's Grotesques Heads. Prolegomena to Their Study*, in *Leonardo. Saggi e Ricerche*, a cura di G. Castelfranco, Roma, Istituto Poligrafico dello Stato, 1954, later recalled in Id., *Il metodo di analisi e permutazione di Leonardo da Vinci. Le teste grottesche*, in *L'eredità di Apelle. Studi sull'arte del Rinascimento*, Torino, Einaudi, 1986.

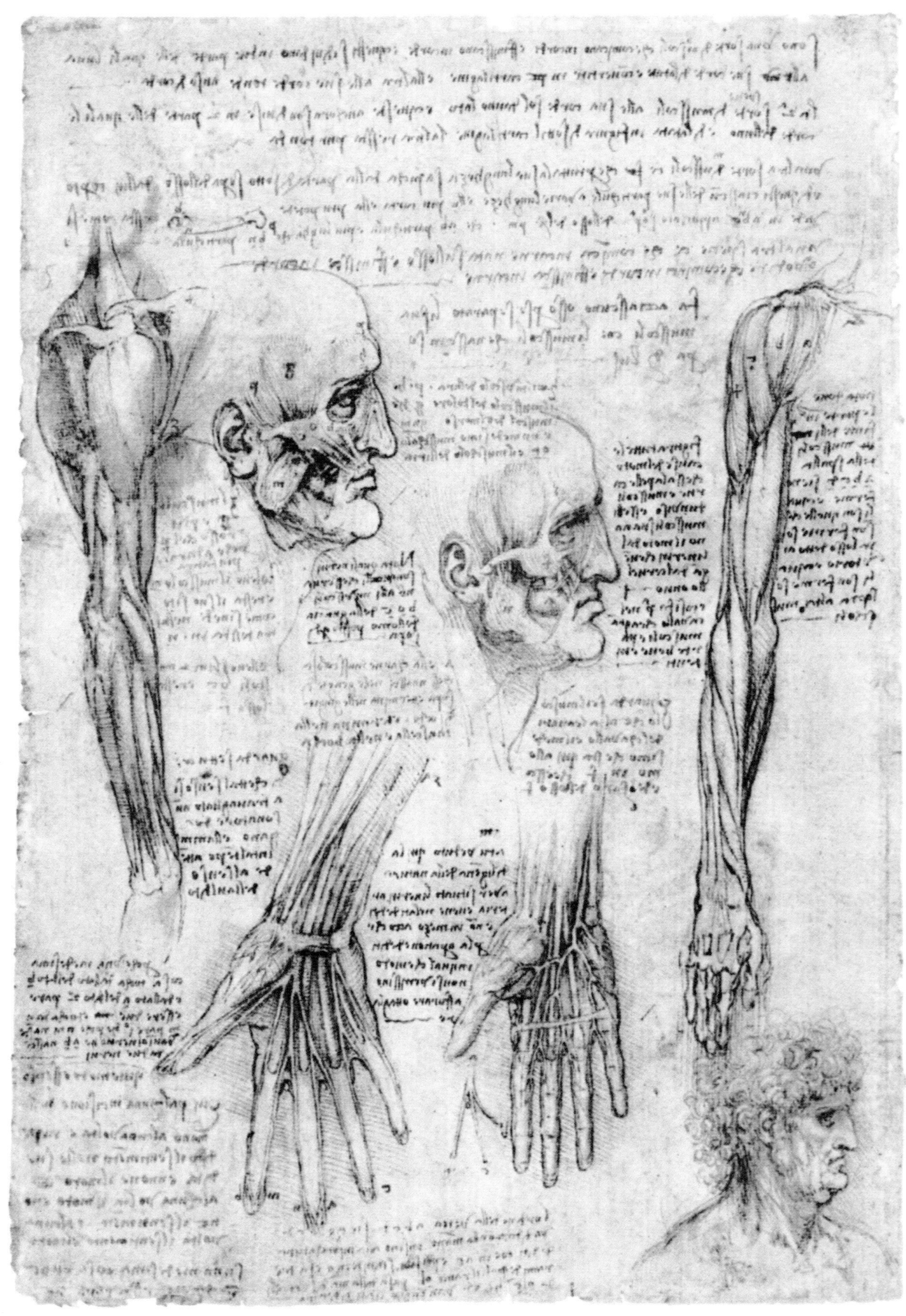

Leonardo da Vinci, *Study on the muscles of the arm, of the hand and of the face. Profile of a man*, 1510. Pen and tawny ink, watercolour on traces of charcoal, 228 x 200 mm. Windsor, RL 19012 *v*

ing deformation of the «frustrated ideal of his youth»,[30] sign of a singular scientific interest for «the aberrations of the human species» to the eyes of Eugène Müntz, that saw Leonardo as a forerunner of Darwin, as he would have been of the Freudian unconscious, according to Flavio Caroli,[31] who has considered him also as the inventor of the physiognomic portrait, following his influences up to the grotesque drawings of the brothers Agostino (1557-1602) and Annibale Carracci (1560-1609), that operated in Bologna and in Rome, between the end of the sixteenth and the beginning of the seventeenth century, making the most, for their own admission, in relation to the motion and the action of the figures as well as to the graded expression of feelings and passions of the various personages, of the reading of the theoretical reflections contained in the *Trattato della Pittura* by Leonardo.[32] It would have been precisely André Félibien, in his *Entretiens sur les vies et les ouvrages des plus excellens peintres anciens et modernes* [33] (1672), to testify that Annibale Carracci was used to repeat that «if in his youth he had read those precepts that the golden book of Lionardo contains, he would have saved to himself twenty years of work». If, for Adolfo Venturi, in those drawings «the scientist got the upper hand over the painter»,[34] with Wilhelm Suida they begun to be interpreted as studies on the human character imprinted in grotesque faces.[35] Michael W. Kwakkelstein,[36] aligning himself to the position of Hans Klaiber,[37] has instead assumed in those studies of physiognomy the leonardian attempt of giving an artistic shape to the «mental motions», for didactic reasons. Also U. Reisser, even though emphasizing the imitative value of those portraits, has brought to light the objective research of Leonardo in defining, through drawing, all the emotional possibilities of the human face.[38] While, more recently, Domenico Laurenza has confirmed, extending the theses of Ludwig H. Heydenreich,[39] that the physiognomic and anatomical researches, they are anything but «the faces of a same plan of study of the human figure», where Leonardo achieved his most original moment with his cranial studies (*c.* 1489), establishing the direct connection between the common sense and the shape of bones.[40] As regards the passion of Leonardo to portray accurately grotesque and caricatural heads, it was the same Vasari to remind it and to testify that he had come into possession of some examples made in pen and charcoal, later kept in his «Book of Drawings», mentioned in the text of the second edition of the *Lives* (1568): «On this side you can see many heads both of females and of males, and I have drawn many of them with my own hand with the pen, in our book of drawings so many times mentioned, as it was that one of Amerigo Vespucci, which it is a most beautiful head of an old man made in coal and similarly the one of Scaramuccia, captain of the Gypsies, that then had Master Donato Valdambrini of Arezzo canon of San Lorenzo and that was left to him by Giambullari».[41] From these information, we learn that the large portrait of the «Scaramuccia, captain of the Gypsies», made in charcoal (cm 38 x 26,5), between 1500 and 1505, and at present kept in the collections of the Governing Body, Christ Church Library of Oxford, belonged to the canon Donato Valdambrini of Arezzo.[42] This drawing,

[30]   See A. E. POPHAM, *The Drawings of Leonardo da Vinci*, London, Cape, 1946.
[31]   See E. MÜNTZ, *Leonard da Vinci: Artist, Thinker, and Man of Science*, 2 vols, London/New York, Heinemann, 1898.
[32]   See F. CAROLI, *Leonardo. Studi di fisiognomica*, Milano, Leonardo, 1991; ID., *Storia della Fisiognomica*, Milano, Leonardo, 1995; ID., *Fisiognomica come nuovo umanesimo*, «Achademia Leonardi Vinci. Journal of Leonardo Studies and Bibliography of Vinciana», VIII, Firenze, Giunti, 1995; ID., *L'Anima e il Volto. Ritratto e fisiognomica da Leonardo a Freud*, catalogo mostra, Milano, Electa, 1998. For the relationship of Annibale Carracci with the *Trattato della Pittura* of Leonardo see C. PEDRETTI, *The Dart Caster*, «Achademia Leonardi Vinci. Journal of Leonardo Studies and Bibliography of Vinciana», IX, Firenze, Giunti, 1996.
[33]   «Essays about the lives and the works of the most excellent ancient and modern painters», Tr. N.
[34]   See A. VENTURI, in «L'Arte», XXV, 1922.
[35]   See W. SUIDA, *Leonardo und sein Kreis*, München, Bruckmann, 1929.
[36]   See M. W. KWAKKELSTEIN, *Leonardo da Vinci's grotesque heads and the breaking of physiognomic mould*, in «Journal of the Warburg and Courtauld Institutes», IV, London, Warburg Institute, University of London, 1991; ID., *The Lost Book on 'moti mentali'*, «Achademia Leonardi Vinci. Journal of Leonardo Studies and Bibliography of Vinciana», VI, Firenze, Giunti, 1993; ID., *Teste di vecchi in buon numero*, «Raccolta Vinciana», XXV, Milano, 1993; ID., *Leonardo da Vinci as a physiognomist, Theory and drawing practise*, Leiden, Primavera Pers, 1994.
[37]   See H. KLAIBER, *Leonardo da Vinci's Stellung in der Geschichte der Physiognomik und Mimik*, in «Leonardostudien», Strasburg, Heitz, 1905.

[38]   See U. REISSER, *Physiognomik und Ausdruckstheorie der Renaissance. Der Einfluss charakterologischer auf Kunst und Kunsttheorie des 15. Und 16 Jahrhunderts*, München, Scaneg, 1997.
[39]   See L. H. HEYDENREICH, *Leonardo da Vinci als Klassiker der Kunst*, in «Kritische Berichte zur Kunstgeschichtlichen Literatur», III-IV, 1930-32; ID. *Leonardo*, Berlin, 1943. The author emphasized the relationship between the grotesque figures and the planned treatise of anatomy, in which also the subjects of the human expressiveness, the physiognomy, the muscular contractions and the canons of proportion would have been dealt with.
[40]   See D. LAURENZA, *La 'Fisonomia naturale' di Leonardo: una traccia giovanile e alcuni sviluppi*, «Achademia Leonardi Vinci. Journal of Leonardo Studies and Bibliography of Vinciana», IX, Firenze, Giunti, 1996; ID., *La 'composizione del corpo'. Fisiognomica ed embriologia in Leonardo*, «Nuncius. Annali di storia della scienza», XIII, Firenze, Olschki, 1998; ID., *Uomini bestiali. Leonardo da Vinci e le sue fonti*, «Micrologus», VIII, 2000; ID., *De Figura Umana…*, 2001, op. cit.
[41]   PIERFRANCESCO GIAMBULLARI (1495-1555), after having been, as Donato Valdambrini, canon of San Lorenzo (1515), where the two perhaps were on good terms of friendship, was one of the intellectuals nearer to Cosimo I, celebrating him with madrigals and intervals since the day of the wedding with Eleonora from Toledo (6 July 1539), daughter of the viceroy of Naples. He was therefore an enthusiastic supporter of the «Florentine Academy» (1541) and composed, beyond to *De 'l sito, forma e misure dello Inferno di Dante* (1544) and to the *Lezzioni* (1551), the *Gello* (1546). The narration of the arrival from Egypt of Hercules in Tuscany, that becomes a mediator as a cosmic force between the natural elements and the organized life of men, would have legitimated the dominion of Cosimo on the entire region, as his heir and modern ruler. See A. D'ALESSANDRO, *Il «Gello» di Pierfrancesco Giambullari…1980, op. cit.*
[42]   With relation to the chronological problem of the dispersion of the drawings of the collection, we know that some of them were already sold from Giorgio Vasari, grandson of the much more illustrious homonymous, others, as remembers Pietro Vasari, were donated, on 29 June 1574, to Francesco I: «Which book

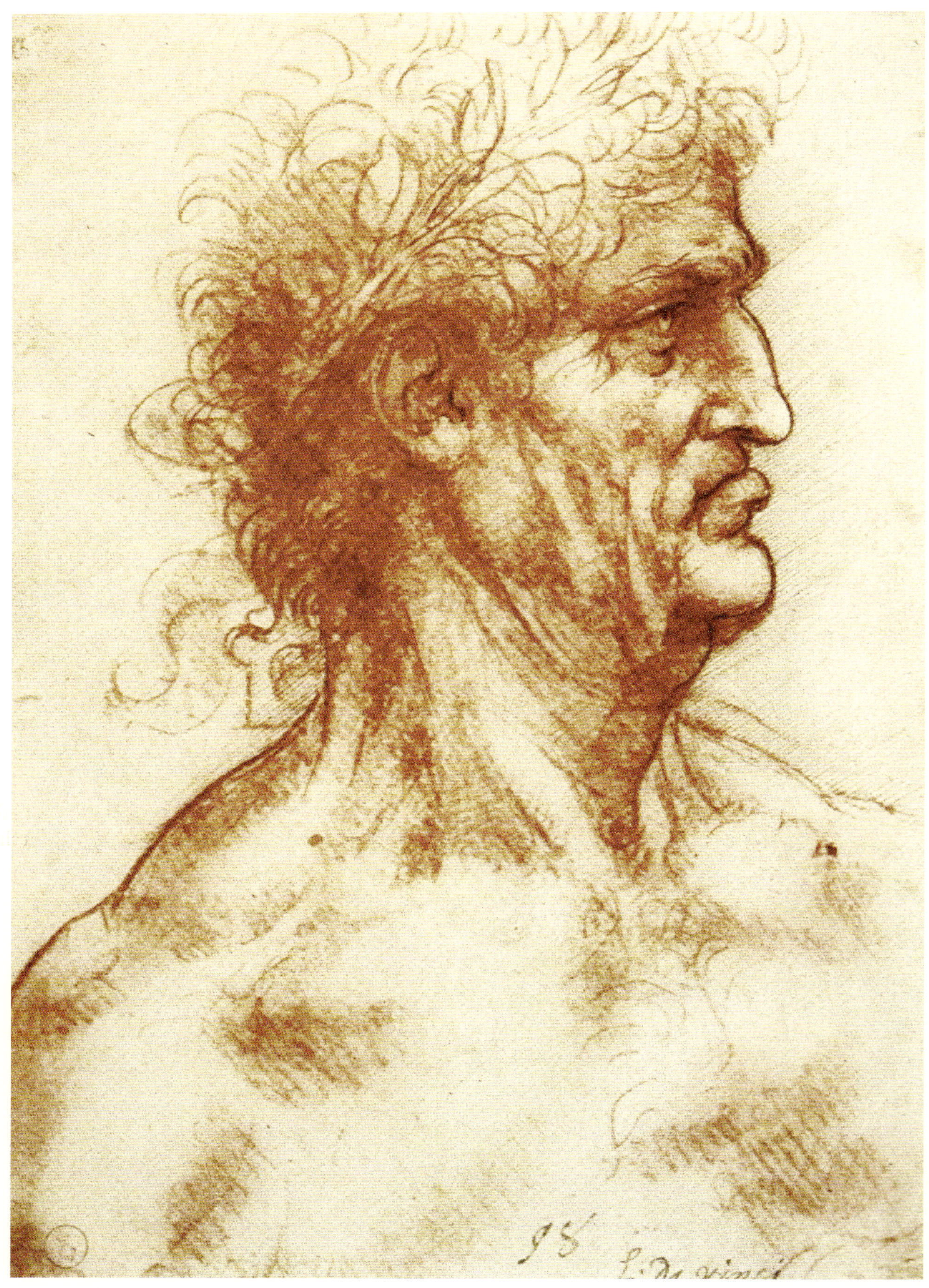

Leonardo da Vinci, *Profile and bust of a man, c.* 1506. Turin, Biblioteca Reale

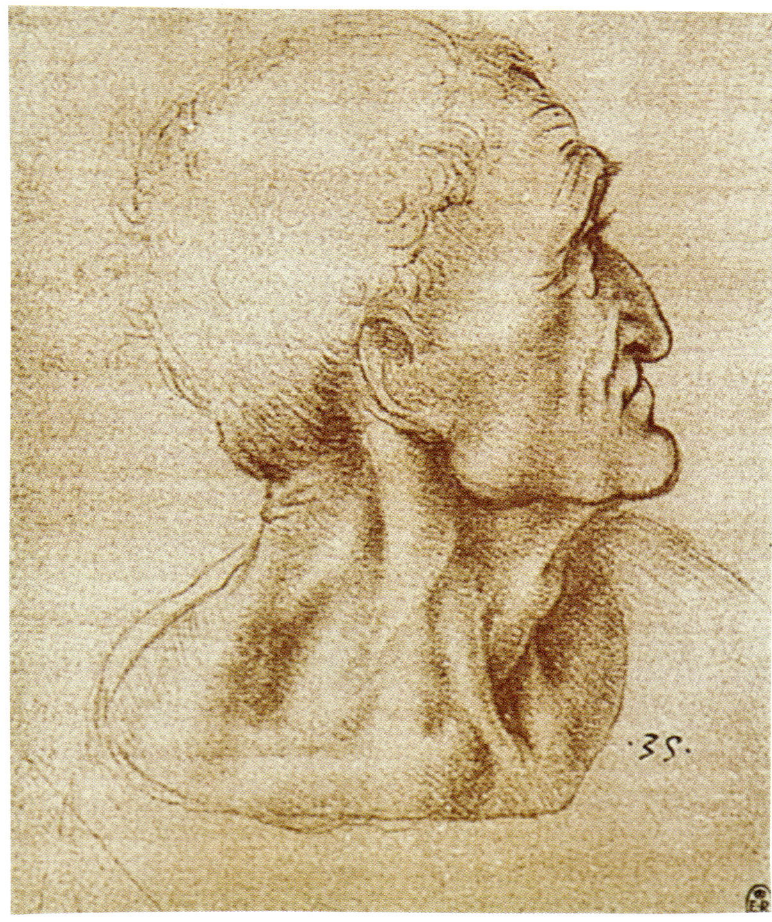

LEONARDO DA VINCI, *Study of a head for the Last Supper (Judas)*, *c.* 1495. Sanguine on prepared red–orange paper, 180 x 150 mm. Windsor, RL 12547

identified by Bernard Berenson like the head of Scaramuccia the captain of the Gypsies, arrived to Oxford thanks to

was a rare joy and we bring it to His Highness, because he sent to ask for it through the Seignior Bart.o Concini and master Tanai de' Medici and together we brought him the model of the cupola of S. Maria del Fiore […] which things both the book and the model were much appreciated by His Highness and he promised us for the memory of our uncle that we shall be always recommended to him». See FRITS LUGT, *Les marques de collection des dessins et d'estampes*, Amsterdam, *Supplément*, La Haye, 1921, II *Suppl.*, The Hague, 1956; B. BERENSON, *I disegni dei pittori fiorentini*, 3 voll., Milano, Electa, 1961; E. PANOFSKY, *La prima pagina del «Libro» del Vasari*, in *Il significato delle arti visive*, Torino, Einaudi, 1962; B. DEGENHART, A. SCHMITT, *Methoden Vasaris bei der Gestaltung seines Libro. in Studien zur toskanischen Kunst, Festschrift für L. H. Heydenreich*, München, Lotz and Möller, 1964; J. BYAM SHAW, *The Collection of Drawings at Chist Church Oxford*, «Master Drawings», VI, 3, 1968; L. RAGGHIANTI COLLOBI, *Il Libro de' Disegni del Vasari*, Firenze, Vallecchi, 1974. The information transmitted by L. FAGANS (*Collectors' Marks*, London, 1883) and took up again by T. MIOTTI (*Il collezionista di disegni*, Venezia, Neri Pozza, 1962) turns out to be entirely without foundation, according to which the «famous book of drawings made up by Vasari» would have been in possession of the Bishop of Arezzo, Mons. Giovan Matteo Marchetti, at the beginning of the eighteenth century, and that such collection, that would have numbered a conspicuous amount of important works, would have been sold by a grandson of his, in 1710, to Lord John Somers, whose collection was put up for auction in Paris on 10 December 1759.

the Duke of Guise, patron of the Christ Church, that would have acquired it from the famous Franco-Dutch collector and supplier Salomon Gautier, ready to recover the drawings of the Vasari of the famous *Book* between the end of the seventeenth and the beginnings of the eighteenth century on the market of Amsterdam or in England, like the drawings of Leonardo for the *Recueil de testes de caractère*, arrived to him from the Arundel family, after the passage in the collection both of Sir Peter Lely and of the van der Schelling family. In fact, its belonging to the «Book» of Master Giorgio would be justified not only by the residues of the edge with a declared «fifteenth century» simplicity, but also by the employment of the name in capital letters that appears there and by the tracing over made by another hand and according to the use of the Vasari. The drawing furthermore turns out to have been pierced for pouncing, so that it can be assumed that it has been used for a painting now lost.

The grotesque profile of this man, curiously portrayed from the back, is marked with a strong realism, above all for the attachment of the «nutcracker-like» nose on the strong over-

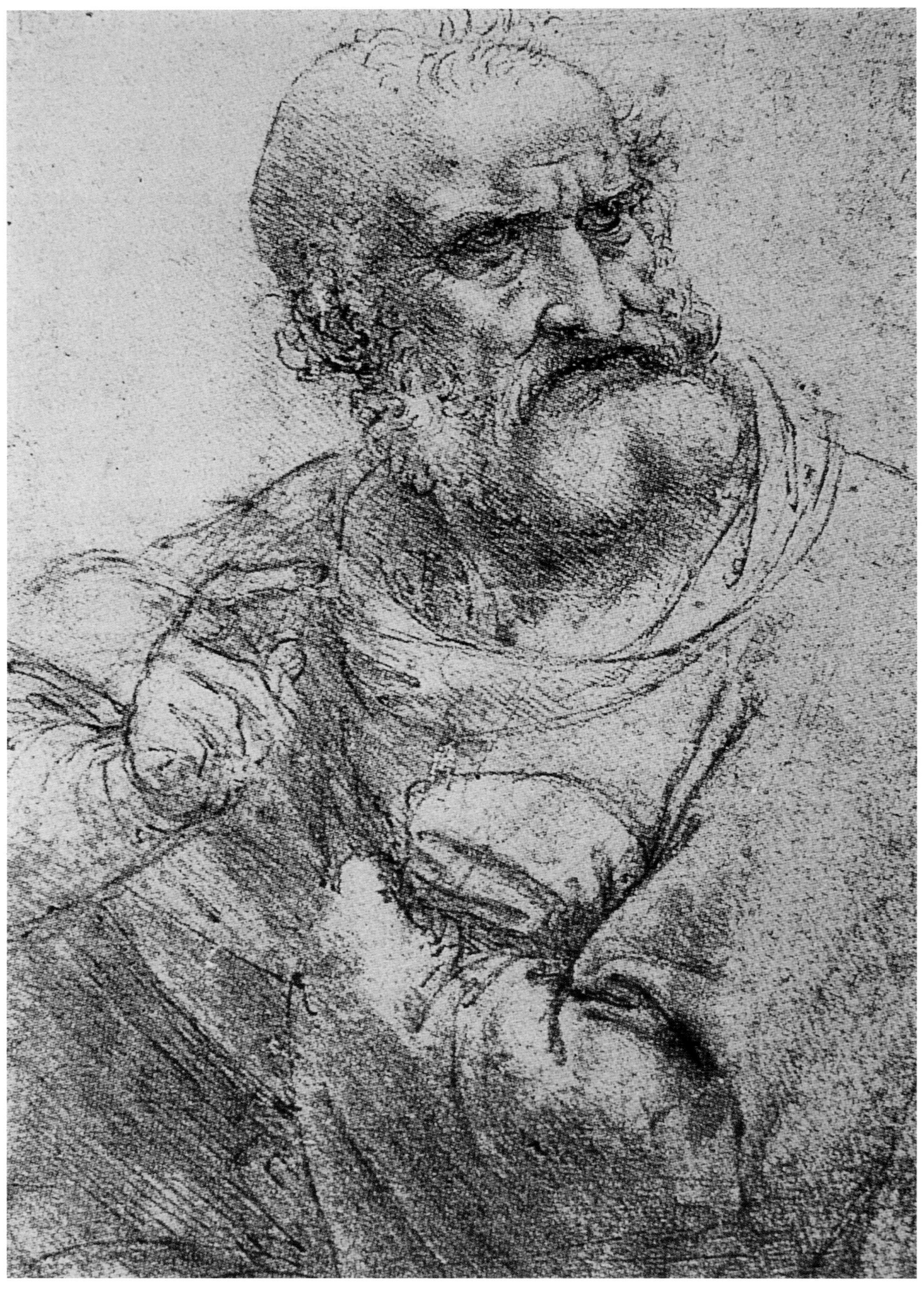

LEONARDO DA VINCI, *Study of a virile figure for the Last Supper (Peter?)*, *c.* 1495. Silver point, pen and ink on prepared blue paper, 146 x 113 mm. Vienna, Graphische Sammlung Albertina, n. 17614

CARLO STARNAZZI

orbital projection and for the contraction of the chin that emphasizes in an exaggerated way the expansion and the swelling up of the lips protruding as a beak. Aspects even more emphasized by the development of the double bag of his chinstrap and by the vitalist expression of his thick, curly and ruffled hair. Physiognomic characters that send back to the psychosomatic connection of a particular irascible temperament, that develops the leonardian concept of the potential human animality, as instinctual and arrogant force of nature, related to a human subject of «little reason».

In Leonardo, hair too, in the analogy between man and earth, turn out to be expression of a particular character and, if it is smooth it is manifestation of shyness, if bristly and curly of great natural force,[43] while its flowing is anchored to the secret motions of universal life (Windsor, RL 12579 r):

> *Notice the motion of the veil of water, which behaves in the way of hair, that it has two motions, of which one follows the weight of the veil, the other the aligning of the vaults; therefore water has its vertiginous vaults of which a part follows the strength of the main course, the other one follows the incident and reflected motion.*

Previous to it, turns out to be the so-called «Vasari Sheet» (cm 49,3 x 37,3) that, once property of the great biographer of Arezzo and now at the Albertina of Vienna, contains drawings of figures in half-length, of heads alone or of profile, made in pen, bistre and watercolour, that seem to send back to the the first Florentine period, when the young Leonardo still inspired, for practice, to the celebrated nudes drawn in pen by Pollaiolo (Florence, Uffizi, Gabinetto dei Disegni e delle Stampe; Paris, Louvre, Cabinet des Dessins), above all as regards the image, placed at the centre on the left margin, for who observes, as it has well demonstrated Domenico Laurenza (1996; 2001).

Among the drawings of the Albertina belonged to the «Book» of Vasari there is also the famous profile of an old man, encircled by an evocative chiaroscuro and contained in a most elegant square border decorated with large masks and allegorical figures, that many have identified with Savonarola, but that does not seem to be attributable to Leonardo (as its heading would like to credit: «Dessein de Leonardo da Vinci tiré du Cabinet de M. Crozat et originairement du Livre de Vasari»). They turn out to be instead of sure leonardian autography the six caricatures placed along the margins of the «Vasari Sheet», that the historian of Arezzo could acquire during his activity of documentary search, with a consisting number of other drawings.

The «Sheet», that brings in the scroll the writing «Lionardo da Vinci» and that in its shape is divided by frames inspired to decorated walls, with elements that recall the classic world and much beloved in the sixteenth century, as volutes, draperies, fantastic animals and marble frames, arrived to the Albertina passing first in the collection of prince Charles de Ligne and of Anne Claude Philippe Thubière, that is the Earl of Caylus (1692-1795), engraver, collector and archaeologist, author of the *Recueil d'Antiquités* (1759), supporter of a new aesthetics of classic inspiration, friend of Pierre Jean Mariette (1694-1774) and perhaps responsible for having cut and pasted in one only sheet, for their thematic singularity, four caricatures of heads, already possessed by Pierre Crozat (1661-1740), that boasted one of the richest French graphical collections.[44]

Alien to the leonardian style turn out to be, instead, the head of the woman and the young Saint John the Baptist, inserted in the «Sheet» during the eighteenth century, and both attributable to Lorenzo di Credi.

The Earl of Caylus had also engraved the reproductions of the drawings of Leonardo contained in the *Recueil de testes de caractère* of Mariette, that, in the introductory *Lettre* (reproduced with translation in Italian also by Bottari, 1822-25), sustained: «Lionardo, that had the nobler intentions, made them in order to study passions. A quick-tempered, scornful, stupid man, has always his character painted on his face. Lionardo by means of this study had become a great physiognomist».

If truth has to be told, the theory of the interrelation between physical aspect and emotional state, that will turn out to be also subsequently a recurrent theoretical and artistic motive, from the engravings by Jacques Callot (1592-1635) to the paintings by William Hogarth (1697-1764), it is already present in Leonardo in the mimic of certain juvenile caricatures and it will persist up to the creation of the splendid grotesque heads, realized around 1494 and later on.

Hogarth had derived, as reference of his composition, from the *Last Supper* of Leonardo and the attitude of the Apostles for some of his figurations saturated of refined sarcasm as in *The Banquet* of 1754, where, beyond to the thirteen guests, placed round to a rectangular table and a round one, the cobbler that clasps the hand of the old candidate reminds the group of Judas, Peter and John. But already in his engrav-

---

[43]   Leonardo, in his theory on the «variety» of art (*Libro di Pittura*, ff. 59v-60, *cap.* 178), mentions briefly the consequential relationship between character and hair: «In the stories there must be men of various complexions, age, flesh-colour, attitudes, fatnesses, thinnesses; outsized, thin, large, small, fat, skinny, proud, urban, old, young, strong and muscular, weak and with little muscles, cheerful, melancholic, and with hair curly and extended».

[44]   See G. Bottari, S. Ticozzi, *Raccolta di lettere sulla pittura, scultura ed architettura, scritte da' più celebri personaggi dei secoli XV, XVI e XVII e continuata fino ai nostri giorni da Stefano Ticozzi*, Milano, Silvestri, 1822-25.

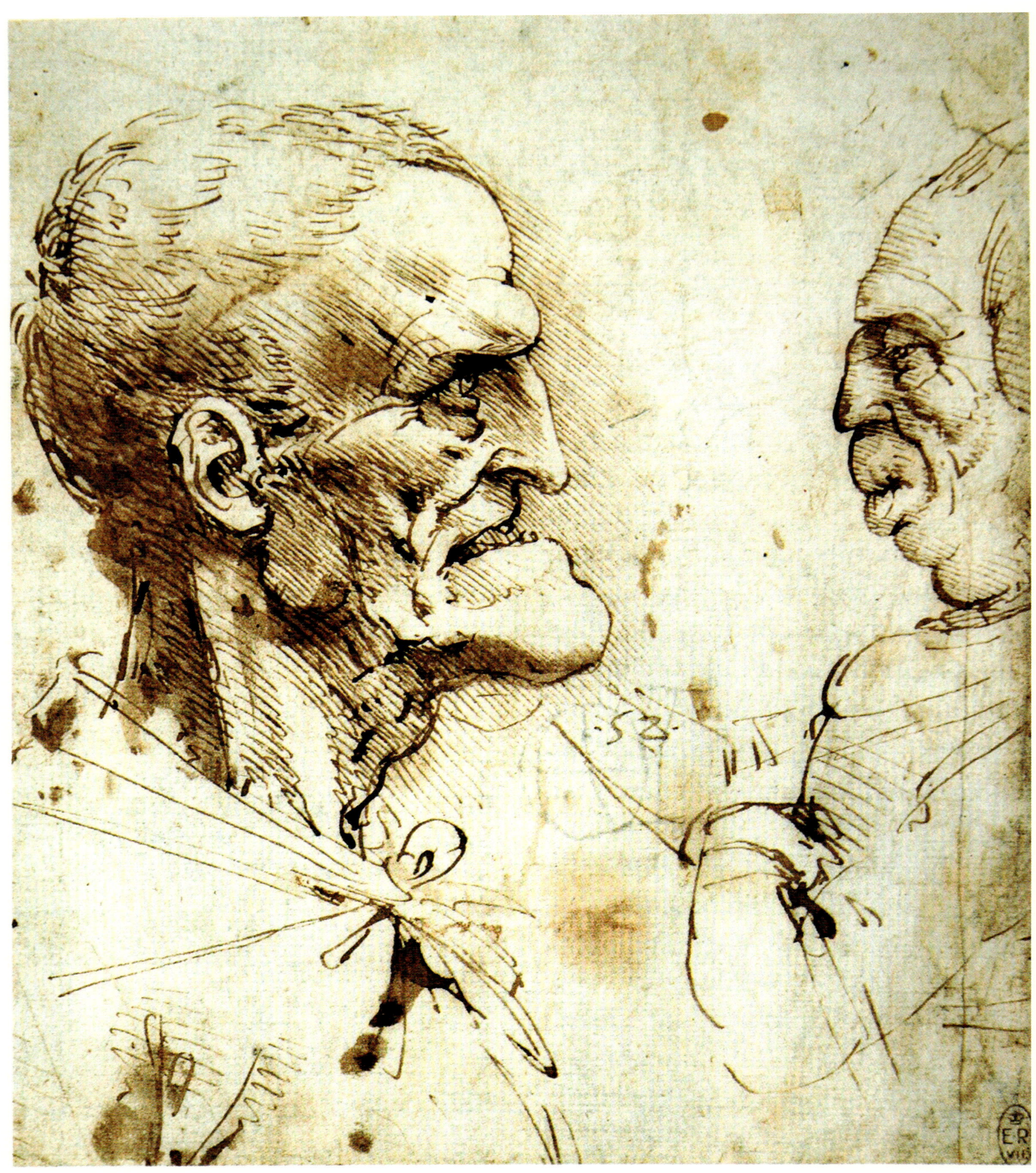

Leonardo da Vinci, *Two facing grotesque profiles*, *c.* 1487–90. Pen and ink and watercolour, 163 x 143 mm. Windsor, RL 12490

Carlo Starnazzi

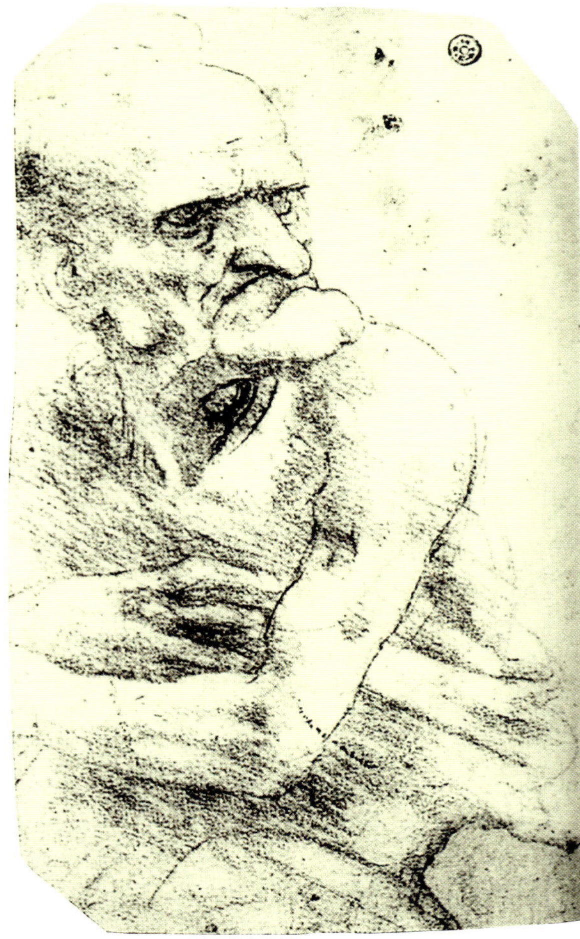

LEONARDO DA VINCI, *Caricatural study of an old man, c.* 1490-95. Rome, Gabinetto Nazionale Disegni e Stampe, n. 8 *r*

ings, with refined and grotesque effects, he reveals his dependency from certain caricatured heads of Leonardo, well recognizable in the last figures on the right of the *Grotesque* sheet. In fact, beyond to a certain knowledge of the precepts contained in the *Trattato della Pittura*, translated for the first time in England in 1721 and commonly used in copies that circulated among artists and lovers of humanities, he could have a precise idea of Leonardo as a draughtsman from the reproductions of the bookseller and printer Cooper, that had diffused in England about ten of his grotesque drawings, just around 1720.

Hence the many caricatures, scattered between the collection of the Castle of Windsor and the sheets of the Codex Atlanticus,[45] would have met a great success during the sev-

enteenth century, when they were copied, reinterpreted and spread in a series of prints, of which, the first, the etchings executed by Wenceslaus Hollar (1607-1677), from 1645 to 1651 («one hundred» according to the edition of Mariette of 1730 and «ninety», according to the one of 1767), perhaps in Antwerp, great economic and cultural centre of the Low Countries, where a diffused political and religious spirit of tolerance reigned too and where art with its bourgeois values had significantly changed its tastes, addressing them any more towards subjects celebrating a confessional client, but towards realistic portraits, faraway from whatever sort of idealization. Here, the artist, that had worked for the king Charles I, could shelter during the English civil war, and here again met Lord

---

[45] At the Ambrosiana there are kept twenty-seven original drawings of Leonardo which are part of funds F 263 inf., F 271 inf., F 274 inf., and of the Codex Resta, many of which have as a topic the study of profiles of old people and of

caricatures. See G. BORA, *I disegni del Codice Resta*, Milano, Silvana, 1978; M. ROSSI, *I disegni di Leonardo e della sua scuola*, in *L'Ambrosiana e Leonardo*, a cura di P. C. Marani, M. Rossi, A. Rovetta, introduzione di G. Ravasi, Novara, Tipografia San Gaudenzio, 1998.

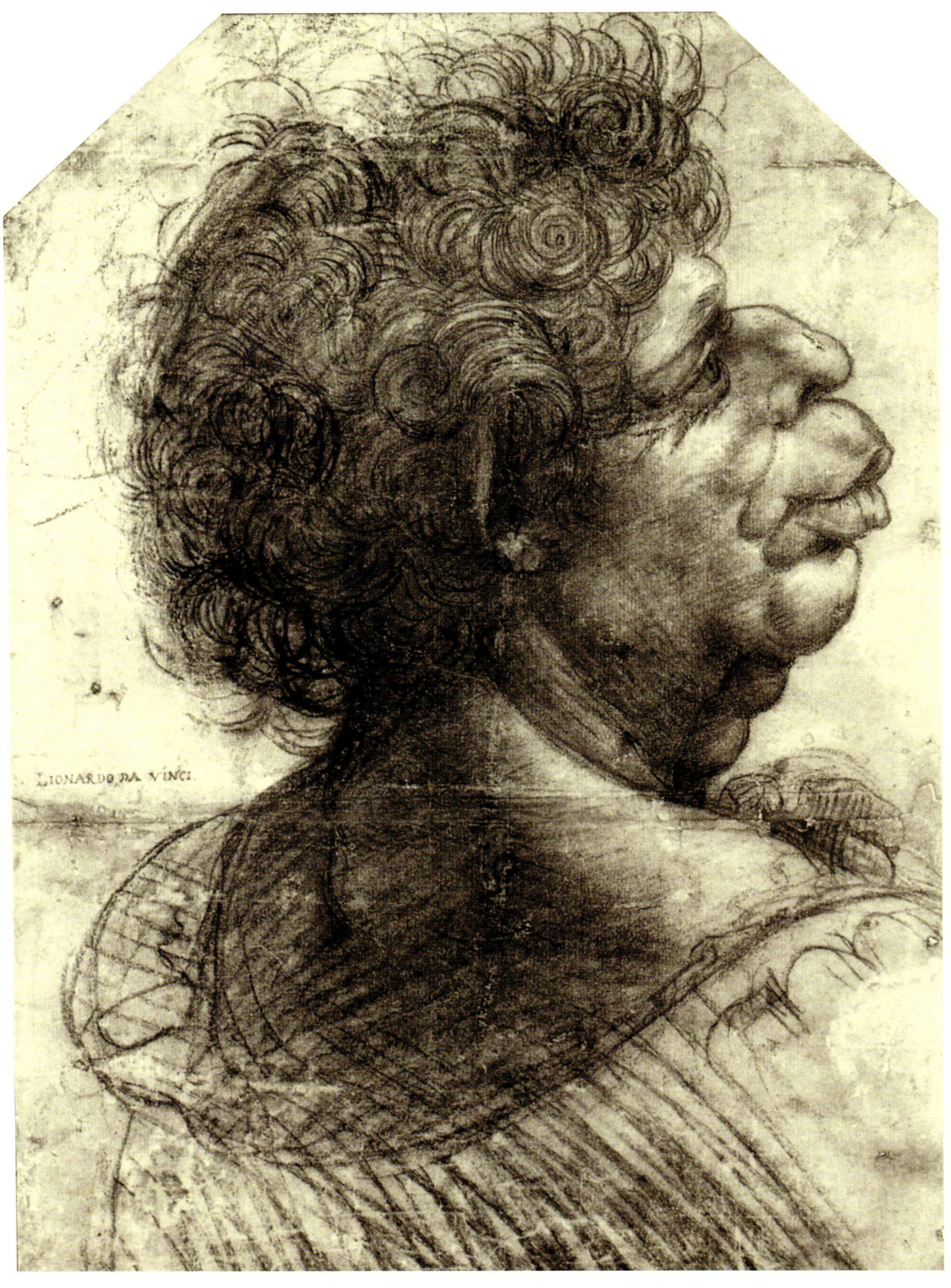

Leonardo da Vinci, *Grotesque portrait of Scaramuccia, captain of the Gypsies, c.* 1500-05. Charcoal, 390 x 280 mm. Oxford, The Governing Body, Christ Church, n. 0033

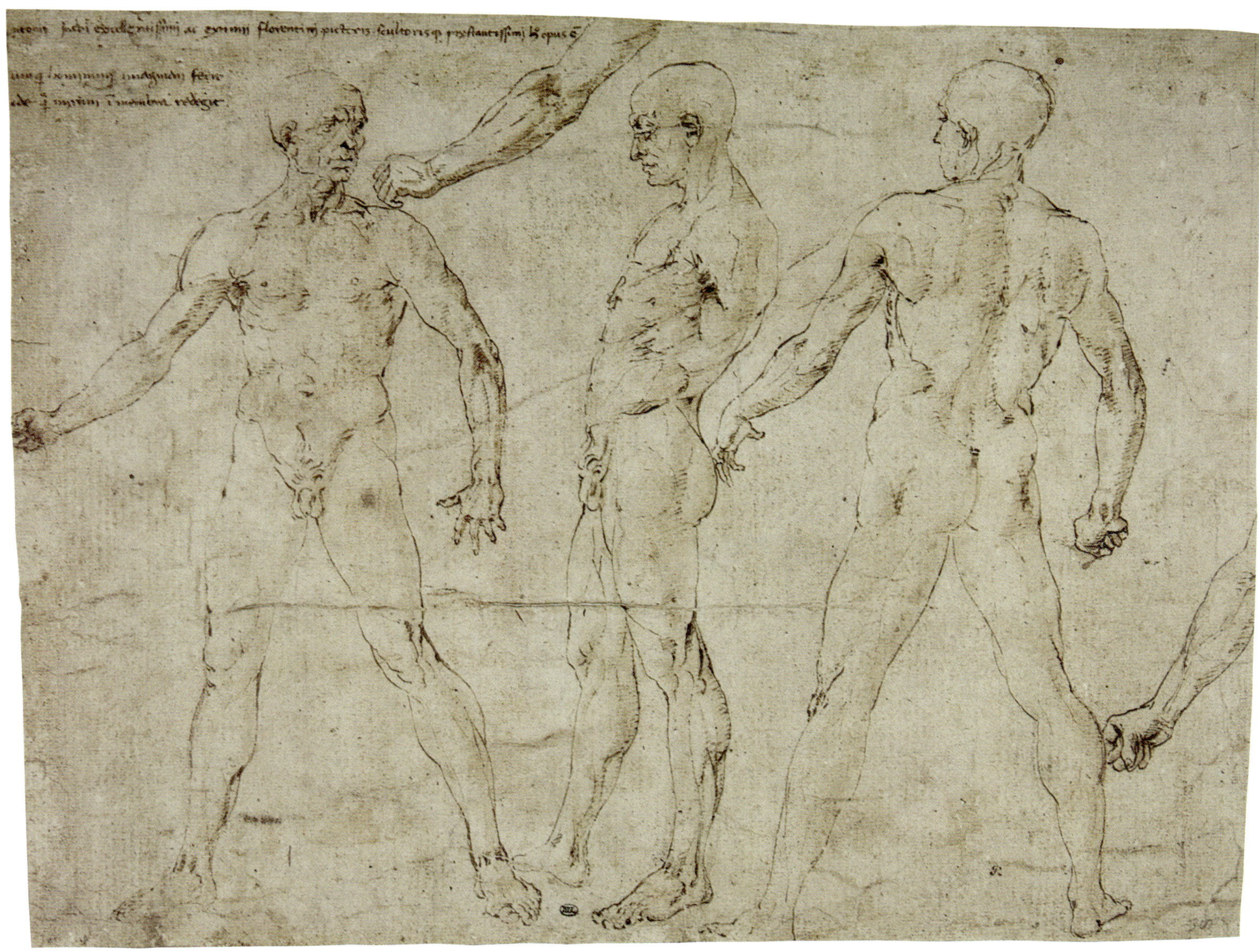

Antonio Pollaiolo, *Study of male nudes, c.* 1475. Paris, Musée du Louvre, Cabinet des Dessins, n. 1486

Thomas Howard, Earl and Marshal of England and of Arundel (1585-1646), his old patron and without doubt the greatest collector of England of the time (in fact almost all the etching caricatures of Hollar have drawn inspiration «Ex Collectione Arundeliana», probably from copies of drawings of Leonardo, previously seen in the private residence of the Earl of Arundel in London, to whose service the Bohemian artist remained from 1636 to 1641).

Sir Thomas Howard, a personage very much in the public eye in the Court of James I and Charles I, that had assigned him important charges of state and diplomatic missions, had enriched his imposing private collection with works of art acquired during his travels in Europe or by means of agents accredited at the various Courts like Sir Dudley Carlton, Sir Francis Cottington, Sir Thomas Roe, Lord Walter Aston of Forfar, Sir William Boswell or his «good Mr. Petty» «missus per Italiam ad conquirenda monumenta antiqua a Rege et a Comite Arundelio»[46], in 1635. In January 1636, the same George Conn, papal agent in London, would have informed Cardinal Francesco Barberini, Urban VIII grandson, that Lord Thomas Howard had acquired the Gaddi drawings, already belonged to Vasari, in virtue of the «recommendation of Your Eminence» and Gregorio Panzani reported he had seen, after lunch, «three books large like a Calepini[47], one all

---

[46] «sent by the King and the Earl of Arundel through Italy to get hold of ancient works of art» Tr. N.

[47] Ambrogio da Calepio from Bergamo, known as *Calepino* (*c.* 1435 – 1510),

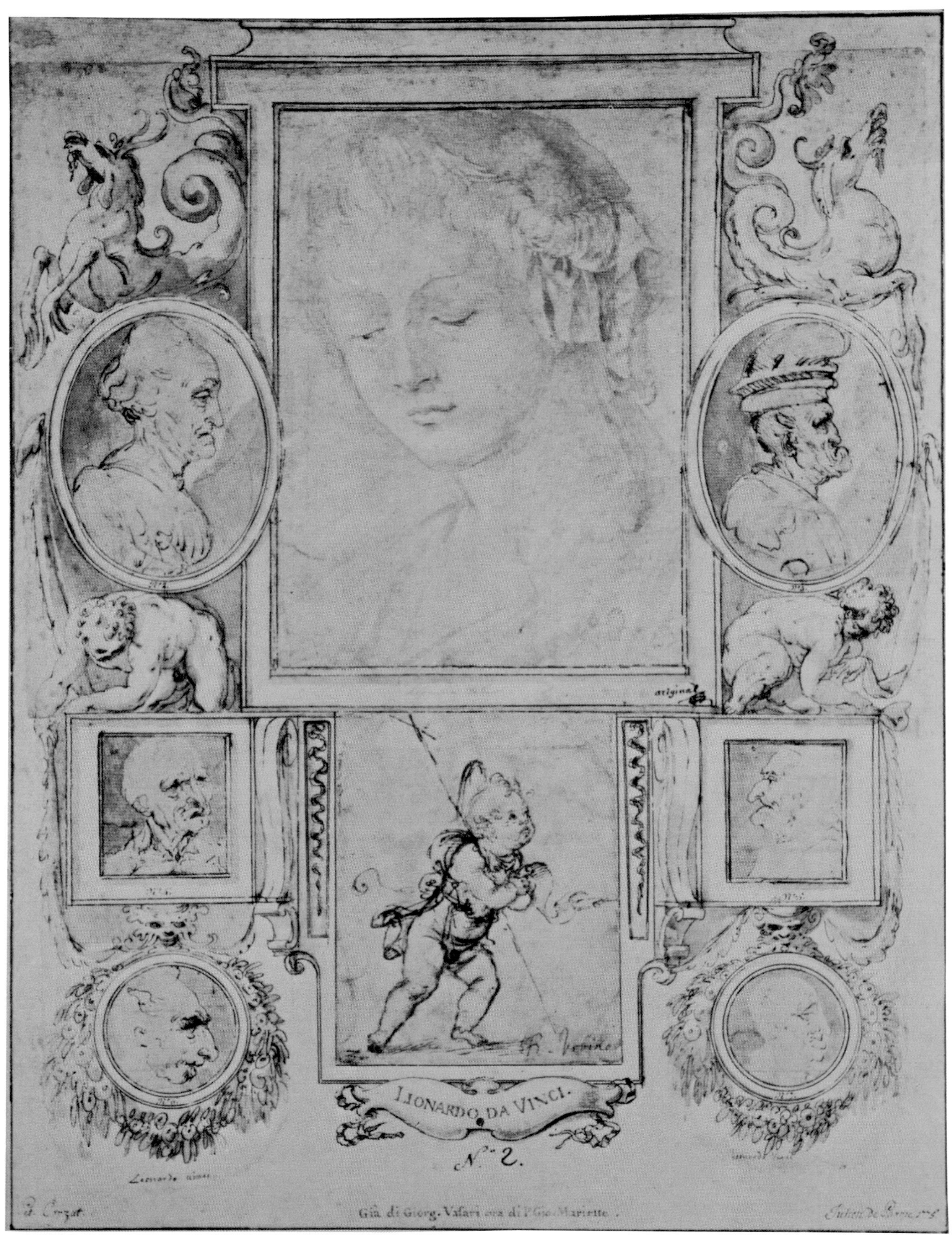

Leonardo da Vinci and Lorenzo di Credi (?), *The «Vasari Sheet»*, c. 1478-80. Pen and ink and watercolour, 493 x 373 mm. Vienna, Graphische Sammlung Albertina, n. 14179

of original drawings of Michelangelo, the other of Raphael, and the other of Leonardo da Vinci», today identifiable with the volume at Windsor. Leonardo was therefore known in England since the first decades of the seventeenth century and was appreciated to the same level of Raphael and Correggio, above all for his drawings, where he had revealed an extraordinary inventiveness in the morphologic variety of the heads. John Evelyn, friend of Lord Arundel, would have remembered in fact in his *Diary* to have seen, on 16 November 1676, at the Lord Chamberlain's, «one head of woman by Leonardo da Vinci».[48] Leonardo in fact had considered the creative force of the painter to be so divine, to transform him in «Lord of every sort of people and of all the things» (*Libro di Pittura, f. 5, cap.* 13), and being provided with «subtle speculation» (*Libro di Pittura, f. 4 v, cap.* 12), he was also the philosopher who knew how to pick and to make understand the upsetting of all the things in their contrary, since «the beautiful things with the ugly ones seem to be more powerful the one because of the other» (*Libro di Pittura, f.* 51, *cap.* 139). Therefore, the art duty was not only the Apollonian and celebrative invention of every equivalent aspect of the truth, but, under the push of a pessimistic impulse, its ability to know how to deform the truth until reaching, with mental and artistic amusement, a type of «eccentric ugliness»,[49]

a taste for the ridicule and the deformed, so widespread as a mask, in the theatre of life, where tragedy and comicality tend to finely co-penetrate.

Those faces, distorted and asymmetric, exasperated in their ugliness according to a delighted popular taste, that goes back to medieval iconography, met the interest of Leonardo for the errors of nature and for the human deformities, nonetheless vibrating of life and psychosomatic motion, in their qualities and defects. The opposition collected between the two categories of ugliness and beauty, after all, turned out to be expression of the entire development of human life. But Leonardo, as a theorist of the physiognomy and of the mimesis, had also suggested to the «good painter» to imitate the gestures of the persons that, lacking in voice, are forced by nature to avail themselves, not only of the motion of the eyes and of the eyelashes, but also of the gestures of the hands to express the inner signs of their mind, that is to say emotions and thoughts:[50]

Of the movements and of the various opinions. The figures of men must have an action appropriate to their operation so that, seeing them, you understand what they believe or say; which things will be well learnt <by> those who will imitate the motions of the dumb, which speak with the movements of the hands, and of the eyes and eyelashes and of all the persons, in the desire to express the concept of their mind, and do not laugh of me, because I appoint you a preceptor without tongue which has to teach you that art that he does not know how to make; because he will teach you better with facts, than

---

Augustinian monk, was the author of a celebrated *Dictionum interpretamenta* (published in Reggio Emilia in 1502), both Dictionary of the Latin language and Encyclopedia of the Classic world. Thanks to the popularity and most of all to the dimensions of his work, all the Dictionaries were once called in Italy «calepini». Tr. N.

[48] See *Characaturas by Leonardo da Vinci from Drawings by Wenceslaus Hollar out of the Portland Museum*, London, J. Clarke, 1786; A. E. POPHAM, *Leonardo's Drawings at Windsor*, «Atti del Convegno di Studi Vinciani», Firenze, Olschki, 1953; S. ALEXANDRE, *Wenzel Hollar*, in *Livres d'images. Images du livre. L'illustration du livre de 1501 à 1831 dans les collections de l'Université de Liège*, Bruxelles, Crédit Communal-Group Dexia, 1998; N. SCHNEIDER, *L'art du portrait. Les plus grandes oeuvres européennes 1420-1670*, Cologne, Taschen, 2000. For reports about the fame of Leonardo in England and more pieces of information about Lord Thomas Howard, see: J. EVELYN, *Memoires illustrative of the life and writings of John Evelyn comprising his diary from the yar 1641 to 1705-1706 and a selection of his familiar letters*, a cura di W. Bray, 2 vols, London, Colburn, 1818; A. GASQUET, *A History of the Venerable English College, Rome, an account of its origins and work from the earliest times to the present day*, London, Longmans Green, 1920; M. F. S. HERVEY, *The Life, Correspondence and Collections of Thomas Howard Earl of Arundel 'father of Vertu in England'*, Cambridge, Cambridge Univ. Press, 1921; D. SUTTON, *The Earl of Arundel as a Collector of Drawings*, «Burlington Magazine», I, Gennaio 1947; II, Febbraio 1947; III, Marzo 1947; D. HOWARTH, *Lord Arundel as an entrepreneur of the Arts*, «Burlington Magazine», CXXII, 1980; B. BARRYTE, *The 'Ill-Matched Couple'*, «Achademia Leonardi Vinci. Journal of Leonardo Studies and Bibliography of Vinciana », III, Firenze, Giunti, 1990; C. PEDRETTI, C. VECCE, *Leonardo da Vinci. Il Codice Arundel 263 nella British Library. Edizione in fac-simile nel riordinamento cronologico dei suoi fascicoli*, Firenze, Giunti, 1998. The Arundel House, Highgate, had given hospitality also to the philosopher Sir FRANCIS BACON, friend of Sir Thomas, when, suddenly taken ill during a travel, there he died on 9 April 1626.

[49] CHARLES BAUDELAIRE, expressing his opinion on the comedian-grotesque artistic manner of Leonardo, formulated the following conclusion: «All the artists know the caricatures of Leonardo da Vinci, are real portraits indeed. They do not lack in cruelty in their off-putting coldness but do so in comical quality; without abandonment, without a pleasant heartiness, the great artist worked with icy se-

riousness, as a geometrician, sage, or professor of natural history at the anatomical table. He took great care not to omit the smallest wart, the smallest hair. In the end it might well be that he did not have any intention to make caricatures but simply he wanted to look around himself and to copy examples of eccentric repulsiveness». See C. BAUDELAIRE, *Curiosités esthétiques*, Paris, Aubry, 1946; ID., *Scritti sull'arte*, Torino, Einaudi, 1992.

[50] In the *Last Supper*, beyond to the studies about the Apostles, Leonardo has left us some annotations on their attitudes, which let us catch a glimpse of the first starting plans of the fresco: «One that drank and left the cup in its place, and turned the head towards the speaker. Another interlaces the fingers of his hands and with rigid eyebrows turns to the companion. The other with his open hands shows the palms of those and raises his shoulders towards the ears and opens the mouth in wonder. Another one speaks in the ear to the other, and the one who is listening to him twists towards him and offers the ears holding a knife in one hand and in the other the bread divided in half by such knife. Another, turning himself while holding a knife in his hand, turns with such hand a cup over of the table. The other puts down the hands over the table and watches. The other blows on his mouthful. The other is bending in order to look at the speaker and shades with the hand his eyes. The other places himself behind the bending one and looks at the speaker between the wall and the bending one». J. P. RICHTER, *The Literary Work of Leonardo da Vinci…*, 1883, *op. cit.*; C. PEDRETTI, *Così si «maravigliava» Leonardo da Vinci*, 2005, *op. cit.*: according to the art historian, the expression of wonder is rendered by Leonardo with fixed eyebrow and tighten mouth, as in the representation of the apostle Andrew who «with his opened hands, shows the palms of those, and raises the shoulders towards the ears and opens the mouth in wonder». But in the *Last Supper*, as a sign of astonishment, we have also opened and half-closed mouths, as in the case of the apostle James the Greater, on the right of Christ.

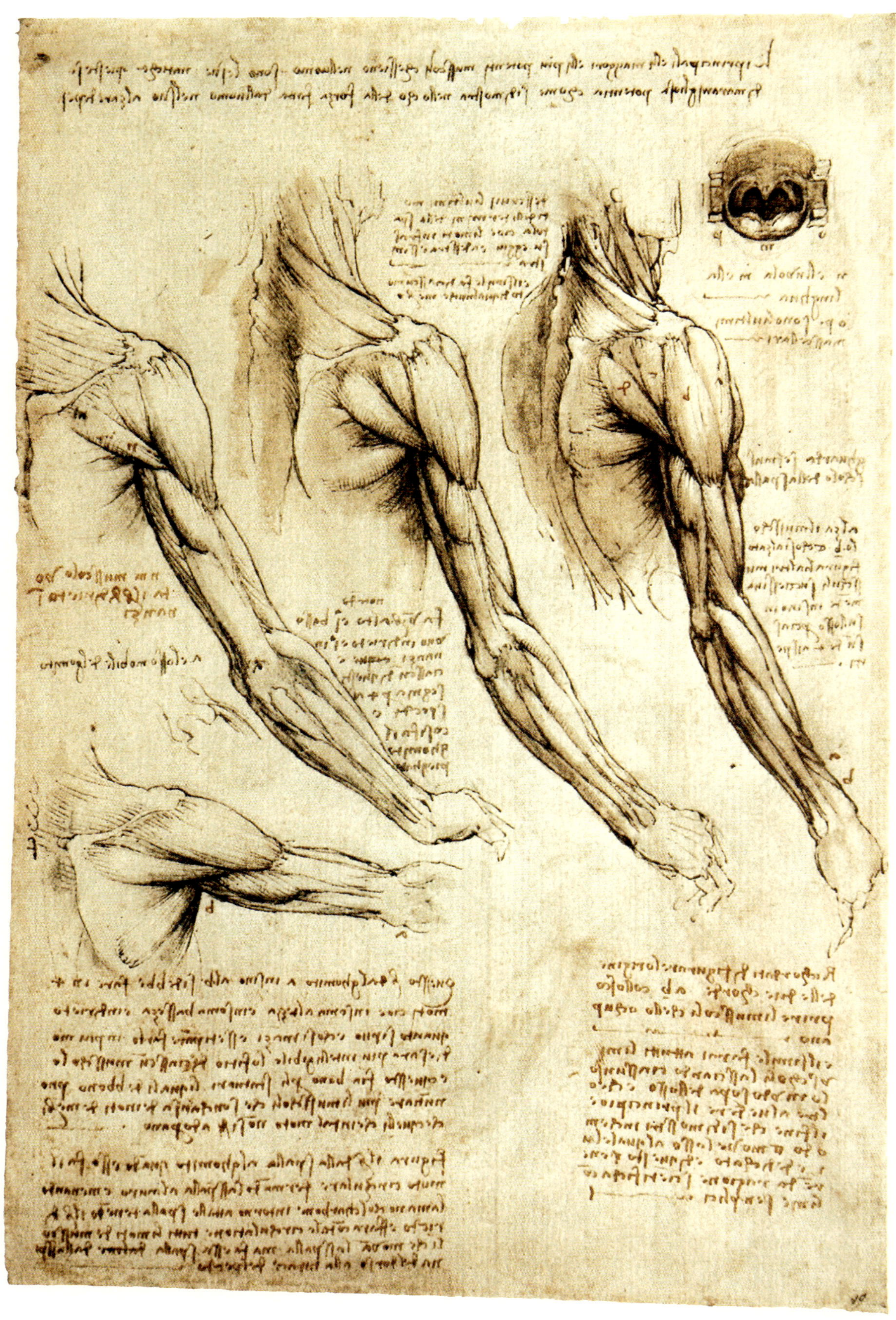

Leonardo da Vinci, *Study on the muscles of the arm, c. 1510-11.* Pen and tawny ink, watercolour on traces of charcoal, 228 x 200 mm. Windsor, RL 19005 *v*

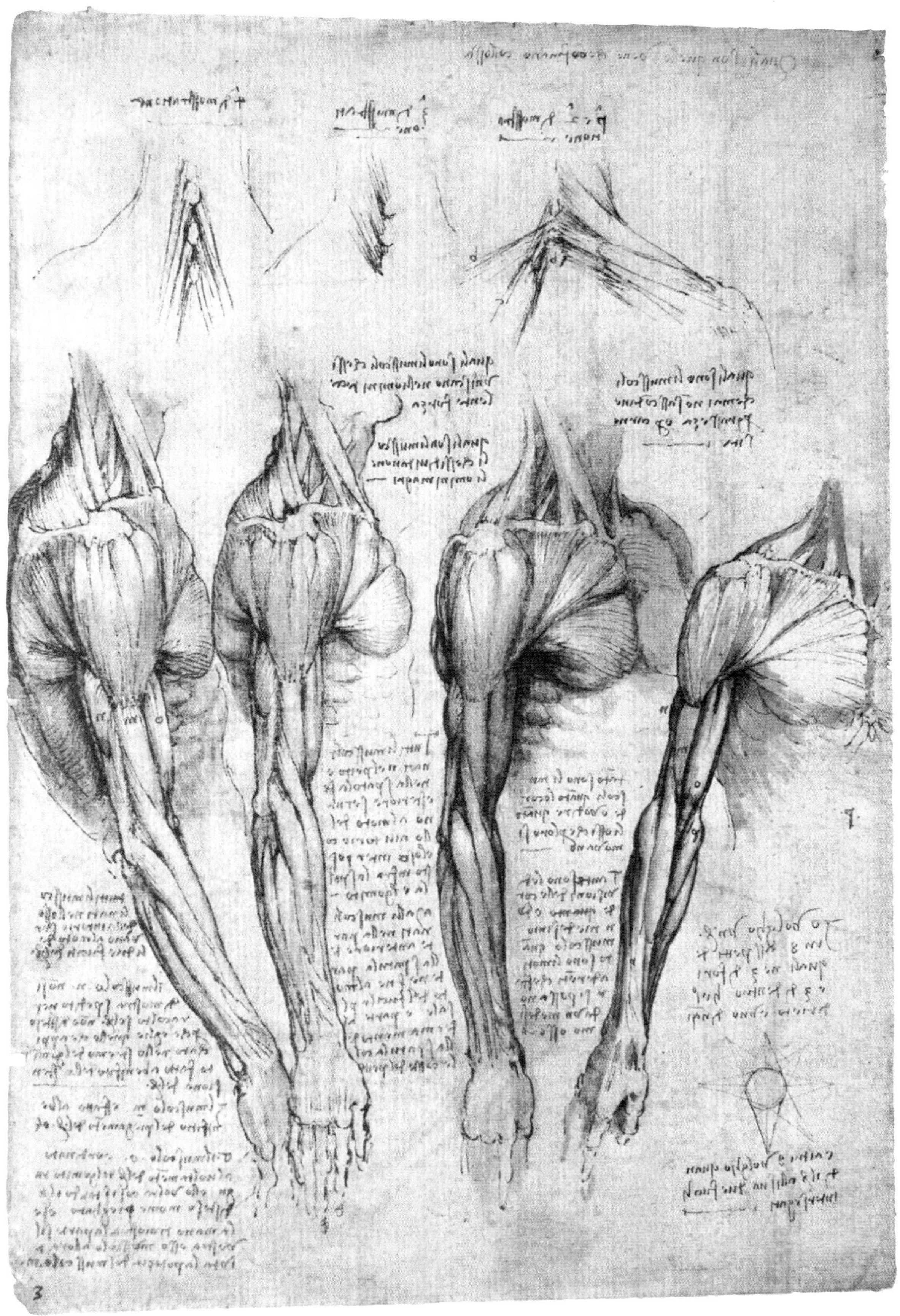

Leonardo da Vinci, *Study on the muscles of the right arm, c.* 1510-11. Pen and tawny ink, watercolour on traces of charcoal, 228 x 201 mm. Windsor, RL 19008 *v*

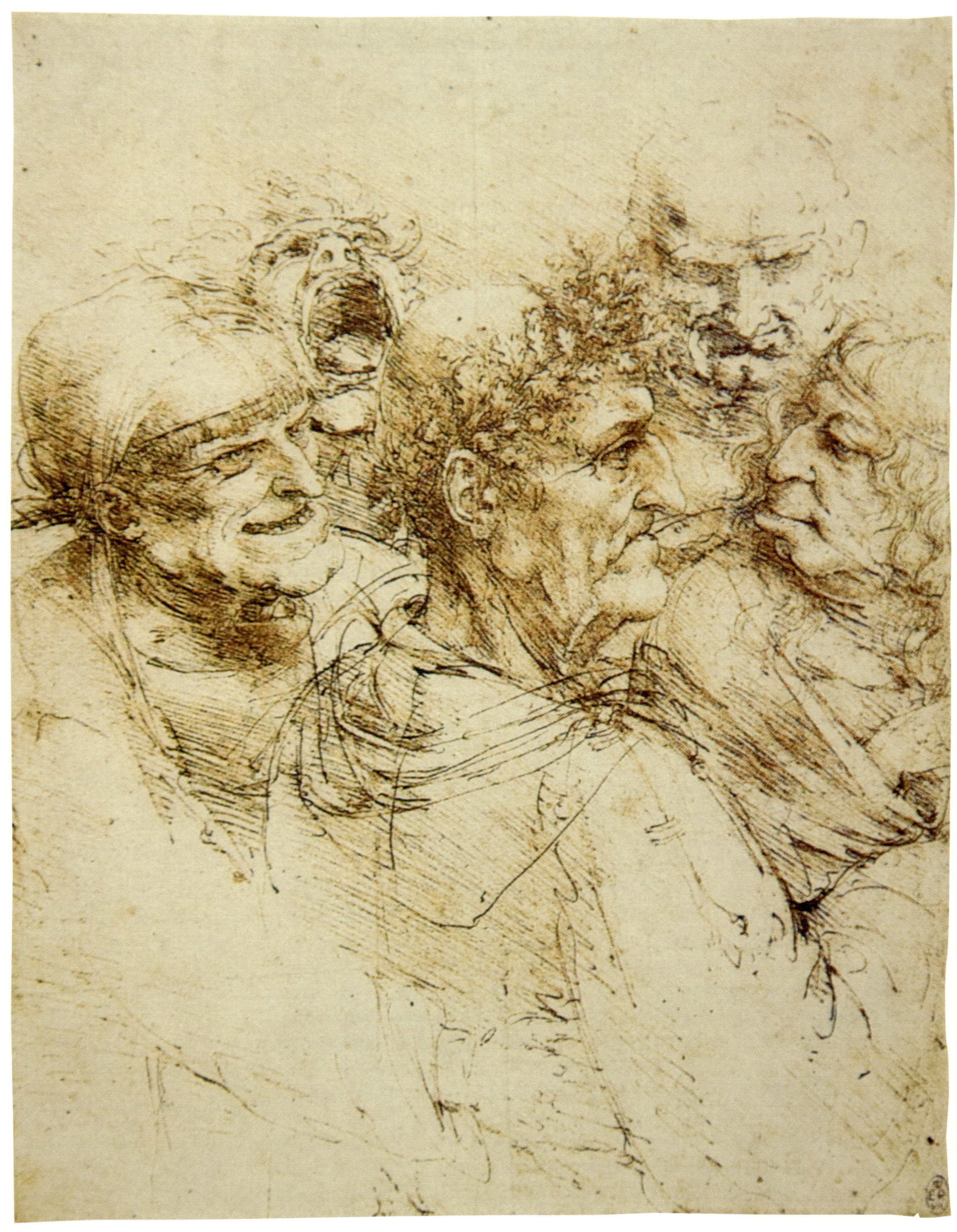

Leonardo da Vinci, *Five grotesque heads*, c. 1490. Pen and ink, 261 x 206 mm. Windsor, RL 12495 *r*

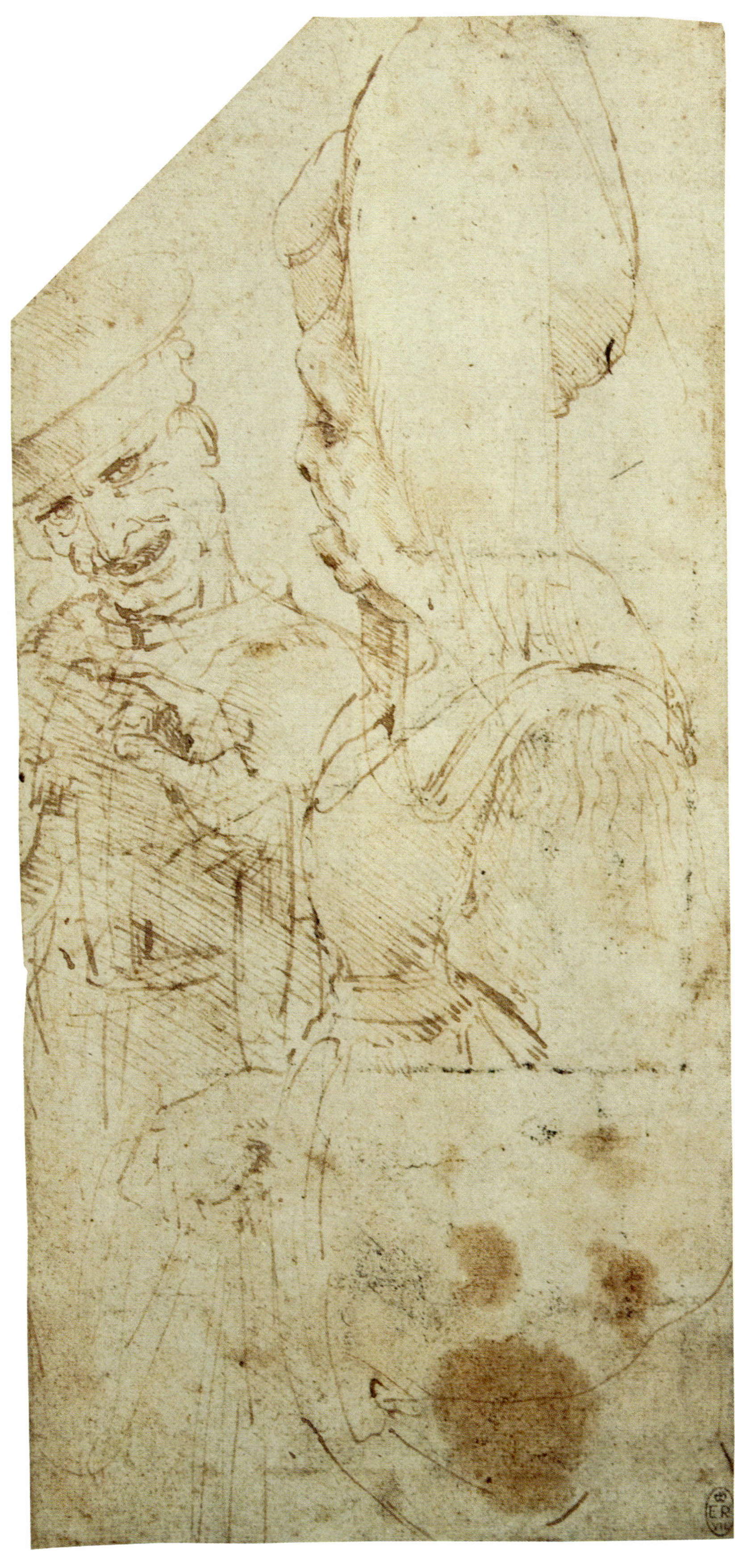

Leonardo da Vinci, *Deform couple*, c. 1490. Pen and ink, 262 x 123 mm. Windsor, RL 12449

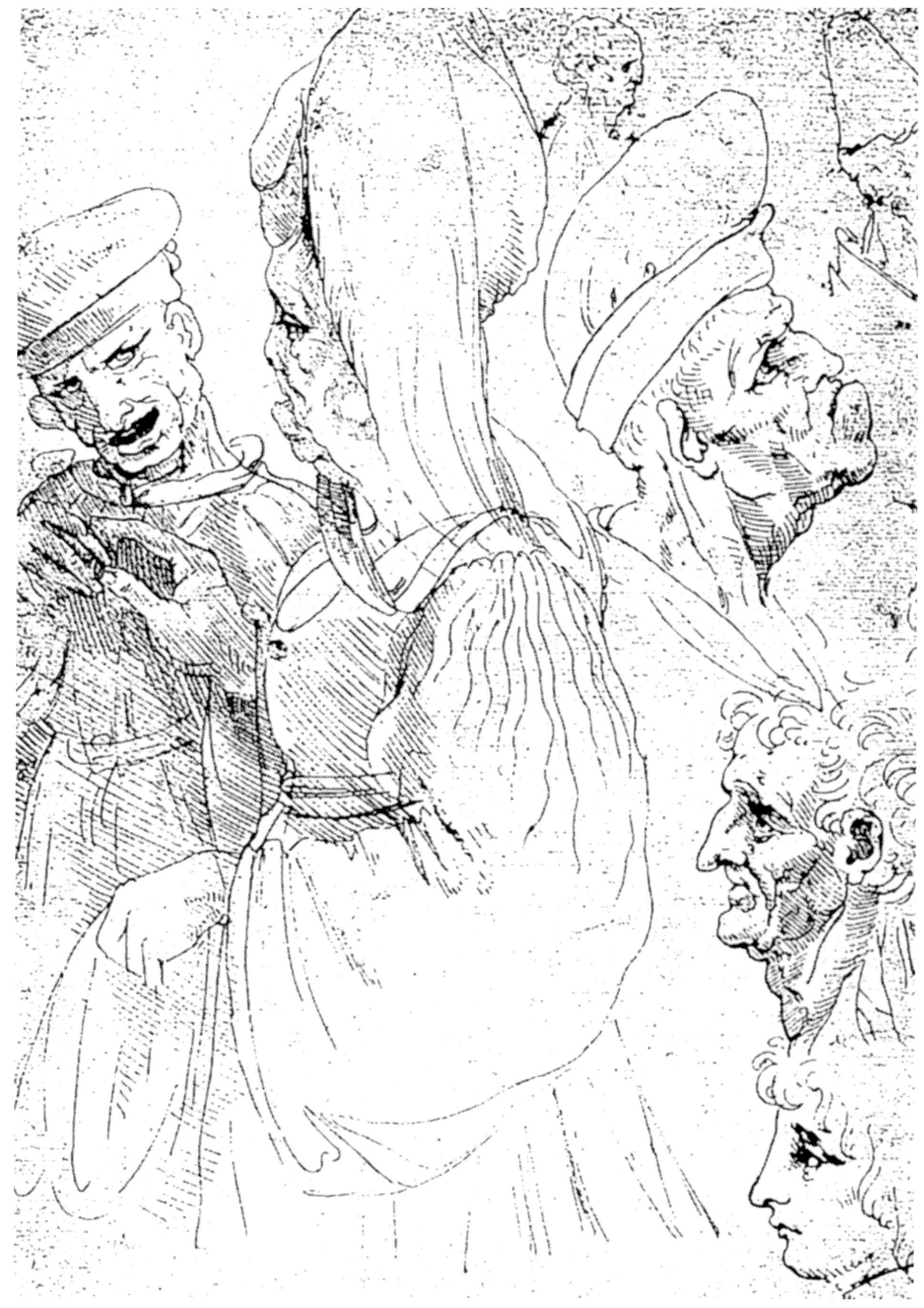

all the others with words; and do not despise such advices, because they are the masters of the movements and understand from far away what one is talking about, when he matches the motions of his hands with the words, (Libro di Pittura, cap. 115).

The five celebrated grotesque heads of Windsor (RL 12495 r), drawn with elegant chiaroscuro outline, reveal, in the morphologic variety of the faces and against every kind of improvisation, the elaboration of a careful figurative study of the expression, connected to a precise psychological investigation. Once again it would emerge, in his anatomical research, the call back to the poetic of the opposite ones, the antithesis between the severe haughtiness of the central figure, crowned with leaves of oak and ideal symbol of the dignity of who has distinguished himself for civil virtues, and the humoral negativeness of the «foolish multitude» that, in its mean instinctivity, mocks at him, reacting with different and graceless physiognomic expression.

Subordinated to a variety of points of view, those deformed faces, like the anatomical drawings of the muscles of the shoulder and of the arms (Windsor, RL 19005 v; 19008 v), suggested a simultaneous mimetic animation and a graduated kinetic variation of posture in time and space. Leonardo had devised there a nearly theatrical figurative narration, that developed, through sequences, recognizable physiognomic expressions.[51] It seems that the same artist, in the back of the sheet, had the intention to comment the scene with the bitterness of an autobiographical reflection:

And if there is someone amongst them, that has some goodness, not otherwise than me they are treated by the other men, and to this purpose I have this conclusion, that it is bad if they are enemies and it is worse if they are friends.

Deformities of faces and psychological implications animate also the subject of the «ill-formed couple», where the old woman with a grotesque profile, but with showy elegance and indecorous vanity, shows a ring to the young man that, pretending to please her, betrays in his malicious and rapacious grin his badly hidden greed (Windsor, RL 12449). The portrait of the «old harridan» will have a great success in the following centuries, so much as to be soon known by Quentin Massys (Matsys or Metsys, c. 1466-1530) that, adopting the grotesque heads of Leonardo for his pictures, painted a variant of it in his *Ugly Duchess* now at the National Gallery of London, while Pieter Paul Rubens, around 1603, will make a copy of it together with others celebrated vincian grotesque figures (Vienna, Albertina). Also Wenceslaus Hollar will draw from it inspiration for his «Queen of Tunis» and John Tenniel (1820-1914) for his «Ugly Duchess» (1865), in his illustrations for *Alice in Wonderland* by Lewis Carroll (1832-1898).[52] Therefore the vincian caricatures have turned out to be an upsetting world, rich of extraordinary interest for the deep innovations of method and thought contained in them, and capable to fascinate in their artistic effects the most refined and shrewd collectors of Europe, from Giorgio Vasari to Pierre-Jean Mariette.[53]

In fact Pierre Jean Mariette, playing a very important role in the European love for making collections, collected prints and drawings, of which a great amount arrived to the Louvre Museum. It is famous his *Recueil de testes de caractère & de charges, dessinées par Léonard de Vinci, Florentin, et gravées à l'eau forte en 1730 par M. le C. de C.*, which Mariette premises with a *Lettre*, considered by the scholars one of the most important critical interventions on Leonardo during the eighteenth century, but it must also be remembered his famous *Abécédario de P. J. Mariette et autres notes inédites de cet amateur sur les arts et sur les artistes*, (Paris, Chennevières et Montaiglon, 6 voll., 1851-60). Mariette moreover had such a highest esteem of Giorgio Vasari, as an historian and as an inventor of the modern critic of art and as a collector (a little less as an artist), to deserve him in such perspective the following praise: «Son nom ne s'est conservé qu'à la faveur de son grand et utile ouvrage sur la vie des Peintres et de son beau Recueil de Desseins des grands Maîtres».

---

[51]   W. SUIDA, beyond indicating the classic character of the central head, taken in its Roman «gravitas», thought that the other four faces illustrated the four human temperaments. Of great interest also the observation of E. H. GOMBRICH, when he takes into consideration the hypothesis that this drawing, of which a copy was known in the Low Countries at the time of Quentin Metsys (1466-1530), passionate mediator between Flemish painting and Italian models, had been examined also by Hieronymus Bosch. He would have found there inspiration for the dramatic and alarming expressions of the faces of the slave-drivers of Christ. W. SUIDA, *Leonardo und sein Kreis*, 1929, *op. cit.*; E. H. GOMBRICH, *Le teste grottesche*, 1986, *op. cit.* The study of the attitudes, that «naturally» are part of the show of life, pressed the same Lomazzo to consider Leonardo as a perfect model also in the representation of some peasants, singled out in the moment of an indecorous and flabby laugh: «being then become familiar with the help of some of his friends, he made a banquet, and he, sitting nearby, began telling the craziest and most ridicule things of the world, so that he made them, even though they did not know of what, laugh to split their sides. Whence he, observing quite diligently he imprinted in his mind all the gestures that they made together with those ridicule sayings and then, after that they were gone, he withdrew to his room and drew them perfectly in such a way that they moved not less to laughing those who watched them than had moved them the novels of Leonardo in the banquet», (*Trattato*, II, 1).

[52]   See E. H. GOMBRICH, *Arte e illusione…*, 1965, *op. cit.*; M. CLAYTON, *Leonardo da Vinci. One hundred Drawings from the collection of Her Majesty the Queen*, London, Merrell Holberton, 1997; ID., *Leonardo da Vinci. The Divine and the Grotesque*, London, The Royal Collection, 2002.

[53]   See K. T. STEINITZ, *Pierre-Jean Mariette & le Comte de Caylus and their Concept of Leonardo da Vinci in the Eighteenth Century*, Los Angeles, Zeitlin & Ver Brugge, 1974; M. V. GUFFANTI, *Il Conte di Caylus e le caricature di Leonardo*, «Raccolta Vinciana», 29, 2001.

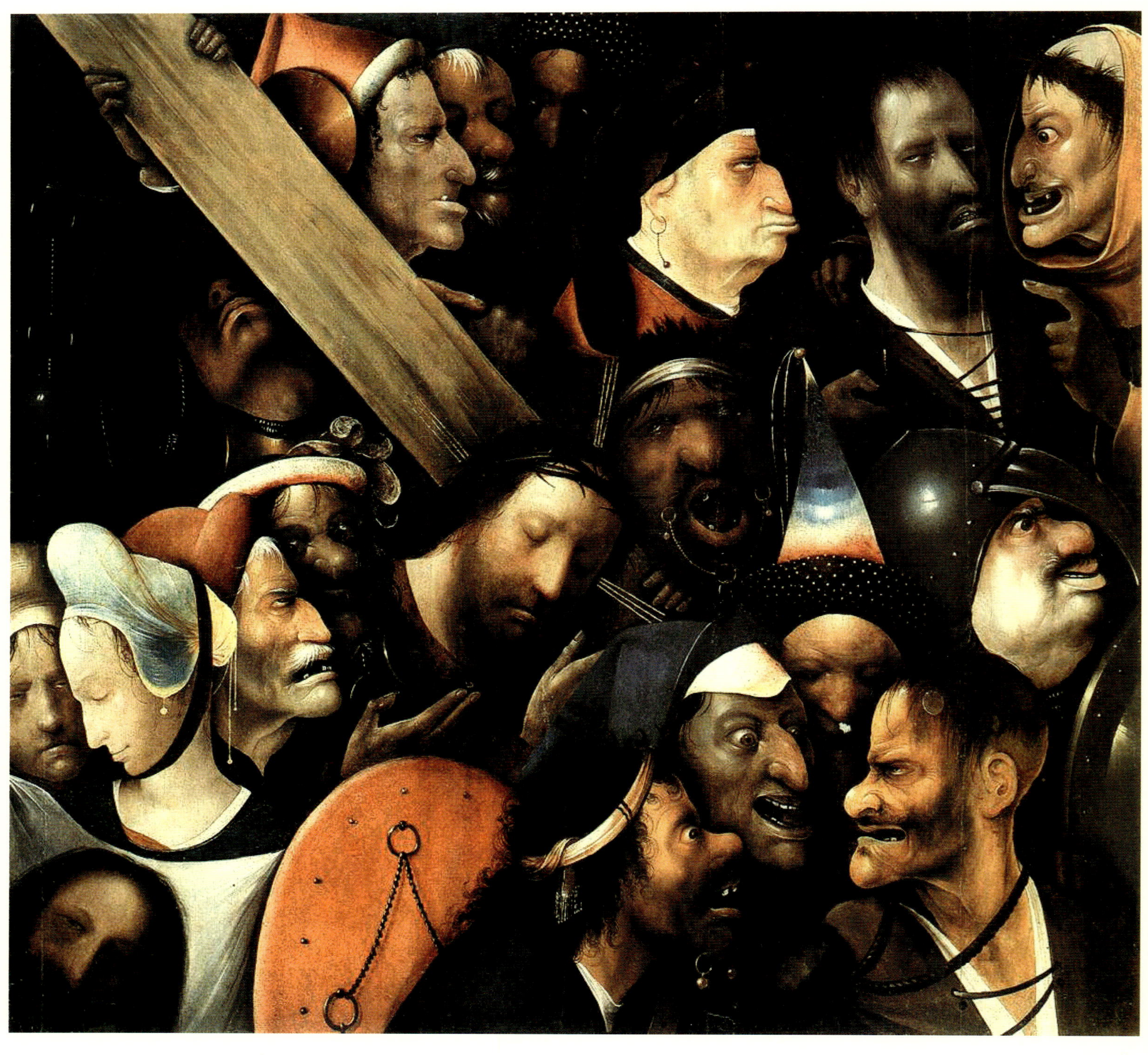

Hyeronymus Bosch, *Rise to the Calvary*, *c.* 1515–16. Oil on table, 76,7 x 83,5 cm. Gand, Musée des Beaux Arts

Bibliography

ACKERMAN J., *Leonardo's Eye*, «Journal of the Warburg and Courtauld Institutes», XLI (1978).

AGGHÁZY M. G., *La statuette équestre de Léonard de Vinci*, «Bulletin du Musée Hongrois des Beaux-Arts», Budapest, Nepmuvelesi Propaganda Iroda, 1971.

ALBERICI C., *Leonardo e l'incisione*, Milano, Electa, 1984.

ALBERICI C., *Leonardo e l'incisione. Stampe derivate da Leonardo e Bramante dal XV al XIX secolo*, Milano, Electa, 1984.

ALBERICI C., *Ritratti di Leonardo*, in *Leonardo e l'incisione: qualche aggiunta*, «Raccolta Vinciana», XXIV (1992).

ALBERTI DE MAZZERI S., *Leonardo. L'uomo e il suo tempo*, Milano, Rusconi, 1983.

AMES-LEWIS F., *Leonardo's Botanical Drawings*, «Achademia Leonardi Vinci. Journal of Leonardo Studies and Bibliography of Vinciana», X, Firenze, Giunti, 1997.

AMES-LEWIS F., *La matita nera nella pratica di disegno di Leonardo da Vinci*, «Lettura Vinciana», XLI, Firenze, Giunti, 2002.

AMORETTI C., *Memorie storiche su la vita, gli studj e le opere di Lionardo da Vinci*, in *Trattato della Pittura*, Milano, Editori de' Classici italiani, 1804.

ANGIOLILLO M. L., *Leonardo. Feste e teatri*, presentazione di C. Pedretti, Napoli, Società Editrice Napoletana, 1979.

ANONIMO FIORENTINO, *Il Codice Magliabechiano. Notizie sopra l'arte degli antichi e dei fiorentini da Cimabue a Michelangelo Buonarroti*, [1537-42], Firenze, Horne, 1909.

ARASSE D., *Le Détail: Pour une histoire rapprochée de la peinture*, Paris, Champs-Flammarion, 1996.

ARASSE D., *Léonard de Vinci. Le rythme du monde*, Paris, Hazan, 1997.

ARGAN G. C., *5 d'aghossto 1473*, in ID., *Classico anticlassico. Il Rinascimento da Brunelleschi a Bruegel*, Milano, Feltrinelli, 1984.

ARSLAN J., *Il romanticismo del paesaggio leonardesco*, «Arte cristiana», VII, 6 (1919).

BABINGER F., *Eine Brücke von Galata nach Stambul: wollte Leonardo in die Dienste des Sultans treten?*, «Die neue Zeitung», 87-88 (1952).

BABINGER F., HEYDENREICH L. H., *Vier Bauvorschläge Lionardo da Vincis an sultan Bajezid II. 1502-3*, «Nachrichten der Akademie der Wissenschaften in Göttingen», Phil.-hist. Klasse, 52 (1952).

BALDACCI A., *Leonardo da Vinci botanico e fondatore del metodo sperimentale*, «Memorie della R. Accademia delle Scienze dell'Istituto di Bologna, Cl. di Sc. Fis., Sez. delle Sc. Natur.», VII, I (1915).

BAMBACH CAPPEL C., *Leonardo, Tagliente and Dürer: "la scienza del far di gruppi"*, «Achademia Leonardi Vinci. Journal of Leonardo Studies and Bibliography of Vinciana», IV, Firenze, Giunti, 1991.

BARATTA M., *Leonardo da Vinci e i problemi della terra*, Torino, Bocca, 1903.

BARATTA M., *Leonardo da Vinci negli studi per la navigazione dell'Arno*, «Bollettino della Società Geografica Italiana», VI, 10-11 (1905).

BARATTA M., *Leonardo da Vinci e la cartografia*, Voghera, Officina d'arti grafiche, 1912.

BARATTA M., *Sopra le fonti cartografiche di Leonardo*, «Atti dell' VII Congresso Geografico Italiano di Firenze», Firenze, Alinari, 1923.

BARATTA M., *Leonardo da Vinci e la Val di Chiana*, «La Geografia», V, 3-4 (1927).

BARATTA M., *I Manoscritti e i Disegni di Leonardo da Vinci pubblicati dalla Reale Commissione Vinciana. I disegni conservati nel Castello di Windsor*, Fascicolo unico, Roma, La Libreria dello Stato, 1941.

BARATTA G., *Musica, figurazione delle cose invisibili. Sul Paragone delle Arti*, in *Tutte le opere non son per istancarmi, Raccolta di scritti per i settant'anni di Carlo Pedretti*, a cura di F. Frosini, Roma, Edizioni Associate, 1998.

BARNI L., *Ricerche intorno all'opera di Leonardo e del Bramante in Vigevano*, «Annuario della R. Scuola Complementare G. Ribecchi in Vigevano», Vigevano, 1928

BAROLSKY P., *The Mysterious Meaning of Leonardo's Saint John the Baptist*, «Source», 8 (1989).

BATKIN L. M., *Leonardo da Vinci*, Roma-Bari, Laterza, 1988.

BECK J. H., *Leonardo's rules of painting: an unconventional approach to modern art*, New York, Viking Press, 1979.

BECK J. H., *Leonardo's rapport with his father*, «Antichità viva», XXVII, 5-6 (1988).

BECK J. H., *I sogni di Leonardo*, «Lettura Vinciana», XXXII, Firenze, Giunti, 1993.

Béguin S., *Léonard de Vinci au Louvre*, Paris, RMN, 1983.

Béguin S., *Leonardo: tutta la pittura*, Firenze, Nardini, 1988.

Beltrame G., *Leonardo, i Navigli milanesi e i disegni Windsor RL 12399 e Ms H, f. 80 r*, «Raccolta Vinciana», XXII (1987).

Beltrami L., *Leonardo da Vinci e la sala delle « Asse » nel Castello di Milano*, Milano, Allegretti, 1902.

Beltrami L., *«Il musicista» di Leonardo da Vinci*, «Raccolta Vinciana», II (1906).

Beltrami L., *L'aeroplano di Leonardo*, in *Leonardo da Vinci. Conferenze fiorentine*, Milano, Treves 1910.

Beltrami L., *Documenti e Memorie riguardanti la Vita e le Opere di Leonardo da Vinci in ordine cronologico*, Milano, Treves, 1919.

Beltrami L., *Leonardo e i disfattisti suoi*, Milano, Treves, 1919.

Beltrami L., *Il volto di Leonardo*, «Emporium», 49 (1919).

Beltrami L., *La vigna di Leonardo*, Milano, Allegretti, 1920.

Beltrami L., Fumagalli G., *Disegni di Leonardo e della sua scuola alla Biblioteca Ambrosiana*, Milano, Montabone, 1904.

Berdini F., *La Gioconda chi è*, Roma, TOMO, 1989.

Berenson B., *The Study and Criticism of Italian Art*, 2 vols, London, Bell and Cos, 1901.

Berenson B., *The Drawings of the Florentine Painters, classified, criticised and studied as documents in the history and appreciation of Tuscan Art*, 2 vols, London, Murray, 1903.

Berenson B., *Italian Pictures of the Renaissance*, Oxford, Clarendon, 1932.

Berenson B., *Verrocchio e Leonardo. Leonardo e Lorenzo di Credi*, «Boll. d'arte», III (1933-34).

Berenson B., *I disegni dei pittori fiorentini*, 3 voll., Milano, Electa, 1961.

Berenson B., *Italian Painters of the Renaissance. Central Italian and North Italian Schools*, London/New York, Phaidon, 1968.

Bertacchi L., in *Zenale e Leonardo*, Milano, Electa, 1982.

Bertelli C., *Verso il vero Leonardo*, in *Leonardo e Milano*, a cura di G. A. Dell'Acqua, Milano, Banca Popolare di Novara, 1982.

Bertelli C., *Il Cenacolo vinciano*, in *Santa Maria delle Grazie in Milano*, Milano, Banca Popolare di Milano, 1983.

Blanc C., *La Joconde de Léonard de Vinci gravée par Calamatta*, «Gazette des Beaux-Arts», février, 1859.

Bode W. von, *Leonardo's Bildnis der Ginevra dei Benci*, «Zeitschr. für bild. K.», XIV (1903).

Bode W. von, *Studien über Leonardo da Vinci*, Berlin, Grote, 1921.

Bologna G., *Leonardo a Milano*, Novara, De Agostini, 1982.

Bonnaffé E., *Sabba da Castiglione. Notes sur la curiosité italienne de la Renaissance*, «Gazette des Beaux-Arts», XXX, 1884.

Bonnamen R., *La question de la Joconde. Problèmes vinciens*, Lyon, Legendre, 1908.

Bora G., *Per un catalogo dei disegni dei leonardeschi lombardi: indicazioni e problemi di metodo*, «Raccolta Vinciana», XXII (1987).

Bora G., *Due tavole leonardesche. Nuove indagini sul Musico e sul San Giovanni dell'Ambrosiana*, Vicenza, Pozza, 1987.

Bossi G., *Del Cenacolo di Leonardo da Vinci*, Milano, Stamperia Reale, 1810.

Bossi G., *Scritti sulle arti*, a cura di R. P. Ciardi, Firenze, SPES, 1982.

Bottari G., *Raccolta di lettere sulla Pittura, Scultura et Architettura*, Roma, Barbiellini, 1754.

Brambilla Barcilon P., *Il Cenacolo di Leonardo. Storia, condizioni, problemi*, Ivrea, Olivetti, 1984.

Brambilla Barcilon P., Marani P. C., *Leonardo. L'ultima cena*, Milano, Electa, 1999.

Bramly S., *Leonardo: the artist and the man*, New York, Penguin, 1994.

Brizio A. M., *Scritti scelti di Leonardo da Vinci* (a cura di), Torino, UTET, 1952.

Brizio A. M., *Delle acque*, in *Leonardo. Saggi e ricerche*, a cura di G. Castelfranco, Roma, Istituto Poligrafico dello Stato, 1954.

Brizio A. M., *Leonardo e Bramante alla corte di Ludovico il Moro*, in *Studi Bramanteschi. Atti del Congresso Internazionale. Milano-Urbino-Roma, 1970*, a cura del Comitato Nazionale per le Celebrazioni Bramantesche, Roma, 1974.

Brizio A. M, *Leonardo l'artista*, Firenze, Giunti Barbèra, 1981.

Brown D. A., *The London Madonna of the Rocks in Light of two Milanese Adaptations*, in *Collaboration in Italian Renaissance Art*, ed. by W. Stedman Sheard and J. T. Paoletti, New Haven, Yale University Press, 1978.

Brown D. A., *Leonardo and the idealized portrait in Milan*, «Arte Lombarda», 67 (1983).

Brown D. A., *Leonardo's Last Supper*, Washington, National Gallery of Art, 1983.

Brown D. A., *Madonna Litta*, «Lettura Vinciana», XXIX, Firenze, Giunti Barbèra, 1990.

Brown D. A., *Raphael, Leonardo and Perugino*, in *Leonardo, Michelangelo, and Raphael in Renaissance Florence from 1500 to 1508*. Symposium in Fiesole, Washington, Georgetown University Press, 1992.

Brown D. A., *Il Cenacolo di Leonardo: la prima eco a Venezia*, in *Leonardo & Venezia*, catalogo della mostra, Milano, Bompiani, 1992.

Brown D. A., *Leonardo da Vinci. Origini di un Genio*, Milano, Rizzoli, 1999.

Brown D. A., *Leonardo apprendista*, «Lettura Vinciana», XXXIX, Firenze, Giunti, 2000.

Brugnoli A. M., *Notizie e ipotesi sulla scultura di Leonardo*, in *Leonardo Saggi e Ricerche*, a cura di G. Castelfranco, Roma, Istituto Poligrafico dello Stato, 1954.

Brugnoli M.V., *Lo scultore*, in *Leonardo. L'artista*, Firenze, Giunti Barbèra, 1981.

Bruschi A., *Bramante, Leonardo e Francesco di Giorgio a Civitavecchia*, in *Studi Bramanteschi. Atti del Congresso internazionale. Milano, Urbino, Roma, 1970*, a cura del Comitato Nazionale per le celebrazioni Bramantesche, Roma, 1974.

Bruschi A., *Pareri sul tiburio del Duomo di Milano. Leonardo, Bramante, Francesco di Giorgio*, in *Scritti rinascimentali di architettura*, Milano, Il Polifilo, 1978.

Bruschi M., *La fede battesimale di Leonardo: ricerche in corso e altri documenti: Vinci e Anchiano*, Firenze, Giunti, 1997.

Calvi G., *Leonardo da Vinci e il conte di Ligny e altri appunti su personaggi vinciani*, in «Raccolta Vinciana», III (1907).

Calvi G., *Introduzione al Codice Leicester di Leonardo da Vinci*, Milano, Cogliati, 1909.

CALVI G., *I Manoscritti di Leonardo da Vinci in ordine cronologico, storico e biografico*, Bologna, Zanichelli, 1925.

CALVI G., *Vita di Leonardo*, Brescia, Morcelliana, 1936.

CALVI G. L., *Notizie dei principali Professori di Belle Arti che fiorirono in Milano durante il governo dei Visconti e degli Sforza*, Parte III, *Leonardo da Vinci*, Milano, Borroni, 1869.

CALVI I., *L'architettura militare di Leonardo da Vinci*, Milano, Libreria Lombarda, 1943.

CAMESASCA E., *Leonardo. Trattato della pittura*, Milano, TEA, 1995.

CAMPIONI R., *Leonardo artista delle macchine e cartografo* (a cura di), presentazione di C. Pedretti, Firenze, Giunti, 1994.

CARAMELLA S., *Scritti scelti*, «Scrittori italiani, sez. filosofica e pedagogica», Milano, Marzorati, 1972.

CARMINATI F., *Storia della fisiognomica*, Milano, Mondadori, 1995.

CARMINATI M., *Cesare da Sesto*, in *I leonardeschi: l'eredità di Leonardo in Lombardia*, Milano, Skira, 1998.

CARMINATI M., *Il maestro legge, pensa e prende appunti*, «Il sole-24 ore. Domenica», 307, 8 novembre 1998.

CARMINATI M., *Leonardo da Vinci, la Gioconda*, Cinisello Balsamo, Silvana Editoriale, 2003.

CAROLI F., *Leonardo. Studi di fisiognomica*, Milano, Leonardo, 1991.

CAROLI F., *Storia della Fisiognomica. Arte e psicologia da Leonardo a Freud*, Milano, Mondadori, 1995.

CAROLI F., *Il Cinquecento lombardo: da Leonardo a Caravaggio* (a cura di), Milano, Skira, 2000.

CARPICECI A. C., *Leonardo architetto. Per una nuova architettura. Per il tempio ideale*, Firenze, 1977.

CARPICECI A. C., *L'architettura di Leonardo. Indagine e ipotesi su tutta l'opera di Leonardo architetto*, Firenze, Bonechi, 1978.

CARPICECI M., *I meccanismi musicali di Leonardo*, «Raccolta Vinciana», XXII (1987).

CARUSI E., *Quel che c'è di Leonardo nel mappamondo a lui attribuito*, in *I disegni geografici di Leonardo da Vinci*, Bergamo, Istituto Italiano d'Arti Grafiche, 1919.

CARUSI E., *Ancora di Salaì*, «Raccolta Vinciana», XIII (1926-1929).

CARUSI E., *Lettere di Galeazzo Arconato e Cassiano dal Pozzo per lavori su manoscritti di Leonardo da Vinci*, «Accademie e Biblioteche d'Italia», III, VI (1929-30).

CARUSI E., FAVARO A., *Del moto e misura dell'acqua: libri nove ordinati da F. Luigi Maria Arconati*, editi sul codice archetipo barberiniano (a cura di), Bologna, Zanichelli, 1923.

CASSIRER E., *Individuo e Cosmo nella filosofia del Rinascimento*, Firenze, La Nuova Italia, 1935.

CASTELFRANCO G., *Il canale Firenze-mare nei progetti di Leonardo*, «Civiltà delle macchine», III, 1955.

CASTELFRANCO G., *La pittura di Leonardo da Vinci*, Milano, Scheiwiller, 1956.

CASTELFRANCO G., *Le due versioni della Vergine delle Rocce*, «Raccolta Vinciana», XVIII (1960).

CASTELFRANCO G., *Scritti vinciani*, Roma, De Luca, 1966.

CASTIGLIONE B., *Il Cortegiano*, [1528], Milano, Garzanti, 1987.

CECCHI A., *Niccolò Machiavelli o Marcello Virgilio Adriani? Sul programma e l'assetto compositivo delle 'battaglie' di Leonardo e Michelangelo per la Sala del Consiglio Maggiore in Palazzo Vecchio*, «Prospettiva», 83-84 (1997).

CERMENATI M., *Leonardo da Vinci in Valsassina. Riproduzione e illustrazione critica di un foglio del «Codice Atlantico»*, Milano, Cogliati, 1910.

CERMENATI M., *Leonardo a Roma nel periodo leoniano*, «Nuova Antologia», CI (1919).

CHASTEL A., *Arte e umanesimo a Firenze ai tempi di Lorenzo il Magnifico*, Torino, Einaudi, 1964.

CHASTEL A., *I centri del Rinascimento*, Milano, Rizzoli, 1965.

CHASTEL A., *Les notes de Léonard de Vinci sur la peinture d'après le nouveau manuscrit de Madrid*, «Revue de l'Art», 15 (1972).

CHASTEL A., *Le Madonne di Leonardo*, «Lettura Vinciana», XVIII, Firenze, Giunti Barbèra, 1979.

CHASTEL A., *Une grande inimitié: Léonard/Michel-Ange (1500-1516)*, in ID.: *Chronique de la peinture italienne, 1280-1580*, Paris-Friburg, Office du Livre, 1983.

CHASTEL A., *Le Cardinal Louis d'Aragon. Un voyageur princier de la Renaissance*, Paris, Fayard, 1987.

CHASTEL A., *Raffaello e Leonardo*, in *Studi su Raffaello*, «Atti del Convegno Internazionale di studi: Urbino-Firenze, 6-14 aprile 1984» a cura di M. Sambucco Hamoud e M. L. Strocchi, Urbino, Quattro Venti, 1987.

CHASTEL A., *La Gioconda. L'illustre incompresa*, Milano, Leonardo, 1989.

CHASTEL A., *Leonardo da Vinci*, Torino, Einaudi, 1995.

CHASTEL A., GALLUZZI P., PEDRETTI C., *Leonardo*, «Art Dossier», 12, Firenze, Giunti, 1987.

CIANCHI M., *Le macchine di Leonardo*, introduzione di C. Pedretti, Firenze, Becocci, 1982.

CIANCHI M., *Leonardo da Vinci*, Firenze, Giunti, 1996.

CIANCHI M., *Leonardo. Anatomia*, Firenze, Giunti, 1997.

CIANCHI R., *Vinci, Leonardo e la sua famiglia (con appendice di documenti inediti)*, Milano, Museo Nazionale della Scienza e della Tecnica, 1953.

CIANCHI R., *Figure del mondo vinciano. Paolo e Vannoccio Biringuccio da Siena*, «Raccolta Vinciana», XX, 1964.

CIANCHI R., *Un acquisto mancato*, «La Nazione», 24 novembre 1967.

CIANCHI R., *Ricerche e documenti sulla madre di Leonardo. Notizie inedite. La dimora dell'Accattabriga e della Caterina in Campo Zeppi a San Pantaleo di Vinci. Un'antica chiesetta da salvare*, Firenze, Giunti Barbèra, 1975.

CIANCHI R., *Sul testamento di Francesco da Vinci a favore di Leonardo*, «Nouvelles de la république des lettres», I (1984).

CIARDI R. P., *Gian Paolo Lomazzo. Scritti sulle arti*, 2 voll., Firenze, Marchi & Bertolli, Centro DI, 1973-75.

CIARDI R. P., *L'immagine di Leonardo*, «Lettura Vinciana», XXXIII, Firenze, Giunti, 1994.

CIARDI R. P., SISI C., *L'immagine di Leonardo. Testimonianze figurative dal XVI al XIX secolo* (a cura di), Firenze, Giunti, 1997.

CIARDI R. P., *Leonardo: autoritratti inesistenti e ritratti immaginati*, in *Leonardo da Vinci: la vera immagine. Documenti e testimonianze sulla vita e sull'opera*, mostra a cura di V. Arrighi, A. Bellinazzi, E. Villata, Firenze, Giunti, 2005.

CLARK K., *Leonardo da Vinci. An Account of His Development as an Artist*, Cambridge, Cambridge University Press, 1939.

CLARK K., *Leonardo and the Antique*, in *Leonardo's Legacy*. An International Symposium, Berkeley/Los Angeles, University of California Press, 1969.

CLARK K., *Mona Lisa*, «Burlington Magazine», CXV, 840 (1973).

CLARK K., *Leonardo e le curve della vita*, «Lettura Vinciana», XVII, Firenze, Giunti Barbèra, 1979.

CLARK K., PEDRETTI C., *The Drawings of Leonardo da Vinci in the Collection of Her Majesty the Queen at Windsor Castle*, 3 vols, London, Phaidon, 1969.

CLAYTON M., *Leonardo da Vinci. A Curious Vision*, London, Merrell Holberton, 1996.

CLAYTON M., *Leonardo da Vinci. One hundred Drawings from the collection of Her Majesty the Queen*, London, Merrell Holberton, 1996.

CLAYTON M., *Leonardo da Vinci. The Divine and the Grotesque*, London, Merrell Holberton, 2002.

CLÉMENT C., *Michel-Ange, Léonard de Vinci, Raphaël*, Paris, Levy, 1861.

COGLIATI ARANO L., *Disegni di Leonardo e della sua cerchia alle Gallerie dell'Accademia di Venezia* (a cura di), Milano, Arcadia Electa, 1980.

COGLIATI ARANO L., *Disegni di Leonardo e della sua cerchia alla Biblioteca Ambrosiana di Milano* (a cura di), Milano, Arcadia Electa, 1981.

COGLIATI ARANO L., *Da Leonardo a Goethe*, «Raccolta Vinciana», XXXII (1987).

COGLIATI ARANO L., *Leonardo e la rappresentazione della terza età*, «Lettura Vinciana», XXXI, Firenze, Giunti, 1992.

COOK H., *La Madone Bénois et les oeuvres de jeunesse de Léonard de Vinci*, «Gazette des Beaux Arts», I (1914).

CORBEAU A., *Les manuscrits de Léonard de Vinci. – Contributions hispaniques à leur histoire*, «Raccolta Vinciana», XX (1964).

CREMANTE S., *Leonardo da Vinci, genio delle macchine*, con introduzione di M. Lombardi e presentazione di C. Pedretti, Firenze, Cartei e Becagli, 2005.

CREMANTE S., *Leonardo da Vinci. Artista, Scienziato, Inventore*, Firenze, Giunti, 2005.

CROCE B., *Leonardo*, Milano, Treves, 1939.

CROWE G. B., CAVALCASELLE J. A., *A new history of painting in Italy from the second to the sixteenth century*, [1864-66], Firenze, Le Monnier, 1886-1908.

D'ANNUNZIO G., *La Gioconda*, in *Tragedie, sogni e misteri*, Firenze, Sansoni, 1950.

DALLI REGOLI G., *Lorenzo di Credi*, Cremona, Edizioni di Comunità, 1966.

DALLI REGOLI G., *Il "Piegar de' Panni"*, «Critica d'arte», XXII, 150 (1976).

DALLI REGOLI G., *La Madonna di Piazza: '…Ce n'è d'assai più belle, nessuna più perfetta'*, in *Scritti di storia dell'arte in onore di Federico Zeri*, 2 voll., Milano, Electa, 1984.

DALLI REGOLI G., *Mito e scienza nella Leda di Leonardo*, «Lettura Vinciana», XXX, Firenze, Giunti, 1991.

DALLI REGOLI G., *Lorenzo di Credi. Madonna col Bambino in trono, fra San Giovanni Battista e San Donato d'Arezzo*, in *Maestri e Botteghe. Pittura a Firenze alla fine del Quattrocento*, a cura di M. Gregori, A. Paolucci, C. Acidini Luchinat, Firenze 16 settembre 1992-10 gennaio 1993, Cinisello Balsamo, Silvana Editoriale, 1992.

DALLI REGOLI G., *Leonardo e Michelangelo: il tema della 'Battaglia' agli inizi del Cinquecento*, «Achademia Leonardi Vinci. Journal of Leonardo Studies and Bibliography of Vinciana», VII, Firenze, Giunti, 1994.

DAVIES M., *Leonardo da Vinci: The Virgin of the Rocks, in the National Gallery*, London, Balding and Mansell, 1947.

DAVIES M., *The earlier Italian Schools*, London, National Gallery Catalogues, 1951.

DE BLASI N., *Antologia di scritti letterari, meditazioni sulle arti, prose scientifiche* (a cura di), Roma, Curcio, 1962.

DE LORENZO G., *Le pessimisme de Léonard de Vinci et de Michel-Ange*, «Nouvelle Revue d'Italie», XVI, 5 (1919).

DE LORENZO G., *Leonardo da Vinci e la geologia*, Bologna, Zanichelli, 1920.

DE MANDACH C., *Léonard de Vinci et les pierres gravées antiques*, «Chronique des Arts», 40 (1904).

DE MICHELI M., *L'uomo e la natura* (a cura di), Milano, Feltrinelli, 1952.

DE SANTI P. M., *La Gioconda rubata*, «Achademia Leonardi Vinci. Journal of Leonardo Studies and Bibliography of Vinciana», III, Firenze, Giunti, 1990.

DE TOLNAY C., *Remarques sur la Joconde*, «Revue des Arts», II, 4 (1952).

DE TOLNAY C., *Les conceptions artistiques de Léonard et leur origine*, Alger, Imbert, 1954.

DE TONI G. B., *Leonardo da Vinci e Luca Paciolo*, «Atti del Regio Istituto Veneto di Scienze, Lettere ed Arti», LXV (1905-1906).

DE TONI G. B., *Frammenti Vinciani X*, «Atti del Regio Istituto Veneto di Scienze, Lettere e Arti», LXXX (1921-1922).

DE TONI G. B., *Le piante e gli animali in Leonardo da Vinci*, Bologna, Zanichelli, 1922.

DE TONI N., *Saggio di onomastica vinciana*, «Raccolta Vinciana», XIV (1934).

DE TONI N., *Repertorio dei passi leonardeschi ai quali attinse l'Arconati per la compilazione del Moto e misura delle acque*, «Raccolta Vinciana», XX (1964).

DE TONI N., *I rilievi cartografici per Cesena ed Urbino nel manoscritto L dell'Istituto di Francia*, «Lettura Vinciana», V, Firenze, Giunti Barbèra, 1965.

DE TONI N., *Frammenti Vinciani XXVI: Contributo alla conoscenza dei Manoscritti 8936 ed 8937 della Biblioteca Nazionale di Madrid*, «Commentari dell'Ateneo di Brescia per il 1966» (ristampato in «Physis», 1, IX, 1967).

DE TONI N., *Ancora sul «Valturio»*, Notiziario Vinciano, 10 (1979).

DE TONI N., *La pianta di Imola e Leonardo*, «Raccolta Vinciana», XXI (1982).

DE VECCHI P. L., *La Vergine delle Rocce*, in *Leonardo e Milano*, a cura di G. A. Dell'Acqua, Milano, Banca Popolare di Milano, 1982.

DEGENHART B., *Di alcuni problemi di sviluppo della pittura nella bottega del Verrocchio, di Leonardo e di Lorenzo di Credi*, «Rivista d'Arte», XIV, 3 (1932).

DEGENHART B., *Dante, Leonardo und Sangallo*, «Römisches Jahrbuch für Kunstgeschichte», 7 (1955).

DIONISOTTI C., *Leonardo uomo di lettere*, «Italia Medievale e Umanistica», V (1962).

DI TEODORO P. F., *Se non che tali ponti caderan in brieve contro al corso del fiume*, «Physis», 1-2, XXVII (1985).

DI TEODORO P. F., *Stupenda e dannosa maraviglia*, «Achademia Leonardi

Vinci. Journal of Leonardo Studies and Bibliography of Vinciana», II, Firenze, Giunti, 1989.

Di Teodoro P. F., *Maestro Piero del Borgo*, «Achademia Leonardi Vinci. Journal of Leonardo Studies and Bibliography of Vinciana», V, Firenze, Giunti, 1992.

Dionisotti C., *Leonardo uomo di lettere*, «Italia Medievale e Umanistica», V (1962).

Dorez L., *Léonard de Vinci et Jean Perréal (Conjectures)*, in *Léonard de Vinci 1519-1919*, «Nouvelle Revue d'Italie», 1919.

Dromard Mairot M. T., *Le fond de la Joconde et l'esthétique de Leonardo de Vinci*, Besançon, Jaque & Demontrond, 1933.

Duhem P., *Études sur Léonard de Vinci. Ceux qu' il a lu et ceux qui l'ont lu*, Paris, Hermann, 1906-1913.

Dumesnil A., *Léonard de Vinci*, [1850], in *L'art italien*, Paris, Giraud, 1854.

Durrieu P., *Les relations de Léonard de Vinci avec le peintre français Jean Perréal*, «Études Italiennes», I (1919).

Eissler R. K., *Leonardo da Vinci. Psychoanalytic Notes on the Enigma*, New York, Int. University Press, 1961.

Eissler R. K., *Léonard de Vinci. Etude psychanalytique*, Paris, PUF, 1980.

Escobar S., *Il tecnico idraulico tra sapere e saper fare*, in *Leonardo e le vie dell'acqua*, Firenze, Giunti Barbèra, 1983.

Fabian B., Marani P. C., *Leonardo. La dama con l'ermellino (a cura di)*, Cinisello Balsamo, Silvana Editoriale, 1998.

Fabrizio-Costa S., *'Elena quando si specchiava'*, «Achademia Leonardi Vinci. Journal of Leonardo Studies and Bibliography of Vinciana», X, Firenze, Giunti, 1997.

Fara A., *Leonardo e l'architettura militare*, «Lettura Vinciana», XXXVI, Firenze, Giunti, 1997.

Farago J. C., *Leonardo's 'Battle of Anghiari': A Study in the Exchange Between Theory and Practice*, «Art Bulletin», 76 (1994).

Favaro A., *Gilberto Govi e i suoi scritti intorno a Leonardo da Vinci*, Roma, Maglione e Strini, 1923.

Favaro A., *Archimede e Leonardo da Vinci*, «Atti del Regio Istituto Veneto di Scienze, Lettere ed Arti», LXXVII (1917).

Favaro G., *Leonardo da Vinci, i medici e la medicina: memoria*, Roma, Maglione & Strini, 1923.

Favaro G., *Gli studi anatomici di Leonardo nei Regesti Vinciani*, «Atti e Memorie della Reale Accademia di Scienze, Lettere e Arti di Venezia», V, III (1938).

Federici Vescovini G., *Premesse a Leonardo: il vocabolario scientifico del 'De pictura' dell'Alberti e la bellezza 'naturale'*, «Achademia Leonardi Vinci. Journal of Leonardo Studies and Bibliography of Vinciana», X, Firenze, Giunti, 1997.

Federici Vescovini G., *Note à propos de la tradition latine des livres de météorologie d'Alkindi et Léonard*, in *Tutte le opere non son per istancarmi. Raccolta di scritti per i settant'anni di Carlo Pedretti*, a cura di F. Frosini, Roma, Edizioni Associate, 1998.

Fehr B., *Walter Pater Beschreibung der Mona Lisa und Théophile Gautier romantischer Orientalismus*, «Archiv für das Studium neuren Sprachen und Literaturen», 135 (1916).

Fehrenbach F., *Licht und Wasser. Zur dynamik Naturphilosophischer leitbilder im Werke Leonardo da Vincis*, Tubingen-Berlin, E. Wasmuth, 1997.

Félibien F., *Entretiens sur les vies et sur les ouvrages des plus excellens peintres*, Paris, Coignard, 1666.

Ferrero L., *Leonardo o dell'arte*, introduzione di Paul Valéry, Torino, Buratti, 1929.

Ferri Piccaluga G., *Le "dispute" teologiche nell'iconografia devozionale di Raffaello*, in *Raffaello e l'Europa*. «Atti del IV Corso Internazionale di Alta Cultura», a cura di M. Fagiolo e M. L. Madonna, Roma, Libreria dello Stato, 1990.

Ferri Piccaluga G., *Σοφία*, «Achademia Leonardi Vinci. Journal of Leonardo Studies and Bibliography of Vinciana», VII, Firenze, Giunti, 1994.

Ferri Piccaluga G., *Una nuova copia della 'Vergine delle Rocce'?*, con un'appendice di D. Chabeaudie Rondanini, in *Tutte le opere non son per istancarmi. Raccolta di scritti per i settant'anni di Carlo Pedretti*, a cura di F. Frosini, Roma, Edizioni Associate, 1998.

Filipczak Z., *New Light on Mona Lisa: Leonardo's Optical Knowledge and his Choice of Lighting*, «The Art Bulletin», LIX (1977).

Fiorio M. T., *Leonardeschi in Lombardia*, Milano, Regione Lombardia Settore commercio e turismo, 1982.

Fiorio M. T., *Leonardo, Boltraffio e Jéan Perréal*, «Raccolta Vinciana», XXVII, Milano, 1997

Fiorio M. T., Marani P. C., *I Leonardeschi a Milano. Fortuna e collezionismo*, Milano, Electa, 1991.

Firpo L., *Leonardo architetto e urbanista*, Torino, UTET, 1971.

Firpo L., *Leonardo architetto militare e civile*, «Lettura Vinciana», XVI, Firenze, Giunti Barbèra, 1976.

Fletcher J., *Bernardo Bembo and Leonardo's Portrait of Ginevra Benci*, «Burlington Magazine», 131 (1989).

Freud S., *Eine Kindheitserinnerung des Leonardo da Vinci*, Leipzig und Wien, Denticke, 1910.

Fritz R., *Zur Ikonographie von Leonardos Bacchus-Johannes*, «Mouseion», 1960.

Frommel C. L., *Leonardo fratello della Confraternita della Pietà dei Fiorentini a Roma*, «Raccolta Vinciana», XX (1964).

Fronza C., *Manoscritti di Leonardo*, in *Leonardo e l'età della ragione*, a cura di E. Bellone e P. Rossi, Milano, Scientia, 1982.

Fumagalli G., *Leonardo omo sanza lettere*, Firenze, Sansoni, 1939.

Fumagalli G., *Eros di Leonardo*, Milano, Garzanti, 1952.

Fumagalli G., *Gli "omini salvatichi" di Leonardo*, «Raccolta Vinciana», XVIII (1960).

Galdi G. P., *Leonardo's Helicopter and Archimedes' Screw. The principle of Action and Reaction*, «Achademia Leonardi Vinci. Journal of Leonardo Studies and Bibliography of Vinciana», IV, Firenze, Giunti, 1991.

Galluzzi P., *Leonardo da Vinci letto e commentato*, «Letture Vinciane I-XII», 1960-1972, Firenze, Giunti, 1974.

Galluzzi P., *La carrière d'un technologue*, in *Léonard de Vinci ingénieur et architecte*, introduzione di C. Pedretti, catalogo della mostra, Montréal, Musée des Beaux-Arts, 1987.

Galluzzi P., *Leonardo e i proporzionanti*, «Lettura Vinciana», XXVIII, Firenze, Giunti Barbèra, 1989.

Galluzzi P., *Prima di Leonardo. Cultura delle macchine a Siena nel Rinascimento*, Milano, Electa, 1991.

Galluzzi P., *Gli ingegneri del Rinascimento, da Brunelleschi a Leonardo da Vinci*, Firenze, Giunti, 1996.

Galluzzi P., *Introduzione*, in *Carlo Pedretti's Publications, 1985-1995, with an Aftermath & a Supplement [1946-1998]*, a cura di N. Guttmann, Firenze, Giunti, 1998.

Galluzzi P., *Presentazione*, in *Nel segno di Masaccio. L'invenzione della prospettiva*, a cura di F. Camerota, Firenze, Giunti, 2001.

Garin E., *La cultura fiorentina nell'età di Leonardo da Vinci*, «Belfagor», Firenze, Olschki, 1952.

Garin E., *Il problema delle fonti del pensiero di Leonardo*, «Atti del Convegno di Studi Vinciani», Firenze, Olschki, 1953.

Garin E., *Universalità di Leonardo*, in Id., *Scienza e vita civile nel Rinascimento italiano*, Bari, Laterza, 1965.

Garin E., *La città in Leonardo*, «Lettura Vinciana», XI, Firenze, Giunti Barbèra, 1972.

Garin E., *Scienza e vita civile nel Rinascimento italiano*, Bari, Laterza, 1972.

Garroni E., *Leonardo e il suo tempo*, «Rassegna di filosofia», IV, 1 (1955).

Gaye G., *Carteggio inedito d'artisti dei secoli XIV, XV, XVI*, Firenze, Molini, 1839.

Gentile C., *Theosophia del Cenacolo: il segreto profetico, la gnosi e l'iniziazione cristica di Leonardo*, «Alba spirituale», IX, 4 (1953).

Gentile G., *Leonardo filosofo*, in Id., *Il pensiero italiano del Rinascimento*, Firenze, Sansoni, 1940.

Giacomelli R., *Gli scritti di Leonardo da Vinci sul volo*, Roma, Bardi, 1936.

Giacomelli R., *Leonardo da Vinci aerodinamico, aerologo, aerotecnico ed osservatore del volo degli uccelli*, «Atti del Convegno di Studi Vinciani», Firenze, Olschki, 1953.

Gibbs-Smith C. H., *Leonardo da Vinci's aeronautics*, London, H.M.S.O., 1967.

Gibbs-Smith C. H., *Le invenzioni di Leonardo*, Milano, Mazzotta, 1979.

Gibbs-Smith C. H., *Aviation. An Historical Survey from its Origins to the End of World War*, II, London, HMSO, 1985.

Gille B., *Leonardo e gli ingegneri del Rinascimento*, Milano, Feltrinelli, 1972.

Goldscheider L., *Leonardo da Vinci. Life and Work. Paintings and Drawings*, London, Phaidon, 1952.

Gombrich E. H., *Leonardo's Grotesques Heads. Prolegomena to Their Study*, in *Leonardo. Saggi e Ricerche*, a cura di G. Castelfranco, Roma, Istituto Poligrafico dello Stato, 1954.

Gombrich E. H., *I precetti di Leonardo per comporre delle storie*, in Id., *Norma e forma*, Torino, Einaudi, 1973.

Gombrich E. H., *Leonardo e i maghi: polemiche e rivalità*, «Lettura Vinciana», XXIII, Firenze, Giunti Barbèra, 1984.

Gombrich E. H., *L'eredità di Apelle. Studi sull'arte del Rinascimento*, Torino, Einaudi, 1986.

Gombrich E. H., *Antichi maestri, nuove letture*, Torino, Einaudi, 1987.

Gordon D., *La leggenda di Leonardo*, in Id., *L'immagine e la parola. Cultura e simboli del Rinascimento*, a cura di S. Orgel, Milano, Il Saggiatore, 1987.

Goukovskj M. A., *Du nouveau sur Léonard de Vinci. Léonard et Janus Lascaris*, «Bibliothèque d'Humanisme et Renaissance», XIX (1957).

Goukovskj M. A., *Leonardo e Galeno*, «Raccolta Vinciana», XX (1964).

Gould C., *Leonardo's Neptune Drawing*, «Burlington Magazine», XCIV (1952).

Gould C., *Leonardo's Great Battle-Piece, a Conjectural Reconstruction*, «Art Bulletin», XXXVI (1954).

Gould C., *Leonardo*, London, Werdenfeld & Nicolson, 1975.

Gould C., *The Newly Discovered Documents concerning Leonardo's 'Virgin of the Rocks' and their bearing on the Problem of the Two Versions*, «Artibus et Historiae», 3, II (1981).

Gould C., *Leonardo's Madonna of the Yarnwinder. Revelations of reflectogram photography*, «Apollo», CXXXVI, 365 (1992).

Gould C., *The Early History of Leonardo's Vierge aux Rochers*, «Gazette des Beaux Arts», 124 (1994).

Green A., *Ange ou Démon?*, «Achademia Leonardi Vinci. Journal of Leonardo Studies and Bibliography of Vinciana», VI, Firenze, Giunti, 1993.

Gregori M., *Uffizi e Pitti: dipinti delle Gallerie fiorentine*, introduzione di A. Paolucci e M. Chiarini, Udine, Magnus, 1994.

Gregori M., Paolucci A., Acidini Luchinat C., *Maestri e botteghe: pittura a Firenze alla fine del Quattrocento* (a cura di), Cinisello Balsamo, Silvana Editoriale, 1992.

Grossmann S., *The Madonna and Child with a Pomegranate and some new Paintings from Circle of Verrocchio*, «Report and Studies in the History of Art», Washington, National Gallery of Art, 1968.

Grossmann S., *Ghirlandaio's "Madonna and Child" in Frankfurt and Leonardo's Beginnings as a Painter*, «Städel-Jahrbuch», VII (1979).

Guerrini M., *Bibliotheca leonardiana, 1493-1989*, 3 voll., Milano, Bibliografica, 1990.

Guillaume J., *Léonard de Vinci, Dominique de Cortone et l'escalier du modèle en bois de Chambord*, «Gazette des Beaux-Arts», s. VI, LXXI (1968).

Guillaume J., De Jonge K., *De l'esquisse au modèle: comment « construire » une église de Léonard*, «Achademia Leonardi Vinci. Journal of Leonardo Studies and Bibliography of Vinciana», I, Firenze, Giunti, 1988.

Guillerm J. P., *Tombeau de Léonard De Vinci. Le peintre et ses tableaux dans l'écriture symboliste et décadente*, Arras, PUL, 1981.

Guttmann N., *A new Madonna of the Yarnwinder*, «Achademia Leonardi Vinci. Journal of Leonardo Studies and Bibliography of Vinciana», IX, Firenze, Giunti, 1996.

Hartt F., *Leonardo and the Second Florentine Republic*, «Journal of the Walters Art Gallery», 41 (1983).

Herzfeld M., *La rappresentazione della 'Danae' organizzata da Leonardo*, «Raccolta Vinciana», XI (1920-22).

Heydenreich L. H., *Studi archeologici di Leonardo da Vinci a Civitavecchia*, «Raccolta Vinciana», XIV, 1930-34.

Heydenreich L. H., *La «Sainte Anne» de Léonard de Vinci*, «Gazette des Beaux-Arts», II (1933).

Heydenreich L. H., *Arte e scienza in Leonardo*, Milano, Bestetti, 1945.

Heydenreich L. H., *Leonardo da Vinci Architect of Francis I*, «Burlington Magazine», X (1952).

Heydenreich L. H., *Leonardo da Vinci*, 2 vols, Basilea-New York, Macmillan-Holbein, 1954.

HEYDENREICH L. H., *Leonardo da Vinci*, «Enciclopedia Universale dell'Arte», VIII, Venezia-Roma, 1958.

HEYDENREICH L. H., *Leonardo architetto*, «Lettura Vinciana», II, Firenze, G. Barbèra, 1962.

HEYDENREICH L. H., *Leonardo and Bramante. Genius in Architecture*, in *Leonardo's Legacy*, ed. by C. D. O'Malley, Berkeley-Los Angeles, University Of California Press, 1969.

HEYDENREICH L. H., *L'architetto militare*, in *Leonardo inventore*, Firenze, Giunti Barbèra, 1981.

HOCHSTETLER MEYER B., *Leonardo's Battle of Anghiari: Proposals for some Sources and a Reflection*, «Art Bulletin», 66, 1984.

HOURS M., *Radiographies des tableaux de Léonard de Vinci*, «Revue des arts», II (1952).

HOURS M., *Étude analytique des tableaux de Léonard de Vinci au Laboratoire du Musée du Louvre*, in *Leonardo. Saggi e ricerche*, a cura di G. Castelfranco, Roma, Istituto Poligrafico dello Stato, 1954.

HOUSSAYE A., *Histoire de Léonard de Vinci*, Paris, Didier, 1869.

HUNTER W., *Two introductory lectures to his last corse of anatomical lectures at his theatre in Windmill Street*, London, Johnson, 1784.

HUOT S., *Hérodiade et la Joconde*, in *Le mythe d'Hérodiade chez Mallarmé. Genèse et évolution*, Pais, 1977.

HUYGHE R., *La Gioconda*, in *Leonardo. La pittura*, introduzione e a cura di P. C. Marani, Firenze, Giunti Martello, 1985.

JASPERS K., *Leonardo filosofo*, Milano, SE, 1988.

JOANNIDES P., *Leonardo da Vinci, Peter-Paul Rubens, Pierre-Nolasque Bergeret and the 'Fight for the Standard'*, «Achademia Leonardi Vinci. Journal of Leonardo Studies and Bibliography of Vinciana», I, Firenze, Giunti, 1988.

KEELE K. D., *The Genesis of Mona Lisa*, «Journal of the History of Medicine and Allied Sciences», XIV, 2 (1959).

KEELE K. D., *Leonardo da Vinci. Elements of the Science of Man*, London, Academic Press, 1983.

KEELE K. D., PEDRETTI C., *Disegni anatomici dalla Biblioteca Reale di Windsor* (a cura di), catalogo mostra, Firenze, Giunti Barbèra, 1979.

KEELE K. D., PEDRETTI C., *Corpus degli studi anatomici nella collezione di Sua Maestà la Regina Elisabetta II nel Castello di Windsor*, Firenze, Giunti, 1980-85.

KEMP M., *"Il concetto dell'anima" in Leonardo's Early Skull Studies*, «Journal of the Warburg and Courtauld Institutes», XXXIV (1971).

KEMP M., *Dissection and Divinity in Leonardo's Late Anatomies*, «Journal of the Warburg and Courtauld Institutes», XXXV (1972).

M. KEMP, *Leonardo's Leda and the Belvedere River-Gods. Roman Sources and a New Chronology*, «Art History», 1980.

KEMP M., *Leonardo da Vinci. Le mirabili operazioni della natura e dell'uomo*, Milano, Mondadori, 1982.

KEMP M., *Les inventions de la nature et la nature de l'invention*, in *Léonard de Vinci ingénieur et architecte*, catalogo della mostra di Montreal, Montreal Museum of Fine Arts, 1987.

KEMP M., *Leonardo e lo spazio dello scultore*, «Lettura Vinciana», XXVII, Firenze, Giunti Barbèra, 1988.

KEMP M., *Leonardo da Vinci. Artist, Scientist, Inventor*, catalogue of exhibition at the Hayward Gallery, ed. by M. Kemp, with essays by E. H. Gombrich, J. Roberts, P. Steadman, London, Yale University Press, 1989.

KEMP M., *'Christo fanciullo'*, «Achademia Leonardi Vinci. Journal of Leonardo Studies and Bibliography of Vinciana», IV, Firenze, Giunti, 1991.

KEMP M., *Leonardo da Vinci. The Mystery of the Madonna Yarnwinder*, with A.T. Crowe, exhibition catalogue, Edinburgh, National Gallery of Scotland, 1992.

KEMP M., *La scienza dell'arte. Prospettiva e percezione visiva da Brunelleschi a Seurat*, Firenze, Giunti, 1994.

KEMP M., *Leonardo's Fossils*, «Natural History», CV, 11 (1996).

KEMP M., *'The Reign of Vanities', A Cloudburst of Material Possessions. A Fantasy on a Drawing by Leonardo da Vinci*, exhibition guide, London, Purdy Hicks Gallery, 1997.

KEMP M., *'In Praise of Model making; from Leonardo to Beuys'*, Demarco: On the Road to Meikle Segie, Kingston University, 2000.

KEMP M., *Leonardo da Vinci*, Oxford, Oxford University Press, 2004.

KHÉRUMIAN R., *Léonard de Vinci et les mystères*, Paris, Nizet, 1952.

KIANG D., *Leonardo and Alchemy. A Bibliographical Note*, «Achademia Leonardi Vinci. Journal of Leonardo Studies and Bibliography of Vinciana », X, Firenze, Giunti, 1997.

KUSTODIEVA K. T., *Madonna Benois e Madonna Litta*, in *Leonardo. La pittura*, introduzione e a cura di P. C. Marani, Firenze, Giunti Martello, 1985.

KUSTODIEVA K. T., *Works from Leonardo da Vinci's school in the Ermitage Collection*, Saint Peterburg, The State Ermitage, 1998.

KUSTODIEVA K. T., *La Madonna Litta. Storia di un capolavoro di Leonardo*, in *Leonardo: la Madonna Litta dell'Ermitage di San Pietroburgo*, Roma, De Luca, 2003.

KWAKKELSTEIN M. W., *Leonardo da Vinci's grotesque heads and breaking of physiognomic mould*, «Journal of the Warburg and Courtauld Institutes», LIV, London, Warburg Institute, University of London, 1991.

KWAKKELSTEIN M. W., *The Lost Book on 'moti mentali'*, «Achademia Leonardi Vinci. Journal of Leonardo Studies and Bibliography of Vinciana », VI, Firenze, Giunti, 1993.

KWAKKELSTEIN M. W., *"Teste di vecchi in buon numero"*, «Raccolta Vinciana», XXV (1993).

LANGLADE J. DE, *Léonard de Vinci, Dante Gabriel Rossetti et les Préraphaelites*, «Bulletin de l'Association Léonard de Vinci», XIII (1974).

LANGTON DOUGLAS R., *Leonardo's Childhood*, «Burlington Magazine», LXXXV (1944).

LAURENZA D., *La «fisonomia naturale» di Leonardo: una traccia giovanile e alcuni sviluppi*, «Achademia Leonardi Vinci. Journal of Leonardo Studies and Bibliography of Vinciana », IX, Firenze, Giunti, 1996.

LAURENZA D., *Il pensiero medico di Leonardo intorno al 1490: Hieronymo Manfredi e altre probabili fonti*, «Achademia Leonardi Vinci. Journal of Leonardo Studies and Bibliography of Vinciana », X, Firenze, Giunti, 1997.

LAURENZA D., *Gli studi leonardiani sul volo. Spunti per una riconsiderazione*, in *Tutte le opere non son per istancarmi, Raccolta di scritti per i settant'anni di Carlo Pedretti*, a cura di F. Frosini, Roma, Edizioni Associate, 1998.

LAURENZA D., *Leonardo. La scienza trasfigurata in arte*, in «Le Scienze», IX (1999).

LAURENZA D., *De figura umana. Fisiognomica, anatomia e arte in Leonardo*, Firenze, Olschki, 2001.

Laurenza D., *Leonardo nella Roma di Leone X (c. 1513-16). Gli studi anatomici, la vita, l'arte*, «Lettura Vinciana», XLIII, Firenze, Giunti, 2004.

Laurenza D., *Leonardo. Il volo*, Firenze, Giunti, 2004.

Lesueur F., *Léonard de Vinci et Chambord*, «Études d'Arts», 8-10, 1953-54.

Ligabue G., *Leonardo da Vinci e i fossili*, Vicenza, Neri Pozza, 1977.

Longhi R., *Difficoltà di Leonardo*, «Paragone», III, 29 (1952).

Lopez G., *La roba e la libertà. Leonardo nella Milano di Ludovico il Moro*, Milano, Mursia, 1982.

Lossky B., *Léonard de Vinci mourant dans les bras de François Ier*, «Bulletin de l'Association Léonard de Vinci», Amboise, 9 (1970).

Luporini C., *La mente di Leonardo*, Firenze, Le Lettere, 1953.

Maccagni C., *Riconsiderando il problema delle fonti di Leonardo: l'elenco di libri ai ff. 2v-3r del cod. 8936 della Biblioteca Nacional di Madrid*, in «Lettura Vinciana», X, Firenze, Giunti, 1971.

Maccurdy E., *Les Carnets de Léonard de Vinci*, Paris, Gallimard, 1987.

Maclagan E., *Leonardo in the consulting room*, «Burlington Magazine», XLII, 1923.

Maïdani J. P., *Alter ego, 1501: l'agneau et le dévidoir*, «Achademia Leonardi Vinci. Journal of Leonardo Studies and Bibliography of Vinciana», VI, 1993.

Maïdani J. P., *Léonard de Vinci. Mythologie ou théologie?*, Paris, PUF, 1994.

Malaguzzi-Valeri F., *Leonardo da Vinci e il tiburio del Duomo di Milano*, «Il Marzocco», 44 (1903).

Malaguzzi Valeri F., *La corte di Ludovico il Moro*, 4 voll., Milano, Hoepli, 1915-23.

Maltese C., *Gusto e metodo scientifico nel pensiero architettonico di Leonardo*, «Lettura Vinciana», Firenze, Giunti Barbèra, 1975.

Mancini F., *Urbanistica rinascimentale a Imola da Girolamo Riario a Leonardo da Vinci (1472-1502)*, Imola, Galeati, 1979.

Marangoni M., *Saper vedere*, Milano, Treves, 1933.

Marani P. C., *Stendhal e il 'Cenacolo' di Leonardo*, «L'Esopo», 3 (1979).

Marani P. C., *Il Codice Ashburnham 361 della Biblioteca Medicea Laurenziana di Firenze. Trattato di Architettura di Francesco di Giorgio Martini (a cura di)*, 2 voll., Firenze, Giunti Barbèra, 1979.

Marani P. C., *Leonardo e l'architettura fortificata: connessioni e sviluppi*, in *Leonardo e l'età della ragione*, a cura di E. Bellone, P. Rossi, Milano, Scientia, 1982.

Marani P. C., *Leonardo, Francesco di Giorgio e il tiburio del Duomo di Milano*, «Arte Lombarda», 62 (1982).

Marani P. C., *Leonardo e le colonne «ad tronchonos». Tracce di un programma iconologico per Ludovico il Moro*, Raccolta Vinciana, XXI (1982).

Marani P. C., *L'architettura fortificata negli studi di Leonardo da Vinci*, Firenze, Olschki, 1984.

Marani P. C., *'Circulo dentato ortogonialmente' (Ms. Madrid 8937, f. 117r). Leonardo, gli ingegneri e alcune macchine lombarde*, «Lettura Vinciana», XXV, Firenze, Giunti Barbèra, 1985.

Marani P. C., *La mappa di Imola di Leonardo*, in *Leonardo: il Codice Hammer e la mappa di Imola*, Firenze, Giunti, 1985.

Marani P. C., *Leonardo. Catalogo completo dei dipinti*, Firenze, Cantini, 1989.

Marani P. C., *Leonardo e i leonardeschi a Brera*, Milano, Electa, 1990.

Marani P. C., *Leonardo*, Milano, Electa, 1994.

Marani P. C., *Tivoli, Hadrian and Antinos. New Evidence of Leonardo's Relation to the Antique*, «Achademia Leonardi Vinci. Journal of Leonardo Studies and Bibliography of Vinciana», VIII, Firenze, Giunti, 1995.

Marani P. C., *Il problema della bottega di Leonardo: la "praticha" e la trasmissione delle idee di Leonardo sull'arte e la pittura*, in *I leonardeschi. L'eredità di Leonardo in Lombardia*, Milano, Skira, 1998.

Marani P. C., *Il Cenacolo. Guida al Refettorio*, Milano, Electa, 1999.

Marani P. C., *Leonardo. Una carriera di pittore*, Milano, Motta, 1999.

Marani P. C., *La Vergine delle Rocce della National Gallery di Londra. Maestro e bottega di fronte al modello*, «Lettura Vinciana», XLII, Firenze, Giunti, 2003.

Marani P. C., *Leonardo. La Gioconda*, «Art Dossier», 189, Firenze, Giunti, 2003.

Marani P. C., *Il ritratto di Leonardo nell'immaginario collettivo e nella tradizione documentaria*, in *Leonardo da Vinci: la vera immagine. Documenti e testimonianze sulla vita e sull'opera*, mostra a cura di V. Arrighi, A. Bellinazzi, E. Villata, Firenze, Giunti, 2005.

Marcolongo R., *Leonardo da Vinci artista-scienziato*, Milano, Hoepli, 1943.

Margat J., *Piccolo trattato di Giocondologia*, «Bizarre», maggio (1959).

Margat J., *Le mythe de la Joconde: déclinaisons sur le tableau le plus emblématique de tous les temps*, Lausanne, Favre, 1997.

Mariani V., *Le idee di Leonardo sulla pittura*, «Lettura Vinciana», VI, Firenze, Giunti Barbèra, 1966.

Mariette P. J., *Recueil de Textes de caractère & de Charges, dessinées par Léonard de Vinci Florentin & gravées par M. le C. de C.*, Paris, Mariette, 1730.

Mariette P. J., *Description sommaire des Pierres Gravées du Cabinet de feu M. Crozat*, Paris, 1741.

Mariette P. J., *Abécédario de P. J. Mariette et autres notes inédites de cet amateur sur les arts et sur les artistes*, 6 voll., Paris, Chennevières et Montaiglon, 1851-60.

Marinoni A., *Tutti gli scritti. Scritti letterari*, Milano, Rizzoli, 1952.

Marinoni A., *I manoscritti di Leonardo da Vinci e le loro edizioni*, in *Leonardo. Saggi e Ricerche*, a cura di G. Castelfranco, Roma, Istituto Poligrafico dello Stato, 1954.

Marinoni A., *I rebus di Leonardo da Vinci raccolti e interpretati. Con un saggio su "Una virtù spirituale"*, Firenze, Olschki, 1954.

Marinoni A., *Il Regno e il Sito di Venere*, in *Il Poliziano e il suo tempo*, «Atti del IV Congresso Internazionale di Studi sul Rinascimento», a cura di V. Fera e M. Martelli, Firenze, Olschki, 1957.

Marinoni A., *L'essere del nulla*, «Lettura Vinciana», I, Firenze, Giunti Barbèra, 1960.

Marinoni A., *Giucco da Gello*, «Raccolta Vinciana», XVIII (1960).

Marinoni A., *Leonardo da Vinci*, «Grande Antologia Filosofica», VI, Milano, Marzorati, 1964.

Marinoni A., *Leonardo, Luca Pacioli e il 'De ludo geometrico'*, «Atti della Accademia Petrarca di Lettere, Arti e Scienze di Arezzo», XL, Arezzo, 1970-1972.

Marinoni A., *Leonardo da Vinci: letture vinciane I-XII (1960-1972)*, Firenze, Giunti Barbèra, 1974.

MARINONI A., *Codice Atlantico*, trascrizione diplomatica e critica 12 voll. (a cura di), Firenze, Giunti, 1975-80.

MARINONI A., *Gli scritti di Leonardo*, in *Leonardo scienziato*, Firenze, Giunti Barbèra, 1980.

MARINONI A., *I manoscritti*, in *Leonardo e Milano*, a cura di G. A. Dell'Acqua, Milano, Banca Popolare di Milano, 1982.

MARINONI A., *La biblioteca di Leonardo da Vinci*, «Raccolta Vinciana», XXII (1987).

MARINONI A., *Leonardo in Romagna*, «Torricelliana», XXXIX, Faenza, Lega, 1989.

MARINONI A., *Leonardo da Vinci. Scritti letterari*, Milano, Rizzoli, 1991.

MARINONI A., *Sulla tipologia dei manoscritti vinciani*, «Raccolta Vinciana», XXIV (1992).

MARSHALL M., *S. M. Eisenstein on Leonardo's Deluge*, «Achademia Leonardi Vinci. Journal of Leonardo Studies and Bibliography of Vinciana», III, Firenze, Giunti, 1990.

MARTIN-DEZÈMIL J., *Léonard de Vinci et les astuces de la construction solognote*, «Revue de l'Art», 87 (1990)

MARTONE T., *Leonardo da Vinci's Reaction Portraits*, «Rivista di Studi italiani» (Univ. di Toronto), II, 2 (1984).

MASUCCI G., *Il disegno territoriale di Leonardo da Vinci. La regione*, in *Tutte le opere non son per istancarmi. Raccolta di scritti per i settant'anni di Carlo Pedretti*, a cura di F. Frosini, Roma, Edizioni Associate, 1998.

MATHÈ J., *Le invenzioni di Leonardo Da Vinci, Disegni e Modelli*, Ginevra-Parigi, Melita, 1989.

MAZENTA G. A., *Le memorie su Leonardo da Vinci di Don Ambrogio Mazenta ripublicate ed illustrate da D. Luigi Gramatica*, Milano, Alfieri & Lacroix, 1919.

MAZZOCCHI DOGLIO M., *Leonardo 'apparatore' di spettacoli a Milano*, in *Leonardo e gli spettacoli del suo tempo*, catalogo della mostra, Milano, Electa, 1983.

MCCURDY E., *The drawings of Leonardo da Vinci*, «Apollo», XII (1930).

MCMAHON A. PH., *Leonardo da Vinci: Treatise on Painting*, introd. by L. H. Heydenreich, Princeton University Press, 1956.

MC MULLEN R., *Les grands mystères de la Joconde*, Paris, Trévise, 1981.

MEI F., *Leonardo e la cultura esoterica*, in *Magia e astrologia nel Cenacolo di Leonardo*, a cura di F. Berdini, Roma, Editalia, 1982.

MELLER P., *Leonardo da Vinci's Drawings to the Divine Comedy*, «Acta Historiae Artium Academiae Scientiarum Hungaricae», 1955.

MELLER P., *Quello che Leonardo non ha scritto sulla figura umana: dall'Uomo di Vitruvio alla Leda*, «Arte Lombarda», 67 (1983-84).

MELLER P., *La Battaglia d'Anghiari*, in *Leonardo. La pittura*, introduzione e a cura di P. C. Marani, Firenze, Giunti Martello, 1985.

MELLER S., *Die reiterdarstellungen Leonardos und sie Budapester Bronzestatuette*, «Jahrbuch der Königlich Preuszischen Kunstsammlungen», XXXVII (1916).

MERCIER MONTGOMERY R., *Tò Mona Lisa smiling (in her portrait in the Louvre)*, «Il Carroccio», VIII (1927).

MERESHKOWSKY D., *La resurrezione degli dei:: Leonardo da Vinci*, Milano, Martello, 1971.

MESSINA F., *Divagazioni su Leonardo scultore*, «L'Osservatore Politico Letterario», II, 1956.

MICHELET J., *La Renaissance*, [1855], Paris, Lemerre, 1887.

MIGLIACCIO L., *Leonardo 'auctor' del genere comico*, «Achademia Leonardi Vinci. Journal of Leonardo Studies and Bibliography of Vinciana», VIII, Firenze, Giunti, 1995.

MIGLIORE S., *Tra Hermes e Prometeo. Il mito di Leonardo nel Decadentismo europeo*, Firenze, Olschki, 1994.

MINICUCCI A., *Quid ex Ovidii operibus in Leonardi Vincii scripta sit derivatum*, «Acta Conventus omnium gentium Ovidianis studiis favendis», Bucurestiis, 1976.

MOFFIT J. F., *The Evidentia of Curling Water and Whirling Wind: Leonardo's Ekphraseis of the Latin Weatherman*, «Achademia Leonardi Vinci. Journal of Leonardo Studies and Bibliography of Vinciana», IV, Firenze, Giunti, 1991.

MÖLLER E., *Wie sah Leonardo aus?*, «Belvedere», Wien, 1926.

MÖLLER E., *Leonardo's Madonna with the Yarnwinder*, «Burlington Magazine», XLIX, 281, 1926.

MÖLLER E., *Leonardo e il Verrocchio. Quattro rilievi di capitani antichi lavorati per Re Mattia Corvino*, «Raccolta Vinciana», XIV, 1930-34.

MÖLLER E., *Ser Giuliano di ser Piero da Vinci e le sue relazioni con Leonardo*, «Rivista d'arte», XVI (1934).

MÖLLER E., *Leonardos Madonna mit der Nelke in der Alteren Pinakothek*, «Münchn. Jahrb. Der bild. K.», XII (1937-38).

MÖLLER E., *Der Geburtstag des Lionardo da Vinci*, «Jahrbuch der preussischer Kulturbesitz», LX (1939).

MONACO M. C., *"…una Leda di marmo, bona, anchora li mancha qualche menbro…". Considerazioni sulle Lede antiche dei tempi di Leonardo*, in *Leonardo e il mito di Leda*, a cura di G. Dalli Regoli, R. Nanni, A. Natali, Vinci 23 giugno-23 settembre, Cinisello Balsamo, Silvana Editoriale, 2001.

MONTI R., *Leonardo*, Firenze, Sansoni, 1966.

MONTI S., *Albero ossia discendenza della famiglia Da Vinci*, Como, Società Storica Comense, 1909.

MONTI S., *Curiosità Letterarie-Storiche-Artistiche* (a cura di), Como, Ostinelli, 1913-16.

MÜLLER HOFSTEDE J., *An Early Rubens Conversion of St. Paul. The Beginning of his Preoccupation with Leonardo's Battle of Anghiari*, «Burlington Magazine», CVI (1964).

MÜNTZ E., *Léonard de Vinci sculpteur. La statue équestre du duc Francesco Sforza*, «Revue Universelle illustrée», I (1888).

MÜNTZ E., *Studi leonardeschi*, «Arch. Stor. dell'arte», III, II (1897).

MÜNTZ E., *Leonardo da Vinci: Artist, Thinker, and Man of Science*, 2 vols, London/New York, Heinemann, 1898.

MÜNTZ E., *Leonardo da Vinci*, Paris, Hachette, 1899.

MURRAY P., *Leonardo and Bramante. Leonardo's approach to anatomy and architecture, and its effect on Bramante*, «Architectural Review», CXXXIV (1963).

NANNI R., *Astrologia e prospettiva. Per lo studio dell'immagine della scienza nel Paragone di Leonardo*, «Raccolta Vinciana», XXVII (1997).

NANNI R., *Osservazione, convenzione, ricomposizione nel paesaggio leonardiano del 1473*, «Raccolta Vinciana», XXVIII (1999).

NANNI R., *Leonardo nella 'tradizione' di Leda*, in *Leonardo e il mito di Leda*, a cura di G. Dalli Regoli, R. Nanni, A. Natali, Vinci 23 giugno-23 settembre 2001, Cinisello Balsamo, Silvana Editoriale, 2001.

NANNI R., *Usi diversi di appunti di paesaggio in Leonardo*, in *Leonardo Genio Cartografo. La rappresentazione del territorio tra scienza e arte*, Arezzo 21 giugno-30 settembre, catalogo a cura di A. Cantile, Firenze, I. G. M., 2003.

NATALI A., *Lo sguardo degli angeli. Verrocchio, Leonardo e il "Battesimo di Cristo"* (a cura di), Cinisello Balsamo, Silvana Editoriale, 1998.

NATALI A., *La natura artefatta*, in *Leonardo a Piombino e l'idea della città moderna tra Quattro e Cinquecento*, a cura di A. Fara, Firenze, Olschki, 1999.

NATALI A., *Dubbi, difficoltà e disguidi nell'Annunciazione di Leonardo*, in *L'Annunciazione di Leonardo. La montagna sul mare*, a cura di A. Natali, Cinisello Balsamo, Silvana Editoriale, 2000.

NATALI A., *Le pose di Leda*, in *Leonardo e il mito di Leda*, catalogo a cura di G. Dalli Regoli, R. Nanni, A. Natali, Vinci 23 giugno-23 settembre 2001, Cinisello Balsamo, Silvana Editoriale, 2001.

NATHAN J., *Some Drawing Practices of Leonardo da Vinci: New Light on the Saint Anne*, «Mitteilungen des Kunsthistorischen Instituts in Florenz», 36 (1992).

NATHAN J., *Kunst und Naturbetrachtung: funktionale Bildformeln im Werk Leonardos*, in *Leonardo da Vinci: Natur und Kunst in Bewegung*, a cura di F. Fehrenbach, München, W. Fink, 2001.

NEPI SCIRÈ G., *La Battaglia di Anghiari*, in *Leonardo & Venezia*, catalogo della mostra, Milano, Bompiani, 1992.

NEPI SCIRÈ G., *Da Leonardo a Canaletto: disegni delle Gallerie dell'Accademia*, Milano, Electa, 1999.

NICODEMI G., *I ritratti di Leonardo da Vinci*, «Raccolta Vinciana», XV-XVI (1935-39)

NICODEMI G., *Leonardo da Vinci: Gemälde, Zeichnungen, Studien*, Leipzig, Fretz & Wasmuth, 1939.

NICODEMI G., *Il volto di Leonardo*, in *Leonardo da Vinci*, Novara, De Agostini, 1980.

NICOLINO F., *Il "Leonardo" freudiano*, in *Indagini su Freud e la psicanalisi*, Napoli, Liguori, 1981.

NOJIA S., *Una frase in turco di mano di Leonardo nel Codice Atlantico*, «Rend. Istit. Lomb.», 110 (1976).

NOSOTTI S., *Leonardo da Vinci: L'intuizione della natura*, catalogo, Museo di Storia Naturale, Milano, Firenze, Giunti Barbèra, 1983.

OLSSON K.-G., *The Vision of a Bridge*, «Achademia Leonardi Vinci. Journal of Leonardo Studies and Bibliography of Vinciana», VI, Firenze, Giunti, 1993.

ORTEGA Y GASSET J., *La Gioconda*, in *La disumanizzazione dell'arte*, a cura di S. Battaglia, Forlì, Ethica, 1964.

OTTINO DELLA CHIESA A., *L'opera completa di Leonardo pittore*, presentazione di M. Pomilio, Milano, Rizzoli, 1967.

PANOFSKY E., *Studies in Ideology: Humanistic Themes In the Art of the Renaissance*, New York, Harper and Row, 1939.

PANOFSKY E., *The Codex Huygens and Leonardo da Vinci's Art Theory. The Pierpont Morgan Library Codex M. A. 1139*, London, The Warburg Institute, 1940.

PANOFSKY E., *Meaning in the visual arts: papers in and art history*, Garden City, N.Y., Doubleday Anchor Books, 1955.

PANOFSKY E., *Idea. Contributo alla storia dell'estetica*, Firenze, La Nuova Italia, 1975.

PAOLUCCI A., *Leonardo dilaga nel "Battesimo"*, «Il Sole-24 ore. Domenica», 140, 24 maggio 1998.

PAOLUCCI A., *La Leda che piaceva a Goering*, «Il Sole-24 ore. Domenica», 200, 22 luglio 2001.

PAOLUCCI A., *Rinascimento: capolavori dei musei italiani* (a cura di), Tokio-Roma, Milano, Skira, 2001.

PAOLUCCI A., *Leonardo e la Madonna Litta: un caso di immedesimazione*, in *Leonardo: la Madonna Litta dell'Ermitage di San Pietroburgo*, Roma, De Luca, 2003.

PAPINI C. M., *Il sorriso della Gioconda. La scrittura fra immaginario e reale*, Roma, Bulzoni, 1989.

PAPINI G., *Leonardo*, in *Ventiquattro cervelli*, Firenze, Vallecchi, 1924.

PAPINI G., *Leonardo e Savonarola*, «Nuova Antologia», LXXXVII, ottobre (1952).

PARRONCHI A., *Nuove proposte per Leonardo scultore*, «Achademia Leonardi Vinci. Journal of Leonardo Studies and Bibliography of Vinciana», II, Firenze, Giunti, 1989.

PARRONCHI A., *Inganni d'ombre*, «Achademia Leonardi Vinci. Journal of Leonardo Studies and Bibliography of Vinciana», IV, Firenze, Giunti, 1991.

PATER W., *Il Rinascimento. Studi d'Arte e di Poesia*, traduzione di A. De Rinaldis, Napoli, Ricciardi, 1925.

PEDRETTI C., *Documenti e memorie riguardanti Leonardo da Vinci a Bologna e in Emilia*, Bologna, Fiammenghi, 1953.

PEDRETTI C., *La macchina idraulica costruita da Leonardo per conto di Bernardo Rucellai e i primi contatori d'acqua*, «Raccolta Vinciana», XVII (1954).

PEDRETTI C., *Un ricordo di Gio. Paolo Lo mazzo su Leonardo scultore*, «L'Arte», XXI (1957).

PEDRETTI C., *Studi Vinciani*, Genève, Droz, 1957.

PEDRETTI C., *Uno studio per la Gioconda*, «L'Arte», LVIII, 24 (1959).

PEDRETTI C., *Il "Neron da Sancto Andrea"*, «Raccolta Vinciana», XVIII (1960).

PEDRETTI C., *Leonardo at Lyon*, «Raccolta Vinciana», XIX (1962).

PEDRETTI C., *Leonardo e Antonio Vinci da Pistoia*, «Raccolta Vinciana», XIX (1962).

PEDRETTI C., *A Chronology of Leonardo da Vinci's Architectural Studies after 1500, In Appendix: A Letter to Pope Leo X on the Architecture of Ancient Rome*, Genève, Droz, 1962.

PEDRETTI C., *Dessins d'une scène, exécutés par Léonard de Vinci pour Charles d'Amboise (1506-1507)*, in *Le lieu théâtral à la Renaissance*, Royaumont 22-27 mars, Paris, CNRS, 1964.

PEDRETTI C., *Leonardo da Vinci On painting. A Lost Book (Libro A) Reassembled from the Codex Vaticanus 1270 and from the Codex Leicester*, Berkeley-Los Angeles, University Of California Press, 1964.

PEDRETTI C., *Leonardo inedito. Tre saggi*, Firenze, Giunti Barbèra, 1968.

PEDRETTI C., *La battaglia di Anghiari di Leonardo*, «L'Arte», I (1968).

PEDRETTI C., *Le note di pittura di Leonardo da Vinci nei manoscritti inediti di Madrid*, «Lettura Vinciana», VIII, Firenze, Giunti Barbèra, 1969.

PEDRETTI C., *Leonardo da Vinci, Manuscripts and Drawings of the French Period 1517-1518*, «Gazette des Beaux-Arts», s. VI, LXXVI (1970).

PEDRETTI C., *Leonardo da Vinci. The Royal Palace at Romorantin*, Cambridge, Mass., The Belknap Press of Harvard University Press, 1972.

PEDRETTI C., *La Verruca*, «Renaissance Quarterly», XXV, 4 (1972).

PEDRETTI C., *Il progetto originario per Santa Maria delle Grazie e altri aspetti inediti del rapporto Leonardo-Bramante*, in *Studi Bramanteschi*. Atti del Congresso internazionale. Milano, Urbino, Roma, 1970, a cura del Comitato Nazionale per le Celebrazioni Bramantesche, Roma, De Luca, 1972.

PEDRETTI C., *Leonardo. A Study in Chronology and Style*, London, Thames and Hudson, 1973.

PEDRETTI C., *The original project for S. Maria delle Grazie*, «Journal of the Society of Architectural Historians», XXXII, 1973.

PEDRETTI C., *New Discovered Evidence of Leonardo's Association with Bramante*, «Journal of the Society of Architectural Historians», III (1973).

PEDRETTI C., *Eccetera: perché la minestra si fredda*, «Lettura Vinciana», XV, Firenze, Giunti Barbèra, 1975.

PEDRETTI C., *Il primo Leonardo a Firenze. L'Arno, la cupola, il Battistero*, Firenze, Giunti Barbèra, 1976.

PEDRETTI C., *Commentary to J. P. Richter's of The Literary Works*, Oxford, Phaidon, 1977.

PEDRETTI C., *Progetti brunelleschiani a Milano nei ricordi di Leonardo*, in *Atti del Convegno internazionale di Studi Brunelleschiani…*, 1977, Firenze, 1978.

PEDRETTI C., *Leonardo architetto*, Milano, Electa, 1978.

PEDRETTI C., *The Codex Atlanticus of Leonardo da Vinci. A Catalogue of Its Newly Restored Sheets*, 2 vols, New York, Johnson Reprint Corporation, Harcourt Brace Jovanovich, 1978.

PEDRETTI C., *Leonardo*, Bologna, Capitol, 1979.

PEDRETTI C., *Leonardo. Il disegno*, «Art Dossier», 67, Firenze, Giunti, 1981.

PEDRETTI C., *Giorgione e Leonardo*, in *Giorgione e l'Umanesimo veneziano*, a cura di R. Pallucchini, Firenze, Olschki, 1981.

PEDRETTI C., *La scientia di questi obbietti è di grande utilità*, «Lettura Vinciana», XXII, Firenze, Giunti Barbèra, 1982.

PEDRETTI C., *Prefazione*, in *Il codice sul volo degli uccelli*, a cura di A. Marinoni, ed. inglese, New York, Harcourt Brace Jovanovich, 1982.

PEDRETTI C., *I cavalli di Leonardo. Studi sul cavallo e altri animali di Leonardo da Vinci dalla Biblioteca Reale nel Castello di Windsor* (a cura di), introduzione di J. Roberts, Firenze, Giunti Barbèra, 1984.

PEDRETTI C., *Leonardo: Il Codice Hammer e la mappa di Imola. Arte e scienza a Bologna, in Emilia e Romagna nel primo Cinquecento* (a cura di), Firenze, Giunti Barbèra, 1985.

PEDRETTI C., *The Mermaid*, «Achademia Leonardi Vinci. Journal of Leonardo Studies and Bibliography of Vinciana», I, Firenze, Giunti, 1988.

PEDRETTI C., *The "libro di medicina di cavalli*, «Achademia Leonardi Vinci. Journal of Leonardo Studies and Bibliography of Vinciana», I, Firenze, Giunti, 1988.

PEDRETTI C., *Disegni di Leonardo e della sua cerchia nella Biblioteca Reale di Torino* (a cura di), Firenze, Giunti, 1990.

PEDRETTI C., *Leonardo and the Antique*, «Achademia Leonardi Vinci. Journal of Leonardo Studies and Bibliography of Vinciana», IV, Firenze, Giunti, 1991.

PEDRETTI C., *The 'Angel in the Flesh'*, «Achademia Leonardi Vinci. Journal of Leonardo Studies and Bibliography of Vinciana», IV, Firenze, Giunti, 1991.

PEDRETTI C., *The Gaddi 'puella'*, «Achademia Leonardi Vinci. Journal of Leonardo Studies and Bibliography of Vinciana», IV, Firenze, Giunti, 1991.

PEDRETTI C., *Paolo di Leonardo*, «Achademia Leonardi Vinci. Journal of Leonardo Studies and Bibliography of Vinciana», V, Firenze, Giunti, 1992.

PEDRETTI C., *Eraclitus and Democritus*, «Achademia Leonardi Vinci. Journal of Leonardo Studies and Bibliography of Vinciana», VI, Firenze, Giunti, 1993.

PEDRETTI C., *"li medici mi crearono e desstrussono"*, «Achademia Leonardi Vinci. Journal of Leonardo Studies and Bibliography of Vinciana», VI, Firenze, Giunti, 1993.

PEDRETTI C., *Leonardo in Sweden*, «Achademia Leonardi Vinci. Journal of Leonardo Studies and Bibliography of Vinciana», VI, Firenze, Giunti, 1993.

PEDRETTI C., *Leonardo. Il ritratto*, «Art Dossier», 138, Firenze, Giunti, 1998.

PEDRETTI C., *Il teatrino di Leonardo*, «Il Sole-24 Ore. Domenica», 27 giugno 1999.

PEDRETTI C., *Leonardo da Vinci. La Battaglia di Anghiari e le armi sofisticate*, Firenze, Grantour, 2000.

PEDRETTI C., *Presentazione*, in *Leonardo da Vinci. Il codice Atlantico della Biblioteca Ambrosiana di Milano nella trascrizione critica di Augusto Marinoni*, Firenze, Giunti, 2000.

PEDRETTI C., *Caterina, Ludovico e Leonardo. Ipotesi di lavoro*, in *Caterina Sforza. Una donna del Cinquecento. Storia e Arte tra Medioevo e Rinascimento*, catalogo a cura di L. Andalò, Imola, La Mandragora, 2000.

PEDRETTI C., *Leonardo e Perugino in Lombardia. Quelle figure a "semicircoli"*, «Art Dossier», 170, Firenze, Giunti, 2001.

PEDRETTI C., *Cesenatico e il Leonardo di Marino Moretti*, Cesena, Sintini, 2002.

PEDRETTI C., *Leonardo: dalla pianta centrale allo spazio sferico*, in *La chiesa a pianta centrale, tempio civico del rinascimento*, a cura di B. Adorni, Milano, Electa, 2002.

PEDRETTI C., *Gioconda in volo*, in P. C. Marani, *Leonardo. La Gioconda*, «Art Dossier», 189, Firenze, Giunti, 2003.

PEDRETTI C., *In piedi o seduta?* in *Leonardo: la Madonna Litta dell'Ermitage di San Pietroburgo*, Roma, De Luca, 2003.

PEDRETTI C., *Le macchie di Leonardo*, «Lettura Vinciana», XLIV, Firenze, Giunti, 2004.

PEDRETTI C., *Leonardo e l'arte sacra*, «L'Osservatore Romano», Domenica 12 Settembre 2004.

PEDRETTI C., *Così si "maravigliava" Leonardo*, «L'Osservatore Romano», CXLV, 62, 16 marzo 2005.

PEDRETTI C., *Un «mirabile artificio» in omaggio al re di Francia*, «L'Osservatore Romano», Giovedì 26 Maggio 2005.

Pedretti C., *Leonardo. La pittura*, «Art Dossier», 215, Firenze, Giunti, 2005.

Pedretti C., *Paleografia vinciana*, in *Leonardo da Vinci: la vera immagine. Documenti e testimonianze sulla vita e sull'opera*, mostra a cura di V. Arrighi, A. Bellinazzi, E. Villata, Firenze, Giunti, 2005.

Pedretti C., Cianchi M., *Leonardo. I codici*, «Art Dossier», 100, Firenze, Giunti, 1995.

Pedretti C., Dalli Regoli G., *I disegni di Leonardo da Vinci e della sua cerchia nel Gabinetto Disegni e Stampe della Galleria degli Uffizi a Firenze*, Firenze, Giunti Barbèra, 1985.

Pedretti C., Roberts J., *Leonardo da Vinci: Drawings of Horses and Other Animals from the Royal Library at Windsor Castle*, Catalogo, Washington, National Gallery of Art, 1985.

Pedretti C., Trutty-Coohill P., *The Drawings of Leonardo da Vinci and his Circle in America,* Firenze, Giunti, 1993.

Pedretti C., Vecce C., *Libro di Pittura. Codice Urbinate lat. 1270 nella Biblioteca Apostolica Vaticana*, Firenze, Giunti, 1995.

Pedretti C., Vecce C., *Leonardo da Vinci. Il Codice Arundel 263 nella British Library. Edizione in fac-simile nel riordinamento cronologico dei suoi fascicoli*, Firenze, Giunti, 1998.

Péladan J., *Léonard de Vinci et les sciences occultes*, «Revue universelle», II (1902).

Pescio C., *Leonardo arte e scienza* (a cura di), Introduzione di C. Pedretti, Firenze, Giunti, 2000.

Petrioli Tofani A., *Gabinetto disegni e stampe degli Uffizi. Inventario. 1. Disegni esposti* (a cura di), Firenze, Olschki, 1986.

Petrioli Tofani A., *Il disegno fiorentino del tempo di Lorenzo il Magnifico* (a cura di), Cinisello Balsamo, Silvana Editoriale, 1992.

Pidcock M., *The Hang Glider*, «Achademia Leonardi Vinci. Journal of Leonardo Studies and Bibliography of Vinciana», VI, Firenze, Giunti, 1993.

Piel F., *Tavola Doria: Leonardo da Vincis modello zu seinem Wandgmälde der "Anghiarischlacht"*, Monaco, Mäander, 1995.

Piumati G., *Il codice Atlantico di Leonardo da Vinci nella Biblioteca Ambrosiana di Milano, riprodotto e pubblicato dalla Regia Accademia dei Lincei. Trascrizione diplomatica e critica di G. Piumati*, Milano, Hoepli, 1894-1903.

Piumati G., Sabachnikoff T., *Codice sul volo degli uccelli e varie altre materie* (a cura di), Paris, Rouveyre, 1893.

Pizzorusso A. C., *Leonardo's geology: a key to identifying the works of Boltraffio, d'Oggiono and other artists*, «Raccolta Vinciana», XXVII (1997).

Planche G., *Étude sur l'art et la poésie en Italie: Léonard de Vinci*, «Revue des deux mondes», 20 (1850).

Poggi G., *Leonardo da Vinci: la Vita di Giorgio Vasari nuovamente commentata e illustrata con 200 tavole*, Firenze, Pampaloni, 1919.

Pope-Hennessy J., *Italian Renaissance Sculpture*, London, Phaidon, 1958.

Pope-Hennessy J., *The interaction of Painting and Sculpture in Florence in the Fifteenth Century*, «Journal of the Royal Society of Arts», 117 (1969).

Popham A. E., *The Drawings of Leonardo da Vinci*, London, Cape, 1946.

Popham A. E., *Les dessins de Léonard de Vinci: introduction, notes et catalogue*, Bruxelles, Éditions de la Connaissance, 1947.

Popham A. E., *Leonardo's Drawings at Windsor*, «Atti del Convegno di Studi Vinciani», Firenze, Olschki, 1953.

Popham A. E., *The Dragon Fight*, in *Leonardo Saggi e Ricerche*, a cura di G. Castelfranco, Roma, Istituto Poligrafico dello Stato, 1954.

Pozzi L., *Leonardo da Vinci e il disegno del duomo di Pavia*, «Bollettino della Società pavese di storia patria», III, 1903.

Praz M., *Leonardo in Inghilterra*, «Ulisse», V, 17 (1952-53).

Ragghianti C. L., *Inizio di Leonardo*, «Critica d'Arte», I (1954).

Raggianti Collobi L., *Il Libro de' Disegni del Vasari*, Firenze, Vallecchi, 1974.

Ragghianti C. L., Dalli Regoli G., *Firenze 1470-1480. Disegni dal modello*, Università di Pisa. Istituto di Storia dell'Arte, Pisa, Lischi, 1975.

Raimondi G., *Leonardo erotico*, «Il Mondo», 25 aprile 1953.

Ramacciotti Donato V., *I decadenti e la Gioconda: ambiguità e polivalenza di un simbolo*, «Studi francesi», gennaio-agosto (1977).

Ravaisson Mollien C., *Les écrits de Léonard de Vinci*, «Gazette des Beaux-Arts», ser. 2, 23 (1881).

Regteren Altena van J., *Rubens as a Draughtsman, I, Relations with Italian Art*, «Burlington Magazine», LXXVI (1940).

Reinach S., *Répertoire de Peintures du Moyen Age et de la Renaissance (1280-1580)*, III, Paris, Leroux, 1905.

Reti L., *«Non si volta chi a stella è fiso». Le Imprese di Leonardo da Vinci*, «Bibliothèque d'Humanisme et Renaissance», XXI (1959).

Reti L., *Helicopters and Whirligigs*, «Raccolta Vinciana», XX (1964).

Reti L., *The Two Unpublished Manuscripts of Leonardo da Vinci in the Biblioteca Nacional of Madrid*, «Burlington Magazine», CX (1964).

Reti L., *Tracce di progetti perduti di Filippo Brunelleschi nel Codice Atlantico di Leonardo da Vinci*, «Lettura Vinciana», IV, Firenze, Giunti Barbèra, 1965.

Reti L., *The Leonardo da Vinci Codices in the Biblioteca Nacional of Madrid*, «Technology and Culture», VIII (1967).

Reti L., *Leonardo* (a cura di), Milano, Mondadori, 1974.

Ricci C., *Leonardo in Vaticano*, «Raccolta Vinciana», X (1919).

Richter I., *Selections from the notebooks of Leonardo*, Oxford, University Press, 1977.

Richter J. P., *Lionardo da Vinci im Orient*, «Zeitschrift fur bildende Kunst», XVI (1881).

Richter J. P., *The Literary Work of Leonardo da Vinci Compiled and Edited from the Original Manuscripts* (ed. by), 2 vols, London, Low-Marston-Searle and Rivington, 1883, *Commentary* by C. Pedretti, Oxford, Phaidon, 1977.

Roberts J., *Il Codice Hammer di Leonardo da Vinci* (a cura di), presentazione di C. Pedretti, Firenze, Giunti Barbèra, 1982.

Roberts J., *Master drawings in the Royal Collection: from Leonardo da Vinci to the present day*, London, Collins Harvill in association with The Queen's Gallery, 1986.

Roberts J., *Il collezionismo dei disegni di Leonardo*, in *Leonardo & Venezia*, catalogo della mostra, Milano, Bompiani, 1992.

Roberts J., Pedretti C., *Drawings by Leonardo da Vinci at Windsor Newly Revealed by Ultraviolet Light*, «Burlington Magazine», CXIX (1977).

Rocchi V., *Leonardo da Vinci e i suoi studi nell'Ospedale di Santo Spirito*, «Giornale di Medicina e Chirurgia», Roma, 1912.

Rogers C., *A Collection of Prints in imitation of Drawings to which are an-*

nexed the lives of their authors with explanatory and critical notes, 2 vols, London, Nichols, 1778.

ROSAND D., *The Meaning of the Mark: Leonardo and Titian*, VIII, The Franklin D. Murphy Lectures, Spencer Museum of Art University of Kansas, 1988.

ROSCI M., *Leonardo*, Milano, Mondadori, 1976.

ROSHEIM M. E., *L'automa programmabile di Leonardo*, «Lettura Vinciana», XL, Firenze, Giunti, 2001.

RUDEL J., *Tecnica di Leonardo*, «SeleArte», III (1954).

RUDEL J., *Il Bacco e San Giovanni Battista*, in *Leonardo. La pittura*, introduzione e a cura di P. C. Marani, Firenze, Giunti, 1985.

SAITO Y., *Nuova ipotesi interpretativa sulla "Vergine delle Rocce" di Leonardo da Vinci*, «Atti e Memorie della Accademia Petrarca di Lettere, Arti e Scienze», LVII, 1995, Arezzo, 1997.

SALMI M., *Il "Cenacolo" di Leonardo da Vinci e la Chiesa delle Grazie a Milano*, Milano, Treves, 1926.

SALMI M., *Mito e realtà di Leonardo*, «Lettura Vinciana», VII, Firenze, Giunti Barbèra, 1968.

SANTI B., *Leonardo da Vinci*, Firenze, Becocci/Scala, 1975.

SANTI P. M., *La Gioconda rubata − "Tu non saprai giammai perché sorrido*, «Achademia Leonardi Vinci. Journal of Leonardo Studies and Bibliography of Vinciana», III, Firenze, Giunti, 1990.

SASSOON D., *La Gioconda. L'avventurosa storia del quadro più famoso del mondo*, Roma, Carocci, 2002.

SCAGLIA G., *Alle origini degli studi tecnologici di Leonardo: la sega idraulica e le macchine per la palla e croce*, «Lettura Vinciana», XX, Firenze, Giunti Barbèra, 1981.

SCAGLIA G., *Leonardo's Non-inverted Writing and Verrocchio's Measured Drawing of a Horse*, «Art Bulletin», LXIV (1982).

SCAGLIA G., *Leonardo e Francesco di Giorgio a Milano*, in *Leonardo e l'età della ragione*, a cura di E. Bellone, P. Rossi, Milano, Scientia, 1982.

SCHOFIELD R., *Amadeo, Bramante and Leonardo and the Tiburio of Milan Cathedral*, «Achademia Leonardi Vinci. Journal of Leonardo Studies and Bibliography of Vinciana», II, Firenze, Giunti, 1989.

SCHOFIELD R., *Leonardo's Milanese Architecture*, «Achademia Leonardi Vinci. Journal of Leonardo Studies and Bibliography of Vinciana», IV, Firenze, Giunti, 1991.

SCIOLLA G. C., *Da Leonardo a Rembrandt: disegni della Biblioteca Reale di Torino*, Torino, Allemandi, 1989.

SCIOLLA G. C., *Leonardo e Pavia*, «Lettura Vinciana», XXXV, Firenze, Giunti, 1996.

SÉAILLES G., *L'esthétique et l'art de Léonard de Vinci*, «Revue des deux Mondes», LXII, 3 (1892).

SÉAILLES G., *Léonard de Vinci. L'artiste et le savant. Essai de biographie psychologique*, Paris, Perrin, 1892.

SEGRE C., *La descrizione al futuro: Leonardo da Vinci*, in ID., *Semiotica filologica*, Torino, Einaudi, 1979.

SEMENZA G., *L'automobile di Leonardo*, «Archeion», IX, 1 (1928).

SEVERI F., *Introduzione*, in *Leonardo. Saggi e ricerche*, a cura di G. Castelfranco, Roma, Istituto Poligrafico dello Stato, 1954.

SEVERI F., *Leonardo*, Roma, Studium, 1954.

SEVERI F., *Scienza ed arte. (A proposito di Leonardo da Vinci)*, Arezzo, Zelli, 1955.

SHAPIRO M., *Leonardo and Freud: an Art-historical Study*, «Journal of the History of Hideas», XVII (1956).

SHELL J., *Léonard de Vinci*, Paris, RMN, 1993.

SHELL J., SIRONI G., *Documents for Copies of the 'Cenacolo' and the 'Virgin of the Rocks'*, «Raccolta Vinciana», XXIII (1989).

SHELL J., SIRONI G., *Salaì and Leonardo's Legacy*, «Burlington Magazine», CXXXIII, 1055 (1991).

SCHELL J., SIRONI G., *Salaì and the Inventory of his Estate*, «Raccolta Vinciana» XXIV (1992).

SHELL J., SIRONI G., *Un nuovo documento di pagamento per la 'Vergine delle Rocce' di Leonardo*, in *Hostinato rigore. Leonardiana in memoria di Augusto Marinoni*, a cura di P. C. Marani, Milano, Electa, 2000.

SIRONI G., *Nuovi documenti riguardanti la Vergine delle Rocce*, introduzione di P. L. de Vecchi, Firenze, Giunti Barbèra, 1981.

SMIRAGLIA SCOGNAMIGLIO N., *Ricerche e documenti sulla giovinezza di L. da Vinci*, Napoli, Marghieri, 1900.

SMITH C. H., *Venice and Emergence of the High Renaissance in Florence: Observations and Questions*, in *Florence and Venise. Comparisons and Relations*, «Atti del convegno», Firenze, Villa I Tatti, 1976-1977.

SNOW-SMITH J., *Leonardo's Virgin of the Rocks (Musée du Louvre), A Franciscan Interpretation*, «Studies in Iconography», XI (1987).

SOLARI E., *Gli arcani occultati di Leonardo*, Bologna, Saval, 1989.

SOLMI E., *Studi sulla filosofia naturale di Leonardo da Vinci: gnoseologia e cosmologia*, Modena, Vincenzi, 1898.

SOLMI E., *«La festa del Paradiso» di Leonardo da Vinci e Bernardo Bellincioni (13 gennaio 1490)*, «Archivio Storico Lombardo», XXXI, 1904.

SOLMI E., *Frammenti letterari e filosofici di Leonardo da Vinci*, Firenze, Barbèra, 1904.

SOLMI E., *La resurrezione dell'opera di Leonardo*, in *Leonardo da Vinci. Conferenze fiorentine*, Milano, Treves, 1910.

SOLMI E., *Leonardo e la sollevazione d'Arezzo del 1502*, «Raccolta Vinciana», VII (1911).

SOLMI E., *Partecipazione di Leonardo da Vinci alla sollevazione di Arezzo e della Val di Chiana nel giugno del 1502*, «Archivio Storico Italiano», ser. V, vol. L (1912).

SOLMI E., *Leonardo (1452-1519)*, Firenze, Barbèra, 1913.

SOLMI E., *Le fonti dei Manoscritti di Leonardo (1908)*, e *Nuovi contributi alle fonti dei manoscritti di Leonardo (1911)*, in ID., *Scritti vinciani. Le fonti dei Manoscritti e altri studi*, presentazione di E. Garin, Firenze, La Nuova Italia, 1976.

SOÓS G., *Antichi modelli delle statue equestri di Leonardo da Vinci*, «Acta Historiae Artium Academiae Scientiarum Hungaricae», IV (1957).

STARNAZZI C., *Leonardo in terra di Arezzo*, «Studi per l'Ecologia del Quaternario», 17, Firenze, 1995.

STARNAZZI C., *La Gioconda nella Valle dell'Arno*, «Archeologia Viva», XV, 58, Maggio-Giugno, Firenze, Giunti, 1996.

STARNAZZI C., *Leonardo da Vinci, la rappresentazione cartografica e pittorica* del paesaggio Toscano, «L'Universo», LXXVI, 5, Settembre-Ottobre, Firenze, I.G.M., 1996.

STARNAZZI C., *Leonardo da Vinci e la Preistoria del Valdarno*, «Studi per l'Ecologia del Quaternario», 19, Firenze, 1997.

STARNAZZI C., *Leonardo da Vinci: un cartografo tra Euclide e Tolomeo*, «L'Universo», LXXVIII, 4, Luglio-Agosto, Firenze, I. G. M., 1998.

STARNAZZI C., *Leonardo da Vinci e la Battaglia di Anghiari*, «Atti e Memorie dell'Accademia Petrarca di Lettere, Arti e Scienze», LIX, Arezzo, 1997-98.

STARNAZZI C., *Dalle carte di Leonardo: il lago Trasimeno e le Chiane nei sogni di un ingegnere idraulico*, «L'Universo», LXXX, 4, Luglio-Agosto, Firenze, I. G. M., 2000.

STARNAZZI C., *Leonardo ad Arezzo. A. D. 2000. La Madonna dei fusi di Leonardo da Vinci e il paesaggio del Valdarno Superiore* (a cura di), con un contributo di C. Pedretti, Tiferno, Città di Castello, 2000.

STARNAZZI C., *Leonardo in Casentino*, in *Leonardo in Casentino. L'Angelo incarnato tra archeologia e leggenda*. Mostra ideata e curata da C. Starnazzi, Stia, 1 luglio-28 ottobre, catalogo a cura di C. Pedretti. Firenze, Grantour, 2001.

STARNAZZI C., *Leonardo. Acque e terre*, presentazione di C. Pedretti, libro-catalogo e mostra a Cesenatico a cura di C. Starnazzi, 6 luglio-8 settembre, Firenze, Grantour, 2002.

STARNAZZI C., *Scenografie per Charles d'Amboise, governatore di Milano*, in *Leonardo da Vinci. Il Foglio del teatro*, catalogo e mostra a cura di C. Starnazzi, Arezzo, 1 giugno-30 settembre, Arezzo, Badiali, 2002.

STARNAZZI C., *Leonardo e gli spettacoli di corte*, in *Leonardo da Vinci. Il Foglio del teatro*, catalogo e mostra a cura di C. Starnazzi, Arezzo, 1 giugno-30 settembre, Arezzo, Badiali, 2002.

STARNAZZI C., *Leonardo e Poliziano nella Valle dell'Arno*, in *Leonardo da Vinci. Il Foglio del teatro*, catalogo e mostra a cura di C. Starnazzi, Arezzo, 1 giugno-30 settembre, Arezzo, Badiali, 2002.

STARNAZZI C., *Anghiari. Leonardo e la battaglia*, «Archeologia Viva», XXI, 93, Firenze, Giunti, 2002.

STARNAZZI C., *Leonardo cartografo*, introduzione di C. Pedretti, supplemento a «L'Universo», n. 2/2003, Firenze, I. G. M., 2003.

STARNAZZI C., *Le mappe di Leonardo: un nuovo concetto di spazio*, in *Leonardo genio e cartografo. La rappresentazione del territorio tra scienza e arte*, Arezzo 21 giugno-30 settembre, catalogo a cura di A. Cantile, Firenze, I. G. M., 2003.

STARNAZZI C., *Leonardo e le acque. Le Chiane, l'Arno e le paludi Pontine*, in *Le acque interne dell'Italia Centrale*. Studi offerti a G. Moretti, a cura di A. Batinti, M. Bonino, E. Gambini, Perugia, SIFA, 2004.

STARNAZZI C., *Masaccio e Leonardo nelle balze del Valdarno*, «L'Universo», LXXXIV, 5, Settembre-Ottobre, Firenze, I. G. M., 2004.

STARNAZZI C., *Cupola di Cortona. La ideò Leonardo?*, «Archeologia Viva», XXIV, 112, Firenze, Giunti, 2005.

STARNAZZI C., *Leonardo e la Terra di Arezzo. Storia, Miti e Paesaggi*, presentazione di C. Pedretti, Cortona, Calosci, 2005.

STARNAZZI C., *Leonardo. Codici e Macchine*, presentazione di C. Pedretti, Firenze, Cartei e Bianchi, 2005.

STEINITZ K. T., *A Reconstruction of Leonardo da Vinci's Revolving Stage*, «The Art Quarterly», XII (1949).

STEINITZ K. T., *Leonardo da Vinci's 'Trattato della Pittura'. A Bibliography of the Printed Editions (1651-1956)*, foreword by E. Belt, Copenhagen, Munksgaard, 1958.

STEINITZ K. T., *Le dessin de Léonard de Vinci pour la représentation de la Danae de Baldassarre Taccone*, in *Le lieu théâtral à la Renaissance*, Royaumont 22-27 mars, Paris, CNRS, 1964.

STEINITZ K. T., *Leonardo architetto teatrale e organizzatore di feste*, «Lettura Vinciana», IX, Firenze, Giunti Barbèra, 1969.

STITES R. S., *The Sublimations of Leonardo da Vinci*, Washington, Smithsonian Institution Press, 1970.

STRONG D. S., *The Painter in Despair: 'Trasparentia' and 'Rilievo' in Leonardo's Treatise on Painting*, «Achademia Leonardi Vinci. Journal of Leonardo Studies and Bibliography of Vinciana», I, Firenze, Giunti, 1988.

SUIDA W., *Leonardo und sein Kreis*, München, Bruckmann, 1929.

SUIDA W., *Leonardos Madonna mit dem Kreuzstab (oder dem Garnwinder)"*, in *Miscellanea di studi lombardi in onore di Ettore Verga*, a cura di Caterina Santoro, Milano, Castello Sforzesco, Archivio Storico Civico, 1931.

SUIDA W., *La scuola di Leonardo*, in *Leonardo da Vinci*, a cura di S. Piantanida e C. Baroni, Novara, De Agostini, 1939.

SUIDA W., *Leonardo's Activity as a Painter. A Sketch*, in *Leonardo. Saggi e ricerche*, a cura di G. Castelfranco, Roma, Istituto Poligrafico dello Stato, 1954.

SUTER K., *A Copy in Colour by Rubens of Leonardo's Battle of Anghiari*, «Burlington Magazine», LVI (1930).

SUYEUX J., *Le Testament de Léonard*, «Le Gnomon: Revue internationale d'histoire du notariat», 88 (1993).

TAINE H., *Voyage en Italie*, Paris, Hachette, 1874.

TANAKA H., *Leonardo's Isabella d'Este. A New Analysis of the Mona Lisa in the Louvre*, «Annali dell'Istituto Giapponese di Cultura in Roma», 13 (1976-77).

TANAKA H., *Leonardo da Vinci. La sua arte e la sua vita,* presentazione di C. Pedretti, Tokyo, Centro di Cultura Suwa, 1983.

TESTAFERRATA E., *La Leda di Leonardo: compendio di un'invenzione*, in *Leonardo e il mito di Leda*, a cura di G. Dalli Regoli, R. Nanni, A. Natali, Vinci 23 giugno-23 settembre 2001, Cinisello Balsamo, Silvana Editoriale, 2001.

TICOZZI S., *Dizionario dei Pittori dal rinnovamento delle belle arti fino al 1800*, Milano, Ferrario, 1818.

TISSONI BENVENUTI A., *Il teatro volgare della Milano sforzesca*, in *Milano nell'età di Ludovico il Moro*. «Atti del Convegno Internazionale», 28 febbraio-4 marzo 1983, Milano, Il Comune: Archivio storico civico e Biblioteca Trivulziana, 1983.

TURNER R., *Words and pictures: the birth and death of Leonardo's Medusa*, «Arte Lombarda», 3 (1983).

UCCELLI A., *Leonardo e l'automobile*, «Raccolta Vinciana», XV-XVI (1935-39).

UCCELLI A., *Leonardo da Vinci. I libri di meccanica, nella rivoluzione ordinata di A. Uccelli*, Milano, Hoepli, 1940.

UCCELLI A., ZAMMATTIO C., *I libri del volo di Leonardo da Vinci*, Milano, Hoepli, 1952.

UZIELLI G., *Ricerche intorno a Leonardo da Vinci. Serie prima*, Firenze, Pellas, 1872.

UZIELLI G., *Ricerche intorno a Leonardo da Vinci. Serie seconda*, Roma, Salviucci, 1884.

UZIELLI G., *Leonardo da Vinci e le Alpi*, Torino, Candeletti, 1890.

UZIELLI G., *Ricordi in Firenze a Leonardo da Vinci e a Paolo Toscanelli, Le Armi della famiglia da Vinci e del comune di Vinci: un fratello di Leonardo Lanaiolo in Firenze e il suo "confessionale"*, Firenze, Stabilimento Tipografico Fiorentino, 1895.

VALENTINER W. R., *Leonardo's relation to Verrocchio*, «The Art Quarterly», I, IV (1941).

VALENTINER W. R., *Studies of Italian Renaissance Sculpture*, London, Phaidon, 1050.

VALERY P., *Introduction à la méthode de Léonard de Vinci*, Paris, Éditions de la Nouvelle Revue Française, 1919.

VALÉRY P., *Les divers essais sur Léonard de Vinci de Paul Valéry: commentés et annotés*, Paris, Éditions du Sagittaire, 1931.

VALLESE G., *Leonardo's Malinchonia*, «Achademia Leonardi Vinci. Journal of Leonardo Studies and Bibliography of Vinciana», V, Firenze, Giunti, 1992.

VASARI G., *Le Vite de' più eccellenti Architetti, Pittori et Scultori Italiani da Cimabue insino a' tempi nostri*, Firenze presso Lorenzo Tormentino, III (1550).

VASARI G., *Le vite de' più eccellenti Pittori, Scultori et Architettori*, Firenze, presso i Giunti, 1568. Altre edizioni: Milanesi G., [1879], Firenze, Sansoni, 1906; Ragghianti C. L., Milano-Roma, Rizzoli, 1945.

VASOLI C., *La lalde del sole di Leonardo da Vinci*, «Lettura Vinciana», XII, Firenze, Giunti Barbèra, 1972.

VASOLI C., *Note su Leonardo e l'alchimia*, in *Leonardo e l'età della ragione*, a cura di E. Bellone e P. Rossi, Milano, Scientia, 1982.

VECCE C., *La Gualanda*, «Achademia Leonardi Vinci. Journal of Leonardo Studies and Bibliography of Vinciana», III, Firenze, Giunti, 1990.

VECCE C., *Leonardo da Vinci. Scritti* (a cura di), Milano, Mursia, 1992.

VECCE C., *Libreria di Sancto Marco*, «Achademia Leonardi Vinci. Journal of Leonardo Studies and Bibliography of Vinciana», V, Firenze, Giunti, 1992.

VECCE C., *Leonardo e il gioco*, in *Passare il tempo. La letteratura del gioco e dell'intrattenimento dal XII al XVI secolo*, Roma, Salerno, 1993.

VECCE C., *«Piglia da Gian di Paris»*, «Achademia Leonardi Vinci. Journal of Leonardo Studies and Bibliography of Vinciana», X, Firenze, Giunti, 1997.

VECCE C., *Leonardo e il «cantico delle acque»*, in *Acqua. Storia di un simbolo tra vita e letteratura*, a cura di G. Garufi e A. Santori, Ancona, Transeuropa, 1997.

VECCE C., *Leonardo*, Roma, Salerno, 1998.

VECCE C., *Le biografie antiche di Leonardo*, in *Leonardo da Vinci: la vera immagine. Documenti e testimonianze sulla vita e sull'opera*, mostra a cura di V. Arrighi, A. Bellinazzi, E. Villata, Firenze, Giunti, 2005.

VENTURI A., *Authentic Leonardo Sculpture*, «Times», 17 (1923).

VENTURI A., *Grandi artisti italiani: Antonello da Messina, Giambellino, Sandro Botticelli, il Bramantino, Bernardo Cavallino, Francesco Laurana, Leonardo da Vinci*, Bologna, Zanichelli, 1925.

VENTURI A., *I Disegni di Leonardo da Vinci*, Roma, Danesi [Libreria dello Stato], 1928.

VENTURI A., *Leonardiana*, «L'Arte», XXVI (1936).

VENTURI A., *Leonardo e la sua scuola*, Novara, De Agostini, 1942.

VENTURI J. B., *Essai sur les ouvrages physico-mathématiques de Léonard de Vinci, avec des fragments tirés de ses manuscrits apportés d'Italie*, Paris, Duprat, 1797.

VENTURI L., *La critica e l'arte di Leonardo da Vinci*, Bologna, Zanichelli, 1919.

VENTURI L., MARTINELLI V., *Lezioni di storia dell'arte moderna: Leonardo da Vinci*, Roma, Edizioni dell'Ateneo, 1952.

VERGA E., *Bibliografia vinciana, 1493-1930*, 2 voll., Bologna, Zanichelli, 1931.

VERTOVA L., *La barba di Leonardo. Osservazioni in margine all'autoritratto*, in *Da Leonardo a Rembrandt. Nuove ricerche in margine alla mostra*, a cura di G. C. Sciolla, Torino, Fondazione San Paolo, 1991.

VEZZOSI A., *Leonardo dopo Milano. La Madonna dei fusi (1501)*, Con il contributo di G. Dalli Regoli e con una nota di P. Galluzzi, Introduzione di C. Pedretti, Firenze, Giunti Barbèra, 1982.

VEZZOSI A., *Leonardo e il leonardismo a Napoli e a Roma*, Testi introduttivi di C. Pedretti, Firenze, Giunti Barbèra, 1983.

VEZZOSI A., *Toscana di Leonardo*, Firenze, Becocci, 1984.

VEZZOSI A., *Leonardo: scomparso e ritrovato* (a cura di), con i contributi di M. Calvesi [et al.], Firenze, Giunti, 1988.

VEZZOSI A., *Leonardo da Vinci. Arte e scienza dell' universo*, Milano-Parigi, Electa/Gallimard, 1996.

VEZZOSI A., *Leonardo e lo sport*, Firenze, Giunti, 2004.

VIATTE F., *Léonard de Vinci: les études de draperie*, Paris, RMN, 1989.

VIATTE F., *«Della figura che va contro il vento». Il tema del soffio nell'opera di Leonardo da Vinci*, «Lettura Vinciana», XLV, Firenze, Giunti, 2006.

VILLATA E., *Il San Giovanni Battista di Leonardo: un'ipotesi per la cronologia e la committenza*, «Raccolta Vinciana», XXVII (1997).

VILLATA E., *Due precisazioni e una ipotesi sul San Giovanni Bacco di Leonardo*, in *Tutte le opere non son per istancarmi. Raccolta di scritti per i settant'anni di Carlo Pedretti*, a cura di F. Frosini, Roma, Edizioni Associate, 1998.

VILLATA E., *Leonardo da Vinci. I documenti e le testimonianze contemporanee*, Milano, Ente Raccolta Vinciana, 1999.

VILLATA E., *Leonardo e gli uomini di lettere*, in *Leonardo da Vinci: la vera immagine. Documenti e testimonianze sulla vita e sull'opera*, mostra a cura di V. Arrighi, A. Bellinazzi, E. Villata, Firenze, Giunti, 2005.

VILLOT F., *Notices des tableaux exposés dans les Galeries du Musée National du Louvre*, Paris, 1852.

VULLIAUD P., *La pensée ésotérique de Léonard de Vinci*, [1906], Paris, Odette, 1945.

WASSERMANN J., *A Re-discovered Cartoon by Leonardo da Vinci*, «Burlington Magazine», CXII, 805 (1970).

WASSERMANN J., *The Dating and Patronage of Leonardo's Burlington House Cartoon*, «Art Bulletin», 53 (1971).

WEIL-GARRIS BRANDT K., *Leonardo e la scultura*, «Lettura Vinciana», XXXVIII, Firenze, Giunti, 1999.

Winternitz E., *Leonardo da Vinci as a musician*, New Haven, Yale University Press, 1982.

Wittkower R., *Nati sotto saturno: la figura dell'artista dall'antichità alla Rivoluzione francese*, Torino, Einaudi, 1967.

Woodson Goodson M., *Mona Lisa*, «Il Carroccio», III (1928).

Zammattio C., *Acque e Pietre: loro meccanica*, in *Leonardo scienziato*, Firenze, Giunti Barbèra, 1981.

Zöllner F., *Rubens rework Leonardo: "The Fight for the Standard"*, «Achademia Leonardi Vinci. Journal of Leonardo Studies and Bibliography of Vinciana», IV, Firenze, Giunti, 1991.

Zöllner F., *Leonardo's portrait of Mona Lisa del Giocondo*, «Gazette des Beaux-Arts», 1490 (1993).

Zöllner F., *L'uomo vitruviano di Leonardo da Vinci, Rudolf Wittkower e l'Angelus Novus di Walter Benjamin*, «Raccolta Vinciana», XXVI (1995).

Zöllner F., *La Battaglia di Anghiari di Leonardo da Vinci fra mitologia e politica*, «Lettura Vinciana», XXXVII, Firenze, Giunti, 1998.

Zöllner F., *Leonardo da Vinci. The Complete Paintings and Drawings*, Köln, Taschen, 1999.

Zöllner F., Nathan J., *Leonardo da Vinci. The Complete Paintings and Drawings*, Köln, Taschen, 2003.

Zoubov V. P., *Léon-Battista Alberti et Léonard de Vinci*, «Raccolta Vinciana», XVIII (1960).

Zoubov V. P., *Leonardo da Vinci*, Cambridge (Mass.), Harvard University Press, 1968.

Boreau G.: 13, 231, 240

Borgia Cesare, also known as Valentino: 55, 60, 76, 135, 210

Borgia Lucrezia: 208

Borsi F.: 204

Borsi S.: 204

Bosch Hieronymus: 279, 280

Boswell William: 271

Bottari G.: 267

Botticelli Sandro: 161, 166, 175, 256

Bracciolini Poggio: 39

Bramante Donato: 13, 73, 76, 80, 91, 106, 118, 132, 155, 157, 158, 165, 251

Brizio A. M.: 123, 165

Brown D.: 236

Brown D. A.: 82, 103, 115, 161, 233

Brown G. M.: 175

Brunelleschi Filippo: 13, 117, 123, 127, 129, 130, 140

Bruni Leonardo: 39, 103

Bruschetti P.: 149

Bruschi A.: 74, 124

Bryan A.: 195

Buckminster Fuller R.: 131

Buonamici G.: 146

Buonarroti Filippo: 146

Buonarroti Michelangelo: 73-6, 95, 99, 145, 162, 175, 179, 182, 211, 213, 273

Buonarroti Michelangelo the Younger: 211

Buoninsegni Domenico: 39, 40, 60

Byam Shaw J.: 265

Caetani Guglielmo, Duke of Sermoneta: 85

Calco Bartolomeo: 132

Callot Jacques: 267

Calvi G.: 29, 243

Camesasca E.: 161, 233

Campbell M.: 73

Camporeale G.: 149

Campori G.: 143

Canfora Iacopo: 239

Canuti F.: 161, 166, 179, 181

Caprotti Giangiacomo, also known as Salaì: 165, 179, 240, 243

Caputo C.: 261

Caputo G.: 146

Caradosso, Cristoforo Foppa known as: 132

Cardano Gerolamo: 124

Carlton Dudley: 271

Caroli F.: 263

Caroti S.: 259

Carpiceci A. C.: 123

Carracci Annibale: 263

Carroll Lewis: 279

Carusi E.: 91

Castelfranco G.: 68, 261

Castelli P.: 261

Castiglione Baldassarre: 89, 236

Castiglione Sabba: 124

Cecchi A.: 100

Cellini Benvenuto: 210, 231

Cesariano Cesare: 251

Charles I, King of England: 243, 269, 271

Charles VIII, King of France: 70, 203, 204, 208, 233

Chastel A.: 29, 80, 108, 127, 155, 203, 208

Ciaffini Silvestro di Giuliano: 118

Cianchi M.: 17

Cianchi R.: 143

Ciardi R. P.: 13, 231, 255

Ciocca Alvise: 179

Cipriani G.: 146

Clark K.: 15, 115, 165, 261

Clayton M.: 89, 103, 106, 279

Clément C.: 233

Cogliati Arano L.: 256

Colantonio: 203

Colleoni Bartolomeo: 253

Conn George: 271

Cottington Francis: 271

Cozens Alexander: 256

Cristofani M.: 149

Croysant Guillaume: 240

Crozat Pierre: 267

Ctesybius of Alexandria: 17

D'Alessandro A.: 146, 263

D'Arrigo A.: 195

Dalli Regoli G.: 103

Dan Pierre: 243

Danti Giovan Battista: 193

Darwin Ch.: 263

Davies M.: 115

De Beatis Antonio: 208-10, 243

De Croy J.: 203, 217

De Jonge K.: 124

De Pagave Venanzio: 240

De Toni G. B.: 210

Degenhart B.: 265

Dei Giambattista: 240

Delacroix Eugène: 162

Del Pozzo Cassiano: 244

Della Porta Giovan Battista: 20, 261

Della Porta Guglielmo: 155

Della Torre Marcantonio: 239

Democritus: 91, 251

Desiderio da Settignano: 115

Di Napoli G.: 239

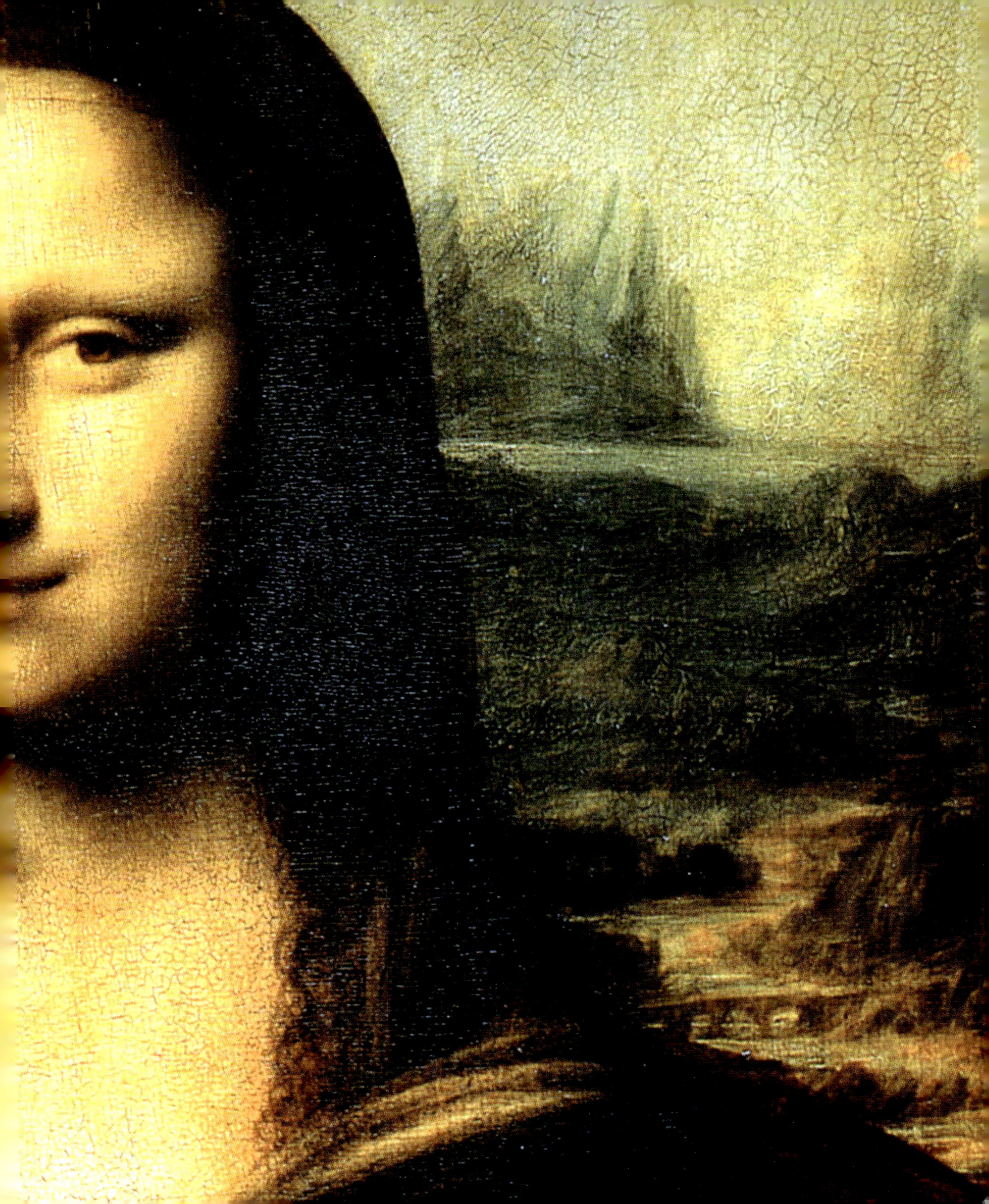

Printed in Italy
by CMF of Foligno
for Cartei & Bianchi Publishers
in the month of July 2008